DERIVATIVE SECURITIES

SECOND EDITION

ROBERT JARROW
Finance Faculty
Johnson Graduate School of Management
Cornell University

STUART TURNBULL
Canadian Imperial Bank of Commerce

South-Western College Publishing
Thomson Learning™

Australia • Canada • Denmark • Japan • Mexico • New Zealand • Philippines
Puerto Rico • Singapore • South Africa • Spain • United Kingdom • United States

Derivative Securities, 2e by Robert Jarrow and Stuart Turnbull

Vice President/Publisher: Jack W. Calhoun
Acquisitions Editor: Michael B. Mercier
Developmental Editor: Thomas S. Sigel
Marketing Manager: Lisa Lysne
Production Editor: Kara ZumBahlen
Manufacturing Coordinator: Charlene Taylor
Cover Design: Michael H. Stratton
Cover Illustration: ArtVille/David Wasserman
Production House: Beckwith Bookworks
Compositor: A & B Typesetting
Printer: R.R. Donnelley

Printed in the United States of America
2 3 4 5 02 01 00

For more information contact South-Western College Publishing, 5101 Madison Road, Cincinnati, Ohio, 45227 or find us on the Internet at http://www.swcollege.com

For permission to use material from this text or product contact us by
• **telephone: 1-800-730-2214**
• **fax: 1-800-730-2215**
• **web: http://www.thomsonrights.com**

Library of Congress Cataloging-in-Publication Data

Jarrow, Robert A.
      Derivative Securities/Robert A. Jarrow, Stuart M. Turnbull.—
      2nd ed.
          p. cm.
      Includes bibliographical references and index.
      ISBN 0-538-87740-5 (hard: alk. paper)
      1. Derivative securities. I. Turnbull, Stuart M.   II. Title.
      HG6024.A3J37 2000   99-046348
      332.63′2—dc21

This book is printed on acid-free paper.

To our wives.

ABOUT THE AUTHORS

Robert A. Jarrow is the Ronald P. and Susan E. Lynch Professor of Investment Management at the Johnson Graduate School of Management, Cornell University. He is also a managing director and the director of research at Kamakura Corporation. He was the 1997 IAFE/SunGard Financial Engineer of the year. He is a graduate of Duke University, Dartmouth College, and the Massachusetts Institute of Technology. He is an IAFE Senior Fellow. Professor Jarrow is renowned for his pioneering work on the Heath-Jarrow-Morton model for pricing interest rate derivatives. His current research interests include the pricing of exotic interest rate options and other credit derivatives as well as investment management theory. His publications include four books, *Options Pricing, Finance Theory, Modelling Fixed Income Securities and Interest Rate Options*, and *Derivative Securities*, as well as over 70 publications in leading finance and economic journals. Professor Jarrow is a founding co-editor of *Mathematical Finance* and a co-editor of *The Journal of Derivatives*. He is an associate editor of the *Journal of Financial and Quantitative Analysis, Review of Derivatives Research, Journal of Fixed Income, The Financial Review, The Journal of Risk*, and *The Review of Futures Markets*. He is an advisory editor for *Asia-Pacific Financial Markets*.

Stuart M. Turnbull is Vice President of Global Analytics, the Canadian Imperial Bank of Commerce. He is in charge of developing the next generation of credit and market risk management models. Prior to joining the Bank, he was the Bank of Montreal Professor of Banking and Finance, Queen's University (Canada), and a Research Fellow, Institute for Policy Analysis (Toronto). He is a graduate of the Imperial College of Science and Technology (London) and the University of British Columbia. He is the author of *Option Valuation*, and (with Robert A. Jarrow) *Derivative Securities*. He has published over 30 articles in major finance and economic journals, and in law and economics journals, as well as many articles in practitioner journals. He is co-author with Robert Jarrow of the J-T model of pricing credit derivatives, which is widely used by financial institutions. He has been a consultant to many financial institutions. He is an associate editor of *Mathematical Finance*, the *Journal of Financial Engineering*, the *International Journal of Theoretical and Applied Finance*, and has served as an associate editor for the *Journal of Finance*.

CONTENTS

PART II The Binomial Model

9   EXTENSIONS TO THE BLACK-SCHOLES MODEL   251

10   REPLICATION AND RISK EXPOSURE WITH MODEL MISSPECIFICATION   272

PART IV INTEREST RATE CONTRACTS, THE HJM MODEL, AND EXTENSIONS

13 INTEREST RATE CONTRACTS   386

18   CREDIT RISK   556

PREFACE

Our purpose in writing this text is to make the theory and practice of pricing and hedging derivative securities accessible to undergraduates and MBA students, as well as practitioners. We have five explicit objectives.

First, the book reflects both *option* pricing theory and practice and *futures* pricing theory and practice. In practice, options on an underlying asset are often hedged with futures on the same underlying asset. This is because futures are viewed as more liquid than the underlying asset. For example, in the over-the-counter swap market Eurodollar futures are considered the preferred instrument for hedging, and in the stock index options market futures on the same stock index are the preferred hedging vehicle.

Current pricing theory, which is based on martingale methods, adopts a unified approach to all forms of derivatives, such as options and futures. Thus theory and practice dictate a new approach to teaching derivative securities. In this text we adopt this new direction, presenting a unified approach to pricing and hedging derivative securities. As such, our text differs from existing books, which either concentrate on options with little or no futures material or on futures with little or no options material.

Second, the book covers diverse areas such as equity and index derivatives, foreign currency derivatives, and commodity derivatives, as well as interest rate derivatives. Given the recent expansion in the trading of exotic options, any relevant text must include this material.

Third, the book addresses the issue of how to incorporate credit risk into the pricing and risk management of derivatives. Our text provides a clear, self-contained explanation of how to incorporate credit risk and gives many numerical examples.

Fourth, the book is a useful guide for pricing and hedging any derivative security, included in the text or not. To achieve this goal, the book includes all proofs and/or necessary references. As such, the level of detail included is higher than that contained in other books in this area, but without any additional mathematical complexity.

Fifth, the book integrates user-friendly software that allows the reader to price equity, foreign currency, and interest rate derivatives, as well as many types of exotic options. This software can be downloaded from our web page, located at *http://jarrow.swcollege.com.*

We believe that in satisfying our five objectives, our textbook offers a unique and comprehensive treatment of derivatives accessible to undergraduates, MBA students, executives, and regulators.

The accessibility of our textbook to students with various backgrounds is facilitated by the organizational design. We explore two key modeling paradigms: (1) the discrete time binomial model, and (2) the continuous time models of Black-Scholes and Heath-Jarrow-Morton. We use the discrete time binomial model to introduce all the relevant concepts. This is done because of its mathematical simplicity. We provide detailed proofs of all the key results. We include numerous examples, each highlighted and isolated from the text for easy reference and identification.

The continuous time models of Black-Scholes and Heath-Jarrow-Morton are provided for two reasons. First, they are used extensively in the industry, so consequently any serious student of derivatives must know this material. Second, they provide closed form solutions for many types of options and futures. These solutions can be programmed on a computer and quickly calculated. This facilitates an understanding of the different properties of financial derivatives. We include numerous examples using the software provided with the text.

Changes and New Components

The present edition has been revised with an eye toward improving presentation, streamlining the internal design for easier reading, and updating the applications and data, as well as including the latest developments in the field. New features include:

- Simplified notation.
- Simpler and more intuitive proofs.
- A new section explaining Ito's lemma (Chapter 8).
- A proof of the restriction that no-arbitrage imposes when modeling the evolution of forward interest rates. This restriction is used in the Heath-Jarrow-Morton model (Chapter 16).
- A new section (Chapter 18) on some of the recent disasters associated with derivative securities, including Barings Bank and Kidder Peabody & Co. This section includes a description of the Tinkerbell phenomenon first identified by Lee Wakeman (1997).

In addition, a web site now accompanies and supports this second edition. Visit *http://jarrow.swcollege.com* to access the following:

- **Spreadsheet software**   This downloadable software gives students the opportunity to implement techniques presented in the text.
- **Test bank**   Written by Arkadev Chatterjea from Indiana University, this new component provides instructors with multiple choice, true or false, and essay questions. Many questions are based upon the Chartered Financial Analyst (CFA) examinations administered by the Association for Investment Management and Research (AIMR). The test bank is password protected.
- **PowerPoint slides**   Prepared by Robert Jarrow and Arkadev Chatterjea, these comprehensive slides may be used by instructors and students to reinforce concepts presented in the book.

- **Thomson Investors Network**   Thomson Investors Network provides instructors, students, and individual investors with a wealth of information and tools, including portfolio tracking software, live stock quotations, and company and industry reports. Instructors can use Thomson Investors Network to create handouts with real-world company and industry data, or they can use it live in the classroom as a pedagogical aid. A preview of this invaluable tool is available by visiting *http://www.thomsoninvest.net*. Contact your ITP sales representative for more information about this feature.

Other Ancillary Materials

Instructor's Manual (ISBN 0-324-003854)   Written by the authors, this manual contains the solutions to the end-of chapter problems and computer exercises. It also contains suggestions for additional exercises.

Flexibility for Using This Text in Different Class Environments

The joy of this second edition is that it can be used in different class environments giving instructors great flexibility in preparing lectures. For courses with students who are new to finance or who have little technical background, the instructor can stress the chapters on the binomial model. We recommend going through the examples in class, leaving the abstract theory for student self-reading. The continuous time models should be explored in class using the computer software that is downloadable from our web site. A possible course outline would include the following: Chapter 1 through Chapter 5, and Chapters 8, 9, 10, 11, 15, 16, and 17.

For courses containing students who have had previous finance electives, or who have strong analytic backgrounds, the instructor can stress the theory sections in class lectures, leaving the examples for student self-reading. For these more advanced students, most of the textbook can be handled within a semester course.

Acknowledgments

This textbook is based on courses taught to undergraduates, MBA students, and executives. We thank our students for their many comments and suggestions. We also are grateful to our colleagues who offered help and advice. In particular, we would like to thank the following:

Paul Bolster, Northeastern University
Robert Brooks, Financial Risk Management, Inc.
Mark Cassano, SUNY College at Stony Brook
Don Chance, Virginia Tech
Eric Chang, Georgia Institute Tech
Jennifer Conrad, University of North Carolina–Chapel Hill
Michel Crouhy, Canadian Imperial Bank of Commerce

Richard DeFusco, University of Nebraska
Donald Fehrs, University of Notre Dame
Richard Flavell, Lombard Risk Systems Limited
Louis Gagnon, Royal Bank of Canada
Bruce Grundy, Wharton School of Business/Australian Graduate School of
   Management
Chandrasekhar Gukhal, Cornell University
Edmond Levy, HSBC Midland Bank
Dean Leistikow, Fordham University
Robert Mark, Canadian Imperial Bank of Commerce
Joseph McCarthy, Bryant College
Tom McCurdy, University of Toronto
Thomas Miller, Kennesaw State University
Ieuan G. Morgan, Queen's University
Edwin H. Neave, Queen's University
M. Nimalendran, University of Florida
Joseph Ogden, SUNY at Buffalo
Hun Park, University of Illinois
Eduardo Schwartz, UCLA
Adel Turki, Purdue University
Robert Trevor, Macquarie University
John Wisbey, Lombard Risk Systems Limited
Guofu Zhou, Washington University

The following people deserve special thanks:

Phelim Boyle, University of Waterloo
Peter Carr, Nations Bank, Montgomery Securities
Arkadev Chatterjea, Indiana University
Dilip Madan, University of Maryland
Angelo Melino, University of Toronto
Frank Milne, Queen's University
Lee Wakeman, Risk Analysis and Control

Credit for the design and implementation of the input and output screens for the software goes to Warren Tom (UBS, Connecticut). We are very grateful to Warren for his many suggestions and dedication. We thank Barb Drake, Linda Freeman, and Donna Phoenix for a wonderful job in typing the manuscript. And special thanks go to our editors Mike Mercier, Thomas Sigel, and Kara ZumBahlen without whom this revised textbook would still only be in manuscript form.

Robert A. Jarrow   Stuart M. Turnbull
Cornell University   Canadian Imperial Bank of Commerce

PART I

THE BASICS

CHAPTER

INTRODUCTION TO DERIVATIVE SECURITIES

1.0 INTRODUCTION

A **derivative security** is a financial contract whose value is derived from the value of an underlying asset, hence the name. The underlying asset may be a stock, Treasury bill/bond, a foreign currency, or even another derivative security. For example, a stock option's value depends upon the value of a stock on which the option is written; the value of a Treasury bill futures contract depends upon the price of the underlying Treasury bill; the value of a foreign currency forward contract depends upon the value of the foreign currency; and the value of an option on a swap (a swaption) depends upon the value of the underlying swap contract. These are all derivative securities.

Two types of derivative securities—futures and options—are actively traded on organized exchanges. These contracts are standardized with regard to the description of the underlying asset, the rights of the owner, and the maturity date. We will discuss later why it is necessary to standardize these contracts. Forward contracts are not standardized, each contract being customized to its owner's specifications. They are traded on what is called the interbank market. Options can be found embedded in other securities, such as convertible bonds and extendible bonds. A convertible bond contains a provision that gives the owner an option to convert the security into common stock. An extendible bond contains a provision that gives the owner an option to extend the maturity of the bond. Once we understand simple derivative securities such as forward contracts, futures contracts, call options, and put options, it will be relatively easy to define and understand more complicated examples.

Derivative securities can be used by individuals, corporations, and financial institutions to hedge an exposure to risk, which can take many forms. For example, an individual may be concerned about the risk that a stock she owns may suffer a major price decline. She could sell the stock or purchase an insurance policy providing protection against a price decline. A put option written on the stock provides this type of protection. A second example is that of a corporation that issues floating rate debt in a foreign currency. Given the nature of its cash flows, the company would prefer to have fixed rate debt payable in the domestic currency. So the company enters into a

foreign currency exchange swap, which is a derivative security. These examples illustrate derivative securities being used to reduce risk exposure.

Derivative securities can also be used to increase one's exposure to risk speculation. For every investor who buys a put option, there must be someone willing to sell a put option. If the individual or financial institution that sells the put option has no offsetting assets, then selling the put option increases their exposure to risk. Hedging—risk reduction—and speculation—risk augmentation—are flip sides of the same coin.

In this chapter, we explain simple derivative securities such as forward contracts, futures contracts, call options, and put options. We will describe the basic characteristics of these different contracts and some of the institutional details. A more detailed discussion of the properties of these contracts will be given in later chapters.

1.1 FORWARD CONTRACTS

A **forward contract** is an agreement to buy or sell a specified quantity of an asset at a specified price, with delivery at a specified time and place. The specified price is referred to as the **delivery price**. At the time the contract is written, the delivery price is set such that the value of the forward contract is zero. This is done by convention so that no cash is exchanged between the parties entering into the contract. As such, the delivery price yields a "fair" price for future delivery of the underlying asset. We will explain how the delivery price is determined later. The party that agrees to buy the underlying asset is said to have a **long position**. The party that agrees to sell the underlying asset is said to have a **short position**.

A forward contract is settled at the delivery date, sometimes called the maturity date or expiration date. The holder of the short portion delivers the specified quantity of the asset at the specified place and in return receives from the holder of the long position a cash payment equal to the delivery price. No cash exchange occurs prior to the delivery date.

EXAMPLE **Foreign Currency Forward Contract**

To illustrate why forward contracts are useful as hedging tools, consider a U.S. company that is planning to buy some equipment from a German manufacturer. The assistant manager in the Treasury Department of the U.S. company has been asked to analyze the consequences of entering into a forward contract to reduce the company's exposure to foreign exchange risk.

The domestic currency is dollars, and the current quotes on Deutsche marks (denoted by DM) available from a large commercial bank are

Spot ($/DM)	0.5611
30-day forward	0.5623
90-day forward	0.5641
180-day forward	0.5669.

The first quote means that the company can buy or sell marks today at the exchange rate of 0.5611 $/DM—that is, one mark can be exchanged for 0.5611 dollars. In practice, there is a bid/ask spread: The company can buy at one rate (the ask price) and sell at another rate (the bid price). For the purposes of this illustration, we will ignore this bid/ask spread. The second quote, $0.5623/DM, gives the forward price to buy or sell marks 30 days in the future. The third quote, $0.5641/DM, is to buy or sell marks 90 days in the future, and the last quote, $0.5669/DM, is to buy or sell marks 180 days in the future.

The company is purchasing equipment costing 10 million Deutsche marks and must make payment in 30 days' time. The company decides to enter into a 30-day forward contract to buy 10 million Deutsche marks at the exchange rate of $0.5623/DM. The counterparty to the contract is a large commercial bank willing to sell this quantity of Deutsche marks to the company. The company knows today that the equipment will cost $5,623,000 in 30 days. By entering into the forward contract, the company has removed all the foreign exchange risk from this transaction.

Let us skip ahead 30 days in time and examine what might have happened if the company had not entered into the forward contract. Suppose that the spot exchange rate in 30 days time is $0.65/DM, implying that the dollar has fallen against the mark. To buy 10 million Deutsche marks would have cost the company $6.5 million. The company saved $877,000 by using the forward contract; conversely, the commercial bank that agreed to sell the Deutsche marks lost $877,000. However, if the dollar had appreciated against the mark, to say $0.50/DM, then buying 10 million Deutsche marks would cost $5 million. In this case, the company would have saved $623,000 by *not* entering into the forward contract. The U.S. company avoided these gains and losses by using this contract.

In summary, under a forward contract, the company is obligated to buy Deutsche marks at the agreed-upon delivery price. The cost to the company is fixed at $5,623,000. On the other side of the transaction, the dollar inflow to the commercial bank is also fixed at $5,623,000.   ∎

Formalization

We now introduce a few algebraic symbols to represent the above transaction. This allows us to economize on time by studying many different examples at once, using a generic terminology. Figure 1.1 gives the key dates of the forward contract, the initiation date (t) and the delivery date (T).

Suppose that the company enters into the forward contract today, at date t. The forward contract matures at date T. Let $F(t)$ ($/DM) denote the forward price at date t for the contract with delivery date T. When the contract is initiated, by definition the forward price equals the delivery price, denoted by K. The delivery price is determined so that no cash is exchanged at this time. The delivery price is fixed over the life of the contract.

FIGURE 1.1   *Time Scale of a Forward Contract*

t	*T*
Initiation date of	Delivery date of
the contract	the contract

FIGURE 1.2   *Value of a Long Forward Contract at Delivery*

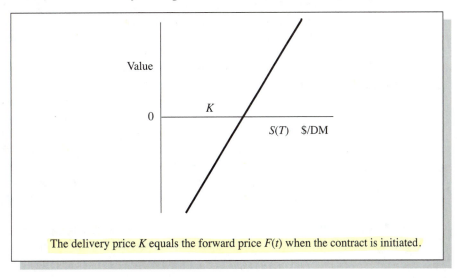

The delivery price *K* equals the forward price *F(t)* when the contract is initiated.

Let $S(t)$ denote the spot exchange rate (\$/DM) at date t. When the contract matures at date T, the spot exchange rate is denoted by $S(T)$. This spot exchange rate, unknown when the forward contract is initiated, is called a random variable. The value of the forward contract at the delivery date T to the long position[1] initiated at date t for one unit of the currency is

$$S(T) - K.$$

The value of the forward contract at delivery equals the value of the foreign currency $S(T)$ less the delivery price paid K.

As illustrated in the above example, the value of the forward contract at delivery can be either positive or negative. A graph of the possible values is shown in Figure 1.2. If the spot exchange rate at the delivery date is less than the delivery price, $S(T) < K$, the value of the forward contract is negative; otherwise, it is zero or positive.

---

[1]The term "long position" means that the party intends to buy the asset.

The delivery price equals the prevailing forward price, $K = F(t)$, when the contract is initiated. Once the contract is written, the delivery price is fixed over the life of the contract. The forward price, which represents the delivery price of newly written contracts, of course can change. If you contracted with a financial institution tomorrow, date $t + 1$, about buying Deutsche marks for delivery at date T, there would be a new delivery or forward price $F(t + 1)$.

This completes the institutional description of forward contracts. We will return to these contracts again in subsequent chapters when we analyze pricing and hedging.

1.2 FUTURES CONTRACTS

A **futures contract** is an agreement to buy or sell a specified quantity of an asset at a specified price and at a specified time and place. This part of the definition of a futures contract is identical to that of a forward contract. But futures contracts differ from forward contracts in four important ways.

First, futures contracts allow participants to realize gains and losses on a daily basis, while forward contracts are cash settled only at delivery. In essence, the delivery price is paid via a sequence of installments over the life of the contract. The sizes of these installments are random and unknown at the time the contract is written. Second, futures contracts are standardized with respect to the quality and the quantity of the asset underlying the contract, the delivery date or period, and the delivery place if there is physical delivery. In contrast, forward contracts customize all these factors to meet the needs of the two counterparties. Third, futures contracts are settled through a **clearing house**. The clearing house acts as a middleman to each transaction, which minimizes credit risk because the second party to a futures contract is always the clearing house. The fourth difference is that futures markets are regulated, while forward contracts are unregulated. We now discuss each of these differences in more detail.

Standardization

The contract specifications for the Chicago Board of Trade (CBOT) 100 troy ounce Gold Futures contract are given in Table 1.1. Each contract is for 100 troy ounces of gold. The **tick size** refers to the value of the minimum price change; in this case it is $0.10 per troy ounce. The exchange can set a daily price limit, which puts bounds on the maximum price change permitted per day; in this case it is $50 per troy ounce. Why set price limits? They are an attempt to reduce "hysteria" trading and price volatility by forcing market participants to "cool off" when dramatic price moves occur. If the limit price is reached, trading stops. It is not clear whether this trading halt will produce the desired result because the exchange may widen the price limit if it so desires. In fact, if the price limit is reached on a number of successive days, the exchange may remove the price limit altogether. Price limits do not apply on the last day of trading in the delivery month, and not all futures contracts have price limits.

TABLE 1.1 *Contract Specifications*

CBOT 100-OUNCE GOLD FUTURES	
Trading unit	100 troy ounces
Tick size	10 cents per troy ounce ($10 per contract)
Daily price limit	$50 per troy ounce ($5,000 per contract) above or below the previous day's settlement price
Contract months	Current month and the next two calendar months and February, April, June, August, October, December
Trading hours	7:20 A.M. to 1:40 P.M. (Chicago time), Monday through Friday. Evening trading hours are from 5 to 8:30 P.M. (Chicago time), or from 6 to 9:30 P.M. (Central Daylight Savings time), Sunday through Thursday.
Last trading day	The fourth to last business day of the delivery month
Deliverable grades	Refined gold in the form of one 100-ounce bar or three 1-kilo gold bars assaying not less than 995 fineness. The total pack cannot vary from a 100-troy-ounce weight by more than 5 percent.
Delivery	By vault receipt issued by a CBOT-approved vault in Chicago or New York

The contract months identify the expiry cycle of delivery dates. For the gold futures, the contract months are the current month, the next two months, plus February, April, June, August, October, and December. The quality of the gold is specified such that the short has some choice in the quality of the gold delivered, though there are offsetting payments to compensate the long.[2] In this case the gold must be at least 995 fineness and cannot deviate from 100 troy ounces by more than 5 percent. The place of delivery is also described by the contract. For gold futures, this is either Chicago or New York City in a vault specified by the CBOT.

Selling or writing of a futures contract is an obligation to deliver the underlying commodity sometime during the contract's expiration period. Buying a futures contract—going long—entails the obligation to accept delivery of the underlying commodity. The obligation to deliver or to accept delivery remains binding unless there is an offsetting transaction, called a **closing transaction**, which can be done at any time. Delivery procedures are initiated by the seller, who may tender a delivery notice any time during a contract's expiration month. Clearing houses generally do not make or

---

[2]The term "short" refers to the party who has written the futures contract, and "long" refers to the party who owns the futures contract.

take delivery of the actual commodity; they only specify the mechanism under which sellers make delivery to qualified buyers. The actual delivery process, although similar in structure, varies from exchange to exchange. We now discuss a typical delivery process.

A futures contract specifies a **First Notice Day**, **Last Notice Day**, and **Last Trading Day**. The First Notice Day is the first day on which a notice of intention to make delivery by the short can be submitted to the exchange; the Last Notice Day is the last such day. The Last Trading Day occurs generally a few days before the Last Notice Day.

To provide an example of this procedure, suppose that a seller decides to make delivery. The three-day delivery process as required by the rules of the Chicago Board of Trade is as follows:[3]

Day 1 (Position Day)
The brokerage firm representing the seller notifies the Board of Trade Clearing Corporation that its customer wants to deliver on a futures contract.

Day 2 (Notice Day)
Prior to the market opening on Day 2, the Board of Trade Clearing Corporation matches the seller with the buyer holding the oldest reported long position, and then notifies both parties.

Day 3 (Delivery Day)
Upon receiving a check from the buyer's brokerage firm, the seller's brokerage firm gives the appropriate ownership receipts to the buyer's brokerage firm.

The vast majority of futures contracts (97 to 99 percent) are closed out with an offsetting transaction before maturity.[4] To close out a futures contract, an investor enters into an offsetting contract with the same maturity date.

Clearing House

Suppose that on Monday morning an individual, A, decides to enter into a futures contract to buy 100 troy ounces of gold at the futures price of $366 per troy ounce. For every buyer there must be a seller (writer), that is, there must be an individual, B, willing to sell 100 troy ounces of gold. In contrast to a forward contract, the two parties need not know each other, because immediately after the trade is completed the clearing house steps in with offsetting positions. Thus with respect to individual A the clearing house writes (sells) a contract, and with respect to individual B the clearing house buys a contract. See Figure 1.3.

---

[3]See *The Commodity Trading Manual*, 1989, pp. 69–70.
[4]*The Commodity Trading Manual*, p. 69.

FIGURE 1.3 *The Clearing House Function*

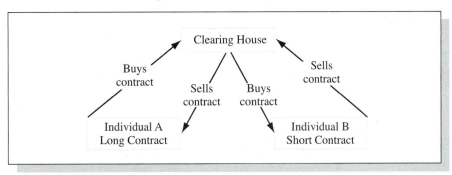

This intervention by the clearing house implies that the futures market has no counterparty risk. Both individuals A and B look to the clearing house to fulfill the contract. The clearing house is thus the counterparty to every contract. The clearing house, having financial reserves to guarantee that its contracts are executed, is considered default-free.[5] It accepts the risk that a counterparty may default on a contract and in return receives a small fee for each contract executed. To minimize counterparty risk, it only accepts contracts from "qualified traders" and it sets margin accounts. The net position of the clearing house is always zero, so that the only risk the clearing house bears is the credit risk that one party to a contract may default.

Settlement Price

A futures contract is marked-to-market each day. At the close of trading, the exchange on which the futures contract trades establishes a settlement price. This settlement price is used to compute the gains or losses on the futures contract for that day, which means that the change in the futures price over the day is credited (debited) to the account of the long (short) if the change is positive. If the change is negative, the account of the long (short) is debited (credited).

---

[5]This is an oversimplification of the issues. For each futures contract the clearing house has purchased, it has written a futures contract with the identical terms, implying that the clearing house has a matched book and no direct market exposure. However, the clearing house has a credit risk that a counterparty may default on its obligations to the clearing house. Market movements may have a significant effect on the size of this credit risk. A similar issue arises for options.

The American Stock Exchange, the Chicago Board Options Exchange, the National Association of Dealers, the New York Stock Exchange, the Pacific Stock Exchange, and the Philadelphia Stock Exchange have equal interests in the Options Clearing Corporation, which is the clearing house for securities options traded on U.S. securities markets. The Options Clearing Corporation has an AAA rating from Standard and Poor's Corporation. See Standard and Poor's *Creditweek* (1993).

Daily Settlement and Margins

When a person enters into a futures contract, the individual is required to deposit funds with the broker in what is called a **margin account.** Although the exchange sets the minimum margin required, the broker can set higher margin limits if he or she is concerned about the individual's ability to cover losses. The margin account may or may not earn interest. Often brokers will pay money market interest rates on margin accounts, at least for large accounts. The economic role of a margin account is to act as collateral in order to minimize the risk of failure by either party in the futures contract.

There are two types of margins: the **initial margin**, which is the initial amount put into a margin account to establish a futures position; and the **maintenance margin**, which is the minimum amount that must be kept in a margin account. The mechanics of these margin accounts are best explained with an example.

EXAMPLE | **Initial and Maintenance Margin Accounts**

Consider an individual, A, who on February 4 enters into a futures contract to buy 100 troy ounces of gold at the futures price of $365 per troy ounce. The initial margin for the contract is set at $2,000 and the maintenance margin is set at 75 percent of the initial margin, or $1,500.

Table 1.2 follows A's margin account over an eight-day period. On February 4, A establishes the initial margin by paying $2,000. On February 5, the futures price drops $3 per troy ounce to $362, implying that A's margin account is reduced to $1,700 = $2,000 − $3 × 100. On February 6, there is a further drop of $3, implying A's margin account at the beginning of the day, $1,400, is below the required maintenance margin of $1,500. There is a margin call of $600 made to individual A to reestablish the initial margin of $2,000. If A refuses to forward the required funds, the broker will close A's futures position.

Excess margin can be withdrawn from the margin account. For example, on February 7, the futures price rises to $364, implying that a gain of $500 is deposited into the margin account. Individual A can withdraw $500 at this time if he or she so wishes. Table 1.2 has individual A withdrawing all gains on the futures contract. ■

TABLE 1.2   *Margins and Marking-to-Market, in Dollars*

DATE	FUTURES PRICE	CASH FLOW	BEGINNING MARGIN	CASH WITHDRAWAL	ENDING MARGIN
2/4	365	0	0	−2,000	2,000
2/5	362	−300	1,700	0	1,700
2/6	359	−300	1,400	−600	2,000
2/7	364	+500	2,500	+500	2,000
2/8	365	+100	2,100	+100	2,000
2/11	367	+200	2,200	+200	2,000

Regulation

A major difference between futures and forward markets is that futures markets are regulated, but the forward markets are not. In the United States, the Commodity Futures Trading Commission (CFTC) was established in 1974 under an amendment to the Commodity Exchange Act of 1936 to regulate futures markets. The CFTC was given exclusive jurisdiction over trade on all organized U.S. futures markets with authority to approve new contracts and to amend the rules and regulations of commodity exchanges. However, since the introduction in 1974 of financial futures, the Securities Exchange Commission (SEC) and the Federal Reserve (Fed) have expressed concern about overlapping jurisdictions. This concern remains unresolved at this time.

The CFTC is required to consider at least two factors before approving a new futures contract proposal: (1) Does the contract serve a useful social function? and (2) Can the contract be manipulated? The issue of whether a contract serves a useful social function can be broken down into two areas. First, hedgers should be able to use the contract to reduce risk exposure; this is known as the insurance motive. For this situation to occur, the contract must also be attractive to speculators (those not trading for the purposes of risk reduction). Speculators must expect to earn an appropriate return for bearing the risk the hedgers shed; this is known as the speculation motive. Second, the proposed futures contract should help market participants predict the future spot price of the asset on which the contract is written, which is referred to as the **price discovery** role of futures markets.

The CFTC also needs to ensure that newly proposed futures contracts cannot be subject to price manipulation, an illegal action which occurs when a trader executes a sequence of trades designed to manipulate the price to his or her advantage. For example, one important form of price manipulation is a **corner** and **short squeeze**. To form a corner, a trader goes long the futures contract in excess of the immediately deliverable supply. By keeping this long position open, the trader will eventually acquire all the deliverable supply, that is, the trader has a monopoly position. A short squeeze occurs to those individuals with short positions. The long demands delivery, but the shorts cannot find any supply to cover their positions except from the long. The long can now extract a high price for the asset when selling to the shorts.

Under CFTC regulations, to break corners the CFTC can order the long trader to liquidate his or her position. For example, this happened with the Hunt brothers' holdings of silver futures in 1979 and 1980. To stop short squeezes, the CFTC can suspend trading and force settlement at a "fair" price set by the exchange issuing the contract. Contract provisions are also designed to increase the deliverable supply, which minimizes the likelihood of manipulation, by allowing variation in the quality of the asset delivered (with appropriate price adjustments) and by allowing a long delivery period.

Why Standardization? Why Daily Settlement?

If you want to establish a market in which there is large trading volume for each type of contract listed in order to maximize the exchange's revenue, how do you design a contract? First, to establish frequent trading, you must design contracts to minimize

the level of transaction costs. In this regard, if each trade involves a unique contract, there will be significant costs in specifying the details of each trade. Nonstandardization also implies that a secondary market where trading of issued contracts occurs will be difficult to establish because every contract must be specific to the individuals involved, hence demand for this contract by others is limited. Second, even if contracts are standardized, we still have the problem of determining whether the counterparty to each contract has the financial resources to fulfill his or her obligations. Traders want to be sure their contracts are fulfilled. As discussed earlier, the clearing house substantially reduces, but does not eliminate, the problem. The clearing house reduces this risk exposure by using margin accounts and daily settlements.

Basis

Before giving a formal definition of the basis, we want to introduce a few more symbols. Let $\mathcal{F}(t)$ denote the futures price at date t for delivery at date T. Let the contract be written on an asset with spot price $S(t)$. In a well-functioning market, the futures price equals the prevailing spot price at the delivery date of the futures contract. Indeed, the futures price at date T for immediate delivery is equivalent to purchasing the asset in the spot market, therefore

$$\mathcal{F}(T) = S(T).$$

Prior to maturity, the spot price need not equal the futures price. The difference between these two prices, the **futures-spot** basis, is defined by[6]

$$\text{Basis} \equiv \mathcal{F}(t) - S(t).$$

FIGURE 1.4 *Basis*

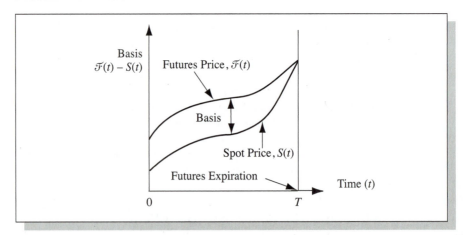

---

[6]Note that the futures spot basis is sometimes defined as $S(t) - \mathcal{F}(t)$.

TABLE 1.3   *Futures Newspaper Quote*

	OPEN	HIGH	LOW	SETTLE	CHANGE	LIFETIME HIGH	LIFETIME LOW	OPEN INTEREST
GOLD (Cmx.Div.NYM)-100 troy oz.; $ per troy oz.								
June	293.70	294.20	292.30	292.70	− 1.00	489.50	281.50	22,007
July	....	....	294.10	− .80	295.00	294.50	3
Aug	296.00	297.00	295.30	295.60	− .60	403.80	284.50	56,602
Oct	298.90	299.50	297.50	297.80	− .60	347.80	290.00	5,955
Dec	300.60	301.30	299.30	299.80	− .60	505.00	287.00	20,097
Fb99	301.50	301.50	301.50	301.50	− .60	349.50	294.50	9,309
Apr	304.00	304.00	304.00	303.30	− .60	351.20	291.50	7,974
June	304.50	306.40	304.40	305.10	− .60	520.00	295.40	11,830
Aug	307.80	308.00	307.80	306.90	− .60	327.00	305.00	391
Oct	....	....	308.70	− .60	....	....	200
Dec	311.00	311.00	311.00	310.50	− .60	506.00	299.50	6,484
Ju00	....	....	316.00	− .60	473.50	309.50	4,549
Dec	....	....	321.60	− .60	474.50	312.40	4,944
Ju01	....	....	327.10	− .60	447.00	347.00	2,152
Dec	....	....	332.40	− .60	429.50	320.00	4,856
Ju02	....	....	338.00	− .60	385.00	335.00	1,474
Dec	....	....	343.60	− .60	....	....	205

Est vol 90,000; vol Wd 81,945; open int 159,032, +9,254.

Exchange Abbreviations:
CMX—Chicago Mercantile Exchange
NYM—New York Mercantile Exchange

Source: *The Wall Street Journal*, May 29, 1998.

A typical pattern is shown in Figure 1.4. In this example, at date 0 the basis is shown to be positive. However, this is not always the case. The basis can be negative when significantly positive cash flows or benefits are received via storage of the spot commodity. As the futures contract matures, the basis converges to zero as the futures price converges to the spot price. This is seen in Figure 1.4 where the two curves intersect at the futures delivery date, date *T*. This relationship between the spot price and futures price will be examined in more detail in Chapter 2.

Newspaper Quotes

Table 1.3 gives an example of quoted futures prices, as reported as *The Wall Street Journal* on May 29, 1998. The figures refer to the trading that took place the day before (in this case May 28, 1998). The contract is identified as the gold 100 troy ounce contract traded on the Chicago Mercantile Exchange (CMX).

Expiry cycle

Every contract is given an expiry cycle by the exchange on which the contract is traded. These are listed in the first column on the left side of the page. The first date is June (1998), the second date is July (1998), and so forth. When the delivery date is reached (the last four business days of the delivery month), the contract is dropped from the table.

Open

The Open column refers to the price at which the first contract of the day was transacted. For the June (1998) contract, the open price was $293.70. This open price will in general be different from the previous day's settlement price. The previous day's settlement price can be determined by using the Change column (discussed below).

High and low

The High and Low columns refer to the contract's highest and lowest prices for the day. For the first June contract which opened at $293.70, the futures price during the day never went above $294.20 or below $292.30.

Settle

The Settle column refers to the settlement price. This is the futures price used to adjust all investors' margin accounts for the daily change in futures prices. For the June (1998) contract, the settle price is $292.70.

Change

The Change column refers to the change in the settlement price from the previous day. For the June (1998) contract, the change is $-$1.00. This means that the previous day's settlement price was $293.70. For an investor with a long position in one contract, his or her margin account would be debited $100 ($= -100 \times$1.00$).

Lifetime high and low

The Lifetime High/Low column refers to the highest and the lowest futures price ever observed in the trading for a particular contract. For the June (1998) contract, the highest recorded futures price for this contract was $489.50 per ounce and the lowest price recorded was $281.50.

Open interest

The Open Interest refers to the total number of contracts outstanding. For the gold futures contract this is 159,032 contracts.

Est. vol.

The "Est vol" refers to the estimated volume of trading in all futures for this contract. For gold futures this volume is 90,000 contracts. Also given is the estimated volume for the previous day and the total open interest.

This completes the institutional description of futures contracts. We will return again in subsequent chapters to futures contracts when we analyze their pricing and hedging.

1.3 OPTIONS

There are two basic types of option contracts: **call** options and **put** options. A call option gives the holder the right to buy an asset at a stated price (called the exercise or strike price) on or before a stated date (called the maturity or expiration date). Conversely, a put option gives the holder the right to sell an asset at a stated price on or before a stated date.

The names "call" and "put" come from the actions potentially taken by the holders of the contracts (the long position). Call options give the holder the option to buy, that is, to **call** the asset away from someone. Put options give the holder the option to sell, or to **put** the asset to someone else.

The **premium** is the price paid for an option. Because each option can be viewed as a type of insurance contract for hedging risks, the terminology is analogous to that used for the price paid to purchase (life) insurance contracts.

In general, call and put options are defined in one of two ways: American or European. A European option can only be exercised at the maturity date of the option, whereas an American option can be exercised at any time up to and including the maturity date. The definitions of a call and of a put option given above are of the American type. Because these adjectives—European and American—refer to when the exercise of the option can occur, the names have no relation to geographic considerations. European options trade on the American continent, and American options trade in Europe.

Call Options

Consider first a European call option written on an asset with spot price $S(t)$ where t denotes the current date. The option is assumed to mature at date T. The exercise price (strike price) of the option is denoted by K.

Let us consider the payoff to the option at its maturity date. The call option gives its owner the right to buy the asset at the exercise price K. If the asset price at this date, $S(T)$, is less than the exercise price, the call option is worthless. This is because the owner can buy the asset more cheaply in the market than she can by exercising the option. For example, if the asset's price at maturity is $20 and the strike price is $25, the option is worthless. The option holder would be better off buying the asset in the spot market. If the asset's price at maturity $S(T)$ is greater than the exercise price K, the option owner can exercise the option and obtain the asset at the exercise price saving $S(T) - K$. For example, if the asset's price at maturity is $27 and the strike price is $25, the option is worth $2.

We can write the call option's payoff at maturity in the form[7]

$$c(T) \equiv \begin{cases} S(T) - K & \text{if} \quad S(T) \geq K \\ 0 & \text{if} \quad S(T) < K. \end{cases}$$

This is sometimes called the call option's **boundary condition**. This payoff is shown in Figure 1.5. The payoff curve starts at a 0 value when the asset price is zero and runs horizontally at zero until the asset's price rises to K. At this time, the curve increases in value one dollar for each dollar increase in the asset's price. When the asset's price exceeds K, the call option is said to be **in-the-money**. Gains from holding the call option are unlimited. Losses are bounded below by zero. The option's profit is the payoff minus the initial cost of the option, thus the maximum one can lose from owning a call option is the initial cost.

Having defined call options, we can now compare them to futures contracts. The first important difference between an option and a futures contract is that the option owner has the right, but not the obligation, to exercise the contract. For a futures contract, the owner is obligated to execute the contract. The second important difference is the fact that the payoff function for options is truncated below while the futures contract's payoff is not. Compare Figure 1.5 to Figure 1.2. In Figure 1.5, the truncated payoff arises because if the asset price is less than the exercise price, the option owner need

FIGURE 1.5 *Payoff to the Owner of a Call Option at Maturity*

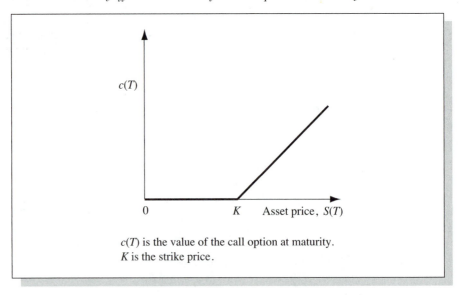

$c(T)$ is the value of the call option at maturity.
K is the strike price.

---

[7]A shorthand way of expressing this payoff is $c(T) = \text{Max}\{S(T) - K, 0\}$. Suppose that $K = 25$ and $S(T) = 20$, implying $S(T) - K = -5$. The maximum of -5 and 0 is 0. The value of the option is $c(T) = 0$. If $S(T) = 27$, then $S(T) - K = 2$ and the maximum of 2 and 0 is 2.

FIGURE 1.6 *Payoff to the Writer of a Call Option at Maturity*

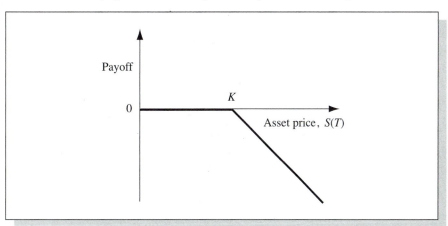

not exercise the option. The maximum the option owner can lose is the initial cost of buying the option. In contrast, the futures contract's losses are unlimited below. This brings us to the third important difference: when you buy an option, there is an up-front payment (the **premium**). This differs from a futures contract that has—ignoring margin requirements—zero initial value and a zero initial cash flow. The final difference is that futures contracts have marking-to-market (daily cash flows) and options do not.

Options, like futures, are written (issued) by individuals. For every buyer, there must be a seller, or writer. Such a contract is said to be in **zero net-supply**. Figure 1.6 shows the payoff to the writer of the call option considered in Figure 1.5. The payoff to the written call is similar to that of the long call, but reflected across the horizontal axis. If the option expires worthless—the asset price being less than the exercise price—the option writer is happy. The option writer has the initial premium and no additional obligation. If the option expires in-the-money, the option writer is unhappy. The option is worth $S(T) - K$, which must be paid by the writer. What is the maximum amount the writer can lose? Theoretically, the loss is unlimited! The writing of an option without any offsetting position in an underlying asset is referred to as writing a **naked option**. Writing a call option, while simultaneously owning the underlying stock, is called a **covered call**.

Put Options

Now consider a European put option written on the same asset. Let the option mature at date T and the exercise price (strike price) be K. Consider the option's payoff at maturity. If the asset's price at maturity is greater than the exercise price, the option is worthless. Suppose the exercise price is $25 and the asset's price at maturity is $27. A put option gives you the right to sell the asset at $25, but this right is worthless because the asset is selling for $27.

Next, if the asset's price $S(T)$ is less than the exercise price K then exercising the put is optimal. Selling the asset at the exercise price generates a profit of $K - S(T)$. For example, if the asset's price is $19, the option to sell the asset for $25 is worth $6 ($= \$25 - 19$). We can write the option's payoff in the form[8]

$$p(T) \equiv \begin{cases} 0 & \text{if} \quad S(T) > K \\ K - S(T) & \text{if} \quad S(T) \leq K. \end{cases}$$

This is sometimes called the put option's boundary condition. The payoff is shown in Figure 1.7. The payoff to the put option starts at its highest value of K dollars if the asset is worthless at maturity. It then decreases one dollar in value for each dollar increase in the asset's price until it has zero value. This occurs when the asset's price equals the exercise price of K dollars. For higher asset values, the put is worthless and the put is said to be **out-of-the-money**.

Contrary to one's first impression, a put option's payoff is not equivalent to the payoff from a written call option, as a comparison of Figures 1.6 and 1.7 shows. Although both positions are **bearish** on the asset's price, that is, they increase in value when the asset price declines, their payoffs are quite different. A key distinction is that both the gains and losses to the put option are bounded. This is not the case, however, with a written call. A written call has bounded gains and unbounded losses. It

FIGURE 1.7   *Payoff to the Owner of a Put Option at Maturity*

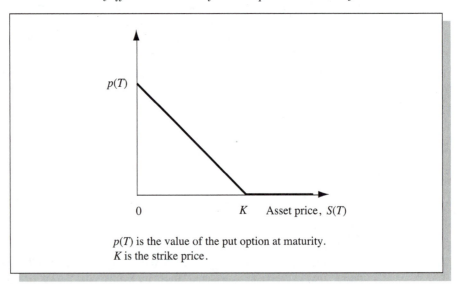

$p(T)$ is the value of the put option at maturity.
K is the strike price.

---

[8] A shorthand way of expressing this payoff is $p(T) = \text{Max } \{K - S(T), 0\}$. Suppose that $K = 20$ and $S(T) = 15$, implying that $K - S(T) = 5$. The maximum of 5 and 0 is 5. If $S(T) = 24$, then $K - S(T) = -4$ and the maximum of -4 and 0 is 0.

FIGURE 1.8   *Payoff to the Writer of a Put Option at Maturity*

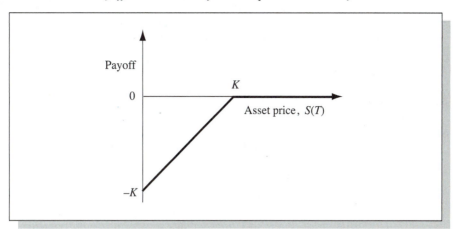

is this distinction that makes the valuation of an American-type put option more difficult than the valuation of an American-type call option. This insight will be explained in Chapter 7.

A European put option is one of the easiest derivative securities to understand, as it is directly analogous to an insurance policy written on the asset. The insurance policy can only be cashed in at its maturity date. The put's price (the **premium**) is the fee paid to ensure the value of the asset to K dollars. If the asset's value at maturity drops below K dollars, the put (insurance) is exercised (cashed in), and one receives K dollars for the asset. If the asset's value at maturity is above K dollars, the put (insurance) is discarded as worthless. This insight that a put option is equivalent to an insurance contract on the underlying asset will be useful to us later in Chapter 3 when we study put–call parity, the relation between call and put options.

What is the payoff to the writer of a put option at maturity? Suppose that the asset price $S(T)$ is greater than the exercise price. The owner of the put option is unhappy, of course, because the option is worthless. The writer is pleased because there is no payout to the owner. If the asset's price at maturity was less than the exercise price, the option is worth $K - S(T)$ to its owner. This represents a loss to the writer of the option. This payoff is graphed in Figure 1.8. The maximum gain to the owner occurs if the asset's price at maturity is zero. If this happens the value of the option is K, thus the maximum loss to the writer is K dollars, the exercise price.

American versus European Options

Remember that American and European options differ with respect to when the contracts can be exercised. An American option allows for an extra degree of freedom. The holder of an American option can exercise the option any time he or she wishes. In contrast, a European option can only be exercised at maturity. This additional flexibility

makes the American option at least as valuable as its European counterpart. More will be said about this later in Chapter 7.

The majority of options traded on organized exchanges are American options. Examples of traded European options are the Chicago Board Options Exchange's (CBOE) Standard and Poor's 500 Index Options (SPX), options on 13-week U.S. Treasury bills (IRX), and options on long-term rates (LTX).

1.4 ORGANIZED OPTION MARKETS

Options are traded in the over-the-counter (OTC) market and on organized exchanges. OTC markets are markets conducted via phones and computers between various commercial and investment banks. In contrast, organized exchanges have a physical location at which trades take place. The first time options traded on an organized exchange occurred in April 1973 at the Chicago Board Options Exchange (CBOE). Coincidentally, this timing coincided with the landmark publications on option pricing by Black and Scholes and by Merton. Today there are organized option markets in all the major financial centers of the world. Option contracts traded on an organized exchange are standardized as to (1) the exercise prices available, (2) the maturity dates, (3) the number of units of the asset that can be purchased (call) or sold (put) per option contract, and (4) the procedures dealing with stock splits and dividends. We shall discuss these standardized provisions for stock options listed on the CBOE. All these options are of the American type.

Exercise (strike) prices

Exercise (strike) prices are generally spaced around the current price of the stock. The spacing is at $2.50 intervals for a stock price between $5 and $25, at $5 intervals for a stock price in the range $25 to $200, and at $10 intervals for stock prices above $200. When options are first listed, strike prices are spaced to surround the current stock price. If the stock price moves outside this range, new stock options are issued to ensure that this spacing is preserved. The trading volume in options is usually the highest for strikes near the current stock price. Options that are deep-in- or deep-out-of-the-money usually have very little trading volume associated with them. This is why new stock options are listed when the stock price moves a lot.

Maturity dates

The exchange assigns a particular stock to an expiry cycle. For a particular cycle, there are three expiry dates, each separated by a three-month period. For example, January, April, and July options expire on the third Friday of the expiry month, either January, April, or July. For options expiring in January, new options are issued with an expiry date in October.

After 1985, these rules were changed in order to allow more expiry months. Now, for each stock, options can be traded over the nearest two months and the next

two months of the original expiry cycle. For example, at the start of February, stocks that are in an April, July, October cycle can have options that mature in February, March, April, and July; stocks that are in a February, May, August cycle can have options that mature in February, March, May, and August; and stocks that mature in a March, June, September cycle can have options that mature in February, March, June, and September.

Size of contract

For stock options, each option contract is for 100 shares of stock. This may be adjusted if there is a stock split or stock dividend. Option premiums are quoted on a per share basis.

Stock splits and dividends

Listed stock options are not adjusted for regular cash dividends, but they are adjusted for stock splits and stock dividends. The adjustment for stock splits and stock dividends is made on the ex-dividend day or ex-split day, the same day the actual stock price reflects the stock dividend or stock split on the stock exchange. The rules for a split or stock dividend are complicated and depend upon whether the split or stock dividend is an integer multiple, such as 2 for 1, or fractional, such as 3 for 2.

Let us consider the first case. Suppose the XYZ Company declares a 3 for 1 split. Now consider an investor who owns a call option with exercise price $60. On the ex-distribution day, the number of options will be increased by a factor of 3 and the exercise price will be reduced by a factor of 3. The aggregate exercise price before the split was $100 \times \$60 = \$6,000$. After the split, the aggregate exercise price is $3 \times 100 \times \$20 = \$6,000$. These are the same. This adjustment makes the option contract neutral with respect to a stock split.

For the second case, suppose there is a 3 for 2 split. The exercise price of the option is divided by the split ratio (in this case 1.5), and rounded to the nearest one-eighth of a point. However, instead of adjusting the number of contracts, the number of shares represented by each contract is multiplied by the split ratio. Before the split, the exercise price is $60. After the split, the price becomes $40 ($= 60/1.5$) and the number of shares 150 ($= 100 \times 1.5$). The aggregate exercise price before the split was $6,000. After the split, the aggregate exercise price is $150 \times \$40 = \$6,000$. Again, this adjustment makes the option contract neutral with respect to a stock split. Note that this is the ideal case. Occasionally, the rounding to a nearest one-eighth of a point can cause some difficulty. For example, suppose that the exercise price is $55. After the split, the price becomes $36\frac{5}{8}$ rounding to the nearest $\frac{1}{8}$. The aggregate exercise before the split was $100 \times \$55 = \$5,500$ and after the split $150 \times \$36\frac{5}{8} = \$5,493\frac{3}{4}$, a reduction of $\$6\frac{1}{4}$. The option contract in this case is reduced in value because of the stock split.

1.5 OPTION NEWSPAPER QUOTES

Table 1.4 gives an example of quoted stock option prices as reported in the May 29, 1998 issue of *The Wall Street Journal*. The figures refer to the trading that took place the previous day.

Stock identification

The first column identifies the stock on which the options are written. For example, the first group of options is written on AT&T, the second group is written on Aames, and so forth.

Option and NY close price

The price listed under the company's name in the first column refers to the closing price of the stock on Thursday, May 28, 1998. For AT&T, the closing stock price was $60\frac{1}{2}$. There is one exception. Look at Aames; there is only one option contract recorded on this stock. Consequently, all the information is given on one line and the stock's closing price is omitted.

TABLE 1.4   *Option Newspaper Quotes*

OPTION	STRIKE	EXP.	CALL VOL.	CALL LAST	PUT VOL.	PUT LAST
AT&T	55	Oct	291	$7\frac{3}{4}$	25	$1\frac{11}{16}$
$60\frac{1}{2}$	60	Jun	483	2	57	$1\frac{1}{4}$
$60\frac{1}{2}$	60	Jul	335	$2\frac{5}{8}$	132	$2\frac{1}{16}$
$60\frac{1}{2}$	60	Oct	193	$4\frac{3}{4}$	10	$3\frac{7}{8}$
$60\frac{1}{2}$	65	Jun	321	$\frac{3}{8}$	20	$4\frac{3}{4}$
$60\frac{1}{2}$	65	Jul	201	$\frac{7}{8}$	60	$5\frac{1}{2}$
$60\frac{1}{2}$	70	Jan	258	$2\frac{1}{2}$	...	...
Aames	$12\frac{1}{2}$	Jul	250	$1\frac{13}{16}$	...	...
Adaptc	15	Oct	714	$3\frac{1}{8}$	40	$1\frac{3}{4}$
16	15	Jan	4	$3\frac{5}{8}$	2020	$2\frac{1}{8}$
AdobeS	45	Jul	178	$1\frac{3}{8}$	10	5
$41\frac{7}{8}$	45	Oct	154	$3\frac{1}{4}$	...	...
A M D	20	Jun	156	$1\frac{3}{8}$	122	1
$20\frac{1}{8}$	$22\frac{1}{2}$	Jun	539	$\frac{9}{16}$	23	$2\frac{7}{8}$
$20\frac{1}{8}$	$22\frac{1}{2}$	Jul	324	$1\frac{1}{8}$	657	$3\frac{3}{8}$
$20\frac{1}{8}$	25	Jun	960	$\frac{1}{4}$	628	$4\frac{7}{8}$
$20\frac{1}{8}$	25	Jul	153	$\frac{9}{16}$	20	$5\frac{1}{8}$
$20\frac{1}{8}$	25	Jan	152	$2\frac{1}{2}$	3	6
Agourn	30	Jul	200	$4\frac{5}{8}$	...	...

Source: *The Wall Street Journal*, May 29, 1998.

Strike price

The second column refers to the strike or exercise price of the option. The first option for AT&T has an exercise price of $55. The second row is for another option on AT&T with a strike price of $60, and so forth. Note that the strikes listed surround the current stock price of 60\frac{1}{2}$.

Expiry cycle

The remaining rows refer to the expiry months. Stock options expire on the third Friday of their expiry month.

Premiums

The figures under the column labeled "Last" are the closing prices for the different options. For example, the AT&T October call option with exercise price $55 closed at 7\frac{3}{4}$ and the put option at 1\frac{11}{16}$.

1.6 INTEREST RATES AND BOND PRICES

In this section we collect the definitions for various interest rates used throughout the text. These interest rates will be for default-free investments of various maturities. The notation may be somewhat confusing, but the basic concept is simple. Each interest rate corresponds to a different way of quoting a zero-coupon bond's price.

Different markets have different conventions for quoting interest rates. For example, Treasury bills are quoted differently from Eurodollar deposits. We must be aware of these differences to understand the various markets. First we discuss zero-coupon bond prices, then discount rates, simple interest rates, discretely compounded rates, and continuously compounded rates. All of these rates are used in this text. We will give a related discussion in Chapter 12.

Zero-Coupon Bond Prices

A **zero-coupon bond** is a bond that makes no coupon or interest payment over its lifetime. It is purchased at an initial price, and the interest earned is determined by the bond's payoff at maturity. Let $B(0, T)$ denote today's (time 0) value of a zero-coupon bond that pays one dollar at its maturity date T. The **face value** of the bond is the amount paid at maturity, one dollar. The relationship between zero-coupon bond prices ($B(0, T)$) and their maturities (T) is called the term structure of zero-coupon bond prices and it implies a **term structure of interest rates**.

An example of a term structure of zero-coupon bond prices is given in Table 1.5. Listed are the prices of zero-coupon bonds for four different maturities. We see that today, at date 0, it costs 0.9560 dollars to receive one dollar in one year's time. It costs 0.9117 dollars today to receive one dollar in two years' time. As the maturity of the

TABLE 1.5   *An Example of a Term Structure of Zero-Coupon Bond Prices*

MATURITY (YEARS)	PRICE $B(0,T)$
1	0.9560
2	0.9117
3	0.8685
4	0.8250

bond increases, the less expensive its price is today. This relationship is often called "the time value of money." Most individuals would prefer a dollar sooner than later. Hence, the maturity of a bond is inversely related to its cost. The prices in Table 1.5 are the discount factors used to compute present values of known cash flows at future dates. Because of this, these zero-coupon bonds and their prices will be fundamental to the concepts in this text.

The relation between maturity and the price of a zero-coupon bond is often analyzed by transforming prices into interest rates. A number of different interest rates are used in different markets. We will describe many of these interest rates, which differ for various reasons. One reason is that in the various markets there are different conventions with respect to the number of days in a year. In some markets, such as the Treasury bill market, the usual convention is a 360-day year. In Eurodollar markets, both a 360- and a 365-day year convention are used.

Discount Rates

Discount rates are used in the Treasury bill market where instruments have maturities of a year or less. The discount rate i_d over the period $[0, T]$, expressed on a per annum basis, is implicitly defined by

$$B(0,T) = 1 - i_d \frac{T}{360},\tag{1.1}$$

where T is the maturity of the zero-coupon bond expressed in days. Notice that a 360-day year is assumed. There is no compounding of interest in Expression (1.1). Rearranging this expression and quoting the discount rate in percentage form gives[9]

$$i_d = 100[1 - B(0,T)](360/T).\tag{1.2}$$

---

[9]Formally, the discount rate in Expression (1.2) should depend on the maturity date T. We omit this dependence for simplicity.

EXAMPLE   **Discount Rates**

Using the Treasury bill prices in Table 1.6, we have

30 days	$i_d = 100[1 - 0.9967](360/30) = 3.96$ percent
60 days	$i_d = 100[1 - 0.9931](360/60) = 4.14$ percent
90 days	$i_d = 100[1 - 0.9894](360/90) = 4.24$ percent
180 days	$i_d = 100[1 - 0.9784](360/180) = 4.32$ percent

For this table, discount rates are increasing with term to maturity. This is an **upward sloping** term structure of interest rates and is the most commonly observed shape for such rates.   ■

Simple Interest Rates

Simple interest rates are often used in the specification of interest rate derivative contracts like caps or swaps in the over-the-counter markets. The simple interest rate over the period [0, *T*], expressed on a per annum basis, is implicitly defined by

$$B(0,T) = \frac{1}{1 + i_S \times \dfrac{T}{365}}, \qquad (1.3)$$

where *T* is the maturity of the zero-coupon bond expressed in days. In Expression (1.3), a 365-day year is assumed. Notice that this expression assumes no compounding of interest. Rearranging this expression and quoting the simple interest rate in percentage form gives

$$i_S = 100\left[\frac{1}{B(0,T)} - 1\right]\left(\frac{365}{T}\right). \qquad (1.4)$$

TABLE 1.6   *Treasury Bill Prices*

MATURITY *T* (DAYS)	PRICE $B(0,T)$
30	0.9967
60	0.9931
90	0.9894
180	0.9784

EXAMPLE

Simple Interest Rates

Using the Treasury bill prices in Table 1.6, we have

30 days	$i_S = 100 \left[\dfrac{1}{0.9967} - 1 \right] (365/30) = 4.03$ percent
60 days	$i_S = 100 \left[\dfrac{1}{0.9931} - 1 \right] (365/60) = 4.23$ percent
90 days	$i_S = 100 \left[\dfrac{1}{0.9894} - 1 \right] (365/90) = 4.34$ percent
180 days	$i_S = 100 \left[\dfrac{1}{0.9784} - 1 \right] (365/180) = 4.48$ percent

Again, the simple interest rates indicate an upward sloping term structure of interest rates. ■

Discretely Compounded Interest Rates

Discretely compounded interest rates are used for valuing long dated coupon-bearing bonds. A discretely compounded interest rate over the period $[0, T]$ is defined as the interest rate earned per period, before compounding, on the zero-coupon bond. This is expressed in the form

$$B(0,T) = \frac{1}{[1 + i_c]^T}. \tag{1.5}$$

Compounding occurs T times in Expression (1.5) because there are T time periods over which the discount rate applies. The following example will clarify this concept.

EXAMPLE

Yearly Compounded Interest Rates

Using the data in Table 1.5, we want to compute the yearly compounded annual rate of interest for the one-year zero-coupon bond:

$$B(0,1) = 0.9560 = \frac{1}{1 + i_c},$$

implying

$$i_c = 4.60 \text{ percent.}$$

Yearly compounding means that the interest earned is compounded once a year.

For the two-year zero-coupon bond, the two-year annual rate of interest is defined by

$$B(0,2) = 0.9117 = \frac{1}{[1 + i_c]^2},$$

implying

$$i_c = 4.73 \text{ percent.}$$

Over the two years, compounding occurs twice, implying that interest is earned on interest once. By investing \$0.9117 for two years, the total value of the principal plus interest at the end of the first year is $0.9117 + 0.9117 \times 0.0473 = \$0.9548$. The total value of the investment at the end of the second year is $0.9548 + 0.9548 \times 0.0473 = \$1.00$.

For the three-year zero-coupon bond, the three-year annual rate of interest is defined by

$$B(0,3) = 0.8685 = \frac{1}{[1 + i_c]^3},$$

implying

$$i_c = 4.81 \text{ percent.}$$

We leave it to you to verify that, for the four-year zero-coupon bond, the four-year annual rate of interest is

$$i_c = 4.93 \text{ percent.}$$

Again, the term structure of these interest rates is upward sloping. ∎

The previous example has compounding once each year. However, compounding is sometimes done on a more frequent basis. For coupon-bearing bonds, it is done on a semiannual basis. If semiannual compounding is used, the annual rate of interest over the period $[0, T]$ is defined by

$$B(0,T) = \frac{1}{\{1 + i_c(1/2)\}^{2T}}. \tag{1.6}$$

The yearly rate i_c applies to half a year, hence it is necessarily multiplied by a $(1/2)$ in the denominator. The number of compounding periods is $2T$, which explains the exponent in Expression (1.6). Note that our notation for i_c does not differentiate the number of compounding periods utilized. The reader is forewarned to be careful when seeing this notation to determine the number of compounding periods involved. It is usually not a problem.

EXAMPLE   **Semiannually Compounded Interest Rates**

Using the data in Table 1.5, we compute the rate of interest on a per-year basis using semiannual compounding. For the one-year zero-coupon bond:

$$B(0,1) = 0.9560 = \frac{1}{\{1 + i_c(1/2)\}^2},$$

implying

$$i_c = 4.55 \text{ percent.}$$

For the two-year zero-coupon bond:

$$B(0,2) = 0.9117 = \frac{1}{\{1 + i_c(1/2)\}^4},$$

implying

$$i_c = 4.68 \text{ percent.}$$

We leave it to you to check that

$$i_c = 4.76 \text{ percent}$$

and

$$i_c = 4.87 \text{ percent.}$$

This term structure of interest rates is upward sloping.   ■

Banks often compound daily when paying interest on demand deposits. This necessitates studying more frequent compounding intervals. If compounding is done m times each year, the annual rate of interest over the period $[0, T]$ is defined by

$$B(0,T) = \frac{1}{\{1 + i_c(1/m)\}^{mT}}. \tag{1.7}$$

Here there are m periods per year, so the appropriate rate per period is the yearly rate divided by m, or i_c/m. There are $m \cdot T$ compounding periods over the discounting horizon T. This explains the exponent in Expression (1.7).

EXAMPLE **Quarterly Compounded Interest Rates**

Using the data in Table 1.5, we want to compute the annual rate of interest, using quarterly compounding. For the one-year zero-coupon bond:

$$B(0,1) = 0.9560 = \frac{1}{\{1 + i_c(1/4)\}^4},$$

implying

$$i_c = 4.53 \text{ percent.}$$

We leave it to you to check that

for 2 years, $i_c = 4.65$ percent;
for 3 years, $i_c = 4.73$ percent;

and

for 4 years, $i_c = 4.84$ percent. ∎

Continuously Compounded Interest Rates

Sometimes commercial banks quote interest rates on demand deposit accounts using continuously compounded interest rates. Continuously compounded rates are also useful for pricing derivatives in continuous time models. A continuously compounded rate of interest over the period $[0, T]$ is implicitly defined by

$$B(0,T) = e^{-rT}, \tag{1.8}$$

implying

$$r = -\{\ln[B(0,T)]\}/T. \tag{1.9}$$

EXAMPLE **Continuously Compounded Interest Rates**

Using the data in Table 1.5, we compute the continuously compounded rate of interest. For the one-year zero-coupon bond:

$$B(0,1) = 0.9560 = e^{-r},$$

implying

   $r = 4.50$ percent.

For the two-year zero-coupon bond:

   $B(0,2) = 0.9117 = e^{-r2}$,

implying

   $r = 4.62$ percent.

For the three-year zero-coupon bond:

   $B(0,3) = 0.8685 = e^{-r3}$,

implying

   $r = 4.70$ percent.

For the four year zero-coupon bond:

   $B(0,4) = 0.8250 = e^{-r4}$,

implying

   $r = 4.81$ percent.   ■

1.7 SUMMARY

In this chapter we have given a brief introduction to forward contracts, futures contracts, and options. Forward contracts are over-the-counter contracts. Futures contracts are traded on organized exchanges and are standardized. Futures contracts, unlike forward contracts, are marked-to-market at the end of each trading date. Option contracts are traded both in organized markets and over-the-counter. There are two types of option contracts, calls and puts. Call options convey the right to buy, while put options convey the right to sell. Option contracts can be exercised at the discretion of the option owner, unlike forward or futures contracts, which are contractual obligations. Finally, we discussed some of the interest rates that will be used throughout the text.

REFERENCES

Chicago Board of Trade, 1989. *The Commodity Trading Manual.*
Standard and Poor's *Creditweek* (February 1, 1993), 52–54.

QUESTIONS

Short Questions

1. What is hedging? What is speculation? Explain the differences between the actions.
2. A financial institution writes a forward contract to sell 10 million pounds sterling at the delivery price of $1.6247 per pound in 30 days' time. At the end of the contract the spot exchange rate was $1.65 per pound. What was the profit to the financial institution?
3. What is the difference between shorting a stock and writing a call option?
4. Suppose you have written 100 futures contracts on gold. How can you use call options to provide insurance against a decline in the value of net position?
5. Suppose that you have written a forward contract on a market index, such as the S&P 500. How can you use call and put options to completely offset the risk?

Question 1

a) What are the four differences between forward contracts and futures contracts?
b) Of the two types of contracts, forwards and futures, which contract has more counterparty risk? Why?

Question 2

Consider a futures contract on an asset with spot price $S(t)$. Let $\mathcal{F}(t)$ denote the futures price at date t for delivery at date T.

a) What is the basis?
b) What must the basis be at the delivery date? Why?

Question 3

Consider a European call option on an asset with price $S(t)$, strike price K, and maturity T.

a) What is the payoff to this call option at date T?

Consider a European put option on the same asset $S(t)$ with strike price K and maturity T.

b)   What is the payoff to this put option at date T?
c)   Is the payoff to the call option exactly opposite to the payoff to the put option? Explain.

Question 4

Consider a portfolio composed of two options written on the same stock:

(1)   long a call option with a strike price K.
(2)   short a put option with a strike price K.

Both options mature at date T.

a)   What is the value of this portfolio at date T?
b)   What other derivative has the same type of payoff?

Question 5

Suppose LMN Company has calls traded on the Chicago Board of Options Exchange with strike 100 and maturity nine months.

a)   If LMN declares a 2-for-1 stock split, how will the call's provisions be adjusted?
b)   If LMN declares a 4-for-3 split, how will the call's provisions be adjusted?
c)   Are the adjustments neutral in (a) and (b)?

Question 6

Consider the zero-coupon bond prices:

ZERO-COUPON BOND PRICE	MATURITY (DAYS)
0.999182	30
0.996750	60
0.992738	90
0.980844	180

a)   Compute the discount rates i_d for these bonds.
b)   Compute the simple interest rates i_S for these bonds.
c)   Compute the discretely compounded rate per year, i_c, for these bonds.

d) Compute the continuously compounded rate of interest r for these bonds.

e) Compare these rates in a table. Is there any relationship between i_d and i_s? Is there any relationship between i_c and r?

(Assume a 365-day year in all cases.)

Question 7

The discount rate is 5.85 percent for a 135-day zero-coupon bond, assuming a 360-day year. What is the discount rate assuming a 365-day year?

Question 8

The simple interest rate for an 85-day instrument is 4.95 percent, assuming a 360-day year. What is the simple interest rate assuming a 365-day year?

Question 9

The discount rate is 4.75 percent for a 97-day instrument, assuming a 360-day year. What is the simple interest rate assuming a 360-day year?

Question 10

The simple rate for a 117-day instrument is 5.15 percent, assuming a 365-day year. What is the discount rate assuming a 360-day year?

Simple Arbitrage Relationships for Forward and Futures Contracts

2.0 INTRODUCTION

In this chapter, we discuss the determinants of forward prices and futures prices. We use simple arbitrage arguments to understand (1) the relationship between the forward price and the spot price of the underlying asset, and (2) the relationship between the futures price and the spot price of the underlying asset. Forward contracts are generally easier to analyze than futures contracts because with forward contracts there is only a single payment at the maturity date. Consequently, much of our discussion focuses on forward contracts. We will show that the relationship between forward prices and spot prices depends upon whether the underlying asset is held solely for investment purposes by the majority of investors, such as with forward contracts on foreign currencies, or whether it is primarily held for productive purposes, such as with forward contracts on commodities. It also depends upon whether it is possible to store the underlying asset. For financial assets, storage costs are minimal. For commodities such as oil, gold, and wheat, storage costs can be substantial. For assets such as electricity, storage costs can be infinite, because with current technology it is not possible to store large amounts of electricity for extended periods of time.

We start by defining arbitrage, a key concept underlying most of the results in this text. We then apply this concept to determine the forward price for a variety of different assets. The same basic argument is repeated for each type of asset. The chapter finishes by considering the relationship between forward and futures contracts. We show that if interest rates are deterministic, forward and futures prices must be equal. However, if interest rates are stochastic (uncertain), forward prices differ from futures prices.

2.1 DEFINITION OF ARBITRAGE

Arbitrage is any trading strategy requiring no cash input that has some probability of making profits without any risk of a loss. To clarify the meaning of this definition, consider starting out with zero cash. You formulate an investment strategy involving a portfolio of securities. Because you have zero cash, the purchase of any securities

must be financed by borrowing or short selling other securities. You cleverly design this investment strategy such that the worst possible outcome will leave you where you started—with zero cash—but in other possible outcomes, the strategy generates positive profits. Although it is uncertain how much your wealth will increase, there is no risk of a loss. This is a key characteristic of the investment strategy; such a trading strategy is called an **arbitrage opportunity**.

If arbitrage opportunities exist, the actions of **arbitrageurs** (those who take advantage of arbitrage opportunities) will eventually cause prices to adjust until arbitrage is no longer possible. One cannot expect to continually earn arbitrage profits in well-functioning capital markets. Why not? Because if prices remained unchanged, arbitrageurs would make unlimited profits, implying that the parties trading opposite the arbitrageurs would incur unlimited losses. Such a transfer of wealth cannot persist indefinitely.

From an economic perspective, the existence of arbitrage opportunities implies that the economy is in an **economic disequilibrium**. An economic disequilibrium is a situation in which traders are unsatisfied with their current portfolio positions, and they trade. Their trading causes prices to change, moving them to a new economic equilibrium, at which point traders must be satisfied with their portfolios, and arbitrage opportunities no longer exist. Otherwise, they would continue to trade and prices would adjust until the motivation for trading vanishes. In summary, the existence of arbitrage opportunities induces trading and price adjustments until an economic equilibrium is reached, with no arbitrage opportunities left in the economy.

This chapter and, in fact, the entire textbook is concerned with pricing derivatives such that there are no arbitrage opportunities available in the economy. Such arbitrage-free prices are reasonable because they are consistent with an economic equilibrium and well-functioning financial markets.

2.2 ASSUMPTIONS

Throughout this book, we will impose the following four assumptions. The quality of any theory is a direct result of the quality of the underlying assumptions. The assumptions determine the degree to which the theory matches reality. Be sure to understand the content of each of the following assumptions.

Assumption A1. There are no market frictions. That is, there are no transaction costs, no bid/ask spreads, no margin requirements, no restrictions on short sales, and no taxes.

Assumption A2. Market participants entail no counterparty risk. That is, counterparties will not default on any contracts they undertake.

Assumption A3. Markets are competitive. Market participants act as price takers.

Assumption A4. Prices have adjusted so that there are arbitrage opportunities.

Assumption A1, frictionless markets, is imposed for simplicity and as a starting point for the subsequent analysis. There are two justifications for assumption A1. First, for large market participants such as financial institutions, this is a reasonable first approximation. Transaction costs are small for financial institutions. Financial institutions can often trade within the bid/ask spread,[1] they are unrestricted by either margin requirements or short sale constraints, and all their trading profits are taxed at the same rate, as short-term gains. Thus if financial institutions determine market prices, then as a descriptive theory assumption A1 will provide a reasonable approximation. Second, we cannot hope to understand financial markets under market frictions unless we first understand how markets behave without these frictions. As a normative theory for "small" traders, understanding pricing under assumption A1 will provide the necessary insights for understanding pricing under its relaxation. This is an active area of current research. We will not relax this assumption in this text.

For the same two reasons, assumption A2, the lack of counterparty risk between market participants, is also a reasonable first approximation. It implies, for example, under assumption A1 that there is no difference between borrowing and lending rates because there is no difference in default risk between the borrower and lender. For options and futures contracts that trade on organized exchanges, due to the clearing house, this is a reasonable assumption (see Chapter 1). For OTC derivatives, it is less so. Collateral requirements written into some OTC derivatives, especially for low-rated counterparties, is an attempt to guarantee the satisfaction of this assumption. Understanding the modifications to our theory under the relaxation of this assumption is becoming more and more important and forms the content of Chapter 18.

Assumption A3, competitive markets, is a standard postulate of modern finance. In fact, because it is such an accepted part of the field, it is often implicitly imposed without adequate discussion. This assumption implies that traders can buy or sell as much of any security as they wish without influencing the security's price; that is, buying one share is no different than buying one million shares because there are no quantity effects on prices. The larger the market, the more likely this assumption will be satisfied. But, even for large markets, it is only an approximation. Large purchases or sales do change prices. For example, block sales (purchases of 10,000 shares or more) of common stock on the New York Stock Exchange are transacted at different prices than are odd-lot orders (orders for less than 100 shares). The relaxation of this assumption is an area of current research and involves the study of strategic trading and market manipulation. We will not relax this assumption in this text.

Lastly, we impose assumption A4, no arbitrage opportunities. We have already discussed the justification for this assumption. We view assumption A4 as the "variable" assumption underlying our analysis. The remaining three, Assumptions A1–A3, are "fixed" or "maintained." By this we mean the following: we will price futures,

---

[1]In actual markets, there is the price at which you can buy a security (the **ask** price) and a price at which you can sell a security (the **bid** price). They differ so that the market makers (those who hold inventories to satisfy market demands or sales of the security) can earn a living.

forwards, and options under assumptions A1–A4 and develop a "fair" or "theoretical" price. We then compare our theoretical price to the actual market price. If there is a difference, we attribute the difference to a violation of the "variable" assumption and *not* the "maintained" assumptions. Thus we would take this as evidence of an arbitrage opportunity and develop the theory to exploit this difference. In fact, practical applications of the theory often mimic this approach. If we subsequently discover, to our chagrin, that it was not assumption A4 that was violated but rather one of assumptions A1–A3, we would go back and modify our theory to incorporate more realistic "maintained" assumptions. Why? Because the purpose of the analysis is to identify and exploit arbitrage opportunities.

2.3 FORWARD AND SPOT PRICES

We now examine the relationship between forward prices and spot prices. First we analyze the determination of forward prices written on financial assets. For simplicity, we initially assume that over the life of the forward contract the underlying asset does not have any cash flow—neither dividends nor coupon payments.

No Cash Flows on the Underlying Asset Over the Life of the Forward Contract

Consider forward contracts written on financial assets that provide no cash flow over the life of the contract. This class of forward contracts is important. Examples of such financial assets would be non-dividend paying stocks and zero-coupon Treasury bonds. Before giving a formal derivation, we consider a simple example.

EXAMPLE   **Cash-and-Carry**

This example illustrates the "cash-and-carry" strategy for generating a forward contract synthetically. Creating a contract **synthetically** means constructing a portfolio of traded assets that duplicates the cash flow and value of the contract under consideration.

Let the price of a non-dividend paying stock today be $25. Let the risk-free simple interest rate be 7.12 percent per year. First we determine the forward price for a six-month contract on the stock. Suppose that the investor buys the stock for $25 and writes a six-month forward contract, with forward price F. By **writing** we mean that the investor agrees to sell the stock at the forward price in six months' time. To have no initial cash flow, the investor finances the purchase of the stock by borrowing at the risk-free simple interest rate 7.12 percent per annum, implying that the investor must pay $25 [1 + 0.0712 \times (1/2)]$ in six months' time.[2]

---

[2]This is a simple interest rate as defined in Chapter 1.

Now consider the outcomes from this strategy in six months' time. Letting $S(6)$ denote the stock price after six months, we can now illustrate the payouts of this investment strategy at maturity.

The payoff at maturity to this cash-and-carry strategy is

a)	Stock investment	$S(6)$
b)	Forward contract	$-[S(6) - F]$
c)	Repay borrowing	$-25[1 + 0.0712 \times (1/2)]$
	Net payoff	$F - 25[1 + 0.0712 \times (1/2)]$.

The minus sign for the payoff of the forward contract arises because the investor has written the forward contract.

The net payoff to the investment strategy in six months is

$$F - 25[1 + 0.0712 \times (1/2)],$$

which is known today because it is independent of the final stock price, $S(6)$. The initial outlay for the investor was zero. Recall that the purchase of the stock was financed by borrowing and that the initial value of the forward contract was zero. Thus to avoid arbitrage the net payoff must be zero. Otherwise, one can generate positive cash flows at date T with no initial investment and no risk. Therefore,

$$F = 25[1 + 0.0712 \times (1/2)] = 25.89.$$

This must be the arbitrage-free forward price.

Besides determining the forward price, this argument also demonstrates how to synthetically construct the forward contract with the cash-and-carry strategy. The cash-and-carry strategy consists of the following actions: (1) buy the stock through borrowing (cash), and (2) hold it until the delivery date of the forward contract (carry). At the delivery date, the initial borrowing is paid off. As shown above, this strategy replicates the forward contract's cash flows at the delivery date. Indeed, it generates total ownership of the stock at the delivery date when the borrowing is paid off. The "purchase price" at maturity is determined at the date the strategy is initiated. We will use this cash-and-carry strategy again for other commodities in subsequent sections. ∎

In Chapter 1 we stated that the forward price is set such that the initial value of the forward contract is zero. Similarly, in the above example we claim that the initial value of the forward contract is zero. This is because the value of the forward contract today can be determined by computing the present value of its payoff in six months' time, $[F - S(6)]$. The first term, (F), is known today, so its present value is determined by discounting at the risk-free rate of interest. The second term, $S(6)$, is the stock price in six months' time. The present value of the stock price in six months'

time, $S(6)$, must be the stock price today, given that the stock pays no dividends over the life of the forward contract. Thus the value of the forward contract today is

$$(F/[1 + 0.0712 \times (1/2)]) - 25 = 0,$$

after substituting for F.

Formal Derivation (Cash-and-Carry)

The previous cash-and-carry strategy readily generalizes to an arbitrary forward contract, with delivery date T on a spot commodity with no cash flows over the forward contract's life. The formal derivation simply replaces the numbers in the previous example with symbols and then repeats the same logic.

We need to introduce some minimal notation to present the cash-and-carry strategy, some of which we have seen before. Let $S(t)$ denote the stock price at time t, where t will often by either 0 or T. Let $F(t, T)$ denote the forward price at time t for a contract with delivery date T. Let $B(t, T)$ represent the value at date t of a Treasury bill that pays \$1 at date T.

We introduce the two arguments in the notation for the forward price in order to increase transparency in the subsequent formulas. Given this notation, we can now revisit the cash-and-carry strategy.

Portfolio Today (Date 0)—Cash	Net Outflow
a) Buy one share, at cost $S(0)$	$S(0)$
b) Finance purchase of share by borrowing at the risk-free simple rate of interest, i_S	$-S(0)$
c) Write one forward contract, maturity T, forward price $F(0, T)$.	0
Total	0

Portfolio at Date T—Carry	Net Inflow
a) Value of share	$S(T)$
b) Repay borrowing	$- S(0)[1 + i_S \times T]$
c) Value of forward	$- [S(T) - F(0, T)]$
Total	$F(0, T) - S(0)[1 + i_S \times T]$

The date T value of this portfolio is known at date 0 because it is independent of the stock price, $S(T)$, and thus involves no uncertainty. Therefore, to avoid arbitrage the payoff must be zero, because otherwise one can generate positive cash flows at date T with no initial investment and no risk. This implies

$$F(0, T) = S(0)[1 + i_S \times T]. \tag{2.1}$$

The above is called the cash-and-carry relationship between the spot and forward price, an implication of which is that when there are no cash flows on the underlying asset, the forward price is never less than the spot price. We will see later that for commodities with cash flows, this is not always the case.

We can write the above in a slightly different way, which will aid our understanding of extensions of this cash-and-carry relationship. Performing some simple algebra on Expression (2.1) gives

$$S(0) = F(0,T)/(1 + i_S \times T) = F(0,T) B(0,T), \tag{2.2}$$

where

$$B(0,T) \equiv \frac{1}{1 + i_S \times T}.$$

See Chapter 1 for a discussion of zero-coupon bonds and simple interest rates.

For an arbitrary date t between 0 and T, the same argument generating Expression (2.2) yields

$$S(t) = F(t,T)B(t,T). \tag{2.3}$$

EXAMPLE

Exploiting a Cash-and-Carry Mispricing

Consider a forward contract written on a non-dividend paying stock. Let the current stock price be \$45 and the quoted forward price be \$46.54. Let the maturity of the contract be 90 days and the simple interest rate for this period be 4.85 percent per annum assuming a 365-day year (see Chapter 1). The theoretical forward price using Expression (2.1) is

$$F(0, 90) = 45[1 + 0.0485 \times (90/365)] = 45.54.$$

The theoretical forward price is less than the quoted price, which implies that there is an arbitrage opportunity.

If we sell the overvalued forward contract, the resulting position is risky because we can lose money if the spot price falls. To offset the risk, we buy the stock borrowing to finance our purchase. By construction, the net outflow of funds is zero. At the maturity of the forward contract, our position's value is

Short forward contract	$- [S(T) - 46.54]$
Long stock	$S(T)$
Repay borrowing	$- 45[1 + 0.0485 \times (90/365)]$
Net profit	$46.54 - 45.54$
	$= 1.00.$

Note that net profit is riskless, being independent of $S(T)$. This is an arbitrage opportunity! The initial cost of the position is zero, and we end up making \$1 for sure when the positions are closed out at the maturity of the forward contract. If current prices did not change as a result of our trade, we could repeat this strategy and reap additional benefits.   ■

Value of a Forward Contract

When a forward contract is initiated, by market design, its value is zero. After initiation its value can fluctuate and be either positive or negative. This happens because the spot price of the underlying asset changes, either increasing or decreasing, making the existing forward contract's value either increase or decrease. A simple argument, given below, determines the value of the forward contract at any time in its life.

Suppose that at date 0 you enter into a forward contract to buy an asset at date T with a forward price of $F(0, T)$. Denote the value of this forward contract at date t by $V(t)$.

By construction, the forward price is set such that the initial value of the forward contract is zero; that is, at date 0:

$$V(0) \equiv 0.$$

As shown earlier, the value of the forward contract when it matures is the difference between the spot price at date T and the initial forward price (delivery price):

$$V(T) \equiv S(T) - F(0, T).$$

To determine the value of the forward contract at some intermediate date t, we need to take the present value of this last expression as of date t. To do this, we take the present value of each term.

The present value of the asset's price, $S(T)$, at date t is $S(t)$, given that there are no cash flows from it. The present value of the fixed delivery price is $B(t, T) F(0, T)$. Combined, we get

$$V(t) = S(t) - B(t, T) F(0, T). \tag{2.4}$$

Substitution of Expression (2.3) into (2.4) yields

$$V(t) = [F(t, T) - F(0, T)]B(t, T). \tag{2.5}$$

Both Expressions (2.4) and (2.5) give the easy-to-use final results. Before discussing these results, let us revisit the previous example (Cash-and-Carry).

EXAMPLE   **Forward Contract's Value**

Recall the previous Cash-and-Carry example. The initial forward price was $25.89 and the delivery date was in six months.

Suppose now that time has passed and the time remaining until maturity is three months. Let the stock price with three months until maturity be $23 and the three-month simple interest rate be 8.08 percent per annum using a 365-day year. The forward price for a *new* contract maturing in three months' time can be computed via Expression (2.3):

$$f(3, 6) = 23[1 + 0.0808 \times (1/4)] = 23.46.$$

The value of the original forward contract is (via Expression (2.5))

$$V(3) = (23.46 - 25.89)1/[1 + 0.0808 \times (1/4)] = -\$2.38.$$

The forward contract has a negative value equal to $-\$2.38$. To close out this contract, one would need to pay the counterparty $2.38. On the other hand, the *short* forward contract position has gained a positive $2.38.   ∎

This simple numerical example demonstrates three important points about Expression (2.5). First, the value of the original contract after initiation and prior to delivery depends upon the new forward price for a newly issued contract with the same delivery date. From Expression (2.3) we see that this new forward price depends upon the prevailing spot price and the three-month simple interest rate. Second, in calculating the value of the forward contract, it is necessary to know the current three-month simple interest rate. Third, the value of the contract can be positive or negative. The value will be negative (positive) if the forward price for a newly issued forward contract is less than (greater than) the delivery price. These same three points will be seen to apply to forward contracts on the different commodities discussed in subsequent sections.

2.4 KNOWN CASH FLOWS TO THE UNDERLYING ASSET

Let us now study the relation between forward prices and spot prices when the underlying asset has known cash flows. If the underlying asset has known cash flows over the life of the forward contract such as a dividend or interest payment, it will affect the forward price because ownership of a forward contract does not entitle the holder to the asset's cash flows. However, ownership of the underlying asset does. Since the current value of the asset reflects the present value of all future cash flows, the simple relationship between the forward and spot price as represented by Expression (2.3) will no longer hold.

Since the timing and the amount of the cash flows paid over the life of the forward contract are known, there is a simple adjustment to the previous results, which the following example illustrates.

EXAMPLE   **Forward and Spot Prices with Known Cash Flows**

This example has a Treasury bond as the underlying asset. A Treasury bond pays known coupons at known dates. Let the price of a twelve-month Treasury bond with face value $1,000 be $1,021.39. The bond has a coupon of 10 percent per annum, paid on a semiannual basis. The next coupon payment of $50 is due in six months' time.

We want to determine the forward price for a nine-month forward contract written on the twelve-month Treasury bond. Let the six-month simple interest rate be 7.18 percent per annum, the nine-month simple interest rate be 7.66 percent per annum, and the twelve-month simple interest rate be 7.90 percent per annum. The price of the Treasury bond is determined by discounting the coupon payments plus the principal repayment.

Let $B_c(0, 12)$ denote the date 0 value of the coupon-paying Treasury bond with maturity in twelve months (the subscript c denotes that the Treasury bond pays a coupon). Then

$$B_c(0, 12) = \frac{50}{[1 + 0.0718 \times (1/2)]} + \frac{50 + 1,000}{[1 + 0.0790]} = \$1,021.39.$$

Consider two investment strategies.

Strategy one (date-zero cash flows)
   a) Buy the Treasury bond at a cost of $1,021.39.
   b) Borrow for six months the present value of the coupon payment; that is,

   borrow $50/[1 + 0.0718 \times (1/2)]$.
   Total cost = $1,021.39 - 50/[1 + 0.0718 \times (1/2)]$.

Strategy two (date-zero cash flows)
   a) Go long a nine-month forward contract with forward price $F(0, 9)$.
   b) Invest the present value of the forward price for nine months in a riskless investment. The initial investment is $F(0,9)/[1 + 0.0766 \times (9/12)]$.

   Total cost = $F(0,9)/[1 + 0.0766 \times (9/12)]$.

Now consider the payoff of these two investment strategies in nine months' time.

Strategy one (nine-month cash flows)

You own the Treasury bond and you receive the $50 coupon in month 6. This coupon payment is used to repay the amount borrowed. Therefore, the total value of the strategy is the market value of the Treasury bond in month 9, $B_c(9,12)$.

Strategy two (nine-month cash flows)

a)   The payoff to the forward contract is $B_c(9,12) - F(0,9)$.
b)   The payoff to the investment is $F(0, 9)$.

Net value of the strategy is $B_c(9, 12)$.

The payoffs from both investment strategies in nine months are identical. To avoid arbitrage, the date 0 costs of the two strategies must be the same. This implies

$$1{,}021.39 - 50/[1 + 0.0718 \times (1/2)] = F(0,9)/[1 + 0.0766 \times (9/12)].$$

The first term on the left side is the current market value of the Treasury bond. The second term is the present value of the coupon paid during the life of the forward contract. The minus sign arises because the holder of the forward contract has no claim to or responsibility for the coupon payment. Therefore, after some simple algebra, the forward price is

$$F(0, 9) = 1{,}029.03. \qquad \blacksquare$$

Formal Derivation

This section formalizes the previous example. The formal derivation involves little more than replacing the numbers with symbols. Consider a forward contract that matures at date T. Let the forward contract be written on an asset with current spot price $S(0)$, which pays a known cash flow of $d(t_1)$ at date t_1 during the life of the forward contract. The timing and magnitude of this cash payment are known as of date 0.

Consider two investment strategies.

Strategy one (date-zero cash flows)

a)   Buy the underlying asset at a cost of $S(0)$.
b)   Borrow for a period of t_1 the present value of the cash flow $d(t_1)$. The present value is given by $d(t_1)B(0,t_1)$, which implies that at date t_1 an amount $d(t_1)$ will have to be repaid.

Total cost $= S(0) - d(t_1)B(0,t_1)$.

Strategy two (date-zero cash flows)
a)   Go long a T-period forward contract with forward price $F(0, T)$.
b)   Invest in the T-period riskless asset the present value of the forward price for T periods, cost $F(0, T)B(0, T)$.

Total cost $= F(0, T)B(0, T)$.

Now consider the payoff from both of these strategies at date T.

Strategy one (date-T cash flows)
The cash flow that you receive at date t_1 is used to repay the amount borrowed. These two date-t_1 cash flows offset each other. Hence, the total value of the investment strategy at date T is simply the value of the asset, $S(T)$.

Strategy two (date-T cash flows)

a) Value of forward contract	$S(T) - F(0, T)$
b) Value of the riskless investment	$F(0, T)$
Total	$S(T)$

The two investment strategies have identical payoffs. Therefore, to avoid arbitrage the cost of the two strategies at date 0 must be identical. This implies

$$F(0, T)B(0, T) = S(0) - d(t_1)B(0, t_1). \tag{2.6}$$

The right side is the spot price minus the present value of the known cash flow at date t_1.

This relationship holds for an arbitrary date prior to the cash flow payment date, $t < t_1$:

$$F(t, T)B(t, T) = S(t) - d(t_1)B(t, t_1). \tag{2.7}$$

If there is more than one cash flow, the above argument generalizes and Expression (2.7) becomes

$$F(t, T)B(t, T) = S(t) - PV_t \text{ [of all cash flows over the remaining life of the forward contract]}, \tag{2.8}$$

where $PV_t[\cdot]$ represents the date-t present value of the cash flows within the brackets. For example, if there are two known dividends paid at dates t_1 and t_2 prior to T, then

$$F(t, T)B(t, T) = S(t) - [d(t_1)B(t, t_1) + d(t_2)B(t, t_2)].$$

The present value of dividend $d(t_1)$ at date t_1 plus the dividend $d(t_2)$ at date t_2 compose the term inside the square brackets on the right side of the above expression. Given this forward price relation, we can now value the forward contract itself.

Value of a Forward Contract

We now focus on the value of a forward contract on an underlying asset with known cash flows over the forward contract's life. The value of a forward contract at date t, after it has been initiated, can be determined using the same argument described previously.

Suppose that at date 0 you have a forward contract to buy the underlying asset at date T for a forward price of $F(0, T)$. By market design, the initial value of the forward contract is zero. At date t, before the contract matures, the value of the original forward contract, represented by $V(t)$, equals the present value of the date-T cash flow, that is, the present value of $S(T) - F(0, T)$:

$$V(t) = PV_t[S(T) - F(0, T)] = PV_t[S(T)] - F(0, T)B(t, T).$$

But the present value of the stock price at date T is the stock price at date t less the present value of all the cash flows to the stock paid between dates t and T, that is,

$$PV_t[S(T)] = S(t) - PV_t \text{ [all cash flows over the remaining life}$$
$$\text{of the forward contract]}.$$

Substitution yields

$$V(t) = S(t) - PV_t \text{ [all cash flows over the remaining life}$$
$$\text{of the forward contract]}$$
$$- F(0, T)B(t, T).$$

Using Expression (2.8) gives an alternate form of the final result:

$$V(t) = [F(t, T) - F(0, T)]B(t, T). \tag{2.9}$$

The date t value of the forward contract is seen to be the discounted change in the forward price between date 0 and date t. This expression is identical to Expression (2.5). The presence of cash flows does not explicitly enter into this relationship because a forward contract has no claim to or responsibility for the payment of cash flows over the life of the contract. The presence of the cash flows does, of course, affect the actual forward price, as shown by Expression (2.6). We have completed the discussion for the case of known cash flows paid to the underlying asset. The next section extends the analysis to particular types of random cash flows.

2.5 FORWARD CONTRACTS ON CONSTANT DIVIDEND YIELD AND INTEREST-PAYING ASSETS

For many assets, cash flows occur at discrete intervals; for example, dividends for a common stock are usually paid quarterly. Some assets' cash flows, however, are better approximated by a continuous payment stream. For example, a broadly based index such as the Standard and Poor's 500 stock index has dividends that may be approximated as being paid on a continuous basis, proportional to the level of the index. This implies that the dividend yield (dividend divided by the stock index) is a constant. The total dividends paid, however, are random because they depend on the level of the stock index that itself is random.

Let us study the adjustments to the cash-and-carry relationship that occur when the cash-flow stream to an asset is approximated by a continuous and proportionate flow. To illustrate the principles, we use the examples of a stock index forward contract and foreign currency forward contract. Both examples are important in their own right.

Forward Contracts on a Stock Index

The presence of dividends on the stock index affects the forward price in a manner similar to that shown in the last section. From Expression (2.8),

$$F(0,T)B(0,T) = I(0) - PV_0 \text{ [of all dividends over the life of the forward contract]},$$

where $I(0)$ is the date-0 value of the index.

The last term on the right side is the present value of all the dividends paid over the life of the forward contract. The assumption of a constant dividend yield implies that[3]

$$F(0,T)B(0,T) = I(0)e^{-d_y T}, \tag{2.10}$$

where d_y is the dividend yield. Intuitively, the right side of Expression (2.10) gives the percentage of the stock index's value represented by the dividends occurring after date T.

---

[3] A proof is given in the Appendix of this chapter.

EXAMPLE   ## Forward Price of a Stock Index

Consider a 120-day forward contract written on the S&P 500 index. Let the current dividend yield be 2.80 percent per annum. The current index value is 436.00 and the simple rate of interest is 3.50 percent per annum based on a 365-day year.

The present value of receiving $1 for certain in 120 days' time is

$$B(0, 120) = 1/[1 + 0.035 \times (120/365)]$$
$$= 1/1.0115 = 0.9886$$

and

$$e^{-d_y T} = e^{-0.028 \times (120/365)} = 0.9908.$$

Substitution into Expression (2.10) gives

$$F(0, 120) = 436.00 \times 0.9908/0.9886 = 436.97$$ ∎

Foreign Exchange Forward Contracts

A similar (and perhaps more transparent) cash-and-carry argument holds for foreign currency forward contracts, for which there is a large and active over-the-counter market. Let us first consider an example.

EXAMPLE   ## Foreign Currency Forward Prices

A U.S.-based company wants to buy some goods from a firm in Switzerland. The cost of the goods is 62,500 Swiss francs (SF). The firm must pay for the goods in 120 days.

The current spot exchange rate is 0.7032 $/SF. The company is concerned about the Swiss franc appreciating against the dollar. For example, if the exchange increased to 0.7532 $/SF, the dollar cost of buying the goods increases by $3,125 [= 62,500 \times (0.7532 - 0.7032)]. In order to hedge this risk, the company enters into a forward contract to buy 62,500 SF in 120 days' time at the forward exchange rate denoted by $F(0, 120)$ ($/SF). The forward rate is set such that the initial value of the contract is zero.

What is the forward exchange rate? To answer, we need some additional information. The domestic 120-day, default-free simple rate of interest is 3.25 percent per annum, and the Swiss simple rate of interest is 4.50 percent per annum, both assuming a 365-day year. Consider two investment strategies.

Strategy one (date 0)

Go long in a forward contract to buy the foreign currency. The initial cost is zero. Note that the contract is to buy 62,500 Swiss francs.

Strategy two (date 0)

a) Buy $62,500/[1 + 0.045 \times (120/365)]$ Swiss francs and invest them in the Swiss riskless asset for 120 days. Note that it will be worth 62,500 SF with certainty in 120 days' time, given that the 120-day default-free Swiss simple interest rate is 4.5 percent per annum. The dollar cost of this investment is

$$0.7032 \times \left[\frac{62,500}{1 + 0.045 \times (120/365)} \right].$$

b) Borrow the present value of the forward price in dollars, $62,500 \times F(0, 120)/[1 + 0.0325 \times (120/365)]$ at the domestic simple interest rate of 3.25 percent per annum for 120 days.

Note that in 120 days, it will be necessary to pay back $62,500 \times F(0, 120)$ dollars.

The total cost of both parts (a) and (b) of strategy two is

$$0.7032 \times \left[\frac{62,500}{1 + 0.045 \times (120/365)} \right] - \frac{62,500 \times F(0, 120)}{1 + 0.0325 \times (120/365)}.$$

Now consider the payoff of these two strategies in 120 days' time when the forward contract matures. Let $S(120)$ denote the spot exchange rate at that time ($/SF).

Strategy one (date 120 days)

Value of forward contract	$62,500 \times [S(120) - F(0, 120)]$ dollars

Strategy two (date 120 days)

a) Pays 62,500 Swiss francs	or	$62,500S(120)$ dollars
b) Repay amount borrowed		$-62,500\,F(0, 120)$ dollars
Net payoff		$62,500[S(120) - F(0, 120)]$ dollars

The payoffs for the two strategies are the same in 120 days. Therefore, to avoid arbitrage the cost of the two strategies must be the same at date 0.

The cost of the first strategy at date 0 is zero, implying that the cost of the second must be zero at date 0 as well:

$$0.7032\left[\frac{62,500}{1 + 0.045 \times (120/365)}\right] = F(0, 120)\left[\frac{62,500}{1 + 0.0325 \times (120/365)}\right]$$

Therefore, algebra gives

$$F(0, 120) = 0.7004 \ (\$/SF).$$ ∎

Formal derivation (foreign currency forward prices)

The above example is now generalized by replacing numerical values with symbols. The foreign currency is taken to be sterling. Let $S(0)$ denote the current $\$/£$ spot exchange rate, and $B_£(0, T)$ the price in sterling of a zero-coupon bond that pays £ for certain at date T. A forward contract allows you to buy or sell a specified amount of a foreign currency at the forward price.

To determine the forward price, consider two investment strategies.

Strategy one (date 0)

Go long in a forward contract to buy the foreign currency. Initial cost is zero.

Strategy two (date 0)

a) Buy a foreign Treasury bill for a cost $B_£(0, T)$ pounds or $S(0)B_£(0, T)$ dollars.
b) Borrow for a period T the present value of the forward price, receiving $F(0, T)B(0, T)$ dollars.

Total cost of Strategy Two = $S(0)B_£(0, T) - F(0, T)B(0, T)$.

Now consider the payoffs of these two strategies at the delivery date of the forward contract.

Strategy one (date T)

Value of forward contract in dollars $S(T) - F(0, T)$

Strategy two (date T)

a) Dollar value of foreign treasury bill	$S(T)$
b) Repay amount borrowed	$-(F(0, T)$
Net payoff	$S(T) - F(0, T)$

The payoffs for these two strategies at date T are the same. Therefore, to avoid arbitrage, the costs of the strategies at date 0 must be the same, which implies

$$0 = S(0)B_\pounds(0,T) - F(0,T)B(0,T)$$

or

$$F(0,T)B(0,T) = S(0)B_\pounds(0,T). \tag{2.11}$$

This expression determines the forward price, and it is similar in form to Expression (2.10).

To see the equivalence, note that $B_\pounds(0,T) = e^{-r_\pounds T}$ where $r_\pounds$ is the foreign T period interest rate, assuming continuous compounding. In both cases the forward price is reduced by the presence of these foreign currency interest payments. The value of the forward contract is given by Expression (2.9).

In international finance, Expression (2.11) is known as **interest rate parity**. Interest rate parity links together the spot and forward prices and interest rates in both the domestic and foreign economies. For example, if interest rates in the domestic country are lower than those in the foreign country, implying that $B(0,T)$ is greater than $B_\pounds(0,T)$, then the forward price $F(0,T)$ is less than the spot exchange rate $S(0)$. Conversely, if interest rates in the domestic country are higher than those in the foreign country, implying that $B(0,T)$ is less than $B_\pounds(0,T)$, then the forward price $F(0,T)$ is greater than the spot exchange rate $S(0)$.

EXAMPLE   **Revised Foreign Currency Interest Rate Parity**

Using the numbers in the last example, the dollar zero-coupon bond price is

$$B(0,120) = \frac{1}{1 + 0.0325 \times (120/365)} = 0.9894\ \$,$$

and the equivalent Swiss default-free instrument is

$$B_{\text{SF}}(0,120) = \frac{1}{1 + 0.045 \times (120/365)} = 0.9854\ \text{SF}.$$

Therefore, given that the spot exchange rate is $S(0) = 0.7032(\$/\text{SF})$, the forward price is

$$F(0,120) = 0.7032 \times (0.9854/0.9894) = 0.7004(\$/\text{SF}).$$

This result agrees with the forward price obtained earlier. ∎

2.6 FORWARD CONTRACTS ON COMMODITIES

Up to this point we have only considered forward contracts on financial assets. For nonfinancial assets such as gold, silver, or corn, the cash-and-carry strategy must consider the costs of storing such commodities.

Consider a forward contract to buy or sell silver at date T. To determine the forward price, we use the same cash-and-carry argument: Write a forward contract, buy the quantity of silver specified in the contract, and borrow to finance the purchase. In the purchase of silver, we incur the additional cost of storing it until the delivery date. For financial assets such as Treasury bonds, there are no storage costs. We now show how to adjust the previous cash-and-carry arguments to adjust for these storage costs.

Storage Costs

Let G denote the present value of the total cost of storage for some commodity over the time period $[0, T]$. We will make two assumptions concerning these storage costs. Both of these assumptions are made to simplify the analysis.

First, let the total storage costs be known with certainty at date 0. This assumption can be relaxed. Second, let the total storage costs be paid at date 0. This assumption can also be easily relaxed. To pay the storage costs, we will borrow at the risk-free rate of interest.

The cash-and-carry strategy is as follows:

Initial portfolio (date 0)	**Net Outflow**
a) Write forward contract, with forward price $F(0, T)$.	0
b) Buy the asset and pay the storage costs.	$S(0) + G$
c) Finance purchase of asset and storage costs by borrowing at the simple risk-free rate of interest, i_S.	$-[S(0) + G]$
Total	0

Portfolio at date T	
a) Value of forward contract	$-[S(T) - F(0, T)]$
b) Value of asset	$S(T)$
c) Repay borrowing	$-[S(0) + G](1 + i_S \times T)$
Total	$F(0, T) - [S(0) + G](1 + i_S \times T)$

This date T payoff is known at date 0. Therefore, it is riskless. To avoid arbitrage, the payoff must be zero, implying

$$F(0, T) = [S(0) + G](1 + i_S \times T) \tag{2.12}$$

or

$$F(0, T)B(0, T) = S(0) + G,$$

as

$$B(0, T) = 1/(1 + i_S \times T). \tag{2.12'}$$

In comparing Expression (2.12) with Expression (2.6), we see that the storage costs can be interpreted as a **negative dividend**. In other words, storage costs can make the

forward contract more valuable than purchasing and storing the commodity. Therefore, the forward price needs to increase by the future value of the storage costs. If storage costs vary over the life of the contract and are proportional to the spot price, then from Expression (2.10) we get

$$F(0,T)B(0,T) = S(0)e^{gT}, \tag{2.13}$$

where g represents a proportional storage cost.

Expression (2.12) is also referred to as the **cost-of-carry** formula (instead of the cash-and-carry formula). As the name suggests, it involves buying the underlying asset on which the forward contract is written and holding it for the duration of the contract. In holding the asset, certain costs are incurred. The first is the cost of borrowing to finance the purchase of the asset, $S(0)(1 + i_S \times T)$, and the second is the storage cost, $G(1 + i_S \times T)$.

Suppose that it was observed that

$$F(0,T)B(0,T) < S(0) + G,$$

implying that the forward price is too low and the forward contracts are undervalued. How can we take advantage of this? One way is to buy forward, sell short the underlying asset, and invest the proceeds in the riskless asset.[4] The net outflow at date 0 is zero. The value of our portfolio at maturity T is

a)	Value of forward	$S(T) - F(0,T)$
b)	Close short position	$-S(T)$
c)	Payoff from lending	$[S(0) + G](1 + i_S \times T)$
		$[S(0) + G](1 + i_S \times T) - F(0,T).$

Hence the payoff of this portfolio at date T is riskless and positive. It is positive due to the original observation. Because our portfolio did not require any investment, this is an arbitrage opportunity.

EXAMPLE   **Forward Price with Storage Costs**

Consider a forward contract to buy 100 troy ounces of gold in 180 days' time. The current gold price is $368 per ounce and storage costs are $2.25 per troy ounce payable at the maturity of the forward contract. The 180-day simple interest rate is 3.875 percent per annum. What is the forward price?

We cannot substitute directly into Expression (2.12), because, in deriving Expression (2.12), we assumed that the storage costs were payable at the start.

---

[4]We are assuming that competitive pressures are such that the lender of the asset passes the saving on to the borrower.

To use Expression (2.12) we need to calculate G, the present value of the storage costs. This is accomplished by discounting the storage costs to date 0:

$$G = 2.25B(0, 180),$$

where $B(0, 180) = 1/[1 + i_s \times T]$. Thus, $2.25 = G[1 + i_s \times T]$. Substitution into Expression (2.12) yields

$$
\begin{aligned}
F(0, 180) &= S(0)(1 + i_s \times T) + 2.25 \\
&= 368[1 + 0.03875 \times (180/365)] + 2.25 \\
&= \$377.28.
\end{aligned}
$$

Suppose that you observed the forward price to be $390. What arbitrage opportunity presents itself? You could buy 100 troy ounces of gold for $36,800, borrowing to finance this purchase, and write a forward contract to sell 100 troy ounces of gold in 180 days' time.

At the maturity of the forward contract, letting $S(180)$ denote the price of gold in 180 days, the net value of your position is

Value of gold	$100S(180)$
Forward contract	$-100[S(180) - 390]$
Pay storage	-225
Repay borrowing	$-36,800[1 + 0.03875 \times (180/365)]$
Net profit	$39,000 - 225 - 37,503$
	$= \$1,272.$

This amount represents 100 times the difference in the forward price less the arbitrage-free price ($390 - 377.28 = 12.72$). It represents an arbitrage opportunity. ■

Convenience Yield

The example above assumes that the asset underlying the forward contract can be stored and lent out for short sales. In a short sale, the lender gives up the commodity and gets it back later. There are many commodities held not for investment purposes but inventoried for reasons of usage, such as in production. Good examples of such commodities include copper, gasoline, and crude oil. One way to interpret this productive usage is that there is a benefit or implicit dividend from holding such an asset, called a **convenience yield**. This benefit needs to be incorporated in the cost-of-carry relationship.

Including this convenience yield, Expression (2.12) can be written in the form

$$F(0, T) = [S(0) + G - Y(0, T)](1 + i_s \times T), \tag{2.14}$$

where $Y(0, T)$ represents the date-0 present value of the convenience yield from holding the asset. The above equation is often expressed in the form

$$F(0, T) = S(0) e^{(r-y)T}, \qquad (2.15)$$

where y is referred to as the **net convenience yield** and r is the continuously compounded interest rate.

The Implied Repo Rate

It is common usage "on the street" to think in terms of rates earned on a cash-and-carry strategy rather than prices, leading to the notion of an **implied repo rate**, defined as a simple interest rate that equates the forward price and the spot price. Formally, the implied repo rate, i_I, is defined by

$$F(0, T) = S(0)(1 + i_I \times T).$$

To illustrate its use, consider the case of a forward contract written on an asset that does not pay any dividend and for which there are no storage costs. Expression (2.1) gives the theoretical forward price, which we rewrite as

$$F(0, T) = S(0)(1 + i_S \times T).$$

Suppose that the implied repo rate is greater than the simple interest rate, $i_I > i_S$, implying that the observed forward price is greater than the theoretical forward price. This inequality further implies the existence of an arbitrage opportunity.

One should write forward contracts, buy the underlying asset, and finance the purchase by borrowing. There are no intermediate cash flows, and the net payoff at the maturity of the contract is

$$
\begin{aligned}
& -[S(T) - F(0, T)] + S(T) - S(0)(1 + i_S \times T) \\
&= F(0, T) - S(0)(1 + i_S \times T) \\
&= S(0)(1 + i_I \times T) - S(0)(1 + i_S \times T) \\
&= S(0)[i_I - i_S] \times T \\
&> 0,
\end{aligned}
$$

because the implied repo rate exceeds the simple interest rate, $i_I > i_S$. The payoff at date T is a known positive amount. Given that this strategy involves no net outflow of funds at date 0, we have an arbitrage opportunity.

Forward Contracts on Electricity

Derivative securities on electricity are now traded in a new and growing market. At the moment, electricity derivatives are primarily traded over-the-counter and they usually involve physical delivery. The simplest form of an electricity derivative is a

forward contract. However, the simple cost-of-carry argument does not apply; given current technology, it is not possible to store large quantities of electricity for extended periods of time. To derive a relationship between the forward and spot price of electricity, therefore, a more complicated analysis is required that includes the cost of producing and shipping electricity over the existing power grid. Unfortunately, the analysis is too complicated to be included in this text.

2.7 FORWARD AND FUTURES PRICES COMPARED

The previous sections analyzed forward contracts using the simple cash-and-carry strategy. Unfortunately, it is not possible to use such a simple strategy to replicate a futures contract. Consequently, our argument must be more involved. To make the logic simple, we consider a two-period example with simple interest rates, as specified in Figure 2.1. The same argument will also apply to more realistic situations with longer time horizons.

The two time periods are $[0, 1]$ and $[1, 2]$. The short-term rate, known as date 0, is i_S^1 and corresponds to the simple interest one can earn on riskless investing over the period $[0, 1]$. The long-term rate, also known as date 0, is j_S and corresponds to the simple interest one can guarantee today on riskless investing over the period $[0, 2]$. These rates can differ because interest rates are random, said to be **stochastic**, and they can change over time.

Thus, investing for two periods at date 0 can provide a different return than investing for one period at date 0 and rolling it over. If one waits until date 1, the "new" short-term simple interest rate at that date is i_S^2. This is the interest rate one can earn on riskless investing over the period $[1, 2]$. When viewed from date 0, however, i_S^2 is random. It is this fact that makes the analysis for futures contracts more complex than for forward contracts.

Consider both a forward contract and a futures contract with delivery at date 2 on a commodity whose date 2 spot price is denoted by $S(2)$. Let the forward price be denoted $F(0, 2)$ and the futures price $\mathscr{F}(0, 2)$.

Figure 2.1   *Simple Interest Rates*

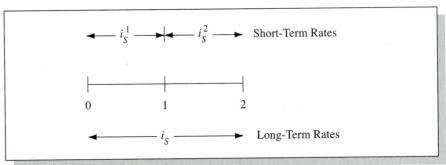

TABLE 2.1   *Cash Flows to Forward and Futures Contracts*

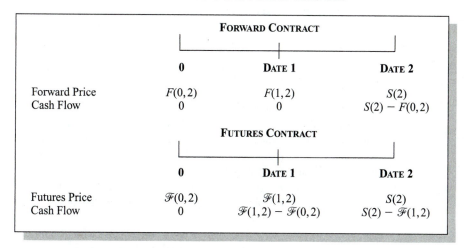

	0	**DATE 1**	**DATE 2**
Forward Price	$F(0,2)$	$F(1,2)$	$S(2)$
Cash Flow	0	0	$S(2) - F(0,2)$

	0	**DATE 1**	**DATE 2**
Futures Price	$\mathscr{F}(0,2)$	$\mathscr{F}(1,2)$	$S(2)$
Cash Flow	0	$\mathscr{F}(1,2) - \mathscr{F}(0,2)$	$S(2) - \mathscr{F}(1,2)$

The cash flows to these contracts are given in Table 2.1. The forward contract only has a cash flow at date 2, while the futures contract has a cash flow at dates 1 and 2 due to marking-to-market. The cash flow to the futures contract at each date is the change in the futures price over the previous day.

To compare the two contracts, we start from an initial position of zero wealth and consider two investment strategies. In the first strategy, we go long in a forward contract at date 0. The forward price is $F(0,2)$.

Strategy one (forward contract)
Go long in a forward contract at date 0 with an initial cost of 0. At date 2, the value of the forward contract is

$$S(2) - F(0,2). \tag{2.16}$$

Strategy two (futures contract)
Go long in the future contract at date 0 until the contract matures at date 2. The initial futures price is $\mathscr{F}(0, 2)$. At date 1, the futures contract is marked-to-market, generating a cash flow of

$$\mathscr{F}(1,2) - \mathscr{F}(0,2),$$

where $\mathscr{F}(1, 2)$ is the futures price at date 1.

If this amount is positive, we invest it in the riskless asset over the period $[1, 2]$. If it is negative, we borrow at the risk-free simple interest rate. The total value of the strategy at date 2 is

$$S(2) - \mathscr{F}(1,2) + [\mathscr{F}(1,2) - \mathscr{F}(0,2)] \times [1 + i_S^2], \tag{2.17}$$

where i_S^2 is the simple interest rate between date 1 and date 2. The first term is the marking-to-market that occurs at date 2. The second term is the marking-to-market that occurs at date 1 multiplied by 1 plus the simple interest rate.

Rearranging this term gives

$$S(2) - \mathscr{F}(0,2) + [\mathscr{F}(1,2) - \mathscr{F}(0,2)]i_S^2, \tag{2.18}$$

Comparing this value at date 2 with that of the forward contract strategy given in Expression (2.16), we see that the difference is given by the last term, the interest gained or lost on the date 1 marking-to-market of the futures contract. When viewed from date 0, this interest adjustment is random due to the changing simple interest rates (i_S^2) and unknown futures prices ($\mathscr{F}(1, 2)$).

The difference in date 2 cash flows shows that these contracts have different risks. The futures contract has the "risk" of reinvesting cash flows; this risk can be a benefit or cost, depending upon the correlation between futures prices and interest rates. For example, if i_S^2 increases (over i_S^1) on average when futures prices increase $[\mathscr{F}(1,2) - \mathscr{F}(0,2)]$, the cash flow to a futures contract at date 2 will, on average, exceed the cash flow to a forward contract. This gives a benefit (on average), which would make the futures contract a more "valuable" contract than the forward contract and would tend to *increase* futures prices relative to forward prices.

Conversely, if changes in short-term interest rates are negatively correlated to changes in futures prices, the futures contract's date 2 cash flow will, on average, be inferior to the forward contract's payoff. It results in a negative difference (on average) and would tend to *reduce* futures prices relative to forward prices.

This argument can be illustrated algebraically by computing the present values of Expressions (2.16) and (2.18) at date 0. Denote the present value at date 0 by the symbol $PV_0[\cdot]$. The present value of the forward contract is

$$V_F(0) = PV_0[S(2)] - F(0,2)B(0,2).$$

The present value of the futures contract, using Expression (2.18), is

$$V_{\mathscr{F}}(0) = PV_0[S(2)] - \mathscr{F}(0,2)B(0,2) + PV_0[[\mathscr{F}(1,2) - \mathscr{F}(0,2)]i_S^2].$$

At date 0, both contracts have zero value, which implies

$$0 = PV_0[S(2)] - F(0,2)B(0,2)$$

and

$$0 = PV_0[S(2)] - \mathscr{F}(0,2)B(0,2) + PV_0[(\mathscr{F}(1,2) - \mathscr{F}(0,2))i_S^2].$$

Solving for $PV_0[S(2)]$ in the first expression, and then substituting the result into the second expression, yields

$$F(0,2) = \mathscr{F}(0,2) - [1 + j_S \times 2]PV_0[[\mathscr{F}(1,2) - \mathscr{F}(0,2)]i_S^2],$$

where j_S is the simple interest rate from time 0 to time 2 and $B(0, 2) = 1/[1 + j_S \times 2]$.

This expression gives the relationship between forward prices and futures prices. The forward price equals the future price minus an adjustment term for the present value of the interest earned or owed from marking-to-market. This present value could be either positive, zero, or negative.

If interest rates are constant over the life of a futures contract, the present value of this interest earned or owed should be zero and there should be no difference between forward and futures prices. The intuition behind this statement is straightforward. If interest rates are uncorrelated to futures prices, then on average the net interest earned or owed from marking-to-market is zero. Therefore, the futures price will be identical to the forward price. This intuition can be more formally proven using an arbitrage-type argument.

Equality of Forward and Futures Prices

Let us assume that interest rates are non-random, and that j_S is known at date 0. While interest rates are known over the life of the contract, the term structure may be of any shape. We need to evaluate the relationship between the one-period simple rate of interest and the two-period simple rate of interest in a world with known interest rates.

Suppose that we start with one dollar. Consider two possible investment strategies. In the first strategy, we invest in the two-period bond and earn $V_1 \equiv [1 + j_S \times 2]$ for certain at the end of the second period.

In the second strategy, we invest in the one-period bond and earn, at the end of the first period, $[1 + i_S^1]$ for certain. We reinvest this amount at date 1 in the one-period bond, so that at the end of the second period we earn a total of

$$V_2 \equiv [1 + i_S^1][1 + i_S^2].$$

Given the absence of risk, the value of the two strategies must be equal, $V_1 = V_2$, implying

$$[1 + j_S \times 2] = [1 + i_S^1][1 + i_S^2]. \tag{2.19}$$

Thus the return from investing for two periods must equal the return from investing for one period and rolling it over.

We will consider a portfolio in which we go long futures contracts to buy the commodity and we write forward contracts. The initial value of the portfolio is zero. Any proceeds (positive or negative) generated by the marking-to-market of the futures contracts are invested (we borrow if a debit occurs) at the prevailing one-period simple interest rate. We want to design this portfolio such that the final payoff involves no risk.

Initial portfolio (date 0)

Part A (forward contracts)
Short n forward contracts with forward price $F(0,2)$, where $n = [1 + j_S \times 2]$.

Part B (futures contracts)
Go long m futures contracts with futures price $\mathscr{F}(0,2)$, where $m = [1 + i_S^1]$.

    Note that the initial value of this portfolio (Part A plus Part B) is zero because each contract has zero value.

    After one period, at date 1, the futures contracts are marked-to-market. This generates a credit or debit of

$$m[\mathscr{F}(1,2) - \mathscr{F}(0,2)].$$

This credit is reinvested at the prevailing one period simple interest rate, i_S^2. Had it been a debit, we would borrow at the same rate. At the end of the second period the total value of the investment will be

$$m[\mathscr{F}(1,2) - \mathscr{F}(0,2)][1 + i_S^2]$$

    At date 1, we increase our futures position, so that we now have a total of $m_1 \equiv m[1 + i_S^2]$ futures contracts.

Payoff at maturity (date 2)

Part A (forward contracts)
The value of the position in forward contracts is

$$-n[S(2) - F(0,2)] = -[1 + j_S \times 2][S2) - F(0,2)],$$

where $S(2)$ is the prevailing asset price. The minus sign arises because we have written the forward contracts.

Part B (futures contracts) (using $m_1 = m[1 + i_S^2]$ and $m = [1 + i_S^1]$)
The value of futures contracts position is $[1 + i_S^1][1 + i_S^2][S(2) - \mathscr{F}(1,2)]$. The funds generated at $t = 2$ by the marking-to-market process at $t = 1$ are

$$[1 + i_S^1][1 + i_S^2][\mathscr{F}(1,2) - \mathscr{F}(0,2)].$$

The combined total of these two cash flows is

$$[1 + i_S^1][1 + i_S^2][S(2) - \mathscr{F}(0,2)] = [1 + j_S \times 2][S(2) - \mathscr{F}(0,2)].$$

This uses from Expression (2.19) the result that $[1 + i_S^1][1 + i_S^2] = [1 + j_S \times 2]$. Therefore, the total payoff of Part A and Part B at date 2 is

$$-[1 + j_S \times 2][S(2) - F(0,2)] + [1 + j_S \times 2][S(2) - \mathscr{F}(0,2)]$$
$$= [1 + j_S \times 2][\mathscr{F}(0,2) - \mathscr{F}(0,2)].$$

This payoff depends only on quantities that are known at date 0 and therefore are riskless. Given that this portfolio was constructed with zero initial investment to avoid arbitrage, the final payoff must be identically zero. Therefore, the forward price must equal the futures price. This completes the argument.

For a generalization of this argument to many periods, see Cox, Ingersoll, and Ross (1981) and Jarrow and Oldfield (1981). This argument only works because we can deduce the simple interest rate at date 1 and create a portfolio of futures that duplicates the forward contracts. This argument breaks down if interest rates are random.

Note that the above analysis implicitly incorporated assumption A2, that there is no default risk with the forward contract and the futures contract. Given that failure of financial institutions is not a rare event—for example, Barings Ltd. in 1995—think about the empirical robustness of this assumption.

Empirical Evidence

Two essential differences exist between forward and futures contracts. First, futures contracts are marked-to-market, which implies that randomness in short-term interest rates will affect the futures price. The second difference is default risk. Futures contracts are traded on organized exchanges and the clearing house guarantees the contracts. The default risk is the risk that the clearing house will be unable to honor its commitments. Forward contracts are over-the-counter contracts and the default risk is that the parties involved may default. The effects of differential default risk between forward and futures contracts have been ignored in most empirical studies.

Ideally, for empirical work one would like, at a given point in time, say Tuesday at 11:23 A.M., to observe the futures price and forward price for contracts written on the same asset, having the same maturity, and having the same default risk. In practice, this is rarely possible because these contracts are not traded in the same market. This problem gives rise to what is referred to as a non-simultaneity measurement problem. Nonetheless, the evidence is as follows.

Rendleman and Carabini (1979) concluded that, for Treasury bill contracts, the differences between forward and futures prices are economically insignificant. Theoretical work by Flesaker (1993) and Musiela, Turnbull, and Wakeman (1993) reached the same conclusion provided the contracts are short-term.

Cornell and Reinganum (1981) and Chang and Chang (1990) examined the differences between forward and futures prices in the foreign exchange markets. For the five currencies they examined—British pounds, Canadian dollars, Deutsche marks, Japanese yen and Swiss francs—they found the differences between futures and forward prices to be small. Dezhbakhsh (1994) contradicted these results and found significant divergence for several currencies.

For five commodities—gold, silver, silver coins, platinum, and copper—Park and Chen (1985) found a statistically significant difference between forward and futures prices.

Although these studies investigated the differences between forward and futures prices and most found them to be slight, we emphasize that forward contracts are different contracts than are futures contracts. In subsequent chapters, we will show that futures contracts are hedged differently than are forward contracts, even under constant interest rates. This difference is economically significant and should not be overlooked. It is due to the marking-to-market of futures contracts and the different cash flows this provides.

2.8 SUMMARY

Here we have studied the relationship between the spot price and forward price for an underlying asset, and the relationship between forward and futures prices. When a forward contract is initiated, the forward price is set such that the value of the contract is zero. We have used simple arbitrage arguments to establish the relationship between the spot price of the asset on which the forward contract is written and the forward price. This relation is called cash-and-carry. The results are summarized in Table 2.2.

After a forward contract is initiated, the value of the contract may be either positive or negative. We derive a general expression for the value of a forward contract in terms of the initial forward price $F(0,T)$ and the current forward price $F(t,T)$. It is shown in Expressions (2.5) and (2.9) that the value of a contract is

$$V(t) = [F(t,T) - F(0,T)]B(t,T).$$

TABLE 2.2   *Spot-Forward Price Relationships Summary of Results*

CASE	FORWARD/SPOT RELATIONSHIP	REFERENCE EXPRESSION
No dividend/coupon	$F(0,T)B(0,T) = S(0)$	(2.2)
Known dividend, d_1 at date t_1	$F(0,T)B(0,T) = S(0) - d_1B(0,t_1)$	(2.6)
Constant dividend yield, d_y	$F(0,T)B(0,T) = I(0)\exp(-d_yT)$	(2.10)
Foreign exchange	$F(0,T)B(0,T) = S(0)B_f(0,T)$	(2.11)
Commodity, with net convenience yield, y	$F(0,T)B(0,T) = S(0)\exp(-yT)$	(2.15)

$F(0,T)$ is the forward price at date 0 for a contract that matures at date T; $S(0)$ is the spot price at date 0; $I(0)$ is the stock index value at date 0; $B(0,T)$ is the value at date 0 of a Treasury bill that pays \$1 with certainty at date T; and $B_f(0,T)$ is the value at date 0 in terms of the foreign currency of a claim that pays one unit of the foreign currency with certainty at date T.

We demonstrate that forward prices and futures prices are, in general, not equal. This difference is due to the randomness of short-term interest rates and the reinvestment risk inherent in marking-to-market. If there is no uncertainty about future interest rates, we have also shown that forward and futures prices are equal.

SUGGESTIONS FOR FURTHER READING

Empirical research concerning forward and futures prices:

Chang, C., and J. Chang, 1990. "Forward and Futures Prices: Evidence from Foreign Exchange Markets." *Journal of Finance* 45, 1333–1336.

Cornell, B., and M. Reinganum, 1981. "Forward and Futures Prices: Evidence from Foreign Exchange Markets." *Journal of Finance* 36, 1035–1045.

Dezhbakhsh, H., 1994. "Foreign Exchange Forward and Futures Prices: Are They Equal?" *Journal of Financial and Quantitative Analysis* 29, 75–87.

French, K., 1983. "A Comparison of Futures and Forward Prices." *Journal of Financial Economics* 12, 311–342.

Park, H. Y., and A. H. Chen, 1985. "Differences Between Futures and Forward Prices: A Further Investigation of Marking to Market Effects." *Journal of Futures Markets* 5, 77–88.

Rendleman, R., and C. Carabini, 1979. "The Efficiency of the Treasury Bill Futures Markets." *Journal of Finance* 34, 895–914.

The theoretical relationship between forward and futures prices:

Cox, J. C., J. E. Ingersoll, and S. A. Ross, 1981. "The Relation Between Forward Prices and Futures Prices." *Journal of Financial Economics* 9, 321–346.

Jarrow, R. A., and G. S. Oldfield, 1981. "Forward Contracts and Futures Contracts." *Journal of Financial Economics* 9, 373–382.

Richard, S., and M. Sundaresan, 1981. "A Continuous Time Model of Forward and Futures Prices in a Multigood Economy." *Journal of Financial Economics* 9, 347–372.

The theoretical relationship between forward and futures interest rate prices:

Flesaker, B., 1993. "Arbitrage Free Pricing of Interest Rate Futures and Forward Contracts." *Journal of Futures Markets* 13, 77–91.

Jarrow, R., 1997. *Modelling Fixed Income Securities and Interest Rate Options.* McGraw-Hill: New York.

Musiela, M., S. M. Turnbull, and L. M. Wakeman, 1993. "Interest Rate Risk Management." *Review of Futures Markets* 12, 221–261.

QUESTIONS

Short Questions

1. List all the forward contracts that are traded on financial assets and commodities.
2. What futures contracts are traded on financial assets and commodities?
3. Use a newspaper to compare forward and futures prices on the Japanese yen. Why do these prices in general differ?

Question 1

The current spot exchange is 0.6676 ($/DM). The price of a domestic 180-day Treasury bill is $98.0199 per $100 face value, and the price of the equivalent German instrument is DM 96.4635 per DM 100 face value. The 180-day forward exchange rate is 0.66 ($/DM). There are no transaction costs and markets are assumed to be perfect.

a) What is the theoretical forward exchange rate?
b) Given that the current forward exchange rate is greater than the theoretical forward exchange rate, describe an arbitrage strategy given zero wealth. Assume the contract size is 100 DM.

Question 2

On June 3, 1994, a company enters into a forward contract to buy 10 million Deutsche marks at the forward rate F_0 ($/DM). The contract expires June 4, 1995. On September 5, 1994, the company enters into a forward contract to sell 10 million Deutsche marks on June 4, 1995. The forward exchange rate is F_1 ($/DM). Describe the payoff from this strategy. What is the value of the June 3, 1994 forward contract on September 5, 1994?

Question 3

Consider a forward contract written on a non-dividend paying asset. The current spot price is $65. The maturity of the contract is 90 days and the simple interest rate for this period is 4.50 percent per annum.

a) Determine the forward price. What is the value of the contract?
b) A corporate client wants a 90-day forward contract with the delivery price set at $60. What is the value of this contract?

(Assume a 365-day year.)

Question 4

Three months ago you entered into a forward contract to buy stock. The forward contract matures in 100 days' time and the delivery price is $50.25. Given a change of circumstances, you no longer want the forward contract. To offset the initial forward contract, you enter into a new forward contract to sell stock. The current stock price is $45, the rate of interest is 4.75 percent per annum, expressed as a simple interest rate and assuming a 365-day year. The stock will not pay any dividends over the life of the option.

a) What is the forward price for this new contract?
b) What is the value of your net position when the two forward contracts mature?
c) What is the present value today of your net position?

Question 5

The current dollar/Deutsche mark spot exchange rate is 0.5685. If you invested $1 for three months in the domestic riskless asset you would earn $1.0101, and if you invested 1 DM for three months in the German riskless asset you would earn 1.0113 marks.

A corporation wants a three-month forward contract to buy 1 million marks at the exchange rate of 0.54 dollars/mark. What is the value of this contract?

Question 6

You are given the following information about Japanese yen forward exchange rates.

| | FORWARD EXCHANGE RATE | |
MATURITY (DAYS)	$/YEN	U.S. DISCOUNT RATE*
30	0.011047	5.46
90	0.011123	5.77
180	0.011249	5.96
Spot Rate	0.011009	

*Expressed as a discount rate assuming a 360-day year.

a) Determine the price of U.S. 30-day, 90-day, and 180-day Treasury bills.
b) Determine the 30-day, 90-day, and 180-day Japanese discount rates.

Question 7

A one-year forward contract is written on a dividend-paying stock. The current stock is $63\frac{3}{8}$, and it is known that the stock will pay a dividend of $1.50 per share in one month and a dividend of $2 per share in seven months' time. The price of a one-month Treasury bill is 0.9967, a seven-month Treasury bill 0.9741, and a twelve-month Treasury bill 0.9512, assuming a face value of $1. What is the forward price?

Question 8

You are given the following information about the S&P 500 futures price.

MATURITY (DAYS)	FUTURES PRICE	DISCOUNT RATE*
94	497.40	5.74
192	501.85	5.90
276	506.50	5.93
Spot Index Value	492.89	

*Expressed as a discount rate assuming a 360-day year.

a) Determine the 94-day, 192-day, and 276-day Treasury bill prices.
b) Ignoring the difference between forward and futures prices, determine the implied dividend yield, assuming a 360-day year.

Question 9

The current value of the S&P 500 index is 495.00. The dividend yield is 2.50 percent per annum, assuming continuous compounding, and a 365-day year.

a) What is the 95-day forward price? The 95-day discount rate is 5.75 percent, assuming a 360-day year.
b) One day later the index is at 493. What is the value of the forward contract? The 94-day discount rate is 5.75 percent.
c) Suppose that one day later, after the forward contract was initiated, the index is at 493 and the 94-day discount rate is 5.65 percent. What is the value of the forward contract?
d) Is the difference in your answers to parts (b) and (c) what you would expect?

Question 10

You are given the following information about silver futures (Comex, Division of the New York Mercantile Exchange). The contract size is 5,000 troy ounces, and prices are quoted in terms of cents per troy ounce.

CONTRACT	MATURITY (MONTHS)	FUTURES PRICE (CENTS PER TROY OUNCE)	DISCOUNT RATE*
May	2	472.0	5.71
July	4	477.4	5.78
September	6	482.5	5.88
December	9	490.4	5.93
Spot Price		468.1	

*Expressed as a discount rate assuming a 360-day year.

Ignoring the difference between forward and futures prices, use Expression (2.15) to determine the implied net convenience yield for each futures contract.

APPENDIX: PRESENT VALUE OF DIVIDENDS OVER LIFE OF FORWARD CONTRACT

To compute the present value of the dividends, consider two indices, one without dividends, $\tilde{I}(t)$, and one with dividends, $I(t)$. Let $\tilde{I}(0) = aI(0)$, where a is constant and

$$d \ln[I(t)] = d \ln[\tilde{I}(t)] - d_y dt.$$

This implies

$$I(t) = a\tilde{I}(t)\exp(-d_y t).$$

The present value of the index without dividends is

$$PV_0[\tilde{I}(t)] = \tilde{I}(0).$$

Consider the present value of the index with dividends:

$$\begin{aligned} PV_0[I(t)] &= PV_0[a\tilde{I}(t)\exp(-d_y t)] \\ &= aPV_0[\tilde{I}(t)]\exp(-d_y t) \\ &= a\tilde{I}(0)\exp(-d_y t) \\ &= I(0)\exp(-d_y t) \end{aligned}$$

Given that

$$I(0) = PV_0[I(t)] + PV_0[\text{dividends over } (0, t)],$$

we get

$$PV_0[\text{dividends over } (0, t)] = I(0)[1 - \exp(d_y t)].$$

Simple Arbitrage Relationships for Options

3.0 INTRODUCTION

In the last chapter, we studied the synthetic construction of forward and futures contracts via trading in the underlying spot commodity and riskless borrowing or lending. This ability to synthetically construct forward and futures contracts enables investment banks to make markets in these securities and to offset their risks. Similarly, to make markets in call and put options, investment banks need to know how to synthetically construct these securities. This chapter provides the initial insights into this synthetic construction. Here, we concentrate only on the most fundamental relationships between call and put options written on the same underlying asset.

We use simple arbitrage arguments to establish some general results for option prices without making any explicit assumptions concerning the probability distribution for the future value of the underlying asset. In particular, we will establish upper and lower bounds for call and put option prices. Should an option price lie outside these bounds, this indicates a possible arbitrage opportunity. To keep our discussion simple, we assume that over the life of an option the underlying asset has no cash flows. The extension to assets with cash flows is straightforward and we leave this discussion to subsequent chapters.

3.1 CALL AND PUT OPTIONS

We now establish some basic results for call options using simple arbitrage arguments. To fix the discussion, we let the underlying asset be a common stock. However, we emphasize that these arguments apply to other assets as well. Let $C(0)$ represent the time-zero value of an American call option on a stock with current price $S(0)$, expiration date T, and strike price K.[1]

---

[1]A capital C will be used to denote an American call option and a small c will be used to denote a European call option. For simplicity, we suppress the stock price, strike price, and maturity date in this notation. Where necessary, we will make these explicit.

Result 1

If the stock price is zero, then the value of an American call option must be zero, that is,

if $S(0) = 0$ then $C(0) = 0$.

PROOF   The proof of this result is straightforward. Recall that the stock price reflects the present value of all future cash flows accruing to shareholders. If the stock price is zero, there are never any future cash flows. Consequently, at the expiration date, the stock price will be zero as well, and thus the option will expire worthless.   ∎

Result 2

The minimum value of an American call option is given by zero or $S(0) - K$, whichever is greater:

$$C(0) \geq \text{Max}\{0, S(0) - K\}.$$

PROOF   The proof of this result has two parts. First, the option cannot have a negative value due to its limited liability. Limited liability implies that one can always discard the option, thus we must have

$$C(0) \geq 0. \tag{3.1}$$

Second, suppose that $S(0)$ is greater than K. If $C(0)$ was less than $S(0) - K$, arbitrage is possible: Simply buy the option at a cost of $C(0)$, and immediately exercise generating a cash flow of $S(0) - K$. The net profit is

$$S(0) - K - C(0) > 0.$$

Thus to avoid arbitrage, we must have:

$$C(0) \geq S(0) - K. \quad ∎ \tag{3.2}$$

EXAMPLE   ### Result 2

Let the value of an American call option that matures in 90 days' time be $2. Let the stock price be $50 and let the strike price be $45.

This contradicts Result 2 because

$$C(0) = 2,$$

yet

$$S(0) - K = 50 - 45 = 5,$$

implying that arbitrage is possible.

The arbitrage opportunity is to buy the option and immediately exercise it. The total cost is $47 (= 2 + 45). Since the stock is worth $50, our profit is $3. Clearly this is a money machine that can be repeated until prices change and Result 2 holds. ■

Result 3

An American call option can never be worth more than the underlying asset:

$$S(0) \geq C(0).$$

PROOF   If this result is false, an arbitrage opportunity would exist. The arbitrage opportunity would be to buy the stock and sell the call. The difference is a positive cash flow at date 0. If the call is ever exercised, we can deliver the stock and receive the strike price of K dollars. Otherwise, we own the stock. In either circumstance, the future cash flow is positive or zero. To avoid this arbitrage, Result 3 must hold. ■

The above three results are illustrated in Figure 3.1. These results establish upper and lower bounds for an American call option. If an American call option lies outside these bounds, arbitrage is possible. To obtain these results, we make no assumptions about the probability distribution describing future movements of the stock's price.

FIGURE 3.1   *American Call Option Valuation*

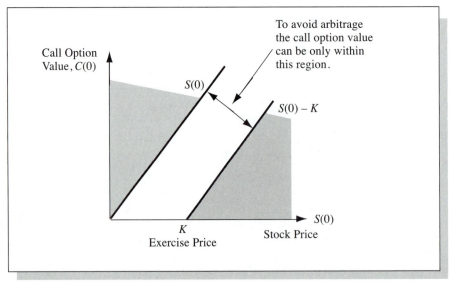

Result 2 establishes a lower bound for American call options using an argument that relies upon the flexibility of prematurely exercising the option. We can establish a similar lower bound for a European call option. Denote the European call's value by $c(0)$, given a current stock price of $S(0)$, expiration date T, and strike price K. Remember that we use capital C to denote the value of an American option and small c to denote the value of a European option.

Result 4

Assume that the underlying stock pays no dividends. The minimum value of a European option is zero or $S(0) - KB(0, T)$, whichever is greater:

$$c(0) \geq \text{Max}\{0, S(0) - KB(0, T)\},$$

where $B(0, T)$ is the price of a default-free zero-coupon bond that pays \$1 at date T.

PROOF

The proof of this result is given in two parts. First, because the European option is of limited liability, $c(0) \geq 0$. Second, consider two investment strategies. We will show that the payoff to the first strategy is never less than the payoff to the second. Consequently, the cost of the first strategy is never less than the cost of the second.

Strategy one (date 0)

Purchase a European call option at a cost of $c(0)$.

Strategy two (date 0)

Purchase a forward contract with delivery price K. The forward contract is written on the same stock and with the same maturity date as the option. From Expression (2.4), the value of the forward contract is[2]

$$S(0) - KB(0, T).$$

Now consider the value of the two strategies at date T:

	$S(T) < K$	$S(T) \geq K$
Strategy One (Date T) Long Call Option	0	$S(T) - K$
Strategy Two (Date T) Long Forward Contract	$S(T) - K$	$S(T) - K$

The payoff to the call option dominates the payoff of the forward contract when the asset price is less than K because the value of the option is zero while the value of the forward contract is negative. When the stock price exceeds K, the

---

[2]The delivery price is not necessarily the prevailing forward price.

option and forward contract have identical values. Therefore, the option cannot be worth less than the forward contract:

$$c(0) \geq S(0) - KB(0, T).$$

Combined, these values give the result.   ■

EXAMPLE   **Result 4**

It is instructive to compute the lower bound for a European call option.

Suppose the stock price is $55 and the exercise price is $50. Let the option mature in three months' time and let the three-month simple interest rate be 8.90 percent. Let the stock pay no dividends over the next three months. Therefore, the lower bound for a European call is

$$S(0) - KB(0, T) = 55 - 50/[1 + 0.089 \times (3/12)]$$
$$= 6.09.$$

Suppose that the option price is $4, implying that the lower bound is violated, which in turn implies that the option is undervalued. Consider the investment strategy in which you buy the option for $4 and write a forward contract with a delivery price of $50. The value of this forward contract, using Expression (2.4), is

$$55 - 50/[1 + 0.089 \times (3/12)] = 6.09.$$

The investment strategy generates an initial *inflow* of $2.09 (= 6.09 − 4.00).

The value of this investment strategy, when the option and forward contracts mature, is

	$S(T) < 50$	$S(T) \geq 50$
Long Option	0	$S(T) - 50$
Short Forward	$-[S(T) - 50]$	$-[S(T) - 50]$
Net	$50 - S(T)$	0

implying that no matter what happens, we cannot lose. The strategy is a money machine.   ■

Result 5

An American call option can never be worth less than a European call option:

$$C(0) \geq c(0).$$

PROOF The proof of this result is very simple: Anything you can do with a European call option you can do with an American call option. Furthermore, with an American call option you have the added flexibility of being able to exercise it at any time until the maturity date. This flexibility cannot have a negative value, though it can have a zero value. Therefore, an American call option cannot be worth less than a European call option. ∎

There are a set of conditions, given in Result 6, under which an American call option has equal value to a European call option.

Result 6

Given no dividends on the underlying stock and positive interest rates, that is, $B(0, T)$ < 1 for all $T > 0$, an American call option will never be prematurely exercised, implying that an American option will be priced as a European option:

$$C(0) = c(0).$$

PROOF The proof of this property follows by combining Results 4 and 5. From these we have

$$C(0) \geq c(0) \geq \text{Max}\{0, S(0) - KB(0, T)\},$$

implying

$$C(0) \geq S(0) - KB(0, T).$$

The value of an American call option, if exercised, is $S(0) - K$. Now $B(0, T)$ < 1 by assumption, therefore

$$S(0) - KB(0, T) > S(0) - K,$$

and

$$C(0) > S(0) - K,$$

implying that the option is worth more "alive" than "dead." ∎

Under the conditions of Result 6, you will not exercise an American call option until it matures. Because of this fact, its value will be identical to that of a European call option, a useful result that we will use later.

This result may seem counterintuitive at first reading. The reader might ask: If the stock's value is currently above K but we believe that it is going to fall below K,

then shouldn't we exercise the call? The answer is no. You would be better off by selling the call option. To understand this point, note that if you exercise the call you get $S(0) - K$, but if you sell it you get $C(0)$. From Result 6, we have $C(0) > S(0) - K$. You get more dollars by selling than by exercising.

The intuition is straightforward. By exercising early you take possession of the stock and pay K dollars. You now bear the risk of the stock falling below K, and you lose the interest you would have earned on the strike price K from waiting to exercise. There are only costs to exercising early, and because the stock pays no dividends there are no benefits. Early exercise is suboptimal.

This argument does not follow if there are dividends paid on the stock over the life of the option. If dividends are paid, it may be optimal to prematurely exercise a call option just before the dividend payment because the benefits of receiving the dividend may exceed the interest lost on the strike K and the cost of giving up the downside protection. We will discuss this possibility in Chapter 7.

Result 7

If two American call options have the same exercise price and are written on the same stock, the option with the longer maturity date cannot be worth less than the other option:[3]

$$\text{if} \quad T_1 > T_2 \quad \text{then} \quad C(0; T_1) \geq C(0; T_2).$$

PROOF   Let us consider the situation at date T_2 when the option with the shorter maturity expires. Anything you can do with this option you can do with the option that matures at date T_1; moreover, with the longer maturity option you have the added flexibility of postponing exercise until a later date. The added flexibility cannot have a negative value, thus the result. ■

3.2 PUT OPTIONS

We now derive similar arbitrage-based restrictions for put options. As the proofs are similar, the exposition will be brief to avoid redundancy. Let $P(0)$ denote the price of an American put option[4] with expiration date T and strike price K on a stock with current price $S(0)$. The next result is analogous to Result 1 for call options.

Result 8

If the stock price is zero, the value of an American put must be its exercise price:

$$\text{if} \quad S(0) = 0, \quad \text{then} \quad P(0) = K.$$

---

[3]Note that we augment the notation for the call value to include the maturity date.
[4]A capital P will be used to denote an American put option and a small p will be used to denote a European put option.

PROOF

> The proof of this result is straightforward. If the stock price is zero, exercising the option immediately provides its maximum payoff. Waiting only loses the interest one can earn on the strike price K. ∎

Result 9

The minimum value of an American put option is either zero or $K - S(0)$, whichever is greater:

$$P(0) \geq \text{Max}\{0, K - S(0)\}.$$

PROOF

> The proof of this result is similar to the proof of Result 2. Suppose that this is not true and $K - S(0) > P(0)$. We could then buy the option and exercise immediately, making a profit $K - S(0) - P(0) > 0$. Thus to avoid arbitrage we must have $K - S(0) \leq P(0)$. The put's value is also non-negative due to its limited liability. ∎

EXAMPLE

> ### Result 9
>
> Let the value of an American put option that matures in 78 days' time be \$3. Let the stock price be \$50 and the strike price be \$55.
>   Note that this contradicts Result 9 because
>
> $$P(0) = 3$$
>
> and
>
> $$K - S(0) = 55 - 50 = 5,$$
>
> implying that arbitrage is possible.
>   The arbitrage opportunity is to buy the put option and exercise it immediately, making a profit of \$2 ($= 5 - 3$). ∎

The next result gives the maximum value for an American put option.

Result 10

The maximum value of an American put option is its exercise price, that is:

$$K \geq P(0).$$

PROOF This result follows because the maximum payoff to the American put option is the strike price K, which occurs if the stock price is zero. For any positive stock price, the option must be worth less than the maximum. ■

Clearly, if you own a put option the maximum you can earn is the strike price, which occurs if the stock price is zero. Put options provide insurance against bad news. The cost of the insurance is the cost of the option.

The previous three results are illustrated in Figure 3.2 and establish upper and lower bounds for an American put option. If these bounds are violated, arbitrage opportunities exist.

EXAMPLE ### Results 9 and 10

If the stock price is $50 and the strike price is $50, then using Results 9 and 10 the value of an American put must be between zero and $50:

$$0 \leq P(0) \leq 50.$$

While we have established upper and lower bounds, these bounds can be large and not very useful in generating arbitrage opportunities. ■

We now investigate similar results for European put options. Let $p(0)$ denote a European put option's value given that the current stock price is $S(0)$, the expiration date is T, and the strike price is K. Remember that we use capital P to denote the value

FIGURE 3.2   *American Put Option Valuation*

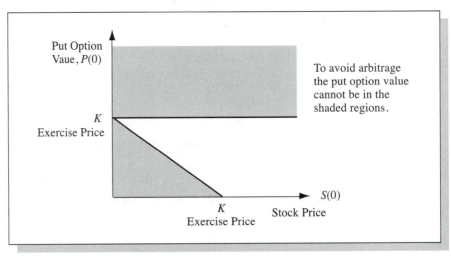

of an American put option and small p to denote the value of a European put option. The next result is analogous to Result 4 for European call options.

Result 11

Assume that the stock pays no dividends. For a European put option,

$$p(0) \geq \text{Max}\{0, KB(0,T) - S(0)\}.$$

PROOF

The proof for this result is similar to the proof given for Result 4. Limited liability guarantees $p(0) \geq 0$. In addition, the European put option has more flexibility than being short a forward contract on the stock, with delivery price K. The written forward contract has current value $KB(0,T) - S(0)$. The European put is worth at least this much since it need not be exercised at maturity, but the forward contract must be exercised at maturity, even if its value is negative. Thus

$$p(0) \geq KB(0,T) - S(0).$$

Combined, these values give the desired result. ∎

EXAMPLE

Result 11

Consider a three-month European put option with a strike price $50. Let the stock price be $45. Let the three-month simple rate of interest be 8.90 percent. The stock pays no dividends over the next three months.

The lower bound for the European put is:

$$50/[1 + 0.089 \times (3/12)] - 45 = 3.91.$$

Suppose that the option price is $3, implying that the lower bound is violated. This implies that the option is undervalued. Consider an investment strategy in which you buy the option for $3 and go long in a *new* forward contract.

The forward price is, using Expression (2.3):

$$F(0,3/12) = 45 \times [1 + 0.089 \times (3/12)]$$
$$= 46.0,$$

which is different from the strike price of the option. By construction, the value of this forward contract is zero. You borrow the present value of the difference between the strike price of the option and the forward price:

$$(50 - 46)/[1 + .089 \times (3/12)] = 3.91.$$

This investment strategy generates a cash inflow at date 0 equal to

Amount Borrowed   3.91
Cost of Option   3.00
─────
Net Inflow   0.91.

The value of this investment strategy when the option and forward contracts mature is

	$S(T) \leq 50$	$S(T) > 50$
Put Option	$50 - S(T)$	0
Forward Contract	$S(T) - 46$	$S(T) - 46$
Repay Amount Borrowed[5]	-4	-4
Net Amount	0	$S(T) - 50$

Thus, by implication, no matter what happens you cannot lose. This is clearly a money machine. ∎

The next result relating American and European put options is analogous to Result 5 for call options.

Result 12

An American put is worth at least as much as a European put:

$P(0) \geq p(0).$

The argument is similar to that used for Result 5 and is left to the reader to work through.

Unlike the situation for an American call option, even in the absence of dividends, it may be optimal to prematurely exercise an American put option. This happens when the stock price falls low enough so that any potential benefit received from the likelihood that it falls more is less than the interest gained on the cash received from immediately exercising the option.

EXAMPLE   **Early Exercise**

This example illustrates a situation in which early exercise of a put option is optimal. Let the exercise price be $25, the stock price be $1, the maturity be six months and the six-month simple rate of interest be 9.50 percent.

─────────

[5]Amount borrowed $= 3.91 \times [1 + 0.089 \times (3/12)]$
                $= 4.0.$

If the option is exercised immediately, you would receive $24. Investing this amount for six months at 9.50 percent will generate $25.17. However, the maximum possible value of the put option is $25, using Result 10, and it may never be obtained. Thus you would be better off by prematurely exercising the option and investing the proceeds in a riskless asset. ■

Recall that for American call options, if there are no dividends on the stock, the call should never be exercised early. This is not the case for put options. This difference between the premature exercise of an American call option versus an American put option exists because of the differences in their payoff diagrams. The call option has unlimited upside potential, so there is always some additional benefit of waiting to exercise, namely, more profits are possible. However, it is not true for the American put, the upside potential of which is limited by the strike price K. Hence, if the upper limit is "close," it is better to exercise and earn interest on the proceeds than to wait.

3.3 RELATIONSHIP BETWEEN EUROPEAN CALL AND PUT OPTIONS

This section derives relationships between European call and put options. Unlike Results 1–12, which are most useful for developing an understanding of options, the following results can provide some profit opportunities for option traders. As will be shown, there is an intrinsic relationship between the value of a European call option and a European put option with the same maturity date and with the same strike price. This relationship is called **put-call parity**. For simplicity, it is assumed that the underlying stock pays no dividends over the life of the option. The addition of dividends is a straightforward exercise and is left to the end of the chapter.

Result 13: European Put-Call Parity

For European options there is a simple relation between call and put options:

$$p(0) = c(0) + KB(0,T) - S(0).$$

PROOF   To prove this result, consider two portfolios.

Portfolio A.   Buy one put option, cost $p(0)$.

Portfolio B.   Buy one call option, buy K of the $B(0,T)$ bonds, and short one share of the stock. The total cost is

$$c(0) + KB(0,T) - S(0).$$

Now consider the payoff of these two portfolios at maturity.

	$S(T) \leq K$	$S(T) > K$
Portfolio A Put	$K - S(T)$	0
Portfolio B Call Option Bond Short Stock	0 K $-S(T)$	$S(T) - K$ K $-S(T)$
Total	$K - S(T)$	0

Irrespective of the terminal stock price $S(T)$, the payoffs for the two portfolios are identical. Therefore, to avoid arbitrage we must have identical time-0 values:

$$p(0) = c(0) + KB(0, T) - S(0). \quad \blacksquare$$

The logic underlying the proof of Result 13 is given in Figure 3.3, in which we consider a portfolio consisting of:

Buy one call option.	$c(0)$
Buy K of the $B(0, T)$ bonds.	$KB(0, T)$
Short one stock $S(0)$.	$-S(0)$
Total cost	$c(0) + KB(0, T) - S(0)$

At maturity the payoff to this portfolio is seen to be equal to that of a put option. To avoid arbitrage, the costs of the portfolio and the put option must be the same:

$$p(0) = c(0) + KB(0, T) - S(0).$$

This equality is put-call parity.

Put-call parity is an important relationship for understanding calls and puts. Rewritten, it says:

$$c(0) = p(0) + S(0) - KB(0, T).$$

In words, a call option is equivalent to a levered position in the stock [$S(0) - KB(0, T)$] with an insurance policy on the stock's price set at K. The value of this insurance policy is $p(0)$. By "levered," we mean the portfolio consists of the stock plus borrowing. This basic intuition is useful for understanding various trading strategies involving options.

FIGURE 3.3   *Put-Call Parity*

Consider a portfolio of:
  a) long a European call option;
  b) long a Treasury bill with face value *K;*
  c) short stock *S*(0).

At the maturity of the option the payoffs are:

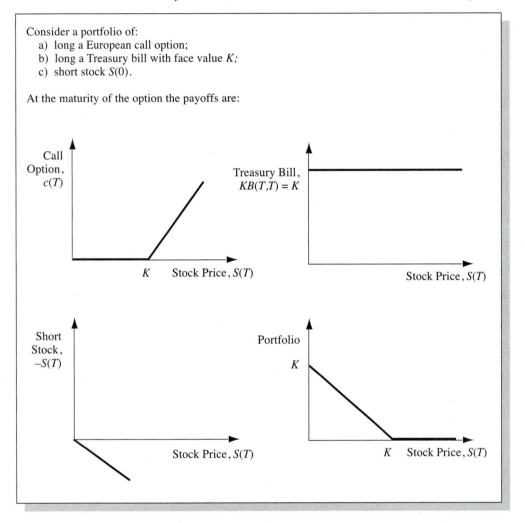

EXAMPLE   **Use of Put-Call Parity**

Suppose we have special information that the stock's price will increase significantly over the next month. How do we take advantage of this information? Do we buy calls, sell puts, buy the stock, or buy the stock with borrowing?

   Put-call parity gives us the answer. If you believe the stock price cannot fall, you should buy the stock with borrowing. Do not buy a call because by put-call parity this involves purchasing an insurance policy you do not need. On the other hand, you could simultaneously buy calls and write puts, but again by put-call parity this is the same as a levered stock position.   ∎

3.4 RELATIONSHIP BETWEEN AMERICAN CALL AND PUT OPTIONS

For the relative pricing of American call and put options, we want to determine a put-call parity relationship. In the absence of dividends, while it is never optimal to prematurely exercise an American call option, it may be optimal to prematurely exercise an American put option. Consequently, the argument we used for the put-call parity relationship for European options does not hold. However, it is "approximately" true for American options, that is:

call option $\approx$ put option + stock + borrowing.

The symbol "$\approx$" means approximately. Although an equality does not hold, the basic intuition is still approximately correct. An American call option is approximately equal to taking a levered position in the stock, plus holding an insurance policy on its value. The formal statement of the relationship is contained in Result 14. The best we can obtain are two inequalities.

Result 14: American Put/Call Parity

Assume that over the life of the option the stock pays no dividends, then

i) $P(0) + S(0) - KB(0, T) \geq C(0)$

and

ii) $C(0) \geq P(0) + S(0) - K.$

The proof consists of two parts. Part One proves the first inequality, and Part Two proves the second.

PROOF   **Part One**

To prove the first inequality, we know from Result 12 that the price of an American put cannot be less than the price of a European put:

$P(0) \geq p(0).$

But, using put-call parity for European options,

$P(0) = c(0) - S(0) + KB(0, T).$

Substituting this result and rearranging gives

$P(0) + S(0) - KB(0, T) \geq c(0).$

We know from Result 6 that, in the absence of any dividend payments, the value of an American option is equal to the value of a European option:

$$c(0) = C(0).$$

Combining this result gives

$$P(0) + S(0) - KB(0, T) \geq C(0).$$

completing the proof of Part One.

Part Two

To prove Part Two, consider the following portfolio: Buy one call, sell one put, short the stock, and hold K dollars in cash. The cost is

$$C(0) - P(0) - S(0) + K.$$

Since we sold the put, it could be exercised against us. As we own the call, we decide its early exercise strategy. Let us never exercise it early. We now examine the cash flows to our portfolio.

If the put is exercised early, say at date t^*, our position is

$$C(t^*) - [K - S(t^*)] - S(t^*) - K \geq 0$$

with strict inequality if $S(t^*) > 0$. We liquidate our position.

If the put is not exercised early, our position at date T is zero, as the following table shows.

PORTFOLIO POSITION	$S(T) \leq K$	$S(T) > K$
Long call	0	$[S(T) - K]$
Short put	$-[K - S(T)]$	0
Short stock	$-S(T)$	$-S(T)$
Long K cash	K	K
Total	0	0

The payoff to our portfolio, no matter which event occurs, is either zero or positive. Thus to avoid arbitrage, the initial cost must be non-negative:

$$C(0) - P(0) - S(0) + K \geq 0.$$

completing the proof of Part Two, and the proof of the theorem. ∎

The previous put-call parity theorems for both European and American options are for stocks that pay no dividends. The adjustment to the put-call parity theorem to account for dividends differs for European and American options.

For European options, in Result 13 the current stock price $S(0)$ is replaced by the present value of the stock price at date T, that is, $PV_0(S(T))$. For example, if the stock price pays a known dividend of $d(t_1)$ at date t_1, then $PV_0(S(T)) = S(0) - d(t_1)B(0, t_1)$ replaces the current stock price $S(0)$. This makes sense because European options can be exercised only after the dividend is paid.

For American options, Result 14(i) remains unchanged, given dividends. The logic is that the American call could be exercised immediately, making the call effectively equal to the stock (including all future dividends). Result 14(ii) changes. The stock price $S(0)$ is again replaced by $PV_0(S(T))$. The logic for this modification is that, in the worst scenario, the put is not exercised prior to date T. Therefore, we lose all the dividends on the short stock position. The necessary modifications for dividends are now complete.

3.5 SUMMARY

In this chapter, we discussed some general results for call and put options, using simple arbitrage arguments. We did not need to make any assumptions about the probability distribution of the underlying asset. Consequently, our results are robust to the levels of uncertainty that characterize financial markets. We show that, in the absence of dividends, it is never optimal to exercise an American call option early. This result does not hold for American put options. There is also an intrinsic relationship between the value of a European call option and a European put option, referred to as put-call parity. The relationship is useful for option traders.

This put-call parity relationship was extended to American options. However, for American options it is only possible to establish two inequalities. The basic intuition obtained from put-call parity is that a call option is approximately equal to a levered position in the stock plus an insurance policy on its value, an intuition sometimes useful for understanding various trading strategies.

SUGGESTIONS FOR FURTHER READING

The theoretical properties for options are derived in:

Merton, R. C., 1973. "Theory of Rational Option Pricing." *Bell Journal of Economics and Management Science* 4, 141–183.

Smith, C. W., 1976. "Option Pricing: A Review." *Journal of Financial Economics* 3, 3–52.

Boundary condition tests are described in:

Halpern, P. J., and S. M. Turnbull, 1985. "Empirical Tests of Boundary Conditions for Toronto Stock Exchange Options." *Journal of Finance* 40, 481–500.

QUESTIONS

Short Questions

1. List all of the different types of financial options that are traded on organized options exchanges.
2. An investor buys a put option and sells a call option on the same stock with the same strike price. Describe the investor's position. If the strike price is equal to the forward price of the stock, what can we say about the relative prices of the call and put options?
3. Explain why brokers may require margins from clients who sell options, but not when they buy options. Under what conditions would a broker not require margins?

Question 1

A stock is trading at $50. You purchase a call option with an exercise price of $45 and write a call option with an exercise price of $55. Both options mature in three months. Draw a diagram showing the value of this portfolio when the two options mature. Justify your answer by describing the value of the portfolio for different values of the stock. (This combination of options is known as a bullish vertical spread or price spread.)

Question 2

A stock is trading at $30. Suppose you write a call with an exercise price of $25 and buy a call with exercise price $35. Both options mature at the same date. Draw a diagram showing the value of this portfolio when the two options mature. Justify your answer by describing the value of the portfolio for different values of the stock. (This combination of options is known as a bearish vertical spread.)

Question 3

A stock is trading at $50. You write two call options with an exercise price of $50 and purchase two call options: one with an exercise price of $45 and the other with an exercise price of $55. All options mature in three months. Draw the payoff diagram for this portfolio of options. (This combination of options is known as a butterfly spread.) What is the relationship of a butterfly spread to a bullish vertical spread and a bearish vertical spread? If instead of using call options you use put options, what would be the payoff diagram? Justify your answers.

Question 4

A stock price is $25. Suppose you buy a call option and put option each with a strike price of $25 and same maturity date. Draw the payoff diagram at the maturity date of the options.

Instead of buying options with the same strike price, you buy a call option with a strike price of $27 and a put option with a strike of $23. The options have the same

maturity date. Draw the payoff diagrams. Justify your answers. (This combination of options is known as a bottom straddle.)

Question 5

Consider a three-month European call option. The strike price of the option is $50. The three-month simple rate of interest is 8.90 percent per annum. The stock price is $55, and over the life of the option it is known that the stock will not pay any dividends.

a) Calculate the lower bound for the option.
b) Suppose the option price is $4, implying that the lower bound is violated. Consider an investment strategy in which you buy the option for $4 and write a new forward contract, with a delivery price equal to the forward price. The value of this contract is zero. The maturity of the forward contract is identical to that of the option. You also borrow the present value of the difference between the forward price and the strike price.

What is the initial cash inflow of this investment? What is the value of this strategy when the option and forward contracts expire?

Question 6

Part A

Consider a portfolio containing two European call options: long a call option with a strike price of 50 and short a call option with a strike price of 55. The two options have a maturity of three months.

i) At maturity, what is the value of the portfolio if the stock price, $S(3)$, is less than or equal to 50? What is the value of the portfolio if $50 < S(3) \leq 55$? What is the value of the portfolio if $S(3) > 55$? Ignore the initial cost of the portfolio.
ii) If $c[0; K]$ denotes the value of a European call option with maturity T and strike price K, prove that

$$0 \leq c[0; 50] - c[0; 55] \leq 5B(0, T).$$

Part B

Consider a portfolio containing two European put options: short a put option with a strike price of 50 and long a put option with a strike of 45. The two options have a maturity of three months.

i)   At maturity, what is the value of the portfolio if the stock price, $S(3)$, is greater than or equal to 50? What is the value of the portfolio if $45 \leq S(3) < 50$? What is the value of the portfolio if $S(3) < 45$? Ignore the initial cost of the portfolio.

ii) If $p[0; K]$ denotes the value of a European put option with a maturity T and strike price K, prove that

$$- 5B(0, T) \leq - p[0; 50] + p[0; 45] \leq 0.$$

Part C

Consider the following portfolio: long one share of stock, short a call option with strike of 55, long a put option with strike of 45, and short 50 Treasury bills, each bill having a face value of \$1 and maturity of three months. All options are European and have a maturity of three months. The initial cost of this portfolio is

$$S(0) - c[0; 55] + p[0; 45] - 50B(0, T),$$

where $T = 3$ months.

What is the relationship of this portfolio to the portfolios considered in Part A and Part B? Justify your answer.

Question 7

Let $F(t; n)$ denote the forward price at date t for a contract that matures at date $n (t \leq n)$. The payoff to a European call option that matures at date $m (\leq n)$ is defined by:

$$c[F(m; n), 0; K] = \begin{cases} [F(m; n) - K]B(m, n) & \text{if} \quad F(m; n) \geq K \\ 0 & \text{if} \quad F(m; n) < K, \end{cases}$$

where K is the strike price. The payoff to a European put option is

$$p[F(m; n), 0; K] = \begin{cases} 0 & \text{if} \quad F(m; n) \geq K \\ [K - F(m; n)]B(m, n) & \text{if} \quad F(m; n) < K. \end{cases}$$

i)   Prove that for a European call option written on a forward contract,

$$c[F(0; n), m; K] \geq \text{Max}\{0, [F(0; n) - K]B(0, n)\}.$$

Do not use (iii) in your proof. (Hint: The proof is similar to the proof for a lower bound for a European call option written on a stock.)

ii) Prove that for a European put option written on a forward contract,

$$p[F(0, n), m; K] \geq \text{Max}\{0, [K - F(0; n)]B(0, n)\}.$$

Do not use (iii) in your proof.

iii) Prove that:

$$c[F(0; n), m; K] + KB(0, n) = p[F(0; n), m; K] + F(0; n)B(0; n).$$

Question 8

Suppose you construct the following portfolio.

a) long 1 call, strike price 40
b) short 1 call, strike price 50
c) short 1 call, strike price 70
d) long 1 call, strike price 80

All options are written on the same stock and mature at the same time. Without the aid of diagrams, describe the total value of the portfolio when the options mature.

Question 9

A pension fund manager expects to receive an inflow of funds in 60 days' time. The manager would like to use these funds to buy a stock that is currently trading at $25 per share. The manager is concerned that the stock price might increase over the next 60 days. The maximum the manager would be prepared to pay for the stock is $30.

A financial institution offers the company the following contract. In 60 days' time, if the stock price is above $30 the institution will compensate the fund manager for the difference between the spot price and $30. If the stock price is below $22, the fund manager will pay the institution the difference between $22 and the spot price.

Please identify the options in this contract and provide a clear explanation to justify your answer.

Question 10

A stock price is $50. The value of a European call option with a strike price of $47\frac{1}{2}$ and maturity of 100 days is $4\frac{3}{8}$. The 100-day default-free discount rate is 5 percent, assuming a 360-day year.

a) For a put option with a strike price of $47\frac{1}{2}$ and maturity of 100 days, you are quoted a price of $2\frac{1}{8}$. Is this consistent with the absence of arbitrage? Please justify your answer.
b) If your answer to (a) is that arbitrage is possible, how would you construct an arbitrage portfolio to take advantage of the situation?

PART II

THE BINOMIAL MODEL

CHAPTER

ASSET PRICE DYNAMICS

4.0 INTRODUCTION

In Chapter 3 we derived upper and lower bounds for option prices using simple arbitrage arguments. Although these bounds limit the price of the option, they can be quite large. For example, consider a European call option with a strike price of 100, maturity date in six months, and an underlying asset price of 100. Let the interest rate be 6 percent. Using Results 3 and 4 in Chapter 3, we know that the value of the option must be less than 100 or greater than 2.96. This leaves us with lots of room in which to maneuver. To price options more precisely, we must make additional assumptions about the probability distribution describing the possible price changes in the underlying asset.

The purpose of this chapter is to study a model for the evolution of asset prices. The model needs to be simple enough to facilitate analysis, but complex enough to provide a reasonable approximation to the actual evolution of asset price movements. The model selected for presentation, with these characteristics in mind, is the lognormal distribution model, the "workhorse" for the subsequent options/futures pricing theory. It underlies the Black-Scholes model for pricing equity derivatives (Chapter 8) as well as the pricing of foreign currency derivatives (Chapter 11) and the special cases of the Heath-Jarrow-Morton model studied in Chapters 16 and 17. The following section provides a complete analysis of the lognormal distribution and justifies its selection as the basic model for asset price dynamics.

The lognormal distribution is well suited for continuous trading models and the use of calculus. Nonetheless, it is our experience that continuous trading models (and the use of calculus) is less intuitive than discrete trading models (and the use of algebra). For this reason we also introduce the binomial model.

The binomial model is cast in discrete time, and it is a very useful teaching tool for understanding the pricing and hedging of options/futures. Furthermore, if the binomial model is carefully constructed it can also serve as an approximation to the lognormal distribution and is useful in practice. In fact, in applications such as American option valuation, the binomial approximation to the lognormal distribution is the model of choice for many financial institutions.

Because of its simplicity, we will utilize the binomial model in this text to explain the arguments underlying the various options/futures pricing theories. Nonetheless, the lognormal distribution will always be lurking in the background, motivating and calibrating the models used in the various applications.

To fix discussion, the asset under consideration in this chapter will be called a stock. The analysis, however, applies equally well to most other assets and commodities addressed in this text.

4.1 THE LOGNORMAL DISTRIBUTION

A lognormal distribution for stock price returns is the standard model used in financial economics. Why? The answer is the topic of this section.

We show that given some reasonable assumptions about the random behavior of stock returns, a lognormal distribution is implied. These assumptions, in fact, characterize the lognormal distribution in a very intuitive manner. This intuition is important for our understanding because, to reiterate, the lognormal distribution is the "workhorse" for the subsequent derivative securities theory.

To motivate the analysis, consider a typical stock price chart as illustrated in Figure 4.1. A stock price evolution is usually very jagged, with peaks and valleys, sometimes separated by trend-like rises or declines. As all stock analysts and portfolio managers know, the future price of a stock is uncertain and very difficult to predict. For illustrative purposes, we have subdivided the time horizon $[0, T]$ into n equally spaced intervals of length Δ. By understanding the stock price process over each interval, we can understand it over the total horizon.

FIGURE 4.1   *A Typical Stock Price Chart*

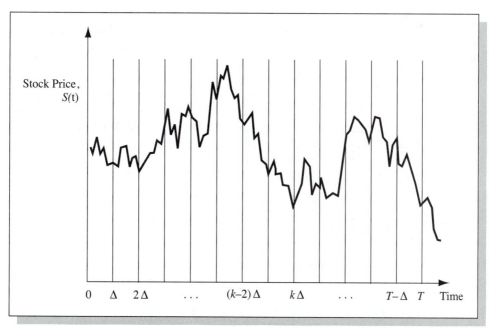

We start by developing some notation. Let $S(t)$ be the stock's price at date t. Define z_t to be the continuously compounded return on the stock over the time interval $[t - \Delta, t]$, that is,

$$S(t) = S(t - \Delta)e^{z_t}. \tag{4.1}$$

To analyze the stock price process over the horizon $[0, T]$, we divide the period into n intervals of length Δ, when $T = n\Delta$. The stock price at the end of the first interval is denoted by $S(\Delta)$, at the end of the second interval by $S(2\Delta)$ and so forth, and at the end of the nth interval by $S(T)$. We can write the stock price $S(T)$ as the product of the ratios of the intervening stock prices:

$$S(T) = \left[\frac{S(T)}{S(T - \Delta)}\right]\left[\frac{S(T - \Delta)}{S(T - 2\Delta)}\right] \cdots \left[\frac{S(2)}{S(\Delta)}\right]\left[\frac{S(\Delta)}{S(0)}\right]S(0). \tag{4.2}$$

This follows because on the right side of this expression, we are always multiplying and dividing by the same stock prices. Next, substituting the definition of the continuously compounded return into Expression (4.2) gives the desired result:

$$S(T) = S(0)e^{z_\Delta + z_{2\Delta} + \cdots + z_{T-\Delta} + z_T}. \tag{4.3}$$

To define:

$$Z(T) = z_\Delta + z_{2\Delta} + \cdots + z_{T-\Delta} + z_T. \tag{4.4}$$

$Z(T)$ represents the continuously compounded return on the stock over the horizon $[0, T]$.[1]

$Z(T) = \ln[S(T)/S(0)]$ is seen to be the sum of the continuously compounded returns over the n intervals. This simple linear relationship is the reason for working with continuously compounded returns rather than with discretely compounded returns. For discretely compounded returns, a much more complex relationship applies.

To obtain a lognormal distribution for stock prices, we now impose some conditions on the probability distributions for the continuously compounded returns z_t.

These conditions are motivated by the empirical evidence. First, stock returns over successive intervals have been observed to be approximately statistically independent of each other. Second, over each interval, stock returns appear to be generated by the same distribution. Formally, we impose two assumptions:

Assumption A1.   The returns $\{z_t\}$ are independently distributed.

Assumption A2.   The returns $\{z_t\}$ are identically distributed.

The first assumption, A1, implies that the return over the interval $[t - \Delta, t]$, z_t, is of no use in predicting the return $z_{t+\Delta}$ over the next interval.

---

[1]This can be seen by substituting Expression (4.4) into (4.3) to obtain $S(T) = S(0)e^{Z(T)}$.

The second assumption, A2, implies that the return z_t does not depend upon the previous stock price $S(t - \Delta)$.

These two assumptions together imply that stock prices follow a **random walk**.[2] This characteristic of stock prices has often been associated with "efficient market" theory.[3]

Given these two assumptions, we now describe how the return changes as the size of the time interval Δ declines. We want to ensure that the characteristics of the return over each interval, as described in Assumptions A1 and A2, remain intact as the size of the time interval becomes smaller. To achieve this end, we add two more assumptions:

Assumption A3.   The expected continuously compounded return can be written in the form

$$E[z_t] = \mu\Delta,$$

where μ is the expected continuously compounded return per unit time.

Assumption A4.   The variance of the continuously compounded return can be written in the form

$$\text{var}[z_t] = \sigma^2\Delta,$$

where σ^2 is the variance of the continuously compounded return per unit time.

Assumption A3 states that the expected value of the continuously compounded return equals a constant μ times the length of the interval Δ.

Assumption A4 states that the variance of the continuously compounded return equals a constant σ^2 times the length of the interval Δ.

Both the expected return and the variance of the return are seen to be proportional to the length of the time interval. Thus, as the length of the time interval decreases, these two moments of the stock return's distribution decrease proportionately.

Technically, these assumptions ensure that as the time interval decreases, the behavior of the distribution for $Z(T)$ does not explode nor degenerate to a fixed point. It remains random and similar in appearance to any other size interval, appropriately magnified.

Given these four assumptions, the expected continuously compounded return over the horizon $[0, T]$ is

$$
\begin{aligned}
E[Z(T)] &= E(z_\Delta) + E(z_{2\Delta}) + \ldots + E(z_t) \\
&= \sum_{j=1}^{n} \mu\Delta \qquad \text{using Assumptions A2 and A3} \\
&= \mu T.
\end{aligned}
$$

(4.5)

---

[2]A random walk does not imply any particular probability distribution for stock price changes.
[3]The efficient market theory is described in Fama (1970, 1991).

The variance of the continuously compounded return over the horizon $[0, T]$ is

$$\text{var}[Z(T)] = \text{var}(z_\Delta) + \text{var}(z_{2\Delta}) + ... + \text{var}(z_T)$$

$$= \sum_{j=1}^{n} \sigma^2 \Delta \qquad \text{using Assumptions A2 and A4}$$

$$= \sigma^2 T. \qquad\qquad (4.6)$$

At this point it may appear as if we have not made any restrictive assumptions about the probability distribution for each continuously compounded return z_t and thus $Z(T)$. But, Assumptions A1 to A4 are quite powerful and imply that for infinitesimal time intervals, the distribution for the continuously compounded return z_t has a normal distribution with mean $\mu\Delta$ and variance $\sigma^2\Delta$. The proof of this result relies on the Central Limit Theorem from probability theory. Because the proof provides no additional insight, we leave it to interested readers to pursue the proof in the references (see Cox and Miller, 1990). This result, in turn, can be shown to imply that stock prices are lognormally distributed.

Let us summarize what we have achieved. Given a horizon $[0, T]$, we divided it into n intervals of length Δ and examined the distribution of the continuously compounded returns over each interval. We imposed Assumptions A1 through A4 on the nature of these returns based on empirical considerations. The assumptions implied that for infinitesimal intervals, returns are normally distributed. Since the sum of n independent normally distributed random variables is itself normally distributed, using Expression (4.4), we see that $Z(T) = \ln[S(T)/S(0)]$ is normally distributed with mean μT-expression (4.5) and variance $\sigma^2 T$-expression (4.6). But, this is equivalent to stating that the stock price $S(T)$ is *lognormally distributed*.

In fact, Assumptions A1 through A4 characterize the lognormal distribution for stock returns. Why? If $Z(T)$ has a normal distribution, z_t will satisfy Assumptions A1 through A4 as well. Thus we have obtained our "workhorse" model for the evolution of stock prices, as exhibited in Figure 4.1.

EXAMPLE | **Lognormally Distributed Stock Prices**

Suppose that the expected return, expressed on a continuously compounded basis, is 15 percent per year and the volatility of the return is 25 percent per year. The distribution for the continuously compounded return over a two-year period is normally distributed with a mean of $15 \times 2 = 30$ percent and volatility of $25 \times \sqrt{2} = 35.36$ percent. ∎

Figure 4.2 displays typical shapes for a normal and a lognormal distribution. Part A shows the distribution for the continuously compounded returns. Note that these returns can be negative, given that the normal distribution is defined for both positive

FIGURE 4.2   *Part A: Normal Distribution for Logarithm of the Price Relative, Z(T)*
Part B: Lognormal Distribution for S(T)

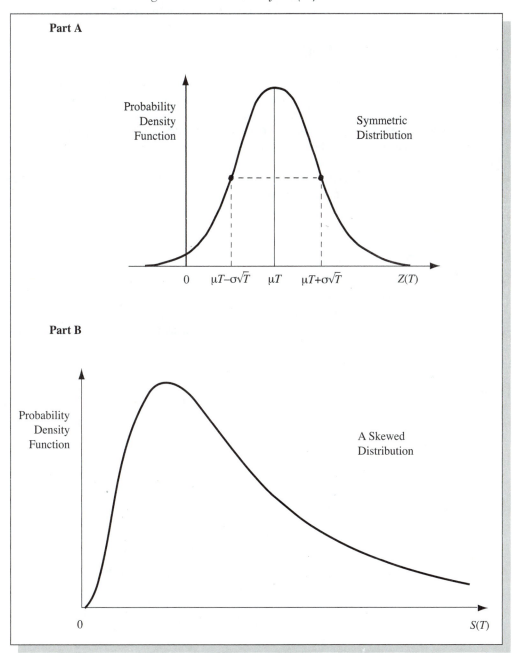

and negative values.[4] Part B shows the distribution for the stock price at date T. The lognormal distribution is only defined for positive values.[5]

If the stock price at date T is described by a lognormal distribution, the expected stock price at date T given today's price can be shown to be

$$E[S(T) \mid S(0)] = S(0)\exp(\mu T + \sigma^2 T/2). \tag{4.7}$$

A proof of this result is given in the chapter Appendix; we will use it in Chapter 5.

The assumption that stock prices are lognormally distributed is a convenient assumption and one that we will use extensively. It allows us to derive relatively simple expressions for different types of derivative securities. For example, this assumption is used in the Black-Scholes option model, which is the standard basic model for pricing equity options. However, simple convenience is not necessarily a sufficient justification for employing a particular assumption, and this is why we motivated this assumption based on four intuitive and empirically verifiable assumptions. This issue is briefly discussed again in Section 4.5.

4.2 THE BASIC IDEA (BINOMIAL PRICING)

Given that the lognormal distribution for stock price movements has been discussed, we now consider another related model, the binomial model. The binomial model is useful as a teaching tool in understanding options/futures pricing and hedging theory. We will subsequently relate this binomial model back to the lognormal distribution.

FIGURE 4.3   *Binomial Pricing*

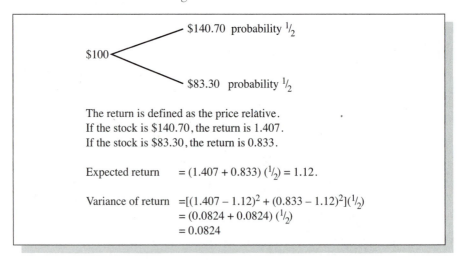

$100

$140.70 probability $\frac{1}{2}$

$83.30 probability $\frac{1}{2}$

The return is defined as the price relative.
If the stock is $140.70, the return is 1.407.
If the stock is $83.30, the return is 0.833.

Expected return $= (1.407 + 0.833)\,(\frac{1}{2}) = 1.12.$

Variance of return $=[(1.407 - 1.12)^2 + (0.833 - 1.12)^2](\frac{1}{2})$
$= (0.0824 + 0.0824)\,(\frac{1}{2})$
$= 0.0824$

---

[4]The normal distribution is defined from minus infinity to plus infinity.
[5]The lognormal distribution is defined from zero to plus infinity.

FIGURE 4.4   *Multiperiod Extension*

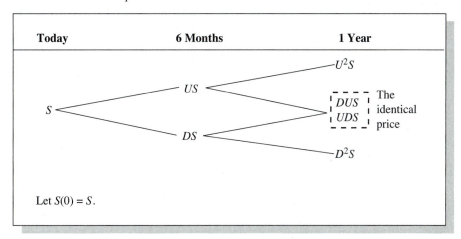

Let $S(0) = S$.

To be concrete, we must first consider a numerical example. Let the price of a stock today be $100. We are interested in the stock's price in a year. For simplicity, assume that the stock does not pay any dividends over this period and that at the end of the year, the stock's price can take on only one of two possible values: either $140.70 with probability $\frac{1}{2}$ or $83.30 with probability $\frac{1}{2}$ (see Figure 4.3).

The expected dollar return on the stock is 1.12, where the **dollar return** is defined to be the price relative (one plus the percent return).

We can represent the stock price at the end of one year, $S(1)$, in the following manner:

$$S(1) = \begin{cases} U_0 S(0) & \text{if the stock price moves "up"} \\ D_0 S(0) & \text{if the stock price moves "down,"} \end{cases}$$

where $S(0)$ is the initial stock price, $100. U_0 is called the **up-factor** with $U_0 = 1.407$, and D_0 is called the **down-factor** with $D_0 = 0.833$.

The assumption that the stock price can take only one of two possible values at the end of each interval is referred to as the **binomial model**. We could have alternatively assumed that at the end of each interval the stock price could have one of three (or more) possible values. The restriction to the binomial model is made for two reasons. The first is for simplicity. Jumping ahead, Figure 4.4 shows that even the binomial model gets complicated. Had we assumed that the stock could take one of three possible values at the end of each interval, then Figure 4.4 would be even more cluttered and complex. Second, for most purposes, as the time interval between price movements declines, this assumption is not as restrictive as it appears. We will show later that the binomial model can be used to approximate a lognormal distribution.

Regardless, you might argue that it is unrealistic to assume that the stock price can have only one of two possible values in a year. Given the multitude of events that may happen, one might expect a large number of possible values. We agree. As a first step toward accommodating this possibility, let us divide the one-year period into two subintervals of length six months. At the end of each of these six-month periods, it is now assumed again that the stock price can take on one of two possible values:

$$S(t + 1) = \begin{cases} US(t) & \text{if the stock price moves "up"} \\ DS(t) & \text{if the stock price moves "down,"} \end{cases}$$

where $S(t)$ is the stock price at date t, and U and D are constants, U being greater than D.

The range of possible outcomes is shown in Figure 4.4. There are now three possible prices at the end of the year (U^2S, UDS, D^2S). Such a figure is referred to as a **lattice**.

We wish to make a number of comments about Figure 4.4. First, what are the values of U and D? A complete answer will be given in the next section. For the moment, notice that it is unreasonable to expect the initial values for the up and down factors, $U = 1.407$ and $D = 0.833$, to remain unchanged as the number of intervals increases. Because, if they remained unchanged, then as the number of periods increased the magnitude of the largest stock price would explode (approach infinity). To avoid this result, the size of the up and down factors must depend on the number of intervals.

Second, we assumed that the up and down factors do not depend on time and are state independent.[6] These assumptions imply that the lattice recombines at the end of each interval, giving a total of three distinct possible prices for the stock at year end. If we had n intervals per year, n being a positive integer, there would be ($n + 1$) possible stock prices at year end. We could relax the assumptions of time and state independence, but it would result in an increase in the complexity of the lattice. An illustration of this complexity occurs when we talk about the pricing of interest-rate derivative securities in Chapter 15.

4.3 FORMAL DESCRIPTION (BINOMIAL PRICING)

In order to formalize[7] the description of the lattice, we divide the horizon [0, T] into n periods of equal length Δ, where $T \equiv n\Delta$. Let $S(t)$ denote the stock price at date t, where $t = 0, \Delta, 2\Delta, \dots, n\Delta$. Remember that $S(0)$ denotes today's stock price. All future stock prices are uncertain.

At some intermediate date t, the stock price next period, date $t + \Delta$, would take the values

---

[6]By state independent, we mean that the up and down factors do not depend on the level of the stock price.
[7]This is not intended to be a rigorous derivation. We want to concentrate on the underlying economics without getting too involved in the mathematics. For more rigor, see the references.

FIGURE 4.5   *Multiperiod Bionomial Pricing*

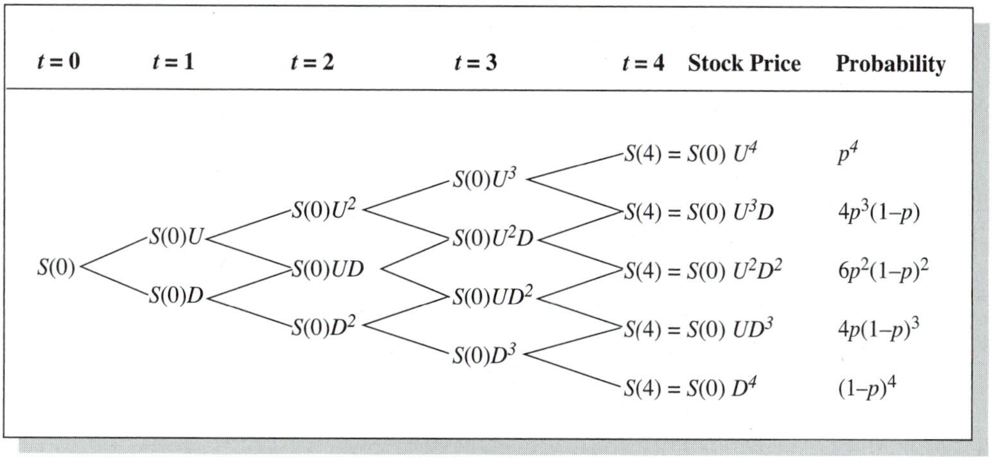

$$S(t + \Delta) = \begin{cases} S(t)U & \text{with probability } p \\ S(t)D & \text{with probability } 1 - p. \end{cases} \tag{4.8}$$

Taking $\Delta = 1$, a lattice of four intervals is shown in Figure 4.5. Observe that at the end of four intervals, the stock price $S(4)$ can have one of five possible values.

The probabilities are determined by considering the number of up and down transitions along all the feasible paths through the lattice. At date T, after n intervals, there are $(n + 1)$ possible values for the stock price $S(T)$. These values and their associated probabilities are listed in Table 4.1 on the next page. The probabilities are easily computed, and the resulting distribution for the time T stock price is known as a **multinomial distribution**. Tables for its values can be readily found in standard statistical software.

The formal description of the binomial model is now complete. To use this model in applications, the specification of the factors U and D is crucial. Different choices of U and D will generate different models for the stock price. Next we will show how to specify U and D so that the lattice of stock prices will approximate the lognormal distribution.

4.4 THE BINOMIAL APPROXIMATION TO THE LOGNORMAL DISTRIBUTION

We now show how to use the binomial model of the previous section to approximate the lognormal distribution of Section 4.1. It is done by choosing the up (U) and down (D) magnitudes in a clever fashion.

TABLE 4.1 *Stock Prices at Date T for a Lattice with n Intervals*

$S(T)$	PROBABILITY
$S(0)U^n$	p^n
$S(0)U^{n-1}D$	$\binom{n}{1}p^{n-1}(1-p)$
$S(0)U^{n-2}D^2$	$\binom{n}{2}p^{n-2}(1-p)^2$
$\vdots$	
$S(0)UD^{n-1}$	$\binom{n}{n-1}p(1-p)^{n-1}$
$S(0)D^n$	$(1-p)^n$

where the binomial coefficient $\binom{n}{k}$ is defined by

$$\binom{n}{k} = \frac{n \times (n-1) \times (n-2)\ldots 2 \times 1}{[k \times (k-1) \times \ldots \times 2 \times 1][(n-k) \times (n-k-1) \times \ldots \times 2 \times 1]}.$$

For example, when $n = 4$, the values for $k = 3$ and 2 are:

$$\binom{4}{3} = \frac{4 \times 3 \times 2 \times 1}{[3 \times 2 \times 1] \times 1} = 4 \quad \text{and} \quad \binom{4}{2} = \frac{4 \times 3 \times 2 \times 1}{[2 \times 1] \times [2 \times 1]} = 6.$$

Recall that the binomial representation assumes that, at the end of each interval, the stock's return can take only one of two possible values. Let us rewrite the binomial representation as

$$\ln[S(t)/S(t-\Delta)] \equiv z_t = \begin{cases} \mu\Delta + \sigma\sqrt{\Delta} & \text{with probability } \frac{1}{2} \\ \mu\Delta - \sigma\sqrt{\Delta} & \text{with probability } \frac{1}{2}. \end{cases} \tag{4.9}$$

With probability $\frac{1}{2}$ the stock's (continuously compounded) return goes "up" to $\mu\Delta + \sigma\sqrt{\Delta}$, and with probability $\frac{1}{2}$ the stock's return goes "down" to $\mu\Delta - \sigma\sqrt{\Delta}$. The choice of the probability of an upward movement to be $\frac{1}{2}$ is justified subsequently.

The expected return over $[t - \Delta, t]$ is

$$E[z_t] = (\mu\Delta + \sigma\sqrt{\Delta})(\tfrac{1}{2}) + (\mu\Delta - \sigma\sqrt{\Delta})(\tfrac{1}{2})$$
$$= \mu\Delta$$

and the variance is

$$\text{var}[z_t] = (\sigma\sqrt{\Delta})^2(\tfrac{1}{2}) + (-\sigma\sqrt{\Delta})^2(\tfrac{1}{2})$$
$$= \sigma^2\Delta.$$

The expected return, $\mu\Delta$, is often called the **drift** because it is the value to which the stock return drifts before it is shocked by $+\sigma\sqrt{\Delta}$ or $-\sigma\sqrt{\Delta}$ (see Expression (4.9)). The square root of the term σ^2 is often called the stock's **volatility** (σ) because it reflects the size of the random shocks in the stock's return as it moves through time.

We now argue that Expression (4.9) approximates a lognormal distribution. Note that, by construction, Expression (4.9) satisfies Assumptions A1 through A4 in Section 4.1. First, z_t is independently and identically distributed since the probabilities ($\tfrac{1}{2}$), the drift μ, and the volatility σ do not change with t (Assumptions A1 and A2). Second, Assumptions A3 and A4 are seen to be satisfied by the expected return and variance of Expression (4.9). They are both proportional to the length of the time period Δ. Thus, by the argument used in Section 4.1, for infinitesimal intervals (as Δ tends to zero), z_t is approximately normally distributed.[8]

This is an important observation because it implies (as argued earlier) that the binomial representation in Expression (4.9) *approximates a lognormal distribution.*

Using Expression (4.9), the stock price at date t can be written in the form

$$S(t) = S(t - \Delta) \begin{cases} \exp(\mu\Delta + \sigma\sqrt{\Delta}) & \text{with probability } \tfrac{1}{2} \\ \exp(\mu\Delta - \sigma\sqrt{\Delta}) & \text{with probability } \tfrac{1}{2}. \end{cases} \qquad (4.10)$$

Given this expression, we can easily identify the up and down factors in Figure 4.4 in terms of the instantaneous expected return per unit time, μ, the instantaneous volatility per unit date, σ, and the length of the interval, Δ. They are

$$U = \exp(\mu\Delta + \sigma\sqrt{\Delta})$$

and

$$D = \exp(\mu\Delta - \sigma\sqrt{\Delta}).$$

A final comment is in order. Because we are only interested in approximating a lognormal distribution as Δ gets small via a binomial representation, the representation of stock price movements in Expression (4.10) is not uniquely determined. There are other ways of representing stock price movements that satisfy Assumptions A1 through A4.[9]

---

[8]A formal proof is given in Cox and Miller (1990, Chapter 5).

[9]The representation used in Cox, Ross, and Rubinstein (1979) is

$$S(t) = S(t - \Delta) \begin{cases} \exp(\sigma\sqrt{\Delta}) & \text{with probability } [1 + (\mu/\sigma)\sqrt{\Delta}]/2 \\ \exp(-\sigma\sqrt{\Delta}) & \text{with probability } [1 - (\mu/\sigma)\sqrt{\Delta}]/2. \end{cases}$$

EXAMPLE   **Binomial Lattice Approximation to the Lognormal Distribution**

Suppose that the expected return μ is 11 percent per year and the volatility σ is 25 percent per year. These numbers can be calibrated to market data.

In Figure 4.6 the horizon is one year. In Part A we have split this into two six-month intervals, implying the number of periods, $n = 2$, and the length of each interval, $\Delta = \frac{1}{2} = 0.5$. Therefore, the expected drift is

$$\mu\Delta = 0.11 \times .05 = 0.055$$

and the volatility over the interval is

$$\sigma\sqrt{\Delta} = 0.25 \times \sqrt{0.5} = 0.1768.$$

Hence, from Expression (4.9) the one-period continuously compounded returns can be written as

$$z_t = \begin{cases} 0.2318 & \text{with probability } \frac{1}{2} \\ -0.1218 & \text{with probability } \frac{1}{2}, \end{cases}$$

FIGURE 4.6   *Binomial Stock Price Lattices*

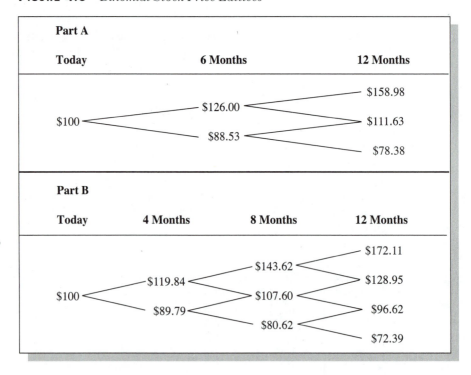

TABLE 4.2 *Size of the Up and Down Factors*

NUMBER OF INTERVALS	LENGTH OF INTERVALS	UP FACTOR	DOWN FACTOR
n	Δ	U	D
1	1	1.4333	0.8694
2	1/2	1.2609	0.8853
3	1/3	1.1984	0.8979

and from Expression (4.10), the binomial model is

$$S(t + \Delta) = S(t) \begin{cases} 1.2609 & \text{with probability } \frac{1}{2} \\ 0.8853 & \text{with probability } \frac{1}{2}. \end{cases}$$

In Figure 4.6, it is assumed that the initial stock price is $100.

In Part B we have divided the twelve-month interval into three subperiods. As an exercise, check that you can reproduce the numbers in Part B. In this case, the binomial model is

$$S(t + \Delta) = S(t) \begin{cases} 1.1984 & \text{with probability } \frac{1}{2} \\ 0.8979 & \text{with probability } \frac{1}{2}. \end{cases}$$

Both these binomial models approximate the lognormal distribution, but the model with $n = 3$ does a better job than does the model with $n = 2$. The approximation improves as n increases. ■

Note two points from this example. The size of the up and down factors, U and D, change as the length of the interval changes. This relationship of U and D to the time interval Δ is summarized in Table 4.2. As the length of the interval Δ decreases, the size of the up factor U decreases toward 1 and the size of the down factor D increases toward 1. It is always the case that the size of the up factor U is greater than the size of the down factor D. This model will be utilized repeatedly later on in the text to understand the pricing and hedging of options and futures.

EXAMPLE | **Lognormal Approximation**

We use Expression (4.10) to generate binomial stock price movements, which approximate a lognormal distribution. A random sequence of coin tosses is used to determine whether the stock price goes up or down each interval. If the current stock price is $S(t)$ and the coin toss is "heads," the stock price next interval is

$$S(t + \Delta) = S(t) \exp(\mu\Delta + \sigma\sqrt{\Delta}).$$

FIGURE 4.7   *Pattern of Price Movements*

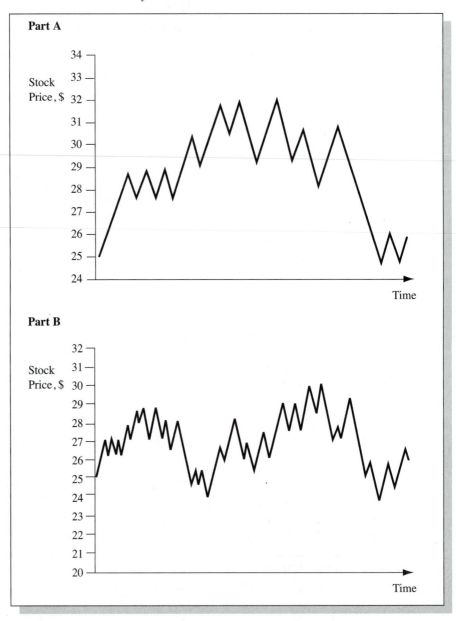

> If the coin toss is "tails," the stock price next interval is
>
> $$S(t + \Delta) = S(t)\exp(\mu\Delta - \sigma\sqrt{\Delta}).$$
>
> In Figure 4.7, Part A, a three-day interval is used, so $\Delta = 3/365$. In Part B, a one-day interval is used, so $\Delta = 1/365$. You should compare these figures to Figure 4.1.   ■

4.5 EXTENSIONS

We now discuss generalizations of the lognormally distributed stock price process. Recall that the lognormal distribution is characterized by Assumptions A1 through A4. Changing any of these assumptions will imply a different stock price distribution; the two assumptions most often modified are Assumptions A3 and A4. For example, the mean return μ and the variance of the return σ^2 can both be made functions of the stock price. This modification changes the stock price process to a non-lognormal distribution.

There are many reasonable distributions for which the return's variance depends upon the stock price level. For example, in some markets it is observed that the variance of price changes increases as the stock price increases. In terms of returns, it implies that the variance of the stock's return decreases as the stock price increases. We can incorporate this idea by assuming that

$$\text{var}[z_t] = \eta^2\Delta/S(t),$$

where η is the "new" volatility term.

This modification of Assumption A4 yields a **stochastic volatility model** for the stock price, which causes a number of complications. First, the lattice may not recombine, implying that in Figure 4.4 we would have four different price levels at the terminal time.[10] This condition can cause computing problems when the number of intervals is large. Second, successive price changes will no longer be independently distributed, which complicates the statistical procedures employed when estimating the parameters μ and η.

4.6 STOCHASTIC DIFFERENTIAL EQUATION REPRESENTATION

To read the academic literature on option pricing, one must be acquainted with the stochastic differential equation representation of lognormally distributed stock prices. We hereby provide a simple introduction.

---

[10]See Nelson and Ramaswamy (1990) for a description of how to use binomial processes to approximate different types of processes.

An elegant way to represent Assumptions A1 through A4 for continuous compounded returns is[11]

$$z_{t+\Delta} = \mu\Delta + \sigma[W(t + \Delta) - W(t)],$$

where $[W(t + \Delta) - W(t)]$ is a normally distributed random variable with zero mean and variance Δ.

The above equation is usually expressed in terms of stock price changes. Recall that, by definition,

$$z_{t+\Delta} = \ln[S(t + \Delta)/S(t)] = \ln S(t + \Delta) - \ln S(t).$$

Hence we can write Assumptions A1 through A4 alternatively as

$$\ln S(t + \Delta) - \ln S(t) = \mu\Delta + \sigma[W(t + \Delta) - W(t)]. \tag{4.11}$$

Replacing discrete changes with infinitesimal changes, that is, $dt \cong \Delta$, $d\ln S(t) \cong \ln S(t + \Delta) - \ln S(t)$, and $dW(t) \cong W(t + \Delta) - W(t)$, we obtain

$$d\ln S(t) = \mu dt + \sigma dW(t). \tag{4.12}$$

Expression (4.12) is the form by which Assumptions A1 through A4 most often appear in the literature.

For distributions more complex than the lognormal, Expression (4.12) can be generalized to

$$d\ln S(t) = \mu[t, S(t)]dt + \sigma[t, S(t)]dW(t), \tag{4.13}$$

where $d\ln S(t)$ represents the change in the natural logarithm of the stock price from date t to $t + dt$, with dt being an infinitesimal change in time. $\mu[t, S(t)]$ is the instantaneous expected return per unit time, and $dW(t)$ is a Brownian motion.

A **Brownian motion**, by definition, is a random variable that is normally distributed with zero mean, variance dt, and has independent increments (that is, $dW(t)$ and $dW(t + dt)$ are independently distributed).

Note that, in this general form, both the mean and volatility are functions of date t and the current stock price, $S(t)$. Expression (4.13) is called a differential equation

---

[11]The expected value of z_t is

$$E[z_t] = \mu\Delta$$

and the variance is

$$\begin{aligned} \text{var}[z_t] &= \sigma^2\text{var}[\Delta W(t)] \\ &= \sigma^2\Delta. \end{aligned}$$

because the stock price $S(t)$ is only defined implicitly by describing its changes through time.

Different assumptions about the form of the volatility give rise to different solutions $S(t)$ to this stochastic differential equation. The standard assumption is to assume that μ and σ are constants, which is the form of the equation implied by Expression (4.12). The solution for $S(t)$ in this case is a lognormal distribution. It is the stock price distribution underlying the Black-Scholes option pricing model and the special cases of the Heath-Jarrow-Morton model studied later.

4.7 COMPLICATIONS

We now consider various complications to the preceding theory.

Lognormal Distribution

If we look at the empirical distribution of continuously compounded returns, we find that the tails of the distribution are fatter than those expected by a normal distribution. This condition is inconsistent with a lognormal distribution for stock prices. By examining the dynamic properties of stock price changes, there is also some evidence that the volatility of the distribution changes,[12] which is inconsistent with a lognormal distribution for stock prices because stochastic volatility causes the distribution of returns to have fat tails. There is a growing literature using stochastic volatility stock price models to price derivative securities. We will return to this point shortly.

Continuous Trading

In the binomial model approximation to the lognormal, the length of the trading period Δ decreases in size as we increase the number of intervals. In the limit, the length of the trading period becomes infinitesimal and implies that trading is approximated as being continuous. This, of course, is not true because there are holidays and weekends on which markets close.

The closing of markets on weekends and holidays can cause Assumptions A1 through A4 to be violated. In particular, French (1980) has documented that over weekends the volatility of returns differs from that during the week, violating Assumption A4, which assumes a constant volatility. If we know the different volatilities during the different periods, we can introduce these complications into our description of stock price movements via the generalizations discussed in Section 4.5.

The tradeoff for increased realism will be increased complexity. The choice between the two (realism versus simplicity) is made with the use of the models in mind.

---

[12]See Schwert (1989) and Haugen, Talmor, and Torous (1991).

Trading rooms often prefer realism, while corporate treasury departments often prefer simplicity.

Continuously Changing Prices

Assumptions A3 and A4 imply that for infinitesimal time intervals, returns are normally distributed with a variance approaching zero. It implies that stock price changes will be quite small, and in the limit, continuously changing. Unfortunately, an institutional feature of most markets is the existence of minimum allowed price changes. For example, in equity markets the minimum price change is usually $\frac{1}{16}$ per share. We have ignored this institutional feature, and for most of the book we will continue to ignore it because, for large dollar positions, continuously changing prices is a reasonable approximation.

However, this institutional feature may affect how we estimate different parameters and test the models. For example, academic studies often ignore deep-out-of-the-money options near expiration because option prices are near zero, and $\frac{1}{16}$ can be a large percent of the option's value. Traders also recognize these difficulties and will often refrain from trading deep-out-of-the-money options near expiration.

4.8 SUMMARY

To price derivative securities, we need a way of representing the evolution of the future prices of an asset. We need a model that is simple enough to perform analysis but complex enough to provide a realistic approximation. The lognormal distribution is our selection.

However, to facilitate understanding we study the binomial model. We show how to specify the up and down factors such that as the number of intervals increases—or equivalently, the length of each interval decreases—the binomial model approximates a lognormal distribution. The binomial form of this representation will also be the model used to explain the pricing and hedging of equity, stock index, foreign currency, commodity, and interest rate derivatives in subsequent chapters.

REFERENCES

References for the material on convergence:

Cox, D. R., and H. D. Miller, 1990. *The Theory of Stochastic Processes*. London: Chapman Hall.

Cox, J., S. Ross, and M. Rubinstein, 1979. "Option Pricing: A Simplified Approach." *Journal of Financial Economics* 7, 229–264.

Hoel, G. H., S. C. Port, and C. H. Stone, 1971. *Introduction to Probability Theory*. Boston: Houghton Mifflin Company.

Nelson, D. B., and K. Ramaswamy, 1990. "Simple Binomial Approximations in Financial Models." *Review of Financial Studies* 3, 393–430.

References for properties of asset price distributions:

French, K. R., 1980. "Stock Returns and the Weekend Effect."*Journal of Financial Economics* 9, 55–69.

Haugen, R. A., E. Talmor, and W. N. Torous, 1991. "The Effect of Volatility Changes on the Level of Stock Prices and Subsequent Expected Returns." *Journal of Finance* 46, 985–1007.

Richardson, M., and T. Smith, 1993. "A Test for Multivariate Normality in Stock Returns." *Journal of Business* 66, 295–321.

Schwert, G. W., 1989. "Why Does Stock Market Volatility Change Over Time?" *Journal of Finance* 44, 1115–1153.

For a relatively simple explanation of the properties of the lognormal distribution, see:

Ingersoll, J. E., 1987. *Theory of Financial Decision Making*. New Jersey: Rowman & Littlefield Publishers, pp. 14–15.

References about efficient market theory:

Fama, E., 1970. "Efficient Capital Markets: A Review of Theory and Empirical Work." *Journal of Finance* 25, 383–417.

Fama, E., 1991. "Efficient Capital Markets: II." *Journal of Finance* 46, 1575–1617.

Jarrow, R. A., 1988. *Finance Theory*. Englewood Cliffs, NJ: Prentice-Hall.

QUESTIONS

Question 1

What are the four assumptions that characterize a lognormal distribution for stock price returns?

Question 2

The expected value of a continuously compounded rate of return is 12 percent per year and its volatility is 30 percent per year.

a) What is the expected return and volatility over a one-month period?
b) What is the expected return and volatility over a two-month period?
c) What is the expected return and volatility over a three-month period?
d) What is the expected return and volatility over a six-month period?

Question 3

What is the dollar expected return and standard deviation of the dollar return over $[t, t + \Delta]$ for the stock price in Expression (4.8)?

Question 4

Consider the following binomial model for a stock S_t, for $t = 0, 1, 2$.

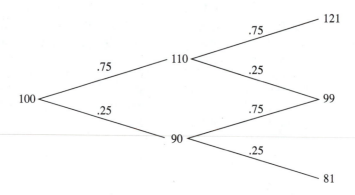

a)   What is the probability that $S_2 = 121$?
b)   What is the probability that $S_2 = 99$?
c)   What is the probability that $S_2 = 81$?
d)   What is the expected stock price at date 1?
e)   What is the variance of the stock price at date 1? At date 2? Is the stock price variance increasing, decreasing, or constant across time?

Question 5

Consider a lognormal distribution with mean return per year of $\mu = 0.05$ and return standard deviation per year of $\sigma = 0.2$.

a)   What are the up (U) and down (D) magnitudes for the binomial approximations to this lognormal distribution for an arbitrary set size Δ?
b)   Compute the values in a) for $\Delta = 1, 1/2, 1/4, 1/8$. What happens to U and D as Δ decreases?
c)   Using $\Delta = 1$, construct the binomial tree for two time steps. Let the initial stock price be $100.

Question 6

The expected value of the continuously compounded rate of return is 12 percent per annum and its volatility is 30 percent per annum. The current stock price is $100.

a)   If the interval Δ is chosen to be one day, that is, $\Delta = 1/365$, use Expression (4.10) to compute the binomial distribution of stock prices over the interval.
b)   Calculate the expected value of the stock price relative.
c)   Calculate the volatility of the stock price relative. What relationship does your computed value have with the value of $\sigma\sqrt{\Delta}$?

Question 7

The expected value of the continuously compounded rate of return is 15 percent per annum and its volatility is 30 percent per annum. The current stock price is $100.

a) If the time interval is chosen to be one week, that is, $\Delta = 7/365$, use Expression (4.10) to compute a binomial lattice of stock prices over three weeks.
b) Compute the expected stock price at the end of one week.
c) Compute the expected stock price at the end of two weeks.
d) Compute the expected stock price at the end of three weeks.
e) How does your answer to part d) compare to the expected stock price computed using Expression (4.7)?

Question 8

The expected value of the continuously compounded rate of return is 18 percent per year and its volatility is 35 percent per year. The return is normally distributed. Below you are given the outcome of tossing a fair coin with outcomes Heads (H) or Tails (T).

Sequence	1	2	3	4	5	6	7	8	9	10
Outcome	T	T	H	T	H	H	T	H	H	H

The current stock price is $25.

a) If the interval is 5 days, that is, $\Delta = 5/365$, use Expression (4.10) to generate a random sequence of stock prices.
b) Repeat this exercise with the interval being one day, $\Delta = 1/365$.

Question 9

Given the information in Question 8, you are now given the values of a random drawing from a normal distribution with zero mean and variance Δ, where $\Delta = 1/365$.

Sequence	ΔW
1	−0.0604
2	−0.0219
3	0.0178
4	−0.0174
5	0.0244
6	0.0538
7	−0.0230
8	0.0152
9	0.0467
10	0.0396

a) Use Expression (4.11) to generate a random sequence of stock prices.
b) Compare your answers to those in Question 8b).

Question 10

Suppose the stock price is described via the stochastic differential equation

$$d\ln S(t) = \mu dt + \sigma dW(t).$$

a) What distribution does the stock price follow?
b) This description implicitly assumes that trading takes place continuously in time. What problems are there with this assumption?
c) This description implies that stock prices change continuously. What problems are there with this implication?

APPENDIX: THE EXPECTED VALUE OF THE FUTURE STOCK PRICE

We want to prove

$$E[S(T)\,|\,(S(0)] = S(0)\exp(\mu T + \sigma^2 T/2). \tag{A1}$$

PROOF   From Expression (4.4) we have

$$S(T) = S(0)\exp[Z(T)],$$

where $Z(T)$ is normally distributed with mean μT, using Expression (4.5), and variance $\sigma^2 T$, using Expression (4.6). The probability density function for $Z(T)$ is

$$\frac{1}{\sigma_1\sqrt{2\pi}}\exp\left[-\frac{1}{2}\left(\frac{z-\mu_1}{\sigma_1}\right)^2\right],$$

where z is a realized value of $Z(T)$, $\mu_1 = \sigma T$, and $\sigma_1^2 = \sigma^2 T$.

The expected value of $S(T)$ conditional upon knowing $S(0)$ is

$$E[S(T)\,|\,S(0)] = S(0)\frac{1}{\sigma_1\sqrt{2\pi}}\int_{-\infty}^{+\infty}\exp(z)\exp\left[-\frac{1}{2}\left(\frac{z-\mu_1}{\sigma_1}\right)^2\right]dz. \tag{A2}$$

Completing the square gives

$$z - \frac{1}{2}\left(\frac{z-\mu_1}{\sigma_1}\right)^2 = \mu_1 + \sigma_1^2/2 - \frac{1}{2}\left[\frac{z-(\mu_1+\sigma_1^2)}{\sigma_1}\right]^2,$$

so that

$$E[S(T) \mid (S(0)] =$$
$$S(0)\exp(\mu_1 + \sigma_1^2/2)\frac{1}{\sigma_1\sqrt{2\pi}}\int_{-\infty}^{+\infty}\exp\left\{-\frac{1}{2}\left[\frac{z-(\mu_1+\sigma_1^2)}{\sigma_1}\right]^2\right\}dz. \quad (A3)$$

Let $u \equiv [z - (\mu_1 + \sigma_1^2)]/\sigma_1$ so that

$$E[S(T) \mid (S(0)] = S(0)\exp(\mu_1 + \sigma_1^2/2)\frac{1}{\sqrt{2\pi}}\int_{-\infty}^{+\infty}\exp\left(-\frac{1}{2}u^2\right)du. \quad (A4)$$

Now the last term on the right side is the area under the normal probability density function and equals unity:

$$\frac{1}{\sqrt{2\pi}}\int_{-\infty}^{+\infty}\exp\left(-\frac{1}{2}u^2\right)du = 1. \quad (A5)$$

Therefore, after substituting for μ_1 and σ_1^2, we have the required result:

$$E[S(T) \mid (S(0)] = S(0)\exp(\mu T + \sigma^2 T/2). \quad (A6)$$

■

THE BINOMIAL PRICING MODEL

5.0 INTRODUCTION

I
n this chapter, we describe the binomial pricing model. This model provides a simple yet powerful approach for understanding the pricing and hedging of derivative securities. To explain the basic idea, we will first consider a call option written on a stock. For this application, the binomial model (of Chapter 4) assumes that at the end of each interval the stock price can take only one of two possible values. Therefore, in this model, the call option will also take only one of two possible values.

We will price the call option via a **synthetic construction**. That is, to price the call option, we will construct a portfolio of the stock and a riskless investment to mimic, or replicate, the value of the option. This portfolio is called a **synthetic call option**, which must, by the absence of arbitrage, equal the price of a traded call option. Otherwise, profit opportunities will arise because there are two distinct ways to obtain the same cash flows. The procedure of synthetic construction not only gives us a way to price call options but also provides a way to hedge.

The binomial approach to the valuation of call options yields important insights into the pricing and hedging of other derivative securities. Indeed, if you understand the basic logic of this approach, you will also understand the underlying logic of the majority of derivative security models in use today. As an illustration, this chapter will also use the binomial pricing model to characterize futures prices for futures contracts written on the stock. In some ways, futures contracts are the most fundamental derivative securities studied in this text. Consequently, the analysis of futures contracts is important in its own right. We will show how to determine futures prices and how to use futures contracts for hedging.

In Chapter 4, we discussed the binomial representation for stock price changes. This chapter uses that representation as the model for stock prices. As before, we initially assume for simplicity that the stock does not pay any dividends over the life of the option or futures contract. Dividends will be introduced when we describe how to price American options in Chapter 7. Of course, we will need the standard assumptions discussed in Chapter 2. To refresh your memory, they are as follows:

Assumption A1.   There are no market frictions.

Assumption A2.   Market participants entail no counterparty risk.

Assumption A3.   Markets are competitive.

Assumption A4.   There are no arbitrage opportunities.

For a detailed elaboration of these assumptions, see the discussion in Chapter 2.
For this chapter we also add an additional assumption that is standard in this setting:

Assumption A5.   There is no interest rate uncertainty.

This assumption is introduced to reduce the complexity of the pricing problem. For short-dated options or futures contracts, say, less than a year, this may be a reasonable approximation. It is also reasonable if the underlying asset's price is not very sensitive to changes in interest rates. It will be relaxed in Chapter 15 when we discuss interest rate options and futures.

5.1 SINGLE-PERIOD EXAMPLE

To understand the logic behind this model, we start with a single-period example and then gradually generalize it. Suppose we want to price a European call option with maturity at one year. Let the strike price of the option be 110, and let the option be written on a stock whose value today is 100. We will assume that at the end of the year the stock price can take only one of two possible values, 127.12 or 85.21; see Figure 5.1. Note that to generate the stock prices at each point in the lattice, we have used Expression (4.10) from Chapter 4. A discussion of the parameter values used in (4.10) is given in Section 5.5.

In one year the option matures. At maturity, conditional upon knowing the stock price, we can determine the option's value. If the stock price is 127.12, the option must be worth 17.12. Why? The call option allows you to buy stock at the strike price of 110. Given that the stock price is above the strike price, the option is in-the-money and worth the difference ($127.12 - 110 = 17.12$). If the stock price is 85.21, the call option expires out-of-the-money and is worthless. (If this is not clear, go back to

FIGURE 5.1   *Stock Price Dynamics*

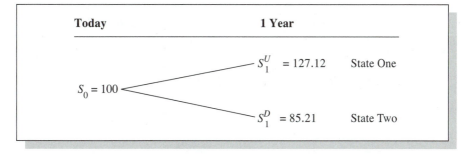

Today	1 Year	
	S_1^U = 127.12	State One
$S_0 = 100$		
	S_1^D = 85.21	State Two

Chapter 1 and check the definition of a call option.) The call option values are shown in Figure 5.2.

We have determined the option values at maturity, but we still do not know the option value today. To determine today's value, we can use a simple arbitrage argument. Consider forming a portfolio that mimics or replicates the payoff of the call option. This portfolio, the synthetic call option, will consist of investments in the underlying asset—the stock—and a riskless asset. We will assume that if we invest one dollar in the riskless asset, in one year our investment will be worth 1.0618 dollars.

At this point in the analysis we need to ensure that the stock and riskless asset are priced correctly with respect to one another—that is, the stock does not dominate the riskless asset as an investment or vice versa. To do this, note that the dollar return on the stock in the up state is $127.12/100 = 1.2712$, which is greater than the dollar return on the riskless asset, 1.0618, which is greater than the dollar return on the stock in the down state, $85.21/100 = 0.8521$. Thus the dollar return on the riskless asset lies between the return on the stock in the up and down states. This condition is, in fact, an arbitrage-free pricing relation necessarily satisfied by the stock and riskless asset. If it is violated, an arbitrage opportunity can be constructed. We encourage the reader to try to prove this assertion. The justification for this assertion is given later in this chapter.

Given that the economy is arbitrage-free, we can now continue with the construction of the synthetic call. Suppose we buy m_0 *shares* of stock and invest B_0 *dollars* in the riskless asset. The value of our portfolio today is

$$V(0) \equiv m_0 100 + B_0. \tag{5.1}$$

But what must m_0 and B_0 be to mimic the payoffs of the option?

Suppose at the end of the year the stock price is 127.12; then the option value is 17.12. By design, our portfolio must also be worth 17.12. This gives the first condition:

$$m_0 127.12 + B_0 1.0618 = 17.12. \tag{5.2}$$

FIGURE 5.2   *Call Prices*

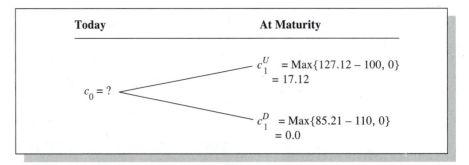

Today	At Maturity
	$c_1^U = \text{Max}\{127.12 - 100, 0\}$ = 17.12
$c_0 = ?$	
	$c_1^D = \text{Max}\{85.21 - 110, 0\}$ = 0.0

The first term on the left side of Expression (5.2) is the dollar value of the investment in the stock. The second term is the dollar value of our investment in the riskless asset. Recall that every dollar invested in the riskless asset yields 1.0618 dollars at the end of the year.

If the stock price is 85.21 at the end of the year, the call option is out-of-the-money and expires worthless. Thus, in this case, we want our portfolio to have zero value, which gives our second condition:

$$m_0 85.21 + B_0 1.0618 = 0. \tag{5.3}$$

Note that at the end of the year the dollar value of our investment in the riskless asset is still $B_0 1.0618$ because the payoff is not affected by the stock price.

Can we design a portfolio to satisfy these two conditions? In general, the answer is yes. We have two linear equations in two unknowns, hence we simply need to solve for m_0 and B_0. The solution is

$$m_0 = 17.12/(127.12 - 85.21) = 0.4085$$

and

$$B_0 = -m_0 85.21/1.0618 = -32.78.$$

The minus sign for B_0 implies that we must borrow 32.78 at the simple interest rate of 6.18 percent.

The value of our replicating portfolio or synthetic call option today is determined by substituting into Expression (5.1):

$$\begin{aligned} V(0) &= 0.4085 \times 100 - 32.78 \\ &= 8.07. \end{aligned} \tag{5.4}$$

We claim that this is the arbitrage-free value of the traded call option. By design we have constructed a portfolio of the stock and riskless investment that mimics the payoff of the traded call option. If the stock price goes up to 127.12, the traded option is worth 17.12 and the synthetic option is also worth 17.12. If the stock price goes down to 85.21, the traded option is worthless and so is the synthetic option. Given that the payoffs of the traded option and synthetic option are the same in one year, the two values must be the same today. That is, the traded option's value must also be 8.07. Otherwise, there would be arbitrage.

However, suppose that is not the case, and the traded call option is priced at 10. What can we do? The traded option is overvalued. Therefore, it is worthwhile for us to write traded call options receiving 10 for each. But this position is risky. How can we offset the risk? By constructing and adding to our portfolio a synthetic call option that mimics the payoff of the traded call option.

We do this by buying 0.4085 shares of stock at a cost of 40.85 and borrowing 32.78. The cost of this synthetic call option is 8.07, so our net position is $10 - 8.07 = 1.93$. We receive an immediate cash inflow of \$1.93. At the maturity of the traded

call option, if the stock price is 127.12 the traded call option is worth 17.12. Given that we have written the traded call option, it is a liability. However, the value of the synthetic call option is 17.12, so our net position is zero. If the stock price is 85.21 the traded call option is worthless and our synthetic call option also has zero value. Again, our net position is zero. Hence we have generated 1.93 today and all future cash flows net to zero, so our position is completely riskless and is clearly a "free lunch." Eventually, prices should adjust until the option trades at 8.07.

Suppose that the traded call option is priced at 7, implying that it is undervalued. Can we design an investment strategy that is completely riskless and will provide us with a free lunch? For a start, we want to buy the undervalued traded call options at 7. But it is a risky position. We can construct a synthetic call option by selling short 0.4085 shares of the stock, which provides an immediate cash inflow of 40.85. We also must invest 32.78 in the one-year riskless asset. Hence the net position today is an inflow of 40.85 and an outflow of 39.78 (7 + 32.78 = 39.78), yielding a net cash inflow of 1.07. But what about our position at year end when the call option matures? If the stock price is 127.12, the traded call option is in-the-money and worth 17.12. Our portfolio also has a negative value of 17.12, so our net position is zero. If the stock price is 85.21, the call option is worthless and our portfolio has zero value, so again our net position is zero. We have made a profit today of 1.07 and all future cash flows net to zero, so our position is completely riskless. Again, we have a free lunch.

This numerical example illustrates three important points. First, the argument is explicitly independent of the probabilities of the up or down movement in stock prices. At no point did we specify the probability of an up or down state occurring. There is an important implication. Consider two individuals, one an optimist and the other a pessimist. The optimist believes that the probability[1] of the stock price going up to 127.12 is 90 percent and the probability of the stock going down to 85.21 is 10 percent. On the other hand, the pessimist believes that the probability of the stock price going up is 10 percent and the probability of the stock going down is 90 percent. Provided that these two individuals agree that the stock price today is worth 100, that the stock price in the up state is 127.12, and that the stock price in the down state is 85.21, then they both will agree that the traded option's value today is 8.07. This argument follows because our replication works independently of whether the stock price moves up or down.

Second, we assume in the binomial model that the stock price can take only one of two possible values at year end, implying that the traded option can have only one of two possible values. To form a replicating portfolio to match the payoffs of the traded option, we only need two assets: the underlying stock and a riskless asset. These are the only other traded assets in our model. Thus the binomial model plays an important role. The model enables us to construct a replicating portfolio because the number of possible stock price outcomes is less than or equal to the number of assets

---

[1]The probability of each state occurring must be positive for both the pessimist and optimist; otherwise, extreme positions would be taken and the stock market would break down.

traded in our model. If this condition does not hold, our argument will not follow and our methodology will fail.

Third, we value the traded option by considering its possible values at maturity and then work backward in reverse chronological time to price the traded option today. All option pricing models follow this procedure, which is called **backward induction**. It is necessary because the only date that we know the value of the option for sure (given the stock price) is the option's expiration date, and it is this value on expiration that determines the value of the option today.

5.2 MULTIPERIOD EXAMPLE

Now that we have mastered the single-period example, we can move on. It is unrealistic to assume that only two possible values for the stock price exist at the end of the year. We initially relax this assumption by dividing one year into two six-month intervals. We illustrated this technique in Chapter 4. We still retain the binomial model so that at the end of each six-month interval the stock price can have only one of two possible values (see Figure 5.3). Note that to generate the stock prices at each node in the lattice, we have used the approximation to the lognormal distribution from Expression (4.10) in Chapter 4. For the moment, we will postpone discussion of what values we have used for the drift parameter μ and volatility σ in (4.10).

We assume that interest rates are constant and the term structure of interest rates is flat. Since the lognormal distribution is based on continuous trading and thus continuous time, we use continuous compounding in our selection of interest rates (see Chapter 1). If r denotes the continuously compounded rate of interest per annum, then if we invest one dollar in the riskless asset for the period Δ we will earn an

FIGURE 5.3   *Stock Price Dynamics*

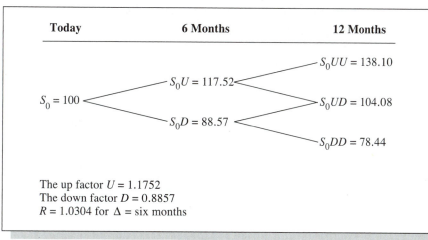

The up factor $U = 1.1752$
The down factor $D = 0.8857$
$R = 1.0304$ for Δ = six months

amount R, where $R \equiv \exp(r\Delta)$. If we invest one dollar in the riskless asset for a period of six months ($\Delta = 1/2$) and the continuously compounded rate of interest is 6 percent per annum, we earn

$$R = e^{0.06 \times 0.5}$$
$$= 1.0304. \tag{5.5}$$

Finally, we need to guarantee over each six-month period that, for each possible stock price, the stock is not dominated by the riskless asset or, conversely, the riskless asset by the stock. The guarantee is made by checking that the dollar return on the stock, if it moves up, exceeds the dollar return on the riskless asset for that period, and if the stock moves down, the dollar return is less than the dollar return on the riskless asset for that period.

This calculation is verified by noting that in Figure 5.3, $U = 1.1752 > R = 1.0304 > D = 0.8857$, a no-arbitrage condition. Although this condition seems trivial here, when we study interest rate options in Chapter 15 the analogous condition becomes quite difficult to ensure.

How do we price the traded call option? To answer that question, we simply repeat the logic used before. We start at the maturity of the traded call option. From Figure 5.3 we see that there are three possible stock prices. If the stock price is 138.10, the traded call option is worth 28.10. The traded call option is out-of-the-money and worthless if the stock price is 104.08 or 78.44.

Now let us move backward in time so that we are standing six months before maturity. The stock price can have only one of two possible values: 117.52 or 88.57. If the stock price is 88.57, the traded call option must be worthless because six months later, the stock price could be 104.08 or 78.44. In either case, the traded call option is worthless. If we are at the up state where the stock price is 117.52, to determine the value of the traded option we use exactly the same logic as before.

We form a portfolio to construct a synthetic option by buying m_1 shares of stock and investing B_1 dollars in the riskless asset. The cost of the investment is

$$V_1 \equiv m_1 117.52 + B_1. \tag{5.6}$$

By design, the portfolio must be constructed to create the cash flows to the traded call option.

If the stock price at maturity is 138.10, the traded call option is worth 28.10 and our portfolio's value must equal 28.10. Thus our first condition is

$$m_1 138.10 + B_1 1.0304 = 28.10. \tag{5.7}$$

If the stock price is 104.08, the traded call option is worthless and our portfolio's value must also equal 0, which gives our second condition:

$$m_1 104.08 + B_1 1.0304 = 0. \tag{5.8}$$

Solving for the unknowns gives

$$m_1 = 0.8260 \tag{5.9}$$

and

$$B_1 = -83.43.$$

The cost of constructing the synthetic option at date 1 can now be computed. It is

$$m_1 S_0 U + B_1 = 0.8260 \times 117.52 - 83.43$$
$$= 13.64. \tag{5.10}$$

To avoid arbitrage, the value of the traded option at date 1 must be

$$c_1 = 13.64.$$

What is the traded option worth today? Repeating the same logic gives

$$m_0 = 0.4712$$
$$B_0 = -40.50. \tag{5.11}$$

The initial cost of constructing the synthetic call option is

$$m_0 S_0 + B_0 = 0.4712 \times 100 - 40.50 = 6.62, \tag{5.12}$$

so the traded call option must be worth

$$c_0 = 6.62.$$

You should check these figures for yourself. The details are summarized in Figure 5.4.

Three important implications can be gleaned from Figure 5.4. First, today we set up a replicating portfolio and six months later the portfolio has to be rebalanced; in other words, we have to alter our positions in the stock and in the riskless asset. As a result, our portfolio is seen to be **self-financing**, having no additional cash inflow or outflow.

To see this, suppose at the end of the first six months we are in the up state where the stock price is 117.52. Our portfolio, which was formed at date 0, holds 0.4712 units of the stock and we have borrowed 40.50. The value of this portfolio at the end of the first six months is 13.64. We rebalance our portfolio at date 1 in the up state to hold 0.8260 units of the stock and borrow a total of 83.43. The rebalanced position is worth 13.64, which is the same as the value of the portfolio before it was revised. Thus it is self-financing.

If our portfolio was not self-financing, it would not replicate the cash flows of the traded call option. The traded call option has no cash flows prior to maturity.

FIGURE 5.4   *European Call Option Values*

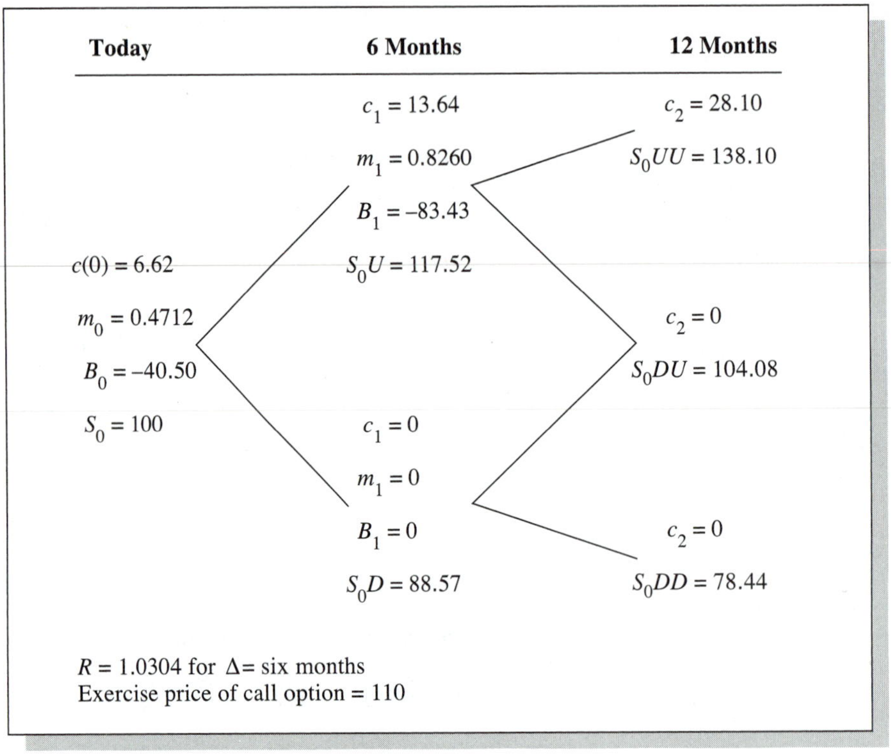

Today	6 Months	12 Months
	$c_1 = 13.64$	$c_2 = 28.10$
	$m_1 = 0.8260$	$S_0 UU = 138.10$
	$B_1 = -83.43$	
$c(0) = 6.62$	$S_0 U = 117.52$	
$m_0 = 0.4712$		$c_2 = 0$
$B_0 = -40.50$		$S_0 DU = 104.08$
$S_0 = 100$	$c_1 = 0$	
	$m_1 = 0$	
	$B_1 = 0$	$c_2 = 0$
	$S_0 D = 88.57$	$S_0 DD = 78.44$

$R = 1.0304$ for $\Delta =$ six months
Exercise price of call option = 110

If the stock price follows a binomial model such as that described in Figure 5.3, it is always possible to form a self-financing portfolio that replicates the cash flows and payout to the traded call option. Given these conditions, to avoid arbitrage the cost of constructing the synthetic call option must equal the value of the traded call option.

Second, you will notice that in Figure 5.4 the value of the synthetic call option is 6.62. When we had only one interval of length twelve months, the value of the synthetic call option from Expression (5.4) was 8.07. Why do these values differ? Compare Figures 5.1 and 5.3; they differ because we are imposing different assumptions about the distribution of the stock price at the maturity of the option.

Third, in Figure 5.4 you will notice that when the traded option matures, three possible stock prices exist. Although we have only two assets in our replicating portfolio, by rebalancing our portfolio at date 1 we are still able to replicate the option's value at date 2 in the three possible states. This is the "flip side" of the self-financing discussion we had earlier.

By now, it should be clear that we can generalize this model to an arbitrary number of time periods. If we have divided the one year into n intervals ($n = 1, 2,$

3, 4, ...), then there would be $n + 1$ possible stock prices at the end of the year and $n + 1$ possible option prices. By rebalancing our portfolio at the end of each interval in a self-financing manner, we can replicate the value of the traded option in each of these ($n + 1$) states. Thus with only two securities—the stock and the bond—we are still able to replicate the traded option's values across the ($n + 1$) states.

This is referred to as **dynamically completing** the market. *Dynamic* refers to the condition that there is more than one period; *complete* describes the portfolio's ability to match the option's values at maturity. In this example, the market is dynamically complete because of the binomial model: At the end of each interval the stock's price and thus the option's value can have only one of two possible values. We need two assets in our replicating portfolio, one for each possible value. We have two assets trading, the stock and riskless asset, and are thus able to construct a synthetic option.

5.3   THE BINOMIAL PRICING MODEL

Let us formalize the previous examples. For the most part, this will involve little more than replacing numbers with symbols. Given that many people find symbols cold, abstract, or "too mathematical," why formalize? The answer is that by formalizing the examples we can see that a general principle is involved in the pricing of derivative securities.

The Binomial Model

Referring to Figure 5.3, let S_0 denote today's stock price ($= 100$) and let the stock price in six months' time be represented by S_1 with $S_0 U = 117.42$ and $S_0 D = 88.57$.

When the option matures in twelve months, let the stock price be represented by S_2, with $S_0 UU = 138.10$, $S_0 UD = 104.08$ and $S_0 DD = 78.44$.

S_2 can also be rewritten as ($S_1 U = S_0 UU$ and $S_1 D = S_0 UD$) or ($S_1 U = S_0 DU$ and $S_1 D = S_0 DD$), depending on the starting position of S_1. For simplicity of exposition we will employ the latter representation. There should be no confusion because the position on the lattice will uniquely identify the relevant stock price S_1.

One plus the riskless return over each six-month period is represented by R, where Δ denotes six months. If r denotes the continuously compounded rate of interest, then

$$R = e^{r\Delta}.$$

Furthermore, to avoid arbitrage between the stock and riskless asset, we must have the condition

$$U > R > D. \tag{5.13}$$

This inequality states that the dollar return on the stock in the up state exceeds the riskless return that exceeds the dollar return on the stock in the down state. Neither investment dominates the other.[2]

Constructing the Synthetic Option

Now consider constructing the replicating portfolio in six months' time, when the stock price is S_1. The cost of the replicating portfolio is

$$V_1 \equiv m_1 S_1 + B_1. \tag{5.14}$$

For this equation, m_1 is the number of shares of the stock held in the portfolio when the stock price is S_1, and B_1 is the dollar investment in the riskless asset. Comparing Expression (5.14) with Expression (5.6), you will observe that all we have done is replace numbers with symbols.

Now, after the next six-month period, the stock price will be either $S_1 U$ or $S_1 D$ and the traded option's value will be either c_2^U or c_2^D. If the stock price is $S_1 U$, the value of the replicating portfolio must be chosen such that

$$m_1 S_1 U + B_1 R = c_2^U. \tag{5.15}$$

If the stock price is $S_1 D$, the value of the replicating portfolio must be chosen such that

$$m_1 S_1 D + B_1 R = c_2^D. \tag{5.16}$$

Solving for m_1 and B_1 gives

$$m_1 = (c_2^U - c_2^D)/(S_1 U - S_1 D) \tag{5.17}$$

and

$$B_1 = -(S_1 D c_2^U - S_1 U c_2^D)/[R(S_1 U - S_1 D)]. \tag{5.18}$$

EXAMPLE   **Figure 5.4**

This example illustrates the use of the preceding formulas. Refer back to Figure 5.4. To check that we have not made a mistake, substitute the values for $S_1 U$ and $S_1 D$, c_2^U and c_2^D, and R and compare your computed values with Expressions (5.9) and (5.10).

---

[2]Suppose $U > D > R$. In this case, no one would buy the riskless asset because you always earn more by investing in the stock. This implies an arbitrage situation. You would borrow at the riskless rate and invest the proceeds in the stock. No matter what state occurred at the end of the year, you can pay off the loan. Suppose that $R > U > D$; it would again imply arbitrage. Therefore, you must have $U > R > D$ to avoid arbitrage.

At the up node at time 1, substituting into Expression (5.17) gives

$$m_1 = (28.10 - 0)/(138.10 - 104.08)$$
$$= 0.8260.$$

Substituting into Expression (5.18) gives

$$B_1 = -(104.08 \times 28.10 - 138.10 \times 0)/[1.0304(138.10 - 104.08)]$$
$$= -83.43.$$

These numbers match the previous computations.   ∎

Next, we need to determine the cost of constructing the synthetic option at date 1. Substituting for m_1 and B_1 into Expression (5.14), using Expressions (5.17) and (5.18), respectively, gives

$$V_1 = \left[(c_2^U - c_2^D)S_1 - \frac{1}{R}(S_1 D c_2^U - S_1 U c_2^D) \right] \frac{1}{(S_1 U - S_1 D)}. \tag{5.19}$$

This represents the cost of constructing the synthetic option at date 1 when the stock price is S_1. To avoid arbitrage, the traded option must have this value:

$$c_1 = V_1 \tag{5.20}$$

EXAMPLE   **Figure 5.4**

This example illustrates the use of the preceding formulas. Again, standing at the up node at time 1, substitute the values from Figure 5.4 into Expressions (5.19) and (5.20). Doing so gives

$$V_1 = \left[(28.10 - 0) \times 117.52 - \frac{1}{1.0304}(104.08 \times 28.10 - 138.10 \times 0) \right]$$
$$\times \frac{1}{(138.10 - 104.08)}$$
$$= 13.64 = c_1.$$

This computation matches the previous value.   ∎

After the first six months the value of c_1 is described by Expression (5.20), depending on whether S_1 is US_0 or DS_0. To determine the value of the traded option today, we repeat the same logic. The cost of the replicating portfolio is

$$V(0) = m_0 S + B_0. \tag{5.21}$$

By construction, the value of our replicating portfolio must equal the value of the traded option at the end of the subsequent interval:

$$m_0 S_0 U + B_0 R = c_1^U \qquad (5.22)$$

and

$$m_0 S_0 D + B_0 R = c_1^D. \qquad (5.23)$$

Solving for m_0 and B_0 gives

$$m_0 = (c_1^U - c_1^D)/(S_0 U - S_0 D) \qquad (5.24)$$

and

$$B_0 = -(S_0 U c_1^U - S_0 D c_1^D)/[R(S_0 U - S_0 D)]. \qquad (5.25)$$

Note that these equations are identical to Expressions (5.14)–(5.18) with the exception that the time subscript changes from 1 to 0. Substituting Expressions (5.24) and (5.25) into Expression (5.21) gives the final result:

$$V(0) = \left[(c_1^U - c_1^D)S_0 - \frac{1}{R}(S_0 D c_1^U - S_0 U c_1^D)\right]\frac{1}{(S_0 U - S_0 D)}. \qquad (5.26)$$

To avoid arbitrage the cost of constructing the synthetic option must equal the value of the traded call:

$$c(0) = V(0). \qquad (5.27)$$

EXAMPLE

Figure 5.4

This example illustrates the use of Expression (5.26). Substituting numerical values from Figure 5.4 into (5.26) gives

$$c(0) = \left[(13.64 - 0) \times 100 - \frac{1}{1.0304}(88.57 \times 13.64 - 117.52 \times 0)\right]$$

$$\times \frac{1}{(117.52 - 88.57)}$$

$$= 6.62.$$

This result agrees with Expression (5.12). ∎

Risk-Neutral Valuation

The previous analysis showed how to construct a synthetic option using the stock and riskless investment. To avoid arbitrage, the cost of constructing the synthetic option must equal the value of the traded option. This logic leads to the valuation Expressions (5.20) and (5.27), some algebraic manipulation of which leads in turn to an important insight in option pricing, called the **risk-neutral valuation** principle.

Returning to the valuation formula for the traded call, Expressions (5.19) and (5.20), we see that

$$c_1 = \left[(c_2^U - c_2^D)S_1 - \frac{1}{R}(S_1 D c_2^U - S_1 U c_2^D) \right] \frac{1}{S_1 U - S_1 D)} . \tag{5.28}$$

Now we can rewrite the above equation in a more compact form:

$$c_1 = [\pi c_2^U + (1 - \pi)c_2^D]/R, \tag{5.29}$$

where

$$\pi \equiv [RS_1 - S_1 D]/[S_1 U - S_1 D] = [R - D]/[U - D]. \tag{5.30}$$

EXAMPLE   **Computation of π**

This example illustrates the computation of π in Expression (5.30). The numerical value of π is

$$\pi = (1.0304 - 0.8857)/(1.1752 - 0.8857)$$
$$= 0.5001.$$

Note that this value differs from $\frac{1}{2}$.   ■

To avoid arbitrage, recall that $U > R > D$. This implies that π is between zero and one, so we can interpret π as a probability. This observation is important and deserves attention. Furthermore, given the assumption that the up-and-down factors U and D do not depend on the level of the stock price, the value of π also does not depend on the price level. This simplification facilitates computation.

Three observations need to be made about Expressions (5.29) and (5.30). First, Expression (5.29) for the value of the option depends on the parameter π. While there may be optimists and pessimists with different beliefs about the probability of occurrence of each state, everyone agrees about the value of π. The probability π depends upon U, D, and R, and there is no disagreement about these quantities.

Second, using the probabilities π and $(1-\pi)$, the term inside the square bracket in Expression (5.29) is simply the expected value of the option at the end of the period. We use the risk-free rate of interest to discount the date-2 expected cash flows to date-1 values. This equation is what is referred to as **risk-neutral pricing**. The probabilities π and $(1-\pi)$ are often referred to as risk-neutral probabilities. This terminology is misleading, however, because we are not really assuming that people are risk-neutral.[3] For this reason we prefer the term **equivalent martingale probabilities**. This may sound like jargon, but as will be explained in the next chapter, it is quite descriptive.

---

[3]The term **risk-neutral** refers to individuals who make their decisions only on the basis of expected values. They do not consider the dispersion of a distribution. To determine the present value of a future cash flow, a risk-neutral individual would first determine the expected value of the cash flow and then discount it using a risk-free rate of interest.

Third, looking at Expression (5.29), we have used c_2^U and c_2^D to represent the traded option values in the up and down states. Although we were talking about call options, we might have been talking about put options because the argument is the same. This insight implies that the equivalent martingale probabilities π and $(1-\pi)$ do not depend on the identity of the derivative security we are pricing. This can be seen by examining the definition of π in Expression (5.30), which does not refer to whether we are pricing a call or a put option.

EXAMPLE

Figure 5.4

This example illustrates the use of Expression (5.29) to compare our results with the numerical values in Figure 5.4. Recall that $\pi = 0.5001$. At the up state at time 1, substituting into Expression (5.29) gives

$$c_1 = \frac{1}{1.0304}[\pi \times 28.10 + (1 - \pi) \times 0.0]$$

$$= 13.64.$$

This agrees with Expression (5.10). At the down state at time 1, substituting into Expression (5.29) gives

$$c_1 = 0. \quad \blacksquare$$

Finally, the value for the traded option at date 0 is given in Expression (5.27) as

$$c(0) = [(c_1^U - c_1^D)S_0 - \frac{1}{R}(S_0 U c_1^U - S_0 D c_1^D)]\frac{1}{S_0 U - S_0 D}. \qquad (5.31)$$

We can write the above expression in the form

$$c(0) = [\pi c_1^U + (1 - \pi)c_1^D]/R, \qquad (5.32)$$

where

$$\pi = [R - D]/[U - D]. \qquad (5.33)$$

Expression (5.32) is similar to Expression (5.29), and Expression (5.33) is identical to Expression (5.30).

EXAMPLE

Figure 5.4

This example illustrates the use of Expressions (5.32) and (5.33). Substituting the numerical values from Figure 5.4 into Expression (5.32) gives

$$c(0) = \frac{1}{1.0304}[0.5001 \times 13.64 + 0.4999 \times 0] = 6.62.$$

This equation agrees with Expression (5.12). $\quad \blacksquare$

If we substitute Expression (5.28) for both the up and down states of time 1 into Expression (5.32), we obtain an alternative expression for the option's value:

$$c(0) = [\pi^2 c_2^{UU} + 2\pi(1 - \pi)c_2^{UD} + (1 - \pi)^2 c_2^{DD}]/R^2. \tag{5.34}$$

The term inside the square bracket on the right side is the expected value of the traded option's price at the end of the second period using the martingale probabilities. The expectation is taken with respect to all three outcomes (c_2^{DD}, $c_2^{DU} = c_2^{UD}$, c_2^{DD}) possible at date 2. The probability of getting c_2^{UD} is π^2, the probability of getting $c_2^{DU} = c_2^{UD}$ is $2\pi(1-\pi)$, and the probability of getting c_2^{DD} is $(1-\pi)^2$. These probabilities can be obtained by multiplying together the probabilities on the branches on the lattice leading to these outcomes. The advantage of this formulation is the ease of calculation.

EXAMPLE

Figure 5.4

This example illustrates the use of Expression (5.34). Given the values of c_2^{UU}, c_2^{UD}, and c_2^{DD} from Figure 5.4 and the value of π,

$$c(0) = \frac{1}{(1.0304)^2} (\pi^2 \, 28.10)$$

$$= \frac{1}{1.0618} (7.0178)$$

$$= 6.62.$$

This value agrees with those previously obtained. ∎

Expression (5.34) readily extends to models with an arbitrary number of time intervals. For the n-step binomial model of Section 4.2 in Chapter 4, it can be shown that

$$c(0) = \left\{ \sum_{j=0}^{n} \binom{n}{j} \pi^j (1 - \pi)^{n-j} \text{Max}[S_0 U^j D^{n-j} - K, 0] \right\} \frac{1}{R^n}, \tag{5.35}$$

where K is the strike price and $\binom{n}{j}$ the binomial coefficient.

This expression represents the expectation of the $(n + 1)$ outcomes for the call option at expiration, discounted to date 0. The expectation uses the martingale probabilities. The $(n + 1)$ outcomes for the call option at expiration are identified by the term $\text{Max}[S_0 U^j D^{n-j} - K, 0]$, which corresponds to the value of the call at date T given that the stock price is $S_0 U^j D^{n-j}$. If exercised, the call is worth $S_0 U^j D^{n-j} - K$; otherwise, it is worthless. This stock price was obtained starting at S_0 and having j up movements and $(n - j)$ down movements occurring subsequent to date 0.

The probability of obtaining the value $\text{Max}[S_0 U^j D^{n-j} - K, 0]$ is

$$\binom{n}{j} \pi^j (1 - \pi)^{n-j}.$$

This probability is determined by multiplying together the probabilities on a path of the lattice leading to this stock price outcome, and summing across all possible paths that lead to this particular outcome.

This closed-form solution for the call option's value is easily programmed on a computer. Next to Black-Scholes, it is perhaps the most widely known expression for a European call option's value.

Given the assumption that interest rates are constant, the value today of a two-period zero-coupon bond is

$$B(0,2) = \frac{1}{R^2}.$$

An abstract way of writing Expression (5.34) is

$$c(0) = B(0,2)E^{\pi}[c(2)], \qquad (5.36)$$

where $E^{\pi}[c(2)]$ denotes the expected value of the terminal payoff to the traded option at time 2, $c(2)$.

We use the superscript π as a reminder that we are calculating the expected value using the equivalent martingale probabilities. This abstract expression is the one that is most easily generalized to other derivative securities and other sets of assumptions concerning the random evolution of the underlying asset's price and the term structure of interest rates. We will encounter Expression (5.36) again later in the text.

Put Options

We now value put options. The same logic used for calls can be used to price put options, hence our discussion will be brief.

Suppose that the put's exercise price is 100, the put's maturity is one year, and the put option is European (can only be exercised at maturity). Divide the one-year life of the put option into two six-month intervals. The stock price lattice is the same as that shown in Figure 5.3 and is reproduced in Figure 5.5.

If the stock price at maturity is 78.44, the traded put option is worth 21.56. If the stock price is 104.08 or 138.10, the put option is worthless. Why? Having established the traded put option's prices at maturity, let us move back six months.

If the stock price is 117.52, the value of the traded put option is zero:

$$p_1^U = 0.$$

If the stock price is 88.57, the value of the traded put option is derived using Expression (5.29), appropriately modified:

FIGURE 5.5 *Put Prices at Maturity*

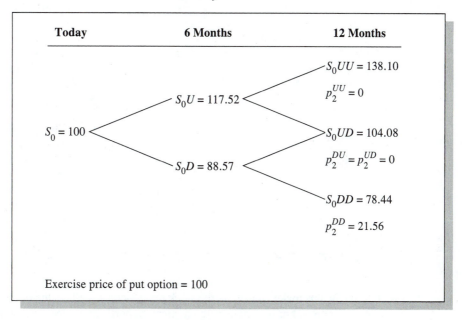

Today	6 Months	12 Months

$S_0 = 100$

$S_0U = 117.52$

$S_0D = 88.57$

$S_0UU = 138.10$

$p_2^{UU} = 0$

$S_0UD = 104.08$

$p_2^{DU} = p_2^{UD} = 0$

$S_0DD = 78.44$

$p_2^{DD} = 21.56$

Exercise price of put option = 100

$$p_1^D = \frac{1}{1.0304}[\pi \times 0 + (1 - \pi) \times 21.56]$$

$$= 10.46,$$

where $\pi = 0.5001$.

Today the value of the traded option is given again by using Expression (5.32), appropriately modified:

$$p_0 = \frac{1}{1.0304}[\pi \times 0 + (1 - \pi) \times 10.46]$$

$$= 5.08.$$

The initial position in the stock needed to construct the synthetic put option is given by

$$m_0 = (p_1^U - p_1^D)/(S_0U - S_0D)$$
$$= (0 - 10.46)/(117.52 - 88.57)$$
$$= -0.3613.$$

This position is a negative number, which means that we must sell short 0.3613 shares of the stock with full use of the proceeds invested in the riskless asset.

FIGURE 5.6   *Summary of European Put Prices*

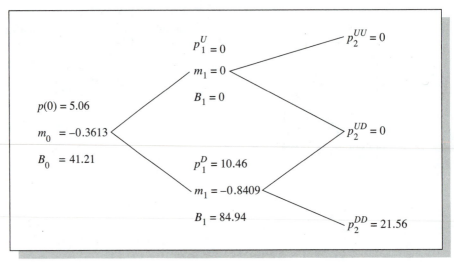

Intuitively, this makes sense. As the stock price increases, the value of the traded put option declines. For the value of the replicating portfolio to decline, we must therefore short the stock.

A summary of the option prices and replicating portfolio positions are given in Figure 5.6. If you are still unsure about using Expression (5.32), try constructing the replicating portfolio and verifying the numbers given in Figure 5.6.[4]

---

[4]For example, if the stock price is 88.75, the value of the replicating portfolio is

$$m88.75 + B,$$

where m is the number of shares and B is the investment in the riskless asset. If the stock price goes to 104.08, the option is worthless, hence

$$m104.08 + B1.0304 = 0.$$

If the stock price goes to 78.44, the option is worth 21.56 and

$$m78.44 + B1.0304 = 21.56.$$

Solving gives

$$m = -21.56/25.64$$
$$= -0.8409$$

and

$$B = 84.9316.$$

Thus the value of the replicating portfolio is

$$p_1 = -0.8409 \times 88.57 + 84.9316$$
$$= 10.45.$$

This number agrees with the value in Figure 5.6 if we ignore the small error due to round-off.

5.4 HEDGE RATIO (DELTA)

Let us examine the concept of an option's delta. Deltas and delta hedging are the most important concepts that the previous theory produces.

Consider replicating a European call option. The number of shares of the underlying stock to use in the replicating portfolio is given by Expression (5.17) and is of the form

$$m_t = (c^U_{t+1} - c^D_{t+1})/(S_t U - S_t D). \tag{5.37}$$

This number is referred to as the **hedge ratio**. It is the difference in the price of the option at the end of the period divided by the difference in the price of the stock at the end of the period. Referring to Figures 5.4 and 5.6, note that the hedge ratio changes at each node in the lattice because the ending values of the call option change at these nodes.

An alternative interpretation can be given to the hedge ratio. Recall that the cost of constructing the synthetic option today is given by

$$c(0) = m_0 S_0 + B_0.$$

Now suppose that the stock price changes by an infinitesimal amount ΔS. What would be the change in the option price if everything else is kept constant?

To answer this question, note that from the above equation we can write

$$\Delta c(0) = m_0 \Delta S_0.$$

The change in B_0 is zero because ΔS has no impact on it. Thus,

$$m_0 = \Delta c(0)/\Delta S_0.$$

We can imply from this equation that the hedge ratio m_0 measures the change in the option price for an infinitesimal change in the stock price, keeping everything else fixed. For this reason, the hedge ratio is often referred to as the option's **delta**. The term *delta* is borrowed from its use in calculus.

5.5 LATTICE PARAMETERS

Now we will see why the stock's drift parameter (μ) is not needed to price options. This is an important characteristic of the model because the stock's drift is a difficult quantity to accurately estimate.

In Chapter 4, we showed how the binomial model can be used to approximate a stock price with a lognormal distribution. This approximation is described by Expression (4.10). This expression depends on the stock's volatility, σ, and the expected return of the stock, μ.

Fortunately, our approach to pricing options avoids the need to estimate the stock's expected return. The trick is to determine the "expected return" on the stock using the equivalent martingale probabilities. It is the only "expected return" required for pricing derivatives, as the actual probabilities never enter the calculation.

To see why this is true, consider Expressions (5.34) or (5.36). They hold for an option with an arbitrary exercise price, and in particular they hold for an option with an exercise price of zero. But, from Chapter 1, recall that the value of a call option with a zero exercise price is simply the value of the stock. Thus we can also calculate the current stock price using risk-neutral valuation.

Let us now do just that. From Expression (4.7) in Chapter 4, we know that the expected value of the terminal stock price using the equivalent martingale probabilities is given by

$$E^{\pi}[S(T) \mid S(0)] = S(0)\exp(\tilde{\mu}T + \sigma^2 T/2), \tag{5.38}$$

where $\tilde{\mu}$ is the expected return per unit time (under the martingale probabilities π).

Risk-neutral valuation implies that if we discount this quantity at the continuously compounded risk-free rate of interest r, it must equal the current stock price:

$$S(0) = e^{-rT}E^{\pi}[S(T) \mid S(0)]. \tag{5.39}$$

Substituting Expression (5.38) into the right side of Expression (5.39) gives

$$S(0) = S(0)\exp[(\tilde{\mu} + \sigma^2/2 - r)T]. \tag{5.40}$$

The implication is that the drift of the stock in the risk-neutral setting must be equal to

$$\tilde{\mu} = r - \sigma^2/2. \tag{5.41}$$

This condition may appear to be quite mysterious, if not completely mystifying. On the left side we have the instantaneous expected rate of return on the stock using the equivalent martingale probabilities, which we have set equal to the continuously compounded risk-free rate minus half the stock return's variance.

To understand why Expression (5.41) only involves r and σ, remember that we are using the equivalent martingale distribution to compute the value of the option with a zero exercise price. We have already argued in the derivation of (5.36) that while pessimists and optimists may disagree about the probability of a particular state occurring, there is no disagreement about the equivalent martingale probabilities. This reasoning implies that the expected terminal value of the stock under the equivalent martingale probabilities is known and computable from r and σ^2 alone.

Thus, to value an option under the lognormal approximation, we specify the binomial stock price movements using Expressions (5.41) and (4.10) to be

$$S_{t+1} = S_t \begin{cases} \exp[(r - \sigma^2/2)\Delta + \sigma\sqrt{\Delta}] & \text{with probability } \pi \\ \exp[(r - \sigma^2/2)\Delta - \sigma\sqrt{\Delta}] & \text{with probability } 1 - \pi. \end{cases} \quad (5.42)$$

From the definition given in Expression (5.30) and using Expression (5.42), the probability π can be written (after some simplification)

$$\pi = [\exp(\sigma^2\Delta/2) - \exp(-\sigma\sqrt{\Delta})]/[\exp(\sigma\sqrt{\Delta}) - \exp(-\sqrt{\Delta})].$$

It can be shown that, as Δ decreases to zero,

π approaches $^1/_2$.

EXAMPLE

Computation of Figures 5.1 and 5.3

Expression (5.42) is used to generate the numbers in Figure 5.1. Using discrete compounding, the value of investing one dollar for one year yields a total of 1.0618 dollars. This was based on a continuously compounded interest rate of $r = 0.06$ and $\Delta = 1$, that is,

$$\exp(r \times 1) = 1.0618.$$

The volatility is 20 percent ($\sigma = 0.2$) and the interval is one year, hence

$$U = \exp\{[0.06 - (0.2)^2/2] + 0.2\} = 1.27124$$
$$D = \exp\{[0.06 - (0.2)^2/2] - 0.2\} = 0.85214$$

and

$$\pi = 0.5003.$$

In Figure 5.3, the interval Δ is six months or 0.5 years, so that

$$U = \exp\{[0.06 - (0.2)^2/2]0.5 + 0.2\sqrt{0.5}\} = 1.17518$$
$$D = \exp\{[0.06 - (0.2)^2/2]0.5 - 0.2\sqrt{0.5}\} = 0.88566$$

and

$$\pi = 0.5001. \quad \blacksquare$$

If we divide the horizon $[0, T]$ into n intervals, and then increase the value of n while keeping T fixed (so $\Delta = T/n$), we know from Chapter 4 that the terminal distribution converges to a lognormal distribution.

TABLE 5.1   *Convergence*

NUMBER OF INTERVALS	CALL OPTION PRICE	HEDGE RATIO
1	8.064	0.409
2	6.617	0.471
3	6.784	0.451
4	6.697	0.470
5	6.520	0.458
6	6.677	0.469
7	6.407	0.461
8	6.649	0.469
9	6.345	0.463
10	6.619	0.469
11	6.305	0.464
12	6.594	0.469
24	6.496	0.468
48	6.407	0.468
96	6.453	0.469
192	6.433	0.469
Black-Scholes	6.437	0.470
Maturity	1 year	
Volatility	20 percent	
Rate of Interest (Continuous Compounding)	6 percent	
Exercise Price	110	
Asset Price	100	

Table 5.1 examines the convergence of the option prices[5] from the above example as we increase the number of intervals, n, and thus decrease the length of each interval Δ.

Two points should be noted. First, the option values do seem to converge, but there is oscillation. Second, the hedge ratio also seems to converge. But what do these values converge to? One would think that the option's value should converge to the value of an option in an economy with a lognormal distribution for stock prices. In fact this is true, and it is the topic of the next section.

---

[5]The rate of interest expressed as a discount rate is 5.8235 percent, assuming a 365-day year. The program Binomial/Pricing European Option/No Dividends is used to compute the binomial call option prices.

5.6 THE BLACK-SCHOLES OPTION PRICING MODEL

The Black-Scholes option pricing model assumes that the terminal distribution of the stock prices is described by a lognormal probability distribution. We now compute the value of the call option in this setting. The value of a call option at maturity is given by its boundary condition:

$$c(T) = \begin{cases} S(T) - K & \text{if} \quad S(T) \geq K \\ 0 & \text{if} \quad S(T) < K. \end{cases}$$

Therefore, the expected value of the option using the equivalent martingale probabilities for a lognormal distribution is[6]

$$\begin{aligned} E^\pi[c(T)] &= E^\pi[S(T) - K \mid S(T) \geq K] \\ &= \exp(rT)S(0)N(d) - KN(d - \sigma\sqrt{T}), \end{aligned}$$

where $d \equiv \{\ln[S(0)/KB(0, T)] + \sigma^2 T/2\}/\sigma\sqrt{T}$, $B(0, T) = e^{-rT}$ is the value today of a zero-coupon bond that pays one dollar for sure at date T, and $N(\cdot)$ is the cumulative normal distribution function.[7]

Discounting the expected value using the risk-free rate of interest gives the risk-neutral pricing formula

$$\begin{aligned} c(0) &= B(0, T)E^\pi[c(T)] \\ &= S(0)N(d) - KB(0, T)N(d - \sigma\sqrt{T}), \end{aligned} \tag{5.43}$$

which is the famous Black-Scholes formula.

The above result is directly analogous to Expression (5.1). Consider the first term on the right side. We have today's stock price and the term $N(d)$. By comparison to Expression (5.1), the term $N(d)$ is simply the hedge ratio. Notice for the second term we have a minus sign. Again, by comparison with Expression (5.1), the second term is the amount we must borrow to construct the replicating portfolio.

Thus we now have our answer. The binomial option pricing model using the parameters from the lognormal approximation will approach the Black-Scholes option model as given in Expression (5.43), and the hedge ratio will approach $N(d)$. We will return to the Black-Scholes formula again in Chapters 8 and 9.

---

[6]A proof of this result is given in Chapter 8, Appendix B.

[7]This value is the probability that a standardized normal random variable will be less than or equal to d; it can quickly be calculated using a computer. See Abramowitz and Stegun (1972).

5.7 FORWARD AND FUTURES PRICES

We can use the same arbitrage arguments found in the previous sections to characterize futures prices. Futures contracts are basic derivative securities that are used as hedging instruments. Consequently, we need to understand how futures prices change as the underlying asset price changes.

We construct a replicating portfolio using the stock and riskless asset to match the value and cash flow of a futures contract. This synthetic futures contract has a futures price the magnitude of which must equal the magnitude of the futures price of the traded futures contract. Otherwise, an arbitrage opportunity would exist.

At the start of each trading period the futures price is set such that the value of a contract is zero. At the end of the trading day, the contract is marked-to-market. This characteristic leads to simplifications both in the construction of the synthetic futures contract and in the identification of the futures price. These insights are emphasized below. We illustrate the arguments with a two-period numerical example.

Consider a futures contract written on the stock. Let the futures contract mature in one year. For simplicity, we will divide the one-year period into two six-month intervals. The initial futures price is denoted by $\mathcal{F}(0,2)$. At $t = 1$, the contract is marked-to-market and a new futures price $\mathcal{F}(1,2)$ is established. At $t = 2$, the contract matures and the final settlement price is the spot price of the asset, $S(2)$.

The stock price lattice is the same as shown in Figure 5.3 and is reproduced in Figure 5.7. Using this lattice, we now want to construct a synthetic futures contract using shares of the stock and the riskless asset.

At $t = 2$, when the futures contract matures, the futures price is the spot price of the asset:

$$\mathcal{F}(2,2) = S(2). \tag{5.44}$$

See Figure 5.7. Thus the cash flow to the futures contract at date 2 from marking-to-market will be $S(2) - \mathcal{F}(1,2)$.

FIGURE 5.7   *Stock and Futures Price Dynamics*

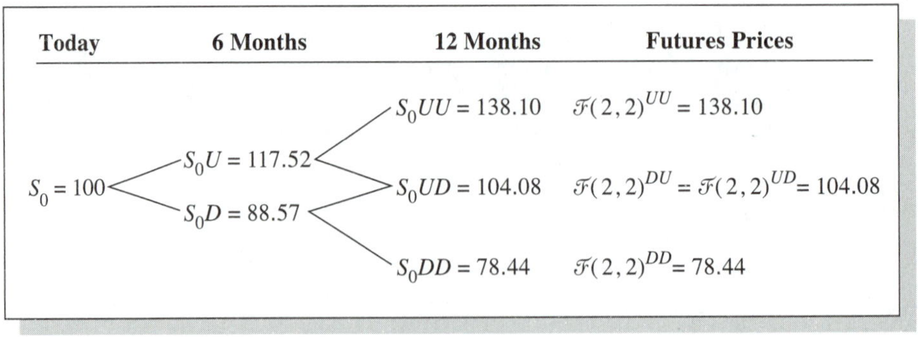

We proceed as we did before. Consider the cost of the replicating portfolio at $t = 1$. Suppose that we are at the up node where the stock price is $S_1 = 117.52$. The replicating portfolio's cost at date 1 is

$$V_1 = m_1 S_1 + B_1. \tag{5.45}$$

In this equation, m_1 is the number of shares of the stock and B_1 is the dollars invested in the riskless asset.

At $t = 2$, if the stock price is $S_1 U = 138.10$ the cash flow to the traded futures contract is $\mathscr{F}(2,2)^U - \mathscr{F}(1,2)$, where $\mathscr{F}(2,2)^U = 138.10$ and $\mathscr{F}(1,2)$ denotes the futures price at $t = 1$ when the stock price is 117.52.

The futures price $\mathscr{F}(1,2)$ is also unknown and needs to be determined by this procedure.

If the stock price moves up, the value of the synthetic futures contract portfolio at date 2, by construction, must satisfy

$$m_1 138.10 + B_1 1.0304 = 138.10 - \mathscr{F}(1,2). \tag{5.46}$$

If the stock price at $t = 2$ moves down to $S_1 D = 104.08$, then the value of the replicating portfolio must be equal to

$$m_1 104.08 + B_1 1.0304 = 104.08 - \mathscr{F}(1,2). \tag{5.47}$$

This gives us two equations in *three* unknowns.

We need another equation to solve this system. This equation is obtained from Expression (5.45) because the cost of the replicating portfolio at date 1 must be zero. Why? When entering into a traded futures contract, the futures price is determined such that the value of the contract is zero. To avoid arbitrage, the synthetic futures contract and the traded futures contract must have identical values. Therefore,

$$V_1 = 0 = m_1 S_1 + B_1,$$

so that

$$0 = m_1 117.52 + B. \tag{5.48}$$

This is our third equation.

To solve this system, subtract Expression (5.47) from Expression (5.46) to yield

$$m_1(138.10 - 104.08) = 138.10 - 104.08,$$

implying

$$m_1 = 1.$$

Substituting $m_1 = 1$ into Expression (5.48) gives

$$B_1 = -117.52.$$

The futures price $\mathcal{F}(1,2)$ now can be determined by substituting for m_1 and B_1 in either Expression (5.46) or Expression (5.47). The solution is

$$\mathcal{F}(1,2) = 117.52 \times 1.0304$$
$$= 121.09. \tag{5.49}$$

We now repeat this procedure at $t = 1$ if we are at the down node and the stock price is $S_1 = 88.57$. Using the identical argument, we ask you to verify that $m_1 = 1$ and $B_1 = -88.57$. The futures price is given by

$$\mathcal{F}(1,2) = -B_1 1.0304$$
$$= 91.26. \tag{5.50}$$

These results can be verified using our knowledge from Chapter 2, in which we showed that under deterministic interest rates, forward prices are equal to futures prices. We also derived a cash-and-carry argument to determine the forward price. Combined, these two insights give us an alternative way to determine the futures price for this example.

Consider a forward contract on the stock with delivery at date 2. From Expression (2.2), based on cash-and-carry, the forward price is

$$F(1,2)B(1,2) = S(1).$$

To use this equation, we need to determine $B(1, 2)$. Given a flat term structure,

$$B(1,2) = 1/R$$
$$= 1/1.0304.$$

Using the forward price equation at time 1 in the up node with $S_1 = 117.52$ gives

$$F(1,2) = 117.52 \times 1.0304$$
$$= 121.09,$$

which agrees with $\mathcal{F}(1,2)$. Similarly, at time 1 in the down node,

$$F(1,2) = 88.57 \times 1.0304$$
$$= 91.26,$$

which agrees with $\mathcal{F}(1,2)$.

The verification of the futures price at date 1 using the alternative cash-and-carry argument is now complete. This argument, however, only works under deterministic interest rates. It will be of no use when interest rates are random. We now move backward to date zero.

To replicate the value and cash flow to the futures contract over the first period, we repeat the same argument. The date-0 cost of the replicating portfolio is

$$V_0 = m_0 S_0 + B_0, \tag{5.51}$$

where $S_0 = 100$.

At $t = 1$, if the stock price is 117.52, the new futures price is 121.09. The date-1 cash flow to a futures contract initiated at $t = 0$ is, by definition, the difference in futures prices: $121.09 - \mathscr{F}(0,2)$. Therefore, we must set

$$m_0 117.52 + B_0 1.0304 = 121.09 - \mathscr{F}(0,2). \tag{5.52}$$

If the stock price at $t = 1$ is 88.57, we set

$$m_0 88.57 + B_0 1.0304 = 91.26 - \mathscr{F}(0,2). \tag{5.53}$$

These are our first two equations.

To avoid arbitrage, the cost of the synthetic futures contract when initiated at $t = 0$ must be the value of a traded futures contract, which is zero. Therefore, we get our third equation:

$$V_0 = m_0 100 + B_0 = 0.$$

Subtracting the first two equations gives

$$
\begin{aligned}
m_0 &= (121.09 - 91.26)/(117.52 - 88.57) \\
&= 1.0304.
\end{aligned}
$$

Using the third equation gives

$$
\begin{aligned}
B_0 &= -1.0304 \times 100 \\
&= -103.04.
\end{aligned}
$$

The futures price $\mathscr{F}(0,2)$ is determined by substituting m_0 and B_0 into either (5.52) or (5.53), giving the solution

$$\mathscr{F}(0,2) = 106.17. \tag{5.54}$$

We can also verify this futures price using the previously mentioned insight from Chapter 2.

The forward price $F(0,2)$, from the cash-and-carry strategy in Chapter 2, is given by

$$F(0,2)B(0,2) = S(0).$$

Now, from Expression (5.6) we get

$$B(0,2) = \frac{1}{1.0618},$$

implying

$$F(0,2) = 1.0618 \times 100$$
$$= 106.18.$$

Ignoring the small round-off error, this value is identical to the futures price $\mathscr{F}(0,2)$ derived from the synthetic futures contract procedure. We emphasize again that this alternative approach only works under deterministic interest rates.

The construction of the synthetic futures contract is now complete. Because this construction was more complex than that for option contracts, we review the procedure and point out some important, but subtle, observations.

Although we derived the replicating portfolio in a backward inductive fashion, we now explain how to implement it moving forward in time, starting from date 0. At date 0, our synthetic futures contract is formed by buying $m_0 = 1.0304$ shares of the stock and borrowing $B_0 = -103.04$ dollars to do so. The initial cost of this portfolio is zero, matching the value of the traded futures contract. We hold this portfolio until date 1.

At date 1, there are two possibilities. If the stock price moves up to $S_0 U = 117.52$, the value of our portfolio is

$$m_0(117.52) - 103.04(1.0304) = 121.09 - 106.18 = 14.91.$$

We liquidate this portfolio to get a cash flow that matches the cash flow received from marking-to-market of the traded futures contract. After liquidation, the value of our synthetic futures contract is again zero, matching the value of the traded futures contract at date 1.

Next, we form a new portfolio to construct the synthetic futures contract over the next time interval by buying $m_1 = 1$ shares of the stock and borrowing $B_1 = -117.52$ dollars to do so. The cost of this portfolio is zero, matching the value of the traded futures contract. We hold this portfolio until date 2, at which time its value, when liquidated, again matches the cash flow to the traded futures contract at delivery. We leave the verification of this statement to you.

If, instead, at date 1 the stock price moves down to $S_0 D = 88.57$, a similar analysis shows that the synthetic futures contract, when liquidated, again matches the cash flow to the traded futures contract. Liquidation resets the value of the portfolio to zero, matching the date-1 value of the traded futures contract. A new portfolio is then

formed at date 1 to construct the synthetic futures contract over the next interval, at which time the traded futures contract matures.

As evidenced by the above discussion, a synthetic futures contract matches both the traded futures contract's *cash flows* and *values* across time and states. The cash flow matching occurs by liquidation and then recomposition of the synthetic futures. This liquidation differs from the argument used to construct synthetic options that had no intermediate cash flows. It is this liquidation that makes the synthetic futures contract distinct, and important to understand.

Formalization

Let us formalize the previous example. In essence, we simply need to replace numbers with symbols. However, this formalization will generate a very important insight: The futures price today equals its expected value tomorrow under the martingale probabilities π. Stated differently, futures prices are martingales under the martingale probabilities π.

We start our argument at date 0. At $t = 0$, the cost of the replicating portfolio is, from Expression (5.51),

$$V_0 = m_0 S_0 + B_0 = 0. \tag{5.55}$$

The cost of the replicating portfolio must be zero because the value of the traded futures contract is zero. From Expression (5.55), we see that our investment in the stock is financed by borrowing, that is,

$$B_0 = -m_0 S_0. \tag{5.56}$$

At $t = 1$, if the stock price is $S_0 U$ the value of the replicating portfolio must be set so that

$$m_0 S_0 U + B_0 R = \mathscr{F}(1,2)^U - \mathscr{F}(0,2). \tag{5.57}$$

Compare this equation with Expression (5.51). If, instead, the stock price is $S_0 D$, the value of the replicating portfolio must be set so that

$$m_0 S_0 D + B_0 R = \mathscr{F}(1,2)^D - \mathscr{F}(0,2). \tag{5.58}$$

Compare this equation with Expression (5.53). Up to the present point, all we have done is to replace numbers with symbols.

We now have our three equations, (5.56) through (5.58), in three unknowns, m_0, B_0, $\mathscr{F}(0,2)$. To solve these equations, first subtract Expression (5.58) from Expression (5.57) to give

$$m_0(S_0 U - S_0 D) = \mathscr{F}(1,2)^U - \mathscr{F}(1,2)^D$$

or

$$m_0 = [\mathscr{F}(1,2)^U - \mathscr{F}(1,2)^D]/(S_0 U - S_0 D). \tag{5.59}$$

Next, rewrite Expression (5.57) in the form

$$\mathcal{F}(0,2) = \mathcal{F}(1,2)^U - m_0 S_0 U - B_0 R.$$

Using Expressions (5.56) and (5.59) to eliminate m_0 and B_0 from the above equation yields

$$\begin{aligned}\mathcal{F}(0,2) &= \mathcal{F}(1,2)^U - m_0[S_0 U - R S_0]\\&= \pi \mathcal{F}(1,2)^U + (1 - \pi)\mathcal{F}(1,2)^D,\end{aligned} \qquad (5.60)$$

where $\pi = [R - D]/[U - D]$.

This result is key. We see here that today's futures price equals the expected date-1 futures price using the probabilities π and $(1 - \pi)$ to make the calculation.

At $t = 1$ we can repeat the identical argument to show that

$$\mathcal{F}(1,2) = \pi \mathcal{F}(2,2)^U + (1 - \pi)\mathcal{F}(2,2)^D. \qquad (5.61)$$

We leave this derivation as an exercise for the reader. Again, Expression (5.61) demonstrates that the futures price at date 1 is its date-2 expectation using the martingale probabilities π and $(1 - \pi)$ to make the calculation. Let us illustrate this computation with an example.

EXAMPLE   **Futures Prices**

This example illustrates the use of Expressions (5.60) and (5.61).

At the up state at time 1, given $\pi = 0.5001$, $\mathcal{F}(2,2)^U = 138.10$, and $\mathcal{F}(2,2)^D = 104.08$, using Expression (5.60) yields

$$\begin{aligned}\mathcal{F}(1,2) &= \pi 138.10 + (1 - \pi)104.08\\&= 121.09,\end{aligned}$$

which agrees with Expression (5.49).

At the down state at time 1, given $\mathcal{F}(2,2)^U = 104.08$ and $\mathcal{F}(2,2)^D = 78.44$, Expression (5.61) yields

$$\begin{aligned}\mathcal{F}(1,2) &= \pi 104.08 + (1 - \pi)78.44\\&= 91.26,\end{aligned}$$

which agrees with Expression (5.50).

Finally, the initial futures price, using Expression (5.60), is

$$\begin{aligned}\mathcal{F}(0,2) &= \pi 129.09 + (1 - \pi)91.26\\&= 106.18.\end{aligned}$$

This result agrees with (5.54), ignoring a small round-off error. As illustrated, the use of these formulas greatly simplifies the computations involved in determining futures prices. ■

In order to calculate $\mathcal{F}(0,2)$ via Expression (5.60), the futures price today, we first calculated $\mathcal{F}(1,2)^U$ and $\mathcal{F}(1,2)^D$, the futures prices tomorrow. If we are only interested in calculating the date-0 futures price, we can avoid these intermediate calculations. This simplification can be obtained with some simple algebra.

Substituting Expression (5.61) into Expression (5.60) gives

$$\mathcal{F}(0,2) = \pi \mathcal{F}(2,2)^{DD} + 2\pi(1 - \pi)\mathcal{F}(2,2)^{UD} + (1 - \pi)^2\mathcal{F}(2,2)^{DD}. \qquad (5.62)$$

The right side of the above expression is simply the expected value of the futures price at $t = 2$ under the equivalent martingale probabilities $\{\pi\}$. Not only is the futures price today its expected value tomorrow, but it is also equal to its expected value two periods from now!

We can rewrite Expression (5.62) in a more compact form:

$$\mathcal{F}(0,2) = E^\pi[\mathcal{F}(2,2)]. \qquad (5.63)$$

This form of Expression (5.63) is the one most easily generalized to alternative assumptions about the evolution of stock price movements or the term structure of interest rates. In fact, Expression (5.63) can be shown to hold under random interest rates, although the derivation is more complex; we will use it later in the text.

Expression (5.63) also has a probabilistic interpretation. A random variable that satisfies an equation like (5.63) is said to be a **martingale**. Thus futures prices are martingales under the equivalent martingale probabilities $\{\pi\}$. This definition is one justification for the name we have been using for the probabilities $\{\pi\}$.

EXAMPLE   **Futures Prices Revisited**

This example illustrates the use of Expression (5.62). Substituting the previous example's numbers into Expression (5.62) gives

$$\mathcal{F}(0,2) = \pi^2\,138.10 + 2\pi(1 - \pi)104.08 + (1 - \pi)^2\,78.44$$
$$= 106.18.$$

This number matches the value of $\mathcal{F}(0,2)$ computed earlier. ■

Expression (5.63) is a very important result; in fact, it can be given another interpretation. Note that, at maturity, the futures price equals the spot price:

$$\mathcal{F}(2,2) = S(2).$$

Thus we can write Expression (5.63) as

$$\mathcal{F}(0,2) = E^{\pi}[S(2)]. \tag{5.64}$$

Expression (5.64) shows that the futures price is the expected spot price at delivery, computing the expectation using the martingale probabilities $\{\pi\}$. However, care must be exercised in interpreting this equation. It does not say that the futures price is an unbiased estimator of the future spot price. We are calculating the expectation using the equivalent martingale probabilities; consequently, the right side of (5.64) will in general be quite different from the expected stock price using the empirical or actual probabilities. This is an important distinction. Expression (5.64) also generalizes to other assumptions concerning the evolution of the stock price or the term structure of interest rates.

5.8 REPLICATING AN OPTION ON SPOT WITH FUTURES

We now show how to replicate options with other derivatives. In particular, instead of using the stock in the replicating portfolio we can use futures contracts written on the stock.

In practice, there are usually two advantages to using futures contracts for hedging. First, transaction costs associated with the use of futures contracts are usually lower than those associated with the underlying stock. Second, futures contracts are not subject to the market "up-tick rule," as are stocks. For example, if you are replicating a put option, it is necessary to short the stock. The **up-tick rule** is a stock market restriction that allows one to short a stock only on an up-tick, meaning that the last transaction in the stock must be a price increase. There is no such restriction for futures contracts. Of course, if futures contracts on the stock do not trade, then one can use other options on the stock to hedge, and many of the same comments still apply.

EXAMPLE   **Option Replication with Futures**

To demonstrate the use of futures contracts, we use the option values derived in Figure 5.4. The option is a European call, with an exercise price of 110 and maturity of twelve months. The call option, stock, and futures prices are shown in Figure 5.8.

Today, at date 0, consider constructing a replicating portfolio for the option using $m_{\mathcal{F}}$ futures contracts and B dollars in the riskless asset. The initial cost of this portfolio is

$$\begin{aligned} V(0) &= m_{\mathcal{F}} \times 0 + B \\ &= B, \end{aligned}$$

given that the value of the futures contract is zero.

FIGURE 5.8   *Call Option, Stock, and Futures Values*

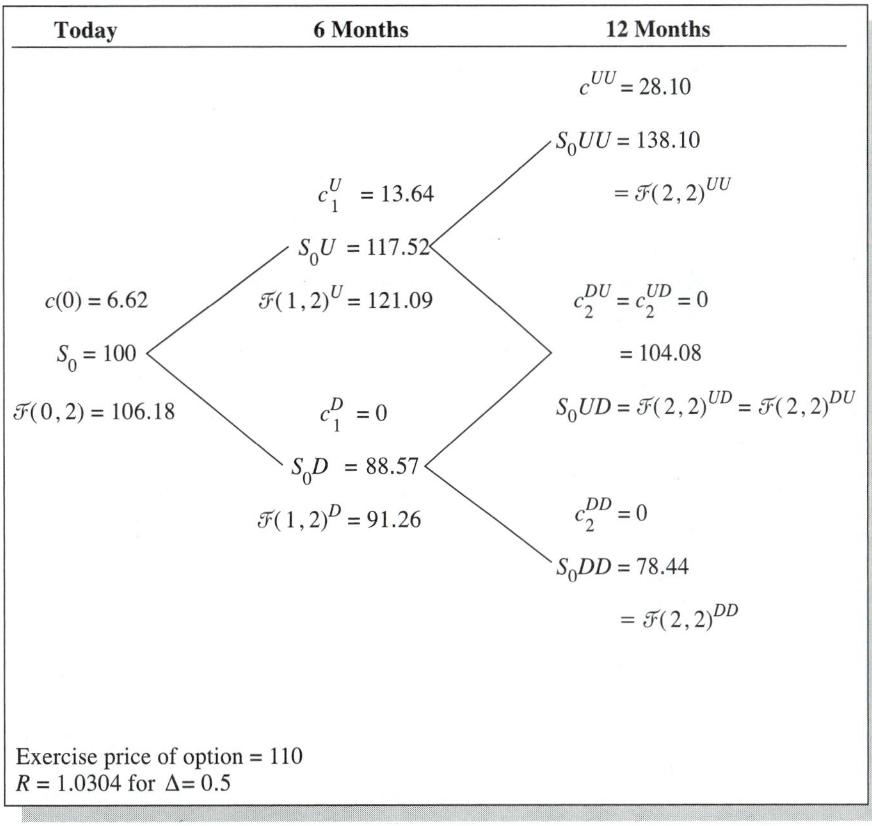

Today	6 Months	12 Months

$$c^{UU} = 28.10$$

$$S_0 UU = 138.10$$

$$c_1^U = 13.64$$

$$= \mathcal{F}(2,2)^{UU}$$

$$S_0 U = 117.52$$

$$c(0) = 6.62$$

$$\mathcal{F}(1,2)^U = 121.09$$

$$c_2^{DU} = c_2^{UD} = 0$$

$$S_0 = 100$$

$$= 104.08$$

$$\mathcal{F}(0,2) = 106.18$$

$$c_1^D = 0$$

$$S_0 UD = \mathcal{F}(2,2)^{UD} = \mathcal{F}(2,2)^{DU}$$

$$S_0 D = 88.57$$

$$\mathcal{F}(1,2)^D = 91.26$$

$$c_2^{DD} = 0$$

$$S_0 DD = 78.44$$

$$= \mathcal{F}(2,2)^{DD}$$

Exercise price of option = 110
$R = 1.0304$ for $\Delta = 0.5$

At date 1, the stock can take on one of two possible values. If the stock price is 117.52, the option value is 13.64, the new futures price is 121.09, and the cash flow to the futures contract is $(121.09 - 106.18)$. By construction, our replicating portfolio must match the option value. This gives the first condition:

$$m_{\mathcal{F}}(121.09 - 106.18) + B1.0304 = 13.64,$$

where for each dollar we invest in the riskless asset we earn 1.0304 dollars over the six-month period.

If the stock price is 88.57, the option is worthless and the cash flow to the futures contracts is $(92.26 - 106.18)$. By construction, the value plus cash flow of our replicating portfolio must be zero. This gives our second condition:

$$m_{\mathcal{F}}(91.26 - 106.18) + B1.0304 = 0.$$

Solving these two equations for the two unknowns gives

$$m_{\mathscr{F}} = 13.64/(121.09 - 91.26)$$
$$= 0.4573$$

and

$$B = 6.62.$$

Given that our portfolio replicates the option, to avoid arbitrage the value of the traded option must equal the cost of the synthetic option, that is,

$$c(0) = B = 6.62,$$

which agrees with the value given in Figure 5.8. ∎

Formalization

Let us formalize the previous example. The formalization involves little more than replacing the numbers in the previous example with symbols. Nonetheless, the formalization generates insight into the differences between hedging with spot versus hedging with futures.

Suppose that the option matures at date T. It is assumed that the futures contract used in the replicating portfolio has delivery at date $T_{\mathscr{F}}$, where $T_{\mathscr{F}}$ may be before or after T.

The cost of the replicating portfolio at date t is given by

$$V(t) = m_{\mathscr{F}} \times 0 + B$$
$$= B. \tag{5.65}$$

In this equation, B represents the amount invested in the short-term interest rate and $m_{\mathscr{F}}$ equals the number of units held of the futures contract.

Next period, under the binomial model, the stock price can take one of two possible values, $S(t)U$ or $S(t)D$, implying two possible futures prices, $\mathscr{F}(t + 1, T_{\mathscr{F}})^{U}$ or $\mathscr{F}(t + 1, T_{\mathscr{F}})^{D}$. The value plus cash flows from the replicating portfolio in the up state are set such that

$$m_{\mathscr{F}}[\mathscr{F}(t + 1, T_{\mathscr{F}})^{U} - \mathscr{F}(t, T_{\mathscr{F}})] + BR = c(t + 1)^{U}.$$

In the down state, they are set such that

$$m_{\mathscr{F}}[\mathscr{F}(t + 1, T_{\mathscr{F}})^{D} - \mathscr{F}(t, T_{\mathscr{F}})] + BR = c(t + 1)^{D}.$$

We have two equations in two unknowns, thus we can solve for $m_{\mathscr{F}}$ and B.

For the present purposes we will only discuss the hedge ratio and solve for $m_{\mathscr{F}}$. Subtracting the two equations gives the hedge ratio:

$$m_{\mathscr{F}} = [c(t + 1)^U - c(t + 1)^D]/[\mathscr{F}(t + 1, T_{\mathscr{F}})^U - \mathscr{F}(t + 1, T_{\mathscr{F}})^D]. \qquad (5.66)$$

Let us compare this hedge ratio to that used if we were using the underlying stock in the replicating portfolio. Rewriting Expression (5.37) with a minor but obvious change in notation gives the hedge ratio on the stock:

$$m_S = [c(t + 1)^U - c(t + 1)^D]/[S(t)U - S(t)D]. \qquad (5.67)$$

As seen by comparing these two expressions, the two hedge ratios will differ. The denominator in Expression (5.66) is the difference in futures prices, while in Expression (5.67) it is the difference in stock prices. The magnitude of $m_{\mathscr{F}}$ versus m_S is discussed in the next section.

Hedge Ratios

Here we relate the hedge ratio using futures contracts for an option on the stock to the hedge ratio using the stock. The argument uses our insights from Chapter 2 regarding forward contracts and futures contracts.

Recall that in Chapter 2 we proved that if interest rates were deterministic, then forward and futures prices are identical, implying

$$\mathscr{F}(t, T_{\mathscr{F}}) = F(t, T_{\mathscr{F}}),$$

where $F(t, T_{\mathscr{F}})$ denotes the forward price at date t for a contract with delivery at date $T_{\mathscr{F}}$.

For a stock paying no dividends we also proved a cash-and-carry relationship:

$$F(t, T_{\mathscr{F}})B(t, T_{\mathscr{F}}) = S(t). \qquad (5.68)$$

We can use these relationships to make our comparison. Substituting Expression (5.68) into (5.66) and comparing the result with Expression (5.67) gives a relationship between the two hedge ratios:

$$m_{\mathscr{F}} = m_S B(t + 1, T_{\mathscr{F}}). \qquad (5.69)$$

The hedge ratio based on futures is the hedge ratio based on spot multiplied by the price of a zero-coupon bond. As $B(t + 1, T_{\mathscr{F}}) \leq 1$, we get

$$m_{\mathscr{F}} \leq m_S.$$

In other words, the hedge ratio with futures is never greater in absolute magnitude than the hedge ratio with stocks. Expression (5.69) can prove useful because it en-

ables one to compute $m_{\mathcal{F}}$ given only knowledge of m_S and interest rates. Unfortunately, this relationship only holds under deterministic interest rates.

5.9 SUMMARY

Using the binomial model for the evolution of the underlying asset's price, we demonstrate how to price derivative securities. To price a derivative security such as an option, we construct a synthetic option using a portfolio of the underlying asset and riskless borrowing/lending. We show how to construct this portfolio so that it perfectly replicates the payoffs to the traded option. To avoid arbitrage, the cost of constructing this synthetic option must equal the value of the traded option.

We use this insight to describe a simple way, called risk-neutral pricing, to value the option as a discounted expectation using equivalent martingale probabilities. Using this technique, we use the binomial model to approximate the Black-Scholes option model.

Futures contracts are also studied. We show that given the lattice specifying the prices of the underlying asset, we can determine the arbitrage-free futures prices for a futures contract written on the underlying asset. We also demonstrate an alternative method of replicating an option that uses a portfolio containing futures contracts and riskless borrowing/lending instead of the underlying stock.

The binomial model is a powerful tool, and it will be used in subsequent chapters for pricing and hedging other derivatives including stock index derivatives, foreign currency derivatives, commodity derivatives, and interest rate derivatives.

REFERENCES

Cox, J., S. Ross, and M. Rubinstein, 1970. "Option Pricing: A Simplified Approach." *Journal of Financial Economics* 7, 229–263.

Rendleman, R., and B. Bartter, 1979. "Two State Option Pricing." *Journal of Finance* 34, 1092–1110.

Sharpe, W. F., 1978. *Investments*. Englewood Cliffs, NJ: Prentice-Hall.

Reference for computing the cumulative normal distribution function:

Abramowitz, M., and I. Stegun, 1972. *Handbook of Mathematical Functions*. New York: Dover Publications.

QUESTIONS

Question 1

A European call option with strike price $50 matures in one year. Divide the one-year interval into two six-month intervals. The continuously compounded risk-free rate of interest is 5.00 percent and the volatility is 30 percent per annum.

a) Using Expression (5.42), determine the up and down factors.
b) Determine the martingale probability of an up state occurring.
c) If the current stock price is $40, determine the value of the option using the martingale probabilities.
d) At each node in the lattice, describe the replicating portfolio, that is, the investment in the stock and riskless asset. Verify your answer to (c).

Question 2

A European put option with strike price $45 matures in one year. Divide the one-year interval into two six-month intervals. The continuously compounded risk-free rate of interest is 4.50 percent and the volatility is 20 percent per annum.

a) Using Expression (5.42), determine the up and down factors.
b) Determine the martingale probability of an up state occurring.
c) If the current stock price is $35, determine the value of the option using the martingale probabilities.
d) At each node in the lattice, describe the replicating portfolio, that is, the investment in the stock and riskless asset. Verify your answer to (c).

Question 3

A futures contract written on the ABC stock matures in 106 days. Divide the 106-day period into two intervals of length 53 days. The continuously compounded risk-free rate of interest is 4.35 percent and the volatility of the return on the stock is 25 percent per annum. The current stock price is $60.

a) Using Expression (5.42), determine the up and down factors. Note: set $\Delta = 53/365$.
b) Determine the martingale probability of an up state occurring.
c) Determine the futures price at each node in the lattice using the martingale probabilities.

Question 4

A futures contract written on XYZ stock matures in one year. A European call option is written on this futures contract. The option matures in six months and its strike price is $60. The payoff to the option at maturity is

$$c(T) = \text{Max}[\mathcal{F}(T, T_{\mathcal{F}}) - 60, 0],$$

where T denotes the date the option matures and $T_{\mathcal{F}}$ the date the futures contract matures.

Divide the one-year interval into two six-month intervals. The continuously compounded risk-free rate of interest is 4.75 percent and the volatility is 20 percent per annum.

a)   Determine the up and down factors for the stock.
b)   Determine the martingale probability of an up state.
c)   If the current stock price is $60, determine the futures prices at each node using the martingale probabilities.
d)   Determine the value of the option.

Question 5

The continuously compounded risk-free rate of interest is 4.80 percent and the volatility of the return on a stock is 25 percent per annum. Compute the up factor, U, the down factor, D, the value of R, and the martingale probability, π, for different values of the interval Δ. Complete the following table.

Δ	R	U	D	π
1				
0.5				
0.25				
0.125				

Question 6   Replicating a Stock

Suppose that a futures contract is written on a stock. The contract matures in twelve months. The current stock price is $100 and the stock's volatility is 25 percent. Divide the one-year period into two six-month intervals. The up factor is defined by

$$U = \exp[(r - \sigma^2/2)\Delta + \sigma\sqrt{\Delta}] = 1.2106.$$

The down factor is defined by

$$D = \exp[(r - \sigma^2/2)\Delta - \sigma\sqrt{\Delta}] = 0.8501.$$

In both equations, σ is the volatility (25 percent), r is the continuously compounded rate of interest (6 percent per annum), and Δ is the length of the interval (0.5).

Construct a portfolio using the futures contract and investing in the riskless asset to replicate the stock. Describe the construction of this portfolio at each node.

Question 7   European Call Options

A European call option with strike price $50 matures in one year. Divide the one-year interval into two six-month intervals. The up and down factors are described by

$$U = \exp[(r - \sigma^2/2)\Delta + \sigma\sqrt{\Delta}] = 1.20460$$

and

$$D = \exp[(r - \sigma^2/2)\Delta - \sigma\sqrt{\Delta}] = 0.84586,$$

where r, the continuously compounded risk-free rate of interest, is 5.00 percent and volatility is 25 percent. The time interval, Δ, is 0.5. Note that if one dollar is invested in the riskless asset for six months, after six months its value is 1.0253. The current stock price is $50.

a) Determine the martingale probability of an up state.
b) Determine the call price by using the equivalent martingale probabilities.
c) How would you hedge this option using futures contracts and the riskless asset? Consider a futures contract that is written on the stock and matures in a year.
d) What is the hedge ratio if you used stocks to hedge?

Question 8 European Put Options

A European put option with strike price $50 matures in one year. Divide the one-year interval into two six-month intervals. The up and down factors are described by

$$U = \exp[(r - \sigma^2/2)\Delta + \sigma\sqrt{\Delta}] = 1.172832$$

and

$$D = \exp[(r - \sigma^2/2)\Delta - \sigma\sqrt{\Delta}] = 0.883891.$$

The risk-free rate of interest, r, is 5.60 percent continuously compounded and the volatility, σ, is 20 percent. The time interval, Δ, is 0.5. The current stock price is $50.

a) Determine the put price by using the equivalent martingale probabilities.
b) If you have written this option, how would you hedge your position using a futures contract and a riskless asset? Consider a futures contract that is written on the stock and matures in a year.

Question 9

Determine the value of a European put option with a strike price of $50 and a maturity of one year. The current stock price is $50 and it is known that over the life of the option no dividends will be paid.

a) Divide the one-year interval into two periods of six months' length. Assume a binomial process for the stock price. The up factor is defined by

$$U = \exp[(r - \sigma^2/2)\Delta + \sigma\sqrt{\Delta}] = 1.245615$$

and the down factor by

$$D = \exp[(r - \sigma^2/2)\Delta - \sigma\sqrt{\Delta}] = 0.814947.$$

The risk-free rate of interest, r, is 6 percent (continuously compounded); the volatility, σ, is 30 percent; and $\Delta = 0.5$. The equivalent martingale probability of an up state occurring is 0.5. Use the equivalent martingale approach to price the option.

b) What is the initial replicating portfolio? Determine the investment in the stock and the investment in the riskless asset.

c) What is the initial value of the replicating portfolio? How is this value related to the value of the put option?

d) If this option was American, what would its value be?

Question 10

Consider the following type of equity contract. In a year's time, if the price of BioBetaMedic (BBM) stock is between $30 and $60, you must pay the going spot price to buy the stock. If the stock price is above $60, you must pay an amount given by the formula

$$60 + 0.1(S - 60),$$

where S is the stock price ($S \geq 60$). If the stock price is below $30, you must pay $30.

a) Draw a diagram showing the amount you must pay for the stock when the contract matures. Ignore the initial cost of the contract.

b) You can construct this payoff by buying the stock plus different options. Identify the options. Justify your answer without the aid of diagrams.

c) Divide the one-year interval into two periods of six months. Assume a binomial process for the stock price. The up factor is defined by

$$U = \exp[(r - \sigma^2/2)\Delta + \sigma\sqrt{\Delta}] = 1.27904$$

and the down factor by

$$D = \exp[(r - \sigma^2/2)\Delta - \sigma\sqrt{\Delta}] = 0.77969,$$

where r is the risk-free rate of interest, 5.85 percent (continuous compounding), the volatility is 35 percent per year, and $\Delta = 0.5$. The current stock price is $45. Use the martingale approach to price this type of contract. The equivalent martingale probability of an up state (down state) is 0.5. What is the value of the portfolio of options?

d) How would you redesign this contract such that the net value of the options is zero?

MARTINGALE PRICING

6.0 INTRODUCTION

I n the last chapter, we demonstrated that in the absence of arbitrage, unique probabilities exist—termed "equivalent martingale probabilities"—that can be used to price options and futures. Using the binomial model we demonstrated (1) the existence of the equivalent martingale probabilities, (2) their uniqueness, and (3) their importance for pricing derivative securities. In this chapter, we want to demonstrate the generality of these results by showing that they hold in economies more complex than that of the binomial model.

First, we collect the results and explain the meaning of the term "equivalent martingale probabilities." Then we will discuss how this result generalizes to economies more complex than those studied in previous chapters. Finally, we show that the assumptions used to specify the lattice of asset prices implicitly define futures prices. There are two important implications. First, we cannot arbitrarily specify the probability distributions for spot prices and futures prices. Second, having specified a lattice of spot (and futures) prices that are consistent with an absence of arbitrage, either the spot asset or futures contract can be used to hedge other derivatives, such as options.

6.1 RELATIVE PRICES AND MARTINGALES

In the binomial option model presented in Chapter 5, we demonstrated the risk-neutral valuation procedure. This procedure shows that the value of an option can be determined by calculating the expected future value of the option using the equivalent martingale probabilities and then discounting at the risk-free rate of interest.

Rewriting Expression (5.32) in a slightly more general form, we have

$$c(t) = [\pi c(t+1)^U + (1-\pi)c(t+1)^D]/R, \tag{6.1}$$

where $c(t)$ is the value of the option at date t, $c(t+1)^U$ is the value of the option at date $t + 1$ in the up state, $c(t+1)^D$ is the value of the option at date $t + 1$ in the down state, π is the equivalent martingale probability of the up state, and R is the return over $[t, t+1]$ from investing one dollar in the riskless asset.

Expression (6.1) is an illustration of the **risk neutral valuation** procedure. The term within brackets is the expected value of the option at date $t + 1$ using the equivalent

martingale probability π. The discount factor is $(1/R)$, based on the risk-free rate of interest. Expression (6.1) easily generalizes to multiple periods. Before we consider the multiperiod extension, it is useful to introduce the idea of a money market account.

The Money Market Account

Suppose we have one dollar today. We want to invest it in the one-period riskless asset, and then roll over our investment next period. This investment strategy duplicates the return one would typically receive on a **money market account**.

Let $A(t)$ denote the date-t value of our account. At the start, our account is worth one dollar, $A(0) = 1$. At the end of the first period, our account's value is

$$A(1) = R,$$

which denotes the original dollar plus interest. At the end of the second period, the investment is worth

$$
\begin{aligned}
A(2) &= R^2 \\
&= A(1)R.
\end{aligned}
$$

The dollar has earned compound interest (interest on the interest). Repeating this argument, we can write the date $t + 1$ value of the investment as

$$A(t + 1) = A(t)R, \tag{6.2}$$

where $t = 0, 1, ...,$ and $A(0) \equiv 1$.

The value of the money market account at date $t + 1$ initialized with a dollar investment at date 0 is given by Expression (6.2). It should be noted that at each date t, we know the current value of the money market account, $A(t)$, and we know how much we will earn over the next period by investing in the one-period riskless asset, R. Consequently, we know the date $t + 1$ value of the money market account $A(t + 1)$ at date t.

Risk-Neutral Valuation

Substituting Expression (6.2) into (6.1) and rearranging, we can write the valuation equation as

$$c(t)/A(t) = [\pi c(t + 1)^U + (1 - \pi)c(t + 1)^D]/A(t + 1). \tag{6.3a}$$

We can rewrite it in a more abstract form:

$$c(t)/A(t) = E^\pi[c(t + 1)/A(t + 1)], \tag{6.3b}$$

where E^π denotes that we are computing the expected value of the option at date $t + 1$ using the equivalent martingale probabilities.

We can use Expression (6.3) at each node on the lattice, working backward from the maturity date of the option until we reach the start of the lattice. We did this in Expressions (5.32) and (5.34) in Chapter 5, which can be rewritten in a slightly more abstract form as

$$c(0)/A(0) = E^\pi[c(2)/A(2)]. \tag{6.4}$$

Again, Expression (6.4) states that the value of an option at date 0 is the expected value of the option at a future date (here at date 2), discounted via multiple compounding at the risk-free rate of interest, $1/A(2)$.

Expression (6.4) is often called the **risk-neutral valuation equation** because (6.4) is the value that the option would have in an otherwise identical economy but in which traders' beliefs are given by the equivalent martingale probabilities and not the actual probabilities. Remember that, by definition, the value of the money market account at date 0—$A(0)$—equals one: $A(0) \equiv 1$.

Expressions (6.3) and (6.4) are the source of the term **equivalent martingale probabilities**. Using these probabilities to compute the expected values, the price of the option today relative to the money market account's value is given by the expected value of the option price at $t = 1$ or $t = 2$ relative to the money market account's value at that date. In probability theory, this is equivalent to stating that relative prices are a **martingale**.[1] Martingales are associated with "fair" gambles because expected values always equal current values. In finance, this sense of fairness translates into prices and a pricing system with no arbitrage opportunities, which will be discussed next.

6.2   MARTINGALES AND NO ARBITRAGE

The typical response to Expressions (6.3) and (6.4) from business students is "So what?" In other words, while the martingale condition represented by these equations is mathematically elegant, does it advance our understanding of pricing derivative securities? The answer is an unequivocal yes. We will first state a general result and then explain its significance.

Proposition: In the binomial model, a necessary and sufficient condition for the absence of arbitrage opportunities between the stock and riskless asset is that an equiv-

---

[1]If $x_0, x_1, x_2, \ldots$ denotes a random process, then $\{x_t\}$ is said to be a martingale if

$$E[x_{t+1} \mid x_0, x_1, x_2, \ldots, x_t] = x_t$$

for $t = 1, 2, \ldots$; it implies that

$$E(x_t) = x_0 \text{ for all } t.$$

We use both expressions in the text. For more details, see Karlin and Taylor (1975, Chapter 6).

alent probability π exists that is unique, such that the stock price $S(t)$ relative to the money market account's value $A(t)$ follows a martingale. This can be written in the form

$$S(t)/A(t) = E^{\pi}[S(t+1)/A(t+1)]. \qquad (6.5)$$

The word "equivalent" means that the probability π is positive when the actual probability is positive (and the converse). We refer to the equivalent probability π as an equivalent martingale probability.

Restating this proposition, a necessary condition for the absence of arbitrage opportunities between the stock and riskless asset is that a unique equivalent probability π exists such that the relative stock price $S(t)/A(t)$ follows a martingale. Surprisingly, the converse is also true. If there exists a unique equivalent martingale probability such that relative prices follow a martingale, it implies the absence of arbitrage opportunities between the stock and riskless asset. A proof of this proposition is given in the Appendix for this chapter.

The importance of this proposition to option pricing cannot be overstated. It takes an economic notion of no arbitrage opportunities and transforms it into a mathematical notion of a martingale. As a mathematical notion, theorems can be proven, formulas derived, and computations performed, which would be impossible using the economic notion alone.

This proposition can, in fact, be generalized to economies more complex than the binomial model,[2] which, in turn, implies that the risk-neutral valuation procedure illustrated in Expression (6.4) may also be generalized. Expressions (6.3) and (6.4) were derived from the binomial option model, which assumes that interest rates are deterministic. The risk-neutral valuation condition (6.4) can be generalized to economies in which future interest rates are random. Second, Expression (6.4) applies to any traded asset, not just options; thus Expression (6.4) can be used to value instruments such as interest rate derivatives, equity options when interest rates are stochastic, commodity derivatives, and foreign currency derivatives.

This proposition can also be used to check that a stock price process is arbitrage-free. Let us check the lattice values in Figure 6.1, which are identical to those used in Figure 5.3 of Chapter 5, to see if the stock price evolution is arbitrage-free.

EXAMPLE   **Arbitrage-Free Verification**

This example illustrates how to verify that an asset price lattice is arbitrage-free. One simply checks to see that Expression (6.5) is satisfied at every node on the lattice. To show (6.5), we show equivalently that

$$S(t) = E^{\pi}[S(t+1)/A(t+1)]A(t).$$

---

[2]In generalizations of the binomial model, the existence of the equivalent martingale probabilities is related to the absence of arbitrage in stock and bond markets, while uniqueness of the equivalent probabilities is related to market completeness. See Harrison and Pliska (1981) and Jarrow, Jin, and Madan (1999, in press).

FIGURE 6.1   *Stock Price Dynamics*

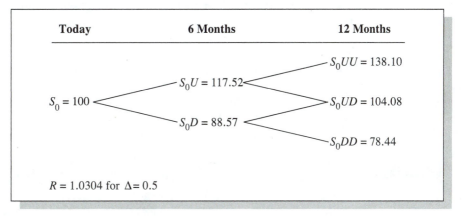

We first need to compute the value of the money market account at each date. Recall that

$$A(0) = 1, A(1) = R = 1.0304$$

and

$$A(2) = A(1)R = A(1)1.0304.$$

At date $t = 1$, if we are at the upper node in the lattice, we use our modification of Expression (6.5) to compute the stock price, that is,

$$E^{\pi}[S(2)]\frac{A(1)}{A(2)}$$
$$= [\pi 138.10 + (1 - \pi)104.08]\frac{1}{1.0304}$$
$$= 117.52,$$

using the equivalent martingale probability $\pi = 0.5001$ [see (5.31)]. It matches $S_0 U$. A similar computation at the down node shows that $S_0 D = 88.57$ satisfies (6.5).

So, the specification of the stock prices at date 1 in the tree is arbitrage-free. For the current stock price we compute

$$E^{\pi}[S(1)]\frac{A(0)}{A(1)}$$
$$= [\pi 117.52 + (1 - \pi)88.57]\frac{1}{1.0304}$$
$$= 100.00.$$

Again, this is the stock price at date 0 in Figure 6.1. As every node in the lattice satisfies Expression (6.5), there are no arbitrage opportunities for this tree. ■

Conversely, we can use the proposition and Expression (6.5) in the opposite way. If we know that a lattice is arbitrage-free, we use Expression (6.5) to determine the (unique) martingale probabilities π. They in turn can be used to price derivatives (as in Expression (6.4)) and to identify arbitrage possibilities in other traded derivatives.

EXAMPLE   **Computation of π Using Expression (6.5) and Pricing a Call Option**

Consider the stock and option prices shown in Figure 6.2. According to Expression (6.5), if the stock and bond market are arbitrage-free, there exist unique equivalent probabilities such that relative stock prices follow a martingale. Therefore, to be arbitrage-free, it must be that for the stock

$$S_1 = E^{\pi}[S_2]\frac{1}{1.0304}, \qquad \text{or}$$

$$117.52 = [138.10 \times \pi + 104.08 \times (1 - \pi)]\frac{1}{1.0304}.$$

This equation has one unknown—π. Solving this equation for π implies that $\pi = 0.5$.

Next, given we know π, we can now price other derivatives on the stock. For example, consider a European call option on the stock with strike price 100

FIGURE 6.2   *Arbitrage Possibilities*

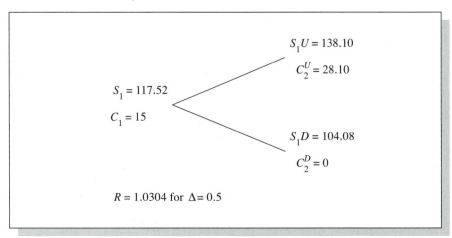

and maturity date 2. This option's payoffs at time 2 are given in Figure 6.2. If the up node occurs, it is in-the-money with value 28.10. If the down node occurs, it is worthless.

The arbitrage-free value of the traded option can now be computed using π and Expression (6.4):

$$c_1 = \frac{1}{1.0304}[28.10 \times 0.5 + 0 \times (1 - 0.5)]$$

$$= 13.64.$$

In this example, the traded option is seen to be mispriced at 15. Can you construct a portfolio that will generate a free lunch? ■

6.3 FUTURES PRICES

Let us now examine the arbitrage-free pricing of futures contracts. The material in Chapter 5 is generalized to a stochastic interest rate economy.

Recall that the futures price for a new contract on an asset is determined such that the initial value of the futures contract is zero. With this market feature, the risk-neutral valuation equation, Expression (6.4), can be used to determine the arbitrage-free futures price.

We will first consider the simple example shown in Figure 5.3 of Chapter 5, reproduced in Figure 6.3, where interest rates are constant over the life of the futures contract. Nonetheless, this example can still be used to illustrate the arguments that apply under stochastic interest rates.

FIGURE 6.3   *Spot and Futures Prices*

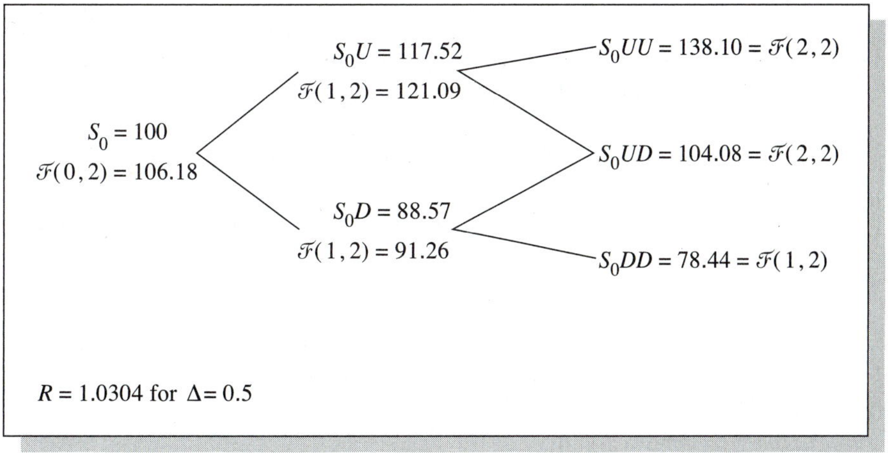

$S_0U = 117.52$
$\mathcal{F}(1,2) = 121.09$

$S_0UU = 138.10 = \mathcal{F}(2,2)$

$S_0 = 100$
$\mathcal{F}(0,2) = 106.18$

$S_0UD = 104.08 = \mathcal{F}(2,2)$

$S_0D = 88.57$
$\mathcal{F}(1,2) = 91.26$

$S_0DD = 78.44 = \mathcal{F}(1,2)$

$R = 1.0304$ for $\Delta = 0.5$

In Figure 6.3, the futures contract matures at $t = 2$. The contract is to buy one unit of an asset with time t spot price denoted by $S(t)$.

The initial futures price is denoted by $\mathcal{F}(0,2)$. At date $t = 1$, the futures contract is marked-to-market and a new futures price $\mathcal{F}(1,2)$ is established. At date $t = 2$, the futures contract matures and the final settlement price is given by the spot price of the asset:

$$\mathcal{F}(2,2) = S(2). \tag{6.6}$$

From Figure 6.3 we see that there are three possible stock prices at date 2. Thus there are three possible futures prices at date 2.

At the time period prior to maturity, suppose we are at the up node where the spot price $S_1 = 117.52$. Let $V[1]$ denote the value of this futures contract. By market convention, the futures price $\mathcal{F}(1,2)$ is determined such that the value of the futures contract is zero, that is,

$$V[1] = 0. \tag{6.7}$$

The cash flow to this futures contract at $t = 2$ is the change in futures prices when the contract is marked-to-market. In symbols, the cash flow is given by

$$\mathcal{F}(2,2) - \mathcal{F}(1,2). \tag{6.8}$$

If the spot price at date 2 goes up to 138.10, the cash flow to the futures contract is

$$138.10 - \mathcal{F}(1,2). \tag{6.9a}$$

If the spot price at date 2 goes down to 104.08, the cash flow to the futures contract is

$$104.08 - \mathcal{F}(1,2). \tag{6.9b}$$

Using the risk-neutral valuation Expression (6.4), the arbitrage-free value of the futures contract at date 1 is

$$V[1]/A(1) = E^{\pi}\{[\mathcal{F}(2,2) - \mathcal{F}(1,2)]/A(2)\}. \tag{6.10}$$

The left side is zero given the market convention (6.7), so Expression (6.10) becomes

$$0 = E^{\pi}\{[\mathcal{F}(2,2) - \mathcal{F}(1,2)]/A(2)\}.$$

Now, $A(2)$ is given by

$$A(2) = A(1)R.$$

At date $t = 1$, we know the values of both $A(1)$ and R, implying that $A(2)$ is a constant. Therefore, we can pull $A(2)$ outside the expectation and multiply both sides of the equation by it to get

$$0 = E^\pi \{ \mathcal{F}(2,2) - \mathcal{F}(1,2) \}. \tag{6.11}$$

Substituting Expressions (6.9a) and (6.9b) into Expression (6.11) gives

$$0 = \pi[138.10 - \mathcal{F}(1,2)] + (1 - \pi)[104.08 - \mathcal{F}(1,2)].$$

Solving for the futures price $\mathcal{F}(1,2)$ yields

$$\begin{aligned} \mathcal{F}(1,2) &= \pi 138.10 + (1 - \pi)104.08 \\ &= 121.09, \end{aligned}$$

where $\pi = 0.5001$.

If we are in the down node at date 1 where the spot price is 88.57, repeating the same argument gives

$$0 = \pi[104.08 - \mathcal{F}(1,2)] + (1 - \pi)[78.44 - \mathcal{F}(1,2)],$$

which implies

$$\begin{aligned} \mathcal{F}(1,2) &= \pi 104.08 + (1 - \pi)78.44 \\ &= 91.26. \end{aligned}$$

To determine the futures price at date 0, the same argument is repeated. The initial value of the futures contract is zero:

$$V[0] = 0. \tag{6.12}$$

At the end of the first period, this contract is marked-to-market, so the date-1 cash flow is the change in the futures prices:

$$\mathcal{F}(1,2) - \mathcal{F}(0,2). \tag{6.13}$$

If the spot price at date 1 goes up to 117.52, the cash flow is

$$121.09 - \mathcal{F}(0,2) \tag{6.14a}$$

and if the spot price at date 1 goes down to 88.57, the cash flow is

$$91.26 - \mathcal{F}(0,2). \tag{6.14b}$$

Using risk-neutral valuation, we have

$$V[0]/A(0) = E^\pi\{[\mathscr{F}(1,2) - \mathscr{F}(0,2)]/A(1)\}. \tag{6.15}$$

Now, from Expression (6.12), the left side of Expression (6.15) is zero. The value of the money market account is

$$A(1) = A(0)R,$$

which is constant across both the up and down states and can be factored outside the expectation calculation. Therefore, Expression (6.15) simplifies to

$$0 = E^\pi\{\mathscr{F}(1,2) - \mathscr{F}(0,2)\}.$$

Using Expressions (6.14a) and (6.14b) gives

$$0 = \pi[121.09 - \mathscr{F}(0,2)] + (1 - \pi)[91.26 - \mathscr{F}(0,2)].$$

Solving for the date-0 futures price gives

$$\begin{aligned}
\mathscr{F}(0,2) &= \pi 121.09 + (1 - \pi)91.26 \\
&= 106.18.
\end{aligned} \tag{6.16}$$

These results are shown in Figure 6.3.

We can check the above results. Recall that in Chapter 2 we proved that if interest rates are constant over the life of a futures contract, then futures and forward prices are the same. We also proved, using a cash-and-carry argument, that

$$F(0,T)B(0,T) = S(0),$$

where $F(0,T)$ is the date-0 forward price of a forward contract delivering the stock at date T and $B(0,T)$ is the date-0 price of a sure dollar paid at date T.

Let us calculate the forward price:

$$F(0,2)/1.0618 = 100,$$

which implies

$$F(0,2) = 106.18.$$

This value matches the futures price, $\mathscr{F}(0,2)$, confirming our earlier calculations.

Formal Description

We now generalize the previous example to stochastic interest rates. The formal description involves little more than replacing the numbers in the previous example with symbols.

Let $\mathcal{F}(t,T)$ denote the futures price at date t of a contract that matures at date T. Let $V[t]$ denote the date-t value of this futures contract.

We determine the futures price by starting at the delivery date of the contract and work backward until we reach time t. This is called backward induction. At the delivery date of the contract, date T, the futures price equals the spot price of the underlying asset:

$$\mathcal{F}(T,T) = S(T). \tag{6.17}$$

At date $T - 1$, the futures price $\mathcal{F}(T - 1, T)$ is determined such that the initial value of the futures contract is zero:

$$V[T-1] = 0. \tag{6.18}$$

The cash flow from marking-to-market is the difference in the futures prices:

$$\mathcal{F}(T,T) - \mathcal{F}(T - 1, T). \tag{6.19}$$

Using the risk-neutral valuation Expression (6.4), the arbitrage-free value of the futures contract at date $T-1$ is

$$\begin{aligned} &V[T - 1]/A(T - 1) \\ &= E^{\pi}\{[\mathcal{F}(T,T) - \mathcal{F}(T - 1, T)]/A(T)\}. \end{aligned} \tag{6.20}$$

The left side is zero because of Expression (6.18). The value of the money market account $A(T)$ is given by

$$A(T) = A(T - 1)R_{T-1}, \tag{6.21}$$

where R_{T-1} is the return over $[T - 1, T]$ from investing one dollar in the riskless asset. This value is of course known at date $T - 1$, implying that $A(T)$ is known.

Thus $A(T)$ is a constant in the calculation of the expected value at date $T - 1$. Factoring $A(T)$ out of Expression (6.20) simplifies it to

$$0 = E^{\pi}\{\mathcal{F}(T,T) - \mathcal{F}(T - 1, T)\}. \tag{6.22}$$

It is important to stress that we are not assuming that interest rates are constant. This simplification occurs because when we calculate the expected value in Expression (6.22) at date $T - 1$, $A(T)$ is known.

At date $T-1$, $\mathcal{F}(T-1,T)$ is also a constant, so we can write

$$\mathcal{F}(T-1,T) = E^\pi[\mathcal{F}(T,T)]. \tag{6.23}$$

The date $T-1$ futures price is seen to be equal to its expected value at date T using the equivalent martingale probabilities.

We can repeat the above argument to determine the futures price at date $T-2$:

$$\mathcal{F}(T-2,T) = E^\pi[\mathcal{F}(T-1,T)] \tag{6.24}$$

and, in general,

$$\mathcal{F}(t,T) = E^\pi[\mathcal{F}(t+1,T)]. \tag{6.25}$$

This result should have been anticipated given our discussion in Section 5.7 in Chapter 5 (see Expression (5.63)). If we compare the general form of Expression (6.25) with the general form of Expression (6.4) we see that, using the equivalent martingale probabilities, futures prices follow a martingale.

This statement usually causes some confusion because, in Expression (6.5), we stated that the relative asset price follows a martingale. The source of the confusion lies within the terminology that is used to describe futures contracts. The terms *futures price* and *value of a futures contract* refer to different concepts. When you enter into a futures contract, the futures price is set such that the value of the futures contract is zero. In Expression (6.4), we are referring to the relative value of an asset. The futures price is just a contractual condition, the price agreed to today for future delivery. It does not correspond to the value of the futures contract.

This source of confusion often generates the question "What has happened to the money market account terms $A(t)$ and $A(t+1)$?" The valuation Expression (6.20) definitely includes the money market account's terms. However, the money market account's value $A(T-1)$ disappears. Why? When the futures price is established, the value of a new contract is zero. The left side of Expression (6.20) is therefore zero. The $A(T)$ is constant in the calculation of the expected value, because at date $T-1$ the value of $A(T)$ is known and it can thus be pulled outside the expectation sign and cancelled (also because the left side is zero). This leads to Expression (6.25), which provides a convenient and simple way to calculate futures prices.

6.4 SUMMARY

The proposition that, in the binomial model, there is no arbitrage in the stock and bond market if, and only if, there exist unique equivalent martingale probabilities such that the relative stock price is a martingale, is a result that forms the foundation for derivative pricing models. This result was anticipated in Chapter 5, where we

demonstrated that there exist unique equivalent martingale probabilities π and $1 - \pi$ such that, for a call option,

$$c(t)/A(t) = \pi[c(t + 1)^U/A(t + 1)] + (1 - \pi)[c(t + 1)^D/A(t + 1)].$$

We derived this result in Chapter 5 assuming that interest rates were deterministic. This expression actually holds under more general assumptions concerning the evolution of the underlying asset's price and the term structure of interest rates. This proposition and the risk-neutral valuation procedure will be used in subsequent chapters for pricing foreign currency, stock index, commodity, and interest rate derivatives.

REFERENCES

Harrison, J. M., and S. Pliska, 1981. "Martingales and Stochastic Integrals in the Theory of Continuous Trading." *Stochastic Processes and Their Applications* 11, 215–260.

Jarrow, R., X. Jin, and D. Madan, 1999. "The Second Fundamental Theorem of Asset Pricing." *Mathematical Finance*, in press.

Karlin, S., and H. M. Taylor, 1975. *A First Course in Stochastic Processes*, Second Edition. New York: Academic Press.

QUESTIONS

Question 1   A Paylater Option

A European paylater call option is defined to have the following payoff at maturity:

$$C_P[T] \equiv \begin{cases} S(T) - K - \bar{c} & \text{if} \quad S(T) > K \\ 0 & \text{if} \quad S(T) \leq K, \end{cases}$$

where K is the strike price; $S(T)$ is the asset price at the maturity date T; and $\bar{c}$ is the initial premium, which is positive. When the option is initiated, the premium is set such that the value of the option is zero. The premium is paid at maturity only if the stock price is greater than the strike. Draw a diagram showing the payoff at maturity.

A European digital option is defined to have the following payoff at maturity:

$$c_D[T] \equiv \begin{cases} 1 & \text{if} \quad S(T) > K \\ 0 & \text{if} \quad S(T) \leq K. \end{cases}$$

Carefully explain how you could replicate a paylater call option with an ordinary call option and digital options.

Question 2   A Leveraged Option

A European call option matures at date T. The strike price of the option is K, and the option is written on a stock that does not pay any dividends over the life of the option. At maturity, the value of the option is defined by

$$c_L[T] \equiv \begin{cases} kS(T) - K & \text{if} \quad S(T) \geq K \\ 0 & \text{if} \quad S(T) < K, \end{cases}$$

where k is a constant.

Prove that the value of the option at date zero can be written as a combination of standard European call options with strike K and European digital call options with strike K.

Question 3

Determine the premium of a European paylater call option (see Question 1 for the definition of a paylater option). The current stock price is \$100 and the strike price is \$100. Recall that the premium is set such that the initial value of the option is zero.

a) Divide the one-year interval into two periods of half a year. Assume a binomial process for the stock price. The up-factor is defined by

$$U \equiv \exp[(r - \sigma^2/2)\Delta + \sigma\sqrt{\Delta}] = 1.245618$$

and the down factor by

$$D \equiv \exp[(r - \sigma^2/2)\Delta - \sigma\sqrt{\Delta}] = 0.814947.$$

The risk-free rate of interest is 6 percent (continuously compounded); the volatility is 30 percent; and $\Delta = 0.5$. The equivalent martingale probability of an up-state occurring is 0.5. Use the equivalent martingale approach to value the option. If you invest one dollar in the riskless asset for six months, you will earn \$1.0305.

b) In practice, these options are difficult to hedge as they approach maturity if the stock price is close to the exercise price. Why?

Question 4

Consider the following type of contract. In a year's time, if the price of ABC Company's stock is between \$25 and \$50, you must pay the going spot price to buy the stock. If the stock price is above \$50, you must only pay \$50. If the stock price is below \$25, then you must pay \$25.

a) Draw a diagram showing the amount you must pay for the stock. You can construct this payoff by buying the stock plus different options. Identify the options. Justify your answer without the aid of diagrams.
b) Divide the one-year interval into two six-month periods. Assume a binomial process for the stock price. The up-factor is defined by

$$U \equiv \exp[(r - \sigma^2/2)\Delta + \sigma\sqrt{\Delta}] = 1.245618$$

and the down factor by

$$D \equiv \exp[(r - \sigma^2/2)\Delta - \sigma\sqrt{\Delta}] = 0.814947.$$

The risk-free rate of interest is 6 percent (continuously compounded); the volatility is 30 percent; and $\Delta = 0.5$. The current stock price is $35. Use the equivalent martingale approach to price the different options.
c) How would you redesign this type of contract such that the net value of the options is zero?

Question 5

The current stock price is $100. The continuously compounded risk-free rate of interest is 6 percent per annum and the volatility of the stock's return is 30 percent. A one-year European option is written on this stock. The strike price is $100.

a) Divide the one-year interval into two six-month intervals. Construct the lattice of spot asset prices.
b) Check that the normalized stock price is a martingale.
c) Given this lattice, the option price is quoted as $14\frac{7}{8}$. Is this consistent with the absence of arbitrage?
d) If your answer to c) is "no," show how to construct a riskless portfolio to take advantage of the situation.

Question 6   *Powered Option*

Consider a European powered call option that expires at date T. The option is written on a stock with price $S(T)$ at date T. At maturity, the value of the call option is defined by

$$c_P[T] \equiv \begin{cases} [S(T) - K] & \text{if} & S(T) \geq K \\ 0 & \text{if} & S(T) < K, \end{cases}$$

where K is the strike price.

Consider a European powered call option that expires in one year. The current stock price is $100 and the strike price is $110. Divide the one-year period into two six-month intervals. The continuously compounded risk-free rate of interest is 4.50 percent, the volatility is 30 percent, and $\Delta = 0.5$.

a) Construct the binomial lattice of stock prices.
b) Calculate the equivalent martingale probability of an up-state occurring.
c) Determine the value of the power option using Expression (6.4).
d) Describe the hedge portfolio.
e) How does the hedge ratio for the position in the stock compare to that for an ordinary option? What are the practical implications?

Question 7

Consider a European return call option that expires at date T. The option is written on a stock with price $S(T)$ at date T. The return over the period T is defined by $R(T) \equiv S(T)/S(0)$, where $S(0)$ is the stock price at date 0. At maturity, the value of the call option is defined by

$$c_R[T] \equiv 100 \begin{cases} R(T) - K & \text{if} & R(T) \geq K \\ 0 & \text{if} & R(T) < K, \end{cases}$$

where K is the strike price.

Consider a European return call option that expires in one year. The current stock price is $64. Divide the one-year period into two six-month intervals. The continuously compounded risk-free rate of interest is 4.75 percent, the volatility is 25 percent per annum, and $\Delta = 0.5$. The strike price of the option is 1.0486.

a) Construct the binomial lattice of stock prices.
b) Calculate the equivalent martingale probabilities of an up-state occurring.
c) Determine the value of the return call option using Expression (6.4).
d) What is the relationship of this type of option to an ordinary option?

Question 8

Given the information in Question 7, the value at maturity of a leveraged return call option is

$$c_{LR}[T] \equiv 100 \begin{cases} R(T)^2 - K & \text{if} & R(T) \geq K \\ 0 & \text{if} & R(T) < K. \end{cases}$$

Consider a European leveraged return call option that expires in one year. The current stock price is $40. Divide the one-year period into two six-month intervals.

The continuously compounded risk-free rate of interest is 5 percent, the volatility is 35 percent per annum, and $\Delta = 0.5$. The strike price of the option is 1.0513.

a)   Construct the binomial lattice of stock prices.
b)   Calculate the equivalent martingale probabilities of an up-state occurring.
c)   Determine the value of the leveraged return call option using Expression (6.4).
d)   A one-year futures contract is traded on this stock. If you have written this option, show how to hedge your position using the futures contract and the money market account.

Question 9

Consider a one-year put option written on a stock. The current stock price is $40 and the current strike price is $40. At month 6, if the stock price is below $35, the strike is lowered to $35; otherwise it remains unchanged.

The continuously compounded risk-free rate of interest is 5 percent and the volatility is 35 percent per annum. Divide the one-year period into two six-month intervals.

a)   Construct the binomial lattice of stock prices.
b)   Construct the binomial lattice of option values using Expression (6.4).

Question 10

Using the information in Question 9, divide the one-year period into four intervals of length 0.25.

a)   Construct the binomial lattice of stock prices.
b)   Determine the current value of the option.
c)   What is the difficulty with valuing this type of option?

APPENDIX: PROOF OF THE PROPOSITION*

PROOF   We first show that no arbitrage implies the existence of unique martingale probabilities satisfying Expression (6.5). In the binomial model, there are two assets trading, a stock and a riskless asset. No arbitrage opportunities between these two assets implies that the return on the stock cannot dominate the riskless asset's return, and the converse, which in turn implies that (using the notation from Chapter 4)

$$U > R > D.$$

*A more general proof is given in Harrison and Pliska (1979).

In words, R always lies between U and D. This relationship implies that there is some unique weighting of U and D that equals R; that is, there exists a unique number π, strictly between 0 and 1, such that

$$\pi U + (1 - \pi)D = R, \tag{A1}$$

which is a simple fact from mathematics. Algebra now gives (6.5). To see this, first multiply both sides of (A1) by $S(t)$:

$$\pi U S(t) + (1 - \pi)D S(t) = R S(t). \tag{A2}$$

Use the fact that $R = A(t + 1)/A(t)$ to rewrite this equation as

$$[\pi U S(t) + (1 - \pi)D S(t)]/A(t + 1) = S(t)/A(t), \tag{A3}$$

which is Expression (6.5) for the binomial model. This completes the proof of the statement that no arbitrage implies the existence of unique equivalent martingale probabilities satisfying Expression (6.5).

We now show that the existence of unique equivalent martingale probabilities satisfying Expression (6.5) implies there are no arbitrage opportunities. Recall that an arbitrage opportunity is a trading strategy with zero initial investment at date 0, and no cash flows, say, until date T. At date T, the value of the trading strategy is always non-negative, and strictly positive with positive probability. This trading strategy is said to be self-financing because it has no cash flows until liquidation.

Let the trading strategy's value at date t be denoted by $V(t)$. If $V(t)$ represents an arbitrage opportunity, then because the money market account's value at dates 0 and T is strictly positive, we have $V(0)/A(0) = 0$, and $V(T)/A(T)$ is non-negative for sure and strictly positive with positive probability.

However, if this is true under the actual probabilities, it is also true under the equivalent martingale probabilities since both are strictly positive. Restated, if $V(t)$ represents an arbitrage opportunity, then

$$V(0)/A(0) = 0, \tag{A4}$$

the initial investment is zero, and

$$E^{\pi}[V(T)/A(T)] > 0, \tag{A5}$$

that is, the expected value of the futures cash flows is strictly positive under the equivalent martingale probabilities.

Combining (A4) and (A5) gives

$$V(0)/A(0) < E^{\pi}[V(T)/A(T)],$$

which states that for an arbitrage opportunity, the trading strategies' relative price, $V(t)/A(t)$, is not a martingale under the equivalent martingale probabilities.

To complete the proof, we show that this inequality can never happen under Expression (6.5); that is, all self-financing trading strategies' relative prices are martingales using the equivalent martingale probabilities.

To understand this point, let the date-t holdings in the stock and money market account be denoted by $\beta(t)$ and $\alpha(t)$, respectively. Thus, *before rebalancing*, at date t we have

$$V(t) = \beta(t - 1)S(t) + \alpha(t - 1)A(t). \tag{A6}$$

After rebalancing, because the holdings in the stock $\beta(t)$ and money market account $\alpha(t)$ in general change, the self-financing condition requires

$$V(t) = \beta(t)S(t) + \alpha(t)A(t). \tag{A7}$$

After dividing by $A(t)$, Expression (A6) becomes

$$V(t)/A(t) = \beta(t - 1)S(t)/A(t) + \alpha(t - 1) \tag{A8}$$

and Expression (A7) becomes

$$V(t)/A(t) = \beta(t)S(t)/A(t) + \alpha(t). \tag{A9}$$

We now show that $V(t)/A(t)$ is a martingale under the equivalent martingale probabilities by taking expectations. First, the relative value of the trading strategy at date $t + 1$ is

$$V(t + 1)/A(t + 1)$$
$$= \beta(t)S(t + 1)/A(t + 1) + \alpha(t)A(t + 1)/A(t + 1). \tag{A10}$$

Taking expectations gives

$$E^\pi[V(t + 1)/A(t + 1) = E^\pi[\beta(t)S(t + 1)/A(t + 1) + \alpha(t)]$$
$$= \beta(t)E^\pi[S(t + 1)/A(t + 1)] + \alpha(t).$$

From Expression (6.5),

$$S(t)/A(t) = E^\pi[S(t + 1)/A(t + 1)]$$

so that

$$E^\pi[V(t + 1)/A(t + 1)] = \beta(t)S(t)/A(t) + \alpha(t). \tag{A11}$$

Using the self-financing condition (A9) gives

$$E^\pi[V(t + 1)/A(t + 1)] = V(t)/A(t) \tag{A12}$$

In summary:

$$E^\pi[V(t + 1)/A(t + 1)] = V(t)/A(t) \text{ for all } t.$$

This equation shows that $V(t)/A(t)$ is a martingale for all self-financing trading strategies and gives the contradiction. Therefore, there can be no arbitrage opportunities.   ∎

We see from the above proof (the second part) that given no arbitrage opportunities in the stock and bond market, any self-financing trading strategy involving the stock and the riskless bond, with value $V(t)$ at date t, is a martingale when normalized by the money market account's value:

$$V(t)/A(t) = E^\pi[V/(T)/A(T)]. \tag{A13}$$

This holds true only under the equivalent martingale probabilities. When markets are complete, any traded derivative can be replicated by such a self-financing trading strategy. This is true, for example, in the binomial model. In that case, as in the derivation of Expression (6.4), Expression (A13) represents the cost of constructing the synthetic derivative. Therefore, to avoid arbitrage, Expression (A13) represents the arbitrage-free price of the traded derivative.

CHAPTER 7

AMERICAN OPTIONS

7.0 INTRODUCTION

I n this chapter we study American options. You will recall from Chapter 3 that American options can be exercised any time up to and including the maturity date of the option. The freedom to exercise at any time implies that understanding the early exercise decision is crucial for the pricing and hedging of American options.

American options are traded on numerous exchanges, for example, the American Stock Exchange, the Chicago Board of Options Exchange, and the Toronto Exchange. The American option feature is often embedded in numerous other financial securities. United States Treasury bonds and corporate bonds often contain call provisions that allow the issuer of the debt to retire the bonds at a predetermined call price, which is an example of an embedded American call option. Many exchange-traded futures contracts contain numerous delivery options that are similar in nature to American options. Convertible bond securities can be converted into common stock, usually after a given period, implying that the option to convert is initially European over a given period and then American.

We first consider call options. From Chapter 3 we know that in the absence of dividends on the underlying stock, it never pays to exercise an American call option early. The American call option is always worth more "alive" than "dead"; by waiting, we save the interest lost by paying the strike price earlier than the maturity date. If dividends are paid to the underlying stock, however, it may be optimal to exercise an American call option early. Early exercise can capture the dividend paid, which may exceed the interest lost. In fact, we will show that an American call option should only be exercised just before the stock goes ex-dividend, or at the maturity date of the option.

We then consider American put options, for which the situation is more complicated. Why is this? The payoff to a put option is bounded above by its strike price (see Result 10 in Chapter 3). This limits the benefit of waiting to exercise, unlike call options. Therefore, even in the absence of dividends, it may be optimal to exercise an American put option early. Early exercise can capture profits sooner, in order to earn interest on the gains. This interest is lost if the put remains unexercised.

This chapter concludes with a section studying options written on forward contracts, which illustrate some of the subtleties of the previous results. Due to the different payoffs to forward contract options, many of the results obtained for stock

options no longer hold. The section on forward contract options can be skipped on a first reading of this material.

The setting of this chapter is similar to Chapter 2, in which we impose the following four assumptions.

Assumption A1.   There are no market frictions.

Assumption A2.   There is no counterparty risk.

Assumption A3.   There are competitive markets.

Assumption A4.   There are no arbitrage opportunities.

It is worth the effort to rethink the meaning of each of these assumptions because all are invoked in the analysis to follow.

7.1 CUM-DIVIDEND/EX-DIVIDEND PRICES

We first study cum-dividend prices, ex-dividend prices, and their relation to each other. For expositional clarity, we refer to the underlying asset as a stock. However, the following analysis is relevant for any traded asset with a cash flow pattern analogous to dividend payments, for example, a coupon-bearing bond.

Consider a stock that pays a known dividend of d_t dollars per share at date t. When the stock goes ex-dividend, we assume that the stock price will fall by the amount of the dividend. This assumption can be shown to hold given no arbitrage opportunities and no differential taxation between capital gains and dividend income.[1]

We write

$$S^c(t) = S^e(t) + d_t,$$

where $S^c(t)$ is the cum-dividend stock price at date t and $S^e(t)$ is the ex-dividend stock price at date t.

The argument that proves this condition is straightforward. If the above condition is violated, that is, $S^c(t) \neq S^e(t) + d_t$, an arbitrage opportunity would result. We consider two cases.

First, suppose that the cum-dividend stock price exceeds the ex-dividend stock price plus dividend, that is, $S^c(t) > S^e(t) + d_t$. The arbitrage strategy is to sell the stock at the cum price and buy it back immediately after the dividend is paid. The profits from this strategy are $S^c(t) - [S^e(t) + d_t] > 0$. We get $S^c(t)$ from selling the stock short; it costs $S^e(t)$ dollars to buy the stock back ex-dividend; and we owe d_t

---

[1]For this statement to hold, we must make some assumptions about the process underlying stock price changes. The statement holds, for example, if the stock price process follows a lognormal distribution. The statement does not hold, however, if the stock price process allows discrete jumps because a jump could occur at the same time as the stock goes ex-dividend, implying $S_t^c \neq S_t^e + d_t$. See Heath and Jarrow (1988) for a formal discussion.

dollars because we shorted the stock and must pay any cash flows to it. These profits will be riskless, or nearly riskless, so long as the variance of the stock price's return between the selling and buying times is zero, or close to zero. This will be true, as shown in Chapter 4, when the stock price process follows a lognormal distribution.[2]

Now for the second case. Suppose that the cum-dividend stock price is less than the ex-dividend stock price plus dividend, that is, $S^c(t) < S^e(t) + d_t$. Then, buying the stock cum-dividend, receiving the dividend, and selling the stock ex-dividend reaps the arbitrage profits $[S^e(t) + d_t] - S^c(t) > 0$.

We see that the only relation consistent with no arbitrage opportunities occurs when $S^c(t) = S^e(t) + d_t$. Figure 7.1 illustrates the theoretical drop that occurs in the stock price when the stock goes ex-dividend. Since the stock price drops by the dividend paid per share, it is not surprising that the value of an option is affected by

FIGURE 7.1   *Stock Price and Dividend Payment*

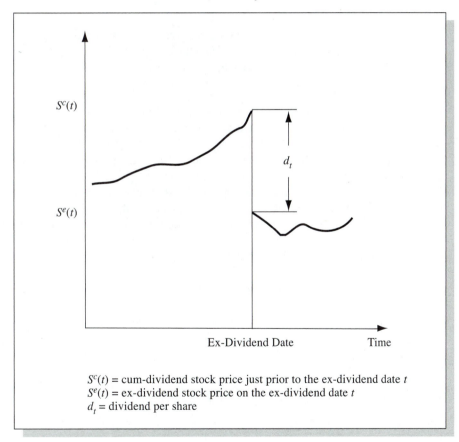

$S^c(t)$ = cum-dividend stock price just prior to the ex-dividend date t
$S^e(t)$ = ex-dividend stock price on the ex-dividend date t
d_t = dividend per share

---

[2]See the discussion in footnote 1.

the payment of a dividend. This cash payment also influences the early exercise decision of American options. This topic is discussed in the next two sections.

7.2 AMERICAN CALL OPTIONS

We now study the early exercise decision of an American call option. As a review, we first consider the case in which the underlying stock pays no dividends over the option's life. Recall from Chapter 3, Result 6, that under this circumstance it is never optimal to exercise an American call option early. To "limber up" our minds, we will repeat the argument. A modification of this argument, in the presence of dividends, shows that it may be optimal to exercise an American call option early to capture the dividend payment. Therefore, early exercise should only occur just before a stock goes ex-dividend. These results do not depend on the binomial model of Chapter 5.

No Dividends

We start our investigation by considering a stock that pays no dividends. Crucial to early-exercise considerations is the notion of the time value of a call option. The next subsection defines the meaning of the time value of a call and discusses some of its properties.

Time value
We introduce the notion of the time value of a call option. First, we need some notation. Let $C(0)$ denote the date-0 value of an American call option that matures at date T, with strike price K, written on a stock with current price $S(0)$. Let $B(0, T)$ be the date-0 value of receiving a sure dollar at date T. Let $PV_0[\cdot]$ represent the time-0 present value of whatever cash flow appears within the brackets.

Now consider the following exercise strategy for the American call. Suppose that we exercise the option at its maturity irrespective of whether the stock price is greater than the strike price. This strategy is obviously suboptimal if the stock price at maturity is out-of-the-money. Nonetheless, the present value of the American call option under this strategy is easily computed, and it equals

$$PV_0[S(T) - K] \equiv S(0) - KB(0, T).$$

This equation holds because, under the given strategy, the American call is equivalent to a forward contract on the stock with delivery price K. The value of a forward contract on the stock with delivery price K equals the stock price less the present value of the delivery price.

The time value of a call option can now be defined. The **time value** of an American call option on a stock paying no dividends is defined by

$$\text{Time Value } (0) = C(0) - [S(0) - KB(0, T)]. \tag{7.1}$$

The time value is that incremental value to the American call option obtained by waiting, perhaps until the maturity date, to decide about exercising the option. The time

value is never negative since the American call need not be exercised at maturity if the stock price is less than the strike price.

We recall from Chapter 3, Result 4, that an American call is at least as valuable as a European call, and that a European call is at least as valuable as a forward contract on the stock with delivery price equal to the strike price of the option, that is,

$$C(0) \geq c(0) \geq \text{Max}\{0, S(0) - KB(0, T)\}. \tag{7.2}$$

where $c(0)$ is the date-0 price of an otherwise equivalent European call option on the stock with maturity date T and strike price K.

Expression (7.2) illustrates that the time value of the American call option, Expression (7.1), exceeds the difference in values between otherwise identical American and European calls. It also shows that the time value is non-negative, as argued previously.

Figure 7.2 illustrates the time value of the call as a function of the stock price. If the current stock price is much less than the strike price, $S(0) \ll K$, the American call option's value will be relatively small, and the time value will be

FIGURE 7.2 *Time Value for a Call Option*

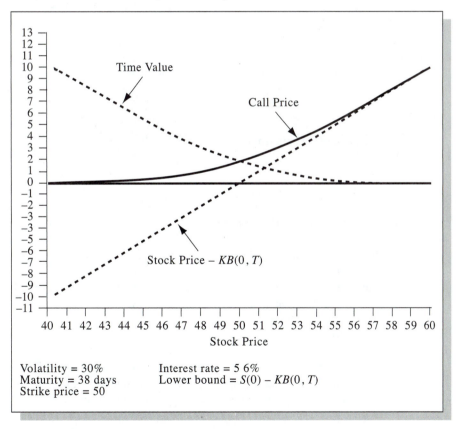

Volatility = 30%   Interest rate = 5 6%
Maturity = 38 days   Lower bound = $S(0) - KB(0, T)$
Strike price = 50

relatively large. On the other hand, if the current stock price is much greater than the strike price so that the probability of the option expiring in-the-money is almost unity, the option value will be only slightly greater than $S(0) - KB(0, T)$, and the time value is relatively small. Our discussion of the call's time value is now complete.

No early exercise

Let us study the early-exercise decision of an American call on a stock that pays no dividends. Our first result was seen earlier in Chapter 3.

Result 7.1

Given strictly positive interest rates and an underlying stock that pays no dividends, it is never optimal to exercise an American call option early.

PROOF   The value of an American call option, if exercised at date 0, is

$$S(0) - K.$$

Assuming positive interest rates gives $B(0, T) < 1$. Therefore,

$$S(0) - KB(0, T) > S(0) - K$$

and, combined with Expression (7.2), we have

$$C(0) \geq \text{Max}\{0, S(0) - KB(0, T)\} > S(0) - K,$$

implying that the option is worth more "alive" than "dead." ∎

Result 7.1 implies that you should not exercise the call option until it matures. If you are bearish on the stock, sell the option rather than exercise it. The logic behind this result is straightforward. If you exercise the option early, you forfeit the interest you could have earned on the strike price by investing it until maturity. There is no offsetting benefit to early exercise, so it should not be done.

Result 7.1 has a further implication for the relation between American and European calls. Because it is never optimal to exercise an American call option early, its value must be identical to that of the European:

$$C(0) = c(0). \tag{7.3}$$

Since European call options are easy to value, Expression (7.3) will prove to be a useful result. We emphasize that it applies to any underlying asset the cash flows of which mimic a stock with no dividends, for example, a zero-coupon Treasury bill.

FIGURE 7.3 *Time of Dividend Payment*

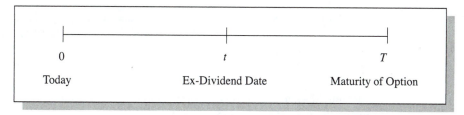

Dividends

Having mastered the situation in which the underlying stock pays no dividends, we now consider the case in which, over the life of the option, one dividend is paid. For simplicity, we suppose that both the dollar amount of the dividend and the ex-dividend date are known.

Timing

First, we consider when during the option's life early exercise may occur.

Result 7.2

Given positive interest rates, it is never optimal to exercise an American call option between ex-dividend dates or prior to maturity.[3]

PROOF

Referring to Figure 7.3, we may ask if we would want to exercise the call option before the ex-dividend date t. Consider two possible strategies:

Strategy (i)   Exercise the option immediately; value is $S(0) - K$.

Strategy (ii)   Wait until just before the ex-dividend date and exercise for sure, even if the option is out-of-the-money. This strategy has a value at date t of $S^c(t) - K$, where $S^c(t)$ is the cum-stock price just before the stock goes ex-dividend. Hence the date-0 value of this strategy is

$$S(0) - KB(0,t).$$

---

[3]For discrete trading models, the optimal exercise decision is made on the last trading date prior to the ex-dividend date. This will be called "just prior to" the ex-dividend date. For continuous trading models, there is no "best" early exercise time, as there is always time remaining before the ex-dividend date. The stock price process is usually assumed to be right continuous, with the ex-dividend price drop causing a discontinuity from the left (see Amin and Jarrow, 1992). This, however, is only a mathematical technicality, which is not relevant in practice when using the discrete-time binomial model.

As $B(0, t) < 1$, the date-0 value of Strategy (ii) is greater than Strategy (i). It is best to wait.

Finally, we may ask if we would want to exercise the call option at any time after the ex-dividend date and prior to maturity. The same argument applies again. Therefore, it is best to wait. ∎

Result 7.2 states that it is never optimal to exercise an American call option between ex-dividend dates or prior to maturity. Again, the logic behind this result is straightforward. Exercising earlier than just before the ex-dividend date loses interest but provides no additional benefit. The only benefit to early exercise is receiving the dividend. Thus we never want to exercise an American call option except just before an ex-dividend date or at maturity.

The exercise decision

Given the above result, let us consider the conditions under which one should prematurely exercise the American call option just before an ex-dividend date. These conditions are obtained by comparing the two possibilities just prior to the ex-dividend date—exercise or not exercise.

The value of the option, if exercised just prior to the ex-dividend date, is

$$S^c(t) - K = S^e(t) + d_t - K.$$

The value of the option not exercised is $C(t)$. This call's value is based on the ex-dividend stock price.

Using Expression (7.1) we have

$$C(t) = S^e(t) - KB(t, T) + \text{Time Value } (t),$$

where $S^e(t) - KB(t, T)$ is the date-t value of exercising the option for sure at the maturity date, and the Time Value (t) is evaluated using the ex-dividend stock price $S^e(t)$.

The option will be exercised just prior to the ex-dividend date if and only if the exercised value exceeds the not-exercised value, that is,

$$S^e(t) + d_t - K > S^e(t) - KB(t, T) + \text{Time Value } (t),$$

which can be simplified to

$$d_t > K[1 - B(t, T)] + \text{Time Value } (t). \tag{7.4}$$

Condition (7.4) states that exercise is optimal at date t if and only if the dividend is greater than the interest lost on the strike price, $K[1 - B(t, T)]$, plus the time value of the call evaluated using the ex-dividend stock price, Time Value (t). Note that as the value at date t of receiving one dollar for sure at a later date T is strictly less than

one, $B(t, T) < 1$, and as Time Value (t) is non-negative, the right side of Expression (7.4) is positive.

Two results immediately follow from Expression (7.4). First, if the stock does not pay any dividends, then it is never optimal to prematurely exercise. This follows because when $d_t = 0$, the left side of Expression (7.4) is zero but the right side is positive, implying that the condition to exercise is not satisfied. This is another proof of Result 7.1. Second, exercise of an American call option is optimal if, and only if, the dividend is large enough to replace the interest lost on the strike price K and the loss of the time value of the call. If the dividend is small, and the time until maturity is large, early exercise will be unlikely.

7.3 AMERICAN PUT OPTIONS

Let us study the early exercise decision of an American put option. The argument for American put options differs significantly from the situation just studied for American call options. The reason for this difference is that the American put option's payoffs are bounded from above by the strike price, limiting the benefit from waiting to exercise. In contrast, the American call's payoffs have unlimited upside potential. The bounded payoff for the American put option makes early exercise optimal (if the stock price gets low enough), even if the underlying stock pays no dividends. The benefit to exercising an American put early is earning interest on the payoff. The cost is giving up any possible additional profit. As the remaining additional profit gets small, this benefit to early exercise can sometimes outweigh the costs. The results of this section do not depend on the binomial model of Chapter 5.

Time Value

We now introduce the time value of an American put. The time value of a put option is defined analogously to the time value of a call option. If the underlying stock pays no dividends, the time value, Time Value (0), of an American put option is defined by

$$\text{Time Value } (0) \equiv P(0) - [KB(0, T) - S(0)], \tag{7.5}$$

where $P(0)$ is the date-0 value of an American put option, and $KB(0, T) - S(0)$ is the date-0 present value of exercising the American put option for sure at the maturity date.

The time value is seen to be the incremental value to the American put option for waiting, perhaps until the maturity date, to decide about exercising the option. The time value is never negative, since one has the flexibility to decide not to exercise at the maturity date if the put option is out-of-the-money.

We recall from Chapter 3 that by combining Results 11 and 12, (i) an American put is at least as valuable as a European put, and (ii) a European put is at least as valuable as

shorting a forward contract on the stock with delivery price equal to the strike price of the option, that is,

$$P(0) \geq p(0) \geq \text{Max}\{0, KB(0, T) - S(0)\},\tag{7.6}$$

where $p(0)$ is the value of an otherwise equivalent European put option on the same stock with strike price K and maturity date T.

Expression (7.6) shows that the time value of the American put, Expression (7.5), exceeds the difference in values between otherwise identical American and European puts. It also shows that the value of a put option is never less than $KB(0, T) - S(0)$, implying that the time value is never negative.

Figure 7.4 illustrates the time value of the put as a function of the stock price. If the current stock price is much greater than the strike price, $S(0) \gg K$, the option value will be relatively small and the time value will be relatively large. On the other hand, if the current stock price is much less than the strike price such that the proba-

FIGURE 7.4   *Time Value for a Put Option*

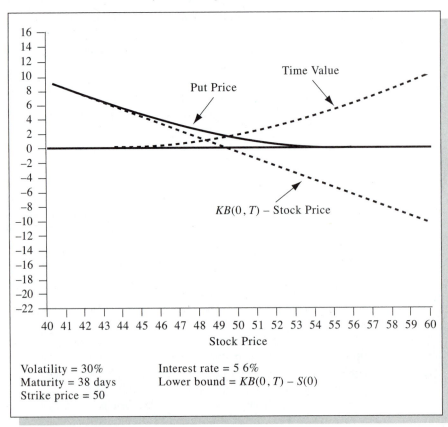

bility of the option expiring in-the-money is almost unity, the option value will be only slightly greater than $KB(0,T) - S(0)$, and the time value will be relatively small.

Dividends

This section examines the impact that dividends have on early exercise of an American put option. As a first cut, suppose that over the life of the option the stock pays a known dividend of d_t per share at date t.

First we need to extend the definition for the time value of a put. The date-0 present value of exercising the American put option for sure at maturity is

$$PV_0[K - S(T)] = KB(0,T) - [S(0) - d_t B(0,t)].$$

It represents the present value of the strike price less the present value of the stock price ex-dividend. The stock price drop due to the dividend payment is added value to this strategy.

The time value of the American put option with dividends is defined by

$$\text{Time Value } (0) \equiv P(0) - \{KB(0,T) - [S(0) - d_t B(0,t)]\}. \tag{7.7}$$

The difference between Expressions (7.7) and (7.5) is the adjustment due to the present value of the dividend paid at date t.

We can now consider the early exercise decision of an American put option. As before, the early exercise decision can be characterized by considering the value of the American put under the two possibilities—exercise or not exercise.

If the American put option is exercised at date 0, its value is

$$K - S(0).$$

Its value if not exercised is $P(0)$. Using Expression (7.7), we can write

$$P(0) = KB(0,T) - [S(0) - d_t B(0,t)] + \text{Time Value } (0).$$

Thus it is optimal to exercise at date 0 if and only if

$$K - S(0) > KB(0,T) - [S(0) - d_t B(0,t)] + \text{Time Value } (0),$$

which simplifies to

$$K[1 - B(0,T)] > d_t B(0,t) + \text{Time Value } (0). \tag{7.8}$$

In words, early exercise is optimal if, and only if, the interest earned on the strike price K exceeds the present value of the dividend lost plus the time value of the put, which is also lost in early exercise.

Expression (7.8) has a number of important implications. We isolate these implications as additional results.

Result 7.3

It may be optimal to prematurely exercise an American put option, even if the underlying stock pays no dividends.

PROOF To prove this result, suppose that d_t is zero, implying that no dividends are paid over the life of the option. Expression (7.8) then simplifies to

$$K[1 - B(0, T)] > \text{Time Value } (0).$$

If the time value is small, which occurs when the stock price is small relative to the exercise price, then the left side can be larger than the right side, implying that it is optimal to prematurely exercise the put option. ∎

This result illustrates a major difference between American call and put options. Given that the underlying stock pays no dividends, it is never optimal to prematurely exercise an American call option. In contrast, Result 7.3 shows that it may be optimal to prematurely exercise an American put option.

Result 7.4

a)   Dividends will tend to delay early exercise of an American put option.
b)   It never pays to exercise an American put option just prior to an ex-dividend date.

PROOF As the magnitude of the dividend increases, it becomes less likely that the magnitude on the left side of Expression (7.8) will be greater than the right side, which implies part a) of the result. For part b), consider two possible exercise strategies:

Strategy 1.   Exercise the put option just before the ex-dividend date. The value of the option is

$$K - [S^e(t) + d_t].$$

Strategy 2.   Exercise the put option just after the ex-dividend date. The value of the option is

$$K - S^e(t).$$

The option is worth more under Strategy 2 than Strategy 1. ∎

This result has two parts. Part a) states that dividends tend to delay early exercise of American puts. This occurs because a future dividend will cause the stock price to fall on the ex-dividend date, and waiting for this drop often increases the value of the American put. Part b) further emphasizes this insight. It states that it is always worthwhile to exercise just after the ex-dividend date rather than just before.

This completes the analysis of American put options[4] without invoking additional distributional assumptions regarding the underlying stock's price movements. Additional distribution assumptions allow one to explicitly determine the time value of the option, hence the early-exercise decision.

7.4 VALUATION

Let us examine procedures for determining an explicit value for American call and put options. Explicit valuation requires more structure than that used in the previous sections. In particular, we need to impose an assumption concerning the distribution for the underlying stock price's movements. The assumption we impose is the binomial model of Chapter 5. We will consider American call options and then American put options.

American Call Options

We first value American call options. There are two cases to consider: The stock pays dividends or the stock pays no dividends. If the stock pays no dividends, it is not optimal to prematurely exercise an American call option. In this case the American call option is valued as a European call option. We have already discussed this situation in Chapter 5. Consequently, we only need to discuss the second case, in which the underlying stock pays dividends. We illustrate the valuation procedure through the use of a simple example.

EXAMPLE   **American Call Option Valuation**

Consider an American call option with one-year maturity written on a stock. The current stock price is $100 and the stock pays a dividend of $5 in six months' time. Both the dividend and the ex-dividend date are known. Let the strike price of the option be $90.

To value this option, we divide the one-year period into two six-month intervals. Using the binomial representation for stock prices, the cum-dividend stock price just prior to the ex-dividend date is 117.52 in the up-state and 88.57

---

[4]Multiple known dividend payments over the life of an American call or put are easily incorporated into the preceding expressions by replacing the present value of the one dividend with the present value of all dividends over the life of the option. This extension is left as an exercise for the reader.

in the down-state (see Figure 7.5[5]). After the dividend is paid, the stock price is assumed to drop by the full amount of the dividend. In the up-state, the ex-dividend stock price is 112.52 (= 117.52 − 5).

Next period prices will be 132.23 (= 1.1752 × 112.52) or 99.65 (= 0.8857 × 112.52).

In the down-state, the ex-dividend stock price is 83.57 (= 88.57 − 5) and stock prices in the next period will be 98.21 (= 1.1752 × 83.57) or 74.01 (= 0.8857 × 83.57).

At the maturity of the option there are four possible stock prices (132.23, 99.65, 98.21, 74.01).

Because of the discrete nature of the model, we need to make a convention concerning the exercising of the option and the receipt of the dividend. We assume that if the option is exercised at time 1, the dividend is received. This assumption can be interpreted as saying that the option is actually exercised after time 0 and just before time 1.

FIGURE 7.5   *Stock Price Dynamics*

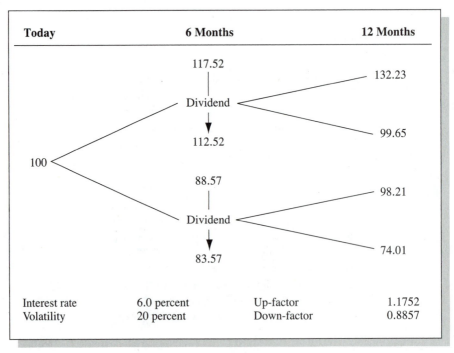

Today	6 Months	12 Months
	117.52	132.23
	Dividend	99.65
	112.52	
100		
	88.57	98.21
	Dividend	74.01
	83.57	

Interest rate	6.0 percent	Up-factor	1.1752
Volatility	20 percent	Down-factor	0.8857

[5]The up-factor is 1.1752 and the down-factor is 0.8857. An investment of one dollar in the riskless asset for six months will yield 1.0304 dollars and for one year 1.0618. The continuously compounded rate of interest is 6.00 percent.

FIGURE 7.6   *Valuation of an American Call Option*

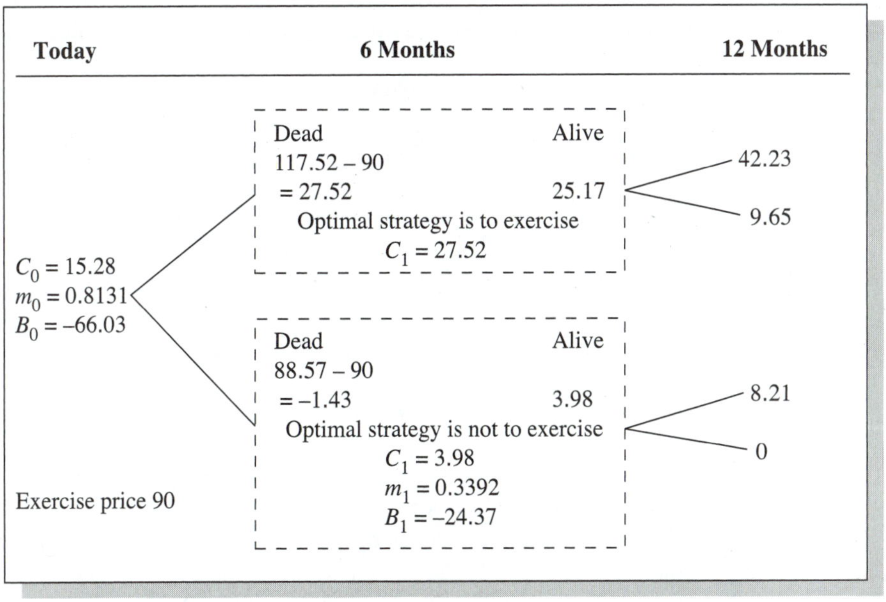

Today	6 Months	12 Months

Dead   Alive

$117.52 - 90$

$= 27.52$ 25.17

Optimal strategy is to exercise

$C_1 = 27.52$

— 42.23

— 9.65

$C_0 = 15.28$
$m_0 = 0.8131$
$B_0 = -66.03$

Dead   Alive

$88.57 - 90$

$= -1.43$ 3.98

Optimal strategy is not to exercise

$C_1 = 3.98$

$m_1 = 0.3392$

$B_1 = -24.37$

— 8.21

— 0

Exercise price 90

The option values are shown in Figure 7.6. If not exercised earlier, at maturity the call option takes on four possible values (42.23, 9.65, 8.21, 0) corresponding to the four possible stock prices.

At each earlier date, to value the call option we need to compare its value under the two possibilities: exercise or not exercise.

Six months prior to maturity, if the ex-dividend stock price is 83.57 in the down-state, the value of the call option if not exercised is given by

$$C_1 \equiv [0.5 \times 8.21 + 0.5 \times 0]/1.0304 = 3.98,$$

where the equivalent martingale probability, π, is 0.5.[6]

The option value C_1 represents the present value of the future cash flows from holding the option "alive." If the option is exercised just prior to the ex-dividend date, its value would be

$$88.57 - 90 = -1.43.$$

The not-exercised value is larger; therefore, the optimal strategy is not to exercise the call, and its value is given by

---

[6]Recall from Chapter 5, Expression (5.30), that

$$\pi = \frac{R - D}{U - D} = \frac{1.0304 - 0.8857}{1.1752 - 0.8857} = 0.5.$$

$$C_1 = \text{Max}\{-1.43, 3.98\} = 3.98.$$

To replicate the call, the synthetic option is obtained by purchasing

$$m_1 = \frac{8.21 - 0}{98.21 - 74.01} = 0.3392$$

shares of the stock, and borrowing

$$B_1 = C_1 - m_1 S_1 = 3.98 - (0.3392)83.57 = -24.3669$$

dollars at the riskless rate. The cost of the synthetic option is

$$m_1 83.57 + B_1 = 3.98.$$

In this construction of the synthetic call, note that the stock price employed at date 1 is the ex-dividend price because the dividend is considered to be paid after date 0 and before the construction of the replicating portfolio at the start of date 1.

If the ex-dividend stock price is 112.52 in the up-state, the value of the call option, if not exercised, is given by

$$C_1 = [0.5 \times 42.23 + 0.5 \times 9.65]/1.0304 = 25.17.$$

On the other hand, if the option is exercised just prior to the ex-dividend date, its value would be

$$117.52 - 90 = 27.52.$$

The optimal strategy is to exercise the option, and the option's value is

$$C_1 = \text{Max}\{27.52, 25.17\} = 27.52.$$

Because the option is exercised here, constructing the synthetic option over the next time period is no longer relevant.

Finally, the value of the option at date 0, if unexercised, is

$$C_0 = [0.5 \times 3.98 + 0.5 \times 27.52]/1.0304 = 15.28.$$

Since there are no dividends at date 0, by Result 7.1 we know that early exercise would not be optimal. As a quick check, note that the exercised value of the option at date 0 is $100 - 90 = 10$, which is less than 15.28. The details are summarized in Figure 7.6.

To replicate the option at date 0, the synthetic call is obtained by purchasing

$$m_0 = \frac{27.52 - 3.98}{117.52 - 88.57} = 0.8131$$

shares of the stock and borrowing

$$B_0 = C_0 - m_0 S_0 = 15.28 - (0.8131)100 = -66.03$$

dollars at the riskless rate. In this construction, the stock price used at date 1 (for the calculation of the option's delta) is the stock price cum-dividend. Why? Purchase of the stock at date 0 gives the owner the dividend cash flow at date 1. ■

Computational Complexity

We briefly discuss here some issues relating to computational complexity with the binomial model when there are dividends paid on the underlying stock.

Looking at Figure 7.6, note that at the maturity of the call option there are four possible stock prices, not three, because after the dividend payment the stock price lattice does not recombine. This additional branching significantly increases computation time.

In general, if there are N possible stock prices at the ex-dividend date, then there will be N new lattices after the dividend payment. This is illustrated in Figure 7.7

FIGURE 7.7 *Lattice Construction*

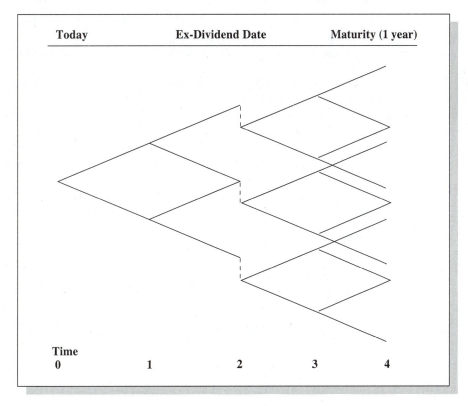

using the preceding example. In Figure 7.7, the one-year period is divided into four intervals. Just prior to the ex-dividend date, at date 2, there are three possible stock prices. When the stock goes ex-dividend, three new sub-lattices are generated. The stock price lattices do not recombine. This increase in the number of lattices causes computing time to increase exponentially as the number of dividends to be paid over the option's life increases. For this reason, efficient computational procedures for computing American option values is an active area of current research.

American Put Options

We next examine the explicit valuation of an American put option under the additional assumption that the stock price follows a binomial model as given in Chapter 5.

We know that even if there are no dividends paid on the stock, it may be optimal to prematurely exercise an American put option. This is due to the fact that the payoff to an American put option is bounded above by the strike price of the option, limiting the benefit of waiting to exercise. Consequently, European put valuation is distinct from American put valuation regardless of dividends. To illustrate the American put valuation procedure, we consider a simple example.

EXAMPLE   **American Put Valuation**

Consider the stock price lattice shown in Figure 7.8. This stock price pays no dividends.

Consider an American put option with a maturity of one year and a strike price of 110.

At maturity, there are three possible stock prices (138.11, 104.09, 78.45). Corresponding to these three stock prices are the put's values at maturity (0, 5.91, 31.55). For example, at a stock price of 138.11, the put is out-of-the-money and worthless.

Prior to maturity, to determine the value of the American put we need to compute the value under the two possibilities—exercise or not exercise—and take the largest.

Six months prior to the option's maturity, if the stock price is 88.57, using the risk-neutral valuation procedure the value of the put option if not exercised is

$$P_1 = [0.5 \times 5.91 + 0.5 \times 31.55]/1.0304 = 18.18.$$

In this calculation, the equivalent martingale probability is $\pi = 0.5$.[7] If the put option is exercised, its value would be

$$110 - 88.57 = 21.43.$$

---

[7]See footnotes 5 and 6.

FIGURE 7.8   *Stock Price Dynamics*

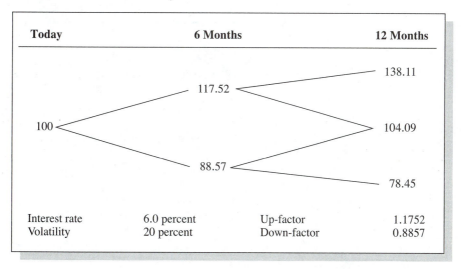

Therefore, it is optimal to prematurely exercise the American put option. Its value at date 1 in the down-state is

$$P_1 = \text{Max}\{21.43, 18.18\} = 21.43.$$

As the put option is exercised, option replication is irrelevant.

If at date 1 the stock price is 117.52, the value of the put option, if not exercised, is

$$P_1 = [0.5 \times 0 + 0.5 \times 5.91]/1.0304 = 2.87.$$

If the put option is exercised, its value would be

$$110 - 117.52 = -7.52.$$

Therefore, it is not optimal to prematurely exercise the put option, and

$$P_1 = \text{Max}\{-7.52, 2.87\} = 2.87.$$

To synthetically construct the American put, sell

$$m_1 = \frac{0 - 5.91}{138.11 - 104.09} = -0.17$$

shares of the stock and invest

$$B_1 = P_1 - m_1(S_1) = 2.87 + 0.17(117.52) = 22.85$$

dollars at the riskless rate.

Finally, the value of the put option at date 0 if not exercised is

$$[0.5 \times 2.87 + 0.5 \times 21.43]/1.0304 = 11.79.$$

If exercised, its value is $110 - 100 = 10$. Thus it is not optimal to exercise, and the put's date-0 value is

$$P_0 = \text{Max}\{10, 11.79\} = 11.79.$$

To synthetically construct the American put at date 0, sell

$$m_0 = \frac{2.87 - 21.43}{117.52 - 88.57} = -0.64$$

FIGURE 7.9   *Valuation of an American Put Option (No Dividends)*

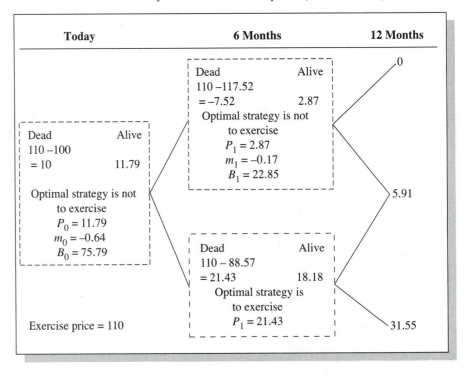

shares of the stock and invest

$$B_0 = P_0 - m_0(S_0) = 11.79 + (0.64)100 = 75.79$$

dollars at the riskless rate.

The details are summarized in Figure 7.9. ∎

The fact that it may be optimal to prematurely exercise an American put option, even if the underlying stock pays no dividends, implies that at each node in the lattice we must check to see if the option should be exercised. This calculation increases the amount of computing time necessary to value the American put option. In a subsequent chapter, we will describe some ways to overcome this problem. Our investigation into the pricing and hedging of standard American call and put options is now complete.

7.5 OPTIONS ON FORWARD CONTRACTS

We now describe the arbitrage-free pricing of options on forward contracts.[8] These options behave differently from standard options because the payoff structure is slightly modified, influencing the early-exercise decision. This section is not fundamental to the remainder of the text and can be skipped on a first reading.

Before studying options on forward contracts, we need to review the valuation of forward contracts themselves.

Consider a forward contract written on some asset with delivery at date T_F. The delivery price is denoted by K. At the time the contract is initiated, the value of the contract is

$$V(0) = [F(0, T_F) - K]B(0, T_F),$$

where $F(0, T_F)$ is the date-0 forward price for delivery at date T_F.

Recall that we proved this valuation formula in Chapter 2. Note that if the delivery price K equals the forward price, the value of the forward contract is zero.

Similarly, at date T, the value of the forward contract is

$$V(T) = [F(T, T_F) - K]B(T, T_F).$$

This relation will prove useful in the following section.

---

[8]This section uses results first derived in Jarrow and Oldfield (1988).

EXAMPLE

Use of Options on Forward Contracts

A company is submitting a bid for the right to sell goods in a foreign market. If successful, the company will have a foreign exchange exposure in nine months' time because of the foreign currency revenues generated by the sale of the goods. The company decides to go short in a forward contract to reduce this exposure. The current forward exchange rate is $F(0,9)$.

In three months' time the company will learn if its bid has been successful. At that date, the value of the forward contract is $-[F(3,9) - F(0,9)]/B(3,9)$. Note the minus sign, because the company has written the forward contract. The value of the forward contract could be positive or negative.

If the company was not successful in its bid, it is exposed to the risk that the value of the forward contract is negative. One way to remove this risk is for the company to buy a put option on the forward contract instead of going short the forward contract. The maturity of the option is three months.   ∎

Call Options

Here we study call options written on forward contracts. In the next section we study put options written on forward contracts. These two sections are independent of the binomial model.

An option written on a forward contract, often referred to as a **forward option**, differs from a standard option in one important way. The difference involves the payoff to the option at maturity.

Consider a call option written on a forward contract, with exercise price K, where the option matures at date T, and the forward contract's delivery date is T_F. The call's payoff at expiry is defined as follows. If the call option is exercised, its owner receives a long forward contract with the delivery price set equal to the exercise price of the option.

The forward option's payoff characterizes the difference between standard options and forward options. For a standard option, the payoff is the value of the asset less the strike price. For a forward option, one gets a forward contract with an adjusted delivery price. This is *not* the value of a forward contract less the strike price.

To illustrate, the value of a European forward call option at its maturity date T with exercise price K, denoted $c(T)$, is

$$c(T) \equiv \begin{cases} [F(T,T_F) - K]B(T,T_F) & \text{if} \quad F(T,T_F) \geq K \\ 0 & \text{if} \quad F(T,T_F) < K. \end{cases}$$

The value of the call when it is in-the-money is the value of the forward contract $[F(T,T_F) - K]B(T_F)$ obtained from the preceding section. Note that K is not the price that a call's owner must pay to exercise the option. Rather, it is the delivery price of the underlying forward contract. There is no cost to exercising the option.

The value of an American call option is similar. If exercised early at time t, one receives the value of the underlying forward contract with the delivery price K, that is,

$$C(t) = [F(t,T_F) - K]B(t,T_F),$$

where $C(t)$ represents the American call option's value.

If exercised at the maturity date of the option, its payoff is identical to the European's payoff.

The payoff to the forward call option, either American or European, can be rewritten as

$$F(t,T_F)B(t,T_F) - KB(t,T_F).$$

Thus a forward call option is like a standard option on the "spot asset" $[F(t,T_F)B(t,T_F)]$ where the "strike price" is $[KB(t,T_F)]$, which increases over time. The previous results on standard American call options only apply to constant strike prices. This is the reason for modifying the previously determined results.

The first result relates the European forward call option to the underlying forward contract with delivery price equal to the exercise price of the option.

Result 7.5

If there is a positive probability of the option being out-of-the-money, that is, $F(T,T_F) < K$, then the value of a European call option must satisfy

$$c(0) > \text{Max}\{0,[F(0,T_F) - K]B(0,T_F)\}. \tag{7.9}$$

PROOF Suppose we were to follow a suboptimal strategy of exercising the call option at maturity, date T, even if it is out-of-the-money. The value of this strategy at date T is $[F(T,T_F) - K]B(T,T_F)$.

The value at date 0 of this strategy is the present value of a forward contract with delivery price K, that is, $[F(0,T_F) - K]B(0,T_F)$. The call's value today must be strictly greater because we would not exercise the option if it is out-of-the-money, or zero.[9] ∎

This result states that a European forward call's value must be at least as great as receiving the forward contract today with delivery price K. After all, it is what one would receive if the forward call were exercised for sure, even if it is out-of-the-money. The option not to exercise has positive value if the forward contract's value can go negative, which explains the additional hypothesis in the statement of the result.

The next result relates the European forward option to an American forward option.

---

[9]For an alternative proof, see Question 10.

Result 7.6

If there is a positive probability of the option being out-of-the-money at maturity, that is, $F(T, T_F) < K$, then it is never optimal to prematurely exercise an American call option on a forward contract.

PROOF   Given Expression (7.9), the proof is identical to that of Result 7.1. Using the fact that an American call option cannot be worth less than a European call option and Expression (7.9), we have

$$C(0) \geq c(0) > \text{Max}\{0, [F(0, T_F) - K]B(0, T_F)\}.$$

Now, given that $[F(0, T_F) - K]B(0, T_F)$ can be negative, zero, or positive, we have

$$\text{Max}\{0, [F(0, T_F) - K]B(0, T_F)\} \geq [F(0, T_F) - K]B(0, T_F).$$

Combining these results gives

$$C(0) > [F(0, T_F) - K]B(0, T_F).$$

The right side is the value of the American option if exercised immediately, implying that it is not optimal to prematurely exercise the American option. ∎

The reason for this result is intuitive. If you exercise the American option early, you get a forward contract with delivery price K. The value of the contract can go negative. If you wait to exercise, you get the value of the same forward contract later, but only if it is positive. Because the forward contract has no intermediate cash flows from exercising early, it pays to wait. This result is useful since it implies that no difference exists between European and American forward call options. This completes the analysis for forward call options.

Put Options

We examine here the arbitrage-free pricing of forward put options. Again, the fact that a forward option can be interpreted as a "standard put option" on the spot asset with a changing strike price implies that all the previous results for standard American put options need to be modified.

The first result relates a European forward put option to the underlying forward contract with delivery price equal to the exercise price of the option.

Result 7.7

If there is a positive probability of the option being out-of-the-money at maturity, that is, if $F(T, T_F) > K$, then the value of a European put option must satisfy

$$p(0) > \text{Max}\{0,[K - F(0,T_F)]B(0,T_F)\}. \tag{7.10}$$

The proof is similar to that of Result 7.5, so it is left as an exercise for the reader.

The logic underlying this result is straightforward. A European put gives the "option" to sell a forward contract with delivery price K. Shorting the forward contract with delivery price K is less valuable because it can have negative value.

The above result implies that it is never optimal to prematurely exercise an American forward put option. See the next result.

Result 7.8

If there is a positive probability of the option being out-of-the-money at maturity, that is, if $F(T,T_F) > K$, then it is never optimal to prematurely exercise an American put option on a forward contract.

PROOF The value of an American put option if exercised is

$$[K - F(0,T_F)]B(0,T_F).$$

But from Result 7.7,

$$P(0) \geq p(0) > \text{Max}\{0,[K - F(0,T_F)]B(0,T_F)\},$$

implying that one should not exercise the option. ∎

At first glance this result seems counterintuitive because we have proven earlier that for a standard American put option written on an asset that pays no dividends, it may be optimal to exercise early. But, the reason here for the difference is that by exercising early, you short the forward contract, with delivery price K, immediately. This contract can have negative value. The American put option gives the "option" not to short the forward contract. This "option" has non-negative value and should not be discarded early. Under this result, there is no difference between European and American forward put options.

Valuation

The preceding results on forward options were independent of the binomial model. To explicitly value these options, we need additional structure. For this structure we impose the binomial model of Chapter 5.

For these forward options, the underlying asset is a forward contract with delivery price equal to the strike price of the option. Thus to value the option we need to construct a lattice for this forward contract's value. It is sufficient to construct a lattice of forward prices. Given that no dividends are paid to the underlying spot asset,

we know from Expression (2.6) of Chapter 2 that there is a simple cash-and-carry relationship between forward and spot prices:

$$F(t, T_F) B(t, T_F) = S(t),$$

where $S(t)$ is the asset's spot price.

This relationship says that the present value of the forward price is the spot price. We can use this relationship to construct a lattice of forward prices.

EXAMPLE   **European Forward Put Option Valuation**

Consider pricing a European put option that matures in twelve months' time. The put option is written on a forward contract with delivery in eighteen months, implying that at the maturity of the option, delivery occurs in six months.

Let the strike price of the option be 40.00. Let the spot asset underlying the forward contract have a current price of 37.50. Let the volatility of the spot asset be 18 percent. Let the spot asset make no dividend payments.

For simplicity of exposition, we divide the one-year period into two intervals of length six months each. Interest rates are assumed to be constant over the life of the option.

Table 7.1 gives information about the term structure of interest rates. The price of a six-month Treasury bill at the maturity of the option is 97.4740—the term structure is assumed to be flat with simple interest rate[10] $R = 1.0259$.

The up-factor, $U = 1.1558$, and the down-factor, $D = 0.8960$, are obtained by using Expression (4.33) of Chapter 4.[11] This equation uses the volatility value of 0.18. The lattice of asset prices is shown in Figure 7.10.

TABLE 7.1   *Term Structure Data*

MATURITY (MONTHS)	PRICE OF TREASURY BILL (FACE VALUE $100)
6	97.4740
12	95.0119
18	92.6119

---

[10]The continuously compounded rate of interest is 5.12 percent per annum, so that

$$R = \exp(0.0512 \times 0.5) = 1.0259,$$

given that $\Delta = 0.5$.

[11]The up-factor is

$$U \equiv \exp[(r - \sigma^2/2\,\Delta + \sigma\sqrt{\Delta}] = 1.1558$$

and the down-factor

$$D \equiv \exp[(r - \sigma^2/2\Delta - \sigma\sqrt{\Delta}] = 0.8960,$$

where $r = 0.0512$, $\sigma = 0.18$, and $\Delta = 0.5$.

FIGURE 7.10   *Pricing a Put Option on a Forward Contract*

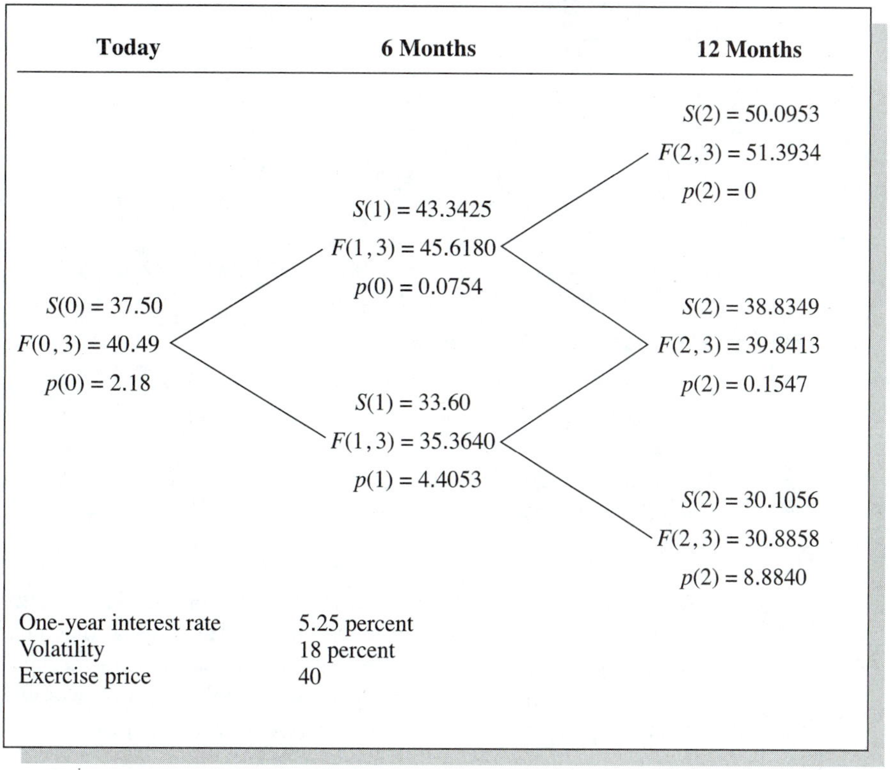

Today	6 Months	12 Months
		$S(2) = 50.0953$
		$F(2,3) = 51.3934$
		$p(2) = 0$
	$S(1) = 43.3425$	
	$F(1,3) = 45.6180$	
	$p(0) = 0.0754$	
$S(0) = 37.50$		$S(2) = 38.8349$
$F(0,3) = 40.49$		$F(2,3) = 39.8413$
$p(0) = 2.18$		$p(2) = 0.1547$
	$S(1) = 33.60$	
	$F(1,3) = 35.3640$	
	$p(1) = 4.4053$	
		$S(2) = 30.1056$
		$F(2,3) = 30.8858$
		$p(2) = 8.8840$

One-year interest rate	5.25 percent
Volatility	18 percent
Exercise price	40

To price the option, we need the forward prices at the maturity of the option. We compute the forward prices using Expression (2.6) of Chapter 2, as shown in Table 7.2.

Using the information from Table 7.2, we can next compute the values of the option at its maturity—see Figure 7.10.

TABLE 7.2   *Forward Prices*

ASSET PRICE $S(2)$	FORWARD PRICE $F(2,3)$	VALUE OF $[K - F(2,3)]B(2,3)$
50.0953	50.0953/0.9747 = 51.3934	−11.1057
38.8349	38.8349/0.9747 = 39.8413	0.1547
30.1056	30.1056/0.9747 = 30.8858	8.8840

$B(2,3) = 0.9747.$

Using the risk-neutral valuation procedure, six months prior to the maturity of the option, if the asset price is 43.34, the forward price is 45.62. The put option's value is

$$p(1) = \frac{1}{1.0259} [\pi \times 0.0 + (1 - \pi)0.1547] = 0.0754,$$

where $\pi = 0.50$ is the martingale probability.[12]

A similar argument at the down node when the spot price is 33.60 gives

$$p(1) = \frac{1}{1.0259} [\pi \times 0.1547 + (1 - \pi)8.8840] = 4.4053.$$

The value of the put at date 0 is

$$p(0) = \frac{1}{1.0259} [\pi \times 0.0754 + (1 - \pi)4.4053] = 2.18.$$

The construction of a synthetic put option is obtained in the standard way and is left as an exercise for the reader.   ■

We can use this example to check whether it is optimal to prematurely exercise an American put option on the forward contract. Result 7.8 says that it is not. Suppose instead that the option in the above example is American. Consider the situation six months prior to the option maturity, as shown in Table 7.3. It is observed in Table 7.3 that it never pays to exercise the American option, which confirms Result 7.8.

TABLE 7.3   *Value of American Put Option*

FORWARD PRICE $F(1,3)$	EXERCISE VALUE $[K - F(1,3)]B(1,3)$	VALUE OF THE AMERICAN OPTION $P(1)$
45.6180	−5.3377	0.0754
35.3640	4.4048	4.4053

$B(1,3) = 0.9501$
$K = 40$

---

[12]Using Expression (5.30), the martingale probability is determined by

$$\pi = \frac{R - D}{U - D}$$

$$= \frac{1.0259 - 0.8960}{1.1558 - 0.8960}$$

$$= 0.5.$$

7.6 SUMMARY

This chapter studies American call and put options. We show that for call options, given no dividends on the underlying stock, it is never optimal to prematurely exercise the option. In the presence of discrete dividends, however, it may be optimal to exercise early to capture the dividend. This should only occur just before the stock goes ex-dividend.

For American put options, the story is more complicated. Even given no dividends, it may be optimal to exercise early because the potential gains for waiting to exercise the put option are bounded by the strike price. If the underlying asset pays dividends over the life of the option, exercise is more likely to occur after the asset goes ex-dividend.

For options written on forward contracts, it is never optimal to prematurely exercise either American call or put options. This is because a forward option is like a standard option on the spot but with a changing strike price. The strike price increases at the rate of interest, making early exercise always suboptimal.

REFERENCES

Amin, K., and R. A. Jarrow, 1992. "Pricing Options on Risky Assets in a Stochastic Interest Rate Economy." *Mathematical Finance* 2, 217–237.

Broadie, M., and J. Detemple, 1996. "American Option Valuation: New Bounds, Approximations, and a Comparison of Existing Methods." *Review of Financial Studies*, 9, 1211–1250.

Heath, D., and R. A. Jarrow, 1988. "Ex-Dividend Stock Price Behavior and Arbitrage Opportunities." *Journal of Business* 61, 95–108.

Jarrow, R. A., and G. S. Oldfield, 1988. "Forward Options and Futures Options." *Advances in Futures and Options Research* 3, 15–28.

QUESTIONS

Question 1

An American put option with a maturity of one year is written on a stock that will not pay a dividend over the life of the option. The current stock price is $60, the volatility is 35 percent, and the continuously compounded riskless rate of interest is 6 percent. The strike price of the option is $70.

Divide the one-year period into two six-month intervals. The up-factor is defined by

$$U \equiv \exp[(r - \sigma^2/2)\,\Delta + \sigma\sqrt{\Delta}] = 1.2800$$

and the down-factor by

$$D \equiv \exp[(r - \sigma^2/2)\,\Delta - \sigma\sqrt{\Delta}] = 0.7803,$$

where σ is the volatility, Δ is the length of the interval, and r the riskless rate of interest.

a)   What is the martingale probability of an up-state occurring next period?
b)   Determine the value of the put option.
c)   If the strike is $50, what is the value of an American put option?
d)   Explain the difference in the exercising strategy for the two options.

Question 2

Use the information in Question 1 to answer the following questions.

a)   What is the value of an American put with a strike of $60 and maturity of one year?
b)   Describe the replicating portfolio at each node. Is the portfolio self-financing? Provide justification for your answer.

Question 3

Use the information in Question 1 to answer the following questions.

a)   What is the value at each node in the lattice of an American call option with a strike of $60 and maturity of one year?
b)   What is the value of a European call option with a strike of $60 and maturity of one year?
c)   What differences, if any, would you expect in your answers to a) and b)?

Question 4

An American call option with a maturity of one year is written on a stock that will pay a dividend of $0.50 per share in six months' time. The current stock price is $50. The volatility is 30 percent and the continuously compounded riskless rate of interest is 5 percent. The strike price of the option is $50.

a)   Divide the one-year period into two six-month intervals. Construct the binomial lattice of stock prices.
b)   Determine the value of the call option.

Question 5

Given the information in Question 4, answer the following questions.

a)   An American put option with a strike of $50 is written on the stock. Construct the binomial lattice of stock prices.
b)   Determine the value of the American put option.
c)   Describe the replicating portfolio at each node.

Question 6

An American call option with a maturity of one year is written on a stock that will pay a dividend of $3.00 per share in six months' time. The current stock price is $50. The volatility is 15 percent and the continuously compounded riskless rate of interest is 5 percent. The strike price of the option is $50.

a) Divide the one-year period into two six-month intervals. Construct the binomial lattice of stock prices.
b) Determine the value of the American call option.
c) Construct the replicating portfolio at each node in the lattice.

Question 7

A European call option with a maturity of one year is written on a forward contract that expires in fifteen months' time. The forward contract is written on a stock that pays no dividends over the life of the forward contract. The current stock price is $65 and the volatility is 25 percent. The term structure of interest rates is flat and the continuously compounded risk-free rate of interest is 5.00 percent. The strike price of the option is $69.

a) Divide the one-year period into two six-month intervals. Construct the binomial lattice of stock prices.
b) Construct the binomial lattice of forward prices.
c) Determine the value of the option.
d) If the option is American, what is its value? Justify your answer by checking if it is optimal to exercise at each node.

Question 8

Given the information in Question 7, answer the following questions.

a) Describe at each node the replicating portfolio using the underlying forward contract and the money market account.
b) Describe at each node the replicating portfolio using the underlying stock and the money market account.

Question 9

Given the information in Question 7, answer the following questions.

a) Determine the value of a European put option, written on the same forward contract, that has the same maturity and strike price as the call option.

b) If the option is American, what is its value? Justify your answer by checking if it is optimal to exercise at each node.

Question 10

Consider a European call option written on a forward contract. The option matures at date T and the forward contract at date T_F. The strike price is K.
    Consider two investment strategies.

Strategy (i)   Go long in a forward contract, forward price $F(0, T_F)$.
                 Buy $F(0, T_F)$ Treasury bills that mature at date T_F.
                 Total cost: $F(0, T_F)B(0, T_F)$.

Strategy (ii)   Buy a European call.
                 Buy K Treasury bills that mature at date T_F.
                 Total cost: $c(0) + KB(0, T_F)$.

By considering the value of these two strategies at date T when the call option matures, show that the value of a European call option written on a forward contract must satisfy

$$c(0) \geq [F(0, T_F) - K]B(0, T_F).$$

Question 11

Consider XYZ Company, which has a share price of $30 on December 31, 1994. XYZ Company declared a dividend of $0.25 per share with an ex-dividend date of April 1, 1995. Let the stock price cum-dividend on April 1, 1995 have the following distribution:

$25 with probability 0.1
$30 with probability 0.1
$31 with probability 0.2
$32 with probability 0.2
$35 with probability 0.2
$40 with probability 0.2

What is the stock price distribution ex-dividend on April 1, 1995?

Question 12

LMN Company has a current stock price of $100. In three months ($\frac{1}{4}$ of a year) it will pay a dividend of $0.50 per share. This is the only dividend to be paid over the next six months. Let the prices today of a sure dollar received in three months be 0.95, and in six months, 0.90.

Consider an American call option on this stock with expiration in six months and strike price 100.

a) Will this American call option be exercised early?
b) What is the largest dividend LMN could pay in three months and still have the answer in a) stay unchanged?
c) Will a European call option with expiration in six months and strike price $100 be priced more, less, or the same as the American call option in a)?

PART III

THE BLACK-SCHOLES MODEL AND EXTENSIONS

8 CHAPTER

THE BLACK-SCHOLES MODEL

8.0 INTRODUCTION

Up to this point, we have emphasized the binomial model for the pricing of derivatives. The binomial model is in discrete time, a natural formulation given that trades take time to execute. Yet, as we argued in Chapter 4, the binomial model is only a reasonable approximation for the evolution of stock prices when the number of trading intervals is large and the time between trades is small. The abstract limit of this construction yields the continuous time setting. In fact, the majority of option theory is formulated in the continuous time setup. Unfortunately, continuous time brings with it a level of mathematics that is quite demanding. Given that some people view mathematics as our forbears viewed the Bubonic Plague, why do we want to study the continuous time framework? This is a pertinent question even if we enjoy mathematics.

Let us examine the benefits of using the continuous time approach. One benefit is that (sometimes) we can derive **closed form solutions**.[1] These solutions imply a saving in computation time, which is important in a trading room where thousands of derivative prices need to be updated regularly. Although the rapid improvements in computing technology are reducing this benefit, at present it is still an important consideration. Another benefit of closed form solutions is that they often provide insight into a pricing and hedging problem. But these two benefits are for closed form solutions and not for the continuous time framework per se.[2] Another benefit of the continuous time framework alone is that it allows the use of stochastic calculus, which, like ordinary calculus, often facilitates the derivation of new and simpler results.

In this chapter we study the best-known continuous time model, the Black-Scholes model.[3] This model, developed by Fischer Black and Myron Scholes in 1973, describes the value of a European option on an asset with no cash flows. The model requires only five inputs: the asset price, the strike price, the time to maturity, the risk-free rate of interest, and the volatility. The Black-Scholes model has become the

---

[1] A closed form solution is a formula that is relatively easy to compute. What constitutes "relatively easy" is a matter of personal judgment.

[2] Closed form solutions can be derived in discrete time. See Brennan (1979) and Turnbull and Milne (1991).

[3] Robert C. Merton and Myron Scholes in 1997 were awarded the Nobel prize in Economics for their work in developing the Black-Scholes formula. Regrettably, Fischer Black died August, 1995.

basic benchmark model for pricing equity options and foreign currency options. It is also sometimes used, in a modified form, to price Eurodollar futures options, Treasury bond options, caps, and floors. We cannot say that we have mastered option pricing theory unless we understand the Black-Scholes formula.

In Chapter 5, we have already provided one derivation of the Black-Scholes model. In Table 5.1, for example, we used the binomial model to approximate a lognormal stock price distribution. The European call option prices from this binomial approximation converged to a price that we later called the Black-Scholes value. Following this demonstration, we then derived the closed form solution for the call's price.

The Black-Scholes model is a continuous time model in which the stock price follows a lognormal probability distribution. We can use these facts directly to give a second derivation of the Black-Scholes formula, slightly more technical in nature than the derivation based on the binomial model. If you are not interested in technical details, you can skip directly to Section 8.5.

The second derivation of the Black-Scholes model requires seven assumptions. It requires the four assumptions imposed in Chapter 2 plus three more. We recall these first four assumptions once again for easy reference. A complete discussion is available in Chapter 2. They are:

Assumption A1. Frictionless markets.

Assumption A2. There is no counterparty risk.

Assumption A3. Competitive markets.

Assumption A4. No arbitrage opportunities.

To these four assumptions we add a fifth:

Assumption A5. Trading takes place continuously in time.

This assumption is necessary for the existence and uniqueness of the equivalent martingale probability distribution discussed in Section 8.4 later.

8.1 CONTINUOUS TIME REPRESENTATION OF STOCK PRICE CHANGES

Here we discuss the sixth assumption necessary for the Black-Scholes formula.

Let $S(t)$ represent the stock price at date t. For simplicity, we assume that the stock price does not pay any dividends. The evolution of the stock price over the time interval t to $t + \Delta$ is given by the expression

$$\Delta \ln S(t) = \mu(S(t),t)\Delta + \sigma(S(t),t)\Delta W(t), \tag{8.1}$$

where $\Delta \ln S(t) \equiv \ln S(t + \Delta) - \ln S(t)$ is the change in the logarithm of the stock price and $\Delta W(t) \equiv W(t + \Delta) - W(t)$ is a normally distributed random variable with zero mean and variance Δ.

The left side of this expression represents the continuously compounded return on the stock over the time interval t to $t + \Delta$. The expected continuously compounded return on the stock price is

$$E[\Delta \ln S(t)] = \mu(S(t),t)\Delta$$

and the variance of the return is

$$\mathrm{var}[\Delta \ln S(t)] = \sigma(S(t),t)^2 \Delta.$$

In this expression, the stock's expected continuously compounded return can depend on the current stock price $S(t)$ and time t. A similar comment applies to the variance of the stock's return. Expression (8.1) is described in greater detail in Chapter 4, Section 4.6.

For the Black-Scholes model we impose two additional simplifying assumptions:

Assumption A6.1.   The instantaneous expected return on the stock per
(constant expected return)   unit time is a constant:

$$\mu(S(t),t) = \mu.$$

Assumption A6.2.   The instantaneous variance of the return on the
(constant volatility)   stock per unit time is a constant:

$$\sigma(S(t),t)^2 = \sigma^2.$$

The first assumption is not necessary; it is made to simplify the argument. The second assumption is crucial and has important implications for the stock price distribution.

The square root of the stock return's instantaneous variance, σ, is called the stock's **volatility**. It is an important parameter in the Black-Scholes model.

Combining these two assumptions, we can rewrite Expression (8.1) as

$$\Delta \ln S(t) = \mu \Delta + \sigma \Delta W(t). \tag{8.2}$$

We demonstrated in Chapter 4 that this equation implies the stock price, $S(t)$, is lognormally distributed.

Expression (8.2) can alternatively be written as

$$S(t) = S(0)\exp[\mu t + \sigma W(t)], \tag{8.3}$$

where $W(t)$ is normally distributed with zero mean and variance t, and $W(0) = 0$. Given the stock price today, $S(0)$, we see that the stock price at date t, $S(t)$ depends on the realized value of the random variable $W(t)$ and the parameters μ and σ.

The last two assumptions can be combined into the sixth assumption, which we list for easy reference:

Assumption A6.   The stock price follows a lognormal probability dis-
(lognormal distribution)   tribution and pays no dividends.

8.2   INTEREST RATES

We now discuss the seventh (and last) assumption underlying the Black-Scholes model. The assumption is imposed upon the riskless rate of interest, which provides the cost of funds needed to construct the synthetic option.

For this model, we need to assume that interest rates are constant.

Assumption A7.   Interest rates are constant.
(constant interest rates)

This assumption could easily be modified to allow interest rates to be deterministic, but this is not much of an improvement. Later, in Chapter 15, we allow interest rates to be stochastic. This generalization, however, changes the entire structure of the model, and it is not an easy extension.

To provide a vehicle for riskless borrowing and lending, we introduce a money market account into the analysis. The money market account is a fund, initialized at a dollar, with value appreciation generated by investing in the short-term riskless interest rate.

Let r denote the continuously compounded spot interest rate. Given that we start with one dollar, the value of the money market account at date t is

$$A(t) = e^{rt}.$$

Note that at date 0, this formula gives $A(0) = e^{r \cdot 0} = 1$, as required. Our discussion of the assumptions underlying the Black-Scholes model is now complete.

8.3   ITO'S LEMMA

We need to introduce a mathematical rule from stochastic calculus called Ito's lemma. This rule is used for computing differentials of functions of stochastic random variables.

Suppose that changes in a stock price can be described as

$$dS(t) = \alpha(t, S(t))dt + \sigma(t, S(t))dW(t),$$

where $dW(t)$ is a normally distributed random variable with zero mean and variance "dt", $\alpha(t, S(t))$ is the drift as a function of $(t, S(t))$, and $\sigma(t, S(t))$ is the volatility as a function $(t, S(t))$. The left side of this expression represents the change in the stock price $dS(t) = S(t + dt) - S(t)$. The random term $dW(t)$ is called a Brownian motion.

The expected change in the stock price is

$$E(dS(t)) = \alpha(S(t), t)dt.$$

The variance of the change in the stock price is $\text{var}(dS(t)) = \sigma(t, S(t))^2 dt$. Both the expected change in the stock price and the variance of the change in the stock price are proportional to the time interval dt.

We know from Chapters 3 and 5 that option values depend on the stock price and time to maturity. We can represent this relation by writing the value of the option in the form $V(t, S(t))$. We want to determine the change in the value of the option over the time interval $[t, t + dt]$. Ito's lemma gives us this result.

(Ito's Lemma):[4]

$$dV(t, S(t)) = \frac{\partial V(t, S(t))}{\partial t} dt + (^1/_2) \frac{\partial^2 V(t, S(t))}{\partial S(t)^2} \sigma^2(S(t), t)dt + \frac{\partial V(t, S(t))}{\partial S(t)} dS(t).$$

The first two terms on the right side represent the drift of $dV(t, S(t))$, while the last term is its stochastic component. The stochastic component is proportional to $dS(t)$. Note that if we had used ordinary calculus, the second term on the right side would not appear.

Ito's lemma can be thought of as a stochastic version of a Taylor series expansion of $V(t + dt, S(t) + dS(t))$ around the points t and $S(t)$. In fact, the proof of Ito's lemma uses exactly this expansion with the appropriate taking of limits.

Ito's lemma will be used later on in this chapter to determine hedge ratios and the Black-Scholes partial differential equation. Before that, however, we illustrate its usefulness by considering an example from Chapter 4. There we derived the process for the logarithm of the stock price

$$d\ln S(t) = \mu dt + \sigma dW(t).$$

But what is the process for the instantaneous return on the stock $dS(t)/S(t)$?

EXAMPLE **Relation between $d\ln S(t)$ and $dS(t)/S(t)$**

This example computes $dS(t)/S(t)$ given a stochastic process for $d\ln S(t)$. Suppose $d\ln S(t) = \mu dt + \sigma dW(t)$ as given in Expression (8.2).

---

[4] $V(t, S(t))$ needs to be once continuously differentiable in t and twice continuously differentiable in $S(t)$.

Let $y(t, S(t)) = \ln S(t)$. Computing the partial derivatives gives

$$\frac{\partial y(t, S(t))}{\partial t} = \frac{\partial \ln S(t)}{\partial t} = 0$$

$$\frac{\partial y(t, S(t))}{\partial S(t)} = \frac{\partial \ln S(t)}{\partial S(t)} = \frac{1}{S(t)}$$

$$\frac{\partial^2 y(t, S(t))}{\partial S(t)^2} = \frac{\partial^2 \ln S(t)}{\partial S(t)^2} = -\frac{1}{S(t)^2}$$

By Ito's lemma,

$$dy = \frac{1}{S(t)} dS(t) - (\tfrac{1}{2}) \frac{1}{S(t)^2} \sigma^2 S(t)^2 dt \qquad \text{or}$$

$$d \ln S(t) = -\frac{\sigma^2}{2} dt + \frac{dS(t)}{S(t)}.$$

Substituting the expression for $d \ln S(t)$ and simplifying gives

$$\frac{dS(t)}{S(t)} = (\mu + \sigma^2/2) dt + \sigma dW(t). \quad \blacksquare$$

8.4 THE EQUIVALENT MARTINGALE PROBABILITY DISTRIBUTION

We know from the binomial model in Chapter 5 that if there are no arbitrage opportunities involving the stock and the money market account, then a unique probability distribution exists under which the normalized stock price follows a martingale. It can be shown that this result is also true under Assumptions A1 through A7 for the Black-Scholes model. We will not prove this result in this text. Instead, we leave the proof of this assertion to the references at the end of this chapter, in particular Heath and Jarrow (1987).

Nonetheless, the intuition for the reasonableness of this result can be obtained from our first derivation, in Chapter 5, of the Black-Scholes model. There we showed that the binomial model, given an appropriate specification of the mean and variance, converges to the lognormal distribution. As this result holds for the binomial model, it is reasonable that it should also hold in the limit, that is, it should hold under the lognormal distribution Assumption A6 as well.

Let π denote the alternative probability distribution under which normalized stock prices follow a martingale. This means that

$$S(t)/A(t) = E^{\pi}[S(T)/A(T)] \tag{8.4}$$

or

$$S(t) = E^{\pi}[S(T)]e^{-r(T-t)}.$$

It also implies that

$$\Delta S(t)/S(t) = r\Delta + \sigma\Delta\tilde{W}(t), \tag{8.5}$$

where $\Delta\tilde{W}(t)$ is a normally distributed random variable with zero mean and variance Δ under the alternative probability distribution π. A proof of Expression (8.5) is given in Appendix A of this chapter.

Expression (8.5) is an important result, as it demonstrates that when we use the probability distribution π, the expected return on the stock is the risk-free rate of interest. The risk-free rate is the equilibrium expected return on the stock that would obtain in an economy otherwise similar to that considered in Assumption A6, but that is populated by risk-neutral investors. As risk-neutral investors care only about expected returns, all traded assets in such an economy (in equilibrium) must have the same expected return. Given one asset's return, the money market account specified in Assumption A7, all remaining returns must equal this rate as well.

For this reason, the term "risk-neutral pricing" is often used to describe the result in Expression (8.5). This terminology can be misleading, because we are not assuming that people are risk-neutral or that the stock's expected return equals the risk-free rate. Rather, our result is only a direct consequence of the fact that, given no arbitrage, there exists an alternative probability distribution π such that normalized stock prices are a martingale. It is a "trick" used to simplify valuation. Expression (8.5) is not a representation of the actual evolution of stock prices for our economy.

To price any derivative security, we need to show that the market is dynamically complete via trading in only the stock and the money market account. That is, given any derivative security, we should be able to replicate its payoffs synthetically using a dynamic and self-financing trading strategy in the stock and the money market account alone. It can be shown[5] under Assumptions A1 through A7 that this continuous-time model is dynamically complete. Again, the validity of this result is motivated by the limit argument used in Chapter 5 to derive the Black-Scholes model.

Next, using a result from probability theory, it can be shown that market completeness implies that the equivalent martingale probability distribution π, described earlier, is unique.[6] This uniqueness allows us to price any derivative security using the risk-neutral valuation procedure discussed in Chapter 6.

The risk-neutral valuation procedure can be described as follows. Given a derivative security with a single payout $V(T)$ at date T, its value at date t is given by

$$V(t) = E^{\pi}[V(T)/A(T)]A(t). \tag{8.6}$$

This value represents the cost at date t of constructing the synthetic derivative. Expression (8.6) is analogous to Expression (6.4) in Chapter 6. In Chapter 6, we as-

---

[5]See Heath and Jarrow (1987). Some additional technical assumptions are also required to rule out doubling strategies.

[6]See Harrison and Pliska (1981), Jarrow, Jin, and Madan (1998, in press), and Battig and Jarrow (1999, in press).

sumed trading took place in discrete time. In this chapter, we have modified these arguments to allow the trading interval to be infinitesimal. The risk-neutral valuation procedure in Expression (8.6) is the basis for the derivation given next.

8.5   EUROPEAN OPTIONS

Now we provide a second derivation of the Black-Scholes formula. The Black-Scholes model (1973) provides closed form solutions for European options. The model only requires that Assumptions A1 through A7 hold over the life of the options.

Recall that the payoff for a European call option at its maturity date T with strike price K is given by

$$c(T) = \text{Max}\{S(T) - K, 0\}.$$

Using the risk-neutral valuation procedure, Expression (8.6), we know that the call's price at date 0 is its expected value at date T appropriately discounted, that is,

$$c(0)/A(0) = E^\pi\{c(T)/A(T)\}. \tag{8.7}$$

After we compute the right side of Expression (8.7), we obtain the desired result:

$$c(0) = S(0)N(d_1) - KB(0,T)N(d_2), \tag{8.8}$$

where $d_1 \equiv \{\ln[S(0)/KB(0,T)] + \sigma^2 T/2\}/(\sigma\sqrt{T})$, $d_2 \equiv d_1 - \sigma\sqrt{T}$, and $N(\cdot)$ is the cumulative normal distribution function.

A formal proof of Expression (8.8) is given in Appendix B of this chapter. Expression (8.8) is the well-known Black-Scholes formula for European call options.

The Black-Scholes formula for European put options is just as easily derived. Recall that the payoff to a put option at its maturity T with strike price K is given by

$$p(T) = \text{Max}\{K - S(T), 0\}.$$

Repeating the above argument yields the desired result:

$$p(0) = KB(0,T)N(-d_2) - S(0)N(-d_1). \tag{8.9}$$

EXAMPLE   **Computation of Black-Scholes Values**

We first want to value an at-the-money European call option. The inputs are shown in Table 8.1, Part A. Note that there are only five inputs: the stock price, the strike price, the maturity, the volatility, and the rate of interest. A discussion of where to get these inputs is postponed until Section 8.7.

TABLE 8.1   *Pricing a European Option*

PART A INPUT DATA	
Stock Price	20
Strike Price	20
Maturity	35 days
Volatility*	25 percent
Discount Rate**	4.25 percent

*A 365-day year is assumed.
**A 360-day year is assumed.

PART B OPTION PRICES*		
TYPE OF OPTION	OPTION PRICE	DELTA
Call	0.6585	0.5367
Put	0.5758	−0.4633

*The program Equity/Pricing European Options/No Dividends is used to calculate these values.

Using the program Equity/Pricing European Options/No Dividends, we can determine the price of the option. The output is given in Table 8.1, Part B, where we also value a put option.

The only complication in computing Black-Scholes values is in computing the terms involving the cumulative normal distribution $N(\cdot)$. Unfortunately, this computation can only be performed with the aid of a table or a computer program. ■

Understanding the derivation of the Black-Scholes formula does not mean that one has mastered this model; it is just a necessary, but small, first step. One still needs to understand how to create synthetic options, how to estimate the model's inputs, how to extend the model to incorporate dividends and early exercise considerations, and how the model is implemented in practice. The study of these considerations comprises the context of the remainder of this chapter, as well as the next two chapters.

8.6 HEDGING

The preceding derivation of the Black-Scholes model used the martingale approach, and it did not explicitly show how to construct the replicating portfolio. This section studies how to hedge an option in continuous time. Unlike the binomial model, one

of the complications with continuous-time models is that the level of mathematics becomes slightly more complicated.

Let $m_s(t)$ denote the number of shares of the stock held in the replicating portfolio. These shares are purchased or sold at date t, held for Δ units of time, and are rebalanced at the end of the interval $t + \Delta$. Let $m_B(t)$ denote the dollar investment in the money market account.

By construction, the synthetic option must replicate the payoffs to the traded option. Therefore, to avoid arbitrage, the cost of constructing the synthetic option, $V(t)$, must equal the value of the traded option, that is,

$$V(t) \equiv m_s(t)S(t) + m_B(t) = c(t). \tag{8.10}$$

Over the time interval t to $t + \Delta$, the change in the value of the replicating portfolio is given by

$$\Delta V(t) = m_s(t)\Delta S(t) + m_B(t)r\Delta. \tag{8.11}$$

The replicating portfolio is rebalanced at date $t + \Delta$ so that $m_s(t)$ and $m_B(t)$ remain unchanged until that time.

At date $t + \Delta$, $V(t + \Delta)$ is rebalanced into $m_s(t + \Delta)$ shares of the stock and $m_B(t + \Delta)$ dollars in the money market account. The rebalancing must be self-financing, so that

$$
\begin{aligned}
V(t) + \Delta V(t) &\equiv V(t + \Delta) \\
&= m_s(t + \Delta)S(t + \Delta) + m_B(t + \Delta).
\end{aligned}
$$

The process continues over the next interval $[t + \Delta, t + 2\Delta]$ in an analogous manner.

In fact, the portfolio construction continues in this fashion until date T, when the boundary condition of the call is matched, that is,

$$V(T) = c(T) = \text{Max}\{S(T) - K, 0\}. \tag{8.12}$$

From the boundary condition, we see that the value of the traded call option depends on the stock price and the time to maturity. By backward induction, this follows at all earlier dates as well.

Using Ito's lemma,[7] over $[t, t + \Delta]$, the change in the value of the traded call option can be written as

$$\Delta c(t) = \frac{\partial c}{\partial t}\Delta + \frac{\partial c}{\partial S}\Delta S + \frac{1}{2}\frac{\partial^2 c}{\partial S^2}\sigma^2 S^2 \Delta \tag{8.13}$$

By construction, the change in the value of the replicating portfolio equals the change in the traded call option price:

$$\Delta V(t) = \Delta c(t).$$

---

[7]In the following notation, we identify $dt = \Delta$, $dS(t) = \Delta S(t)$, and $dc(t) = \Delta c(t)$.

Identifying like terms in Expressions (8.11) and (8.13) gives an equation useful for identifying the number of shares of stock in the synthetic option, that is,

$$\frac{\partial c}{\partial S} \Delta S = m_s(t)\Delta S.$$

Simplification gives the desired result:

$$m_s(t) = \frac{\partial c}{\partial S}. \tag{8.14}$$

This partial derivative is easily computed from the Black-Scholes formula. This computation is given below. The shares in the stock $m_s(t)$ are referred to as the **hedge ratio** or **delta**.

We could also determine $m_B(t)$ in a similar fashion by equating the remaining co-efficients. A simpler procedure, however, uses Expression (8.10):

$$m_B(t) = c(t) - m_s(t)S(t). \tag{8.15}$$

The quantity $m_B(t)$ is the dollar investment in a money market account.

FIGURE 8.1   *Delta for a Call Option*

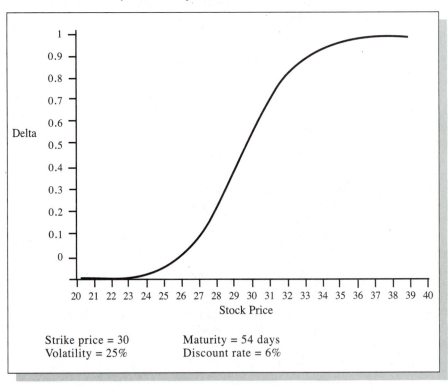

Delta

Stock Price

Strike price = 30   Maturity = 54 days
Volatility = 25%   Discount rate = 6%

Given that we have closed form expressions for the value of a call option and the value of a put option, Expression (8.15) is easily computed. We now turn to the evaluation of Expression (8.14). Standard calculus yields the delta for a call option:

$$\frac{\partial c}{\partial S} = N(d_1). \tag{8.16}$$

This implies that delta lies between zero and one, given that the cumulative normal distribution function, $N(d_1)$, takes value between zero and one.

A graph of delta for a call option is illustrated in Figure 8.1. The delta of the call goes to zero as the stock price goes to zero, which makes sense because as the stock price goes to zero, it is less and less likely that the option will end up in-the-money. By implication, the call option is nearly worthless, so the position in the stock should be near zero as well.

At the other extreme, as the stock price gets very large, the delta goes to one. This is because the call is very likely to be in-the-money. In this case, holding the call is like holding the stock. When the current stock price is near-the-money, the delta is approximately one-half.[8]

EXAMPLE   **Construction of the Synthetic European Call Option**

We know from Table 8.1 that the value of the call option is 0.6585 and its delta is 0.5367. Therefore, Expression (8.10) becomes

$$m_s 20 + m_B = 0.6585,$$

and Expression (8.14) becomes

$$m_s = 0.5367,$$

implying that

$$\begin{aligned} m_B &= 0.6585 - 0.5367 \times 20 \\ &= -10.0755, \end{aligned}$$

using Expression (8.15).

Therefore, a portfolio containing 0.5367 shares of the stock and borrowing -10.0755 dollars is equivalent to a position in the call option. For small changes in the stock price, the value of the traded option and the synthetic option will be almost the same, as demonstrated in Table 8.2, Part A.

If the stock price changes by one cent, the value of the option and the synthetic option are almost identical. If the stock price changes by 10 cents,

---

[8]The common belief that delta for an at-the-money call option is *exactly* one-half is not true. In Table 8.1, Part B, the delta for the at-the-money call option is 0.5367.

TABLE 8.2   *Synthetic Option*

PART A		
STOCK PRICE		VALUE OF SYNTHETIC CALL OPTION
$S(0)$	VALUE OF CALL OPTION*	$0.5367S(0) - 10.0755$
19.90	0.6061	0.6048
19.99	0.6531	0.6531
20.0	0.6585	0.6585
20.01	0.6638	0.6639
20.10	0.7134	0.7122

*The program Equity/Pricing European Options/No Dividends is used to calculate these prices.

PART B CONTRACT SIZE 100 SHARES		
STOCK PRICE		VALUE OF SYNTHETIC CALL OPTION
$S(0)$	VALUE OF CALL OPTION	$54S(0) - 1014.15$
19.90	60.61	60.45
19.99	65.31	65.31
20.0	65.85	65.85
20.01	66.38	66.39
20.10	71.34	71.25

differences can be observed. For example, if the stock goes from $20 to $20.10, the option price now equals $0.7134 while the value of the synthetic portfolio is $0.7122. This difference is due to the discrete changes considered in the stock's price. Recall that the replicating portfolio is theoretically correct only for infinitesimal movements.

In practice, it is not possible to buy 0.5367 shares of stock. A standardized option contract is usually written on 100 shares of stock. In this case, the value of the option contract is $65.85 and its delta 53.67. Rounding off to the nearest integer, the number of shares of stock in the synthetic portfolio becomes

$$m_s = 54,$$

and the dollars invested in the money market account is

$$m_B = 65.85 - 54 \times 20$$
$$= -1,014.15.$$

The performance of the synthetic portfolio is shown in Table 8.2, Part B. In this case, the restriction in treating the number of shares as a whole number produces slightly better results than in Part A for in-the-money options. This is not always the case. ■

We next calculate the delta for a European put option. Using an argument analogous to that used to derive the delta for a European call option gives the delta for the put option:

$$\frac{\partial p}{\partial S} = -N(-d_1). \tag{8.17}$$

This implies that the European put's delta lies between minus one and zero.

A graph of the delta for a European put option is illustrated in Figure 8.2. For stock prices near zero, the put is almost surely to end up in-the-money. Thus holding

FIGURE 8.2 *Delta for a Put Option*

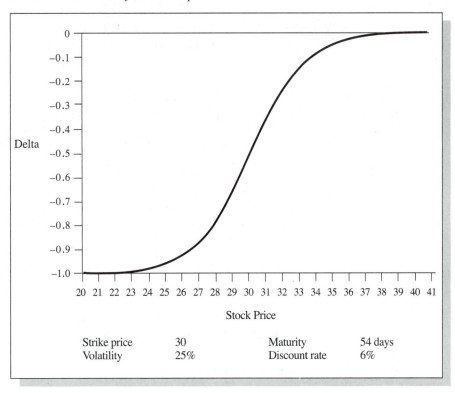

| Strike price | 30 | Maturity | 54 days |
| Volatility | 25% | Discount rate | 6% |

the put is like being short the stock, and the delta has a value of approximately minus one. For large stock prices the put is nearly worthless, and the delta has a value of approximately zero. For stock prices near-the-money, the put's delta is approximately minus one-half.[9]

EXAMPLE

Construction of a Synthetic European Put Option

From Table 8.1, the value of the European put option is 0.5758 and its delta −0.4633. Therefore, Expression (8.10) becomes

$$m_s 20 + m_B = 0.5758$$

and Expression (8.14) becomes

$$m_s = -0.4633,$$

implying that

$$m_B = 0.5758 + 0.4633 \times 20$$
$$= 9.8418,$$

using Expression (8.15). The synthetic portfolio is constructed by shorting 0.4633 shares of stock and lending 9.8418 dollars. ■

8.7 PROPERTIES OF THE BLACK-SCHOLES MODEL

To understand any model, we must understand how the model's value changes when the input parameters change, an analysis we now explore.

The Black-Scholes option value depends on the stock price, the time to maturity, the volatility, and the rate of interest. All these parameters can change over the life of the option. Therefore, we want to determine the sensitivity of the option value to changes in each of these variables. Each of these sensitivities can be determined by taking partial derivatives. We discuss each in turn.

First, the delta, or the hedge ratio, of an option measures the change in the value of the option when there is a unit change in the value of the underlying asset. We can write this in the form

$$\text{Delta} = \frac{\partial c}{\partial S} = \frac{\text{Change in the value of the option}}{\text{Change in the value of the underlying asset}}, \tag{8.18}$$

---

[9]The common belief that delta for an at-the-money put option is *exactly* minus one-half is not true. In Table 8.1, Part B, the delta for an at-the-money put option is −0.4633.

where c is being used in a generic sense to denote the value of an arbitrary option. The option could be a European put or a call.

If we are hedging an option, it is also natural to ask how sensitive our hedge is to changes in the stock price. The sensitivity of delta or the hedge ratio to changes in the value of the underlying asset is called the **gamma**. It is defined by

$$\text{Gamma} = \frac{\partial(\text{Delta})}{\partial S} = \frac{\text{Change in the value of the option's delta}}{\text{Change in the value of the underlying asset}}. \qquad (8.19)$$

Given the definition of delta, it implies that

$$\text{Gamma} = \frac{\partial^2 c}{\partial S^2}. \qquad (8.20)$$

The sensitivity of the option value to changes in the time to expiration is called **theta** and is defined by

$$\text{Theta} = \frac{\partial c}{\partial t} = \frac{\text{Change in the value of the option}}{\text{Decrease in the time to expiration}}. \qquad (8.21)$$

A positive theta indicates that as the time to expiration decreases, the change in the value of the option is positive.

The sensitivity of the option value to changes in the volatility is called **vega** and is defined by

$$\text{Vega} = \frac{\partial c}{\partial \sigma} = \frac{\text{Change in the value of the option}}{\text{Change in the volatility}}. \qquad (8.22)$$

The sensitivity of the option value to changes in the interest rate is called **rho**. We will denote this as rho$D$ because when we discuss foreign currency options, we will talk about the sensitivity of the option to changes in the foreign rate of interest. Formally,

$$\text{RhoD} = \frac{\partial c}{\partial r} = \frac{\text{Change in the value of the option}}{\text{Change in the value of the interest rate}}. \qquad (8.23)$$

Two of the advantages of having a closed form solution are (1) we can readily determine the values for these derivatives, and (2) we can determine whether they are positive, negative, or ambiguous, as shown in Table 8.3.

Table 8.3 gives the various option sensitivities to changes in the underlying input parameters. Both the European call and put derivatives are provided.

Let us consider the call option first. The call's delta lies between 0 and 1, which makes sense because a call is equivalent to a fractional position in the stock. After all, with some probability (less than one and greater than zero) the call will end up as the stock (being in-the-money).

TABLE 8.3 *Derivatives for the Black-Scholes Model*

DERIVATIVE	CALL OPTION	PUT OPTION
Delta $\equiv \dfrac{\partial c}{\partial S}$	$1 \geq N(d_1) \geq 0$	$-1 \leq -N(-d_1) \leq 0$
Gamma $= \dfrac{\partial^2 c}{\partial S^2}$	$\dfrac{1}{S\sigma\sqrt{T}} f(d_1) > 0$	$\dfrac{1}{S\sigma\sqrt{T}} f(-d_1) > 0$
Theta $\equiv \dfrac{\partial c}{\partial t}$	$-\dfrac{Sf(d_1)\sigma}{2\sqrt{T}}$ $- rKB(0,T)N(d_2) < 0$	$-\dfrac{Sf(-d_1)\sigma}{2\sqrt{T}}$ $+ rKB(0,T)N(-d_2) \lessgtr 0$
Vega $\equiv \dfrac{\partial c}{\partial \sigma}$	$S\sqrt{T}f(d_1) > 0$	$S\sqrt{T}f(-d_1) > 0$
RhoD $\equiv \dfrac{\partial c}{\partial r}$	$TKB(0,T)N(d_2) \geq 0$	$-TKB(0,T)N(-d_2) \leq 0$

$f(\cdot)$ is the normal density function.
$N(\cdot)$ is the normal cumulative function.

The call's gamma is positive, which occurs because as the stock price increases, the call is more likely to end up in-the-money. Hence, as the stock price increases, it is equivalent to a larger fraction of the stock, that is, the delta increases.

The theta of the call is negative, that is, as time to maturity increases, the option becomes more valuable. This occurs for two reasons. First, as the time to maturity increases the variance of the stock's return increases ($\sigma^2 T$), making the call more valuable (see vega below). Second, as the time to maturity increases, the cost of exercising (the present value of the strike price) declines, also making the call more valuable.

The vega is positive. As the volatility of the stock increases, the call's value increases, which can be explained as follows. As the volatility increases, the distribution of the stock price at expiration spreads out (widens). But the option only benefits from those stock prices above the strike. As the distribution widens, the probability of stock prices being in-the-money increases, thereby increasing the option's value. Most traders view options as being a "bet on the volatility." The positive vega is the reason why.

Finally, the call option's rhoD is positive because as the risk-free rate increases, the present value of the strike price (the cost of exercising) declines. It increases the option's premium.

The put option's derivatives have similar explanations. The put's delta is between 0 and -1 because at expiration the stock is sold for the strike only with some probability between 0 and 1. Thus the put is equivalent to only a fractional short position in the stock.

The put's gamma is also positive. Thus, as the stock price increases, the delta increases. This occurs because as the stock price increases, the put is less likely to end up in-the-money. As a result, the put's delta declines in absolute value. However, since the put's delta is negative, gamma increases.

The put's theta is ambiguous in sign because there are two opposite effects. As the time to maturity increases, the variance of the stock's return increases, which makes the put more valuable (see the vega below). In the opposite direction, as the time to maturity increases, the present value of the payment for exercise declines, reducing the put's value. On balance, either effect could dominate.

The put's vega is positive. If the volatility of the stock increases, the likelihood that the put ends in-the-money increases, causing the option price to increase.

Finally, the put's rho$D$ is negative. As the interest rate increases, the present value of the strike price, received at expiration (if in-the-money), declines, reducing the value of the put.

EXAMPLE | **Computation of the "Greeks"**

This example illustrates the computation of the option's sensitivity to changes in the underlying parameters. These sensitivities are often called the "Greeks" for obvious reasons.

We can easily demonstrate some of the properties of the Black-Scholes model using the program Equity/Pricing European Options/No Dividends. We want to price a European call option and a European put option for a range of stock prices, given the parameter values in Table 8.1, Part A. We pick a range of stock prices from $15 to $25, increasing by increments of $0.25, so we set

Initial stock price	15
Final stock price	25
Stock price interval	0.25.

One can use the program's graphing facilities to plot how delta, gamma, theta, and RhoD vary as the stock price changes. Note that for the European put option, the sign of theta is ambiguous.

Suppose that the stock price is $15, implying that the option is deep-in-the-money. In this case, theta is positive and equal to 0.0023. If the stock price is $18, so the option is still in-the-money, theta is negative and equal to −0.0014. ∎

8.8 USE OF THE BLACK-SCHOLES MODEL

Given that we understand the model's derivation and its Greeks, the next step is to understand how to determine values for the required inputs. Let us discuss the different inputs and some of the difficulties that arise in obtaining them.

The Black-Scholes model requires five inputs:

1. the stock price;
2. the exercise price;
3. the maturity of the option;
4. the price of a zero-coupon bond, face value one dollar, with the same maturity as the option; and
5. the volatility.

The first four inputs are readily available. The first and fourth inputs are obtainable from market quotes, a potential source being the financial press. The second and third inputs are contractual provisions and readily observed (see Chapter 1). However, the last input, the volatility, cannot be observed directly and must be estimated. The remainder of this section deals with its estimation.

Broadly speaking, there are two general approaches for estimating the volatility: (1) historic volatilities and (2) implied volatilities. We examine each in turn.

Historic Volatility

In Table 8.4 we have recorded a series of daily observations on the closing prices for a stock. The observations are not equally spaced because of weekends and holidays. At the start, we ignore this distinction. To estimate the historic volatility, we first define the price relative:

$$PR(t) \equiv S(t)/S(t - \Delta),$$

where Δ is the time interval between observations. For this example, the time interval is taken to be one day, because we ignore the unequal spacing. The general case is explained in Appendix C of this chapter.

Next, we compute the natural logarithm of the price relative:

$$Lp(t) \equiv \ln[PR(t)].$$

Using Expression (8.3), we can write this as

$$Lp(t) = \mu\Delta + \sigma\Delta W(t), \tag{8.24}$$

where $\Delta W(t) \equiv W(t) - W(t - \Delta)$ is normally distributed with zero mean and variance Δ.

This implies that $Lp(t)$ is a normally distributed random variable and standard statistical techniques can be used to estimate its mean ($\mu\Delta$) and variance ($\sigma^2\Delta$).

To estimate the first term, the mean, we use the arithmetic average:

$$\hat{m} = \frac{1}{n} \sum_{j=1}^{n} Lp(j),$$

TABLE 8.4   *Calculating Volatility Using Historical Data*

NUMBER	DATE	PRICE	PRICE RELATIVE S_t/S_{t-1}	LOGARITHM OF PRICE RELATIVE
	0	34		
1	1	$33\frac{3}{4}$	0.9926	−0.00738
2	2	$34\frac{1}{8}$	1.0111	0.01105
3	3	$33\frac{3}{4}$	0.9890	−0.01105
4	4	$33\frac{1}{2}$	0.9926	−0.00744
5	7	$34\frac{5}{8}$	1.0336	0.03303
6	8	$34\frac{5}{8}$	0.9928	−0.00725
7	9	$34\frac{1}{4}$	0.9964	−0.00364
8	10	$35\frac{5}{8}$	1.0109	0.01089
9	11	$35\frac{1}{8}$	1.0144	0.01434
10	15	$33\frac{7}{8}$	0.9644	−0.03624
11	16	34	1.0037	0.00368
12	17	$33\frac{7}{8}$	0.9963	−0.00368
13	18	$33\frac{5}{8}$	0.9926	−0.00741
14	21	$34\frac{7}{8}$	1.0372	0.03650
15	22	$33\frac{7}{8}$	0.9713	−0.02909
16	23	$33\frac{1}{4}$	0.9816	−0.01862
17	25	$34\frac{1}{8}$	1.0263	0.02598

$$\frac{1}{17} \sum_{j=1}^{17} Lp(j) = 0.000216$$

$$\sum_{j=1}^{17} [Lp(j)]^2 = 0.006431$$

$$\hat{\sigma}^2 = \frac{1}{16} [0.006431 - 17(0.000216)^2] = 0.000402$$

$$\hat{\sigma} = 0.02005$$

where n is the total number of observations.

The variance is estimated by the sample variance, which is normalized by $(n-1)$ to make it an unbiased statistic:

$$\hat{\sigma}^2 = \frac{1}{n-1} \sum_{j=1}^{n} [Lp(j) - \hat{m}]^2$$

$$= \frac{1}{n-1} \left[\sum_{j=1}^{n} Lp(j)^2 - n\hat{m}^2 \right]. \tag{8.25}$$

From Table 8.4 we see that the estimate of the volatility is the square root of the sample variance:

$$\hat\sigma = 0.02005.$$

This number is an estimate of the volatility per time period Δ, which in this case is one day. Volatility, however, is usually quoted on a per-year basis. To convert this number to a per-year basis, since the variance is proportional to the time period Δ, we need only multiply by the number of days in a year, that is,

$$\hat\sigma^2_{\text{Year}} = \hat\sigma^2_{\text{Day}} \text{ (number of days in year)}.$$

The adjusted volatility is therefore

$$\hat\sigma_{\text{Year}} = \hat\sigma_{\text{Day}} \text{ (number of days in year)}^{1/2}.$$

Using a 365-day year gives

$$\begin{aligned}\hat\sigma_{\text{Year}} &= 0.02005\sqrt{365}\\ &= 0.3831.\end{aligned}$$

The historic volatility is 38.31 percent per year.

Some people prefer to use the number of trading days in the adjustment to a per-year volatility:

$$\hat\sigma_{\text{Year}} = \hat\sigma_{\text{Day}} \text{ (number of trading days in year)}^{1/2}.$$

This modification is usually justified by reference to studies by French (1980) and French and Roll (1986). In the 365-day variance adjustment, the variance for a three-day weekend is counted as three times the variance for a one-day return. Some people feel there is less variance over the weekend. In French and Roll, Table 1, the ratio of the two variances is 1.104. Although this result justifies the use of a number of days less than 365, using only the trading days is still a debatable issue. What the result does imply, however, is that the assumption of a constant volatility is questionable.

In using the sample variance, Expression (8.25), a number of issues still remain. First, how many observations should one use? (What is n?) The larger the number of observations, the more accurate is the estimator. Yet, if one believes that the distribution for the stock price relative is changing over time, then one would not want to use a long series of past observations. Why? Observations recorded a "long time ago" may contain little information about the current distribution for the price relative. There is a trade-off. No definitive answer is provided.

Second, what should be the time interval between observations? (What is Δ?) In the above example we used daily observations. We could have used hourly or weekly

observations. Would it make any difference? Under Assumption A6, that stock prices are lognormally distributed, the answer is no. But the assumption of lognormality is only an approximation. Other considerations are relevant, such as noise in the price observations introduced by market microstructure factors like illiquidities and bid/ask spreads. Market microstructure considerations support the use of larger intervals between observations because these market microstructure considerations then have less of an impact. This issue is unresolved at present, and additional research is needed.

Third, in our example we used closing prices. We could have used opening prices, or prices recorded at a particular time of day (say, 2 P.M.). A different approach developed by Parkinson (1980) and extended by Garman and Klass (1980) and Kunitomo (1992) employs the high and low prices for the day. Although high/low estimators are statistically more efficient than close-close or open-close, they are particularly sensitive to reporting errors. If any trade is reported incorrectly during the day, there is a good chance that it will appear as either the high or the low price for the day. Wiggins (1991) confirms this sensitivity of high/low estimators to reporting errors. Again, no definitive answer is provided.

All three considerations are important, and no method currently dominates the others. The use of an approach needs to be determined on a case-by-case basis, taking into account the purpose of the analysis and the data availability of the users.

Implied Volatility

We now describe implied volatility estimation, which is the second approach to estimating volatility. Given an observed option price, we can find the estimate of the volatility that equates the option model price to the observed market price. This value is called the **implied volatility**. Such an implied volatility can always be found—at least in theory—because the Black-Scholes model price is increasing in the volatility. The implicit assumption underlying the validity of this approach is that the option model used is correct.

EXAMPLE   **Implied Volatility Calculation**

Some values for implied volatilities are given in Table 8.5. The mean of the bid-ask prices for each option is used as the observed market option price, and the mean of the bid-ask prices for the stock is used as the market stock price. Given these values, the Black-Scholes option model is used to determine the implied volatility.

In Part A, the maturity of the options is 22 days, and in Part B, the maturity of the options is 50 days. A number of observations can be made. First, the implied volatility seems to depend on whether the option is in/out or at-the-money. In Part A, the implied volatility is lowest for the at-the-money option with a strike price of 95.

TABLE 8.5   *Implied Volatility*†

STOCK PRICE 93.625			
PART A			
TYPE OF OPTION*	**STRIKE PRICE**	**MEAN OPTION PRICE**	**IMPLIED VOLATILITY** (PERCENT)
Call	90	$4^3/_4$	25.46
Call	95	$1^3/_8$	20.22
Call	100	$1/_2$	25.47
Put	90	$1/_2$	20.34
Put	95	$2^7/_8$	24.90

*Maturity 22 days; discount rate 5.12%; a 360-day year is assumed.

**A 365-day year is assumed.

PART B			
TYPE OF OPTION*	**STRIKE PRICE**	**MEAN OPTION PRICE**	**IMPLIED VOLATILITY** (PERCENT)
Call	90	$5^3/_8$	20.18
Call	95	$2^3/_4$	22.24
Call	100	1.00	21.24
Put	90	1.50	23.63
Put	95	$3^3/_4$	24.45

*Maturity 50 days; discount rate 5.15%; a 360-day year is assumed.

**A 365-day year is assumed.

†The program Equity/Implied Volatility European is used to determine these implied volatilities.

The results in Part B show the reverse situation. The implied volatility for calls seems to differ from the implied volatility for puts. This situation is disturbing, because it is not clear what value one should use. ■

The preceding example shows that, for different options on the same stock, implied volatilities differ. One approach to handle these different values is to use them all, in some sort of weighted average. A number of different types of weighting schemes have been proposed.[10] In each one, the at-the-money calls and puts always receive significant weight because they are the options most sensitive to changes in the volatility.

---

[10]See References at the end of the chapter.

There are many reasons why the implied volatility estimates differ. All these reasons are possible explanations as to why the Black-Scholes model is an inappropriate option pricing model. First, we are using the mean of the bid-ask prices. Bid-ask prices are a type of transaction cost. The Black-Scholes option model ignores transaction costs, and we have no guidance as to what adjustment is needed when transaction costs are present.

Second, we are assuming that both the option and stock prices are recorded at the exact same time of the day. Given that these prices are from two different financial markets, there will almost always be observation-time differences, called **non-simultaneous price observations**. This type of error can cause substantial differences in the estimates of implied volatility.

Third, option and stock prices are quoted in terms of discrete values, yet the Black-Scholes model gives continuous values. For deep-out-of-the-money options, these discrete values can cause substantial errors because the minimum price quote for options is $^1/_{16}$ of a dollar.

Referring to Table 8.5, Part A, consider a call option with a strike price of 105, and suppose the volatility is 20.22 percent. Using the Black-Scholes model, the option price is 0.0210. But it will be recorded as $^1/_{16}$. If this value of 0.0625 ($=^1/_{16}$) is used as the correct price, then the implied volatility is 23.80 percent.

For a complete analysis of the implied volatility as a procedure for incorporating these and other model misspecifications, see Jarrow and Wiggins (1989).

8.9   OPTION STRATEGIES

We now use the Black-Scholes model to investigate various option investment strategies. These strategies are useful in modifying the payoff to investment portfolios. The Black-Scholes model can be used to price such combinations and to examine their behavior as the stock price changes.

EXAMPLE   **Long Straddle**

A **long straddle** is a portfolio long a call option and long a put option. The two options have the same strike price and maturity.

Given the pricing information in Table 8.6, we use the program Portfolio/FX European Option Pricing to price this combination of options and to examine the straddle's behavior as the stock price changes.

The current stock price is $90. We want to examine the behavior of this straddle over a range of stock prices. Therefore, we set

Initial asset price	80
Final asset price	100
Asset price interval	1.

TABLE 8.6   *Long Straddle*

	INPUT DATA		
		CALL OPTION	PUT OPTION
Strike Price		90	90
Time to Maturity		60 days	60 days
Stock Price	$90		
Volatility*	25 percent		
Discount Rate**	4.75 percent		
Foreign Discount Rate	0 percent		
*Assuming a 365-day year.			
**Assuming a 360-day year.			

This will price the straddle for the range of stock prices from $80 to $100 in increments of $1.00.

For this range of stock prices, delta goes from 0.6984 to 0.7574, gamma is positive, vega is positive, and theta is negative.

You may want to examine the behavior of this straddle as the time to expiration decreases. Set the maturity to 5 days and look at the graphs of delta, gamma, vega, and theta.   ■

Table 8.7 gives a partial list of common options strategies.

The various option trading strategies include a long (short) call and a long (short) put. These are called **naked** option positions. A **vertical bear (bull) spread** involves two call or put options with different strike prices. A **butterfly spread** is a position that involves both a vertical bull and bear spread. Graphing this position with the software provided reveals the reason for the name; the payoff diagram will resemble a butterfly's wings.

A **straddle** is a position involving buying the call and put, both with the same strike price and expiration date. A **strangle** is buying the put and call, both with the same expiration date but different strikes. More complex option trading strategies include the **condor, seagull,** and **time spread** and involve various combinations of written/purchased calls and puts (See Table 8.7 for a detailed description). These various trading strategies can generate payoff patterns at the expiration of the options that are distinct from simple buy-and-hold positions in the underlying stock.

TABLE 8.7 *Common Option Strategies*

Long call	Purchase a call option.
Long put	Purchase a put option.
Short call	Write a call option.
Short put	Write a put option.
Vertical bear spread	Buy a call (put) option and sell a call (put) option with a lower strike price. All options have the same maturity.
Vertical bull spread	Buy a call (put) option and sell a call (put) option with a higher strike price. All options have the same maturity.
Butterfly spread	A combination of a vertical bull and vertical bear spread with the same expiration date on all options and the same strike price on all short options.
Straddle	Purchase a call and a put, both with the same strike price and time to expiration.
Strangle	A short put and a short call or a long put and a long call with the same expiration date and different strikes.
Condor	Purchase a call option and a put option, both equally out-of-the-money. Write a call option and a put option, both further out-of-the-money than the call option and put option that were purchased. All options have the same time to expiration.
Seagull	Write a call option and a put option, both equally out-of-the-money. Buy an at-the-money call option. All options have the same time to expiration.
Time spread	Write one call (put) and buy another call (put) with a longer time to expiration.

8.10 PARTIAL DIFFERENTIAL EQUATION

In the original derivation of the Black-Scholes model, a partial differential equation was derived the solution for which provided the value to the option. The Black-Scholes model was the solution to this partial differential equation. We now show how to derive the Black-Scholes partial differential equation. For those who are not mathematically inclined, this section can be skipped. It is not used in a substantive manner in the remainder of the text.

Derivation

Let $c(t)$ denote the value of an option at date t. The option matures at date T, and $T - t$ is the time remaining until maturity. The underlying stock price is denoted $S(t)$.

Using the risk-neutral valuation equation, Expression (8.6),

$$c(t)/A(t) = E^{\pi}\{c(T)/A(T)\}. \tag{8.26}$$

By Ito's lemma, it is shown in Appendix D of this chapter that Expression (8.26) leads to the following partial differential equation:

$$\frac{1}{2}\sigma^2 S^2 \frac{\partial^2 c}{\partial S^2} + rS\frac{\partial c}{\partial S} - \frac{\partial c}{\partial t} - rc = 0. \tag{8.27}$$

In deriving Expression (8.27), we did not explicitly consider whether the option was a call or a put. The same equation applies to both types of options.

To solve this equation, we must impose boundary conditions. Moreover, it is these boundary conditions that distinguish the different types of options. The contribution of Black and Scholes was to derive this equation, and to show that Expression (8.8) is a solution for call options and Expression (8.9) is a solution for put options.

It is often impossible to derive a closed form solution to a partial differential equation such as (8.27). In this case, it is therefore necessary to use numerical methods. One approach is to approximate the partial derivatives with finite differences. This leads to a finite difference equation that can be solved using either explicit or implicit methods. These procedures have a voluminous literature regarding their usage.[11]

Delta, Gamma, and Theta

Here we use the partial differential equation described by Expression (8.27) to study delta, gamma, and theta.

Given the definition of delta, Expression (8.18), the definition of gamma, Expression (8.20), and the definition of theta, Expression (8.21), Expression (8.27) can be used to obtain the relation between delta, gamma, theta, and the option value:

$$\frac{1}{2}\sigma^2 S^2 \,\text{Gamma} + rS\text{Delta} - \text{Theta} = rc. \tag{8.28}$$

This relation is useful because it holds for any option that satisfies Expression (8.27). For many non-standard options, the calculation of delta and gamma is relatively easy, while the calculation of theta is difficult. Expression (8.28) provides a quick and easy way to calculate theta. In Chapter 10, we will use Expression (8.28) to show that if we construct a self-financing portfolio to be delta neutral and gamma neutral, then it is also theta neutral.

---

[11]See References at the end of the chapter.

8.11 SUMMARY

In this chapter we studied the Black-Scholes options pricing model. This model has become the standard benchmark model because of its relative simplicity and ease of calculation. It requires five inputs:

1. the stock price
2. the strike price
3. the time to maturity
4. the risk-free rate of interest
5. the volatility.

The only input that cannot be directly observed is the volatility. This can be estimated using historic data, or inferred using traded option prices. In the next chapter, we study extensions to the Black-Scholes model.

REFERENCES

The Black-Scholes model:

Black, F., and M. Scholes, 1973. "The Pricing of Options and Corporate Liabilities." *Journal of Political Economy* 81, 637–659.

Merton, R. C., 1973. "Theory of Rational Option Pricing." *Bell Journal of Economics and Management Science* 4, 141–183.

General:

Battig, R. and R. Jarrow, 1999. "The Second Fundamental Theorem of Asset Pricing—A New Approach," *Review of Financial Studies*, in press.

Harrison, J. M., and S. Pliska, 1981. "Martingales and Stochastic Integrals in the Theory of Continuous Trading." *Stochastic Processes and Their Applications* 11, 215–260.

Heath, D., and R. Jarrow, 1987. "Arbitrage, Continuous Trading, and Margin Requirements." *Journal of Finance* 42, 1129–1142.

Jarrow, R., X. Jin, and D. Madan, 1999. "The Second Fundamental Theorem of Asset Pricing." *Mathematical Finance*, in press.

Discrete time:

Brennan, M. J., 1979. "The Pricing of Contingent Claims in Discrete Time Models." *Journal of Finance* 341, 53–68.

Turnbull, S. M., and F. Milne, 1991. "A Simple Approach to the Pricing of Interest Rate Options." *Review of Financial Studies* 4, 87–120.

Variance estimators:

Ball, C., 1988. "Estimation Bias Induced by Discrete Security Prices." *Journal of Finance* 43, 841–866.

Beckers, S., 1983. "Variances of Security Price Returns Based on High, Low, and Closing Prices." *Journal of Business* 56, 97–112.

Cho, D., and E. Frees, 1998. "Estimation of the Volatility of Discrete Stock Prices." *Journal of Finance* 43, 451–466.

French, K. R., 1980. "Stock Returns and the Weekend Effect." *Journal of Financial Economics* 8, 55–69.

French, K. R. and R. Roll, 1986. "Stock Return Variances: The Arrival of Information and the Reaction of Traders." *Journal of Financial Economics* 17, 5–26.

Garman, M., and M. Klass, 1980. "On the Estimation of Security Price Volatilities from Historical Data." *Journal of Business* 53, 67–78.

Gottlieb, G., and A. Kalay, 1985. "Implications of the Discreteness of Observed Stock Prices." *Journal of Finance* 40, 135–153.

Kunitomo, N., 1992. "Improving the Parkinson Method of Estimating Security Price Violations." *Journal of Business* 65, 295–302.

Marsh, T., and E. Rosenfeld, 1986. "Non-trading, Market Making, and Estimates of Stock Price Volatility." *Journal of Financial Economics* 15, 359–372.

Ohlson, J., and S. Penman, 1985. "Volatility Increases Subsequent to Stock Splits: An Empirical Aberration." *Journal of Financial Economics* 14, 251–266.

Parkinson, M., 1980. "The Extreme Value Method of Estimating the Variance of the Rate of Return." *Journal of Business* 53, 61–66.

Roll, R., 1984. "A Simple Implicit Measure of the Effective Bid–Ask Spread in an Efficient Market." *Journal of Finance* 3, 1127–1139.

Wiggins, J. B., 1991. "Empirical Tests of the Bias and Efficiency of the Extreme Value Variance Estimator for Common Stocks." *Journal of Business* 64, 417–432.

Implied volatility:

Beckers, S., 1981. "Standard Deviations Implied in Option Prices as Predictors of Future Stock Price Variability." *Journal of Banking and Finance* 5, 363–381.

Chiras, D. P., and S. Manaster, 1978. "The Informational Content of Option Prices and a Test of Market Efficiency." *Journal of Financial Economics* 6, 213–234.

Jarrow, R., and J. Wiggins, 1989. "Option Pricing and Implicit Volatilities: A Review and a New Perspective." *Journal of Economic Surveys* 3, 59–81.

Latane, H., and R. J. Rendleman, 1976. "Standard Deviation of Stock Price Ratios Implied by Option Premia." *Journal of Finance* 31, 369–382.

Patell, J. M., and M. A. Wolfson, 1979. "Anticipated Information Releases Reflected in Call Option Prices." *Journal of Accounting and Economics* 1, 117–140.

Schmalensee, R., and R. R. Trippi, 1978. "Common Stock Volatility Expectations Implied By Option Premia." *Journal of Finance* 33, 129–147.

Whaley, R. E., 1982. "Valuation of American Call Options on Dividend Paying Stocks: Empirical Tests." *Journal of Financial Economics* 10, 29–58.

Solving partial differential equations:

Brennan, M. J., and E. Schwartz, 1978. "Finite Difference Methods and Jump Processes Arising in the Pricing of Contingent Claims: A Synthesis." *Journal of Financial and Quantitative Analysis* 13, 462–474.

Schwartz, E., 1977. "The Valuation of Warrants: Implementing a New Approach." *Journal of Financial Economics* 4, 79–94.

Wilmott, P., J. Dewynne, and S. Howison, 1993. *Option Pricing.* Oxford, UK: Oxford Financial Press.

QUESTIONS

Short Questions

1. An at-the-money call option has a delta of one-half and maximum gamma. Do you agree? Please justify your answer. Does this hold for put options?
2. As the maturity of an option increases, its vega increases. Do you agree? Please justify your answer.
3. When is theta for a put option positive?
4. The gamma of a long-dated deep-out-of-the-money call option is smaller than a short-dated at-the-money call option. Is this true? What about vega? What are the implications for hedging? How does theta affect your answer?
5. A risk report for a large derivative book shows the portfolio to have positive gamma and positive theta. Is there anything suspicious here?

Question 1

Use the program Equity/Pricing European Options/No Dividends to price a European call option over a range of stock prices. You are given the following data.

Initial stock price	16
Final stock price	26
Stock price interval	1
Strike price	20
Maturity	30 days
Volatility*	25 percent
Discount rate**	4.25 percent

  *A 365-day year is assumed.
**A 360-day year is assumed.

If the maturity of the option is 90 days instead of 30 days, what effect does it have on the option price and delta?

Question 2

The purpose of this question is to examine how the price of a European put option varies as a function of maturity. To do this, compute the option price over a range of stock prices, exercise prices, and maturities. Fill in the following tables and then answer the questions below.

Volatility	13 percent
Discount rate	4.50 percent

Maturity 30 Days

	Strike Price		
	23	25	27
Stock Price			
23			
25			
27			

Maturity 150 Days

	Strike Price		
	23	25	27
Stock Price			
23			
25			
27			

a) If the option is in-the-money, what is the effect upon the value of the option as maturity increases?
b) If the option is at-the-money, what is the effect upon the value of the option as maturity increases?
c) If the option is out-of-the-money, what is the effect upon the value of the option as maturity increases?
d) If the option was a call option, how would it change your answers?

Question 3

The purpose of this question is to examine how delta (the hedge ratio) varies as a function of maturity, the degree the option is in- or out-of-the-money, and the volatility. To do this, compute delta over a range of stock prices, exercise prices, maturities, and volatilities. Fill in the following tables and then answer the questions below. Use the program Equity/Pricing European Options/No Dividends.

CALL OPTION

Volatility = 20 percent per year
Discount rate = 7 percent per year

Volatility = 30 percent per year
Discount rate = 7 percent per year

Maturity 30 Days

	Strike Price					Strike Price		
	23	25	27			23	25	27
Stock					Stock			
Price					Price			
23					23			
25					25			
27					27			

Maturity 150 Days

	Strike Price					Strike Price		
	23	25	27			23	25	27
Stock					Stock			
Price					Price			
23					23			
25					25			
27					27			

Maturity 270 Days

	Strike Price					Strike Price		
	23	25	27			23	25	27
Stock					Stock			
Price					Price			
23					23			
25					25			
27					27			

PUT OPTION

Volatility = 20 percent per year
Discount rate = 7 percent per year

Volatility = 30 percent per year
Discount rate = 7 percent per year

Maturity 30 Days

	Strike Price					Strike Price		
	23	25	27			23	25	27
Stock					Stock			
Price					Price			
23					23			
25					25			
27					27			

Maturity 150 Days

	Strike Price					Strike Price		
	23	25	27			23	25	27
Stock Price					Stock Price			
23					23			
25					25			
27					27			

Maturity 270 Days

	Strike Price					Strike Price		
	23	25	27			23	25	27
Stock Price					Stock Price			
23					23			
25					25			
27					27			

a) Keeping the stock price fixed, how does the hedge ratio vary as a function of the exercise price?

b) Keeping the exercise price fixed, how does the hedge ratio vary as the stock price increases?

c) Keeping the exercise price and stock price fixed, how does the hedge ratio vary as a function of maturity?

d) How does the hedge ratio vary as volatility increases?

Question 4

A pension fund manager expects to receive an inflow of funds in 90 days' time and would like to invest some of the funds in a certain stock. The stock price today is $25. The fund manager would be very happy if in 90 days' time the stock was selling for $25. The maximum price the manager would pay for the stock is $30.

An innovative financial institution offers the pension fund manager the following type of contract. If the stock price is above $30, the manager can buy the stock at $30. If the stock price is below $X, the manager buys the stock at a price of $X. If the stock price is between X and $30, the manager pays the spot price. The lower bound, X, is set by the financial institution such that the value of the contract is zero.

You are given the following information.

Volatility*   27.25 percent
Discount rate**   6.00 percent

*Assuming a 365-day year.
**Assuming a 360-day year.

a) Identify the two implicit options. What is the financial institution's portfolio of options?
b) Price the option with a strike price of $30. Use the program Equity/Pricing European Options/No Dividends.
c) Determine the lower bound X.
d) Suppose that the volatility is 34 percent. What is the lower bound? What are the practical implications?

Question 5

You are given the following information.

TYPE OF OPTION	MATURITY (DAYS)	STRIKE	OPTION PRICE
Call	38	30	$5\frac{5}{8}$
Call	38	35	$2\frac{1}{8}$
Call	38	40	$\frac{5}{8}$
Call	38	45	$\frac{1}{8}$
Put	38	30	$\frac{1}{2}$
Put	38	35	$1\frac{7}{8}$
Put	38	40	$5\frac{1}{4}$

Stock price $35
Discount rate*   5.65 percent

*Assuming a 360-day year.

Determine the implied volatility for each option. Use the program Equity/Implied Volatility European/No Dividends and assume a 365-day year.

Questions 6 to 12 address different option strategies. Table 8.8 describes the data for these questions.

TABLE 8.8 *Price Information for Questions 6 to 12*

Stock Price	100
Volatility	20.00 percent
Discount Rate	4.50 percent

Price all options over the range $90 to $110 in intervals of $1.00.

Question 6   Vertical Bear Spread

Buy a call option with a strike price of $105 and write call options with a strike price of $95. The maturity of the two options is 60 days. Given the information in Table 8.8, use the program Portfolio/FX European Option Pricing to demonstrate that delta is negative, and that gamma, vega, and theta are ambiguous.

Question 7   Vertical Bull Spread

Buy a call (put) option with a strike price of $95 and write a call (put) option with a strike price of $105. The maturity of the two options is 60 days. Given the information in Table 8.8, use the program Portfolio/FX European Option Pricing to demonstrate that delta is positive, and that gamma, vega, and theta are ambiguous.

Question 8   Butterfly Spread

Write two call (put) options with a strike of $100, buy a call (put) option with a strike of $95, and buy a call (put) option with a strike of $105. All options have the same maturity of 60 days. Given the information in Table 8.8, use the program Portfolio/FX European Option Pricing to demonstrate that delta is positive if the stock is less than $100 and negative otherwise; gamma and vega are initially positive, then negative, and end being positive; and that reverse behavior is observed for theta. Also observe that delta is relatively small in absolute magnitude.

Question 9   Strangle

Buy a put option with a strike of $95 and a call option with a strike of $105. The maturity of the two options is 60 days. Given the information in Table 8.8, use the program Portfolio/FX European Option Pricing to demonstrate that delta is initially negative when the stock price is less than $98 and then positive; gamma and vega are positive.

Question 10   Time Spread

Write a call option with a strike of $100 and maturity of 60 days. Buy a call option with a strike of $100 and a maturity of 90 days. Given the information in Table 8.8, use the program Portfolio/FX European Option Pricing to demonstrate that delta is positive if the stock price is less than $102 and then negative; gamma and theta are ambiguous; vega is positive. Note that delta is relatively small in absolute value.

Question 11   A Condor

Buy a put option with a strike of $95 and buy a call option with a strike of $105. Write a put option with a strike of $92 and write a call option with a strike of $107.

All options have a maturity of 60 days. Given the information in Table 8.8, use the program Portfolio/FX European Option Pricing to demonstrate that delta is negative if the stock is less than $101 and then positive; gamma and vega are positive provided the stock price is between $91 and $109; and that the reverse holds for theta. Also observe that delta is relatively small in absolute value.

Question 12   A Seagull

Write a put option with a strike of $95, buy a call with a strike of $100, and write a call option with a strike of $105. All options have a maturity of 60 days. Given the information in Table 8.8, use the program Portfolio/FX European Option Pricing to demonstrate that delta is positive; gamma and vega are negative; theta is positive.

APPENDIX A

The purpose of this appendix is to show that under the equivalent martingale probability distribution π, the change in stock prices can be represented by

$$dS(t)/S(t) = rdt + \sigma dt \tilde{W}(t),$$

where $d\tilde{W}$ is a normally distributed random variable with zero mean and variance dt.
Let the process describing changes in the stock price be

$$\frac{dS(t)}{S(t)} = \alpha dt + \sigma dW(t)$$

under the empirical probability distribution.
The money market account is given by

$$A(t) = e^{rt}$$

so that

$$dA(t) = rA(t)dt.$$

Let the stock price normalized by the money market account be represented by

$$L(t) \equiv S(t)/A(t).$$

Changes in the normalized stock price are given by

$$dL(t) = \frac{dS(t)}{A(t)} - \frac{S(t)}{A(t)^2} dA(t).$$

Substituting for $dS(t)$ and $dA(t)$ gives

$$dL(t) = L(t)[(\alpha - r)dt + \sigma dW(t)].$$

Under the empirical probability distribution $dW(t)$ is normally distributed with zero mean and variance dt. But under the equivalent martingale distribution π this will no longer be the case. Fortunately, we can use a result called Givsanov's theorem that shows us how to adjust $dW(t)$ so that under the distribution π it is normally distributed with zero mean and variance dt.

Givsanov's theorem implies that $d\tilde{W}(t)$ is a normal distribution with zero mean and variance dt where

$$d\tilde{W}(t) = \lambda dt + dW(t)$$

and λ is a stochastic process often referred to as the market price of risk.

Substituting for $dW(t)$ gives

$$dL(t) = L(t)[(\alpha - r - \lambda\sigma)dt + \sigma d\tilde{W}(t)].$$

Under the equivalent martingale distribution π, we know that $L(t)$ is a martingale. This implies that

$$E^{\pi}[L(t + dt)] = L(t).$$

Consequently,

$$\begin{aligned} E^{\pi}[dL(t)] &= E^{\pi}[L(t + dt)] - L(t) \\ &= L(t) - L(t) \\ &= 0. \end{aligned}$$

Hence

$$\begin{aligned} L(t)(\alpha - r - \lambda\sigma)dt &= 0 \qquad \text{or} \\ \alpha - r - \lambda\sigma &= 0, \end{aligned}$$

implying that the market price of risk is given by

$$\lambda = \frac{\alpha - r}{\sigma}.$$

For the distribution π, the change in the stock price is

$$\begin{aligned} \frac{dS(t)}{S(t)} &= \alpha dt + \sigma[d\tilde{W}(t) - \lambda dt] \\ &= (\alpha - \lambda\sigma)dt + \sigma d\tilde{W}(t) \\ &= r dt + \sigma d\tilde{W}(t). \end{aligned}$$

The proof is complete.

APPENDIX B

This appendix proves both Expressions (8.8) and (8.9). Before proving these results, it is useful to state a lemma.

Lemma

Suppose that X is normally distributed with mean μ and variance σ^2. Then

$$E[\exp(aX) \mid X \geq k] = \exp(a\mu + a^2\sigma^2/2)N(d),$$

where a is constant, and $d \equiv (-k + \mu + a\sigma^2)/\sigma$.

PROOF

Proof of Lemma

Using the definition of the normal density function,

$$E[\exp(aX) \mid X \geq k] = \frac{1}{\sigma\sqrt{2\pi}} \int_k^\infty \exp(aX)\exp\left[-\frac{1}{2}\left(\frac{X-\mu}{\sigma}\right)^2\right]dX.$$

Now, by completing the square, we have

$$aX - \frac{1}{2}\left(\frac{X-\mu}{\sigma}\right)^2 = a\mu + \frac{\sigma^2 a^2}{2} - \frac{1}{2}\left[\frac{X-(\mu+a\sigma^2)}{\sigma}\right]^2.$$

Using this result,

$$E[\exp(aX) \mid X \geq k]$$
$$= \exp(a\mu + a^2\sigma^2/2)\frac{1}{\sigma\sqrt{2\pi}}\int_k^\infty \exp\left\{-\frac{1}{2}\left[\frac{X-(\mu+a\sigma^2)}{\sigma}\right]^2\right\}dX.$$

Let $u \equiv [X - (\mu + a\sigma^2)]/\sigma$ and $K = [k - (\mu + a\sigma^2)]/\sigma$, so that

$$E[\exp(aX) \mid X \geq k] = \exp(a\mu + a^2\sigma^2/2)\frac{1}{\sqrt{2\pi}}\int_K^\infty \exp(-u^2/2)du$$
$$= \exp(a\mu + a^2\sigma^2/2)[1 - N(K)]$$
$$= \exp(a\mu + a^2\sigma^2/2)N(d),$$

where $d \equiv -K = (-k + \mu + a^2\sigma^2)/\sigma$. ∎

PROOF

Proof of Expression (8.8)

The call option will be exercised if

$$S(T) \geq K.$$

Given that we must use the π distribution, this can be written in the form

$$S(0)\exp[\tilde{\mu}T + \sigma\tilde{W}(T)] \geq K$$

or

$$\tilde{W}(t) \geq \{\ln[K/S(0)] - \tilde{\mu}T\}/\sigma \equiv k,$$

where $\tilde{\mu} \equiv (r - \sigma^2/2)$. Using (8.8), recognizing that $A(T)^{-1} = B(0, T)$, and using the above lemma gives

$$\begin{aligned}
c(0) &= B(0,T)E^{\pi}[C(T)]\\
&= B(0,T)E^{\pi}\{S(0)\exp[\tilde{\mu}T + \sigma\tilde{W}(T)] - K \mid \tilde{W}(T) \geq k\}\\
&= S(0)N(d_1) - KB(0,T)N(d_2),
\end{aligned}$$

where $d_1 \equiv \{\ln[S(0)/KB(0,T)] + \sigma^2 T/2\}/\sigma\sqrt{T}$, and $d_2 \equiv d_1 - \sigma\sqrt{T}$.   ■

PROOF   **Proof of Expression (8.9)**

Using the put-call parity theorem,

$$\begin{aligned}
p(0) &= c(0) + KB(0,T) - S(0)\\
&= KB(0,T)[1 - N(d_2)] - S(0)[1 - N(d_1)]\\
&= KB(0,T)N(-d_2) - S(0)N(-d_1).   \quad ■
\end{aligned}$$

APPENDIX C   UNEQUALLY SPACED OBSERVATIONS

To estimate the volatility, we first want to generalize the definition of the price relative:

$$PR(t;n) \equiv S(t)/S(t - n\Delta),$$

where Δ is the minimum interval between observations, and n is a positive integer. Given that we do not have equally spaced observations, n will not be constant. The logarithm of the price relative is

$$Lp(t;n) \equiv \ln[PR(t;n)].$$

Using (8.3) we can write

$$Lp(t;n) = (\mu - \sigma^2/2)n\Delta + \sigma\Delta W(t),$$

where $\Delta W(t) \equiv W(t) - W(t - n\Delta)$ is normally distributed with zero mean and variance $n\Delta$. We would like this variance term to be constant and equal to Δ. We can achieve this by dividing each of the above equations by $\sqrt{n}$:

$$Lp(t;n)/\sqrt{n} = (\mu - \sigma^2/2)\sqrt{n}\Delta + \sigma e(t),$$

where $e(t)$ is normally distributed with zero mean and variance Δ. For convenience, we can write this in the form

$$Y(t) = (\mu - \sigma^2/2)X(t) + \sigma e(t),$$

where $Y(t) \equiv Lp(t;n)/\sqrt{n}$ and $X(t) \equiv \sqrt{n}\Delta$.

Therefore, the estimate of the mean is

$$\hat{m} = \frac{1}{N}\sum_{j=1}^{N} Y(j) / \frac{1}{N}\sum_{j=1}^{N} X(j)$$

and

$$\sigma^2 = \frac{1}{N-1}\sum_{j=1}^{N} [Y(j) - \hat{m}]^2.$$

APPENDIX D

The purpose of this appendix is to derive, using Expression (8.6), a partial differential equation representing the value of an option. Let $V[S(t),t]$ denote the value of a derivative security at date t. The value of this security depends on the value of the underlying stock $S(t)$. For example, V could represent the value of a call option, a put option, or a portfolio of options that are written on the same stock. The value of the derivative security at date t using Expression (8.6) is

$$V(t,S(t))/A(t) = E^\pi\{V(T,S(T))/A(T)\}. \tag{D1}$$

This states that $V(t,S(t))/A(t) = V(t,S(t))e^{-rt}$ is a martingale. Hence

$$E^\pi(d[V(t,S(t))e^{-rt}]) = 0. \tag{D2}$$

Let us apply Ito's lemma to $V(t,S(t))e^{-rt}$ and evaluate the resulting expectation in (D2). The partial derivatives are

$$\partial \frac{[V(t,S(t))e^{-rt}]}{\partial t} = \frac{\partial V(t,S(t))}{\partial t} e^{-rt} - rV(t,S(t))e^{-rt}$$

$$\partial \frac{[V(t,S(t))e^{-rt}]}{\partial S} = \frac{\partial V(t,S(t))}{\partial S} e^{-rt}$$

$$\partial^2 \frac{[V(t,S(t))e^{-rt}]}{\partial S^2} = \frac{\partial^2 V(t,S(t))}{\partial S^2} e^{-rt},$$

so using Ito's lemma gives

$$d[V(t,S(t))e^{-rt}] = \left[\frac{\partial V(t,S(t))}{\partial t} - rV(t,S(t)) + (\tfrac{1}{2})\sigma^2(S(t),t)^2 \frac{\partial^2 V(t,S(t))}{\partial S^2}\right]e^{-rt}dt$$
$$+ \frac{\partial V(t,S(t))}{\partial S}e^{-rt}dS(t).$$

But

$$dS(t) = rS(t)dt + \sigma S(t)d\tilde{W}(t) \text{ under } \pi;$$

see Expression (8.5).

This implies that $\sigma^2(S(t),t) = \sigma^2 S(t)^2$. Substitution gives

$$d[V(t,S(t))e^{-rt}] =$$
$$\left[\frac{\partial V(t,S(t))}{\partial t} - rV(t,S(t)) + (\tfrac{1}{2})\sigma^2 S(t)^2 \frac{\partial^2 V(t,S(t))}{\partial S^2} + rS(t)\frac{\partial V(t,S(t))}{\partial S}\right]e^{-rt}dt$$
$$+ \frac{\partial V(t,S(t))}{\partial S}e^{-rt}d\tilde{W}(t).$$

Taking $E^\pi(\cdot)$ over this expression, noting that $E^\pi(d\tilde{W}(t)) = 0$, dividing by e^{-rt}, and substituting back into (D2) yields

$$0 = -V(t,S(t))r + \frac{\partial V(t,S(t))}{\partial t} + rS(t)\frac{\partial V(t,S(t))}{\partial S} + \frac{1}{2}\sigma^2 S(t)^2 \frac{\partial^2 V(t,S(t))}{\partial S^2}.$$

$$\text{(D3)}$$

If the derivative security is a European call option, then (D3) becomes

$$0 = -c(t)r - \frac{\partial c}{\partial t} + rS(t)\frac{\partial c}{\partial S} + \frac{1}{2}\sigma^2 S(t)^2 \frac{\partial^2 c}{\partial S^2},$$

which we must solve subject to the boundary condition:

$$c(T) = \text{Max}\{S(T) - K, 0\}.$$

If the derivative security is a European put option, then (D3) becomes

$$0 = -p(t)r - \frac{\partial p}{\partial t} + rS(t)\frac{\partial p}{\partial t} + \frac{1}{2}\sigma^2 S(t)^2 \frac{\partial^2 p}{\partial S^2},$$

which we must solve subject to the boundary condition:

$$p(T) = \text{Max}\{K - S(T), 0\}.$$

EXTENSIONS TO THE BLACK-SCHOLES MODEL

9.0 INTRODUCTION

Assumption A6 of the Black-Scholes model assumes that over the life of the option, the underlying asset will not pay dividends. If this is not the case, then the Black-Scholes model will be **misspecified**. Most stocks pay dividends. Let us study the adjustments necessary to the Black-Scholes model when dividends are present.

For European options, the first extension we consider, the **Known Dividend model**, reduces the stock price by the present value of the dividends paid over the life of the option. However, this adjustment is exact only for European options.

For American call options, we know from Chapter 7 that it may be optimal to prematurely exercise the option just before the stock goes ex-dividend. The **Pseudo-American model** attempts to incorporate this possibility of premature exercise. Unfortunately, this model is only an approximation. In the case of one known dividend over the life of an option, it is possible to obtain an exact and closed form solution, known as the **Roll model** for an American call option. We also discuss this model.

The last model we consider is the case of a European option on an asset that pays a constant (known) continuous dividend yield. This model is studied because it has been used extensively in the pricing of European foreign currency options, commodity options, stock index options, and options on futures.

We end the chapter by considering two applications of this model. First, we consider options on futures (the Black model). Such instruments are traded on organized exchanges such as the Chicago Board of Trade and the New York Mercantile Exchange. Second, we consider options on forward contracts, which are used in the over-the-counter market.

9.1 KNOWN DIVIDEND MODEL

The Black-Scholes model was derived using the risk-neutral valuation procedure. This procedure prices European options as the expected discounted value of the stock price at maturity. Thus only the stock price at maturity is relevant in the valuation procedure, and not any intermediate dividend payments. In using the Black-Scholes

model, we substitute into the model the current stock price as the present value of the stock price at maturity. This is fine, because under Assumption A6, we do not expect any dividends to be paid over the life of the option. Now we consider what changes are necessary when dividends are paid over the life of the option.

Consider a European option that matures at date T. Before the option matures, let the stock pay at date t_1 a known dividend of $d(t_1)$ dollars per share. The assumption that the amount and the time of the dividend are known with certainty is reasonable for a company with an established dividend policy, as dividends are paid on a regular basis and companies tend to have stable dividend payments. It is far less reasonable for companies that have substantial volatility in earnings.

This assumption causes a minor technical problem. We can no longer assume that the stock price is lognormally distributed. With a lognormal distribution, the stock price could be less than the present value of the dividends paid over the life of the option. This is impossible. Hence, Assumption A6 needs to be modified.

The modified assumption is that the stock price follows a **displaced lognormal distribution** prior to date t_1. The displaced lognormal distribution is a lognormal distribution shifted along the "x-axis" to the right so that the smallest possible value for the stock at date t_1 becomes $d(t_1)$ (see Figure 9.1).

We can describe this shift algebraically. Define the stock price process $S(t)$ to be

$$S(t) = d(t_1)B(t,t_1) + H(t) \text{ for } t \le t_1$$

and

$$S(t) = H(t) \text{ for } t > t_1,$$

FIGURE 9.1   *Displaced Lognormal Probability Distribution*

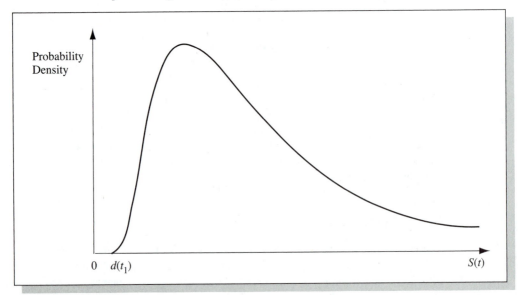

where $H(t)$ is lognormally distributed. This shift of $d(t_1)B(t,t_1)$ reflects the present value of the dividend. We can think of $H(t)$ as the "capital gains" component of the stock price.

The stock price today reflects both the present value of all future dividends and the present value of the stock price at date T. This can be written in the form

$$S(0) = d(t_1)B(0,t_1) + PV_0[S(T)], \tag{9.1}$$

where the last term on the right side is the date-0 present value of the stock price at date T. Note that we discount the dividend $d(t_1)$ at the risk-free rate, given our assumption that both the amount and date of the dividend are known. Expression (9.1) replaces Assumption A6 in the subsequent analysis.

The payoff to a European call option that matures at date T with strike price K is

$$c(T) = \text{Max}\{S(T) - K, 0\}.$$

Using the risk-neutral valuation procedure, we have that

$$c(0) = E^\pi\{c(T)/A(t)\}.$$

Suppose for the moment that $K = 0$, so that the right side becomes

$$E^\pi[S(T)/A(T)] = PV_0[S(T)]$$
$$= S(0) - d(t_1)B(0,t_1).$$

The last equality uses Expression (9.1). It suggests that we should not substitute into the Black-Scholes model the current stock price, but rather the current stock price minus the present value of the dividends paid over the life of the option.

The expression for a call option then becomes

$$c(0) = H(0)N(d_1) - KB(0,T)N(d_2), \tag{9.2}$$

where $H(0) \equiv S(0) - d(t_1)B(0,t_1)$, $d_1 \equiv \{\ln[H(0)/KB(0,T)] + \sigma^2 T/2\}/(\sigma\sqrt{T})$, and $d_2 \equiv d_1 - \sigma\sqrt{T}$. This makes intuitive sense since the European call is an option on the stock at date T, after the dividend has been paid. Thus the underlying asset is not the stock per se, but the stock minus the present value of the dividend, hence Expression (9.2).

Using the same logic, the expression for a put option becomes

$$p(0) = KB(0,T)N(-d_2) - H(0)N(-d_1). \tag{9.3}$$

Expressions (9.2) and (9.3) represent the Known Dividend model.

EXAMPLE **Known Dividend Model Calculation**

Suppose we have a European call option written on a stock that pays a dividend of $1.50 in 31 days' time. The inputs are shown in Table 9.1, Part A.

TABLE 9.1   *Discrete Dividend Payment*

PART A INPUT DATA	
Stock price	25
Strike price	25
Maturity	68 days
Volatility*	25 percent
Discount rate**	6 percent
Dividend	1.5
Date of dividend	31 days

*A 365-day year is assumed.

**A 360-day year is assumed.

PART B OPTION PRICES*	
	OPTION PRICE
Known dividend*	0.5430
Adjusted Black-Scholes**	0.5430

*The program Equity/Pricing European Options/Known Dividends is used.

**The program Equity/Pricing European Options/No Dividends is used.

The term structure is assumed to be flat, so the present value of receiving one dollar for sure in 31 days' time, using a discount interest rate of 6 percent, is

$$B(0,31) = 1 - \frac{6.00}{100} \times \frac{31}{360} = 0.994833.$$

Using the program Equity/Pricing European Options/Known Dividends, we can determine the price of the option. The output is given in Table 9.1, Part B.

The value of the stock minus the present value of the dividend is

$$
\begin{aligned}
H(0) &\equiv S(0) - d(t_1) \times B(0,t_1) \\
&= 25 - 1.50 \times 0.994833 \\
&= 23.5078.
\end{aligned}
$$

We could substitute this value directly into the Black-Scholes model. Using the program Equity/Pricing European Options/No Dividends, the option price is shown in Table 9.1, Part B. The two values are identical, as expected.   ■

9.2 PSEUDO-AMERICAN MODEL

For American call options, it may be optimal to prematurely exercise just before the stock goes ex-dividend. This flexibility makes the American call option more valuable than the European. The Pseudo-American model provides a (lower bound) approximation to the American call's value. It uses the Black-Scholes model to value an American call option that has the following suboptimal exercise policy. At the time the option is written, fix the date at which you decide to exercise the option. This date remains fixed and unchanged over the life of the option.

Obviously this exercise strategy is suboptimal because it may be best to wait until the actual date to decide, and not to precommit, to a particular exercise date beforehand. We will now value this Pseudo-American call.

Consider an option that matures at date T. During the life of the option, the stock pays a known dividend of $d(t_1)$ at date t_1. In this case, the Pseudo-American model has two relevant dates to consider, date t_1 and date T. The decision considers two distinct European call options. The first option matures just before the stock goes ex-dividend at date t_1, and the second option matures at date T. The pseudo-American call option's value is the largest of these two option values. The option with the largest value gives as its maturity date the date precommitted to possibly exercise the American call option in the suboptimal exercise strategy.

Consider the first option with maturity at date t_1. At the maturity of the option, its value is

$$c_1(t_1) = \begin{cases} S_c(t_1) - K & \text{if} \quad S_c(t_1) \geq K \\ 0 & \text{if} \quad S_c(t_1) < K, \end{cases} \tag{9.4}$$

where $S_c(t_1)$ is the cum-dividend stock price. This call option captures the dividend if it is exercised.

From Chapter 7, we have that the cum-dividend price equals the ex-dividend stock price plus the dividend paid, that is,

$$S_c(t_1) = S_e(t_1) + d(t_1),$$

where $S_e(t_1)$ is the ex-dividend stock price. Substituting this result into Expression (9.4), we can write the payoff to the call option in the form

$$c_1(t_1) = \begin{cases} S_e(t_1) - K_1 & \text{if} \quad S_e(t_1) \geq K_1 \\ 0 & \text{if} \quad S_e(t_1) < K_1, \end{cases}$$

where $K_1 \equiv K - d_1(t_1)$.

This is the boundary condition to a call option on the ex-dividend value of the stock with a strike price equal to K_1. It makes sense, as the dividend payment can be used to reduce the cash paid out for the strike price in the event of exercise.

Given that we are expressing the payoff to the option in terms of the ex-dividend value, which follows a lognormal distribution, the Black-Scholes model applies directly to yield the value of the option today as

$$c_1(0) = H(0)N(d_1) - K_1 B(0, t_1) N(d_2),$$

where $d_1 \equiv \{\ln[H(0)/K_1 B(0, t_1)] + \sigma^2 t_1 / 2\}/(\sigma \sqrt{t_1})$, $d_2 \equiv d_1 - \sigma \sqrt{t_1}$, and $H(0) = S(0) - d(t_1)B(0, t_1)$.

The value of the second European call option, which matures at date T, denoted $c_2(0)$, is given by Expression (9.2). This call option does not capture the dividend payment. There are two differences between the call option values $c_1(0)$ and $c_2(0)$:

(i)   their maturity dates differ, and
(ii) their strike prices differ.

Both use $H(0)$ as the current value of the underlying asset.

The Pseudo-American model's value is the maximum of these two European call options' values, that is,

Pseudo-American value = $\text{Max}\{c_1(0), c_2(0)\}$.   (9.5)

The correct value of the American call option cannot be less than either of these two European call option values.

EXAMPLE   **Pseudo-American Call Option Values Calculation**

Using the values given in the previous example,

$$H(0) = 23.5078$$

and the adjusted strike price is

$$K_1 = K - 1.5 = 23.50,$$

so that the first European call's value is

$$c_1(0) = 0.7478.$$

From the previous example, the value of the second option is

$$c_2(0) = 0.5430,$$

which is identical to the value calculated using the Known Dividend model.

The approximate value of the American call option using the Pseudo-American model is

Max{0.5430,0.7478} = 0.7478.

You should check this using the program Equity/Pricing European Options/ Pseudo-American Dividends. ∎

9.3 THE ROLL MODEL

Here we study the Roll model for the pricing of an American call option. A disadvantage of the Pseudo-American model is that it only provides a lower bound for the pricing of American call options. The Roll model provides an exact closed form solution for pricing American call options when one known dividend is paid over the life of the option. In addition, this approach can easily be extended for multiple known dividend payments over the life of the option. This extension is also discussed briefly below.

Consider an American call option that matures at date T. During the life of the option, let the stock pay one known dividend of $d(t_1)$ at date t_1. After the stock goes ex-dividend, we know from Chapter 7 that the next date to consider exercising the option is the maturity date because there are no remaining dividends.

Thus, after date t_1, the option can be valued as a European option and the Black-Scholes model can be used. Thus, for $t > t_1$, the American call's value is

$$c(T) = S_e(t)N(d_1) - KB(t,T)N(d_2), \tag{9.6}$$

where $S_e(t)$ is the ex-dividend stock price at t, $d_1 \equiv \{\ln[S_e(t)/KB(t,T)] + \sigma^2(T-t)/2\}/(\sigma\sqrt{T-t})$, and $d_2 = d_1 - \sigma\sqrt{T-t}$.

Now if we are going to exercise an American call option early, we will do so just before the stock goes ex-dividend at date t_1. If we exercise the option, we receive $S_c(t_1) - K$, where $S_c(t_1)$ is the cum-dividend value of the stock at t_1. If we do not exercise the option, the stock goes ex-dividend and the option value is given by $c(t_1)$ as defined by Expression (9.6). Therefore, the optimal exercise strategy at date t_1 is to pick whichever of these values is the greatest.

The American call option's value at t_1 is given by

$$C(t_1) = \text{Max}\{S_c(t_1) - K, c(t_1)\}.$$

We can define a **critical ex-dividend stock price** S^* such that these two values are just equal, that is,

$$S^* + d(t_1) - K = c(t_1).$$

If $S_e(t_1) > S*$, it will pay to prematurely exercise the option, and if $S* > S_e(t_1)$, the option remains unexercised. If $S* = S_e(t_1)$, then we are indifferent. The critical stock price $S*$ can be easily determined on a computer using a simple numerical search procedure.

Next, stepping back to date 0, we can value the American call option using the risk-neutral valuation methodology on the call's value at time t_1. Therefore, the date-0 value of the option is given by its expected discounted value at date t_1:

$$C(0) = E^\pi\{C(t_1)/A(t_1)\}.$$

The contribution by Roll (1977) and Geske (1979), plus a correction by Whaley (1981), was the explicit evaluation of the above expression. They showed that

$$\begin{aligned}
C(0) = &\ H(0)N(d_1) - K_1B(0,t_1)N(d_2) \\
&+ H(0)N_2(-d_1,a_1,-\sqrt{t_1/T}) \\
&- KB(0,T)N_2(-d_2,a_2,-\sqrt{t_1/T}),
\end{aligned} \tag{9.7}$$

where $H(0) = S(0) - d(t_1)B(0,t_1)$, $K_1 = K - d(t_1)$, $d_1 \equiv \{\ln[H(0)/S*B(0,t_1)] + \sigma^2t_1/2\}/(\sigma\sqrt{t_1})$, $d_2 = d_1 - \sigma\sqrt{t_1}$, $a_1 \equiv \{\ln[S(0)/KB(0,T)] + \sigma^2T/2\}/(\sigma\sqrt{T})$, $a_2 = a_1 - \sigma\sqrt{T}$, and $N_2(a,b,c)$ is the cumulative bivariate normal distribution function with upper limits of integration a and b and the correlation coefficient c.

Expression (9.7) is more complicated than the Black-Scholes formula because there is a possibility of prematurely exercising the call option just before the stock goes ex-dividend at date t_1. For computation purposes, however, Expression (9.7) is no more difficult to utilize than is the Black-Scholes model.

This model can be generalized to more than one dividend paid on the stock over the life of the option. Analogous closed form solutions are available using multivariate (greater than two) cumulative normal distribution functions (see Geske and Shastri (1985)).

There is a large literature studying alternative numerical solutions for valuing American call and put options. These techniques use the equivalent representation of the option's value based on a partial differential equation, subject to boundary conditions, that we studied in Chapter 8, Section 8.10. The numerical procedures are approximations that emphasize efficiency of computation, as these computations are complex and typically take a relatively long time to generate. (See the references at the end of the chapter for more material on these procedures.)

9.4 CONSTANT DIVIDEND YIELD MODEL

We now value a European call option on a stock that pays a continuous dividend with constant dividend yield. The dividend yield is defined as the dividend per share divided by the stock price. A constant dividend yield implies a random dollar dividend per share. It is random because the dollar dividend equals the dividend yield multi-

plied by the stock price, and the stock price magnitude is random and changes through time. This valuation model will prove useful in subsequent sections for pricing foreign currency options, commodity options, stock index options, and options on futures.

To discuss this modification, we need to return to Assumption A6. Assumption A6 is modified here by changing the stock's drift, to reduce it by the continuously paid dividend yield. This is in contrast to the displacement of the lognormal distribution necessary for the known dividend model and the Roll model.

Consider a stock that pays dividends continuously such that the dividend yield d_y per unit time is a constant. One can think of the dividend payment in this case as being paid in a manner analogous to which interest is paid on a savings account at a bank.

The rate of return from holding such a stock from t to $t + \Delta$ is the capital gains plus dividend, that is,

$$[S(t + \Delta) + S(t)d_y\Delta - S(t)]/S(t),$$

where the dividend paid is $S(t)d_y\Delta$ and $S(t)$ is the ex-dividend stock price.

Expression (8.2) of Chapter 8 now becomes

$$\Delta \ln S(t) = (\mu - d_y)\Delta + \sigma\Delta W(t),$$

implying that Expression (8.3) becomes

$$S(t) = S(0)\exp[(\mu - d_y)t + \sigma W(t)].$$

This expression represents the necessary modification to Assumption A6. The term $[\mu - d_y]$ represents the expected capital gains component of the stock's continuously compounded return reduced by the dividend yield.

Under the equivalent martingale distribution, the expected instantaneous rate of return on the stock is the risk-free rate of interest, so that by Expression (5.41) of Chapter 5, Expression (8.5) becomes

$$S(t) = S(0)\exp[(r - d_y - \sigma^2/2)t + \sigma\tilde{W}(t)]. \qquad (9.8)$$

This is the distribution used in the risk-neutral valuation procedure.

The payoff for a European call option with maturity date T and strike price K is

$$c(T) = \begin{cases} S(T) - K & \text{if} \quad S(T) \geq K \\ 0 & \text{if} \quad S(T) < K. \end{cases}$$

Using risk-neutral valuation, the date-0 value of the option is

$$c(0) = \exp(-rT)E^\pi\{c(T)\}.$$

From the Appendix at the end of this chapter, the value of a European call option is

$$c(0) = \exp(-d_y T)S(0)N(d_1) - KB(0,T)N(d_2), \qquad (9.9)$$

where $d_1 \equiv \{\ln[S(0)/KB(0,T)] - (d_y - \sigma^2/2)T\}/(\sigma\sqrt{T})$ and $d_2 \equiv d_1 - \sigma\sqrt{T}$. This is the Black-Scholes call value, where the stock price $S(0)$ is replaced by the stock price less the present value of the dividends paid ($S(0)e^{-d_y T}$).

Analogously, it is easy to show that the value of a European put option is given by

$$p(0) = KB(0,T)N(-d_2) - \exp(-d_y T)S(0)N(-d_1). \qquad (9.10)$$

These European option valuation results were first derived by Merton (1973). The value $S(0)\exp(-d_y T)$ in Expressions (9.9) and (9.10) represents the present value of the stock, $S(T)$, excluding the dividends paid over $[0, T]$. Thus the stock excluding the dividends paid over $[0, T]$ is the "true" underlying asset for the options, and not the stock itself. This is, in fact, the forward price of the stock with delivery at time T as discussed earlier in Chapter 2. It is analogous to the known dividend model for European options studied earlier in this chapter. An example follows.

EXAMPLE

Dividend Yield Model Calculation

This example illustrates the calculation of the constant dividend yield version of the Black-Scholes model.

Suppose we have a European put option written on stock that pays a constant dividend yield of 2.00 percent. The inputs are shown in Table 9.2.

Using the program Equity/Pricing European Options/Constant Dividend Yield, we can determine the price of the put option:

TABLE 9.2   *Constant Dividend Yield*

INPUT DATA	
Stock price	50
Strike price	50
Maturity	38 days
Volatility*	25 percent
Discount rate**	4.50 percent
Dividend yield ***	2.00 percent

  *A 365-day year is assumed.

  **A 360-day year is assumed.

  ***This is continuously compounded. A 360-day year is assumed.

Value of the Put Option = 1.5379
Delta   = −0.4698.

If the dividend yield is zero, the option value is 1.4888 and the delta is −0.4604.

The put option's value is increased by the payment of continuous dividends because it has the effect of lowering the stock price at the maturity of the option.   ■

9.5 OPTIONS ON FUTURES AND FORWARD CONTRACTS

We now study the pricing of futures and forward options under the Black-Scholes Assumptions A1 through A6, modified to include a continuous dividend yield payment.

EXAMPLE   **Put Options on Futures as "Insurance"**

You have purchased 100 futures contracts on the S&P index. If the index goes up, your wealth will increase. If the index goes down, you will be subject to margin calls from your broker. You would like to purchase insurance against declines in the index futures price. One way is to purchase put options written on the index futures.

How do we price such options and what is the appropriate hedge? The answer to this question is what we study next.   ■

We first analyze futures contracts, then forward contracts.

Futures Contracts

Options on futures trade on numerous exchanges throughout the world. Here we examine the pricing of futures options under the modified Black-Scholes assumptions.

Consider a European call option with maturity T and strike price K written on a futures contract that matures at date $T_{\mathcal{F}}$. At the maturity of the call option the payoff is

$$c(T) = \text{Max}\{\mathcal{F}(T; T_{\mathcal{F}}) - K, 0\}, \tag{9.11}$$

where $\mathcal{F}(T; T_{\mathcal{F}})$ is the futures price at date T.

Given Assumption A5 that interest rates are constant, we know from Chapter 2 that forward and futures prices are equal.

If the asset on which the futures contract is written pays a continuous dividend with constant dividend yield, then from the cost-and-carry Expression (2.6) of Chapter 2 the futures price at date T is given by

$$\mathcal{F}(T; T_{\mathcal{F}}) = \exp[(r - d_y)(T_{\mathcal{F}} - T)]S(T),$$

where $S(T)$ is the underlying asset's spot price at date T, d_y is the constant dividend yield, and r is the continuously compounded risk-free rate of interest.

Therefore, by substitution, the payoff to the call option can be written as

$$c(T) = \exp[(r - d_y)(T_{\mathscr{F}} - T)]\text{Max}\{S(T) - k,0\}, \tag{9.12}$$

where $k \equiv \exp[-(r - d_y)(T_{\mathscr{F}} - T)]K$.

There are two differences between Expressions (9.11) and (9.12). First, in Expression (9.11) the underlying asset is the futures price $\mathscr{F}(T, T_{\mathscr{F}})$, while in Expression (9.12) the underlying asset is the spot price $S(T)$. Second, the strike price has been modified in Expression (9.12). The second term on the right side represents the payoff to a European call option on the underlying asset $S(T)$ with a modified strike price of k.

We have already priced this type of option in the preceding section. Therefore, using the constant dividend yield version of Black-Scholes, Expression (9.9), we have

$$c(0) = \exp[(r - d_y)(T_{\mathscr{F}} - T)]\{\exp(-d_yT)S(0)N(d_1) - kB(0,T)N(d_2)\},$$

where $d_1 \equiv \{\ln[S(0)/kB(0,T)] - (d_y - \sigma^2/2)T\}/(\sigma\sqrt{T})$ and $d_2 \equiv d_1 - \sigma\sqrt{T}$.

Using the expression for the modified strike price k and recalling that the futures price at date 0 is given by

$$\mathscr{F}(0; T_{\mathscr{F}}) = \exp[(r - d_y)T_{\mathscr{F}}]S(0)$$

and that the zero-coupon bond's price is

$$B(0,T) = \exp(-rT),$$

we get an alternative form

$$c(0) = B(0,T)[\mathscr{F}(0; T_{\mathscr{F}})N(d_1) - KN(d_2)], \tag{9.13}$$

where $d_1 \equiv \{\ln[\mathscr{F}(0; T_{\mathscr{F}})/K] + \sigma^2T/2\}/(\sigma\sqrt{T})$ and $d_2 \equiv d_1 - \sigma\sqrt{T}$.

This result is referred to as the Black (1976) model. It is used quite regularly in the industry.

For European put options, an analogous argument yields

$$p(0) = B(0,T)[KN(-d_2) - \mathscr{F}(0; T_{\mathscr{F}})N(-d_1)]. \tag{9.14}$$

EXAMPLE   **Computation of the Black Model**

Consider a European put option written on a futures contract. The option matures in 38 days' time and the futures contract also matures on the same date. The futures price is $\mathscr{F}(0,38) = 50.1341$.

Using the data in Table 9.2, and the program Futures/Pricing/European Option, we can determine the price of the option:

Value of Put Option = 1.5379
Delta = −0.4686.

Compared to the last example, two observations can be made. First, the two option values on the spot price and the futures contract are the same, and second, the deltas differ. Why?

Given the assumption that interest rates are constant, forward and futures prices are the same. Using Expression (2.10) of Chapter 2, we have

$$\mathcal{F}(0,T)B(0,T) = S(0)\exp(-d_y T).$$

This identification shows that Expressions (9.10) and (9.14) are identical in value. This equality only holds, however, because the expiration dates of the option and futures contracts coincide.

To verify this relation for this example, we can compute the futures price using the right side. First,

$$B(0,T) = 1 - \frac{4.50}{100} \times \frac{38}{360} = 0.99525$$

and

$$\exp(-d_y T) = \exp(-0.02 \times 38/360) = 0.99789.$$

Given that the stock price is 50,

$$\mathcal{F}(0,38) = (50 \times 0.99789)/0.99525$$
$$= 50.1327.$$

This is the same value given earlier, verifying the expression.

Next we explain the differences in the deltas. In the Black model, as described by Expression (9.14), the delta for a put option on the futures contract is defined as

$$\text{Delta for Put Option on Futures} \equiv \frac{\partial p}{\partial \mathcal{F}}.$$

In the constant dividend yield model, as described by Expression (9.10), the delta for a put option on the spot price is defined as

$$\text{Delta for Put Option on Spot} \equiv \frac{\partial p}{\partial S}.$$

The deltas are with respect to two different underlyings. Using Expression (2.10) of Chapter 2, we see how the deltas relate to each other:

$$\frac{\partial p}{\partial \mathscr{F}} = \frac{\partial S}{\partial \mathscr{F}}\frac{\partial p}{\partial S}$$

$$= \frac{B(0,T)\partial p}{\exp(-d_y T)\partial S}$$

$$= \frac{0.99525}{0.99787} \times (-0.4698)$$

$$= -0.4686.$$

This explains why the two deltas differ.   ∎

Forward Contracts

We now examine the valuation of forward contract options under the modified Black-Scholes assumptions. For those readers who skipped Section 7.5 of Chapter 7 on a similar topic, this section can also be skipped.

In the over-the-counter markets, options on forward contracts are traded. The payoff to these options differs from Expression (9.11).

Consider a European call option with maturity T and strike price K written on a forward contract that matures at date T_F. At the maturity of the option, if the forward price $F(T,T_F)$ is greater than the strike price, the payoff of the option is the value of a forward contract with delivery price K.

From Expression (2.5) of Chapter 2, we know that the value of the forward contract at date T is given by $B(T,T_F)[F(T,T_F) - K]$.

Formally, the payoff to the European call option on a forward contract is defined by

$$c(T) = \text{Max}\{B(T,T_F)[F(T,T_F) - K],0\}.$$

We can write this in the form

$$c(T) = B(T,T_F)\text{Max}\{F(T,T_F) - K,0\}. \tag{9.15}$$

This payoff differs from the payoff to the futures option by the term $B(T,T_F)$. Remember that forward and futures prices are identical, given that interest rates are constant.

Hence, using Expression (9.13), the date-0 value of the European call option on a forward contract is given by

$$c(0) = B(T,T_F)\{B(0,T)[F(0,T_F)N(d_1) - KN(d_2)]\}$$
$$= B(0,T_F)[F(0,T_F)N(d_1) - KN(d_2)], \tag{9.16}$$

where $d_1 \equiv \{\ln[F(0,T_F)/K] + \sigma^2 T/2\}/(\sigma\sqrt{T})$ and $d_2 \equiv d_1 - \sigma\sqrt{T}$.

In this derivation, we use the relation that $B(0,T_F) = B(0,T)B(T,T_F)$, which follows because interest rates are constant.

By an analogous argument, the value of a European put option with maturity T and strike price K on a forward contract with delivery date T_F is given by

$$p(0) = B(0,T_F)[KN(-d_2) - F(0,T_F)N(-d_1)]. \tag{9.17}$$

While the expressions for options on futures and forward contracts look very similar, they do have different implications for the premature exercising of American options.

Consider a deep-in-the-money call futures option where $\mathscr{F}(0,T_{\mathscr{F}}) \gg K$. In this case, Expression (9.13) can be approximated by

$$c(0) \simeq B(0,T)[\mathscr{F}(0,T_{\mathscr{F}}) - K].$$

Now if an American option on the futures is prematurely exercised, its value is $\mathscr{F}(0,T_{\mathscr{F}}) - K$. However,

$$\mathscr{F}(0,T_{\mathscr{F}}) - K > B(0,T)[\mathscr{F}(0,T_{\mathscr{F}}) - K],$$

so it is optimal to prematurely exercise.

Now for a call option on the forward contract, if the option is deep-in-the-money, Expression (9.16) becomes

$$c(0) \simeq B(0,T_F)[F(0,T_F) - K].$$

If an American option on the forward is prematurely exercised, its value is $B(0,T_F)[F(0,T_F) - K]$, so there is no financial gain. It is not optimal to prematurely exercise. This is the same argument underlying the no-exercise Result 7.8 in Chapter 7 for forward options.

9.6 SUMMARY

The Black-Scholes model assumes that over the life of the option the stock does not pay any dividends. In this chapter, we relaxed the dividend payment assumption. For the case in which the stock pays known dividends at discrete dates, three extensions were described: the Known Dividend model, the Pseudo-American model, and the Roll model. In all cases it is assumed that the dates and the amounts of the dividends are known with certainty. The Known Dividend model ignores the possibility of early exercise. The Pseudo-American model attempts to relax the assumption but only provides a lower bound. The Roll model provides an exact valuation formula.

We also considered the case in which the stock pays a continuous and constant dividend yield. This case was utilized in the last section, where the pricing of options on futures contracts and options on forward contracts was discussed. The closed form expression for options on futures contracts is referred to as the Black (1976) model and is used quite regularly in the industry to price various futures options.

REFERENCES

The Black-Scholes model:

Black, F., and M. Scholes, 1973. "The Pricing of Options and Corporate Liabilities." *Journal of Political Economy* 81, 637–659.

Merton, R. C., 1973. "Theory of Rational Option Pricing." *Bell Journal of Economics and Management Science* 4, 141–183.

Extensions to the Black-Scholes model:

Black, F., 1975. "Fact and Fantasy in the Use of Options." *Financial Analyst Journal* 31, 36–72.

Roll model:

Geske, R., 1979. "A Note on the Analytical Valuation Formula for Unprotected American Call Options on Stocks with Known Dividends." *Journal of Financial Economics* 7, 375–380.

Roll, R., 1977. "An Analytical Formula for Unprotected American Call Options on Stocks with Known Dividends." *Journal of Financial Economics* 7, 351–358.

Whaley, R., 1981. "On the Valuation of American Call Options on Stocks with Known Dividends." *Journal of Financial Economics* 9, 207–211.

Black model:

Black, F., 1976. "The Pricing of Commodity Contracts." *Journal of Financial Economics* 3, 167–179.

Numerical approaches to American options valuation:

Barone-Adesi, G., and R. Whaley, 1987. "Efficient Analytic Approximation of American Option Values." *Journal of Finance* 42, 302–320.

Brennan, M., and E. Schwartz, 1977. "The Valuation of American Put Options." *Journal of Finance* 32, 449–462.

Carr, P., R. Jarrow, and R. Mynini, 1992. "Alternative Characterizations of American Put Options." *Mathematical Finance* 2, 87–106.

Geske, R., and K. Shastri, 1983. "Valuation by Approximation: A Comparison of Alternative Option Valuation Techniques." *Journal of Financial and Quantitative Analysis* 20, 45–71.

Geske, R., and K. Shastri, 1985. "The Early Exercise of American Puts." *Journal of Banking and Finance* 9, 207–219.

MacMillan, L. W., 1986. "Analytic Approximation for the American Put Option." *Advances in Futures and Options Research* 1, 119–131.

QUESTIONS

Question 1

Consider a European call option and European put option written on the same stock. The stock price is $50. The options expire in 100 days' time and have a strike price of $50. Over the life of the options, it is known that the stock will pay a quarterly dividend of $0.45 in 48 days' time. The volatility of the return on the stock is 34 percent per annum, assuming a 365-day year. The 100-day discount rate is 5.76 percent, assuming a 360-day year. The value of a 48-day Treasury bill is 99.2440, the discount rate being 5.67 percent.

a) Use the program Equity/Pricing European Options/Known Dividends to price the call and put options.
b) Consider a portfolio containing the put option and one share of stock, which borrows the present value of the dividend. What is the cost of this portfolio and what is its delta?
c) Consider a portfolio containing the call option and the present value of the strike price. What is the cost of this portfolio and what is its delta?
d) What is the relationship between your answers to parts b) and c)?

Question 2

Consider a European call option and European put option written on the same stock. The stock price is $S(0)$. The options expire at date T and have strike price K. Over the life of the options, it is known that the stock will pay a dividend $d(t_1)$ at date t_1. Consider two portfolios.

Portfolio One. Buy the put option, buy the stock, and borrow the present value of the dividend: $d(t_1)B(0,t_1)$. The total cost of this portfolio is

$$p(0) + S(0) - d(t_1)B(0,t_1),$$

where $p(0)$ is the known dividend value of the put option and $H(0) = S(0) - d(t_1)B(0,t_1)$.

a) What is the value of this portfolio at date T when the option expires? Explain carefully how you pay off the amount borrowed.

Portfolio Two. Buy the call option and invest the $KB(0, T)$ in the riskless asset. The total cost of this portfolio is

$$c(0) + KB(0, T),$$

where $c(0)$ is the known dividend value of the call option.

b) What is the value of this portfolio at date T when the option expires?
c) What is the relationship between the cost of Portfolio One and Portfolio Two?

Question 3

You are given the following information about option prices on a stock that pays a quarterly dividend of $0.25 on April 24 (41 days).

| TYPE OF | MATURITY | | STRIKE PRICE | OPTION PRICE |
OPTION	DATE	DAYS		
Call	April 21	38	45	5
Call	April 21	38	50	$1^7/_{16}$
Call	May 19	66	45	$5^3/_8$
Call	May 19	66	50	$2^3/_8$
Put	April 21	38	50	2
Put	May 19	66	50	$2^3/_8$

The 38-day discount rate is 5.65 percent.*
The 66-day discount rate is 5.71 percent.*
The market value of a 41-day Treasury bill is 99.3543.
Stock price is $49.

*A 360-year is assumed.

a) Using the program Equity/Implied Volatility European/No Dividends, determine the implied volatilities for the April options.
b) Using the program Equity/Implied Volatility European/Known Dividends, determine the implied volatilities for the May options.

Question 4

Use the information in Question 1 to answer the following questions.

a) Use the program Equity/Pricing European Options/Pseudo-American Dividends to value the call option.
b) Value a European call option with a maturity of 48 days and a strike price of 49.55. Use the program Equity/Pricing European Options/Known Dividends.
c) Value a European call option with a maturity of 100 days and a strike price of 50. Use the program Equity/Pricing European Options/Known Dividends.
d) Using your answers to parts b) and c), verify your answer to part a).

Question 5

A put option is written on a futures contract. The option expires in 40 days' time and the futures contract in 95 days' time (from today). You are given the following information.

Strike price	517.50
95-day futures price	520.10
Volatility*	18.00 percent
40-day discount rate**	4.65 percent

  *Assuming a 365-day year.
**Assuming a 360-day year.

a) Use the program Futures/Pricing/European Option to determine the value of this option and its delta.
b) If you have written this option, describe the hedge portfolio assuming that you use the underlying futures contract and money market account to hedge.

Question 6

Given the information in Question 5, answer the following questions.
     You decide to hedge the put option using the underlying asset instead of the futures contract. The current value of the asset is 516.63.

a) Determine the implied dividend yield. The 95-day discount rate is 4.70 percent, assuming a 360-day year.
b) Describe the hedge portfolio.

Question 7

Two futures contracts are written on the same asset. The asset pays a continuous dividend with constant dividend yield. The first contract matures at date T_1, and the second contract at date T_2. If forward and futures contracts are treated as being identical, show that if the futures prices for the first contract changes by the amount $\Delta \mathcal{F}(t, T_1)$,

then the second contract changes by the amount $\Delta\mathscr{F}(t, T_2)$ such that

$$\Delta\mathscr{F}(t, T_2) = \Delta\mathscr{F}(t, T_1)\left\{\frac{\exp[-d_y(T_2 - t)]}{B(t, T_2)}\right\}\bigg/\left\{\frac{\exp[-d_y(T_1 - t)]}{B(t, T_1)}\right\},$$

where d_y is the continuously compounded dividend yield and $B(t, T)$ is the value at date t of receiving one dollar for certain at date T.

Question 8

Given the information in Questions 5 and 6, answer the following question. You decide to hedge the put option using both a futures contract that matures in 20 days' time and the money market account. The 20-day discount rate is 4.60 percent and the 95-day discount rate is 4.70 percent, assuming a 360-day year.

Describe the hedge portfolio.

Question 9

You are given the following information about European futures options. Use the program Futures/Implied Volatility/European Options to determine the implied volatility.

STRIKE	CALLS	PUTS
0.8700	0.0180	0.0099
0.8750	0.0153	0.0122
0.8800	0.0127	0.0146
0.8850	0.0107	0.0176
0.8900	0.0088	0.0207
0.8950	0.0072	0.0240
Futures price	0.8781	
Maturity of option	22 days	
22-day discount rate*	5.52 percent	

*Assuming a 360-day year.

Question 10

A call option is written on a futures contract. The option expires in 100 days' time and the futures contract in 127 days (from today). You are given the following information.

Futures price   519
Volatility*   17.00 percent
100-day discount**   4.50 percent

  *Assuming a 365-day year.
**Assuming a 360-day year.

a) Use the program Futures/Pricing to complete the following table.

STRIKE PRICE	VALUE OF EUROPEAN OPTION	VALUE OF AMERICAN OPTION
495		
500		
505		
510		
515		
520		
525		
530		

b) Explain your results.

APPENDIX: CONTINUOUS DIVIDEND YIELD

For the case in which the stock pays a continuous dividend with constant dividend yield, d_y, from Expression (9.8), $\mu = (r - d_y - \sigma^2/2)$. Using the lemma in Appendix B of Chapter 8, the value of the option is

$$c(0) = B(0,T)E^{\pi}\{S(0)\exp[\mu T + \sigma \tilde{W}(T)] - K \mid \tilde{W}(T) \geq K\}$$
$$= \exp(-d_y T)S(0)N(d_1) - KB(0,T)N(d_2),$$

where $d_1 \equiv \{\ln[S(0)/KB(0,T)] - (d_y - \sigma^2/2)T\}/\sigma\sqrt{T}$ and $d_2 \equiv d_1 - \sigma\sqrt{T}$.

REPLICATION AND RISK EXPOSURE WITH MODEL MISSPECIFICATION

10.0 INTRODUCTION

I
n our discussion of hedging, we formed a portfolio that perfectly replicates the payoffs to the traded option we were trying to hedge. This portfolio is called the synthetic option. In the case of the binomial model, we constructed a lattice by specifying the asset price at each node and then deduced the value of the option at each node by backward induction. Once this was done, it was a simple exercise to determine the hedge ratio and thus construct the synthetic option. The ability to form replicating portfolios is the basis for most option models, such as the binomial model and the Black-Scholes option pricing model.

In practice, however, many things can (and do) happen that make it impossible to perfectly replicate an option. For example, a replicating portfolio using the Black-Scholes model assumes that we can continuously adjust the replicating portfolio. In practice, this simply is not possible, and given transaction costs, it is not desirable. This is one form of *model misspecification*. Another form of model misspecification occurs if the assumed stochastic process is in error. For example, in the discrete(finite)-time binomial model, the asset price takes one of two possible values at the end of each interval. In practice, the realized asset price may be different from that specified on the lattice, which leads to inaccurate hedging. This chapter studies the practical modifications of the theory necessary to incorporate these model misspecifications.

10.1 PROBLEMS WITH DELTA HEDGING

This section revisits delta hedging and examines what can go wrong. We illustrate the problems through various examples.

EXAMPLE **Problems with Delta Hedging**

We start with an example that illustrates problems with discrete-time delta hedging in a continuous-time model.

Suppose that we have written 10 European call options on a stock and we want to hedge this portfolio such that the value is insensitive to small changes

TABLE 10.1 *Constructing a Delta Neutral Position*

PART A				
INPUT DATA				
Stock price	50			
Strike price	50			
Maturity	65 days			
Volatility*	25 percent			
Discount rate**	6 percent			

*A 365-day year is assumed.
**A 360-day year is assumed.

PART B				
OPTION PRICE*				
OPTION VALUE	**DELTA**	**GAMMA**	**VEGA**	**THETA**
2.3740	0.5620	0.0747	8.3158	−0.0203

*The program Equity/Pricing European Options/No Dividends is used.

in the stock price. In a continuous-time model this is equivalent to requiring that the portfolio's delta is zero. We also want to make the portfolio self-financing. The self-financing condition is imposed so that all of the examples discussed are comparable, that is, they have identical initial investment—zero dollars. Thus we invest the proceeds from selling (writing) the options in m_s shares of the stock and B dollars in the short-term riskless asset.

To construct the hedged portfolio requires that we calculate the option's delta. This necessitates the use of an option pricing model. We will use the Black-Scholes model.[1] Pricing details are given in Table 10.1.

A standard call option is to buy 100 shares of stock. We have written 10 call options, so the proceeds are $10 \times (100 \times \$2.3740) = \$2,374$, given that the price of the option on a per share basis is \$2.3740.

The value of the initial portfolio is constructed to be zero, that is,

$$0 = -2{,}374 + m_s 50 + B. \tag{10.1}$$

Note that because we have written the 10 European call options, this represents a liability. This is why we place a minus sign in front of the total dollar value of the options.

---

[1]Because the Black-Scholes model is a continuous-time model, this position will remove all risk from the portfolio over an instant in time. Thus, given no model misspecification, we can use the model to generate the synthetic option.

The delta of the portfolio is

$$\text{Delta}_p = -10 \times (100 \times 0.5620) + m_s.$$

This equals the delta of the option position $(-10 \times (100 \times 0.5620))$ plus the delta of the stock (m_s). Given that we want the portfolio's delta to be zero, we set

$$-10 \times (100 \times 0.5620) + m_s = 0. \tag{10.2}$$

Expressions (10.1) and (10.2) then give two linear equations in two unknowns. The solutions are

$$m_s = 562$$

and

$$B = 2,374 - 562 \times 50$$
$$= -\$25,726.$$

To summarize, we have sold 10 call options, receiving $2,374. We have purchased 562 shares of stock at a cost of $28,100 and have borrowed the remainder, $25,726 (= 28,100 − 2,374), to finance the purchase of the stock. The net value of our portfolio is zero. The portfolio's delta is zero, implying that our portfolio is insensitive to small changes in the stock price. Note that we must purchase stock shares in order to hedge our position. This makes intuitive sense: If the stock price increases, it would increase the value of the call options and increase our liability. This is offset by the increase in value of our investment in the stock.

We now want to examine the performance of our hedged portfolio after a period of one day has elapsed. During this period, we incur carrying costs of $4.29, determined as follows. We have borrowed $25,726, so the carrying costs are approximately $25,726 × 0.06 × (1/360) ≈ $4.29, given a discount interest rate of 6 percent.

The value of the portfolio after a day is

$$V(1) \equiv -10 \times (100 \times c(1)) + m_s \times S(1) - (25,726 + 4.29),$$

where $S(1)$ is the stock price and $c(1)$ is the value of the option with a maturity of 64 days and strike price 50.

In Table 10.2, we examine how well our hedged portfolio performs for different possible stock values. These values are calculated using the Black-Scholes model. For example, suppose that there is no change in the stock price from $50. The value of the option will decrease because the time to expiration has de-

TABLE 10.2   *Performance of the Delta Neutral Portfolio One Day Later*

STOCK PRICE	OPTION PRICE	VALUE OF OPTION POSITION	VALUE OF STOCK POSITION	VALUE OF PORTFOLIO
48.00	1.3844	−1,384.40	26,976.00	−138.73
49.00	1.8303	−1,830.30	27,538.00	− 22.59
49.50	2.0824	−2,082.40	27,819.00	6.31
50.00	2.3536	−2,353.60	28,100.00	16.11
50.50	2.6437	−2,643.70	28,381.00	7.01
51.00	2.9521	−2,952.10	28,662.00	− 20.39
52.00	3.6208	−3,620.80	29,224.00	−127.09
Volatility*	25 percent			
Discount rate**	6 percent			

*A 365-day year is assumed.

**A 360-day year is assumed.

creased by one day. The new option price is $2.3536. Given that we have written these options, this reduces our liability. The value of our portfolio is therefore

$$-10 \times (100 \times 2.3536) + (562 \times 50) - 25,730.29$$
$$= \$16.11.$$

It is not zero.

If the stock price decreased by $0.50 to $49.50, the option value will decrease to $2.0824 due to the decrease in the stock price and the time to expiration. The value of our portfolio is then

$$-10 \times (100 \times 2.0824) + (562 \times 49.50) - 25,730.29$$
$$= \$6.31.$$

Again, it is not zero.

If the stock price increases to $50.50 from $50, the option value will increase due to the increase in stock price and decrease due to the decrease in the time to expiration. The net effect is an increase in the option value to $2.6437. The value of our portfolio is

$$-10 \times (100 \times 2.6437) + (562 \times 50.50) - 25,730.29$$
$$= \$7.01.$$

Again, it is not zero.

If the stock price changes by 2.00 to either 48.00 or to 52.00, we incur substantial losses of over $100 in each case.

Although we designed our portfolio to be delta neutral, as Table 10.2 shows, the value of our portfolio changes, even for the case in which the stock price remains unchanged at $50. Why?

The reason is that over a period of one day, we did not revise our portfolio. We designed our portfolio using a continuous-time model that assumes that we should continuously revise our portfolio. We did not, thus generating the hedging error. This is one example of model misspecification, given that in practice, portfolios can only be revised at discrete points in time.

This is not the only difficulty with our hedged portfolio. We next show that the portfolio is not self-financing for the second day's hedge as the synthetic option portfolio requires.

Suppose the stock price is $52.00 at the start of the next day. The value of the portfolio is

$$-10 \times (100 \times 3.6208) + (562 \times 52.00) - 25{,}730.29$$
$$= -\$127.09.$$

We sustained a loss.

We now want to revise our portfolio to again make it delta neutral and have zero value. The delta for the option is now 0.7017.[2] Therefore, we choose

$$m_s = -10 \times (100 \times 0.7017)$$
$$= 702$$

and

$$B = \$3{,}620.80 - 702 \times 52$$
$$= -\$32{,}883.20.$$

By construction, the value of the rebalanced portfolio is now zero, that is,

$$-10 \times (100 \times 3.6208) + 702 \times 52 - 32{,}883.20$$
$$= 0.$$

However, we lost $127.09 prior to rebalancing. In order to rebalance our portfolio we must borrow the amount $127.09. This implies that our portfolio is no longer self-financing. ■

Up to this point, we have assumed that the other parameters that affect the option value—the volatility and the rate of interest—have remained constant. In practice, volatility and interest rates do change. We now investigate what difficulties changes

[2]This value is calculated using the program Equity/Pricing European Options/No Dividends.

in these parameters cause for our hedged portfolio. Again, we illustrate the problems through examples.

EXAMPLE

Change in Volatility

Our second example illustrates the problems caused by changing volatilities. The Black-Scholes model assumes the volatility is constant, hence this is another model misspecification.

TABLE 10.3   *Changes in the Hedged Portfolio Due to Volatility and Discount Rate Changes*

		PART A VOLATILITY INCREASE		
STOCK PRICE	OPTION PRICE	VALUE OF OPTION POSITION	VALUE OF STOCK POSITION	VALUE OF PORTFOLIO
48.00	1.7770	−1,777.00	26,976.00	−531.29
49.50	2.4950	−2,495.00	27,819.00	−406.29
50.00	2.7665	−2,766.50	28,100.00	−396.79
50.50	3.0538	−3,053.80	28,381.00	−403.09
52.00	4.0054	−4,005.40	29,224.00	−511.69
Volatility*	30 percent			
Discount rate**	6 percent			
Maturity	64 days			

		PART B DISCOUNT RATE DECREASE		
STOCK PRICE	OPTION PRICE	VALUE OF OPTION POSITION	VALUE OF STOCK POSITION	VALUE OF PORTFOLIO
48.00	1.3521	−1,352.10	26,976.00	−106.39
49.50	2.0398	−2,039.80	27,819.00	48.91
50.00	2.3077	−2,307.70	28,100.00	62.01
50.50	2.5944	−2,594.40	28,381.00	56.31
52.00	3.5620	−3,562.00	29,224.00	− 68.29
Volatility*	25 percent			
Discount rate**	5 percent			
Maturity	64 days			

*A 365-day year is assumed.

**A 360-day year is assumed.

Suppose that the volatility increases to 30 percent from 25 percent. The effect of this change upon our hedged portfolio is shown in Table 10.3, Part A.

An increase in volatility increases the value of the option, and this increases the value of our liability. In all cases, our portfolio incurs substantial losses. This loss is due to "volatility" risk, a well-known hazard. ∎

EXAMPLE   **Change in Interest Rates**

Our third example illustrates the problems caused by changing interest rates. Again, the Black-Scholes model assumes that interest rates are unchanging, another model misspecification.

Suppose now that the interest rate changes from 6 percent to 5 percent. The volatility of the stock is set at 25 percent. This reduction in the interest rate causes a decrease in the value of the option (see Table 10.3, Part B).

For small price changes, the value of our portfolio increases, though for large price changes the value of our portfolio is negative. This risk is not as large as that due to changing volatilities. For this reason it is often overlooked in practice, at least for short-dated options. ∎

In all these examples, we have considered the simple situation of writing a number of options and then trying to hedge our exposure. We used the Black-Scholes model, which is a continuous-time model. Ideally, if we could continuously revise our portfolio—and given no model misspecification—we could perfectly hedge. But in practice we can only revise our portfolio on a discrete-time basis. This implies the first type of model misspecification. Parameters such as volatility and interest rates, which Black-Scholes assumes to be constant, can also change over the life of the option. Changes in these parameters are the other type of model misspecification that also creates errors in our hedged portfolio.

10.2 A GENERAL APPROACH

We now formalize our previous discussion on hedging using the Black-Scholes model. We start by describing the general problem and then provide examples, which has the advantage of first identifying the issues that have to be addressed. It has the disadvantage that those with limited mathematical backgrounds may be discouraged from pursuing the topic. If you are one of these readers, please do not give up. We give many examples in the following sections. You may want to read those sections first and then come back to this section.

Consider a portfolio of derivatives written on some asset with price S. These derivatives could include forwards, futures, options on the underlying asset, options on futures, options on forwards, and the underlying asset itself. For example, in the previous section, the portfolio contained call options, shares of the underlying asset, and

bonds. Although we are not restricting the types of instruments, we are assuming that the derivatives are written on the same underlying asset.

Now, we know that the value of a derivative depends on the asset price, S; the time to maturity, $T_j - t$, where T_j is the maturity date for the jth derivative and t is today's date; the volatility, σ; and the domestic and foreign interest rates, r and r_f, respectively.[3] Combined, the value of the portfolio will also depend upon all these variables. We can write this in the mathematical form as

$$V = V(t, S, \sigma, r, r_f),\qquad(10.3)$$

where the left side represents the value of the portfolio and the right side identifies the variables upon which it depends.[4]

Let us now study how the value of this portfolio changes as time, asset price, volatility, and interest rates change. From calculus, we can use a Taylor's series expansion to answer this question:[5]

$$\Delta V = \frac{\partial V}{\partial t}\Delta + \frac{\partial V}{\partial S}\Delta S + \frac{\partial V}{\partial \sigma}\Delta\sigma + \frac{\partial V}{\partial r}\Delta r + \frac{\partial V}{\partial r_f}\Delta r_f$$
$$+ \frac{1}{2}\frac{\partial^2 V}{\partial S^2}(\Delta S)^2 + \cdots.\qquad(10.4)$$

Expression (10.4) is a statement about the change in the value of the portfolio caused by changes in the underlying variables. The various terms are: Δ is a change in time; ΔS is a change in the stock price; $\Delta\sigma$ is a change in the volatility; Δr is a change in the domestic interest rate; and Δr_f is a change in the foreign interest rate. The three dots indicate that higher order terms are excluded.

By generalizing some of the definitions we introduced in Chapter 8, we can write Expression (10.4) in a less intimidating way:

$$\Delta V = \text{Theta} \times \Delta + \text{Delta} \times \Delta S + \text{Vega} \times \Delta\sigma + \text{Rho}D \times \Delta r$$
$$+ \text{Rho}F \times \Delta r_f + \tfrac{1}{2} \times \text{Gamma} \times (\Delta S)^2 + \cdots.\qquad(10.5)$$

The left side is the change in the value of the portfolio, and the right side decomposes this change into changes in the underlying variables. The different Greek terms are defined in a slightly more general way than the definitions given earlier in Chapter 8, where we only discussed call and put options. In this chapter, we discuss portfolios of different types of instruments. We therefore need to extend the definitions of these Greek terms for the more general situation.

---

[3]We consider the general situation where the underlying asset may be a foreign currency, hence the inclusion of the foreign rate of interest.

[4]The value of a derivative, say the jth derivative, depends on the time to maturity $T_j - t$, where T_j is the maturity date of the derivative and t is today's date. Note that T_j is fixed; what changes is t. In (10.3), we have omitted reference to T_j.

[5]We are assuming that the function V is infinitely differentiable in all its arguments. We are also assuming that the Taylor's series is convergent.

Theta

$$\text{Theta} \equiv \frac{\partial V}{\partial t} = \frac{\text{Dollar change in } V}{\text{Decrease in the time to expiration}}$$

A negative theta implies price decay or a "negative bias." A positive theta implies a position that increases in value with the passage of time. The partial derivative has the interpretation that we are considering these changes on the value V, with everything else constant.

Delta

$$\text{Delta} \equiv \frac{\partial V}{\partial S} = \frac{\text{Dollar change in } V}{\text{Change in the dollar value of the underlying asset}}$$

If delta is positive (negative), an increase in the value of the underlying asset will result in a positive (negative) change in the value of the portfolio, everything else being constant. We have already discussed the delta in previous chapters.

Vega[6]

$$\text{Vega} \equiv \frac{\partial V}{\partial \sigma} = \frac{\text{Dollar change in } V}{\text{Change in the volatility}}$$

If vega is positive (negative), an increase in volatility will increase (decrease) the dollar value of the portfolio, everything else being constant.

Rho

$$\text{Rho}D \equiv \frac{\partial V}{\partial r} = \frac{\text{Dollar change in } V}{\text{Change in the domestic interest rate}}$$

$$\text{Rho}F \equiv \frac{\partial V}{\partial r_f} = \frac{\text{Dollar change in } V}{\text{Change in the foreign interest rate}}$$

If rho$D$ or rho$F$ is positive (negative), an increase in the interest rate will increase (decrease) the dollar value of the portfolio, everything else being constant.

Gamma

$$\text{Gamma} \equiv \frac{\partial^2 V}{\partial S^2} = \frac{\partial}{\partial S}(\text{Delta})$$

$$= \frac{\text{Change in Delta}}{\text{Change in the dollar value of the underlying asset}}$$

---

[6]This is sometimes referred to as kappa.

If gamma is positive (negative), an increase in the value of the underlying asset will result in a positive (negative) change in the delta of the portfolio, everything else being constant. The gamma is often thought to be the most important of the "Greeks" after the delta, because it indicates how the delta changes if the stock moves in a fashion different than expected.

EXAMPLE   **Use of Expression (10.5)**

A numerical example will illustrate how to use the decomposition of a portfolio's value change given in Expression (10.5).

Consider the call option described in Table 10.1. Now consider the value of the option after the passage of one day. Option values are given in Table 10.2. We want to consider three cases.

Suppose the stock price has increased to 50.50 from 50.00 and the interest rate and volatility have remained unchanged. We have $\Delta S = 0.50$ and $\Delta = 1$, so that from (10.5) the change in the value of the option is

$$\Delta c = \text{Theta} \times \Delta + \text{Delta} \times \Delta S + \tfrac{1}{2} \times \text{Gamma} \times (\Delta S)^2 + \cdots . \quad (10.6)$$

From Tables 10.1 and 10.2, the change in the option price is

$$\Delta c = 2.6437 - 2.3740 = 0.2697.$$

From the right side of Expression (10.6) we have

$$
\begin{aligned}
\text{Theta} \times \Delta &= & 0.0203 \times 1 &= -0.0203 \\
\text{Delta} \times \Delta S &= & 0.5620 \times 0.50 &= 0.2810 \\
\tfrac{1}{2} \times \text{Gamma} \times (\Delta S)^2 &= 0.5 \times 0.0747 \times (0.50)^2 &= 0.0093 \\
& & \text{Total} &= 0.2700
\end{aligned}
$$

The two values differ by only 0.0003 ($= 0.2700 - 0.2697$). This difference is due to the missing higher order terms.

The net sum of the first two terms, theta and delta, explain most of the change in the option price. For small changes in the stock price, the contribution of the gamma term is relatively small compared to the other terms. This is a general result and is due to the fact that for small ΔS, the term $0.50(\Delta S)^2$ is much smaller than the first two terms. For example, if $\Delta S = 0.50$, then $0.50(\Delta S)^2 = 0.125$.

If the stock price had increased to 52.00 from 50.00, the story is more complicated, because gamma now begins to play an important role. In this case, the change in the option price is

$$\Delta c = 3.6208 - 2.3740 = 1.2468.$$

It is the value of the left side of Expression (10.6); the right side of (10.6) is

$$
\begin{array}{lll}
\text{Theta} \times \Delta = & -0.0203 \times 1 = & -0.0203 \\
\text{Delta} \times \Delta S = & 0.5620 \times 2.00 = & 1.1240 \\
\tfrac{1}{2} \times \text{Gamma} \times (\Delta S)^2 = & 0.5 \times 0.0747 \times (2.0)^2 = & 0.1494 \\
& \text{Total} = & 1.2531
\end{array}
$$

The two values now differ by 0.0063 (= 1.2531 − 1.2468), which is an order of magnitude greater than in the last case. The time decay of the option is more than offset by the magnitude of the gamma term.

The last case we consider is when there is no change in the stock price but volatility increases by 5 percent, from 25 percent to 30 percent. From Table 10.3, the change in the option value is

$$
\Delta c = 2.7665 - 2.3740 = 0.3925.
$$

In this case the equation becomes

$$
\Delta c = \text{Theta} \times \Delta + \text{Vega} \times \Delta \sigma + \cdots,
$$

given $\Delta S = 0$. The right side of this expression is

$$
\begin{array}{lll}
\text{Theta} \times \Delta = & -0.0203 \times 1 = & -0.0203 \\
\text{Vega} \times \Delta \sigma = & 8.3158 \times 0.05 = & 0.4158 \\
& \text{Total} = & 0.3955
\end{array}
$$

The left and right sides differ by 0.003 (= 0.3955 − 0.3925). The change due to the vega, for no stock price change, is similar to the error for either of the previous cases. This is called "volatility" risk. ∎

10.3 DELTA HEDGING

We now apply the analysis of the previous section to the problem of delta hedging an option. We can represent the date-0 value of our portfolio as

$$
V(0) \equiv n_1 c + n_2 S + B, \tag{10.7}
$$

where $V(0)$ is the current value of our portfolio, c represents the value of an option, and we have n_1 options. S is the current stock price per share and we have n_2 shares. Finally, B is the dollar amount invested in the short-term riskless asset.

If $n_1 > 0$ this implies that we have purchased the option, and if $n_1 < 0$ this implies that we have sold or written the option.

Given Expression (10.7), taking the partial derivative of both sides with respect to the stock price generates

$$\frac{\partial V}{\partial S} = n_1 \frac{\partial c}{\partial S} + n_2 \tag{10.8}$$

or

$$\text{Delta}_v = n_1 \text{Delta}_c + n_2,$$

given that the delta for the stock is one.

If the delta of the portfolio is positive (negative), then an increase in the value of the underlying asset will increase (decrease) the value of the portfolio. This leads to the following terminology:

$\text{Delta}_v > 0 \Rightarrow$ bullish
$\text{Delta}_v = 0 \Rightarrow$ delta neutral
$\text{Delta}_v < 0 \Rightarrow$ bearish.

A positive delta is a bullish position on the underlying asset, a zero delta is a neutral position on the underlying asset, and a negative delta is a bearish position on the underlying asset.

If we require the portfolio to be self-financing at date 0, we also add

$$V(0) = 0 = n_1 c + n_2 S + B. \tag{10.9}$$

This condition is imposed if we want to take a portfolio position without putting up an initial investment.

The Delta Neutral Position

It is possible to make the portfolio insensitive to small changes in the value of the underlying asset by constructing the portfolio to have a zero delta. With this idea in mind, using Expression (10.8), we require

$$0 = n_1 \text{Delta}_c + n_2.$$

In this case, Expression (10.5) becomes

$$\Delta V = \text{Theta} \times \Delta + \text{Vega} \times \Delta\sigma + \text{Rho}D \times \Delta r + \text{Rho}F \times \Delta r_f$$
$$+ \tfrac{1}{2} \times \text{Gamma} \times (\Delta S)^2. \tag{10.10}$$

The term involving the delta is zero and drops out. The hope in delta hedging is that all the remaining terms are small.[7]

---

[7]In the continuous-time Black-Scholes model, the delta neutral portfolio is held only an instant. Over an instant the theta and gamma terms are non-random. In the Black-Scholes model $\Delta\sigma = \Delta r = \Delta r_f \equiv 0$. Hence a delta neutral portfolio is riskless. This does not hold over finite time intervals.

EXAMPLE

Delta Neutral Portfolio

Suppose that we have written 10 call options. The pricing information is given in Table 10.1. We want to construct a portfolio to hedge our option position, implying that the delta of the portfolio must be zero. The portfolio is also designed to be self-financing, which is done so that we can make comparisons across the examples by keeping the initial investment the same—zero dollars.

In this example, $n_1 = -10$, and substituting into Expression (10.9) gives the zero initial investment condition

$$0 = -10 \times (100 \times 2.3740) + n_2 \times 50 + B.$$

For the portfolio to be delta neutral, using Expression (10.8) we have

$$0 = -10 \times (100 \times 0.5620) + n_2.$$

We must pick n_2 and B to satisfy these two conditions. Therefore,

$$n_2 = 562$$

and

$$B = -25,726.$$

The portfolio is now delta neutral. It is insensitive to small changes in the stock price, as demonstrated in Table 10.2. The portfolio's gamma, vega, and theta are given by

$$
\begin{aligned}
\text{Portfolio's gamma} &= -10 \times (100 \times 0.0747) = -74.70 \\
\text{Portfolio's vega} &= -10 \times (100 \times 8.3158) = -8315.80 \\
\text{Portfolio's theta} &= -10 \times [100 \times (-0.0203)] + B \times (r/360) \\
&= 20.30 - 25,726 \times (0.06/360) \\
&= 20.30 - 4.29 = 16.01.
\end{aligned}
$$

Note that the portfolio's theta is affected by the amount invested in the riskless asset. ■

In the preceding example, we know from Table 10.2 that for large price changes the value of the portfolio will be negative because the portfolio's gamma is negative. In Table 10.2, for intermediate price changes the effect is ambiguous because there are two changes being considered in Table 10.2.

Table 10.2 examines the performance of the delta neutral portfolio *one day later* for different possible stock prices. As time is changing the portfolio's theta is positive. If there is no price change, the change in the value of the portfolio is $16.11, which is very

close to the portfolio's theta of $16.01. If there are changes in the stock price, the portfolio's negative gamma counteracts the portfolio's positive theta. Combined, for small stock price changes, the change is positive. For intermediate stock price changes, the change is ambiguous. For larger stock price changes, however, the gamma dominates.

Formalization

We now formalize the analysis of the previous section to the problem of delta hedging an option.

Let V_1 represent the value of the option that we are hedging and n_1 represent the number of options. If $n_1 > 0$ it implies that we have purchased the option, and if $n_1 < 0$ it implies that we have sold or written the option. For the moment, we want to keep our discussion general, so V_1 could represent either a call option or a put option.

To form a hedged portfolio we want to use two other securities with values V_2 and V_3, respectively. For example, the second security could be the underlying stock and the third security could be a riskless bond. Alternatively, V_2 and V_3 could denote the values of two other different options written on the same stock.

The date-0 value of the delta hedged portfolio is

$$V(0) \equiv n_1 V_1 + n_2 V_2 + n_3 V_3, \tag{10.11}$$

where n_2 represents the number of units of the second security and n_3 the number of units of the third security.

To be delta neutral we require

$$0 = n_1 \text{Delta}_1 + n_2 \text{Delta}_2 + n_3 \text{Delta}_3. \tag{10.12}$$

Note that if our only requirement is to be delta neutral, then we only need one other security, the value of which depends on the value of the underlying stock. The third security is needed only if we want the portfolio to be self-financing at date 0, in which case we would require Expression (10.11) to be identically zero.

EXAMPLE   **Delta Neutral Portfolio Revisited**

This example illustrates the construction of a delta neutral portfolio that is not self-financing.

Suppose that we want to make our portfolio delta neutral *without* any requirement that it be self-financing. The value of the portfolio is

$$V(0) = -10 \times (100 \times 2.3740) + n_2 \times 50.$$

To be delta neutral implies that

$$0 = -10 \times (100 \times 0.5620) + n_2.$$

Therefore,

$$n_2 = 562.$$

The value of the delta neutral portfolio is

$$V(0) = -10 \times (100 \times 2.3740) + 562 \times 50$$
$$= 25,726.$$ ∎

If we require our portfolio to be self-financing, then as mentioned earlier, we also require that

$$V(0) = 0 = n_1 V_1 + n_2 V_2 + n_3 V_3. \tag{10.13}$$

Using Expressions (10.12) and (10.13), we can solve for n_2 and n_3, given that n_1, V_1, V_2, V_3, Delta_1, Delta_2, and Delta_3 are specified.

For some purposes, delta hedging a portfolio leaves too much risk present with respect to large price changes. The next section discusses how to hedge this additional risk.

10.4 DELTA-GAMMA HEDGING

We now discuss delta and gamma hedging a portfolio. If we have designed a portfolio to be delta neutral and the portfolio's gamma is negative, large changes in the stock price will still cause the portfolio to lose money. Recall that the gamma is a measure of the change of delta, given a change in the price of the underlying stock. The larger the absolute value of gamma, the larger will be the change in delta, and this may cause problems with delta hedging in a market characterized by rapid price changes. This arises because a delta neutral portfolio is constructed under the implicit assumption that the delta remains fixed. One way to avoid these types of problems is to design the hedge portfolio to be both delta neutral and gamma neutral.

In designing a self-financing portfolio to be delta neutral, we need two assets. If we add the requirement that the hedged portfolio must also be gamma neutral, then we must add a third asset to the portfolio. An example illustrates this complication.

EXAMPLE **A Delta Neutral and Gamma Neutral Portfolio**

Suppose that we have written 10 call options. Pricing information is the same as that given in Table 10.1 and is reproduced in Table 10.4, Part A.

We want to construct a self-financing portfolio that is delta neutral and gamma neutral. In constructing our portfolio, we will use n_2 shares of stock and n_3 call options written on the same stock. These options have different matu-

TABLE 10.4 *Constructing a Delta-Gamma Neutral Position*

PART A INPUT DATA		
	OPTION TO BE HEDGED	**OPTION 1**
Exercise price	50	55
Maturity (days)	65	100
Type	Call	Call
Stock price	50	
Volatility*	25 percent	
Discount rate**	6 percent	

   *A 365-day year is assumed.
 **A 360-day year is assumed.

PART B OPTION PRICES*					
	PRICE	**DELTA**	**GAMMA**	**VEGA**	**THETA**
Option to be hedged	2.3740	0.5620	0.0747	8.3158	−0.0203
Option 1	1.1466	0.2965	0.0529	9.0510	−0.0136

*The program Equity/Pricing European Options/No Dividends is used.

rity and strike prices than those that we are hedging. Pricing information is given in Table 10.4, Part A. We will also invest B dollars in the riskless asset.

To be self-financing, the date-0 value of the hedged portfolio must be zero. Using the information from Table 10.4 gives

$$0 = -10 \times (100 \times 2.3740) + n_2 \times 50 + n_3 \times 1.1466 + B.$$

To be delta neutral implies

$$0 = -10 \times (100 \times 0.5620) + n_2 + n_3 \times 0.2965.$$

To be gamma neutral implies

$$0 = -10 \times (100 \times 0.0747) + n_2 \times 0 + n_3 \times 0.0529,$$

given that gamma for a stock is zero.

Solving this last equation for n_3 gives

$$n_3 = 74.7/0.0529$$
$$= 1{,}412.10.$$

Solving the second equation for n_2 yields

$$n_2 = 562.0 - n_3 \times 0.2965$$
$$= 143.31.$$

Solving the first equation for B produces

$$B = 2,374.00 - n_2 \times 50 - n_3 \times 1.1466$$
$$= -6,410.75.$$

The portfolio's vega and theta are given by

$$\text{Portfolio's vega} = -10 \times (100 \times 8.3158) + n_3 \times 9.0510$$
$$= 4,465.11$$
$$\text{Portfolio's theta} = -10 \times [100 \times (-0.0203)] + n_3 \times (-0.0136)$$
$$+ B \times (r/360)$$
$$= 20.30 - 19.20 - 1.07$$
$$= 0.03.$$

In Table 10.5, Part A, we examine the value of the delta-gamma neutral portfolio for a range of possible stock prices one day after the portfolio was formed. If the stock price is $48, the value of the portfolio is −$7.62. If the stock price is $52, the value of the portfolio is $7.32. The portfolio's value is still not zero, but these results should be compared to those given in Table 10.2. In comparison, it is seen that the delta-gamma neutral portfolio is far less sensitive to changes in the stock price.

TABLE 10.5   *Performance of the Delta-Gamma Neutral Portfolio One Day Later*

PART A NO CHANGE IN VOLATILITY							
Stock price	48.00	49.00	49.50	50.00	50.50	51.00	52.00
Value of portfolio	−7.62	0.28	0.73	0.06	−0.71	−0.50	7.32
Volatility*	25 percent						

PART B VOLATILITY INCREASE							
Stock price	48.00	49.00	49.50	50.00	50.50	51.00	52.00
Value of portfolio	125.54	184.30	212.80	241.47	270.92	301.79	370.39
Volatility*	30 percent						

*A 365-day year is assumed.

In Table 10.5, Part B, it is assumed that during the period of one day volatility has also increased to 30 percent from 25 percent. Two points should be noted: The value of the delta-gamma neutral portfolio increases, and the changes are significant. If volatility had decreased, the value of the portfolio would have decreased. This is to be expected, given that the portfolio's vega is positive. This shows that even a delta and gamma neutral portfolio still has substantial volatility risk. ∎

Formalization

We now formalize the previous section's analysis on delta and gamma neutral portfolio construction. The formalization involves little more than replacing numbers with symbols.

Let V_1 represent the value of the option we are hedging and n_1 the number of options held. We are going to use three different instruments to form our portfolio. The date-0 value of our portfolio is

$$V(0) = n_1V_1 + n_2V_2 + n_3V_3 + n_4V_4, \tag{10.14}$$

where V_j represents the value of jth instrument that we use to construct our portfolio, and n_j represents the number of units of the jth instrument for $j = 2, 3, 4$.

For the portfolio to be delta neutral, we require that

$$0 = n_1\text{Delta}_1 + n_2\text{Delta}_2 + n_3\text{Delta}_3 + n_4\text{Delta}_4. \tag{10.15}$$

For the portfolio to be gamma neutral, we require that

$$0 = n_1\text{Gamma}_1 + n_2\text{Gamma}_2 + n_3\text{Gamma}_3 + n_4\text{Gamma}_4. \tag{10.16}$$

For the portfolio to be self-financing, we require that

$$0 = n_1V_1 + n_2V_2 + n_3V_3 + n_4V_4. \tag{10.17}$$

Given Expressions (10.15), (10.16), and (10.17), we can solve for n_2, n_3, and n_4, given n_1. We have three linear equations in three unknowns: n_2, n_3, and n_4. It is usually a straightforward exercise to determine the solutions for n_2, n_3, and n_4. For example, many spreadsheet computer programs contain procedures that solve these types of linear equations.

Theta Neutral

Suppose that we construct our portfolio to be delta neutral, gamma neutral, and self-financing. In this case, our portfolio will also be theta neutral. Why? We know from Expression (8.28) of Chapter 8 that for any traded portfolio V, the following equation holds:

$$\tfrac{1}{2}\sigma^2S^2\text{Gamma}_v + rS\text{Delta}_v - rV = \text{Theta}_v. \tag{10.18}$$

For a date-0 self-financing portfolio,

$$V(0) = 0. \tag{10.19}$$

For a delta neutral portfolio,

$$\text{Delta}_v = 0. \tag{10.20}$$

For a gamma neutral portfolio,

$$\text{Gamma}_v = 0. \tag{10.21}$$

Therefore, substituting Expressions (10.19), (10.20), and (10.21) into (10.18) gives the result

$$\text{Theta}_v = 0. \tag{10.22}$$

In the previous example, the theta for the portfolio is almost zero. In the absence of round-off error, it would be zero.

10.5 DELTA-GAMMA-VEGA HEDGING

Let us now study how to augment the hedging portfolio to be not only delta neutral and gamma neutral but vega neutral as well. The hope is that vega hedging will remove volatility risk. The need for this additional risk reduction can be seen in Table 10.5, Part B. The value of the delta-gamma neutral portfolio is seen to be very sensitive to changes in the volatility.

Vega is a measure of the change in the value of an option given a change in the volatility. We can construct our portfolio to have a vega of zero so that it is also insensitive to small changes in volatility. Recall that in designing a self-financing portfolio to be delta-gamma neutral, we need three assets. If we add the requirement that the portfolio is vega neutral, we must add a fourth asset to the portfolio. An example will illustrate this procedure.

EXAMPLE   **Delta-Gamma-Vega Neutral Portfolio**

Suppose that we have written 10 call options. Pricing information is the same as that given in Table 10.1 and is reproduced in Table 10.6, Part A.

We want to construct a self-financing portfolio that is delta neutral, gamma neutral, and vega neutral. In constructing our portfolio, we will use n_2 shares of stock and two different call options written on the same stock. These options are described in Table 10.6, Part A. We will also invest B dollars in the riskless asset.

TABLE 10.6 *Constructing a Delta-Gamma-Vega Neutral Position*

PART A INPUT DATA			
	OPTION TO BE HEDGED	**OPTION 1**	**OPTION 2**
Exercise price	50	55	55
Maturity (days)	65	100	30
Type	Call	Call	Call
Stock price	50		
Volatility*	25 percent		
Discount rate**	6 percent		

*A 365-day year is assumed.

**A 360-day year is assumed.

PART B*					
	PRICE	**DELTA**	**GAMMA**	**VEGA**	**THETA**
Option to be hedged	2.3740	0.5620	0.0747	8.3158	−0.0203
Option 1	1.1466	0.2965	0.0529	9.0510	−0.0136
Option 2	0.1857	0.1105	0.0526	2.7037	−0.0122

*The program Equity/Pricing European Options/No Dividends is used.

To be self-financing, the date-0 value of the hedged portfolio must be zero. Using the information from Tables 10.1 and 10.6 gives

$$0 = -10 \times (100 \times 2.3740) + n_2 50 + n_3 \times 1.1466 + n_4 \times 0.1857 + B.$$

To be delta neutral implies

$$0 = -10 \times (100 \times 0.5620) + n_2 + n_3 \times 0.2965 + n_4 \times 0.1105.$$

To be gamma neutral implies

$$0 = -10 \times (100 \times 0.0747) + n_3 \times 0.0529 + n_4 \times 0.0526.$$

To be vega neutral implies

$$0 = -10 \times (100 \times 8.3158) + n_3 \times 9.0510 + n_4 \times 2.7037.$$

Using the last two equations gives

$$n_3 = 706.92$$

and

$$n_4 = 709.20.$$

Substituting into the second equation gives

$$n_2 = 274.03.$$

Substituting into the first equation gives

$$B = -12,269.83.$$

In Table 10.7, Part A, we examine the value of the delta-gamma-vega neutral portfolio for a range of possible stock prices one day after the portfolio was formed. If the stock price is $48, the value of the portfolio is $-$16.35. If the stock price is $52, the value of the portfolio is $15.97. You should compare these results to those in Table 10.2 and Table 10.5, Part A.

A comparison of Table 10.5, Part A, and Table 10.7, Part A, reveals an interesting observation. The hedging performance of the delta-gamma-vega neu-

TABLE 10.7   *Performance of the Delta-Gamma-Vega Neutral Portfolio*

PART A NO CHANGE IN VOLATILITY							
Stock price	48.00	49.00	49.50	50.00	50.50	51.00	52.00
Value of portfolio	−16.35	0.58	1.58	0.13	−1.55	−1.10	15.97
Volatility*	25 percent						
PART B VOLATILITY INCREASE							
Stock price	48.00	49.00	49.50	50.00	50.50	51.00	52.00
Value of portfolio	−97.37	−37.64	−9.43	19.64	51.13	86.62	175.87
Volatility*	30 percent						
*A 365-day year is assumed.							

tral portfolio is not necessarily superior to that of the delta-gamma neutral portfolio for hedging changes in the stock price.

In Table 10.7, Part B, it is assumed that during the period of a day, volatility has increased to 30 percent from 25 percent. In comparison to Table 10.5, Part B, the hedging performance has improved. If the stock price remains unchanged at $50.00, the value of the portfolio is $19.64. In Table 10.5, part B, it was $241.47. Given that the objective is to make the portfolio insensitive to changes in volatility, the delta-gamma-vega neutral portfolio greatly enhances our ability to hedge against changes in volatility. ■

Formalization

Let us formalize the construction of a delta-gamma-vega neutral portfolio. The formalization involves little more than replacing numbers in the previous example with symbols.

Using the same notation as in Expression (10.14), the date-0 value of our portfolio is

$$V(0) \equiv n_1 V_1 + n_2 V_2 + n_3 V_3 + n_4 V_4 + n_5 V_5. \tag{10.23}$$

Note that in comparison to Expression (10.14), we have added an extra instrument in order to make our portfolio vega neutral.

For the portfolio to be delta neutral, we require that

$$0 = n_1 \text{Delta}_1 + n_2 \text{Delta}_2 + n_3 \text{Delta}_3 + n_4 \text{Delta}_4 + n_5 \text{Delta}_5. \tag{10.24}$$

For the portfolio to be gamma neutral, we require that

$$0 = n_1 \text{Gamma}_1 + n_2 \text{Gamma}_2 + n_3 \text{Gamma}_3 + n_4 \text{Gamma}_4 + n_5 \text{Gamma}_5. \tag{10.25}$$

For the portfolio to be vega neutral, we require that

$$0 = n_1 Vega_1 + n_2 Vega_2 + n_3 Vega_3 + n_4 Vega_4 + n_5 Vega_5. \tag{10.26}$$

For the portfolio to be self-financing at date 0, we require that

$$0 = n_1 V_1 + n_2 V_2 + n_3 V_3 + n_4 V_4 + n_5 V_5. \tag{10.27}$$

Given that we know n_1, we have four linear equations in four unknowns: n_2, n_3, n_4, and n_5. It is usually a straightforward exercise to solve these equations and determine the values of n_2, n_3, n_4, and n_5.

10.6 MODEL MISSPECIFICATION

We have shown how to construct a portfolio to be delta neutral, gamma neutral, and vega neutral. It may seem that we have a procedure to completely hedge an option position. Unfortunately, this is not the case. In all of the examples that we have given, we have used the Black-Scholes model to compute the deltas, gammas, vegas, and so on. The Black-Scholes model is based on the assumption that volatility is constant over the life of the option, interest rates are constant over the life of the option, and the probability distribution of the stock price at the maturity date of the option is lognormal. All of these assumptions are simply approximations of reality. Interest rates are not constant, volatility is not constant, and the probability distribution for the stock price is not lognormal. Consequently, the model that we use for pricing the option and for hedging is misspecified. What this means is that while we may construct a portfolio to be delta neutral, gamma neutral, and vega neutral, its value will still change with small changes in the stock price and/or small changes in volatility.

Hedging errors are not the only negative consequence of a misspecified model. Given a misspecified model, our pricing will also be in error. Indeed, if we use the model to indicate what price to charge for an option, then this price will not compensate us for the risk we have to bear. One way around this pricing error is to use implied volatilities rather than historic volatilities in valuing the options. The implied volatility will partially incorporate the pricing error at date 0. It will not, however, overcome the hedging errors discussed earlier.

These limitations of the Black-Scholes model are well known. Option pricing models exist that relax the assumption of lognormality and incorporate the effects of stochastic interest rates and stochastic volatility. However, even these more complex models may be misspecified.[8] Hence this is the arena of current research in the pricing and hedging of options.

10.7 SUMMARY

In this chapter, we have discussed replication and risk exposure with model misspecification. If we use a continuous-time model, such as the Black-Scholes model, model misspecification will occur when hedging is done at discrete points in time. For both continuous-time models and discrete-time models, such as the binomial model, model misspecification occurs because the assumptions used in constructing the model are violated. We discussed different hedging strategies that are designed to reduce the effects of model misspecification. The effectiveness of these strategies depends on the causes of the model misspecification.

---

[8]The issue of model uncertainty is discussed in Dengler and Jarrow (1996), Melino and Turnbull (1995), and Jacquier and Jarrow (1998, in press).

REFERENCES

Dengler, H., and R. Jarrow, 1996. "Option Pricing Using a Binomial Model with Random Time Steps (A Formal Model of Gamma Hedging)." *Review of Derivatives Research* 1, 107–138.

Jacquier, E., and R. Jarrow, 1998. "Dynamic Evaluation of Contingent Claims Models (An Analysis of Model Error)." *Journal of Econometrics*, in press.

Melino, A., and S. M. Turnbull, 1995. "Misspecification and the Pricing and Hedging of Long Term Foreign Currency Options." *Journal of International Money and Finance* 14, 373–393.

QUESTIONS

Question 1

A financial institution has written 10 European put options and wants to hedge this portfolio to small changes in the stock price. The contract size is for 100 shares. Using the information in Table 10.1:

a) Describe the hedged position using the stock and money market account.
b) Examine the performance of this hedge one day later by completing the following table.

STOCK PRICE	OPTION PRICE	VALUE OF OPTION POSITION	VALUE OF STOCK POSITION	VALUE OF HEDGED* PORTFOLIO
48.00	2.8511			
49.00	2.2969			
49.50	2.0490			
50.00	1.8203			
50.50	1.6104			
51.00	1.4187			
52.00	1.0874			

*Include the cost of carry.

Question 2

In Question 1, suppose that one day later the volatility has changed to 28 percent. Complete the following table. How do your values compare to Question 1?

STOCK PRICE	OPTION PRICE	VALUE OF OPTION POSITION	VALUE OF STOCK POSITION	VALUE OF HEDGED* PORTFOLIO
48.00	3.0861			
49.00	2.5424			
49.50	2.2966			
50.00	2.0680			
50.50	1.8561			
51.00	1.6607			
52.00	1.3167			

*Include the cost of carry.

Question 3

You are given the following information about a European call option.

Maturity	45 days
Volatility*	25 percent
Discount rate**	5.25 percent
Stock price	50.00
Strike price	52.50

*Assuming a 365-day year.
**Assuming a 360-day year.

a) Calculate the value of the option and its delta, gamma, and theta.
b) Suppose that one day later the stock price is $52.50. Calculate the value of the option.
c) Can you explain the change in the option value given its delta, gamma, and theta? Use the program Equity/Pricing European Options/No Dividends.

Question 4

A financial institution has written 10 European call options with a strike price of $65 and maturity of 56 days. The contract size is for 100 shares of stock. The institution wants to construct a hedged position using European put options (written on the same stock) and the money market account. The strike price of the put options is $55 and a maturity of 35 days. You are given the following information.

Stock price	$60
Volatility*	30 percent
35-day discount rate*	5.25 percent
56-day discount rate**	5.40 percent

*A 365-day year is assumed.
**A 360-day year is assumed.

a) Describe the construction of the hedged portfolio. Round off your position in the European put to the nearest integer. Use the program Equity/Pricing European Options/No Dividends.

b) By design, the delta of the hedged portfolio is zero. What is the gamma of the hedged portfolio?

c) One day later the stock price may change. Examine the performance of the hedged portfolio by completing the following table.

STOCK PRICE	VALUE OF CALL* POSITION	VALUE OF PUT* OPTION	VALUE OF HEDGED** PORTFOLIO
57			
58			
59			
60			
61			
62			
63			

*Calculate these values using the program Equity/Pricing European Options/No Dividends.
**Include the cost of carry.

d) Is the performance of the hedged portfolio consistent with the gamma of the hedged portfolio? Justify your answer.

Question 5

Referring to Question 4, suppose that the institution decides to construct a hedged position using European call options and the money market account. The strike price of the call option used to hedge its exposure is $60 and its maturity is 35 days.

a) Describe the construction of the hedged portfolio. Round off your position in the option used in the hedge to the nearest integer. Use the program Equity/Pricing European Options/No Dividends.

b) By design, the delta of the hedged portfolio is zero. What is the gamma of the hedged portfolio?

c) One day later the stock price may change. Examine the performance of the hedged portfolio by completing the following table.

STOCK PRICE	VALUE OF CALL* OPTION, STRIKE $65	VALUE OF CALL* OPTION, STRIKE $60	VALUE OF HEDGED** PORTFOLIO
57			
58			
59			
60			

61

62

63

*Calculate these values using the program Equity/Pricing European Options/No Dividends.

**Include the cost of carry.

d) Is the performance of the hedged portfolio consistent with the gamma of the hedged portfolio? Justify your answer.

e) How does the performance of the hedge compare to that in Question 4?

Question 6

A financial institution has written 40 out-of-the-money calls with a strike price of $65 and maturity 95 days. The current stock price is $55. The institution decides to hedge this portfolio such that the portfolio is delta-vega neutral, using the underlying stock, a short-dated call option with a maturity of 24 days, and the money market account. Relevant pricing details are given below.

	OPTION TO BE HEDGED	OPTION 1
Maturity (days)	95	24
Stock price	65	60
Volatility* (percent)	30	30
Discount rate**	5.25	5.10

 *A 365-day year is assumed.
**A 360-day year is assumed.

The contract size for each option is 100 shares. Use the program Equity/Pricing European Options/No Dividends.

a) Describe the construction of the delta-vega neutral hedge portfolio. Round off your positions in Option 1 and the stock to the nearest integer.

b) What is the gamma and theta of the hedge portfolio?

c) One day later, after the hedge portfolio is formed, the stock price may change. Examine the performance of the hedge portfolio by completing the following table.

STOCK PRICE	OPTION TO BE HEDGED*	OPTION 1*	VALUE OF HEDGE PORTFOLIO
50			
53			
54			
55			

56
57
60

*Use the program Equity/Pricing European Options/No Dividends to price these options.

Question 7

Referring to Question 6, the financial institution decides to hedge its exposure to the call options that it has written by constructing a portfolio that is delta-gamma neutral.

a) Describe the construction of the delta-gamma neutral hedge portfolio. Round off your positions in Option 1 and the stock to the nearest integer.
b) What is the theta and vega of the hedge portfolio?
c) One day later, after the hedge portfolio is formed, the stock price may change. Examine the performance of the hedge portfolio by completing the following table.

STOCK PRICE	OPTION TO BE HEDGED*	OPTION 1*	VALUE OF HEDGE PORTFOLIO
50			
53			
54			
55			
56			
57			
60			

*Use the program Equity/Pricing European Options/No Dividends to price these options.

Question 8

Referring to Question 6, the financial institution decides to hedge its exposure to the call options it has written by constructing a portfolio that is delta-theta neutral.

a) Describe the construction of the delta-theta neutral hedge portfolio. Round off your position in Option 1 and the stock to the nearest integer.
b) What is the gamma and vega of the hedge portfolio? What should the theoretical value of gamma be in this case?
c) One day later after the hedge portfolio is formed, the stock price may change. Examine the performance of the hedge portfolio by completing the following table.

STOCK PRICE	OPTION TO BE HEDGED*	OPTION 1*	VALUE OF HEDGE PORTFOLIO
50			
53			

54
55
56
57
60

*Use the program Equity/Pricing European Options/No Dividends to price these options.

Question 9

A financial institution has written 50 put options with a strike price of $45 and maturity 100 days. The current stock price is $55. The institution decides to hedge this position using two other options and the money market account such that the hedge portfolio is delta-gamma neutral. Relevant pricing details are given below.

Type of Option	Option to Be Hedged European Put	Option 1 European Put	Option 2 European Call
Strike price	45	55	60
Maturity	100	45	16
Volatility*	25%	25%	25%
Discount rate*	5.30%	5.20%	5.05%

*The contract size for each option is 100 shares.

a) For the option to be hedged, determine its value, delta, gamma, theta, and vega.
b) Determine the value, delta, gamma, theta, and vega of Option 1.
c) Determine the value, delta, gamma, theta, and vega of Option 2.
d) Describe the delta-gamma neutral hedged portfolio. Round off your position in Options 1 and 2 to the nearest integer.
e) What is the theta of the hedged portfolio? What should it be theoretically?
f) Immediately after the hedged portfolio is formed, volatility changes to 26 percent per annum. What effect does this have on the value of the hedged portfolio? Is this what you would expect given the portfolio's vega?

Question 10

A financial institution has written 100 put options with a strike price of $50 and 100 call options with the same strike. The maturity of the options is 90 days. The current stock price is $50. The institution decides to hedge this portfolio using the stock and call options with a strike of $55 and maturity of 120 days. Use the following information.

Volatility*	34 percent
90-day discount rate**	4.75 percent

120-day discount rate**   4.77 percent
Option contract size   100 shares

*Assuming a 365-day year.
**Assuming a 360-day year.

a) Describe the delta neutral portfolio. Use the program Equity/Pricing European Options/No Dividends.
b) What is the gamma of the hedge portfolio?

11 CHAPTER

FOREIGN CURRENCY

11.0 INTRODUCTION

Foreign currency derivatives provide a convenient mechanism for companies to alter their response to foreign exchange rate fluctuations. In this chapter, we examine the pricing and hedging of foreign currency derivatives. The pricing of derivatives on foreign currencies is analogous to the pricing of derivatives written on a stock with a constant dividend yield. We examined derivatives with a constant dividend yield in Chapter 9 when considering extensions of the Black-Scholes model. In the next chapter, we will study the pricing and hedging of stock index derivatives and commodity derivatives. The pricing of these contracts is also analogous to the pricing of derivatives written on a stock with a constant dividend yield.

The common structure underlying the pricing of these derivatives is important for both theoretical and practical reasons. In theory, once we understand how to price one of these derivatives—say, an option written on stock with a constant dividend yield—we understand how to price derivatives on foreign currencies, stock indexes, and commodities. In practice, the same computer software can be used to price and hedge derivatives in these different areas.

This chapter is organized as follows. We start by using the binomial pricing model to price foreign currency options. Following the insights of Chapter 5, we then discuss convergence of the binomial model to a lognormal distribution. This motivates the closed form expression for a European option's value based on the lognormal distribution. We next study American options. Here, for both call and put options it may be optimal to exercise early because the interest rate differential between domestic and foreign rates generates an implicit dividend yield. The last part of this chapter discusses the pricing of futures, options on futures, and the use of futures for hedging. In practice, this is an important extension, as futures are often the most liquid instruments available for hedging.

11.1 FOREIGN CURRENCY DERIVATIVES

Before studying pricing and hedging theory, it is important to become acquainted with the foreign currency derivative markets. This section describes the different types of foreign currency derivatives currently available for trade and their common uses. We use the U.S. dollar as the domestic currency, or numeraire; for many traded

derivatives on U.S. exchanges, it is appropriate. However, there exist traded derivatives, especially in the over-the-counter market, for which some other currency, such as Deutsche marks, French francs, or Japanese yen, is the numeraire. If in doubt, you should always seek clarification. The subsequent analysis applies to these foreign currency derivatives as well, but the numeraire must be changed, and the analysis appropriately reinterpreted.

Foreign Currency Options

Here we describe the institutional setting of the existing foreign currency option markets.

Quotes

Table 11.1 shows the closing prices of some of the foreign currency options traded on the Philadelphia Exchange on May 28, 1998. The expiration months for regular options are March, June, September, and December, plus two near-term months. In Table 11.1, we can observe options with expiration dates in June, July, and September. The expiration date is the Friday before the third Wednesday of the expiring month. The settlement date is the third Wednesday of the expiring month and the last trading day is the Friday before the third Wednesday of the expiring month.[1] The size of each contract and the type of option (European or American) are shown. Also notice that one of the contracts is a "cross" currency British pound/German mark option.

TABLE 11.1 *Foreign Currency Option Prices on the Philadelphia Exchange, Thursday, May 28, 1998**

OPTIONS — PHILADELPHIA EXCHANGE

	Calls Vol.	Calls Last	Puts Vol.	Puts Last
Australian Dollar		62.24		
50,000 Australian Dollars-European style.				
62½ Jun	20	0.48	...	...
British Pound		162.57		
31,250 Brit. Pounds-cents per unit.				
159 Jun	...	...	12	0.12
162 Jun	...	...	12	0.72
162 Jul	14	1.85	...	...
163 Jul	...	...	11	1.81
164 Jun	...	...	10	1.40
172 Jun	...	...	7	9.08
British Pound-GMark		289.53		
31,250 British Pound-German Mark cross.				
290 Jul	...	...	2	3.46
Canadian Dollar		68.74		
50,000 Canadian Dollars-European Style.				
69 Jun	10	0.17	...	...
German Mark		56.14		
62,500 German Marks-European Style.				
55 Jun	5	1.31	...	...
55½ Jul	...	...	8	0.40
56 Jul	1	0.81	...	...
57 Jun	5	0.21	...	...
62,500 German Marks-cents per unit.				
56½ Jul	...	...	48	0.89
Japanese Yen		72.10		
6,250,000 J.Yen EOM 100ths of a cent per unit.				
74 Jun	2	0.48	...	...
6,250,000 J.Yen-100ths of a cent per unit.				
70 Sep	...	...	3	0.89
71 Jun	...	...	300	0.15
71 Sep	...	...	12	1.18
71½ Jul	...	...	500	0.23
71½ Jul	...	...	13	0.81
72 Jun	2	0.86	...	...
72 Sep	...	...	24	1.53
73 Jun	5	0.52	10	1.12
73 Jul	...	...	30	1.53
73 Sep	10	2.29	...	...
74 Jun	...	...	237	2.00
75 Jun	...	...	10	2.80
6,250,000 J.Yen-European Style.				
72 Sep	...	...	8	1.45
80 Jun	...	...	5	7.52
Swiss Franc		67.71		
62,500 Swiss Francs-European Style.				
65 Jun	77	2.84	...	...
65 Jul	5	3.08	...	...
67 Jun	...	...	45	0.16
67 Jul	...	...	5	0.45
70 Jun	...	...	45	2.16
74 Jun	...	...	5	6.22

Call Vol 812   Open Int ... 91,904
Put Vol 2,105   Open Int ... 96,297

*Source: *The Wall Street Journal*, Friday, May 29, 1998.

---

[1]These dates can change due to holidays.

Payoff Definitions

In this section, we discuss the payoffs to foreign currency options.

Consider a British pound call option. For options traded on the Philadelphia Exchange, the contract size, or principal, is £31,250 per contract (see Table 11.1).

Let $S(t)$ denote the exchange rate ($/£) at date t. The payoff at maturity, date T, is defined to be

$$C(T) \equiv \text{principal} \begin{cases} S(T) - K & \text{if} & S(T) \geq K \\ 0 & \text{if} & S(T) < K, \end{cases}$$

where K represents the strike price ($/£). All options are settled by delivery of the underlying currency, dollars.

EXAMPLE   **Foreign Currency Options**

This example illustrates the payoff at maturity to a foreign currency call option on the British pound (see Table 11.1).

Suppose the strike price is 163 (cents/£) and the exchange rate at the maturity of the option is 168 (cents/£). We follow the convention shown in Table 11.1 for quoting the exchange rate in terms of cents/pound. The principal of the option is £31,250.

The value of the call option at maturity is

£31,250 $\times$ (168 $-$ 163) cents/100 = \$1,562.50.

We divide by 100 in the above equation because the exchange rate quotations are given in terms of cents/pound.   ■

The payoff to a put option with strike price K at a maturity date T is defined to be

$$P(T) \equiv \text{principal} \begin{cases} 0 & \text{if} & S(T) > K \\ K - S(T) & \text{if} & S(T) \leq K. \end{cases}$$

The principal is in units of the foreign currency.

Cross rate options

Cross rate options are foreign currency options where the numeraire is not the U.S. dollar but rather a foreign currency. For example, in Table 11.1 for the British pound/German mark options, the numeraire is German marks. The option premium is quoted in terms of marks, and the contract size is 31,250 British pounds. Other cross rate options that are traded on the Philadelphia Exchange include the German marks/Japanese yen contract with size 62,500 German marks, and the British pound/Japanese yen contract with size 31,250 British pounds.

The Philadelphia Exchange has introduced a number of recent innovations. In 1994 the Exchange introduced Virtual Currency Options. These options can only be exercised at maturity and are cash settled in dollars. The options have a maturity of two weeks, with a new series listed each week. These options are the first exchange-listed currency options to expire on Monday mornings, making it easier to hedge weekend currency exposures.

On November 14, 1994, the Philadelphia Exchange introduced the United Currency Options Market, which incorporates standardized contracts and customized contracts. For customized contracts the strike price, expiration dates, choice of currency, and choice of premium quotation can all be chosen to suit particular needs. Customized currency options can be traded on any combination of the nine currencies currently available for trading, for a total of 72 currency pairs. These options are an attempt to offer some of the flexibility of the over-the-counter market while minimizing counterparty risk. All contracts are cleared through the Options Clearing Corporation, which has a Standard & Poor's AAA credit rating.

On January 1, 1999, the euro became the legal currency of the eleven participating countries of the European Union. The legacy currencies—Austrian schilling, Belgian franc, Finnish markka, French franc, German mark, Irish punt, Italian lira, Luxembourg franc, Netherlands guilder, Portuguese escudo, and Spanish peseta—became subdenominations of the euro and will coexist with it until the end of the transition period, December 31, 2001. Options on the euro are traded on the Philadelphia Exchange, and futures contracts on Euribor are traded on the London International Financial Futures Exchange.

Options on Foreign Currency Futures

Options on foreign currency futures are very popular traded securities.

Options on futures contracts are characterized by their payoff at maturity. When exercised, the option requires delivery of an underlying futures contract plus a cash settlement. For a call option, the cash settlement is equal to the product of the difference between the current futures price and the exercise price times the contract size. Some notation helps to clarify this payoff.

Let $\mathcal{F}(t, T_{\mathcal{F}})$ denote the futures price at date t for delivery at date $T_{\mathcal{F}}$ ($/foreign currency). The payoff to a call option with maturity date $T < T_{\mathcal{F}}$ and strike price K ($/foreign currency) is

$$C(T) \equiv \text{contract size} \begin{cases} \mathcal{F}(T, T_{\mathcal{F}}) - K & \text{if} & \mathcal{F}(T, T_{\mathcal{F}}) > K \\ 0 & \text{if} & \mathcal{F}(T, T_{\mathcal{F}}) \leq K. \end{cases}$$

The contract size is in units of the foreign currency; it differs for the different currencies.

For a put option, the cash settlement is equal to the product of the difference between the exercise price and the current futures price times the contract size. The

contract size is in units of the foreign currency. The payoff to the put option with maturity $T < T_{\mathscr{F}}$ is

$$P(T) \equiv \text{contract size} \begin{cases} 0 & \text{if} & \mathscr{F}(T, T_{\mathscr{F}}) > K \\ K - \mathscr{F}(T, T_{\mathscr{F}}) & \text{if} & \mathscr{F}(T, T_{\mathscr{F}}) \leq K, \end{cases}$$

where K is the strike price (\$/foreign currency).

Current currency futures quotes are given in Table 11.2. Futures options are traded on many of these currency futures. Table 11.3 contains quotes for currency futures options. We will illustrate the use of these quotes through an example.

TABLE 11.2   *Currency Futures, Thursday, May 28, 1998**

CURRENCY

	Open	High	Low	Settle	Change	Lifetime High	Lifetime Low	Open Interest
JAPAN YEN (CME)-12.5 million yen; \$ per yen (.00)								
June	.7295	.7325	.7212	.7221	− .0078	.9090	.7212	121,563
Sept	.7370	.7398	.7306	.7316	− .0079	.8695	.7306	5,413
Dec	.7450	.7450	.7410	.7412	− .0080	.8445	.7410	712
Mr99	....	....	....	.7509	− .0081	.8315	.7520	1,494
Est vol 20,274; vol Wed 17,181; open int 129,182, +4,592.								
DEUTSCHEMARK (CME)-125,000 marks; \$ per mark								
June	.5615	.5643	.5600	.5624	+ .0007	.5995	.5409	125,321
Sept	.5640	.5670	.5630	.5653	+ .0007	.5944	.5425	8,488
Dec	....	.5691	....	.5680	+ .0007	.5840	.5496	357
Est vol 23,216; vol Wed 61,380; open int 134,166, −11,079.								
CANADIAN DOLLAR (CME)-100,000 dlrs.; \$ per Can \$								
June	.6880	.6886	.6867	.6877	+ .0006	.7470	.6825	59,954
Sept	.6887	.6889	.6878	.6888	+ .0007	.7463	.6845	7,116
Dec	.6895	.6901	.6892	.6899	+ .0006	.7400	.6860	1,686
Mr99	.6904	.6906	.6904	.6910	+ .0006	.7247	.6875	565
June	....	....	....	.6921	+ .0006	.7170	.6910	159
Est vol 4,360; vol Wed 9,188; open int 69,493, −1,194.								
BRITISH POUND (CME)-62,500 pds.; \$ per pound								
June	1.6290	1.6326	1.6204	1.6256	− .0044	1.6940	1.5610	52,137
Sept	1.6150	1.6250	1.6134	1.6188	− .0044	1.6870	1.5690	2,486
Est vol 7,692; vol Wed 13,102; open int 54,808, +2,064.								
SWISS FRANC (CME)-125,000 francs; \$ per franc								
June	.6811	.6813	.6770	.6792	− .0020	.7360	.6560	68,092
Sept	.6853	.6881	.6840	.6860	− .0021	.7420	.6623	6,398
Est vol 13,160; vol Wed 30,657; open int 74,549, +2,243.								
AUSTRALIAN DOLLAR (CME)-100,000 dlrs.; \$ per A.\$								
June	.6205	.6241	.6205	.6225	+ .0027	.7050	.6170	23,193
Est vol 746; vol Wed 1,053; open int 23,470, +165.								
MEXICAN PESO (CME)-500,000 new Mex. peso, \$ per MP								
June	.11250	.11330	.11230	.11242	+ 00020	.11985	.09200	25,518
Sept	.10820	.10905	.10812	.10817	+ 00017	.11680	.08000	12,496
Dec	.10460	.10600	.10425	.10420	+ 00020	.11440	.08000	8,168
Mr99	....	....	....	.10070	+ 00020	.10565	.09900	868
Est vol 9,974; vol Wed 13,327; open int 47,062, +2,242.								

CME = Chicago Mercantile Exchange

*Source: *The Wall Street Journal*, May 29, 1998

TABLE 11.3   *Options on Foreign Currency Futures, Thursday, May 28, 1998**

CURRENCY

JAPANESE YEN (CME)
12,500,000 yen; cents per 100 yen

Strike Price	Calls-Settle Jun	Jly	Aug	Puts-Settle Jun	Jly	Aug
7100	1.39	2.63	....	0.18	0.41	0.84
7150	1.01	....	....	0.30	0.53	....
7200	0.69	....	....	0.48	0.68	1.17
7250	0.46	....	....	0.75	0.86	....
7300	0.28	....	....	1.08	1.08	1.60
7350	0.19	....	....	1.48	1.34	....

Est vol 20,798 Wed 4,005 calls 3,636 puts
Op int Wed 69,122 calls 66,078 puts

DEUTSCHEMARK (CME)
125,000 marks; cents per mark

Strike Price	Calls-Settle Jun	Jly	Aug	Puts-Settle Jun	Jly	Aug
5500	1.28	1.68	....	0.04	0.16	....
5550	0.84	....	....	0.10	0.27	....
5600	0.46	0.93	....	0.22	0.40	0.70
5650	0.21	0.64	....	0.47	0.61	....
5700	0.09	0.44	....	0.85	0.91	....
5750	0.05	0.31	....	1.31	....	....

Est vol 2,601 Wed 1,350 calls 2,856 puts
Op int Wed 66,279 calls 38,021 puts

CANADIAN DOLLAR (CME)
100,000 Can.$, cents per Can.$

Strike Price	Calls-Settle Jun	Jly	Aug	Puts-Settle Jun	Jly	Aug
6800	0.81	....	....	0.04	....	....
6850	0.39	....	....	0.12	....	....
6900	0.13	0.35	....	0.36	0.48	0.64
6950	0.03	....	....	0.76	0.81	....
7000	0.02	....	0.20	1.25	....	1.31
7050	0.01	....	....	1.74	....	....

Est vol 1,176 Wed 668 calls 724 puts
Op int Wed 29,895 calls 9,557 puts

BRITISH POUND (CME)
62,500 pounds; cents per pound

Strike Price	Calls-Settle Jun	Jly	Aug	Puts-Settle Jun	Jly	Aug
16100	1.76	....	....	0.20	1.08	....
16200	1.04	1.42	....	0.48	1.54	....
16300	0.52	1.00	1.60	0.96	2.12	....
16400	0.22	0.66	....	1.66	2.78	....
16500	0.12	0.42	....	2.56	0.00	....
16600	0.06	0.26	0.68	3.50	4.36	....

Est vol 385 Wed 332 calls 249 puts
Op int Wed 16,805 calls 14,549 puts

SWISS FRANC (CME)
125,000 francs; cents per franc

Strike Price	Calls-Settle Jun	Jly	Aug	Puts-Settle Jun	Jly	Aug
6700	1.01	1.84	....	0.09	0.25	....
6750	0.62	....	....	0.20	0.37	....
6800	0.34	1.12	....	0.42	0.53	....
6850	0.17	0.85	....	0.75	0.75	....
6900	0.09	0.63	....	1.17	....	....
6950	0.06	0.45	....	....	....	....

Est vol 1,114 Wed 1,186 calls 212 puts
Op int Wed 13,858 calls 10,874 puts

BRAZILIAN REAL (CME)
100,000 Braz. reais; $ per reais

Strike Price	Calls-Settle Jun	Jly	Aug	Puts-Settle Jun	Jly	Aug
860	....	....	....	0.00	....	....
865	....	....	....	0.00	0.00	....
870	....	....	....	0.00	....	....
875	....	....	....	....	....	....
880	....	....	....	....	....	....
885	....	....	....	....	....	....

Est vol 0 Wed 0 calls 0 puts
Op int Wed 0 calls 2,350 puts

MEXICAN PESO (CME)
500,000 new Mex. pesos; $ per MP

Strike Price	Calls-Settle Jun	Sep	Dec	Puts-Settle Jun	Sep	Dec
1100	2.72	....	....	0.30	3.75	....
1112	1.67	....	....	0.50	5.35	....
1125	0.85	....	....	0.92	....	....
1137	0.57	....	....	1.90	....	....
1150	0.10	0.80	....	2.67	....	....
1162	0.00	....	....	3.82	....	....

Est vol 685 Wed 5 calls 73 puts
Op int Wed 5,433 calls 4,977 puts

CME = Chicago Mercantile Exchange

*Source: *The Wall Street Journal*, May 29, 1998

EXAMPLE **Futures Call Option**

This example illustrates the payoff to a futures call option.

Consider an investor who is long a June Canadian dollar futures call option. The current June futures price is 0.6877 ($/C$) (see Table 11.2).

Suppose that the exercise price of the option is 0.6800 ($/C$) and the contract size is 100,000 Canadian dollars (see Table 11.3). If the option is exercised, the long receives a futures contract with futures price 0.6877 ($/C$) and a cash settlement equal to

$$100{,}000 \, (0.6877 - 0.6800) = \$770.$$

From Table 11.3 we see that this futures option trades for 0.81 ¢/C$ or 0.0081 $/C$. So, the premium for one option contract is .0081 $/C$ × 100,000 C$ = $810. This is $40 more than the value of the option if exercised ($810 − $770).

Note that the value of the futures contract with futures price 0.6877 ($/C$) is zero. This position can be closed out if the investor does not wish to be long in the futures contract. ∎

EXAMPLE **Futures Put Option**

This example illustrates the payoff to a futures put option.

Consider an investor who is long a June British pound futures put option. The current June futures price is 1.6256 ($/£) (see Table 11.2). The exercise price of the option is 1.6300 ($/£) and the contract size is 62,500 pounds (see Table 11.3).

If the put option is exercised, the investor becomes a writer of a futures contract with futures price 1.6256 ($/£) and receives a cash settlement equal to

$$62{,}500 \, (1.63 - 1.6256) = \$275.$$

The put option is currently trading for 0.96 ¢/£ or 0.0096 $/£. A contract's purchase price is then £62,500 (0.0096 $/£) = $600. The put is trading for more than its early exercise value.

Note that the value of the futures contract with futures price 1.6256 ($/£) is zero. This position can be closed out if the investor does not wish to be short in the futures contract. ∎

Uses of Currency Derivatives

Consider a U.S. company that buys machinery costing one million Deutsche marks. The company takes delivery of the machines in four months' time, payment being made on the delivery date. What risk does the company face?

In four months' time the Deutsche mark may appreciate against the dollar, imply-ing that the cost of machinery in terms of dollars may increase. One way to hedge this risk is to go long eight futures contracts, the size of each contract being 125,000 DM, or to enter into a forward contract with a bank to buy one million Deutsche marks.

Alternatively, the company could purchase four-month call options to buy Deutsche marks. The contract size is 62,500 DM so 16 options will be required. Suppose the cost of a European option with maturity date in four months and exercise price 0.64 dollars per mark is quoted to be 0.62 cents per mark. The cost of 16 con-tracts is then $16 \times 62{,}500 \times (0.62/100) = \$6{,}200$.

Table 11.4 shows the dollar cost of the machinery for a range of possible ex-change rates and the net payoffs from using two forms of hedging instruments: (a) a forward contract with forward price 0.6400 \$/DM and (b) the call options described above. From Table 11.4 it is seen that the cost of the machinery when a forward con-tract is used is always \$640,000. In contrast, the cost of hedging with a futures op-tion changes.

If the Deutsche mark appreciates against the dollar so that the exchange rate is, say, 0.66 (\$/DM), the net total cost of purchasing the machinery when hedging with a forward contract is lower than when hedging with an option. If the Deutsche mark depreciates against the dollar, so that the exchange rate is, say, 0.60 (\$/DM), the re-verse is true. The call option provides insurance only against the Deutsche mark ap-preciating against the dollar. The cost of this insurance policy is the premium one pays for the option.

TABLE 11.4   *Use of Different Hedging Instruments*

		FORWARD CONTRACT		OPTION ON SPOT	
POSSIBLE EXCHANGE RATE $/DM	DOLLAR COST OF EQUIPMENT	DOLLAR VALUE OF FORWARD CONTRACT	NET TOTAL $	DOLLAR VALUE OF OPTION	NET TOTAL* $
0.60	600,000	−40,000	640,000	0	606,283
0.61	610,000	−30,000	640,000	0	616,283
0.62	620,000	−20,000	640,000	0	626,283
0.63	630,000	−10,000	640,000	0	636,283
0.64	640,000	0	640,000	0	646,283
0.65	650,000	10,000	640,000	10,000	646,283
0.66	660,000	20,000	640,000	20,000	646,283

*This includes the cost of borrowing to finance the purchase of the options. The borrowing cost is 4 percent, so the total for borrowing for 4 months is

$\$6{,}200[1 + .04 \times (1/3)] = \$6{,}283$.

Note that the two hedging instruments have different implications for the net to-tal cost of buying the machinery and the risk involved. The cost of entering into the forward contract is zero with no additional risk, while the cost of buying the option is the option premium with some residual risk remaining. Deciding which form of hedging instrument to use depends on your preferences about the desired distribution of the net total cost.

11.2 SINGLE-PERIOD EXAMPLE

Here we illustrate the procedure for valuing foreign currency options using the bino-mial model of Chapter 5. We start with a simple numerical example and then gener-alize quickly, for the arguments are almost identical to those used in Chapter 5. It is useful to list here all the assumptions that are necessary.

Assumption A1.   Frictionless markets.

Assumption A2.   There is no counterparty risk.

Assumption A3.   Competitive markets.

Assumption A4.   No arbitrage opportunities.

Assumption A5.   The spot exchange rate is described by a lognormal probabil-ity distribution.

Assumption A6.   The domestic and foreign interest rates are constant over the life of the option, and the term structures for both interest rates are flat.

FIGURE 11.1   *Spot Exchange Rate Dynamics*

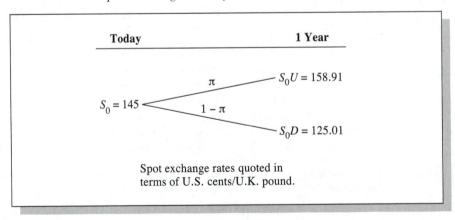

Spot exchange rates quoted in
terms of U.S. cents/U.K. pound.

FIGURE 11.2 *Dollar Value of a British Bond Paying One Pound in 1 Year (The Asset Underlying the Currency Option)*

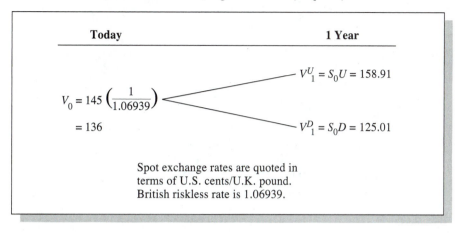

The first four assumptions are identical to those described in Chapter 2. Consequently, we refer the reader to that description.

Together, Assumptions A5 and A6 imply that the only source of uncertainty in valuing foreign currency options is the spot exchange rate. This is a very strong assumption, because in reality interest rates are not constant. Fortunately, for short-dated options, it is a reasonable approximation because the effects of stochastic interest rates on pricing can be shown to be quite minor.[2] The probability distribution describing the spot exchange rate is assumed to be lognormal so that the binomial approximation to the lognormal distribution can be applied. This process eventually leads to the derivation of a modified version of the Black-Scholes model.

Suppose that we want to price a European call option with a maturity of one year. Let the initial spot exchange rate be 145 cents/pound and the strike price be 145 cents/pound. At the end of the year we assume that the spot exchange rate can take only one of two possible values: 158.91 or 125.01, as shown in Figure 11.1. We will discuss later how we determine these values (Figure 11.2).

The option matures in one year's time. At the maturity of the option we can determine its value, conditional upon knowing the spot exchange rate. For simplicity, we assume the principal of the option is one pound (£1). The option's values at maturity are shown in Figure 11.3. If the up-state occurs, the call option is worth 13.91 cents; if the down-state occurs, the call option ends up out-of-the-money and expires worthless.

---

[2]For a full discussion and clarification of what "quite minor" means, see Amin and Bodurtha (1993). The assumption that the term structures are flat can easily be relaxed. Amin and Jarrow (1991) show how to price foreign currency derivatives when interest rates are stochastic.

FIGURE 11.3   *Foreign Exchange Call Prices*

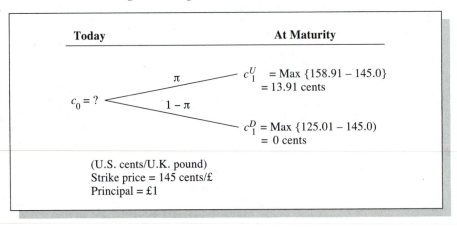

Today   **At Maturity**

$$c_1^U = \text{Max} \{158.91 - 145.0\}$$
$$= 13.91 \text{ cents}$$

$$c_0 = ?$$

$$c_1^D = \text{Max} \{125.01 - 145.0)$$
$$= 0 \text{ cents}$$

(U.S. cents/U.K. pound)
Strike price = 145 cents/£
Principal = £1

Although we have determined the option's values at maturity, we do not know the option's value today. For today's value, we can use a generalization of the arguments described in Chapter 5. We must first determine the martingale probabilities, π and $(1 - \pi)$, given in Figure 11.1. The argument we use to determine these probabilities follows directly from Chapter 6 and is given here. The idea is that the asset underlying the option is *not the spot exchange rate*, but the dollar value of an investment in a British bond paying 1 pound at the maturity date of the option. This follows because the dollar investment in the foreign bond pays the spot price at maturity, the payoff to the option.[3]

This insight is solidified by considering Figure 11.2, the binomial evolution for the dollar values of a British bond paying one pound for sure at time 1. The British pound riskless rate is assumed to be 1.06939.

At time 0, the British bond is worth $(1/1.06939)$ pounds or $145 \times (1/1.06939)$ dollars. The British bond pays one pound back in one year. If the up-state occurs, the bond is worth £1 $\times$ 158.91 ¢/£ = 158.91¢. If the down-state occurs, the bond is £1 $\times$ 125.01 ¢/£ = 125.01¢.

For purposes of risk-neutral valuation, it is the dollar value of the British bond that is a martingale under the probabilities π. Thus we need to determine the specific π that makes this martingale condition hold.

From Figure 11.2, the time-0 dollar value of purchasing a British bond that pays £1 in one year is

$$V(0) \equiv 1.45 \left(\frac{1}{1.06939} \right) = 1.36 \text{ dollars.}$$

---

[3]In these models currency does not trade. So, in fact, the only way that one can trade in the spot exchange rate is by investing in a foreign denominated bond, which is optimal because the foreign bond earns interest while holding currency does not.

The date-1 dollar value of the British bond is

$$V(1) \equiv \begin{cases} 1.5891 \text{ dollars, with martingale probability } \pi \\ 1.2501 \text{ dollars, with martingale probability } 1 - \pi. \end{cases}$$

This value is the spot exchange rate at time 1.

Suppose that for every dollar invested in the domestic (U.S.) one-year riskless asset, the value at the end of the year will be 1.0416 dollars. We know from Chapter 6 that for the relative price of this investment to be a martingale,

$$V(0) = \frac{1}{1.0416} E^{\pi}[V(1)]$$

or

$$136 = \frac{1}{1.0416} [1.5891 \times \pi + 1.2501 \times (1 - \pi)].$$

Hence, solving for π gives

$$\pi = 0.500021. \tag{11.1}$$

This completes the argument determining the martingale probability.

Using the risk-neutral valuation procedure, the value of the option today, from Figure 11.3, is

$$c(0) = \frac{1}{1.0416} [13.91 \times \pi + 0 \times (1 - \pi)]$$

$$= 6.68 \text{ cents}. \tag{11.2}$$

We have now determined a price for this option, but how can we construct a portfolio to replicate the option? By analogy with Chapter 5, it would be tempting to buy sterling and invest in the domestic riskless asset.

Suppose that we buy m pounds at a cost of $m1.45$ dollars and invest B dollars in the domestic riskless asset. The dollar value of the portfolio today would be

$$m1.45 + B,$$

which is similar to Expression (5.1) of Chapter 5. At this point, our argument differs from that given in Chapter 5. Today we have purchased m pounds. It would be imprudent if we simply kept this currency without investing it. Let us invest this currency in a one-year default-free foreign asset. Again, this logic implies that the underlying asset is not sterling but a sterling bond with maturity equal to the maturity date of the option, as in Figure 11.2.

So, our investment is now the purchase of m British bonds paying one pound back at time 1. The cost of each British bond is £$(1/1.0639)$. So, our initial dollar investment is

$$V(0) = m1.45\left(\frac{1}{1.0639}\right) + B$$

$$= m1.36 + B.$$

Note that while this investment is riskless in terms of its value quoted in pounds, it is risky when quoted in terms of dollars.

We want our portfolio to replicate the payoffs of the traded option. Suppose that at the end of the year the spot exchange rate is 158.91 (cents/pound). In this case, the option value is 13.91 cents. By construction, our portfolio must also be worth this amount.

The value of the replicating portfolio in one period in the up-state is therefore

$$m1.5891 + B1.0416 = 0.1391.$$

The first term is the value in dollars of the U.K. riskless investment at time 1. The spot exchange rate 1.5891 ($/£) converts the pounds received on the British bond to dollars. Note that in Figure 11.2 the spot exchange rate is quoted in terms of cents/£. We set this replicating portfolio's value to be equal to the call's payoff in the up-state, which gives us our first equation.

Suppose that at the end of the year the spot exchange rate is 125.01 cents/ pound. In this case, the option expires worthless. The value of the replicating portfolio must be set equal to zero:

$$m1.2501 + B1.0416 = 0.$$

This is our second equation.

Hence, we have two linear equations in two unknowns. Solving for m and B gives

$$m = 0.4103$$

and

$$B = -0.4929.$$

This minus sign for B implies that we must borrow 0.4929 dollars at the domestic riskless rate of 4.16 percent.

The cost of constructing the synthetic option today is

$$V(0) = 0.4103 \times 1.36 - 0.4929$$
$$= 0.0668 \text{ dollars,} \qquad (11.3)$$

which must equal the value of the traded option to avoid arbitrage. It agrees with the value in Expression (11.2). Our simple, single-period example is now complete.

11.3 MULTIPERIOD EXTENSION

We now examine the multiperiod version of the preceding binomial model. We increase the realism of the analysis by dividing the one-year period into two six-month intervals. The lattice of spot exchange rates for this situation is shown in Figure 11.4. We will postpone until later a discussion of the determination of the spot exchange rates in this figure. As before, Assumptions A1 through A6 are maintained. In particular, the interest rates are constant in both the domestic and foreign countries, and the term structures are flat.

If we invest one dollar in the domestic riskless asset for one year, we will earn 1.0416 dollars. Alternatively, we can invest in the domestic riskless asset for six months and roll over our investment. These two strategies must yield the same terminal value given the assumption about constant interest rates. If we invest one dollar for six months, we will earn an amount denoted by R where Δ is the interval (six months). This investment is rolled over, and after a further six months its value is R^2. To avoid arbitrage, the two strategies must have the same value, that is,

$$R^2 = 1.0416,$$

implying

$$R = 1.0206.$$

FIGURE 11.4 *Spot Exchange Rate Dynamics (Cents/Pound) for Two Periods*

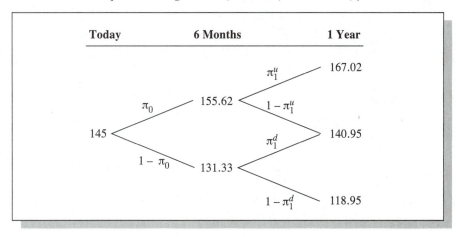

A similar argument is used for the foreign interest rate. Let R_f denote the value, in terms of the foreign currency, of investing one unit of the foreign currency (pounds) for a period Δ (six months). We leave it to you to verify[4] that

$$R_f = 1.0315.$$

We next determine the martingale probability π_0 of an increase in the exchange rate over the first interval. We repeat the argument used to determine Expression (11.1). The evolution of the dollar value of a British bond paying a pound in one year is given in Figure 11.5. The idea is to find the martingale probability in each time-state combination such that the dollar value of the foreign bond, normalized by the dollar money market account, is a martingale.

Over the first interval we have that

$$1.3629 = \frac{1}{1.0206}[1.5087 \times \pi_0 + 1.2732 \times (1 - \pi_0)],$$

implying

$$\pi_0 = 0.499702.$$

Over the second period in the up-state, we get

$$1.5087 = \frac{1}{1.0206}[1.6702 \times \pi_1^u + 1.4095 \times (1 - \pi_1^u)],$$

implying

$$\pi_1^u = 0.499702.$$

Similarly, over the second period in the down-state, we get

$$1.2732 = \frac{1}{1.0206}[1.4095 \times \pi_1^d + 1.1895 \times (1 - \pi_1^d)],$$

---

[4]Recall from Chapter 5 that

$$R \equiv \exp(r\Delta)$$

and

$$R_f \equiv \exp(r_f \Delta),$$

where r is the domestic continuously compounded rate of interest and r_f the foreign continuously compounded rate of interest. In this example, $e^r = 1.0416$ implies that $r = 4.076$ percent per annum, and $e^{r_f} = 1.0639$ implies that $r_f = 6.194$ percent per annum. Thus

$$R = \exp(0.04076 \times 0.5) = 1.0206 \text{ with } \Delta = 0.5$$

and

$$R_f = \exp(0.06194 \times 0.5) = 1.0315 \text{ with } \Delta = 0.5.$$

FIGURE 11.5   *Dollar Value of a British Bond Paying 1 Pound in 1 Year*

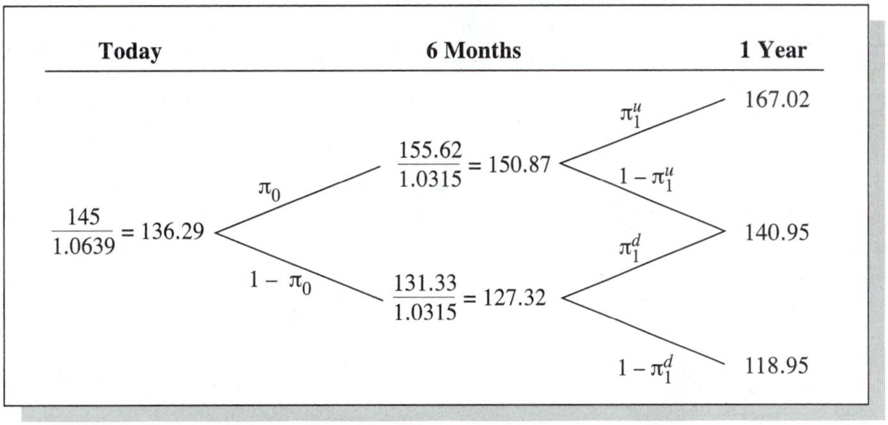

implying

$$\pi_1^d = 0.499702.$$

In this example, all three martingale probabilities are identical:

$$\pi_0 = \pi_1^u = \pi_1^d \equiv \pi.$$

Consider the same European call option with maturity of one year and strike price 145 cents/pound. At maturity, the values of the call option for the three possible spot exchange rates are shown in Figure 11.6. If the spot exchange rate is 167.02 (cents/pound), the call option is worth 22.02 cents. The option is worthless if the spot exchange is either 140.95 cents/pound or 118.95 cents/pound.

Now move backward in time to a point six months before maturity. If the spot exchange rate is 131.33 cents/pound, the call option is worthless. Why?

If the spot exchange rate is at the up node and equal to 155.62, the value of the call option is given by

$$\frac{c_1}{A(1)} = \frac{1}{A(2)} [c_2^U \times \pi + c_2^D \times (1 - \pi)],$$

where $A(t)$ is the value of the domestic money market account at date t. Therefore, as $A(2) = A(1) 1.0206$,

$$c_1 = \frac{1}{1.0206} [22.02 \times \pi + 0 \times (1 - \pi)]$$

$$= 10.78 \text{ cents.}$$

Figure 11.6 *Foreign Exchange European Call Option*

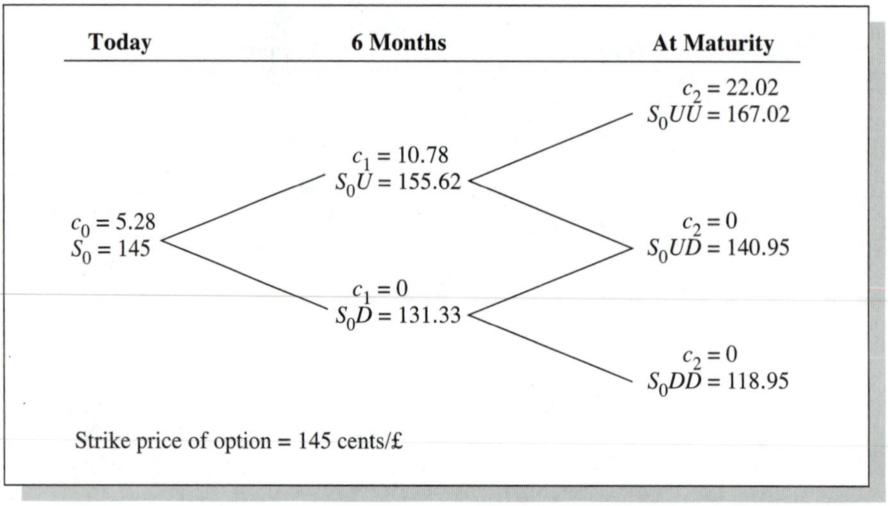

Today	6 Months	At Maturity

$$
c_2 = 22.02 \\
S_0 U U = 167.02
$$

$$
c_1 = 10.78 \\
S_0 U = 155.62
$$

$$
c_0 = 5.28 \\
S_0 = 145
$$

$$
c_2 = 0 \\
S_0 U D = 140.95
$$

$$
c_1 = 0 \\
S_0 D = 131.33
$$

$$
c_2 = 0 \\
S_0 D D = 118.95
$$

Strike price of option = 145 cents/£

The value of the option today is given by

$$
c_0 = \frac{1}{1.0206} \left[10.78 \times \pi + 0 \times (1 - \pi) \right]
$$

$$
= 5.28 \text{ cents.}
$$

The synthetic option is constructed analogously as in the single-period example, and is left to the reader as an exercise.[5] The multiperiod extension of the previous single-period example is now complete.

11.4 FORMALIZATION

We now formalize the valuation procedure illustrated in the previous sections. We start by using the binomial process from Chapter 5 to describe how the spot exchange rate changes over time.

Let the spot exchange rate at date t be denoted $S(t)$, which is quoted in terms of the domestic currency per unit of the foreign currency (d/f). Next period at date $t + 1$, after an interval of length Δ, let the spot exchange rate take one of two values:

$$
S(t + 1) \equiv \begin{cases} S(t)U \text{ with martingale probability } \pi \\ S(t)D \text{ with martingale probability } 1 - \pi, \end{cases} \tag{11.4}
$$

---

[5] At $t = 1$, if $S_0 U = 155.62$, the replicating portfolio is $m_1 = 0.8439$ and $B_1 = -116.65$. At $t = 0$, the replicating portfolio is $m_0 = 0.4621$ and $B_0 = -57.1084$.

U being the up-factor and *D* being the down-factor. Remember that the magnitude of the up- and down-factors depend on the length of the interval Δ. Later we will discuss how *U* and *D* are selected such that this binomial model approximates the lognormality assumption, A5, introduced earlier.

We next introduce the domestic and foreign term structures as given in Assumption A6. We assume that there exists a domestic riskless asset such that every dollar invested yields $R = \exp(r\Delta)$ dollars at the end of the investment interval of size Δ, where *r* is the domestic continuously compounded interest rate. Similarly, we assume that there exists a foreign riskless asset such that every unit of the foreign currency invested yields $R_f = \exp(r_f\Delta)$, where r_f is the foreign continuously compounded interest rate.

For discounting purposes, we need to utilize a money market account denominated in dollars. If $A(t)$ denotes the value of the domestic money market account at date *t*, then the value at date $t + \Delta$ is

$$A(t + 1) = A(t)R. \tag{11.5}$$

These are the basic elements of the model from which we can describe the evolution of the dollar value of a foreign currency bond with maturity *T*. The cost in units of the foreign currency of the foreign currency bond maturing at time *T* is

$$B_f(t,T) = \frac{1}{R_f^{T-t}}.$$

The dollar value of this foreign bond is the spot exchange rate times its cost, that is,

$$V(t) \equiv S(t)B_f(t,T). \tag{11.6}$$

We hold this foreign bond for an interval of length Δ. The value at date $t + \Delta$ of the foreign currency bond in the foreign currency is

$$B_f(t + 1,T) = \frac{1}{R_f^{T-(t+1)}}$$

and in terms of the domestic currency it is

$$V(t + 1) = \begin{cases} S(t)UB_f(t + 1,T) \text{ with martingale probability } \pi \\ S(t)DB_f(t + 1,T) \text{ with martingale probability } 1 - \pi. \end{cases} \tag{11.7}$$

Expression (11.7) gives the binomial process describing the evolution of the foreign bond in dollars. While the foreign currency investment is riskless in terms of the foreign currency, it is risky in terms of dollars because the spot exchange rate at the end of the interval is random. The description of the model structure is complete.

Martingale Pricing

This section shows how to determine the martingale probability π from the no-arbitrage, martingale pricing condition.

From Chapter 6 we know that under the binomial model, no arbitrage implies that normalized prices for the dollar value of the foreign bond must be a martingale, implying

$$\frac{V(t)}{A(t)} = E^\pi \left[\frac{V(t+1)}{A(t+1)} \right].$$

Using Expressions (11.5), (11.6), and (11.7) gives

$$S(t)B_f(t,T) = \frac{1}{R} [S(t)UB_f(t+1,T)\pi + S(t)DB_f(t+1,T)(1-\pi)].$$

Algebra yields the final result:

$$\pi = ([R/R_f] - D)/(U - D). \tag{11.8}$$

Note that if the foreign risk-free rate of interest was zero, implying that $R_f \equiv 1$, then Expression (11.8) is identical to Expression (5.31) of Chapter 5.

Risk-Neutral Valuation

Here we show how to price foreign currency derivatives using the martingale probabilities.

Let $c(t)$ denote the value at date t of a contingent claim written on the spot exchange rate. Next period, at date $t+1$, let the value of this contingent claim be c_{t+1}^U if the spot exchange rate is $S(t)U$, and c_{t+1}^D if the spot exchange rate is $S(t)D$, that is,

$$c(t+1) \equiv \begin{cases} c_{t+1}^U \text{ with martingale probability } \pi \\ c_{t+1}^D \text{ with martingale probability } 1 - \pi. \end{cases} \tag{11.9}$$

Using risk-neutral valuation, the date-t value of the contingent claim is the discounted date-$t+1$ expected value, using the martingale probabilities:

$$c(t) = \frac{1}{R} [c_{t+1}^U \pi + c_{t+1}^D (1-\pi)], \tag{11.10}$$

where π is given by Expression (11.8).

Replicating Portfolio

Given the prices of the foreign currency derivative, we show in this section how to hedge it using the foreign currency bond and the domestic money market account.

The foreign currency bond's price is denoted $B_f(t,T)$ in units of the foreign currency. Since R_f is the foreign riskless rate per period, $B_f(t,T) = 1/R_f^{T-t}$.

To form a portfolio to replicate this contingent claim, we purchase m_t units of the foreign currency bond, which matures at time T (the maturity of the derivative), and we invest B_t units of the domestic currency in the domestic riskless asset. We determine these positions as follows.

The date-t value of the portfolio in units of the domestic currency is

$$V(t) = m_t S(t) B_f(t, T) + B_t.$$

To construct the contingent claim synthetically, we must match the payoffs to the traded contingent claim at date $t + 1$, that is,

$$m_t S(t) U B_f(t + 1, T) + B_t R = c_{t+1}^U$$

and

$$m_t S(t) D B_f(t + 1, T) + B_t R = c_{t+1}^D. \tag{11.11}$$

This gives two linear equations in two unknowns. Solving for m_t and B_t gives

$$m_t = [(c_{t+1}^U - c_{t+1}^D)/(S(t)U - S(t)D)]/B_f(t + 1, T) \tag{11.12}$$

and

$$B_t = -[(S(t)D c_{t+1}^U - S(t)U c_{t+1}^D)/(S(t)U - S(t)D)]/R. \tag{11.13}$$

The quantity m_t is referred to as the hedge ratio, or **delta**. It measures the investment in the foreign bond. If we compare Expression (11.12) with that of (5.18) in Chapter 5, we will notice that they differ in an important way. In Expression (11.12) we have an extra term $B_f(t + 1, T)$, which arises because of the foreign bond. Note that the above derivation is applicable to call options, put options, or futures options. Our discussion of the logic underlying the binomial model for pricing foreign currency derivatives is now complete.

11.5 LATTICE PARAMETERS

Here we show how to determine the specification for the up- and down-factors such that the binomial model gives an approximation to the lognormal distribution for the spot exchange rate as specified in Assumption A5. The argument is similar to that used in Section 5.5 of Chapter 5 and involves some minor technical details. For those who are not technically inclined, proceed directly to the discussion of Expressions (11.14) and (11.15).

Assumption A5 states that the spot exchange rate follows a lognormal probability distribution. The derivation uses the generalized result from Chapter 6 on the existence of equivalent martingale probabilities. Using these martingale probabilities, we can compute the expected value of the spot exchange rate as

$$E^\pi[S(T)] = S(0)\exp[\tilde{\mu}T + \sigma^2 T/2],$$

where $S(T)$ is the spot exchange rate at date T, $\tilde{\mu}$ is the mean return on the continuously compounded spot exchange rate per unit time, and σ is the spot exchange rate's volatility. At this point the argument will differ slightly from that used in Section 5.5 of Chapter 5. The goal of the analysis is to determine $\tilde{\mu}$ in terms of r, r_f, and σ.

Let $B(0, T)$ denote the date-0 value of a domestic zero-coupon bond that pays one dollar for sure at date T. Under Assumption A6, we can represent this value in terms of a continuously compounded interest rate r by

$$B(0, T) = \exp(-rT).$$

Similarly, the date-0 value of a foreign zero-coupon bond that pays one unit of the foreign currency for sure at date T can also be represented in terms of a continuously compounded interest rate r_f as

$$B_f(0, T) = \exp(-r_f T).$$

In terms of dollars, the initial value of this investment is

$$V(0) \equiv S(0) e^{-r_f T}$$

and its value at date T is

$$V(T) = S(T).$$

Its time-T value is exactly the spot exchange rate at time-T.

We know from the generalized theorem on the existence of equivalent martingale probabilities that the normalized dollar value of the foreign denominated bond follows a martingale:

$$V(0) = E^{\pi}[V(T)/A(T)],$$

where $A(T)$ is the value at date T of the domestic money market account and $A(0) \equiv 1$. Given that interest rates are constant,

$$A(T) = \exp(rT).$$

So,

$$V(0) = \exp(-rT)E^{\pi}[V(T)].$$

Substituting for $V(T)$ and $V(0)$ and using the expression for $E^{\pi}[S(T)]$ gives

$$\begin{aligned}
S(0)e^{-r_f T} &= \exp(-rT)E^{\pi}[S(T)] \\
&= \exp(-rT)S(0)\exp(\tilde{\mu}T + \sigma^2 T/2).
\end{aligned}$$

This implies the desired result

$$\tilde{\mu} = r - r_f - \sigma^2/2. \tag{11.14}$$

For martingale pricing, the instantaneous mean return on the spot exchange rate must equal the domestic risk-free rate of interest minus the foreign risk-free rate of interest less half the variance of the spot exchange rate. Hence, we can write

$$S(t) = S(0)\exp[(r - r_f - \sigma^2/2)t + \sigma\tilde{W}(t)], \tag{11.15}$$

where $\tilde{W}(t)$ is a normally distributed random variable under the martingale probabilities with mean 0 and variance t.

Compare this equation with Expression (9.8) of Chapter 9. If we replaced d_y in Expression (9.8) with r_f, we would have Expression (11.15). This transformation makes intuitive sense. The "dividend yield" to the underlying asset, the foreign bond, is the foreign interest rate r_f. This insight is important because although Section 9.4 describes derivatives written on assets that pay a continuous dividend, and this section describes foreign currency derivatives, the two descriptions are equivalent apart from minor differences in terminology and notation. Thus the results derived in Section 9.4 immediately apply here. We use these results to determine the binomial approximation to the lognormal distribution.

To approximate the lognormal distribution for the spot exchange rate, we specify the binomial spot exchange rate movements using Expression (11.14) and Expression (5.42) of Chapter 5 to be

$$S_{t+1} = S_t \begin{cases} \exp[(r - r_f - \sigma^2/2)\Delta + \sigma\sqrt{\Delta}] & \text{with martingale probability } \pi \\ \exp[(r - r_f - \sigma^2/2)\Delta - \sigma\sqrt{\Delta}] & \text{with martingale probability } 1 - \pi. \end{cases} \tag{11.16}$$

It defines the up- and down-factors to be

$$U = \exp[(r - r_f - \sigma^2/2)\Delta + \sigma\sqrt{\Delta}]$$

and

$$D = \exp[(r - r_f - \sigma^2/2)\Delta - \sigma\sqrt{\Delta}].$$

From the definition of π in Expression (11.8), and using Expression (11.6), the probability π can be written after some simplification in the form

$$\pi = [\exp(\sigma^2\Delta/2) - \exp(-\sigma\sqrt{\Delta})]/[\exp(\sigma\sqrt{\Delta}) - \exp(-\sigma\sqrt{\Delta})], \tag{11.17}$$

which is identical to that derived in Section 5.5. It can be shown that as Δ decreases in value, π approaches $1/2$.

Notice that all of the parameters of the binomial approximation—U, D, and π—depend only on the domestic and foreign interest rates (r, r_f) and the spot exchange rate's volatility (σ). Because U, D, and π are all that are needed to price foreign currency derivatives under the risk-neutral valuation methodology, we see that pricing derivatives under the binomial approximation depends only on (r, r_f) and σ, in addition to the defining conditions of the derivative itself. This makes the practical application of these techniques possible because rates (r, r_f) are easily estimated (see Chapter 8 for additional discussion of these issues).

EXAMPLE   ## Lognormal Approximation

In this example we illustrate the computation of the parameter values for the lognormal approximation under the binomial model.

Using discrete compounding, one dollar invested for one year yields 1.0416 dollars. This implies that the continuously compounded domestic rate, r, is determined by

$$\exp(-r1) = \frac{1}{1.0416},$$

giving

$$r = 0.04076 \text{ per year.}$$

The continuously compounded foreign interest rate is given by

$$\exp(-r_f1) = \frac{1}{1.0639},$$

implying

$$r_f = 0.06194 \text{ per year.}$$

The spot exchange rate volatility is 12 percent per annum and the interval is one year, hence

$$(r - r_f - \sigma^2/2)\Delta + \sigma\sqrt{\Delta} = 0.09162$$

and

$$(r - r_f - \sigma^2/2)\Delta - \sigma\sqrt{\Delta} = -0.14838,$$

where $\Delta = 1$. Therefore,

$$U = 1.095945$$

and

$$D = 0.862101.$$

If the date-0 spot exchange rate is $S(0) = 145$, then

$$S_0 U = 158.91 \text{ with martingale probability } \pi = 0.500073$$

and

$$S_0 D = 125.01 \text{ with martingale probability } 1 - \pi = 0.499927,$$

which are the values shown in Figure 11.1.

If the interval is 6 months, then with $\Delta = 0.5$,

$$(r - r_f - \sigma^2/2)\Delta + \sigma\sqrt{\Delta} = 0.070663$$

and

$$(r - r_f - \sigma^2/2)\Delta - \sigma\sqrt{\Delta} = -0.099043,$$

implying $U = 1.073219$ and $D = 0.905704$. These values are used in constructing the lattice shown in Figure 11.4. ∎

11.6 CLOSED FORM SOLUTIONS (MODIFIED BLACK-SCHOLES)

Let us use the results from Chapter 8 to obtain closed form solutions for various European options on the spot exchange rate. To do this, we must add one more assumption to the six assumptions already imposed in Section 11.2. This last assumption is:

Assumption A7.   Trading takes place continuously in time.

These seven assumptions are similar in form to those under which the Black-Scholes model is derived in Chapter 8.

Let us first consider valuing a European call option on the spot exchange rate. The value of a European call option on the spot exchange rate with maturity T and strike price K is

$$c(T) \equiv \begin{cases} S(T) - K & \text{if} \quad S(T) \geq K \\ 0 & \text{if} \quad S(T) < K. \end{cases}$$

Using risk-neutral valuation, the value of the option at date 0 is

$$c(0) = B(0,T)E^\pi[S(T) - K \mid S(T) \geq K]$$
$$= B_f(0,T)S(0)N(d_1) - B(0,T)KN(d_2), \tag{11.18}$$

where $d_1 \equiv \{\ln\{[S(0)B_f(0,T)]/[KB(0,T)]\} + \sigma^2 T/2\}/\sigma\sqrt{T}$, $d_2 \equiv d_1 \, \sigma\sqrt{T}$, and $N(\cdot)$ is the cumulative normal distribution function.

These results follow immediately from Expression (9.9) of Chapter 9, replacing the dividend yield d_y with the foreign interest rate r_f. The justification for this substitution is given by Expression (11.15). The result is a modified Black-Scholes formula. The modification involves replacing the "stock price" with the dollar value of a foreign zero-coupon bond.

The hedge ratio, or delta, for the European call option is

$$\text{Delta} = B_f(0,T)N(d_1) \geq 0.$$

Using an analogous argument, the date-0 value for a European put option on the spot exchange rate, using Expression (9.10) of Chapter 9, is

$$p(0) = B(0,T)KN(-d_2) - B_f(0,T)S(0)N(-d_1). \tag{11.19}$$

Again, this is a modified Black-Scholes formula from Chapter 9, in which the dollar value of the foreign zero-coupon bond replaces the "stock price."

The hedge ratio (delta) for the put option is

$$\text{Delta} = -B_f(0,T)N(-d_1) \leq 0.$$

EXAMPLE   **Modified Black-Scholes**

This example illustrates the computation of Expressions (11.18) and (11.19).

We want to value a European call option and a European put option. The inputs are shown in Table 11.5, Part A. In comparison to the inputs necessary for the Black-Scholes model of Chapter 8, there is one additional input: the foreign interest rate. Also note that the spot exchange rate and strike price are quoted in terms of cents per Deutsche mark, which implies that the option prices will be quoted in terms of cents per Deutsche mark.

The price and delta for the call and put options are shown in Table 11.5, Part B. The contract size is 62,500 Deutsche marks. The cost of the call option is

$$62{,}500(\text{DM}) \times (1.2971 \; (\text{¢/DM})/100) = \$810.69.$$

We divide by 100 to convert the price from cents to dollars.

In Table 11.5, Part C, the options are valued assuming that the spot exchange rate is quoted in terms of dollars per Deutsche mark (0.6408), and the strike price is quoted in terms of dollars per Deutsche mark (0.63). Comparing Part C to Part B, note that for the call and put options, the price is reduced by a

TABLE 11.5 *Pricing European Options*

PART A
INPUT DATA

Spot exchange rate	64.08 cents/DM
Strike price	63.00 cents/DM
Maturity	35 days
Volatility*	8.15 percent
Domestic discount rate**	4.03 percent
Foreign discount rate**	4.40 percent

*A 365-day year is assumed.
**A 360-day year is assumed

PART B
OPTION PRICES*

TYPE OF OPTION	OPTION PRICE (CENTS)	DELTA
Call	1.2971	0.7459
Put	0.2443	−0.2498

PART C
OPTION PRICES*

TYPE OF OPTION	OPTION PRICE (DOLLARS)	DELTA
Call	0.0130	0.7459
Put	0.0024	−0.2498

*The program FX/Pricing/European is used.

factor of 100 while the value of delta remains unchanged. Delta is invariant to changes in the units of the spot exchange rate and strike price. ∎

The binomial option pricing model with Expression (11.16) will converge to the closed form solutions described by (11.18) and (11.19). It is demonstrated in Table 11.6 for call options.[6] The speed of convergence is reasonably fast. For 100 intervals

---

[6]We use the binomial option pricing model for pricing options on stocks with a constant dividend yield. There is a minor conversion of units, which must be undertaken before using the model. The foreign interest rate is expressed as a discount rate. In the binomial model, the constant dividend yield is expressed on a continuously compounded basis. To convert from a discount rate to a continuously compounded basis we must use the relation

$$1 - 0.06 = \exp(-d_y),$$

implying $d_y = 6.1875$ percent. If you find this conversion confusing, please refer to Chapter 1.

TABLE 11.6   *Convergence of the Binomial Option Pricing Model*

NUMBER OF INTERVALS	CALL OPTION PRICE** (CENTS)	DELTA	GAMMA
1	6.6877	0.4109	0.0019
2	5.2867	0.4443	0.0015
50	5.2447	0.4267	0.0217
100	5.2436	0.4266	0.0215
155	5.2336	0.4267	0.0215
200	5.2477	0.4269	0.0215
Closed form solution*	5.2416	0.4268	0.0214

COMMON INPUTS

Spot exchange rate	145 cents/£
Strike price	145 cents/£
Domestic discount rate***	4.00%
Maturity	365 days
Volatility***	12%
Number of days in year	365
Binomial option pricing model	
Constant dividend yield	6.1875
Foreign Discount Rate***	6%

*The program FX/Pricing/European is used.

**The program Binomial/Pricing European Option/Constant Dividend is used.

***A 365-day year is assumed.

the binomial approximation is 5.2436 compared to the correct value of 5.2416. The solution oscillates as it approaches the limiting value. Compare the values at 100, 155, and 200 intervals. The advantage of the closed form solution over the binomial option model is in computational speed.

It is instructive to study these valuation formulas from another perspective. This alternative perspective relates the above solutions to Black's model in Chapter 9. The expressions for the value of these options can be written in terms of the forward exchange rate. From Expression (2.7) of Chapter 2, called interest-rate-parity, we have

$$F(0,T)B(0,T) = S(0)B_f(0,T), \tag{11.20}$$

where $F(0,T)$ is the date-0 forward exchange rate for delivery at date T.

Substituting Expression (11.20) into Expressions (11.18) and (11.19) gives

$$c(0) = B(0,T)[F(0,T)N(d) - KN(d - \sigma\sqrt{T})] \qquad (11.21)$$

and

$$p(0) = B(0,T)[KN(-d + \sigma\sqrt{T}) - F(0,T)N(-d)], \qquad (11.22)$$

where $d \equiv \{\ln[F(0,T)/K] + \sigma^2 T/2\}/\sigma\sqrt{T}$.

The preceding results are an example of Black's model, which we discussed in Chapter 9. Note that the use of the forward rate eliminates the foreign discount exchange rate from the option valuation equations, Expressions (11.21) and (11.22).

EXAMPLE **Black's Model**

In this example we illustrate the valuation of foreign currency options using Black's model. Using the data in Table 11.5, Part A,

$$B(0,35) = (1 - \frac{4.03}{100} \times \frac{35}{360}) = 0.996082$$

and

$$B_f(0,35) = (1 - \frac{4.40}{100} \times \frac{35}{360}) = 0.995722.$$

Substituting into Expression (11.20), the forward exchange rate is

$$F(0,35) = 64.08 \times \frac{0.995722}{0.996082}$$

$$= 64.0569 \text{ cents per Deutsche mark.}$$

Using this forward exchange rate and the data in Table 11.5, Part A, we use the Black model to determine the price of a call option and put option. The results are shown in Table 11.7. These results should be compared to those in Table 11.5, Part B. We observe that the option prices are the same while the deltas differ.

In the Black model, the delta for a call option is

$$\text{Delta} \equiv \frac{\partial c}{\partial F} = \frac{\partial S}{\partial F} \frac{\partial c}{\partial S}.$$

TABLE 11.7 *Using the Black Model**

TYPE OF CALL	OPTION PRICE (CENTS)	DELTA
Call	1.2971	0.7462
Put	0.2443	−0.2499

*The program Futures/Pricing/European Options is used.

Using Expression (11.20),

$$\frac{\partial c}{\partial F} = \frac{B(0,T)}{B_f(0,T)} \frac{\partial c}{\partial S}.$$

Using the value in Table 11.5, Part B, the delta for the call on the spot exchange rate is

$$\frac{\partial c}{\partial S} = 0.7459.$$

Therefore,

$$\frac{\partial c}{\partial F} = \frac{0.996082}{0.995722} \times 0.7459$$

$$= 0.7462,$$

which agrees with the number in Table 11.7. For the put option, the delta is

$$\frac{\partial p}{\partial F} = \frac{0.996082}{0.995722} \times (-0.2498)$$

$$= -0.2499,$$

which agrees with the number in Table 11.7. ∎

11.7 AMERICAN OPTIONS

We now examine the pricing of American options written on a spot exchange rate. Using the analogy between the "dividend yield" on a stock and the foreign interest rate on the spot exchange rate, we see that early exercise of American options is a distinct possibility. We illustrate these issues through an example.

Consider pricing an American call option on a spot exchange rate with a strike price of 130 cents/pound and maturity of one year. Let the lattice of spot exchange rates be as described in Figure 11.7, which is identical to that contained in Figure 11.4. The call option values at maturity are also shown in Figure 11.7. The call option is in-the-money for the top two branches of the tree and out-of-the-money for the third.

Now consider the value of the option six months prior to maturity. Suppose that the spot exchange rate is 131.33. The value of the call option, if not exercised, is

$$\frac{1}{1.0206}[10.95 \times \pi + 0 \times (1 - \pi)] = 5.36,$$

where we have shown earlier that the equivalent martingale probability is 0.4997 (see Section 11.3).

FIGURE 11.7   *Spot Exchange Rates and the American Call Option's*
Characteristics

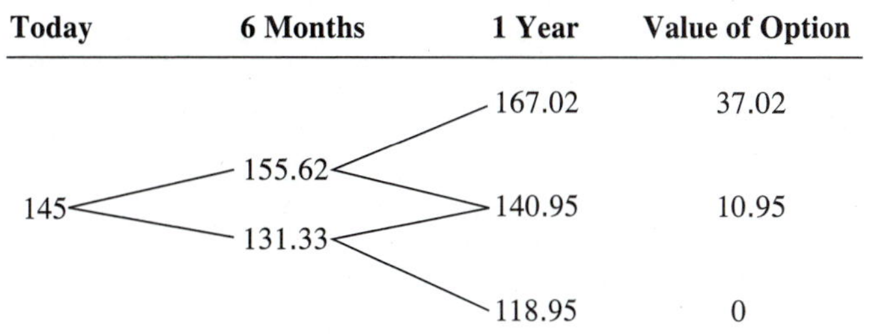

Today	6 Months	1 Year	Value of Option
		167.02	37.02
	155.62		
145		140.95	10.95
	131.33		
		118.95	0

Spot exchange rates are expressed as cents/pound.
Strike price of option is 130 cents/pound.

Because the option is American, it can be exercised early. If it is exercised early, when the spot exchange rate is 131.33 cents/pound, its value would be 1.33 (= 131.33 − 130) cents. Clearly, the optimal strategy is not to exercise.

Next, suppose the spot exchange rate is 155.62 cents/pound. The value of the call option if not exercised is

$$\frac{1}{1.0206} [37.02 \times \pi + 10.95 \times (1 - \pi)] = 23.50.$$

If the option is exercised early, its value is 25.62 (= 155.62 − 130) cents. In this case, the optimal strategy is to exercise the option.

Finally, at date 0 the value of the option, if not exercised, is

$$C_0 = \frac{1}{1.0206} [25.62 \times \pi + 5.36 \times (1 - \pi)]$$

$$= 15.18.$$

If exercised, the value would be (145 − 130) = 15 cents; thus no exercise is optimal. We summarize these results in Figure 11.8.

This simple example illustrates that it may be optimal to prematurely exercise an American call option on a spot exchange rate. Why? Because by exercising early the interest on the foreign riskless asset can be earned, whereas it is lost otherwise. The interest on the foreign riskless asset is analogous to a dividend (see Expression (11.15)).

The construction of the synthetic American call option is similar to that described in Chapter 5 and is left as an exercise for the reader.

FIGURE 11.8   *Prematurely Exercising an American Foreign Currency Call Option*

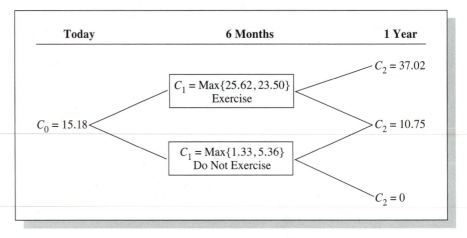

The same point made about early exercise of foreign currency American call options can also be made using the closed form solution, Expression (11.18). Suppose that a call option is deep-in-the-money, $S(0) \gg K$. This implies that $N(d_1) \simeq 1$ and $N(d_2) \simeq 1$, so we can write

$$c(0) \simeq B_f(0, T)S(0) - B(0, T)K.$$

If the foreign interest rate is greater than or equal to the domestic interest rate, then $B_f(0, T) < B(0, T)$ so that

$$c(0) < S(0) - K,$$

implying that it is optimal to prematurely exercise the option to earn the foreign interest rate on the foreign currency.

This result should not be surprising given our discussion in Chapter 7. There we demonstrated that it may be optimal to exercise earlier than maturity an American call option in the presence of dividends. For foreign currency options, the "dividend yield" is the foreign interest rate. Thus it may be optimal to exercise the option early and invest in the foreign riskless asset to earn the higher rate of interest (receive the "dividend yield").

EXAMPLE   **American Call Valuation**

This example illustrates the positive value to early exercise in foreign currency options.

Using the information in Table 11.5, Part A, we value a European call option with a strike price of 60 cents/Deutsche marks, maturity of 35 days, and

with a spot exchange rate of 64.08 cents/Deutsche marks. Using Expression (11.18), the value of the European is

$c(0) = 4.0433$ cents/Deutsche marks.

If this option could be exercised immediately, its value would be

$64.08 - 60 = 4.08$ cents/Deutsche marks,

implying there is value to early exercise. ∎

For pricing American options we can use the binomial option pricing model as just described. However, computation time for this approach tends to be slow. Fortunately, MacMillan (1986) derived an approximate but accurate formula for pricing American options.[7] For illustrative purposes, Table 11.8 compares the binomial option model prices with those derived using the MacMillan approximation, which is described in the Appendix of this chapter.[8] After 150 time steps the binomial model

TABLE 11.8 *Pricing American Foreign Currency Options*

	EUROPEAN	AMERICAN	
EXCHANGE RATE		MACMILLAN APPROXIMATION*	BINOMIAL**
140	3.3735	3.6071	3.5741
145	5.2416	5.6239	5.6138
150	7.6413	8.2564	8.2740
155	10.5518	11.5260	11.5693
160	13.9188	15.4389	15.5077
Strike price	145 cents/£		
Maturity	1 year		
Domestic discount rate	4%		
Foreign discount rate	6%		
Volatility	12%		

*The program FX/Pricing/American Option is used.

**Number of intervals 150. The program Binomial/Pricing American Option/Constant Dividend Yield is used.

[7]See also Barone-Adesi and Whaley (1987).

[8]See Table 11.6 and footnote 6 for the inputs to the binomial model if you want to check these figures for yourself.

TABLE 11.9   *Pricing American and European Call Options*

PART A INPUT DATA	
Spot exchange rate	154.85 cents/British pound
Maturity	35 days
Volatility*	11.95 percent
Domestic**	4.03 percent
Foreign **	4.49 percent

 *A 365-day year is assumed.

**A 360-day year is assumed

PART B OPTION PRICES		
STRIKE PRICE (CENTS/BRITISH POUND)	**AMERICAN OPTION PRICE (CENTS)***	**EUROPEAN OPTION PRICE (CENTS)****
152	3.9137	3.9055
153	3.2656	3.2592
154	2.6850	2.6800
155	2.1737	2.1698

*The program FX/Pricing/American Option is used.

**The program FX/Pricing/European Option is used.

yields values that have two-decimal-place accuracy (see Table 11.6). Thus we can view these values as the "true" values compared to which the MacMillan approximation is accurate to within one decimal place for most spot exchange rate values.

EXAMPLE   **American Versus European Option Values**
We want to compare the prices of European and American options written on the same spot exchange rate. The inputs are shown in Table 11.9, Part A. We value the options for a range of strike prices. The option prices are shown in Table 11.9, Part B. In all cases we observe that the American call is strictly greater in value than the corresponding European call, implying that early exercise has value. ∎

11.8 OPTIONS ON FOREIGN CURRENCY FUTURES

We examine here the pricing of options on foreign currency futures. We first illustrate the analysis using the binomial model of Chapter 5. Following this illustration we examine closed form solutions for options on foreign currency futures under the continuous-time model.

Consider a European call option that matures in six months' time. The option is written on a foreign currency futures contract on the pound that matures in twelve months' time. Let the strike price of the option be 147 cents per pound.

Let us use the two-period binomial lattice described in Figure 11.9, which is identical to that described in Figure 11.5. To price this option, we must first determine the futures prices at each node. Let $\mathscr{F}(t, T_{\mathscr{F}})$ denote the futures price at date t for a contract that matures at date $T_{\mathscr{F}}$.

At the delivery date of the futures contract the futures prices equal the spot exchange rate. This gives the futures prices on the nodes at one year (167.02, 140.95, 118.95).

Six months prior to maturity, suppose that the spot exchange rate is 155.62. We know from Chapter 6 that under the martingale probabilities, futures prices follow a martingale. This implies that the futures price is

$$\begin{aligned}\mathscr{F}(1,2) &= \pi 167.02 + (1 - \pi)140.95 \\ &= 153.99,\end{aligned}$$

where π is the martingale probability, which is 0.499702.

If the spot exchange rate is 131.33, the futures price is analogously determined via

$$\begin{aligned}\mathscr{F}(1,2) &= \pi 140.95 + (1 - \pi)118.95 \\ &= 129.95.\end{aligned}$$

Finally, the futures price at date 0 is

$$\begin{aligned}\mathscr{F}(0,2) &= \pi 153.99 + (1 - \pi)129.95 \\ &= 141.97.\end{aligned}$$

FIGURE 11.9   *Spot Exchange Rate Dynamics (Cents/Pound) and Futures Prices, Two Periods*

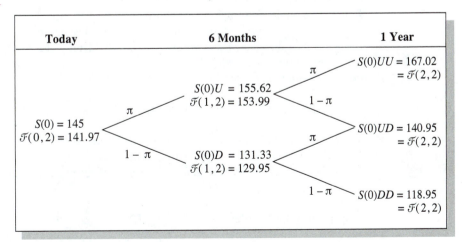

Now consider the value of the European call option at maturity. If the futures price is 129.95, the call option is worthless: $c_1^D = 0$. If the futures price is 153.99, the value of the option is

$$c_1^U = 153.99 - 147$$
$$= 6.99 \text{ cents per pound.}$$

Finally, the date-0 value of the option is

$$c(0) = \frac{1}{A(1)} [c_1^U \pi + c_1^D (1 - \pi)]$$

$$= \frac{1}{1.0206} [6.99\pi + 0(1 - \pi)]$$

$$= 3.42 \text{ cents per pound,}$$

computed using the risk-neutral valuation procedure. The analysis for European options is now complete.

American options on foreign currency futures are handled analogously to American options on the spot exchange rate. The procedure is as follows: The early exercise decision is considered at each node of the lattice in the backward inductive argument. The value of the option under the best decision is placed at each node for analysis at the next step backwards. The procedure stops when date 0 is reached, thus completing the pricing of foreign currency futures options using the binomial model of Chapter 5.

Closed Form Solutions

We now describe closed form solutions for pricing foreign currency futures options under the continuous-time model. Although options on foreign currency futures are American, we initially ignore the possibility of premature exercise and treat the option as being European.

In this case, under Assumptions A1 through A7 we can directly use the results from Chapter 9 to derive closed form solutions. It follows because the spot exchange rate is lognormally distributed, and we can use the "dividend yield" analogy for the foreign interest rate. Thus, using Expression (9.13) in Chapter 9, the value of a European call option on the foreign currency futures is given by

$$c(0) = B(0,T)[\mathcal{F}(0,T_{\mathcal{F}})N(d_1) - KN(d_2)], \tag{11.23}$$

where the option matures at date T, K is the strike price, $d_1 \equiv \{\ln[\mathcal{F}(0,T_{\mathcal{F}})/K] + (\sigma^2/2)T\}/\sigma\sqrt{T}$, and $d_2 \equiv d_1 - \sigma\sqrt{T}$. This is Black's model.

Using Expression (9.14), the value of a foreign currency futures European put option is given by

$$p(0) = B(0,T)[KN(-d_2) - \mathcal{F}(0,T_{\mathcal{F}})N(-d_1)]. \tag{11.24}$$

To value American options under Assumptions A1 through A7, we can either use a binomial lattice approximation to the lognormal and proceed as discussed in the previous section, or we can use the MacMillan (1986) model approximation, illustrated in the following example.

EXAMPLE

American Foreign Currency Futures Option Valuation

We want to value an option written on the Canadian futures contract. The option matures in October. Foreign currency futures contracts mature in March, June, September, and December. Consider the October futures option that is written on the December futures contract. The inputs are shown in Table 11.10, Part A. The December futures price is 72.14 cents/C$.

The MacMillan model is used to price the American options. The price and delta for the call and put options are shown in Table 11.10, Part B. The contract size is 100,000 Canadian dollars. The cost of the call options is

$$100,000 \times (0.4619/100) = \$461.90.$$

Note that we divide by 100 because the option price is quoted in cents. ∎

TABLE 11.10 *Pricing Options on Foreign Currency Futures*

PART A INPUT DATA	
Futures price	72.14 cents/C$
Strike price	72.50 cents/C$
Maturity	71 days
Volatility*	5.00 percent
Discount rate**	4.3 percent

 *A 365-day year is assumed.
**A 360-day year is assumed.

PART B OPTION PRICES*		
TYPE OF OPTION	OPTION PRICE (CENTS)	DELTA
Call	0.4619	0.4121
Put	0.8267	−0.5812

*The program Futures/Pricing/American Option is used.

11.9 REPLICATING OPTIONS ON SPOT WITH FUTURES

Let us now study how to replicate an option on the spot exchange rate with foreign currency futures. It is a practical consideration because the foreign currency futures are often more liquid than the underlying spot exchange rate. We discuss the construction of synthetic options from both the perspective of the binomial model of Chapter 5 and the continuous-time model of Chapter 10.

We first use the binomial model. Consider a European put option written on a foreign currency. Let the maturity of the option be one year and the strike price be 145 cents per unit of the foreign currency. We can use the binomial model described in Section 11.3 to price this option. The details are shown in Figure 11.10. We leave it to the reader to check these figures.

In Section 11.3, we constructed the replicating portfolio using the foreign riskless asset (riskless in terms of the foreign currency) and the domestic riskless asset.

Figure 11.10   *Hedging Options on the Spot Exchange Rate with Futures (Strike Price 145 Cents/Pound)*

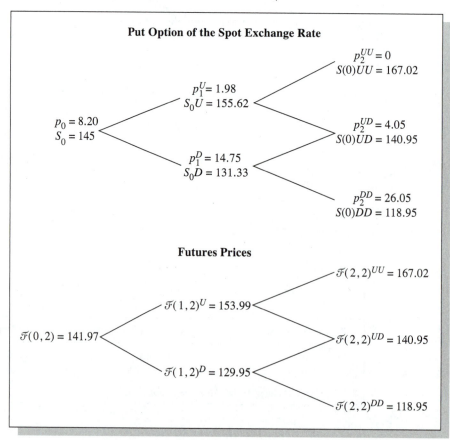

An alternative way to construct this replicating portfolio is to use the foreign currency futures contracts and the domestic riskless asset. Although we have already explained how to do this in Chapters 5 and 6, it is instructive to repeat the arguments here.

Let the synthetic option be constructed by using $m_{\mathscr{F}}$ futures contracts written on the foreign currency with maturity one year and investing B dollars in the domestic riskless asset. The initial value of the replicating portfolio is

$$V(0) = m_{\mathscr{F}} \times 0 + B = B,$$

given that the value of the futures contracts is zero. The futures price is $\mathscr{F}(0,2)$.

One period later, if the up state occurs the value of the option is p_1^U and the value of the replicating portfolio must be constructed such that

$$m_{\mathscr{F}}[\mathscr{F}(1,2)^U - \mathscr{F}(0,2)] + BR = p_1^U$$

and, if the down state occurs,

$$m_{\mathscr{F}}[\mathscr{F}(1,2)^D - \mathscr{F}(0,2)] + B = p_1^D.$$

This gives two equations in two unknowns. Solving for $m_{\mathscr{F}}$ and B gives

$$m_{\mathscr{F}} = (p_1^U - p_1^D)/[\mathscr{F}(1,2)^U - \mathscr{F}(1,2)^D] \tag{11.25}$$

and

$$B = \frac{R^{-1}\{p_1^D[\mathscr{F}(1,2)^U - \mathscr{F}(0,2)] - p_1^U[\mathscr{F}(1,2)^D - \mathscr{F}(0,2)]\}}{[\mathscr{F}(1,2)^U \mathscr{F}(1,2)^D]}. \tag{11.26}$$

EXAMPLE   **Synthetic Option Using Futures**

Here we illustrate how to construct the synthetic option using futures contracts. We use the numbers from Figure 11.10. Direct substitution into Expressions (11.25) and (11.26) yields

$$m_{\mathscr{F}} = [1.98 - 14.75]/(153.99 - 129.95)$$
$$= -0.5312$$

and

$$B = \frac{1}{1.0206} \ \frac{\{14.75[153.99 - 141.97] - 1.98[129.95 - 141.97]\}}{(153.99 - 129.95)}$$

$$= 8.20.$$

In this example, the value of $m_{\mathscr{F}}$ is negative, implying that we must write futures contracts. ∎

Expressions (11.25) and (11.26) show how to construct synthetic options on spot using futures contracts and the domestic riskless asset.

To avoid arbitrage, the cost of constructing the synthetic option must equal the value of the traded option, that is,

$$V(0) = p_0.$$

The analysis using a continuous-time valuation model, such as in Expression (11.18) or (11.19), is best described via a numerical example.

EXAMPLE   **Continuous-Time Model Replication**

This example illustrates continuous-time synthetic option replication with futures contracts.

Consider a financial institution that wants to construct a synthetic European put option to sell 10 million British pounds. The institution wants to use traded futures contracts and the domestic money market account. Relevant details are given in Table 11.11.

Using the program FX/Pricing/European Option, the value of the put option is 4.7998 cents/pound and its delta is -0.5454. Therefore, the value of the synthetic put option is

(4.7998/100) × 10,000,000
= $479,980,

where we divide by 100 to convert the value of the option from cents to dollars.

TABLE 11.11   *Data for Synthetic Put Option*

Spot exchange rate	158.40 cents/British pound
Maturity of option	99 days
Strike price	160 cents/British pound
Volatility*	12.04%
Domestic discount rate**	5.75%
U.K. discount rate**	5.93%
Futures price	1.5831 $/British pound
$B(0,99) = 1 - 0.0575 \times (99/360) = 0.9842$	
$B_f(0,99) = 1 - 0.0593 \times (99/360) = 0.9837$	

  *A 365-day year is assumed.
 **A 360-day year is assumed.

This gives us enough information to compute the investment in the money market account. The initial value of the replicating portfolio must be equal to the value of the put option, that is,

$$479{,}980 = m_{\mathscr{F}} \times 0 + B,$$

implying that the investment in the money market account is $479,980.

To complete the construction, we need to determine the position in the futures contract. The instantaneous change in the value of the synthetic option must equal the instantaneous change in the put option. This condition will enable us to obtain the desired result.

First, the instantaneous change in the value of the put option is

$$\text{Delta} \times \Delta S, \tag{11.27}$$

where ΔS denotes the instantaneous change in the spot exchange rate. Therefore, the instantaneous change is

$$-0.5454 \times 10{,}000{,}000 \times \Delta S. \tag{11.28}$$

Note that we do not divide by 100, because the delta is the same as if we express the spot exchange rate and the strike in terms of cents/pounds or dollars/pounds.

Second, the instantaneous change in the cash flow plus the value of the replicating portfolio is

$$m_{\mathscr{F}} \times 62{,}500 \times \Delta \mathscr{F}, \tag{11.29}$$

where $\Delta \mathscr{F}$ is the instantaneous change in the futures price. We must multiply by 62,500, as this is the size of a traded futures contract.

We need to rewrite Expression (11.29) in terms of the spot exchange rate. Recall that the futures price equals the forward price, given the assumption of constant interest rates. Therefore, using interest-rate parity, we have from Expression (11.20) that

$$\mathscr{F}(0,T) = [B_f(0,T)/B(0,T)]S(0),$$

so that

$$\Delta \mathscr{F} = [B_f(0,T)/B(0,T)]\Delta S. \tag{11.30}$$

Substituting Expression (11.30) into Expression (11.29), the instantaneous change in the value of the replicating portfolio is

$$m_{\mathscr{F}} \times 62{,}500 \times [B_f(0,T)/B(0,T)]\Delta S. \tag{11.31}$$

We can now determine the position in the futures contract $m_{\mathcal{F}}$. Equating the instantaneous change in the value of the put option to the instantaneous change in the value of the synthetic portfolio gives

$$-0.5454 \times 10,000,000 = m_{\mathcal{F}} \times 62,500 \times (0.9837/0.9842),$$

implying

$$m_{\mathcal{F}} = -87.31.$$

The replicating portfolio requires writing 87 futures contracts (rounding off to the nearest integer). ∎

11.10 SUMMARY

This chapter examines the pricing and hedging of foreign currency derivatives. Given Assumptions A1 through A6, the pricing of derivatives on foreign currencies is analogous to the pricing of derivatives written on a stock with a known constant dividend yield. This analogy enables us to show how to construct the binomial lattice of spot exchange rates for these different assets and futures prices. Because an implicit dividend yield exists, it may be optimal to prematurely exercise American call and put options. We also discussed American valuation procedures. Finally, we showed how to construct synthetic options using futures contracts instead of the underlying spot exchange rate for both the binomial and continuous time models. In the next chapter, we study the pricing and hedging of derivatives on stock indices and commodities.

REFERENCES

General:

Barone-Adesi, G., and R. E. Whaley, 1987. "Efficient Analytic Approximation of American Option Values." *Journal of Finance* 42, 301–320.

MacMillan, L. W., 1986. "Analytic Approximation for the American Put Option." *Advances in Futures and Options Research* 1, 119–139.

Merton, R. C., 1973. "Theory of Rational Option Pricing." *Bell Journal of Economics and Management Science* 4, 141–183.

"United Currency Options Market." Philadelphia Stock Exchange (October, 1994).

Options on currencies:

Amin, K. I., and J. N. Bodurtha, 1993. "Stochastic Interest Rates and the American Exercise Feature: With an Application to IMM Contingent Claims." Working Paper, School of Business, University of Michigan.

Amin, K., and R. A. Jarrow, 1991. "Pricing Foreign Currency Options Under Stochastic Interest Rates." *Journal of International Money and Finance* 10, 310–329.

Biger, N., and J. Hull, 1983. "The Valuation of Currency Options." *Financial Management* 12, 24–28.

Bodurtha, J. N., and G. R. Courtadon, 1987. "Tests of an American Option Pricing Model on the Foreign Currency Options Market." *Journal of Financial and Quantitative Analysis* 22, 153–167.

Garman, M. B., and S. W. Kohlhagen, 1983. "Foreign Currency Option Values." *Journal of International Money and Finance* 2, 231–237.

Grabbe, J. O., 1983. "The Pricing of Call and Put Options on Foreign Exchange." *Journal of International Money and Finance* 2, 239–253.

Melino, A., and S. M. Turnbull, 1990. "The Pricing of Foreign Currency Options with Stochastic Volatility." *Journal of Econometrics* 45, 239–265.

Melino, A., and S. M. Turnbull, 1991. "The Pricing of Foreign Currency Options." *Canadian Journal of Economics* 24, 251–281.

Options on futures:

Black, F., 1976. "The Pricing of Commodity Contracts." *Journal of Financial Economics* 3, 167–179.

Brenner, M., G. Courtadon, and M. Subrahmanyam, 1985. "Options on the Spot and Options on Futures." *Journal of Finance* 40, 1303–1317.

Ramaswamy, K., and S. M. Sundaresan, 1985. "The Valuation of Options on Futures Contracts." *Journal of Finance* 40, 1319–1340.

Wolf, A., 1982. "Fundamentals of Commodity Options on Futures." *Journal of Futures Markets* 2, 391–408.

QUESTIONS

Question 1

A corporation enters into a forward contract to buy one million French francs (FF) at date T. The corporation specifies the delivery price $K(\$/FF)$, which differs from the current forward exchange rate $F(0, T)$ ($\$/FF$). Show that the dollar value of this contract is

$$V[0] = 1,000,000[F(0, T) - K]B(0, T).$$

Question 2

Prove that a lower bound for a European call option written on the spot exchange rate $S(0)$ is

$$c[0] \geq \text{Max}\{0, S(0)B_f(0, T) - KB(0, T)\}.$$

The option matures at date T, and K denotes the strike price.

Show that a lower bound for a European put option is

$$p[0] \geq \text{Max}\{0, KB(0,T) - S(0)B_f(0,T)\}.$$

Question 3

Prove that for European foreign currency options, the following relationship must hold:

$$p[0] + S(0)B_f(0,T) = c[0] + KB(0,T).$$

This relationship is called the put-call parity relationship for European foreign currency options. (Hint: Look at the proof of the put-call parity relationship for ordinary stock options given in Chapter 3.)

Question 4 *Identify the Implicit Options*

A company must purchase machinery costing 10 million Deutsche marks in 90 days' time. The current exchange rate is 0.66 $/DM. The company is concerned about the Deutsche mark appreciating against the dollar. The maximum spot exchange rate the company could tolerate is 0.74 $/DM.

A financial institution offers the company the following contract. In 90 days' time, if the spot exchange rate is 0.74 $/DM or greater the company can buy 10 million Deutsche marks at the rate 0.74 $/DM. If the spot exchange rate is X $/DM or less the company must buy marks at the rate of X $/DM. If the spot exchange rate is between X $/DM and 0.74 $/DM, the company buys marks at the spot rate. The financial institution picks the exchange rate X $/DM such that the value of the contract is zero.

Please identify the options in this contract and provide a clear explanation to justify your answer. Also, explain how to determine the exchange rate X $/DM such that the net total cost of the options is zero.

Question 5 *Foreign Currency Options*

a) What is the price of a European call option written on French francs with a maturity of one year? The spot exchange rate is 0.1760 ($/FF), volatility is 12 percent, and the strike price is 0.16. The contract size is 250,000 FF.

Divide the one-year period into two six-month intervals. The up-factor is defined by

$$U \equiv \exp[(r - r_f - \sigma^2/2)\Delta + \sigma\sqrt{\Delta}] = 1.068436$$

and the down-factor by

$$D \equiv \exp[(r - r_f - \sigma^2/2)\Delta - \sigma\sqrt{\Delta}] = 0.901667,$$

where σ is the volatility, Δ is the length of the interval, r is the domestic interest rate, and r_f is the French interest rate. If you invest one dollar for six months in the domestic riskless asset you will earn 1.0151 ($), and if you invest one French franc for six months in the French riskless asset you will earn 1.0305 (FF). For simplicity, assume that the martingale probability of an up state occurring is 0.5.

b)   If the option is American, what is its value? Use the same binomial lattice to determine the answer.

Question 6

The purpose of this question is to examine how the price of a foreign currency option varies as a function of maturity. Compute the option price over a range of spot exchange rates, exercise prices, and maturities. Use the program FX/Pricing/European Option. Fill in the following tables and then answer the question that follows.

CALL OPTIONS / PUT OPTIONS

Maturity 30 Days

CALL OPTIONS				PUT OPTIONS		
	Strike Price				Strike Price	
	23	25	27		23	25	27
Exchange Rate				Exchange Rate		
23				23		
25				25		
27				27		

Maturity 150 Days

CALL OPTIONS				PUT OPTIONS		
	Strike Price				Strike Price	
	23	25	27		23	25	27
Exchange Rate				Exchange Rate		
23				23		
25				25		
27				27		

Volatility	13%
Domestic Discount Rate	4.50%
Foreign Discount Rate	7.25%

a) How does the option value vary with maturity?
b) If the foreign discount rate is zero, would it alter your answer?
c) Suppose now that the foreign discount rate is 4.00 percent. How does this fact affect your answer?

Question 7

The table below contains information about European options written on the Deutsche mark, the U.S. dollar being the numeraire. Compute the implied volatilities using the program FX/Implied Volatility/European Option. What value for the volatility would you use to value other similar options?

TYPE OF OPTION	STRIKE PRICE	MATURITY (DAYS)	OPTION PRICE
Call	75	36	0.21
Call	67	99	4.70
Call	69	99	3.25
Put	69	36	0.51

Spot Exchange Rate	70.62 cents/DM
36-day Domestic Discount Rate*	5.65%
36-day Foreign Discount Rate*	4.46%
99-day Domestic Discount Rate*	5.75%
99-day Foreign Discount Rate*	4.64%

*A 360-day year is assumed.

Question 8

Below is a table of prices for American options on the Deutsche mark.

a) Compute the implied volatilities for these options using the program FX/Implied Volatility/American Option.
b) For the first five options, is there any pattern to the implied volatilities?
c) How do the implied volatilities for the call options differ from those for the put options?
d) How do your estimates for the implied volatility vary with maturity?

TYPE OF OPTION	STRIKE PRICE	MATURITY (DAYS)	OPTION PRICE
Call	66	36	4.91
Call	68	36	3.19
Call	69½	36	2.00

Call	71	36	1.23
Call	71½	36	1.13
Call	71	99	2.13
Call	72	99	1.74
Call	74	99	0.99
Call	75	99	0.61
Put	68	36	0.31
Put	68½	36	0.37
Put	70	99	1.51
Put	70½	99	1.85
Put	71	99	2.06
Put	72	99	2.32

Spot Exchange Rate	70.62 cents/DM
36-day Domestic Discount Rate*	5.65%
36-day Foreign Discount Rate*	4.46%
99-day Domestic Discount Rate*	5.75%
99-day Foreign Discount Rate*	4.64%

*A 360-day year is assumed.

Question 9

Using the information that follows, construct a synthetic foreign currency European put option on Deutsche marks using futures contracts and the domestic money market account. The contract size for the option is 10 million Deutsche marks.

Spot Exchange Rate	70.62 cents/DM
Maturity of Option	99 days
Strike Price	68 cents/DM
Volatility*	13%
Domestic Discount Rate**	5.75%
Foreign Discount Rate**	4.64%
Future Price (maturity 99 days)	70.84 cents/DM

 *A 365-day year is assumed.
**A 360-day year is assumed.

a) What is the value of the put option and its delta? Use the program FX/Pricing/European Option.
b) What is the delta of the futures contract?
c) Describe the synthetic portfolio. Note that one futures contract is for 125,000 DM.
d) Examine the performance of the synthetic option one day later by completing the following table.

Spot Exchange Rate	Futures Price	Value of Contract	Value of Synthetic Option
68	68.20	170,030	
69	69.21	128,000	
70	70.21	94,060	
71	71.21	67,440	
72	72.22	47,160	

Question 10   Index Currency Option Notes (ICONS)

An Australian company plans to issue a 10-year U.S. dollar Eurobond. In this issue, if the spot exchange rate (A\$/\$) is greater than A\$1.45/\$ (= 0.6897\$/A\$), the bond-holder receives the face amount of the \$1,000 (U.S.) note. If the spot exchange rate is less than A\$1.45/\$ the bondholder receives the face value of the note minus an amount given by the formula

$$[1.45S - 1]1,000,$$

where S is the prevailing spot exchange rate, \$/A\$, when the bond matures. Thus, if the spot exchange rate is A\$1.30/\$ (= 0.7692\$/A\$), the amount deducted is

$$[1.45 \times 0.7692 - 1]1,000$$
$$= [1.1154 - 1]1,000$$
$$= \$115.4.$$

The bondholder receives

$$\$1,000 - 115.4$$
$$= \$884.6.$$

Note that ICONS are issued, serviced, and redeemed in U.S. dollars. If the exchange rate is less than A\$0.725/\$ (= 1.45/2), the bondholder receives zero.

Volatility*	8.96%
10-year U.S. Discount Rate**	5.30%
10-year Australian Discount Rate**	6.66%

*Assuming a 365-day year.
**Assuming a 360-day year.

a) Answer these three questions in terms of the spot exchange rate S, \$/A\$, when the bond matures.

    i)   If $S \leq 0.6897$,
        amount deducted =

ii)   If $1.3794 > S > 0.6897$,
    amount deducted =
iii)   If $S \geq 1.3793$,
    amount deducted =

b)   What simple combination of options can be combined to give such a payoff? (Hint: First, consider a European FX call option written on the Australian dollar with an exercise price of 0.6897 $/A$.)
c)   Price the individual options.
d)   Determine a value for the combination.

APPENDIX: THE QUADRATIC APPROXIMATION

The approximate value of an American call option is given by

$$C(S,T) = \begin{cases} c(S,T) + A_1(S/S^*)^{q_1} & \text{if} \quad S \leq S^* \\ S = K & \text{if} \quad S > S^*. \end{cases}$$

Here, $c(S,T)$ is the value of a European call option as given by (11.18):

$q_1 \equiv \{(1 - \beta) + [(1 - \beta)^2 + 4\alpha/K]^{1/2}\}/2;$
$\alpha \equiv 2r/\sigma^2;$
$\beta \equiv 2(r - r_f)/\sigma^2;$
$A_1 \equiv [1 - \exp(-r_f T)N(d^*)]S^*/q_1;$
$d^* \equiv \{\ln[B_f(0,T)S^*/B(0,T)K] + T\sigma^2/2\}/(\sigma\sqrt{T});$

and S^* is defined to be the solution of the equation

$$S^* - K = c(S^*,T) + [1 - \exp(-r_f T)N(d^*)]S^*/q_1.$$

The approximate value of an American put option is given by

$$P(S,T) = \begin{cases} p(S,T) + A_2(S/S^{**})^{q_2} & \text{if} \quad S \geq S^{**} \\ K - S & \text{if} \quad S < S^{**}. \end{cases}$$

Here, $p(S,T)$ is the value of a European put option as given by (11.19):

$q_2 \equiv \{(1 - \beta) - [(1 - \beta)^2 + 4\alpha/K]^{1/2}\}/2;$
$A_2 \equiv [1 - \exp(-r_f T)N(-d^{**})]S^{**}/q_2;$
$d^{**} \equiv \{\ln[B_f(0,T)S^{**}/B(0,T)K] + T\sigma^2/2\}/(\sigma\sqrt{T});$

and S^{**} is defined to be the solution to the equation

$$K - S^{**} = p(S^{**},T) - [1 - \exp(-r_f T)N(-d^{**})]S^{**}/q_2.$$

12 CHAPTER

STOCK INDEXES AND COMMODITIES

12.0 INTRODUCTION

I n this chapter, we examine derivatives on stock market indexes and commodities. Money managers of mutual funds, pension plans, and hedge funds regularly use stock index futures and options to insure fund performance and/or enhance fund returns. For example, buying put options on a stock index provides "portfolio insurance" on the fund's return. In contrast, to enhance fund returns in flat markets, the fund can write call options on the stock index. Analogously, commodity derivatives can be used to hedge future commodity price uncertainties due to production or delivery lags. For example, oil companies regularly use oil futures and options to hedge price risks associated with long-dated, fixed-price contracts to deliver oil to their various customers.

If we wish to gain insight into the uses of stock index and commodity derivatives, we need to understand their pricing and hedging. The pricing and hedging of derivatives on stock indexes and commodities is analogous to the pricing and hedging of derivatives written on foreign currencies. Therefore, our discussion of these derivatives will be brief. We first consider derivatives on stock indexes and then discuss derivatives on commodities.

12.1 DERIVATIVES ON STOCK MARKET INDEXES

A stock market index is a portfolio consisting of a collection of stocks. Table 12.1 shows the diversity of stock indices available. Thirty-eight different stock market indexes are included in this table. For example, the Major Market index (in row seventeen) is composed of twenty New York Stock Exchange (NYSE) blue-chip stocks. The S&P 500 index is composed of 500 common stocks, approximately 77 percent industrials, 8 percent utilities, 4 percent transportation companies, and 11 percent financial institutions. The market value of the 500 companies included is equal to approximately 80 percent of the value of all the stocks traded on the New York Stock Exchange. Alternatively, the New York Stock Exchange composite index (in row twelve) includes all of the more than 1,700 common stocks that trade on the NYSE. The Value Line Composite Average (in row thirty-three) consists of over 1,700 stocks traded on the NYSE, American Stock Exchange, and the over-the-counter market.

TABLE 12.1   *Diversity of Indexes, Thursday, May 28, 1998**

RANGES FOR UNDERLYING INDEXES
Thursday, May 28, 1998

	High	Low	Close	Net Chg.	From Dec. 31.	% Chg.
DJ Indus (DJX)	89.93	89.01	89.70	+ 0.33	+ 10.62	+ 13.4
DJ Trans (DTX)	335.89	331.19	333.70	+ 0.45	+ 8.05	+ 2.5
DJ Util (DUX)	281.15	277.03	280.78	+ 3.36	+ 7.71	+ 2.8
S&P 100 (OEX)	535.08	530.41	534.04	+ 2.04	+ 74.10	+ 16.1
S&P 500 -A.M.(SPX) ..1099.73	1089.06	1097.59	+ 5.36	+ 127.16	+ 13.1	
CB-Tech (TXX)	256.92	253.34	254.86	− 0.59	+ 39.07	+ 18.1
CB-Mexico (MEX)	105.55	104.22	104.53	− 0.78	− 22.45	− 17.7
CB-Lps Mex (VEX)..	10.56	10.42	10.45	− 0.08	− 2.25	− 17.7
MS Multintl (NFT)...	603.64	598.34	601.76	+ 1.14	+ 70.21	+ 13.2
GSTI Comp (GTC) ...	171.36	169.07	170.31	+ 0.05	+ 26.85	+ 18.7
Nasdaq 100 (NDX)....1218.16	1200.24	1214.83	+ 5.37	+ 224.03	+ 22.6	
NYSE (NYA)	567.91	562.67	567.10	+ 3.17	+ 55.91	+ 10.9
Russell 2000 (RUT)..	455.81	450.26	455.81	+ 5.55	+ 18.79	+ 4.3
Lps S&P 100 (OEX) .	107.02	106.08	106.81	+ 0.41	+ 14.82	+ 16.1
Lps S&P 500 (SPX) ..	109.97	108.91	109.76	+ 0.54	+ 12.72	+ 13.1
S&P Midcap (MID) ..	358.63	354.91	358.52	+ 3.58	+ 25.15	+ 7.5
Major Mkt (XMI)	945.83	936.61	943.38	+ 4.10	+ 106.53	+ 12.7
HK Fltg (HKO)..........	173.78	173.78	173.78	− 2.02	− 40.78	− 19.0
HK Fixed (HKD)			174.17	− 2.02	− 40.87	− 19.0
IW Internet (IIX).....	326.39	319.28	324.65	+ 1.64	+ 64.40	+ 24.8
AM-Mexico (MXY) ...	119.33	117.23	117.41	− 1.38	− 24.12	− 17.0
Institut'l -A.M.(XII) ..	610.44	604.79	608.96	+ 1.89	− 441.20	− 42.0
Japan (JPN)...............			163.33	+ 1.31	+ 5.69	+ 3.6
MS Cyclical (CYC) ...	529.65	525.83	527.92	+ 0.30	+ 52.91	+ 11.1
MS Consumr (CMR) .	495.33	489.82	494.52	+ 3.87	+ 48.88	+ 11.0
MS Hi Tech (MSH) ..	556.41	547.79	552.87	− 0.26	+ 105.35	+ 23.5
Pharma (DRG)..........	632.15	626.09	628.92	− 2.60	+ 95.18	+ 17.8
Biotech (BTK)	164.28	160.72	163.67	+ 2.38	+ 1.25	+ 0.8
Comp Tech (XCI)	523.40	516.06	518.55	− 2.10	+ 79.56	+ 18.1
Gold/Silver (XAU)...	76.73	74.90	76.29	+ 1.49	+ 2.10	+ 2.8
OTC (XOC)	881.56	869.79	879.12	+ 3.23	+ 141.17	+ 19.1
Utility (UTY)	308.88	304.45	308.86	+ 4.39	− 1.17	− 0.4
Value Line (VLE)....	951.89	942.89	951.24	+ 8.21	+ 74.40	+ 8.5
Bank (BKX)...............	844.09	835.97	842.70	+ 4.80	+ 87.35	+ 11.6
Semicond (SOX).......	271.09	265.43	267.75	+ 1.09	+ 4.12	+ 1.6
Top 100 (TPX) 1046.94	1037.26	1044.39	+ 3.59	+ 134.77	+ 14.8	
Oil Service (OSX).....	104.67	100.79	104.67	+ 1.90	− 9.70	− 8.5
PSE Tech (PSE)........	336.20	332.14	335.05	+ 1.98	+ 44.49	+ 15.3

*Source: *The Wall Street Journal*, May 29, 1998

Lastly, the Japanese index (in row twenty-three) is composed of 225 companies traded on the Tokyo Stock Exchange. The U.S. dollar/yen exchange rate is fixed in the quotation of the Japanese index's value.

At present there are three different forms of derivatives traded on stock indices: options on the index, futures on the index, and options on stock index futures. We discuss each of these derivatives sequentially in the next three sections.

12.2 STOCK MARKET INDEX FUTURES

Let us examine the pricing and hedging of stock market index futures contracts. Table 12.2 shows closing prices for some of the different index futures contracts. Thirteen different stock index futures contracts are listed in this table. The second futures contract listed is on the S&P 500 index. The contract size for the S&P 500 index futures contract is $250 multiplied by the value of the S&P 500 stock index. The CAC-40 contract is written on a French market index and is traded on the MATIF exchange. The index value is quoted in French francs. The FT-SE 100 is a contract written on a British market index. This contract is traded on the London International Financial Futures and Options Exchange (LIFFE). Its value is quoted in British pounds. Because of futures market regulations, there is usually a minimum price movement on a stock index futures contract; it is best illustrated with an example.

EXAMPLE   **Minimum Price Fluctuation, S&P 500 Index Futures**

Suppose an investor goes long in a June futures contract on the S&P 500. The current index value is 1,100.70 (see Table 12.2). Suppose that when the contract is marked-to-market, the futures price has increased by the minimum trading price change (one "tick") to 1,100.75. The minimum price change in the value of the futures contract is thus

$$\$250 \times (1,100.75 - 1,100.70) = \$12.50.$$

We multiply by 250 because the contract size in dollars is 250 times the S&P 500 stock price index. ■

Futures Prices

Here we study the arbitrage-free determination of futures prices for a stock market index.

Consider a futures contract with delivery at date $T_{\mathcal{F}}$, and let $\mathcal{F}(t,T_{\mathcal{F}})$ denote the stock market index futures price at date t. Under the assumption that interest rates are deterministic, we know from Section 2.5 of Chapter 2 that forward and futures prices are identical. Therefore, using Expression (2.8) from Chapter 2, we can relate the futures price to the value of the spot index via the cost-of-carry relationship, that is,

$$B(0,T_{\mathcal{F}})\mathcal{F}(0,T_{\mathcal{F}})$$

$$= I(0) - PV_0 \left\{ \begin{matrix} \text{of all dividends paid by the stocks in the index} \\ \text{over the life of the futures contract} \end{matrix} \right\},$$

where $I(0)$ is the current value of the index and $B(0,T_{\mathcal{F}})$ is the date-0 value of a Treasury bill that pays one dollar for sure at date $T_{\mathcal{F}}$.

TABLE 12.2 *Futures on Indexes, Thursday, May 28, 1998**

INDEX

DJ INDUSTRIAL AVERAGE (CBOT)-$10 times average

	Open	High	Low	Settle	Chg	High	Low	Open Interest
June	8977	9020	8922	9006	+ 310	9295	7070	12,986
Sept	9050	9110	9018	9097	+ 220	9390	7150	1,292
Dec	9135	9200	9110	9189	+ 230	9480	7677	622

Est vol 13,000; vol Wed 20,535; open int 14,993, +43.
Idx prl: High 8993.12; Low 8900.70; Close 8936.57 +33.63

S&P 500 INDEX (CME)-$250 times index

	Open	High	Low	Settle	Chg	High	Low	Open Interest
June	109700	110320	109110	110070	+ 4.20	114230	864.25	337,881
Sept	110950	111500	110300	111260	+ 4.20	115430	879.20	44,703
Dec	112350	112650	111500	112460	+ 4.10	116590	890.85	10,285
Mr99	....	....	113690	+ 3.90	117840	902.85		1,802
June	....	....	114930	+ 4.00	119260	914.85		192
Dec	....	....	117560	+ 4.00	121980	981.40		486

Est vol 134,108; vol Wed 178,346; open int 395,428, +6,175.
Idx prl: High 1099.73; Low 1089.06; Close 1097.59 +5.36

MINI S&P 500 (CME)-$50 times index

	Open	High	Low	Settle	Chg	High	Low	Open Interest
June	109725	110325	109100	1101.00	+ 4.25	114250	923.75	18,326

Vol Wed 15,891; open int 18,706, +538.

S&P MIDCAP 400 (CME)-$500 times index

	Open	High	Low	Settle	Chg	High	Low	Open Interest
June	357.00	360.10	355.70	359.20	+ 2.60	384.60	299.00	12,394

Est vol 598; vol Wed 1,383; open int 13,319, −63.
Idx prl: High 358.61; Low 354.93; Close 358.52 +358.00

NIKKEI 225 STOCK AVERAGE (CME)-$5 times index

	Open	High	Low	Settle	Chg	High	Low	Open Interest
June	15750.	15790.	15665.	15685.	+ 40	21005.	14620.	17,597

Est vol 809; vol Wed 1,909; open int 18,055, +80.
Idx prl: High 15891.71; Low 15639.01; Close 15796.55 +132.26

NASDAQ 100 (CME)-$100 times index

	Open	High	Low	Settle	Chg	High	Low	Open Interest
June	121200	122450	120150	121850	+ 2.00	130700	963.75	8,615
Sept	123950	123950	122950	123500	+ 1.50	132100	980.50	357

Est vol 3,025; vol Wed 5,879; open int 9,036, −181.
Idx prl: High 1796.73; Low 1775.43; Close 1794.62 +1352.00

GSCI (CME)-$250 times nearby index

	Open	High	Low	Settle	Chg	High	Low	Open Interest
June	156.40	157.20	155.60	156.10	− .40	185.20	155.30	24,778

Est vol 2,824; vol Wed 5,251; open int 27,042, +867.
Idx prl: High 156.97; Low 155.68; Close 156.44 −.44

RUSSELL 2000 (CME)-$500 times index

	Open	High	Low	Settle	Chg	High	Low	Open Interest
June	454.00	458.50	450.00	458.25	+ 6.05	498.00	406.15	8,283

Est vol 544; vol Wed 654; open int 8,833, −86.
Idx prl: High 455.81; Low 450.30; Close 455.80 +5.54

U.S. DOLLAR INDEX (FINEX)-$1,000 times USDX

	Open	High	Low	Settle	Chg	High	Low	Open Interest
June	100.21	100.52	99.95	100.22	+ .11	102.00	97.34	4,410
Sept	99.91	100.28	99.73	99.98	+ .13	101.70	98.23	2,772

Est vol 2,000; vol Wed 3,149; open int 7,205, −193.
Idx prl: High 100.51; Low 99.91; Close 100.25 +.10

ALL ORDINARIES SHARE PRICE INDEX (SFE)
A$25 times index

	Open	High	Low	Settle	Chg	High	Low	Open Interest
June	2695.0	2717.0	2681.0	2717.0	+ 45.0	2921.0	2280.0	164,700
Sept	2709.0	2730.0	2700.0	2732.0	+ 45.0	2930.0	905.0	5,101
Dec	....	....	2744.0	+ 45.0	2920.0	2760.0		1,207
Mr99	....	....	2759.0	+ 45.0	2940.0	2770.0		773
June	....	....	2756.0	+ 45.0	....	....		121

Est vol 11,002; vol Wd 17,492; open int 171,902, +9,789.
The index: High 2716.3; Low 2685.4; Close 2714.4 +27.6

CAC-40 STOCK INDEX (MATIF)-FFr 200 per index pt.

	Open	High	Low	Settle	Chg	High	Low	Open Interest
May	4075.5	4082.5	4013.5	4020.0	+ 12.0	4144.5	3491.0	20,547
June	4056.0	4062.0	3996.5	4000.0	+ 12.5	4123.5	2204.5	39,111
July	4052.0	4052.0	4017.5	4005.0	+ 12.0	4120.5	2750.5	640
Sept	4049.5	4056.0	4046.5	4029.0	+ 12.0	4135.0	2936.0	17,951
Dec	....	....	4064.0	+ 12.0	4174.5	2807.5		2,820
Mr99	....	....	4104.5	+ 12.0	4204.5	2890.0		6,643
Sept	....	....	4115.0	+ 12.0	....	....		1,635

Est vol 47,557; vol Wd 59,254; open int 89,547, +115.

DAX-30 GERMAN STOCK INDEX (DTB)
DM 100 times index

	Open	High	Low	Settle	Chg	High	Low	Open Interest
June	5588.0	5588.0	5475.0	5529.0	+ 1.45	5681.5	3534.0	137,512
Sept	5631.0	5631.0	5526.0	5564.0	+ 1.23	5726.0	4309.0	18,901
Dec	5640.0	5640.0	5586.0	5615.0	+ .95	5742.0	5742.0	1,413

Est vol 28,892; vol Wd 39,316; open int 157,826, −1,199.
The index: High 5579.20; Low 5470.60; Close 5507.36 +.74

FT-SE 100 INDEX (LIFFE)-£10 per index point

	Open	High	Low	Settle	Chg	High	Low	Open Interest
June	5940.0	5941.0	5828.0	5881.0	+ 21.0	6207.0	4761.0	158,336
Sept	6014.0	6014.0	5922.0	5957.0	+ 21.0	6280.5	5823.0	13,899
Dec	....	....	6039.0	+ 21.0	6128.0	5998.0		250

Est vol 24,099; vol Wd 29,469; open int 172,485, +2,010.

This cost-of-carry relationship has three important implications. First, the futures price depends directly upon the level of the stock market index. If the index increases, the futures price increases, everything else being constant. Second, if the stocks in the index increase the level of dividend payments over the life of the futures contract, the futures price will fall, everything else being constant. This happens because the futures contract holder does not receive the dividend payments. Third, if the level of interest rates increases, the futures price will increase, everything else being constant. This occurs because of the multiplication by the discount factor $B(0, T_{\mathscr{F}})$ on the left side of the cost-of-carry relation. If $B(0, T_{\mathscr{F}})$ declines, the present value of the dividends paid by the stocks in the index over the life of the futures contract declines. Because the value of the index remains unchanged, the right side of the cost-of-carry relation increases, implying that the futures price $\mathscr{F}(0, T_{\mathscr{F}})$ must also increase.

This cost-of-carry relation is the basis of **index arbitrage**, a form of **program trading**, often engaged in by various investment banks. Recall that the cost-of-carry relation is based on a no-arbitrage argument. Thus a violation of this cost-of-carry relation indicates the existence of an arbitrage opportunity. For example, if the futures price is too large relative to the spot index's value, then futures contracts are sold and the spot index is purchased (in the appropriate amounts, as discussed in Chapter 2).

Stock index arbitrage is usually executed in sizable quantities, and it is therefore capable of moving the stock index's value and/or the futures price. In fact, the action of index arbitrage has been accused of causing the stock market crash of October 1987. It has also been widely acclaimed as increasing the efficiency of the stock market by keeping futures prices aligned. Whether good or evil, index arbitrage is here to stay and is an important part of market activity.

We can increase our understanding of this cost-of-carry relation by simplifying its form. Under the assumption that the dividend payments to the index can be approximated by a constant dividend yield over the life of the futures contract, we can write the above relation using Expression (2.10) of Chapter 2 as

$$B(0, T_{\mathscr{F}})\mathscr{F}(0, T_{\mathscr{F}}) = I(0)\exp(-d_y T_{\mathscr{F}}), \tag{12.1}$$

where d_y is the dividend yield. Next, expressing the price of the Treasury bill in terms of a continuously compounded interest rate r gives the simpler cost-of-carry relation

$$\mathscr{F}(0, T_{\mathscr{F}}) = I(0)\exp[(r - d_y)T_{\mathscr{F}}]. \tag{12.2}$$

Using this form of the cost-of-carry relation, it is easy to see when the index's value should exceed the futures price, and conversely. If the interest rate r is above the dividend yield, the futures price will be higher than the index value. Conversely, if the interest rate r is less than the dividend yield, the futures price will be lower than the index value.

EXAMPLE **The Implied Dividend Yield**

This example shows how to use Expression (12.1) to determine the implied dividend yield. The S&P 500 index value from Table 12.2 is 1,097.59 and the September futures contract price is 1,112.60. This contract expires in 112 days. The discount rate for a 112-day period is 4.99 percent, assuming a 360-day year, implying that the value of a 117-day zero-coupon bond is

$$B(0,112) = 1 - 0.0499 \times (112/360) = 0.9845.$$

Using Expression (12.1),

$$1,112.60 \times 0.9845 = 1,097.59 \exp[-d_y(112/360)],$$

implying that the implied dividend yield over this 112 days is

$$d_y = 0.66 \text{ percent.} \qquad \blacksquare$$

The sensitivity of stock index futures prices to interest rates is also clarified by Expression (12.2), which implies that if interest rates change, the greater the change in the futures price the longer the maturity of the contract. Indeed, from Expression (12.2) we have that

$$\frac{\Delta \mathcal{F}}{\Delta r} = T_{\mathcal{F}} \times \mathcal{F}(0, T_{\mathcal{F}}). \tag{12.3}$$

The greater $T_{\mathcal{F}}$ is, the larger is $\Delta\mathcal{F}/\Delta r$, everything else being constant. Our discussion of the stock index futures price determination is now complete.

12.3 SPREAD TRADING

Now we look at various trading strategies involving stock index futures. We discussed one such strategy, index arbitrage, in the previous section.

Same Index

First we discuss a trading strategy involving stock index futures contracts that is used as a vehicle for betting on beliefs about interest rates. Suppose that we anticipate rising interest rates. One way to capitalize on this anticipation is to short the nearby stock index futures contract and go long a stock index futures contract with a longer delivery date than the nearby contract, a strategy based on Expression (12.3). For a given change in interest rates, the longer the delivery date the greater will be the impact on the futures price. This difference in sensitivity can be the basis of a profitable trading strategy.

EXAMPLE **Speculating on Rising Interest Rates**

This example illustrates a trading strategy involving stock index futures that is sensitive to changes in interest rates. Using the data in Table 12.2, the June S&P 500 futures contract is trading at 1,100.70 and the September contract at 1,112.60, a spread of 11.90. The S&P 500 index is 1,097.59 (see Table 12.1).

We short the June contract and go long the September contract. Suppose that our view on interest rates is correct, and interest rates increase by 25 basis points. Suppose also that the June futures price moves to 1,100.80 and the September futures price to 1,113.10, the spread increasing to 12.30. The net change in the dollar value of this play is

$$-250(1,100.80 - 1,100.70) + 250(1,113.10 - 1,112.60) = \$100.$$

Suppose that our view on interest rates is incorrect, with interest rates remaining unchanged. Suppose that the June futures price closes at 1,101.70 and the September futures price closes at 1,113.20; the spread is now 2.50. The net change in the dollar value of this play is

$$-250(1,101.70 - 1,100.70) + 250(1,113.10 - 1,112.60)$$
$$= -250.00 + 150.00$$
$$= -\$100.00.$$

The position results in a loss, although the position is insensitive to "small" changes in the index. ■

Different Indexes

The differing constituent nature of indexes provides investors with the ability to trade on the relative performance of one market compared to another. We illustrate this opportunity via an example.

EXAMPLE **Speculating on Relative Changes in Stock Index Values**

This example illustrates the use of different stock index futures to formulate a trading strategy based on beliefs about relative performances.

Suppose an investor believes that given the current economic conditions, blue-chip firms will have on average a relatively sluggish performance compared to smaller firms. To take advantage of this belief, the investor can go long one June futures contract on the S&P Midcap 400 index, current futures price 359.20 and short one June futures contract on the DJ Industrial Average, current futures price 9,006 (see Table 12.2). The spread in dollars is $500 \times 359.20 - \$10 \times 9,006 = \$89,540$.

When the position is closed, suppose the S&P Midcap futures price is 375.00 and the Major Market index futures price is 9,050. The dollar spread has increased to $500 × 375 − $10 × 9,050 = $97,000. The net result is a profit of

$$97,000 - 89,540 = \$7,460. \qquad \blacksquare$$

12.4 INDEX OPTIONS

Now we describe stock index options and illustrate their use in portfolio insurance.

Table 12.3 shows closing prices for a selection of stock index options. The Chicago Board of Options Exchange trades options on the S&P 100 index. The contract size for the S&P 100 stock index option is $100 times the index level. The option is American, that is, it may be exercised any time up to and including its maturity date. S&P 500 stock index options also trade on this exchange. The contract size for the S&P 500 stock index is $100 times the index level. The option is European, that is, it may be exercised only at its maturity date. Traded on various exchanges are LEAPS. The acronym LEAPS means Long-Term Equity Anticipation Securities. These options have maturities of up to three years. LEAPS on the S&P 100 index can be exercised anytime. LEAPS on the S&P 500 index are European. All these index options are settled in cash.

The payoffs to stock index options are similar to the payoffs on standard call and put options. For example, consider a call option written on the S&P 500. Let the option mature at date T and the strike price be K. The value of the option at maturity is defined to be

$$c(T) \equiv \text{contract size} \begin{cases} I(T) - K & \text{if} \quad I(T) \geq K \\ 0 & \text{if} \quad I(T) < K. \end{cases} \qquad (12.4)$$

The contract size is $100 for the S&P 500 index option. If the index exceeds the strike price, the option ends in-the-money, and its value is: (contract size) $\times [I(T) - K]$. Otherwise, it is worthless.

Similarly, the value of a put option with maturity T and strike price K is defined to be

$$p(T) \equiv \text{contract size} \begin{cases} K - I(T) & \text{if} \quad I(T) \leq K \\ 0 & \text{if} \quad I(T) > K. \end{cases} \qquad (12.5)$$

If the index lies below the strike price, the put ends up in-the-money, earning the difference: (contract size) $\times [K - I(T)]$. Otherwise, it ends up out-of-the-money and worthless.

TABLE 12.3 *Index Options, Thursday, May 28, 1998**

Thursday, May 28, 1998

Volume, last, net change and open interest for all contracts. Volume figures are unofficial. Open interest reflects previous trading day. p-Put c-Call

CHICAGO

CB TECHNOLOGY(TXX)

Strike		Vol.	Last	Net Chg.	Open Int.
Jun	265p	5	12	+ 3 3/4	25

Call Vol. ....0 Open Int. 1,401
Put Vol. ....15 Open Int. 2,065

DJ INDUS AVG(DJX)

Strike		Vol.	Last	Net Chg.	Open Int.
Dec	64c	30	27 1/4	+ 1	686
Dec	66p	6	5 7/8	− 7/8	461
Jun	72c	80	17 3/4	− 1 3/4	201
Jun	72p	64	1/16	...	4,370
Dec	72p	110	1 1/8	− 1/8	36,636
Jun	80p	20	1/8	− 1/8	10,031
Sep	80p	9	1 7/16	− 1/4	14,009
Jun	82p	20	1/4	− 1/4	790
Jul	82p	2	13/16	− 1/8	5,965
Jun	84p	10	1/2	− 1/16	1,940
Jul	84p	1	1	− 1/2	3,057
Sep	84p	7	2 1/8	− 1/8	16,070
Dec	84p	20	3 1/4	− 5/8	546
Jun	85c	450	5 1/4	+ 3/8	1,522
Jul	85p	4	1 1/8	− 11/16	75
Jul	86p	2	1 1/2	− 1/8	975
Jun	87p	88	3/4	− 3/16	1,182
Jul	87p	55	1 3/4	− 1/2	140
Jun	88c	26	3	+ 1/8	4,923
Jun	88p	91	15/16	− 1/8	8,638
Jul	88c	1	4	− 1/4	63
Jul	88p	60	1 3/4	− 3/16	1,250
Sep	88p	29	3	− 1 1/8	2,024
Dec	88c	2	8 1/8	− 1 1/4	3,262
Jun	89c	471	2 3/16	+ 1/8	1,179
Jun	89p	603	1 1/4	− 1/4	5,297
Jul	89c	4	3 3/8	...	244
Jul	89p	10	2 1/4	− 3/4	89
Jun	90c	1,042	1 9/16	+ 1/16	7,364
Jun	90p	1,214	1 5/8	− 1/8	13,233
Jul	90c	106	2 5/8	− 1/8	988
Jul	90p	761	2 9/16	− 3/16	4,503
Sep	90c	7	4 3/4	...	1,331
Sep	90p	1	3 7/8	− 1/2	852
Dec	90p	2	5 3/8	− 1/4	366
Jun	91c	356	1	− 1/8	1,276
Jun	91p	90	2 1/8	− 1/8	3,052
Jul	91c	625	2	− 5/16	49
Jun	92c	115	9/16	− 3/16	2,644
Jun	92p	226	2 7/8	...	3,229
Jul	92c	2,715	1 3/4	...	2,857
Jul	92p	2	3 1/4	− 1/2	6,534
Sep	92c	5	3 3/8	− 1/4	1,526
Sep	92p	19	4 7/8	− 3/4	2,371
Jun	93c	34	7/16	...	1,268
Jun	93p	15	3 1/2	− 1/8	779
Jun	94c	300	3/16	− 1/16	1,987
Jun	94p	223	4 1/4	− 1/8	353
Jul	94p	4	4 5/8	− 1/2	206
Jun	95c	40	1/8	...	1,089
Jun	95p	10	5	− 3/8	875
Jun	96c	400	1/16	− 1/16	1,785
Jun	96p	75	6 1/4	+ 1/8	645
Sep	100p	20	9 3/4	− 5/8	165

Call Vol. ....6,943 Open Int. ...117,010
Put Vol. ....3,940 Open Int. ...250,501

DJ TRANP AVG(DTX)

Strike		Vol.	Last	Net Chg.	Open Int.
Jun	310p	25	1/2	+ 1/16	108
Jun	325c	11	10 1/8	− 5 3/8	400
Jun	330c	22	7 7/8	− 7/8	100
Jun	335c	30	6	− 1/2	129
Jun	340c	25	3 5/8	+ 5/8	181
Jun	340p	6	8 5/8	− 1	46
Jul	340c	5	7 5/8	+ 7/8	5

Call Vol. ....93 Open Int. 1,518
Put Vol. ....31 Open Int. 2,015

NASDAQ-100(NDX)

Strike		Vol.	Last	Net Chg.	Open Int.
Jun	900c	6	320	− 70	13
Sep	900c	6	338 3/4	− 24 1/8	13
Jun	1010p	3	1 1/4	− 1 1/8	218
Sep	1010p	20	17 1/8	+ 1 7/8	240
Jun	1020p	10	1	− 7/8	432
Jun	1050p	10	2	− 2 1/2	1,229
Jun	1080p	40	3	− 1/2	531
Sep	1080c	1	182	− 32 1/8	1
Jun	1100p	40	3 3/4	− 5 1/8	255
Jul	1100p	35	14 1/2	− 3 1/2	230
Aug	1100p	1	25 1/8	+ 4 5/8	1
Jun	1110p	10	4 3/8	− 3 7/8	303
Jun	1120p	94	5 1/8	− 2 5/8	388
Jun	1130p	13	6 7/8	− 4 1/8	55
Jun	1140p	1	7 3/4	− 8 3/8	290
Jun	1150p	21	9 3/4	− 1 3/4	2,223
Jun	1160c	2	67 7/8	+ 4 7/8	22
Jun	1160p	49	12	− 3	404
Jun	1170p	3	13	− 5 1/2	170
Jun	1180p	312	15 7/8	− 2 1/8	1,082
Jun	1190c	400	45	+ 1	658
Jun	1190p	2	18 1/8	− 8 5/8	129
Jun	1200c	93	40	+ 2	749
Jun	1200p	107	21	− 3	896
Jul	1200c	10	60 3/4	+ 14 3/4	21
Jul	1200p	100	41 1/2	+ 3/4	273
Jun	1220c	930	26	− 1 1/4	1,739
Jun	1220p	1,739	30	− 12	1,959
Jul	1220p	12	48 1/8	− 3 7/8	135
Jun	1240c	79	18 [illegible]	− 3/4	1,176
Jun	1240p	32	38 1/2	− 4 1/2	819
Jul	1240c	7	39 3/8	+ 5 1/2	9
Jul	1240p	7	58 1/4	− 10 1/8	58
Jun	1260c	292	9 3/4	− 1 7/8	1,383
Jun	1260p	3	53	− 3	762
Jul	1260c	10	30	+ 1	57
Jun	1280c	128	5 1/2	− 1 1/2	1,575
Jun	1280p	259	65	− 11	368
Jul	1280p	3	83	− 12	1,511
Jun	1300c	660	3 1/2	+ 1/8	1,234
Jul	1300c	163	18	+ 1 1/2	139
Jun	1320c	303	1 1/4	+ 9/16	230
Jul	1320c	10	12 1/2	+ 2 7/8	188
Jul	1340c	500	9	+ 2 3/4	27

Call Vol. ....3,600 Open Int......13,572
Put Vol. ....2,926 Open Int......23,938

RUSSELL 2000(RUT)

Strike		Vol.	Last	Net Chg.	Open Int.
Jun	390p	200	9/16	− 6 5/16	50
Jun	420p	20	1 9/16	− 1/8	673
Jun	425p	50	1 3/8	− 1 7/8	1
Jun	435p	25	2 7/16	+ 3/8	50
Jun	440c	200	20	− 1 3/8	440
Jun	445c	115	16 1/4	+ 4 5/8	204
Jul	445p	65	7	...	...
Jun	450c	36	11 1/2	+ 3 1/2	1,050
Jun	450p	35	4 1/2	− 2 3/8	823
Jun	455c	10	8 3/4	+ 3 3/8	203
Jun	455p	43	6 3/8	− 5 3/8	100
Jun	460c	1,133	5 3/4	+ 2 7/8	2,045
Jun	460p	1,102	8 3/8	− 4 5/8	2,307
Sep	460c	700	19 1/2	− 23	235
Sep	460p	700	18	+ 1 3/4	435
Jun	465c	1,026	3	+ 1 3/8	1,015
Jun	465p	1,025	11 1/2	− 5 1/2	1,300
Jul	465p	1	14 5/8	+ 3 1/8	2
Jun	470p	1,000	13 3/8	− 6 1/4	3,349
Jul	475p	1	26 1/2	+ 12 1/4	11
Jun	480c	1,182	1/4	− 1/8	4,284
Jun	480p	182	23	− 9 1/2	3,052
Jun	485p	100	30 7/8	+ 13 1/4	300
Jul	485p	25	30 1/8	− 3 3/4	50
Jul	490p	25	39 1/4	...	...
Aug	490p	25	39 1/4	...	...

Call Vol. ....5,952 Open Int......19,690
Put Vol. ....4,824 Open Int......30,348

S & P 100 INDEX(OEX)

Strike		Vol.	Last	Net Chg.	Open Int.
Jun	440p	487	5/16	− 1/8	5,709
Jun	450p	555	7/16	− 3/16	2,434
Jun	460p	401	9/16	− 1/4	10,525
Jul	460p	173	1 7/8	− 3/4	1,935
Jun	470p	506	3/4	− 1/4	5,232
Jul	470p	37	2 1/2	− 1/2	1,047
Aug	470c	20	72 1/2	+ 4	14
Aug	470p	387	5 3/8	− 1 3/4	807
Jun	480c	10	57	+ 6 1/2	611
Jun	480p	1,569	1	− 3/8	9,348
Jul	480p	761	3 3/8	− 5/8	1,868
Jun	485p	294	1 1/4	− 1/2	4,792
Jun	490c	2	47 1/4	+ 4 5/8	1,574
Jun	490p	965	1 1/2	− 3/8	8,571
Jul	490p	57	4 1/8	− 5/8	6,942
Sep	490p	10	11 5/8	+ 5/8	69
Jun	495p	1,011	1 13/16	− 9/16	3,980
Jun	500c	49	38 3/8	+ 4 7/8	545
Jun	500p	1,093	2 1/8	− 5/8	15,503
Jul	500p	250	6	− 1/2	12,804
Aug	500p	10	10 1/8	− 2 7/8	806
Sep	500p	5	12 3/4	− 4 1/4	69
Jun	505c	9	33 5/8	+ 1 5/8	150
Jun	505p	1,939	2 5/8	− 1/2	21,474
Jul	505p	202	6 3/8	− 1	796
Jun	510c	209	28 1/2	+ 1/8	1,941
Jun	510p	1,904	3 1/8	− 5/8	14,580
Jul	510c	1	34	− 5 1/2	75
Jul	510p	31	7 3/4	− 3/4	10,679
Aug	510p	11	11 7/8	− 7/8	1,023
Sep	510p	25	15	+ 1/8	303
Jun	515p	2,243	3 3/4	− 1	21,288
Jul	515p	347	8 1/2	− 1 1/2	297
Jun	520c	570	19 3/4	...	3,501
Jun	520p	3,100	4 3/4	− 3/4	11,688
Jul	520c	1	27	+ 6 1/8	1,857
Jul	520p	28	10 1/4	− 5/8	3,174
Sep	520p	1	18 1/4	− 1 3/4	583
Jun	525c	530	15 7/8	− 3/4	7,539
Jun	525p	5,324	6	− 7/8	9,917
Jul	525c	14	23 1/4	+ 3/8	2,769
Jul	525p	176	12	− 1	2,573
Jun	530c	2,831	12 3/4	− 3/8	11,180
Jun	530p	7,454	7 1/2	− 1	18,107
Jul	530c	72	19 7/8	+ 1/8	2,445
Jul	530p	175	13 1/2	− 1/2	3,044
Aug	530c	15	25 1/2	− 1/2	909
Aug	530p	57	18	− 2 1/8	1,639
Sep	530c	325	31	+ 2	600
Sep	530p	375	21 1/4	− 3 3/4	1,068
Jun	535c	4,565	9 7/8	...	15,028
Jun	535p	2,936	9 3/8	− 1 3/8	14,132
Jul	535c	100	16	− 1/4	2,094
Jul	535p	51	15	− 1 1/2	1,938
Aug	535p	152	20 1/8	− 1 7/8	33
Jun	540c	8,456	7 1/8	− 1/8	17,843
Jun	540p	4,301	11 1/2	− 1 3/4	18,958
Jul	540c	165	14 3/8	− 1/8	3,151
Jul	540p	70	17 1/2	− 1 1/2	2,217
Aug	540c	2	21	+ 3/8	3,594
Aug	540p	2	23 1/2	− 7/8	3,292
Sep	540p	1	25 5/8	− 4 3/8	1,712
Jun	545c	4,898	4 3/4	− 1/4	10,786
Jun	545p	767	14 1/2	− 1 1/2	2,836
Jul	545c	34	11 1/4	− 1/2	1,666
Jul	545p	10	20 1/4	− 8	1,350
Aug	545c	3	18 1/4	− 3 1/4	26
Aug	545p	2	25 5/8	+ 2 5/8	31
Jun	550c	5,961	3	− 3/8	11,633
Jun	550p	462	19 3/8	...	1,498
Jul	550c	100	9	− 1/8	5,805
Aug	550p	8	28 3/4	− 4 1/4	1,559
Jun	555c	5,030	1 13/16	− 3/8	8,311
Jun	555p	14	23	− 2	110
Jul	555c	26	7	− 1/4	1,555
Aug	555c	5	12	− 1 1/4	940
Jun	560c	4,375	1 1/16	− 3/16	11,615
Jun	560p	81	27	− 1 1/2	464
Jul	560c	303	5 3/4	+ 1/4	4,027
Jul	560p	10	31 1/2	− 8 1/2	110
Aug	560c	7	10 3/8	− 2 1/8	3,714
Sep	560p	11	35 1/4	− 4 1/4	94
Jun	565c	1,898	5/8	− 1/8	7,185
Jun	565p	50	30 1/2	− 9 1/4	133
Jul	565c	65	3 3/4	...	4,118
Aug	565c	10	8 1/2	− 3/4	4,845
Jun	570c	3,372	5/16	− 1/8	10,502
Jun	570p	31	36 3/4	− 1 1/2	44
Jul	570c	54	2 1/2	− 5/8	3,780
Jul	570p	29	38 1/2	+ 1/2	149
Aug	570c	1	7 1/4	+ 1/2	5,646
Sep	570c	25	11 5/8	− 2 3/8	112
Jun	575c	377	1/4	− 1/16	6,508
Jul	575c	31	1 7/8	+ 1/4	1,174
Jul	575p	1	42 5/8	− 10 3/8	43
Jun	580c	1,955	1/8	− 1/16	8,685
Jun	580p	4	47	− 1/4	7
Jul	580c	127	1 1/4	+ 1/16	1,310
Jul	580p	176	46 1/2	1/2	804
Aug	580c	2	4 5/8	+ 5/8	312
Jun	590c	1,677	1/16	− 1/16	6,899
Jul	590c	625	5/8	− 1/4	2,186
Jul	600c	25	3/8	...	2,291
Aug	600c	55	1 15/16	+ 3/8	196

Call Vol.......48,989 Open Int. ...209,473
Put Vol. ......41,132 Open Int. ...273,506

S & P 500 INDEX-AM(SPX)

Strike		Vol.	Last	Net Chg.	Open Int.
Jun	400c	10	693 3/8	− 5	3,525
Jun	400p	10	1/8	+ 1/16	541
Jun	700c	14	400	+ 4 3/4	1,490
Jun	700p	30	1/16	...	6,457
Jun	750p	250	1/16	− 1/16	13,440
Jun	800p	700	1/8	− 1/4	12,974
Jul	800p	145	9/16	− 7/16	3,100
Sep	800p	194	3	− 7/8	5,852
Sep	825p	4	4	− 1/4	3,170
Jun	875p	10	3/8	− 1/8	11,798
Jun	900c	10	195 3/8	+ 10 3/8	37,804
Jun	900p	10	1/4	− 1	29,053
Sep	900p	102	8	− 1 3/4	12,826
Jun	925p	60	3/4	− 7/8	17,893
Jul	925p	10	3 1/4	− 1 7/8	2,693
Jun	940p	22	1	− 3/8	1,458
Jun	950c	5	147 1/2	− 8	12,850
Jun	950p	236	1 1/8	− 7/8	26,681
Jul	950p	30	4 1/2	− 2	2,075
Sep	950p	105	12	− 3	21,050
Jun	975c	2	124 5/8	+ 16 5/8	14,020
Jun	975p	543	1 3/4	− 2 3/4	28,500
Jul	975p	4,152	4 3/4	− 3 1/2	906
Sep	975p	105	14	− 2	11,442
Jun	995p	2,669	2	− 1	22,654
Sep	995p	18	19	− 3	21,449
Jun	1005p	513	2 1/4	− 1	8,919
Jul	1005p	1,723	8	− 1 1/2	2,405
Aug	1005p	205	15	− 1	508
Jun	1010p	100	2 3/4	− 7/8	2,874
Jun	1020p	757	3 1/2	− 3	4,891
Jun	1025c	10	76	+ 11 3/4	8,058
Jun	1025p	510	3 1/2	− 1 3/4	14,956
Jul	1025p	102	10 1/4	− 3 3/4	2,199
Aug	1025p	20	19 3/4	− 4 3/4	998
Sep	1025p	342	23 1/4	− 1 1/4	15,005
Jun	1030p	30	4	− 2	1,711
Jun	1035c	3	68	+ 8 1/2	3
Jun	1035p	324	4 3/8	− 5 5/8	2,179
Jun	1040p	191	5 1/4	− 1 1/4	21,660
Sep	1040p	6	27 1/2	− 2 1/2	586
Jun	1050c	1,611	55 1/4	+ 1 1/4	16,218
Jun	1050p	7,171	6	− 2 1/4	29,576
Jul	1050c	5	65	+ 5 1/2	53
Jul	1050p	6,393	14 3/4	− 2 3/4	8,795
Aug	1050p	10	24	− 2 1/2	53
Sep	1050p	21	28	− 3	18,560
Jun	1055p	13	6 5/8	− 1 7/8	2,170
Jun	1060c	10	46 1/2	+ 1/2	1,881
Jun	1060p	1,675	7 5/8	− 1 7/8	13,010
Jun	1065p	1	8 3/4	...	...
Jun	1075c	3	35	+ 2 3/8	7,817
Jun	1075p	1,592	10 3/4	− 2	20,543
Jul	1075c	2	44 1/2	− 4 7/8	158
Jul	1075p	3,024	21 1/2	− 3	2,410
Sep	1075c	10	73	+ 10 1/2	11,764
Sep	1075p	970	36	− 2	21,248
Jun	1085c	1,434	28 1/2	+ 2 1/8	15,489
Jun	1085p	6,048	13 3/4	− 2 1/4	18,917
Jun	1090c	572	23 1/4	− 3/4	7,468
Jun	1090p	873	14	− 3 1/2	10,016
Jul	1090c	18	39 1/4	+ 3 1/4	254
Jul	1090p	43	24 3/4	− 4 1/4	7,028
Aug	1090p	160	35	− 3	306
Jun	1095c	1,481	20 1/2	− 1/2	1,910
Jun	1095p	1,299	16 3/4	− 4 1/4	6,600
Sep	1095c	7	57 1/2	− 9	76
Sep	1095p	118	42	− 5 3/4	1,800
Jun	1100c	5,269	19	+ 1	33,957
Jun	1100p	5,358	19	− 3	35,153
Jul	1100c	654	31 3/8	+ 1/8	6,152
Jul	1100p	420	29 1/4	− 3 3/4	8,681
Aug	1100c	250	44 3/4	− 1 1/4	202
Aug	1100p	109	38	− 3 1/4	866
Sep	1100c	1,261	56	+ 6 1/4	10,124
Sep	1100p	1,221	45	− 2	15,362
Jun	1105c	37	16	+ 3/4	5,268
Jun	1105p	675	20 1/2	− 5 1/2	5,245
Jun	1110c	369	12 5/8	− 1/8	15,208
Jun	1110p	909	23 1/4	− 3	19,615
Jul	1110c	2	27 1/2	+ 3 1/2	3,076

Table 12.3 *(Continued)*

Strike		Vol.	Last	Net Chg.	Open Int.
Jul	1110 p	18	34 1/2	– 2 1/2	665
Jun	1115 c	1,800	10 3/4	+ 5/8	8,447
Jun	1115 p	3,519	27	– 3	9,615
Jun	1120 c	1,547	9	– 1/4	16,523
Jun	1120 p	821	28 1/2	– 3 1/2	9,793
Jul	1120 c	238	21	– 1/2	5,455
Jul	1120 p	333	37 3/4	– 7 1/4	3,836
Aug	1120 c	252	32	– 3	414
Aug	1120 p	130	48 1/2	+ 7 1/2	21
Jun	1125 c	2,570	6 5/8	– 3/8	39,360
Jun	1125 p	248	32 1/2	– 2 1/2	34,240
Jul	1125 c	40	19 3/4	– 1/4	5,570
Jul	1125 p	521	41 3/4	– 14 1/4	3,895
Sep	1125 c	375	43	+ 1 1/8	16,278
Sep	1125 p	49	55 1/2	– 4 1/2	14,317
Jun	1130 c	1,902	5 3/4	– 1/2	9,883
Jun	1130 p	14	37	– 7 3/4	4,196
Jun	1135 c	4	4	– 1/2	7,933
Jun	1135 p	13	38	– 14 1/2	9,201
Jun	1140 c	372	3 1/8	– 1/8	3,113
Jun	1140 p	16	44	– 3	116
Jul	1140 c	32	12 5/8	+ 2 3/8	534
Jun	1150 c	403	1 7/8	– 1/4	15,770
Jun	1150 p	7	55 3/4	– 16 1/4	2,414
Jul	1150 c	25	9 1/2	– 1	4,329
Jul	1150 p	3	54 1/2	– 6 1/2	260
Sep	1150 c	500	28 3/8	– 1 1/4	6,617
Jun	1160 c	1,876	1 1/16	– 3/16	13,731
Jun	1160 p	6	60	– 10 1/2	237
Jul	1160 c	4,102	8	+ 1/2	361
Jun	1165 c	50	5/8	– 1/8	3,021
Jun	1170 c	2,080	5/8	+ 1/8	986
Jun	1170 p	2	72	+ 21 1/2	7
Jul	1170 c	189	5 1/4	– 1 1/4	1,518
Aug	1170 c	400	14 1/2	– 4 3/4	6
Aug	1170 p	1	75 1/2	– 12 1/2	5
Jun	1175 c	136	1/2	+ 1/16	13,234
Jun	1175 p	2	82	– 3 1/2	1,204
Sep	1175 c	101	21	+ 1/2	4,051
Jul	1180 c	43	4	– 2 3/4	499
Jun	1200 c	502	1/8	– 1/8	15,770
Jun	1200 p	16	101	– 14	4,978
Jul	1200 c	100	1 3/4	+ 1/8	929
Aug	1200 c	160	7 1/4	...	585
Sep	1200 c	1,109	13	– 3/4	15,410
Sep	1225 c	109	8	– 1	1,293
Jul	1250 p	45	147	– 19	565
Sep	1250 c	100	4 1/8	– 1/4	10,801
Sep	1250 p	450	143	– 2	1,910
Sep	1300 c	10	1 1/4	...	2,690

Call Vol. ......36,371 Open Int. ...919,362
Put Vol. ......61,816 Open Int. .1,369,503

AMERICAN

COMP TECH(XCI)

Strike		Vol.	Last	Net Chg.	Open Int.
Jun	510 c	1	20 1/8	+ 4	6
Jun	525 p	1	15 1/8	– 5 3/8	1
Jun	540 c	10	5 3/4	– 1/2	278

Call Vol. ....11 Open Int. 528
Put Vol. ....1 Open Int. 816

HONG KONG INDEX(HKO)

Strike		Vol.	Last	Net Chg.	Open Int.
Jun	190 c	10	1 11/16	– 4 5/16	10

Call Vol. ....10 Open Int. 5,387
Put Vol. ....0 Open Int. 1,653

INSTITUTIONAL-AM(XII)

Strike		Vol.	Last	Net Chg.	Open Int.
Jun	625 c	75	4 1/4	+ 5/8	21
Jun	630 c	20	2 5/8	+ 1/8	90
Jun	635 c	5	1 15/16	...	180

Call Vol. ....100 Open Int. 52,113
Put Vol. ....0 Open Int. 58,475

INTERNET(IIX)

Strike		Vol.	Last	Net Chg.	Open Int.
Jun	300 p	2	3 5/8	– 2 1/2	65
Jun	350 c	3	2 5/8	+ 1 1/8	63
Jul	350 p	2	35 3/8	...	...

Call Vol. ....3 Open Int. 568
Put Vol. ....4 Open Int. 603

JAPAN INDEX(JPN)

Strike		Vol.	Last	Net Chg.	Open Int.
Jul	155 p	2	2 3/4	– 3/4	576
Jun	160 c	7	5 1/8	+ 1 1/8	584
Sep	160 p	10	7 3/4	+ 5/8	308
Jul	165 p	5	6 3/4	– 1	300
Jul	170 c	1	2 9/16	– 15/16	353
Jun	175 c	13	5/16	– 5/16	1,931

Call Vol. ....21 Open Int. 47,912
Put Vol. ....17 Open Int. 19,361

MAJOR MARKET(XMI)

Strike		Vol.	Last	Net Chg.	Open Int.
Jun	860 p	10	2 1/16	...	...
Jun	880 p	10	3 1/8	– 1 1/2	64
Jun	920 c	25	34 7/8	+ 10 7/8	181
Jun	920 p	1	10 3/8	– 5/8	15
Jun	940 p	3	13 3/8	– 11 5/8	44
Jun	950 p	10	17 1/4	– 3 1/8	28
Jun	960 c	6	8 3/8	– 2 1/4	54

Call Vol. ....31 Open Int. 1,526
Put Vol. ....34 Open Int. 1,810

MS HITECH 35(MSH)

Strike		Vol.	Last	Net Chg.	Open Int.
Jun	485 p	20	1 7/16	+ 1/16	120
Jun	495 p	5	1 15/16	– 2 13/16	202
Jun	500 p	1	2 1/16	– 3/16	509
Jul	500 c	100	60	...	...
Jul	500 p	600	8 1/4	...	...
Jul	505 c	100	56	...	...
Jul	510 c	100	52	...	...
Jun	515 p	2	3 3/4	– 2 3/4	171
Jun	520 p	4	4 3/8	– 4 5/8	41
Jul	525 c	100	43 1/2	– 21 3/4	100
Jun	540 c	100	25	– 5/8	760
Jun	540 p	250	9 3/4	– 2 3/4	1,936
Sep	545 p	70	31	– 3	200
Jun	550 c	5	17 1/8	+ 5 1/8	259
Sep	550 c	70	47	+ 2 1/2	425
Sep	550 p	50	34 3/8	– 3 1/8	255
Jun	555 c	1	14 5/8	+ 3/8	68
Jul	555 p	600	25 1/4	+ 1/4	30
Jun	560 c	2	11	– 1 1/2	1,006
Jun	565 c	1	10 7/8	+ 1	102
Jun	565 p	150	19	– 8 1/2	1,000
Jul	565 c	1	21	...	...
Jul	570 c	1	18 1/2	– 18 1/4	5
Jun	580 c	260	5 3/8	+ 1 5/8	715
Jun	580 p	500	32 1/4	– 11 1/4	1,045
Jun	585 p	25	36 1/4	+ 18 5/8	391
Jun	590 c	18	2 3/4	– 3/4	620
Jun	595 c	100	1 7/8	+ 5/8	160
Jun	600 c	521	1 3/16	– 1/2	952
Jun	605 c	1	1 1/4	+ 1/2	270
Jul	610 c	600	5 3/4	...	...
Jul	620 p	5	67 1/4	...	...

Call Vol. ....2,081 Open Int. 11,795
Put Vol. ....2,282 Open Int. 21,892

PHARMACEUTICAL(DRG)

Strike		Vol.	Last	Net Chg.	Open Int.
Jun	580 p	1	2 3/4	– 5/8	22
Jun	620 c	1	20 3/8	+ 2 5/8	150
Jun	620 p	20	9 3/4	– 6 5/8	222
Jun	630 p	1	13 3/4	+ 3 1/8	303
Jun	640 c	30	9 5/8	+ 2 1/8	153
Jun	670 p	20	42 1/8	...	...

Call Vol. ....31 Open Int. 2,188
Put Vol. ....42 Open Int. 1,793

S & P MIDCAP(MID)

Strike		Vol.	Last	Net Chg.	Open Int.
Jul	320 c	1,000	40 1/2	...	...
Jun	360 c	6	4 3/4	+ 1 1/4	6
Jun	365 p	5	8 1/4	+ 1/4	400
Sep	375 p	3	20 1/2	+ 3 1/2	28

Call Vol. ....1,006 Open Int. 9,263
Put Vol. ....8 Open Int. 8,585

LEAPS-LONG TERM

DJ INDUS AVG – CB

Strike		Vol.	Last	Net Chg.	Open Int.
Dec 00	68 p	50	3 1/2	+ 1/4	92
Dec 00	72 p	100	4 1/8	+ 1/8	46331
Dec 00	76 p	208	5	...	35825
Dec 00	84 p	3000	6 3/4	...	9650
Dec 00	92 p	5	9 1/4	+ 3/8	820
Dec 00	95 p	4	11 1/4	+ 3/4	1705
Dec 99	100 c	400	7 5/8	– 7/8	604
Dec 00	100 p	10	12 1/4	– 1/8	950

Call vol. ....400 Open Int. 82,609
Put vol. ....3,377 Open Int. ...153,219

S & P 100 INDEX – CB

Strike		Vol.	Last	Net Chg.	Open Int.
Dec 99	60 p	5	15/16	– 1/16	2562
Dec 99	80 p	4	2 7/8	– 3/8	2878
Dec 98	95 p	5	3 1/8	– 3/8	12686
Dec 99	95 p	1	6 1/4	+ 3/8	335
Dec 98	100 p	1	4 3/8	– 1/8	4321
Dec 99	100 p	1	8	– 1/8	6616
Dec 99	105 p	38	9	+ 1/4	1819

Call vol. ....0 Open Int. 20,328
Put vol. ....55 Open Int. ...110,570

S & P 500 INDEX – CB

Strike		Vol.	Last	Net Chg.	Open Int.
Dec 99	67 1/2 p	145	1 1/4	+ 1/4	8983
Dec 00	70 p	10	2 1/8	– 1/8	6488
Dec 99	72 1/2 p	70	1 1/2	+ 1/16	8535
Dec 98	75 p	232	1/2	+ 1/8	16896
Dec 99	75 p	40	1 7/8	– 1/16	15147
Dec 98	80 p	5	13/16	– 1/16	19204
Dec 99	80 p	20	2 3/8	...	23614
Dec 98	85 p	15	1	– 3/8	11511
Dec 99	85 p	20	3 1/8	– 1/8	10067
Dec 98	90 p	3	1 11/16	...	6337
Dec 00	90 p	1	5 1/4	– 1/4	6793
Dec 99	92 1/2 p	7	4 1/4	– 1/4	4727
Dec 98	95 c	12	18 7/8	– 3 1/8	274
Dec 98	95 p	30	2 1/4	– 7/16	10086
Dec 98	100 p	105	3 1/8	– 1/2	3851
Dec 99	100 c	12	21 3/4	– 3/8	15881
Dec 00	102 1/2 p	5000	7 7/8	– 1/8	2676
Dec 00	107 1/2 p	2	9 5/8	+ 7/8	629
Dec 98	110 p	26	6	– 5/8	1428
Dec 99	110 p	11	9 1/8	– 1/2	1507
Dec 00	110 p	3	10 1/2	– 3/8	11084
Dec 00	115 p	8	12 1/4	...	10694
Dec 98	117 1/2 c	2	4 5/8	+ 1/2	86
Dec 00	120 p	2	13 7/8	– 1/8	5463

Call vol. ....26 Open Int. 81,080
Put vol. ....5,755 Open Int. ...436,916

*Source: *The Wall Street Journal*, May 29, 1998

EXAMPLE

Portfolio Insurance Using Index Put Options

The use of stock index put options as portfolio insurance is to provide protection against the value of a portfolio declining. The simplest case to consider is one in which the portfolio perfectly tracks the index.

Suppose that the value of the portfolio is \$5 million. The portfolio manager wants to protect the value of the portfolio from dropping below \$4,480,000 over the next three months. Put options can provide this protection.

By assumption, the portfolio perfectly tracks the index. Thus, changes in the value of the portfolio are perfectly correlated with changes in the index, implying that we can write

$$V(t) = a + bI(t), \tag{12.6}$$

where $V(t)$ is the value of the portfolio at date t and a and b are constants that must be determined. Suppose that by empirical analysis the manager knows $a = 0.0$ and $b = 4,458$.

Let $I(T)$ denote the value of the index in three months; it is a random variable. Today we do not know what this value will be nor do we know what the value of the portfolio will be, which is given by $V(T) = bI(T)$.

The portfolio manager does not want the value of the portfolio to fall below \$4,480,000. It implies a value of the market index of approximately 1,005, that is, $bI(T) = 4,480,000$ or $I(T) = 4,480,000/b = 4,480,000/4,458 = 1,005$. This is the level of the index the manager should insure against.

The manager decides to buy a number of three-month put options on the S&P 500 index with strike price 1,005. Let the current index value be 1,100.00, and the current cost of each put with strike 1,005 be $15 \times 100 = \$1,500$. We multiply by 100, given the contract's definition. How many options should the manager buy to insure against this contingency?

Since the portfolio is worth $b = 4,458$ times the index $I(T)$ and each option pays off $\$100 \times I(T)$, the manager should choose $n = b/100$ or $n = 44.58$ options.

To show that this provides the appropriate insurance, the payoff to the insured portfolio if the index is below 1,005 is

$$bI(T) + b[1,005 - I(T)] = b \times 1,005 = 4,480,000. \tag{12.7}$$

On the left side, the first term, $bI(T)$, is the value of the portfolio. The second term, $b[1,005 - I(T)]$, is the value of $n = b/100$ put options in-the-money times the contract size of 100. This equals $b \times 1,005$ or 4,480,000, which is the time-T value of the insured portfolio. The value does not fall below 4,480,000.

If the portfolio's return is not perfectly correlated with the return on the index, which is often the case, the use of index options only provides partial insurance. Consider an extreme case. Suppose our portfolio contains only one stock. Consider a situation in which the market goes up so that the index put options expire worthless. However, our stock goes bankrupt and is worthless. The put option on the index is insurance against movements in the index, not movements in the stock.

If we want to use index options for partial portfolio insurance, we need to use the portfolio's Beta.[1] For example, in the numerical example just consid-

---

[1]Beta is a measure of the covariance of the portfolio with the market portfolio. If the market portfolio changes by one percent, the portfolio changes by Beta percent.

ered, if the portfolio's Beta = 0.8 we would alter our purchase of put options to
0.8 × 44.58 = 35.66.   ∎

12.5 PRICING INDEX OPTIONS

We now price options on a stock market index. We discuss both the binomial model
of Chapter 5 and a modification of the continuous-time model of Chapter 8.

The key to our discussion is showing that the pricing of options on a stock market index is similar in nature to pricing foreign currency options. This is the task to
which we now turn.

Consider the case of a stock index paying dividends such that they can be ap-
proximated by a constant dividend yield. We know from the cost-of-carry relation of
Chapter 2 that the relationship between the forward price and spot index value using
Expression (2.10) of Chapter 2 is given by

$$F(0,T)B(0,T) = I(0)\exp(-d_y T),\tag{12.8}$$

where $F(0,T)$ is the forward price today for a contract that matures at date T and d_y is
the constant dividend yield.

Now, compare Expression (12.8) to Expression (11.20) of Chapter 11 relating
the forward price on a foreign exchange contract and the spot exchange rate:

$$F_{FX}(0,T)B(0,T) = S(0)\exp(-r_f T),\tag{12.9}$$

where $F_{FX}(0,T)$ is the forward foreign exchange rate, $S(0)$ is the spot exchange rate
(d/f), and r_f is the continuously compounded foreign rate of interest.

The form of these two expressions is the same. The stock index value is analogous to the spot exchange rate, and the constant dividend yield is analogous to the
foreign rate of interest. This similarity allows us to use the results from the last chapter with the appropriate changes in terminology and notation.

Let the stock market index satisfy the analogous Assumptions A1 through A7
from Chapter 11. In particular, Assumptions A1 through A4 are identical and remain
unchanged. Assumption A5 needs to be modified to state that the index's return follows a lognormal distribution. Assumption A6 now only concerns the domestic spot
rate, assuming it is a constant. Assumption A7 remains unchanged. Finally, we add
one more assumption.

Assumption A8.   The dividend yield for the index is constant over the life of the
option.

Given these modified assumptions, we can now price stock index options using the
results from Chapter 11.

Binomial Pricing Model

We first illustrate option pricing using the binomial model of Chapter 5. Following from Expression (11.6) of Chapter 11, the binomial representation for changes in the stock index value is given by

$$I(t + 1) = I(t) \begin{cases} \exp[(r - d_y - \sigma^2/2)\Delta + \sigma\sqrt{\Delta}] \text{ with martingale probability } 1/2 \\ \exp[(r - d_y - \sigma^2/2)\Delta - \sigma\sqrt{\Delta}] \text{ with martingale probability } 1/2, \end{cases}$$

(12.10)

where Δ is the length of the interval between dates t and $t + 1$, r is the continuously compounded rate of interest, and σ is the return volatility of the stock index.

Using Expression (11.8) of Chapter 11, the martingale probability is

$$\pi = ([R/R_{d_y}] - D)/(U - D),$$

(12.11)

where $R_{d_y} \equiv \exp(d_y \Delta)$.

EXAMPLE   **Stock Index Option Valuation Under the Binomial Model**

Suppose we want to price a call option written on the S&P 500 index. The current value of the index is 458.88. Let the maturity of the option be two months and let the strike price be 460. Let the constant dividend yield be 4.75 percent per annum and the continuously compounded rate of interest be 4.38 percent per annum. Volatility is assumed to be 11 percent per annum.

To implement the model, we divide the two-month interval into two one-month intervals, implying that $\Delta = 1/12$ years. The up-factor, from Expression (12.10), is

$$U \equiv \exp\{[0.0438 - 0.0475 - (0.11)^2/2](1/12) + 0.11\sqrt{1/12}\}$$
$$U = 1.031425$$

and the down-factor is

$$D \equiv \exp\{[0.0438 - 0.0475 - (0.11)^2/2](1/12) - 0.11\sqrt{1/12}\}$$
$$D = 0.967958.$$

The lattice of index values is shown in Figure 12.1.

The martingale probability is computed via Expression (12.11) as

$$\pi = \{\exp[(0.0438 - 0.0475)(1/12)] - 0.967958\}/(1.031425 - 0.967958)$$
$$= 0.500001.$$

FIGURE 12.1   *European Index Call Option*

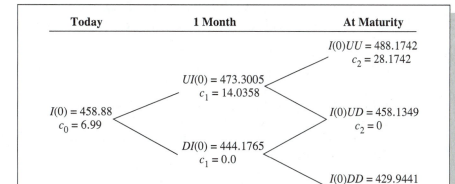

Today	1 Month	At Maturity

$I(0)UU = 488.1742$
$c_2 = 28.1742$

$UI(0) = 473.3005$
$c_1 = 14.0358$

$I(0) = 458.88$
$c_0 = 6.99$

$I(0)UD = 458.1349$
$c_2 = 0$

$DI(0) = 444.1765$
$c_1 = 0.0$

$I(0)DD = 429.9441$
$c_2 = 0$

Strike price of option = 460

Given these parameter values, we can now price the call option. The value of the call option at expiration is easily determined from the value of the index at date 2. The values are (28.1742, 0, 0).

At $t = 1$, if the index value is 473.3005, the value of the option is

$$c_1 = \frac{1}{1.0037}[\pi \times 28.1742 + (1 - \pi) \times 0]$$

$$= 14.0358.$$

The discount factor is $R = \exp[0.0438 \times (1/12)] = 1.0037$ dollars.
If the index value is 444.1765, the call option is worthless:

$$c_1 = 0.$$

At $t = 0$, the value of the call option is

$$c_1 = \frac{1}{1.0037}[\pi \times 14.0358 + (1 - \pi) \times 0]$$

$$= 6.99.$$

The construction of the synthetic call option using a portfolio of the stock index and riskless asset is straightforward. We leave it as an exercise for the reader.   ∎

Closed Form Solutions

Using the continuous-time model of Chapter 11, we can obtain closed form solutions for European call and put options on stock indexes. By analogy with Expression (11.18) of Chapter 11, the value of a European call option on the index is

$$c(0) = \exp(-d_y T)I(0)N(d_1) - B(0,T)KN(d_2), \tag{12.12}$$

where $d_1 \equiv \{\ln[I(0)/KB(0,T)] + (-d_y + \sigma^2/2)T\}\sigma\sqrt{T}$ and $d_2 \equiv d_1 - \sigma\sqrt{T}$. This is a modified Black-Scholes formula.

By analogy with Expression (11.19) of Chapter 11, the value of a European put option on the index is

$$p(0) = B(0,T)KN(-d_2) - \exp(-d_y T)I(0)N(-d_1). \tag{12.13}$$

Again, this is a modified Black-Scholes formula.

EXAMPLE   **Computation of Modified Black-Scholes Values**

This example illustrates the computation of modified Black-Scholes values for European call and put stock index options.

We want to value a European call option and a European put option. The inputs are shown in Table 12.4, Part A. We use the program FX/Pricing/European Option. Note that the foreign interest rate is expressed as a discount rate. Therefore, we must express the dividend yield as a discount rate. The output is shown in Table 12.4, Part B.

We could also have used the program Equity/Pricing European Options/Constant Dividend Yield, in which the dividend yield is expressed as a continuously compounded rate. We must convert our input

$$1 - \frac{5.27}{100} \times \frac{41}{360} \equiv \exp[-d_y(41/360)],$$

implying

$$d_y = 5.2859 \text{ percent.}$$

The output is shown in Table 12.4, Part C. Comparing Parts B and C, observe that the results are identical, as is to be expected. ∎

To price American options we can use a binomial lattice with the parameters selected to approximate a lognormal distribution, as in the previous section. Alternatively, we can use the MacMillan (1986) model or any of the approximations discussed in Chapter 9.

TABLE 12.4   *Pricing European Index Options*

PART A INPUT DATA	
Index value	458.88
Strike price	460
Maturity	41 days
Volatility*	11 percent
Discount rate**	4.36 percent
Dividend yield**	5.27 percent
*A 365-day year is assumed. **A 360-day year is assumed	
PART B* OPTION PRICE	
Call	5.9548
Put	7.5448
*The program FX/Pricing/European option is used.	
PART C* OPTION PRICE	
Call	5.9548
Put	7.5448
*The program Equity/Pricing European Options/Constant Dividend Yield is used.	

Discrete Dividends

We should mention the empirical validity of the constant dividend yield Assumption A8 of the preceding section, and the resulting consequences.

In the United States, companies tend to pay discrete dividends on a quarterly basis, thus there is strong evidence of seasonality in stock index dividend payments. In Japan there is also evidence of seasonality in dividend payouts. This evidence about dividend seasonality has at least two implications.

First, as we know from Chapter 7, it may be optimal to exercise an American call option just prior to a dividend and an American put option just after a dividend. For options such as the CBOT's S&P 100 index options that are American, seasonality of the indexes' dividend payments will be an important consideration in valuing such options.

Second, seasonality implies a discrete nature to the dividend payments, which in turn implies that the assumption of a constant dividend yield is questionable. In Chapter 9, we discussed the Known Dividend model. This model can be used for

pricing European stock index options, taking into account the discrete nature of the stock index payments.

Synthetic Options

Here we examine the construction of synthetic index options using futures contracts. Futures contracts written on the stock index can be used to replicate options on the index. The theory is identical to that described in Section 11.9 of Chapter 11, and is illustrated with an example.

EXAMPLE

Construction of a Synthetic European Put Option

A financial institution wants to construct a synthetic European put option with a strike price of 515 and maturity 63 days. The contract size is 10,000. The value of the option is $14.1031 \times 10,000 = \$141,031$. Relevant pricing data are given in Table 12.5.

Let $m_{\mathscr{F}}$ denote the number of futures contracts and B the investment in the money market account. Using the program Equity/Pricing European Options/Constant Dividend Yield, the price of the option is $14.1031 and its delta is -0.5210. Given the contract size is 10,000, the value of the synthetic option is $141,031. Therefore,

$$141,031 = m_{\mathscr{F}} \times 0 + B,$$

implying the investment in the money market account is $141,031.

To determine the number of futures contracts, the delta of the put contract and the delta of the synthetic put are equated. The delta of the put contract is $-0.5210 \times 10,000 = -5,210$, implying that if the index increases by one unit, the value of the put contract decreases by 5,210 dollars per unit. The

TABLE 12.5 *Synthetic Put Option*

Index value	509.23
Futures price	512.15
Maturity of futures contract	63 days
Maturity of option	63 days
Volatility*	15 percent
Discount rate**	5.56 percent
Dividend yield***	2.32 percent

  *Assuming a 365-day year.

 **Assuming a 360-day year.

***Expressed as a continuously compounded rate, assuming a 360-day year.

money market account is insensitive to changes in the index, implying that its delta is zero.

To determine the delta of the futures contract, we must use Expression (12.8), which we write in the form

$$\mathcal{F}(0, T_{\mathcal{F}}) = [\exp(-d_y T_{\mathcal{F}})/B(0, T_{\mathcal{F}})]I(0).$$

If the index changes by an amount ΔI, the futures price changes by the amount $\Delta \mathcal{F}$, where

$$\Delta \mathcal{F} = [\exp(-d_y T_{\mathcal{F}})/B(0, T_{\mathcal{F}})]\Delta I. \tag{12.14}$$

Now

$$\exp(-d_y T_{\mathcal{F}}) = \exp[-0.0232 \times (63/360)]$$
$$= 0.995948$$

and

$$B(0, T_{\mathcal{F}}) = 1 - 0.0556 \times (63/360)$$
$$= 0.99027,$$

so that the delta of the futures price is

$$0.995948/0.99027 = 1.0057.$$

Alternatively, using Expression (12.8) again, we can write Expression (12.14) in a more convenient form:

$$\Delta \mathcal{F} = [\mathcal{F}(0, T_{\mathcal{F}})/I(0)]\Delta I. \tag{12.15}$$

The delta of the futures price is

$$512.15/509.23 = 1.0057,$$

which agrees with our previous calculation.

If the index changes by the amount ΔI, causing a change in the futures price of $\Delta \mathcal{F}$, the change in the value of the synthetic portfolio is

$$m_{\mathcal{F}} \times 250 \times \Delta \mathcal{F} = m_{\mathcal{F}} \times 250 \times 1.0057\Delta I,$$

where we multiply by 250 because the contract size for futures contracts on the S&P 500 index is 250.

Equating the change in the value of the put contract to the change in the value of the synthetic portfolio gives

$$-5210 = m_{\mathscr{F}} \times 250 \times 1.0057,$$

implying that

$$m_{\mathscr{F}} = -5.18.$$

Rounding off to the nearest integer implies that the institution must write five futures contracts. ∎

There are at least two advantages to using stock index futures rather than a portfolio of stocks to form synthetic options. First, transaction costs are lower for futures contracts when compared to the stock portfolio. Second, the use of futures contracts avoids the up-tick rule. To replicate a put option or to hedge a call option, it is necessary to short the stock portfolio. To be concrete, consider the case of using stock index futures to replicate a put option on an index. If the market falls so that the index falls, it is necessary to increase the short positions of stocks in the index. However, it is a market rule that you can only short a stock on an up-tick; that is, the last price change must be positive before you are allowed to short a stock. No such rule applies for shorting (writing) futures contracts.

The use of derivatives to form synthetic options forms the basis of synthetic portfolio insurance. Assumption A3, competitive markets, underlies the theory used to form synthetic portfolio insurance. This assumption implies that one can buy and/or sell as much of a stock as required without changing its price. In extreme market conditions, such as the crash of October 19, 1987, such an assumption is questionable, implying that in such conditions a synthetic option may be a poor substitute for a real option.[2]

Circuit Breakers

There is an intrinsic relationship—see Expression (12.1)—between the level of a market index and the futures price on the index. If this relationship does not hold, then arbitrage is possible. For example, suppose that the observed futures price is below the theoretical level, implying that futures are "underpriced." To form an arbitrage position, buy futures and short the index. Arbitrating the differences between the spot and futures prices has been automated with computer programs to monitor price differences and to take appropriate positions if arbitrage is possible. It is a type of programmed trading.

---

[2] For a discussion of the role of synthetic options in the market crash, see "Symposium: Brady Commission Report on the Stock Market Crash" (1988).

However, the action of shorting the stocks in the index puts pressure on the stock prices, especially if undertaken in sufficient quantity. Following the stock market crash of October 1987, program trading was blamed for precipitating the crash. While such claims rest on questionable evidence, regulators have introduced circuit breakers.[3] A circuit breaker is described as follows: If price changes in the index or futures are of a certain magnitude, trading in one or both markets is halted for a specified length of time. The idea is that this trading break will allow investors time to reflect upon their actions, and this, it is hoped, will reduce the magnitude of price changes.

The Wildcard Option

Let us discuss an imbedded option within the S&P 100 index option contract. The S&P 100 index option contract traded on the Chicago Board Options Exchange is an American style contract: The option can be exercised any time up to and including its maturity date. The settlement price of the option is set equal to the S&P index level at 3:00 P.M. (Central Standard Time) when the New York Stock Exchange closes. The option holder may postpone the exercise decision until 3:20 P.M., providing the option holder with a twenty-minute window. If there is a major market fall (rise) during this twenty-minute period, the holder of a long call (put) may find it optimal to exercise the option at the higher (lower) settlement price. The twenty-minute window provides the option holder with additional flexibility and is referred to as an end-of-day **wildcard option**. Fleming and Whaley (1994) show how to use the binomial model to value this wildcard option.

12.6 OPTIONS ON INDEX FUTURES

Now we examine the pricing and hedging of options on index futures.

Table 12.6 shows closing prices for a selection of traded index futures options. When we buy an option on a stock index futures contract, we acquire the right to take a position at a specified price in a futures contract written on the underlying index. For a call option we have the right to take a long position at a specified price in a futures contract written on the underlying index. For a put option we have the right to take a short position at a specified price in a futures contract written on the underlying index.

Futures options on the S&P 500 index are American, that is, the option can be exercised any time up to and including its maturity date. If we exercise any of the options that expire within a calendar quarter, we take a position in a futures contract that delivers at the end of the quarter. For example, referring to Table 12.6, if we exercise the June 1090 call option, we take a long position at 1090 in the June futures contract. Exercising a quarter-end S&P option on the last trading day results in a cash settlement because the underlying futures contract terminates trading at the same time.

---

[3]A description of circuit breakers is given in Hasbrouck, Sofianos, and Sosebee (1993).

TABLE 12.6 *Options on Stock Index Futures, Thursday, May 28, 1998**

INDEX

DJ INDUSTRIAL AVG (CBOT)
$100 times premium

Strike	Calls-Settle			Puts-Settle		
Price	Jun	Jly	Aug	Jun	Jly	Aug
88	29.60	....	....	9.05	16.50	....
89	22.35	....	48.65	11.75	19.25	28.75
90	16.35	32.50	....	15.75	22.80	....
91	11.10	26.40	....	20.50	26.45	....
92	7.15	20.75	....	26.50	30.95	....
93	4.35	15.70	....	33.70	....	....

Est vol 1,000 Wd 9,572 calls 16,052 puts
Op int Wed 96,043 calls 217,525 puts

S&P 500 STOCK INDEX (CME)
$250 times premium

Strike	Calls-Settle			Puts-Settle		
Price	Jun	Jly	Aug	Jun	Jly	Aug
1090	25.10	44.70	....	14.40	22.30	33.10
1095	21.80	....	....	16.10	23.80	....
1100	18.70	38.00	49.00	18.00	25.50	36.60
1105	15.90	34.80	....	20.20	27.30	....
1110	13.30	31.90	43.10	22.60	29.40	40.50
1115	11.10	29.00	....	25.30	31.40	....

Est vol 17,532 Wd 1,090 calls 419 puts
Op int Wed 21,395 calls 19,048 puts

*Source: *The Wall Street Journal*, May 29, 1998

EXAMPLE

Use of Index Futures Options

Consider an investor who sold a June S&P futures contract at 1105.00, anticipating the stock market would drop. Today, the June futures price is 1100.70 (see Table 12.2), and the investor has a profit of $1,075.00 (= 250 × 4.3).

TABLE 12.7 *Use of Index Futures Options*

POSSIBLE FUTURES PRICES	FUTURES POSITION	OPTION POSITION*	NET TOTAL PROFIT
1075	30	−15.90	+24.10
1085	20	−15.90	+ 4.10
1095	10	−15.90	− 5.90
1105	0	−15.90	−15.90
1115	−10	− 5.90	−15.90
1125	−20	+ 4.10	−15.90

*Net of original cost.

The investor wants to remain with the short futures position but is concerned that the market might become bullish. To obtain insurance on this position, the investor buys a June futures call option with strike 1105, for a total cost of $3,975 = (250 × 15.90) (see Table 12.6).

The profit profile of this position in June, when the call matures, is shown in Table 12.7. The option provides insurance against a rising market. The largest loss possible is $3,975 = (250 × 15.90). This occurs for all futures prices above 1105. ■

Pricing Index Futures Options

Here we price index futures options. The foreign currency analogy, discussed in Section 12.5, is used to derive the results.

Consider options that mature at date T. The options are written on a futures contract that matures at date $T_{\mathscr{F}}$.

The value of a European call option, from Expression (9.13) of Chapter 9, is given by

$$c(0) = B(0, T) \left[\mathscr{F}(0, T_{\mathscr{F}}) N(d_1) - KN(d_2) \right], \tag{12.16}$$

where K is the strike price, $d_1 \equiv \{\ln[\mathscr{F}(0, T_{\mathscr{F}})/K] + (\sigma^2/2)T\}/\sigma\sqrt{T}$, and $d_2 \equiv d_1 - \sigma\sqrt{T}$. This is Black's model applied to stock index futures.

Similarly, for a European put option,

$$p(0) = B(0, T)[KN(-d_2) - \mathscr{F}(0, T_{\mathscr{F}})N(-d_1)]. \tag{12.17}$$

For pricing American futures options, a binomial lattice approximation to the lognormal model can be used, or the MacMillan model can be applied; see Chapter 11.

EXAMPLE **Pricing European and American Index Futures Options**

This example illustrates the use of Black's model for pricing European stock index futures options and the MacMillan model for pricing American options.

We want to value index futures options. The inputs are shown in Table 12.8, Part A. The prices for American and European options are shown in Table 12.8, Part B. American options are seen to be more valuable, implying that the early exercise privilege has value. The contract size is 500, so the cost of the European call option is $2,811.95 (= 500 × 5.6239). ■

Table 12.8 *Pricing Index Futures Options*

PART A DATA INPUT	
Future price	458.40
Strike price	460.00
Maturity	37 days
Volatility*	11 percent
Discount rate**	4.03 percent

*A 365-day year is assumed.
**A 360-day year is assumed

PART B		
	EUROPEAN PRICE*	AMERICAN PRICE**
Call	5.6239	5.6273
Put	7.2173	7.2218

*The program Futures/Pricing/European Option is used.
**The program Futures/Pricing/American Option is used.

12.7 COMMODITY DERIVATIVES

Now we study the pricing of commodity derivatives. Our presentation will be brief, as the analysis is similar to that given for foreign currency options and stock index options.

Futures Prices

First we discuss commodity futures contracts. Table 12.9 shows some of the futures contracts traded on different commodities. Included are grains and oilseeds, metals and petroleum products, food, and fiber products. The markets for commodity derivatives are expanding and growing in volume.

If it is assumed that interest rates are constant over the life of the futures contract, then forward and futures prices will be equal. Let $\mathscr{F}(0, T_{\mathscr{F}})$ denote the futures price on a contract that matures at date $T_{\mathscr{F}}$ and $S(0)$ denote the spot commodity price. Then, from the cost-of-carry relationship (2.11) of Chapter 2, we have

$$\mathscr{F}(0, T_{\mathscr{F}}) = S(0)\exp[(r - y_N)T_{\mathscr{F}}], \qquad (12.18)$$

where r is the continuously compounded rate of interest and y_N is the net convenience yield.

Comparing Expression (12.18) to (12.9), we see that the net convenience yield is analogous to the foreign interest rate. Given observations of the futures price, spot

TABLE 12.9 *Commodity Futures, Thursday, May 28, 1998**

Thursday, May 28, 1998
Open Interest Reflects Previous Trading Day.

GRAINS AND OILSEEDS

	Open	High	Low	Settle	Change	Lifetime High	Low	Open Interest
CORN (CBT) 5,000 bu.; cents per bu.								
July	237¼	240	237¼	238¼	+ 1½	315½	235¼	138,977
Sept	243	245¾	242¼	243½	....	301	241	41,881
Dec	247¾	249¾	246¾	247¾	....	299½	245¾	126,303
Mr99	256½	258	255½	256	....	305	254	13,078
May	261¼	262½	260½	260¾	+ ¼	299	259	2,472
July	266	267	265	265¾	+ ¼	312	256¼	6,298
Dec	264½	264½	263	263	....	291½	262¾	2,890
Est vol 60,000; vol Wed 82,313; open int 331,900, −3,528.								
OATS (CBT) 5,000 bu.; cents per bu.								
July	127½	129½	127¼	127½	....	184	124½	8,599
Sept	131	133¼	130½	130¾	− ¼	177	129	3,013
Dec	139½	139¼	137¼	137½	− ¼	177½	136	5,505
Mr99	144	144½	143¾	143¾	+ 1¼	166½	142	459
Est vol 1,000; vol Wed 1,429; open int 17,579, −192.								
SOYBEANS (CBT) 5,000 bu.; cents per bu.								
July	617¾	623	617½	618¾	+ 1½	753	611½	61,596
Aug	612	615¾	611	611¼	+ ¼	745	607	17,672
Sept	596½	602	596½	596½	....	723	594	5,238
Nov	590½	594¾	588½	589	− ¾	717	585½	48,084
Ja99	598½	602	596	596¼	− ¼	701½	594	4,078
Mar	607	609½	603	603	− ½	694	602	1,128
May	612	612	607½	607½	+ ¼	671	606	264
July	616	618½	611½	611¾	− 1¼	728	611½	724
Nov	606	606½	603	603	− 1¼	680	606	1,198
Est vol 48,000; vol Wed 82,367; open int 139,990, −4,607.								
SOYBEAN MEAL (CBT) 100 tons; $ per ton.								
July	155.00	158.00	154.50	156.90	+ 2.20	231.50	153.50	56,239
Aug	155.00	157.20	154.50	156.30	+ 1.40	231.50	153.80	21,823
Sept	155.50	157.00	155.00	156.20	+ .80	231.50	154.80	15,496
Oct	154.50	156.00	154.00	154.60	+ .40	226.00	154.00	11,047
Dec	157.00	158.30	156.30	156.60	....	231.00	156.10	27,124
Ja99	159.30	159.30	157.50	157.60	....	215.50	157.50	3,419
Mar	161.00	162.00	160.10	160.10	....	195.00	160.00	2,511
May	164.00	164.00	162.00	162.00	+ .30	192.50	161.70	492
Est vol 26,000; vol Wed 31,836; open int 138,233, −1,044.								
SOYBEAN OIL (CBT) 60,000 lbs.; cents per lb.								
July	26.35	26.75	26.30	26.33	− .01	29.83	24.09	63,204
Aug	26.45	26.87	26.43	26.45	....	29.88	24.03	23,771
Sept	26.80	26.92	26.51	26.51	− .01	29.85	24.15	17,451
Oct	26.50	26.70	26.35	26.35	+ .05	29.55	23.95	8,530
Dec	26.22	26.45	26.12	26.13	+ .05	29.30	24.00	29,940
Ja99	26.20	26.40	26.05	26.07	+ .05	29.05	24.60	3,217
Mar	26.35	26.35	26.05	26.05	+ .07	28.80	24.60	1,687
May	26.15	26.25	25.91	25.91	+ .05	27.50	25.20	776
Est vol 24,000; vol Wed 53,027; open int 148,789, +1,447.								
WHEAT (CBT) 5,000 bu.; cents per bu.								
July	288	293	284¼	284½	− 3	425	282¾	62,245
Sept	297½	301	294¾	295	− 2	403	293¼	16,194
Dec	313½	318	310	310¼	− 2¼	417	308½	25,707
Mr99	329	329	323½	323¾	− 4	384½	323¾	5,420
May	333	333	329	329	− 4	355	329	657
July	340	341½	338	338	− ½	389	334	498
Est vol 21,000; vol Wed 46,760; open int 110,722, −6,134.								
WHEAT (KC) 5,000 bu.; cents per bu.								
July	314	315	311	311	− 1½	408½	309½	25,235
Sept	322	322½	318	318	− 1½	410	317¾	11,417
Dec	333½	334	329½	329¾	− 2¼	418½	329½	12,817
Mr99	341½	342	338½	338½	− 3½	410½	338	2,510
Est vol 7,275; vol Wed 11,457; open int 52,341, +699.								
WHEAT (MPLS) 5,000 bu.; cents per bu.								
July	361	361¼	357	357¾	− 2½	416	355½	8,578
Sept	362	362½	357¾	358	− 3	418	357	6,218
Dec	365	366	362	362½	− 1½	422	361½	3,288
Mr99	368	368	366	366	− ½	398	368	333
Est vol 5,627; vol Wed 4,379; open int 18,423, −47.								
CANOLA (WPG) 20 metric tons; Can. $ per ton								
July	416.20	418.40	415.05	415.70	+ 2.00	437.10	366.00	18,671
Aug	395.50	397.70	394.00	394.00	+ .20	415.50	385.90	2,599
Sept	....	....	376.30	....	+ 1.20	395.50	363.30	1,828
Nov	378.00	380.00	377.80	377.80	+ .70	396.50	362.40	28,201
Ja99	381.00	383.20	380.00	382.00	+ 3.50	400.50	368.00	4,320
Mar	385.50	385.50	384.50	384.50	+ 2.50	390.40	382.00	275
May	....	....	388.00	....	+ 2.00	....	....	100
Est vol 7,225; vol Wed 8,328; open int 55,994, −2,313.								
WHEAT (WPG) 20 metric tons; Can. $ per ton								
July	150.30	150.90	149.70	149.70	− .80	184.50	146.70	2,607
Oct	151.50	151.50	150.60	150.90	− .10	180.50	149.50	2,559
Dec	151.50	151.50	150.50	151.10	+ .10	170.00	149.10	3,252
Mr99	153.00	153.00	152.70	153.00	....	153.00	152.70	264
Est vol 940; vol Wd 717; open int 8,707, −264.								

	Open	High	Low	Settle	Chg	Yield Settle	Open Chg	Interest
BARLEY-WESTERN (WPG) 20 metric tons; Can. $ per ton								
July	131.00	131.00	130.10	130.30	− .40	162.60	127.50	6,219
Oct	132.00	132.00	131.40	131.80	− .20	158.00	128.50	3,518
Dec	134.00	134.00	132.50	132.70	− 1.20	151.50	129.50	1,993
Mr99	....	....	135.00	....	+ .20	142.50	133.00	163
Est vol 800; vol Wd 818; open int 12,192, −124.								

CATTLE-FEEDER (CME) 50,000 lbs.; cents per lb.
Aug	75.50	75.70	75.05	75.20	− .30	83.25	75.05	7,361
Sept	75.40	75.65	75.10	75.20	− .30	83.05	75.10	1,101
Oct	75.65	75.90	75.30	75.40	− .20	83.00	75.30	1,547
Nov	76.20	76.55	76.20	76.20	− .10	83.60	76.20	425
Ja99	76.70	76.70	76.55	76.55	− .15	81.75	76.55	173
Est vol 1,024; vol Wed 1,860; open int 10,676, −2,586.								

CATTLE-LIVE (CME) 40,000 lbs.; cents per lb.
June	64.20	64.80	64.02	64.12	− .30	72.37	64.02	29,259
Aug	66.20	66.95	66.12	66.27	+ .05	72.15	66.12	33,641
Oct	66.50	66.90	66.32	66.47	+ .02	74.05	66.32	16,879
Dec	67.85	68.20	67.80	67.82	− .02	74.20	67.80	6,062
Fb99	69.00	69.15	68.72	68.77	− .22	73.50	68.72	2,138
Apr	70.05	70.25	69.95	70.00	− .10	73.25	69.95	759
Est vol 17,998; vol Wed 18,755; open int 88,782, −438.								

HOGS-LEAN (CME) 40,000 lbs.; cents per lb.
June	60.15	60.60	59.90	60.37	+ .12	73.70	55.25	8,643
July	58.80	59.50	58.75	59.35	+ .32	71.75	55.30	9,876
Aug	55.85	56.70	55.85	56.62	+ .40	69.70	53.02	5,941
Oct	51.70	52.07	51.70	52.02	+ .10	66.00	50.57	3,859
Dec	52.00	52.25	51.80	52.00	....	58.50	50.45	3,412
Fb99	54.52	54.60	53.95	54.55	....	59.50	53.99	799
Apr	54.50	54.50	54.40	54.40	+ .15	58.20	52.25	272
June	63.50	63.60	63.40	63.55	− .30	65.50	61.75	169
Est vol 8,643; vol Wed 10,307; open int 33,003, −404.								

PORK BELLIES (CME) 40,000 lbs.; cents per lb.
July	47.62	49.10	46.90	48.95	+ 1.07	79.00	40.05	4,567
Aug	46.15	47.75	45.60	46.87	+ .22	75.00	39.05	1,863
Est vol 2,333; vol Wed 1,956; open int 6,532, −21.								

FOOD AND FIBER

COCOA (CSCE) 10 metric tons; $ per ton.
July	1,660	1,675	1,660	1,666	− 34	1,835	1,485	25,787
Sept	1,689	1,698	1,686	1,693	− 30	1,836	1,456	16,775
Dec	1,716	1,724	1,712	1,721	− 30	1,863	1,510	16,512
Mr99	1,741	1,742	1,741	1,745	− 29	1,901	1,634	10,346
May	....	....	....	1,762	− 27	1,911	1,685	3,926
July	....	....	....	1,779	− 25	1,850	1,705	1,573
Sept	....	....	....	1,795	− 25	1,858	1,745	956
Dec	1,815	1,815	1,815	1,819	− 25	1,885	1,785	4,724
Mr00	....	....	....	1,849	− 25	1,910	1,882	2,064
Est vol 12,278; vol Wd 5,726; open int 82,663, +164.								

COFFEE (CSCE) 37,500 lbs.; cents per lb.
July	128.50	133.00	128.50	132.40	+ 2.25	191.00	120.00	15,069
Sept	128.25	131.25	128.25	130.50	+ 1.35	186.00	122.00	8,294
Dec	124.25	127.00	124.25	126.50	+ 1.50	157.50	119.75	7,105
Mr99	118.50	122.00	118.00	122.00	+ 1.10	154.00	117.00	2,645
May	118.50	118.50	118.50	120.00	+ 1.10	151.50	115.00	1,115
July	....	....	....	118.00	+ 1.50	131.00	113.75	709
Sept	114.50	114.50	114.50	116.00	+ 1.50	123.00	112.00	487
Est vol 6,266; vol Wd 7,277; open int 35,424, −577.								

SUGAR-WORLD (CSCE) 112,000 lbs.; cents per lb.
July	8.26	8.44	8.25	8.26	− .08	12.11	8.23	77,299
Oct	8.48	8.60	8.42	8.44	− .09	11.97	8.42	59,292
Mr99	9.12	9.17	9.04	9.07	− .05	11.87	9.04	27,446
May	9.15	9.20	9.10	9.11	− .04	11.68	9.09	4,045
July	9.20	9.24	9.12	9.12	− .03	11.68	9.12	3,710
Sept	9.20	9.15	9.15	9.15	....	11.58	9.15	4,233
Mar	9.24	9.24	9.16	9.16	− .02	10.90	9.17	2,020
Est vol 22,911; vol Wd 42,942; open int 178,045, +6,633.								

SUGAR-DOMESTIC (CSCE) 112,000 lbs.; cents per lb.
Sept	22.24	22.25	22.22	22.28	+ .04	22.67	21.79	3,168
Nov	22.26	22.26	22.25	22.25	− .04	22.68	21.95	3,931
Ja99	22.20	22.20	22.20	22.20	....	22.44	22.10	984
Mar	22.20	22.20	22.20	22.20	....	22.42	22.10	922
May	22.24	22.25	22.24	22.25	+ .01	22.37	22.10	463
July	22.38	22.38	22.38	22.38	....	22.40	22.10	370
Sept	22.38	22.38	22.38	22.38	− .02	22.28	22.28	171
Est vol 532; vol Wd 419; open int 12,169, −7.								

COTTON (CTN) 50,000 lbs.; cents per lb.
July	67.90	69.40	67.80	69.33	+ 1.45	79.25	62.35	29,307
Oct	70.30	71.65	70.30	71.60	+ 1.21	78.00	65.60	4,398
Dec	71.20	72.60	71.10	72.55	+ 1.31	76.60	66.90	36,068
Mr99	72.45	73.75	72.45	73.70	+ 1.31	77.25	68.50	7,950
May	73.20	74.00	73.20	74.23	+ 1.28	76.10	69.50	3,743
July	73.75	74.60	73.75	74.78	+ 1.25	77.31	69.80	2,317

	Open	High	Low	Settle	Change	Lifetime High	Low	Open Interest
Oct	73.30	73.40	73.30	73.30	+ .55	77.05	70.80	420
Dec	71.75	72.60	71.75	72.55	+ .50	73.50	70.10	3,241
Est vol 20,000; vol Wed 13,387; open int 87,481, +1,792.								

ORANGE JUICE (CTN) 15,000 lbs.; cents per lb.
July	108.50	108.90	107.10	108.80	− .10	117.00	75.30	21,389
Sept	111.60	112.20	110.80	112.20	− .05	119.50	78.25	6,806
Nov	114.25	114.25	113.15	114.80	− .05	120.90	80.95	4,699
Ja99	....	....	....	116.80	− .05	122.00	83.40	2,170
Mar	....	....	....	119.30	− .05	125.75	86.05	1,027
May	....	....	....	121.80	− .05	125.75	90.80	680
July	....	....	....	124.30	− .05	126.00	109.00	145
Est vol 1,500; vol Wd 1,623; open int 36,921, +101.								

METALS AND PETROLEUM

COPPER-HIGH (Cmx.Div.NYM) 25,000 lbs.; cents per lb.
June	78.00	78.00	75.90	76.35	+ .45	103.65	73.50	3,956
July	76.30	78.70	76.20	76.85	+ .55	104.10	73.50	27,968
Aug	78.50	78.50	77.50	77.20	+ .60	102.00	74.30	2,146
Sept	77.90	79.50	77.00	77.50	+ .65	102.10	74.30	7,490
Oct	78.95	78.95	78.95	77.75	+ .65	99.40	76.00	1,710
Nov	77.70	77.70	77.70	77.85	+ .75	98.80	76.50	1,558
Dec	77.70	79.30	77.70	78.05	+ .75	102.00	75.20	10,894
Ja99	....	....	....	78.30	+ .75	96.80	76.50	1,634
Feb	....	....	....	78.40	+ .80	94.60	76.70	655
Mar	79.40	79.40	79.20	78.45	+ .85	98.20	76.30	2,428
Apr	....	....	....	78.50	+ .80	96.00	77.30	574
May	....	....	....	78.55	+ .75	98.50	76.75	1,401
June	....	....	....	78.65	+ .80	91.00	77.20	490
July	....	....	....	78.80	+ .85	95.75	76.50	1,151
Aug	....	....	....	78.95	+ .90	90.50	77.90	393
Sept	....	....	....	79.20	+ 1.00	94.60	78.00	927
Nov	....	....	....	79.45	+ 1.05	84.90	78.20	249
Dec	....	....	....	79.45	+ 1.05	87.50	78.20	282
Dec	....	....	....	77.60	+ 1.05	84.90	77.30	1,059
Est vol 13,000; vol Wed 5,172; open int 67,490, +149.								

GOLD (Cmx.Div.NYM) 100 troy oz.; $ per troy oz.
June	293.70	294.20	292.30	292.70	− 1.00	489.50	281.50	22,007
July	....	....	....	294.10	− .80	295.00	294.50	3
Aug	296.00	297.00	295.30	295.60	− .60	403.80	284.50	56,602
Oct	298.90	299.50	297.50	297.80	− .60	347.80	290.00	5,955
Dec	300.60	301.30	299.30	299.80	− .60	505.00	287.00	20,097
Fb99	301.50	301.50	301.50	301.50	− .60	349.50	294.50	9,309
Apr	304.00	304.00	304.00	303.30	− .60	351.20	291.50	7,974
June	306.40	306.40	304.40	305.15	− .60	520.00	295.40	11,830
Aug	307.80	308.00	307.80	306.90	− .60	327.00	305.00	391
Oct	....	....	....	308.70	− .60	....	....	200
Dec	311.00	311.00	311.00	310.50	− .60	506.00	299.50	6,484
Ju00	....	....	....	316.00	− .60	473.50	309.50	4,549
Dec	....	....	....	321.60	− .60	474.50	312.40	4,944
Ju01	....	....	....	327.10	− .60	447.00	347.00	2,152
Dec	....	....	....	332.40	− .60	429.50	320.00	4,856
Ju02	....	....	....	338.00	− .60	385.00	335.00	1,474
Dec	....	....	....	343.60	− .60	....	....	205
Est vol 90,000; vol Wed 81,945; open int 159,032, +9,254.								

PLATINUM (NYM) 50 troy oz.; $ per troy oz.
July	371.10	374.10	366.00	367.20	− 6.90	432.00	341.00	9,131
Oct	370.00	370.00	366.00	366.20	− 5.90	425.00	343.00	1,384
Est vol 2,697; vol Wed 2,339; open int 10,582, −478.								

SILVER (Cmx.Div.NYM) 5,000 troy oz.; cents per troy oz.
June	....	....	....	504.0	− 11.8	632.0	508.0	2
July	513.5	522.0	504.0	505.0	− 11.8	738.0	438.0	51,707
Sept	517.0	524.5	508.0	508.6	− 11.8	728.0	453.0	7,840
Dec	521.0	529.0	510.0	512.7	− 11.8	734.0	448.5	13,800
Mr99	524.0	530.0	524.0	517.7	− 11.8	690.0	473.0	3,123
May	532.0	532.0	530.0	513.7	− 11.8	656.0	493.0	775
July	528.0	528.0	525.0	514.7	− 11.8	680.0	472.0	2,487
Dec	525.0	525.0	525.0	516.7	− 11.8	720.0	484.0	2,812
Mr00	....	....	....	516.7	− 11.8	552.5	537.0	101
July	....	....	....	516.7	− 11.8	590.0	538.0	942
Dec	....	....	....	516.7	− 11.8	685.0	535.0	768
Dc01	....	....	....	516.7	− 11.8	680.0	537.0	211
Dc02	....	....	....	516.7	− 11.8	640.0	533.0	195
Est vol 13,000; vol Wd 13,715; open int 84,802, +733.								

CRUDE OIL, Light Sweet (NYM) 1,000 bbls.; $ per bbl.
July	14.99	15.07	14.66	14.85	− .14	21.05	14.02	106,745
Aug	15.47	15.47	15.05	15.33	− .10	21.12	14.43	58,955
Sept	15.85	15.85	15.58	15.74	− .09	20.82	14.78	38,638
Oct	16.05	16.13	15.97	16.07	− .09	20.75	15.07	23,726
Nov	16.28	16.39	16.28	16.35	− .08	20.63	15.32	13,668
Ja99	16.74	16.78	16.74	16.72	− .05	20.30	15.70	26,565
Feb	16.81	16.81	16.81	16.82	− .04	20.32	15.93	11,927
Mar	16.91	16.91	16.90	16.92	− .03	20.04	15.65	9,862
Apr	17.00	17.00	17.00	17.01	− .02	20.27	16.20	5,236
May	....	....	....	17.09	− .02	20.29	16.35	3,001

(continued)

TABLE 12.9   *(Continued)*

	Open	High	Low	Settle	Change	Lifetime High	Lifetime Low	Open Interest
June	17.12	17.15	17.12	17.16	− .02	20.47	16.40	14,256
July	....	....	....	17.23	− .02	20.14	16.75	5,814
Aug	....	....	....	17.30	− .01	19.47	17.05	7,455
Sept	....	....	....	17.35	− .01	20.10	16.60	3,835
Oct	....	....	....	17.40	− .01	20.14	17.30	3,535
Nov	....	....	....	17.45	....	19.90	17.42	1,426
Dec	17.50	17.52	17.49	17.49	....	20.75	16.75	18,100
Dc00	....	....	....	17.69	....	20.75	17.00	10,007
Jan	17.52	17.57	17.52	17.52	....	19.15	17.15	3,061
Feb	....	....	....	17.55	....	20.16	18.70	1,446
Mar	....	....	....	17.56	....	20.10	17.28	507
Apr	....	....	....	17.57	....	19.16	17.33	338
May	....	....	....	17.58	....	19.16	19.16	470
June	....	....	....	17.59	....	20.10	17.25	4,251
July	....	....	....	17.61	....	17.74	17.74	250
Aug	....	....	....	17.63	....	....	....	350
Sept	....	....	....	17.65	....	17.70	17.63	1,921
Dc01	....	....	....	17.72	....	20.98	17.00	4,396
Dc02	....	....	....	17.75	....	21.38	17.15	4,790
Dc03	....	....	....	17.78	....	22.00	16.95	4,291
Dc04	....	....	....	17.81	....	19.07	17.20	3,195

Est vol 92,192; vol Wed 90,080; open int 431,879, −9,919.

HEATING OIL NO. 2 (NYM) 42,000 gal.; $ per gal.

	Open	High	Low	Settle	Change	Lifetime High	Lifetime Low	Open Interest
June	.4000	.4000	.3885	.3898	− .0090	.5755	.3885	17,874
July	.4070	.4090	.3980	.4000	− .0071	.5720	.3960	48,159
Aug	.4165	.4165	.4100	.4120	− .0066	.5750	.4090	20,044
Sept	.4280	.4290	.4250	.4265	− .0056	.5840	.4240	12,384
Oct	.4420	.4430	.4390	.4405	− .0051	.5850	.4380	12,882
Nov	.4560	.4570	.4530	.4535	− .0041	.5905	.4510	10,502
Dec	.4675	.4685	.4650	.4665	− .0031	.5900	.4610	19,413
Ja99	.4775	.4795	.4740	.4775	− .0026	.5950	.4685	17,956
Feb	.4860	.4885	.4835	.4860	− .0021	.5850	.4715	9,542
Mar	.4860	.4910	.4860	.4860	− .0001	.5830	.4690	3,989
Apr	.4820	.4820	.4800	.4800	− .0001	.5900	.4630	2,568
May	.4765	.4765	.4735	.4720	− .0001	.5330	.4600	1,354
June	.4720	.4735	.4720	.4720	− .0001	.5300	.4645	5,783
July	.4760	.4760	.4760	.4740	− .0001	.5290	.4655	1,066
Aug	....	....	....	.4800	− .0001	.5120	.4700	1,147
Sept	....	....	....	.4880	− .0001	.5200	.4860	303
Oct	....	....	....	.4960	− .0001	.5200	.4950	237

Est vol 50,306; vol Wed 46,823; open int 185,342, −839.

GASOLINE-NY Unleaded (NYM)) 42,000 gal.; $ per gal.

	Open	High	Low	Settle	Chg	Yield Settle	Chg	Open Interest
June	.4995	.4995	.4870	.4920	− .0076	.6270	.4620	15,109
July	.5055	.5055	.4965	.5007	− .0059	.6345	.4675	39,136
Aug	.5090	.5090	.5035	.5074	− .0042	.6110	.4710	20,879
Sept	.5050	.5070	.5030	.5062	− .0031	.6150	.4750	15,015
Oct	.4960	.4980	.4955	.4980	− .0028	.5780	.4775	5,168
Nov	.4910	.4910	.4910	.4945	− .0023	.5585	.4850	1,950
Dec	.4940	.4940	.4940	.4945	− .0018	.5450	.4650	3,746
Ja99	.4980	.4980	.4980	.4990	− .0013	.5350	.4890	1,072

Est vol 43,583; vol Wed 63,222; open int 103,297, −5,224.

NATURAL GAS, (NYM) 10,000 MMBtu.; $ per MMBtu's

	Open	High	Low	Settle	Chg	Yield Settle	Chg	Open Interest
July	2.052	2.085	2.035	2.071	+ .025	2.750	1.852	42,746
Aug	2.100	2.140	2.095	2.124	+ .024	2.760	1.845	25,077
Sept	2.140	2.175	2.136	2.168	+ .022	2.740	1.850	19,477
Oct	2.205	2.240	2.200	2.233	+ .018	2.750	1.840	18,778
Nov	2.385	2.410	2.370	2.400	+ .015	2.830	1.915	13,957
Dec	2.555	2.580	2.550	2.567	+ .015	2.940	1.950	19,056
Ja99	2.595	2.620	2.590	2.610	+ .015	2.950	2.085	25,368
Feb	2.495	2.515	2.485	2.500	+ .010	2.770	2.025	13,183
Mar	2.400	2.410	2.380	2.395	− .010	2.600	1.945	9,654
Apr	2.315	2.315	2.285	2.288	+ .008	2.440	1.910	5,225
May	2.270	2.270	2.255	2.248	+ .003	2.380	1.960	5,081
June	2.275	2.275	2.255	2.248	+ .003	2.380	1.860	5,541
July	2.255	2.270	2.255	2.253	+ .003	2.390	1.960	4,308
Aug	2.270	2.290	2.270	2.270	+ .003	2.390	1.975	3,828
Sept	2.291	2.300	2.290	2.284	+ .003	2.375	1.970	3,359
Oct	2.310	2.330	2.310	2.312	+ .003	2.401	2.042	2,621
Nov	2.435	2.450	2.435	2.437	+ .003	2.535	2.140	2,711
Dec	2.585	2.585	2.580	2.569	+ .003	2.680	2.213	4,696
Ja00	2.605	2.605	2.605	2.586	+ .003	2.680	2.295	5,362
Feb	....	....	....	2.471	+ .003	2.565	2.242	1,738
Mar	....	....	....	2.354	+ .003	2.475	2.119	1,841
Apr	2.243	2.243	2.243	2.246	+ .003	2.360	2.015	1,879
May	....	....	....	2.231	+ .003	2.339	1.960	1,261
June	2.233	2.233	2.233	2.236	+ .003	2.320	2.001	1,938
July	....	....	....	2.239	+ .003	2.325	2.005	1,099
Aug	....	....	....	2.252	+ .012	2.320	2.005	917
Sept	....	....	....	2.256	+ .012	2.370	2.150	1,115
Oct	....	....	....	2.277	+ .012	2.346	2.100	747
Nov	....	....	....	2.404	+ .012	2.469	2.240	677
Dec	....	....	....	2.543	+ .012	2.620	2.380	1,338

	Open	High	Low	Settle	Change	Lifetime High	Lifetime Low	Open Interest
Ja01	2.560	2.560	2.560	2.563	+ .012	2.675	2.480	1,217
Feb	2.445	2.445	2.445	2.446	+ .012	2.522	2.400	819
Mar	2.350	2.350	2.350	2.355	+ .014	2.395	2.300	587
Apr	....	....	....	2.255	+ .014	2.311	2.192	911
May	....	....	....	2.243	+ .014	2.238	2.218	425

Est vol 44,908; vol Wed 117,449; open int 254,289, −11,891.

BRENT CRUDE (IPE) 1,000 net bbls.; $ per bbl.

	Open	High	Low	Settle	Change	Lifetime High	Lifetime Low	Open Interest
July	14.05	14.14	13.90	14.13	− .10	19.80	12.72	78,617
Aug	14.31	14.39	14.17	14.37	− .08	19.33	13.13	42,691
Sept	14.54	14.65	14.47	14.63	− .05	19.36	13.50	19,524
Oct	14.80	14.86	14.80	14.91	− .04	19.34	13.79	12,523
Nov	15.06	15.14	15.06	15.16	− .04	19.15	14.08	9,373
Dec	15.30	15.37	15.20	15.37	− .10	18.53	14.37	37,001
Ja99	15.46	15.46	15.40	15.52	− .10	17.95	14.53	17,729
Feb	....	....	....	15.64	− .10	17.35	14.76	8,308
Mar	....	....	....	15.75	− .08	17.80	15.44	3,335
Apr	....	....	....	15.85	− .07	16.15	15.85	1,167
June	15.89	15.89	15.89	16.09	− .06	17.30	15.27	4,160
Sept	....	....	....	16.20	− .05	16.79	16.79	100
Dec	16.29	16.29	16.15	16.31	+ .01	17.80	15.58	7,975
Ju00	....	....	....	16.56	+ .10	16.58	16.58	1,000
Dec	16.54	16.54	16.54	16.66	+ .11	17.63	15.85	1,875

Est vol 51,000; vol Wd 44,786; open int 245,478, −1,085.

GAS OIL (IPE) 100 metric tons; $ per ton

	Open	High	Low	Settle	Change	Lifetime High	Lifetime Low	Open Interest
June	122.50	122.75	121.25	122.25	− .50	183.75	119.75	27,791
July	125.25	126.00	124.25	125.50	− .25	183.25	122.50	19,879
Aug	128.75	129.50	128.25	129.00	− .25	183.00	126.50	12,699
Sept	131.75	132.50	131.75	132.50	− .25	182.00	130.50	11,652
Oct	135.25	136.25	135.25	136.00	− .25	184.00	134.00	15,362
Nov	138.25	138.75	138.25	138.75	− .50	179.75	137.00	9,758
Dec	141.00	141.75	141.00	141.50	− .50	175.00	13850	32,573
Ja99	143.25	144.25	143.25	144.00	− .25	162.00	140.50	8,053
Feb	....	....	....	146.00	− .50	160.50	143.25	4,071
Mar	146.75	146.75	146.75	146.50	− .50	186.00	146.75	3,421
Apr	....	....	....	147.00	− .50	148.75	147.00	411
May	....	....	....	147.50	− .50	149.25	149.25	301
June	....	....	....	147.75	− .50	175.00	143.75	4,684
Sept	....	....	....	151.25	− .50	153.75	152.50	500

Est vol 16,000; vol Wd 16,053; open int 151,155, +1,058.

Source: The Wall Street Journal, May 29, 1998

price, and the continuous rate of interest, Expression (12.18) can be used to infer the net convenience yield.

EXAMPLE   **Computing the Net Convenience Yield**

Suppose that we want to compute the net convenience yield for gold using the August, October, and December futures prices in Table 12.9. The necessary data are summarized in Table 12.10, Part A.

Using Expression (12.18), the net convenience yield for each contract is shown in Table 12.10, Part B. The net convenience yields vary from 1.92 percent for 214 days to maturity to 2.83 percent for 91 days to maturity. ■

Futures Options

Let us examine the pricing of commodity futures options. Table 12.11 shows some of the futures options that are currently traded. Included are options on agricultural commodities, oil, metals, and livestock.

TABLE 12.10   *Net Convenience Yield, Gold Futures*

PART A INPUTS			
Cash price	$294.00 troy oz		
Futures price*	295.60	297.80	299.80
Maturity (days)[†]	91	153	214
Discount rate (percent)	4.91	4.94	5.10
T-Bill price	0.9876	0.9790	0.9697

*These prices are taken from Table 12.9.

[†]The last trading day is the third business day of the maturing delivery month.

PART B NET CONVENIENCE YIELD	
MATURITY (DAYS)	NET CONVENIENCE YIELD* (PERCENT)
91	2.83
153	2.00
214	1.92

*A 365-day year is assumed.

The pricing of commodity futures options is similar to the pricing of index futures options. We only need to modify Assumption A8 as follows.

> Assumption A8.   The net convenience yield is known and constant over the life of the option.

This is analogous to a constant dividend yield on a stock index.

For European options, Expressions (12.16) and (12.17) can be used for pricing. For American futures options, a binomial lattice approximation to the lognormal model can be used, or the MacMillan model can be applied.

EXAMPLE   **Implied Volatilities for Gold Futures Options**

Consider the Comex (CMX) options on gold futures. These options are American, implying that they can be exercised at any time up to and including the expiry date. The last trading day is the second Friday of the month prior to the delivery of the underlying futures contract.

Suppose that for the remaining part of the year, futures contracts expire in October and December. Also, suppose that we obtain the October and

TABLE 12.11 *Options on Commodity Futures, Thursday, May 28, 1998**

AGRICULTURAL

CORN (CBT)
5,000 bu.; cents per bu.

Strike	Calls-Settle			Puts-Settle		
Price	Jly	Sep	Dec	Jly	Sep	Dec
220	....	....	....	⅜	3	4¼
230	10½	....	25½	2⅜	6½	7¾
240	5⅛	15½	20½	6⅞	12	12½
250	2⅜	11½	16¼	14⅛	17¾	18
260	1⅛	9	13	22⅝	25¼	24¾
270	⅝	7⅛	10½	32¼	33⅜	32

Est vol 13,000 Wd 21,330 calls 7,318 puts
Op int Wed 241,351 calls 125,372 puts

SOYBEANS (CBT)
5,000 bu.; cents per bu.

Strike	Calls-Settle			Puts-Settle		
Price	Jly	Aug	Sep	Jly	Aug	Sep
575	44	....	35	⅜	4¾	13½
600	21¼	25	24	2½	14	27
625	7	15½	16½	13¼	28⅝	44⅛
650	2⅜	10½	12	33⅝	49	64½
675	1	6¾	8¾	57⅛	70	86
700	½	4½	6¾	81½	93	109

Est vol 14,000 Wd 34,898 calls 9,008 puts
Op int Wed 166,382 calls 65,984 puts

SOYBEAN MEAL (CBT)
100 tons; $ per ton

Strike	Calls-Settle			Puts-Settle		
Price	Jly	Aug	Sep	Jly	Aug	Sep
145	....	....	....	.60	1.90	3.25
150	8.15	9.60	....	1.25	3.60	4.75
155	4.90	7.00	8.40	3.00	5.80	7.25
160	2.75	5.00	6.50	6.00	8.65	10.25
165	1.60	3.70	5.25	9.70	12.25	....
170	.75	2.75	4.10	13.75	16.15	....

Est vol 4,700 Wd 1,202 calls 1,208 puts
Op int Wed 43,129 calls 30,433 puts

SOYBEAN OIL (CBT)
60,000 lbs.; cents per lb.

Strike	Calls-Settle			Puts-Settle		
Price	Jly	Aug	Sep	Jly	Aug	Sep
2550	.990	....	....	.170	.420	.530
2600	.650	1.050	1.230	.330	.600	.730
2650	.400	.825	....	.600	.845	.990
2700	.250	.665	.820	.940	1.195	1.290
2750	.180	.510	.700	1.360	1.550	1.670
2800	.120	.400	.590	1.770	1.940	2.060

Est vol 5,000 Wd 2,263 calls 1,619 puts
Op int Wed 62,988 calls 43,718 puts

WHEAT (CBT)
5,000 bu.; cents per bu.

Strike	Calls-Settle			Puts-Settle		
Price	Jly	Sep	Dec	Jly	Sep	Dec
260	24½	36½	....	....	....	....
270	15¼	....	43½	¾	3¼	....
280	8	21	36	3½	5¾	6½
290	3⅝	15	30	9	10	10½
300	1⅝	11	24¼	17	16	14½
310	¾	8	19¼	26	23¼	19¼

Est vol 4,500 Wd 4,883 calls 6,423 puts
Op int Wed 86,423 calls 46,330 puts

COTTON (CTN)
50,000 lbs.; cents per lb.

Strike	Calls-Settle			Puts-Settle		
Price	Jly	Oct	Dec	Jly	Oct	Dec
67	2.66	5.48	6.34	.33	.97	1.00
68	1.90	4.69	5.63	.58	1.26	1.26
69	1.29	4.14	4.97	.96	1.60	1.56
70	.33	3.56	4.30	1.50	1.99	1.90
71	.50	3.02	3.79	2.17	2.43	2.29
72	.31	2.54	3.27	2.98	2.93	2.74

Est vol 3,800 Wd 4,062 calls 596 puts
Op int Wed 66,195 calls 42,511 puts

ORANGE JUICE (CTN)
15,000 lbs.; cents per lb.

Strike	Calls-Settle			Puts-Settle		
Price	Jly	Sep	Nov	Jly	Sep	Nov
100	9.80	13.80	16.80	1.05	2.10	3.10
105	5.90	10.30	....	2.30	3.70	4.50
110	3.10	7.50	10.50	4.30	5.60	6.40
115	1.40	5.35	7.60	8.00	8.20	8.80
120	.55	3.40	5.80	12.00	11.20	11.20
125	.25	2.20	3.90	....	14.85	....

Est vol 200 Wd 376 calls 214 puts
Op int Wed 27,104 calls 24,331 puts

COFFEE (CSCE)
37,500 lbs.; cents per lb.

Strike	Calls-Settle			Puts-Settle		
Price	Jly	Aug	Sep	Jly	Aug	Sep
120	12.85	13.90	17.10	.45	3.40	6.60
125	8.35	11.00	14.50	.95	5.50	9.00
130	4.75	8.50	12.50	2.40	8.00	12.00
135	2.50	7.45	10.90	5.00	11.95	15.40
140	1.10	5.95	9.50	8.70	15.45	19.00
145	.45	4.80	8.35	13.05	19.30	22.85

Est vol 3,111 Wd 1,521 calls 916 puts
Op int Wed 32,685 calls 27,224 puts

SUGAR-WORLD (CSCE)
112,000 lbs.; cents per lb.

Strike	Calls-Settle			Puts-Settle		
Price	Jly	Aug	Oct	Jly	Aug	Oct
750	.79	1.07	1.19	.03	.13	.25
800	.38	.67	.83	.12	.23	.39
850	.12	.38	.55	.36	.44	.61
900	.03	.18	.34	.76	.74	.90
950	.01	.08	.20	1.25	1.14	1.26
1000	.01	.03	.11	1.75	1.59	1.67

Est vol 13,041 Wd 11,127 calls 6,572 puts
Op int Wed 124,012 calls 55,631 puts

COCOA (CSCE)
10 metric tons; $ per ton

Strike	Calls-Settle			Puts-Settle		
Price	Jly	Aug	Sep	Jly	Aug	Sep
1550	117	146	155	1	3	12
1600	68	104	115	2	11	22
1650	33	68	85	17	25	42
1700	10	43	65	42	50	72
1750	3	23	42	87	80	99
1800	1	13	31	135	120	138

Est vol 3,170 Wd 441 calls 833 puts
Op int Wed 20,889 calls 16,263 puts

OIL

CRUDE OIL (NYM)
1,000 bbls.; $ per bbl.

Strike	Calls-Settle			Puts-Settle		
Price	Jly	Aug	Sep	Jly	Aug	Sep
1400	1.06	1.63	2.04	.21	.31	.32
1450	.73	....	....	.37	....	.46
1500	.48	1.00	1.37	.63	.67	.64
1550	.30	.74	1.10	.95	.91	.86
1600	.17	.55	.87	1.32	1.22	1.13
1650	.10	.40	.68	1.75	1.56	1.43

Est vol 27,813 Wd 12,147 calls 11,-
178 puts
Op int Wed 299,846 calls 203,157 puts

HEATING OIL No.2 (NYM)
42,000 gal.; $ per gal.

Strike	Calls-Settle			Puts-Settle		
Price	Jly	Aug	Sep	Jly	Aug	Sep
38	....	....	....	.0070	....	....
39	....	....	....	.0105	.0114	.0095
40	.0150	.0271	.0388	.0150	.0152	.0125
41	.0108	.0220	....	.0208	.0200	.0210
42	.0080	.0175	.0215	.0279	.0255	.0250
43	.0055	.0135	....	.0354	.0314	.0325

Est vol 2,208 Wd 435 calls 272 puts
Op int Wed 27,775 calls 18,240 puts

GASOLINE-Unlead (NYM)
42,000 gal.; $ per gal.

Strike	Calls-Settle			Puts-Settle		
Price	Jly	Aug	Sep	Jly	Aug	Sep
47	.0383	....	....	.0077	.0120	.0151
48	.0313	.0426	.0448	.0107	.0154	.0188
49	.0254	.0367	....	.0147	.0194	.0231
50	.0192	.0314	.0337	.0185	.0240	.0275
51	.0150	.0260	....	.0243	.0286	.0331
52	.0115	.0216	.0257	.0307	.0341	.0394

Est vol 2,047 Wed 2,417 calls 501 puts
Op int Wed 46,719 calls 20,147 puts

NATURAL GAS (NYM)
10,000 MMBtu.; $ per MMBtu.

Strike	Calls-Settle			Puts-Settle		
Price	Jly	Aug	Sep	Jly	Aug	Sep
200	....	....	....	.067	.088	.101
205	.112	.183	.239	.090	.109	.122
210	.090	.156	.213	.119	.134	.145
215	.071	.133	.185	.150	.159	.170
220	.055	.114	.164	.184	.190	.196
225	.043	.097	.145	.221	.222	.227

Est vol 11,252 Wd 10,804 calls 6,196 puts
Op int Wed 154,286 calls 110,547 puts

BRENT CRUDE (IPE)
1,000 net bbls.; $ per bbl.

Strike	Calls-Settle			Puts-Settle		
Price	Jly	Aug	Sep	Jly	Aug	Sep
1250	1.65	2.04	2.29	.02	.17	.16
1300	1.19	1.64	1.89	.06	.27	.26
1350	.78	1.27	1.52	.15	.40	.39
1400	.46	.96	1.19	.35	.59	.56
1450	.26	.77	.92	.63	.90	.79
1500	.12	.54	.70	.99	1.17	1.07

Est vol 850 Wd 875 calls 2,400 puts
Op int Wed 16,969 calls 11,514 puts

GAS OIL (IPE)
100 metric tons; $ per ton

Strike	Calls-Settle			Puts-Settle		
Price	Jun	Jly	Aug	Jun	Jly	Aug
105	17.25	10.65	24.55	....	.15	.55
110	12.25	15.90	20.10	....	.40	1.10
115	7.25	11.60	16.00	....	1.10	2.00
120	275	7.90	12.35	.50	2.40	3.35
125	1.30	4.70	9.15	4.05	4.20	5.15
130	.25	2.65	6.50	8.00	7.15	7.50

Est vol 1,000 calls 20 puts
Op int Wed 13,221 calls 3,009 puts

LIVESTOCK

CATTLE-FEEDER (CME)
50,000 lbs.; cents per lb.

Strike	Calls-Settle			Puts-Settle		
Price	Aug	Sep	Oct	Aug	Sep	Oct
73	....	....	....	0.75	....	....
74	2.17	....	....	1.00	1.25	1.45
75	....	....	....	1.45	....	....
76	1.12	1.45	....	1.92	2.25	2.30
77	0.75	....	....	2.52	....	....
78	0.47	0.80	1.00	3.25	3.55	3.55

Est vol 931 Wd 174 calls 418 puts
Op int Wed 2,862 calls 7,727 puts

CATTLE-LIVE (CME)
40,000 lbs.; cents per lb.

Strike	Calls-Settle			Puts-Settle		
Price	Jun	Aug	Oct	Jun	Aug	Oct
62	2.17	....	....	0.05	0.17	0.37
63	....	....	....	0.17	0.30	....
64	0.57	....	....	0.45	0.50	0.80
65	0.22	2.05	....	1.10	0.80	....
66	0.07	1.45	2.00	1.95	1.17	1.52
67	0.05	0.97	....	2.92	1.70	....

Est vol 2,683 Wd 1,394 calls 2,249 puts
Op int Wed 23,772 calls 29,644 puts

HOGS-LEAN (CME)
40,000 lbs.; cents per lb.

Strike	Calls-Settle			Puts-Settle		
Price	Jun	Jly	Aug	Jun	Jly	Aug
58	2.47	2.32	1.20	0.10	0.97	2.55
59	1.62	1.75	....	0.25	1.40	....
60	0.92	1.30	0.60	0.55	1.95	3.92
61	0.45	0.90	....	1.00	2.52	....
62	0.25	0.65	0.30	1.87	3.27	5.62
63	0.15	0.45	....	2.77	4.07	

Est vol 417 Wd 312 calls 351 puts
Op int Wed 10,062 calls 9,628 puts

METALS

COPPER (CMX)
25,000 lbs.; cents per lb.

Strike	Calls-Settle			Puts-Settle		
Price	Jly	Aug	Sep	Jly	Aug	Sep
72	5.75	6.60	7.40	.90	1.45	1.95
74	4.25	5.25	6.10	1.40	2.10	2.65
76	3.00	4.15	5.00	2.15	2.95	3.50
78	2.00	3.15	4.00	3.15	3.95	4.50
80	1.35	2.35	3.20	4.50	5.15	5.65
82	.80	1.75	2.60	5.95	6.50	7.05

Est vol.400 Wd 380 calls 36 puts
Op int Wed 17,584 calls 4,068 puts

GOLD (CMX)
100 troy ounces; $ per troy ounce

Strike	Calls-Settle			Puts-Settle		
Price	Jly	Aug	Oct	Jly	Aug	Oct
285	11.30	13.10	15.80	.90	2.50	4.00
290	6.70	9.60	12.30	2.00	4.00	5.40
295	4.00	6.30	9.90	3.50	5.70	7.40
300	1.70	4.20	7.40	5.70	8.60	9.60
305	.80	2.20	5.30	10.40	11.70	12.10
310	.50	1.40	4.20	15.10	15.80	16.70

Est vol 18,000 Wd 4,840 calls 6,649 puts
Op int Wed 228,798 calls 104,893 puts

SILVER (CMX)
5,000 troy ounces; cts per troy ounce

Strike	Calls-Settle			Puts-Settle		
Price	Jly	Aug	Sep	Jly	Aug	Sep
450	55.9	61.0	65.0	.9	3.4	7.0
475	33.5	41.5	47.5	3.5	8.0	14.2
500	16.2	25.6	33.3	11.2	17.0	24.8
525	7.0	16.0	22.3	27.0	32.3	39.0
550	2.8	10.2	15.3	47.8	51.4	56.7
575	1.5	6.1	10.5	71.5	72.2	76.0

Est vol 2,200 Wd 2,392 calls 2,160 puts
Op int Wed 74,903 calls 30,245 puts

*Source: *The Wall Street Journal*, May 29, 1998

TABLE 12.12 *Implied Volatilities for Gold Futures Options**

| | CALL OPTIONS | | PUT OPTIONS | |
STRIKE PRICE	OCTOBER	DECEMBER	OCTOBER	DECEMBER
360	12.92	9.32	12.53	10.95
370	9.20	10.01	10.73	10.34
380	9.80	9.55	9.80	9.78
390	11.14	10.86	11.21	10.65

*The program Futures/Implied Volatility/American Options is used. A 365-day year is assumed. The numbers are expressed as percentages.

December gold futures prices, the maturity dates of the contracts, and the discount rates as follows.

October gold futures price	381.00
December gold futures price	384.00
Maturity of October option	29 days
Maturity of December option	92 days
Discount rate for 36 days	4.02 percent
Discount rate for 99 days	4.33 percent

Given this data, we use the program Futures/Implied Volatility/American Option to determine the implied volatilities for the October and December options. The results are shown in Table 12.12. ■

12.8 SUMMARY

Given Assumptions A1 through A6, we found that the pricing of derivatives on stock indexes and commodities is analogous to the pricing of derivatives written on foreign currencies. This analogy enabled us to construct the binomial lattice of spot prices for these different assets and futures prices. For many of these types of assets there is an implicit dividend, so it may be optimal to exercise American call and put options earlier than maturity. We discussed valuation procedures for these circumstances. Finally, we showed how to construct synthetic options using futures contracts instead of the underlying spot asset.

REFERENCES

General:

MacMillan, L. W., 1986. "Analytic Approximation for the American Put Option." *Advances in Futures and Options Research* 1, 119–139.

Merton, R. C., 1973. "Theory of Rational Option Pricing." *Bell Journal of Economics and Management Science* 4, 141–183.

"Symposium: Brady Commission Report on the Stock Market Crash," 1988. *Journal of Economic Perspectives* 2, 3–50.

Options on futures:

Black, F., 1976. "The Pricing of Commodity Contracts." *Journal of Financial Economics* 3, 167–179.

Brenner, M., G. Courtadon, and M. Subrahmanyam, 1985. "Options on the Spot and Options on Futures." *Journal of Finance* 40, 1303–1317.

Ramaswamy, K., and S. M. Sundaresan, 1985. "The Valuation of Options on Futures Contracts." *Journal of Finance* 40, 1219–1340.

Wolf, A., 1982. "Fundamentals of Commodity Options on Futures." *Journal of Futures Markets* 2, 391–408.

Options on stock indices

General information:

Chicago Mercantile Exchange, 1990. *Using S&P 500 Stock Index Futures and Options.*

Chicago Mercantile Exchange, 1993. *Stock Index Futures and Options: A Reference Guide.*

Fleming, J., and R. E. Whaley, 1994. "The Value of Wildcard Options." *Journal of Finance* 49, 215–236.

Empirical studies:

Chance, D. M., 1986. "Empirical Tests of the Pricing of Index Call Options." *Advances in Futures and Options Research* 1(A), 141–166.

Harvey, C. R., and R. E. Whaley, 1991. "S&P 100 Index Option Volatility." *Journal of Finance* 46, 1551–1561.

Harvey, C. R., and R. E. Whaley, 1992. "Dividends and S&P 100 Index Option Valuations." *Journal of Futures Markets* 12, 123–137.

MacKinlay, A. C., and K. Ramaswamy, 1988. "Index-Futures Arbitrage and the Behavior of Stock Index Futures Prices." *Review of Financial Studies* 1, 137–158.

Circuit breakers:

Hasbrouck, J., G. Sofianos, and D. Sosebee, 1993. "New York Stock Exchange Systems and Trading Procedures." New York Stock Exchange Working Paper #93.01.

QUESTIONS

Question 1

Today the June S&P 500 index futures price is 512.15 and the September futures price is 516.45. You short the June contract and go long in the September contract. Tomorrow the June futures price is 507.30 and the September futures price is 511.55. What is the profit from your portfolio?

Question 2

An investor is bullish on small firms while pessimistic about the general economy. The investor goes long in June 20 futures contracts on the S&P 400 Midcap index with futures price 186.75. The investor shorts June 15 futures contracts on the S&P 500 index with futures price 512.15. On the next day, the S&P 400 Midcap futures price is 183.65 and the S&P 500 futures price is 507.30. What is the investor's profit?

Question 3

You are given information about European options on the S&P 500 index.

TYPE OF OPTION	MATURITY (DAYS)	STRIKE PRICE	PRICE OF OPTION
Put	36	460	$7/_{16}$
Put	63	470	$1^5/_8$
Put	63	475	$1^3/_4$
Put	63	480	$2^1/_4$
Call	63	480	$34^1/_2$

Index Value	509.23
36-day Discount Rate*	5.50 percent
63-day Discount Rate*	5.56 percent
Dividend Yield**	2.32 percent

*Assuming a 360-day year.

**Expressed as a continuously compounded rate, assuming a 360-day year.

Determine the implied volatility for each option, using the program Equity/Implied Volatility/Constant Dividend Yield.

Question 4

You are given information about American options on the S&P 100 index.

TYPE OF OPTION	MATURITY (DAYS)	STRIKE PRICE	PRICE OF OPTION
Call	36	460	22
Call	36	470	$12\frac{7}{8}$
Call	36	480	6
Call	63	460	$23\frac{7}{8}$
Call	63	470	16
Call	63	480	$8\frac{1}{2}$
Put	36	460	$1\frac{1}{2}$
Put	36	470	$2\frac{7}{8}$
Put	36	480	6
Put	63	460	$3\frac{1}{8}$
Put	63	470	$5\frac{1}{8}$
Put	63	480	$8\frac{3}{8}$

Index Value	478.81
36-day Discount Rate*	5.50 percent
63-day Discount Rate*	5.56 percent
Dividend Yield**	2.32 percent

*Assuming a 360-day year.

**Expressed as a discount rate, assuming a 360-day year.

a)   Determine the implied volatilities for these options. Use the program FX/Implied Volatility/American Option. The dividend yield has been expressed as a discount rate. Substitute this value into the foreign discount rate.

b)   To determine the implied volatility, it is necessary to determine the dividend yield. Given the difficulty of estimating this term, assume that the dividend yield is 2 percent, expressed as a discount rate. Calculate the implied volatilities.

c)   Assume the dividend yield is 2.50 percent, expressed as a discount rate. Calculate the implied volatilities.

d)   Discuss the differences in your answers to parts a), b), and c).

Question 5

A financial institution has written a call option contract on the S&P 500 index. The contract size is 10,000. The institution wants to use futures contracts to hedge its position. Relevant pricing data follows.

Index Value	509.23	
Futures Price	516.45	
Maturity of Futures Contract	155 days	September 14
Maturity of Option	120 days	August 11
Strike Price	515	
Volatility*	14.80 percent	

Discount Rate for 120 Days**	5.64 percent
Discount Rate for 155 Days**	5.67 percent
Dividend Yield***	2.47 percent

*Assuming a 365-day year.

**Assuming a 360-day year.

***Continuously compounded, assuming a 360-day year.

a) Determine the value of the option contract and its delta. Use the program Equity/Pricing European Options/Constant Dividend Yield.
b) Determine the delta for the futures contract.
c) Describe the hedge portfolio. The contract size for the futures contract is 500 times the index.

Question 6

In the following table you are given price data for options on the S&P 500 futures contract.

		MATURITY	
TYPE OF OPTION	MATURITY (DAYS)	MAY	JUNE
Call	500	14.60	16.85
Call	505	10.60	13.20
Call	510	7.10	9.85
Call	515	4.40	7.00
Put	505	3.50	6.10
Put	510	4.95	7.70
Put	515	7.25	9.80
Time to Maturity for May Option	35 days	May 18	
Time to Maturity for June Option	63 days	June 15	
Futures Price Maturing June	512.80		
Discount Rate* for 35 Days	5.50 percent		
Discount Rate* for 63 Days	5.57 percent		

*Assuming a 360-day year.

a) Determine the implied volatility for each option, assuming a 365-day year. Use the program Futures/Implied Volatility/European Options.
b) Is there any difference between the implied volatilities for call options and for put options?
c) These options are in fact American, so determine the implied volatilities using the program Futures/Implied Volatility/American Options. How do your answers compare to those in a)?

Question 7

A financial institution has written 100 May put options on the June S&P 500 futures contract. The institution wants to hedge its position using the June futures contract and the money market account.

June Futures Price	512.80
Index Value	509.23
Strike Price	505.00
Maturity of Option	35 days
Maturity of Futures Contract	63 days
Volatility*	9 percent
Discount Rate** for 35 Days	5.50 percent
Discount Rate** for 63 Days	5.57 percent
Dividend Yield***	1.74 percent

*Assuming a 365-day year.

**Assuming a 360-day year.

***Continuously compounded, assuming a 360-day year.

a) Determine the delta of the May put option and its gamma. Use the program Futures/Pricing/American Option.
b) Determine the delta of the June futures contract.
c) Describe the hedge portfolio.
d) The delta of the hedge portfolio is zero. What is the gamma of the portfolio?

Question 8

A gold processing company approaches a financial institution to buy a 100-troy-ounce call option on gold. The maturity of the option is 120 days and the strike price is 390.00.

a) Using the data in Table 12.10, what is the net convenience yield? The 120-day discount rate is 4.50 percent, assuming a 360-day year.
b) Using the data in Tables 12.10 and 12.12, determine the value of the option. Explicitly identify the additional assumptions that you must make. Use the program Equity/Pricing European Options/Constant Dividend Yield. Examine the sensitivity of your answer to different assumptions about volatility.

Question 9

You are given the following information on CMX call options written on gold futures.

CALL OPTIONS

	MATURITIES (DAYS)		
STRIKE PRICE	44	107	170
420	17.60	25.90	33.70
440	4.80	13.50	21.40
460	0.90	6.20	11.50
Futures Price	434.10	438.20	442.40
Discount Rates	5.12	5.60	5.78

a) Determine the implied volatilities, assuming the options are European. Use the program Futures/Implied Volatility/European Option.

b) Determine the implied volatilities, assuming the options are American. Use the program Futures/Implied Volatility/American Option.

c) Explain the major difference in the results.

Question 10

A mining company is planning a bond issue. Its financial advisors have advised the company to issue gold options along with the bonds. Each option would allow the bondholder to buy 10 troy ounces of gold at $484 per troy ounce. The options have a maturity of 12 months and are European.

Spot gold price	$435.74
Maturity of option	360 days
Discount rate for 360 days	6.11 percent

a) Determine the net convenience yield, expressed as a continuously compounded rate, assuming a 360-day year. Use the data in Question 9. What implicit assumption are you making?

b) Using the data in Question 9, determine the volatility needed to price this option. What implicit assumptions are you making?

c) What is the value of the gold options? Use the program Equity/Pricing European Options/Constant Dividend Yield.

d) What is the maximum liability to the mining company?

e) If the gold price went up to about $550, this could have a serious effect on the company's cash flows. What type of option could the company use to limit its risk?

f) What is the value of the combined options?

PART IV

INTEREST RATE CONTRACTS, THE HJM MODEL, AND EXTENSIONS

INTEREST RATE CONTRACTS

13.0 INTRODUCTION

In our examination of the pricing and hedging of options and futures in Chapter 5 and in Chapter 8 through Chapter 12, we made the strong assumption that interest rates are constant through time. We imposed this assumption in order to simplify our discussion of pricing and hedging. This assumption implies that all default-free securities, and options or futures on default-free securities, are identical from an economic perspective. That is, they are all riskless, and they all earn the same constant interest rate.

The assumption of constant interest rates is obviously an unrealistic assumption. But for short-dated options and futures on underlying assets distinct from and uncorrelated with interest rates (like common stock), it is an acceptable first approximation. For these derivatives, interest rates are only of secondary importance to the analysis. Yet, for options and futures on the term structure of interest rates, this assumption is unreasonable and unacceptable, even as a first approximation.

The next step in our examination of derivatives—Chapter 13 through Chapter 17—is to study the relaxation of this constant interest rate assumption.

Our first task in this chapter is to examine the basic types of traded default-free securities making up the term structures of interest rates, that is, Treasury bills, Treasury notes, Treasury bonds, and the futures contracts written on these instruments. Also necessary is an understanding of related interest rate instruments: Eurodollar forward rate agreements and futures. In subsequent chapters we will examine other interest rate contracts and the pricing and hedging of interest rate derivatives.

13.1 ZERO-COUPON BONDS

First we discuss default-free zero-coupon bonds. We recall that a **zero-coupon bond** is a bond that has no coupon payments. Profits from owning such a security come solely from price appreciation. Zero-coupon bonds are sometimes called **discount bonds** because they are sold at a discount, a price lower than the par or face value of the bond that is paid at maturity.

U.S. Treasury bills are zero-coupon bonds issued by the U.S. government. Because their payment is guaranteed by the taxing power of the U.S. government, they are generally considered to be default-free. Treasury bills (T-bills) are short-term instruments with maturities of a year or less. New Treasury bills are regularly issued

by the U.S. government via competitive auctions. Every Thursday the Treasury auctions new 91-day (13-week) and 182-day (26-week) T-bills, and every fourth Thursday it auctions new 364-day (52-week) T-bills. The minimum face value of a Treasury bill is $10,000. Quotes for T-bills are given in terms of discount rates.

Discount Rates

For U.S. T-bills, the **discount rate**[1], i_d, is defined by

$$B(0, T) = [1 - i_d(T/360)],$$ (13.1)

where $B(0, T)$ is the date-0 value of a T-bill with a dollar payoff at maturity T. The maturity is expressed in days, and it is assumed that there are 360 days in the year. Table 13.1 gives some examples of bid/asked quotes for T-bills.

TABLE 13.1 *Treasury Bill Quotes, Thursday, May 28, 1998**

TREASURY BILLS

Maturity	Days to Mat.	Bid	Asked	Chg.	Ask Yld.
Jun 04 '98	6	4.39	4.35	− 0.05	4.41
Jun 11 '98	13	4.44	4.40	− 0.06	4.47
Jun 18 '98	20	4.46	4.42	− 0.06	4.49
Jun 25 '98	27	4.53	4.49	− 0.06	4.57
Jul 02 '98	34	4.65	4.61	− 0.05	4.69
Jul 09 '98	41	4.67	4.63	− 0.04	4.72
Jul 16 '98	48	4.71	4.67	− 0.05	4.76
Jul 23 '98	55	4.79	4.75	− 0.04	4.85
Jul 30 '98	62	4.81	4.79	− 0.03	4.90
Aug 06 '98	69	4.86	4.84	− 0.04	4.95
Aug 13 '98	76	4.90	4.88	− 0.03	5.00
Aug 20 '98	83	4.94	4.92	− 0.03	5.05
Aug 27 '98	90	4.92	4.91	− 0.03	5.04
Sep 03 '98	97	4.96	4.94	− 0.03	5.08
Sep 03 '98	**97**	**4.97**	**4.96**	**+ 0.01**	**5.10**
Sep 10 '98	104	4.99	4.97	− 0.03	5.11
Sep 17 '98	111	5.00	4.98	− 0.02	5.13
Sep 24 '98	118	4.98	4.96	− 0.03	5.11
Oct 01 '98	125	5.03	5.01	− 0.02	5.17
Oct 08 '98	132	5.04	5.02	− 0.01	5.19
Oct 15 '98	139	5.08	5.06	− 0.02	5.23
Oct 22 '98	146	5.07	5.05	− 0.01	5.23
Oct 29 '98	153	4.95	4.93	− 0.01	5.11
Nov 05 '98	160	5.11	5.09	− 0.01	5.28
Nov 12 '98	167	5.13	5.11	....	5.31
Nov 19 '98	174	5.12	5.10	− 0.01	5.30
Nov 27 '98	182	5.13	5.12	....	5.33
Dec 03 '98	**188**	**5.13**	**5.12**	**− 0.01**	**5.33**
Dec 10 '98	195	5.13	5.11	....	5.32
Jan 07 '99	223	5.11	5.09	....	5.30
Feb 04 '99	251	5.13	5.11	+ 0.01	5.33
Mar 04 '99	279	5.14	5.12	....	5.36
Apr 01 '99	307	5.14	5.12	+ 0.01	5.37
Apr 29 '99	335	5.14	5.12	+ 0.01	5.38
May 27 '99	363	5.14	5.13	+ 0.01	5.41

*Source: *The Wall Street Journal*, May 29, 1998.

---

[1]A good reference for interest rate calculations is Stigum (1981).

For securities such as stocks, the ask price is higher than the bid price. This is not the case for the T-bill quotes, however, due to the inverse relation between the T-bill's price and the discount rate. Thus the ask rate is less than the bid rate. Referring to Table 13.1, consider the Treasury bills that mature on August 20. These T-bills have a maturity of 83 days. The bid rate is 4.94, which exceeds the ask rate of 4.92.

From these rates, however, we can show that the ask price on T-bills does exceed the bid price. Indeed, the bid is a discount rate of 4.94 percent, implying a price of

$$\text{Bid price} = 10{,}000\, B(0, T) = 10{,}000 \left[1 - \frac{4.94}{100} \times \frac{83}{360} \right]$$
$$= \$9{,}886.11,$$

given that Treasury bills trade with a face value (payoff) of $10,000. The ask discount rate is 4.92, implying a price of

$$\text{Ask price} = 10{,}000 \left[1 - \frac{4.92}{100} \times \frac{83}{360} \right]$$
$$= \$9{,}886.57.$$

In terms of dollars, the ask price is greater than the bid price. This completes our discussion of discount rates.

Simple Interest Rates

Here we discuss simple interest rates (see also Chapter 1). The **simple interest rate**, i_S, is defined as

$$B(0, T) \equiv \frac{1}{[1 + i_S\,(T/365)]}, \tag{13.2}$$

assuming a 365-day year. In some cases a 360-day year is used.

The difference between discount rates and simple interest rates is greater the higher the discount rate and the longer the time to maturity. For example, consider a discount rate of 4 percent and a maturity of 30 days. The T-bill price with face value 100 is

$$100\, B(0, T) = 100 \left[1 - \frac{4}{100} \times \frac{30}{360} \right] = 99.6667.$$

This implies an equivalent simple rate of

$$i_S = 1 \left[\frac{1 - B(0, T)}{B(0, T)} \right] \frac{365}{T}$$
$$= 4.069 \text{ percent,}$$

a difference of 0.069 percent. If a 360-day year had been used, the simple interest rate would be 4.013 percent, a difference of only 0.013 percent.

Continuously Compounded Interest Rates

The continuously compounded annual interest rate, r, is defined by

$$B(0,T) = \exp[-r(T/365)], \tag{13.3}$$

assuming a 365-day year.

Referring to the previous example in which

$$B(0,T) = 0.996667,$$

and $T = 30$ days, then

$$r = \{-\ln[B(0,T)]\}(365/T)$$
$$= 4.062 \text{ percent.}$$

The three different interest rates are different ways of expressing dollar prices. They are each important, and each has its own use. For example, discount rates are used in quoting Treasury bill prices and in the T-bill futures markets. Simple interest rates are used in the Eurodollar markets, swaps markets, and foreign currency markets. Continuously compounded rates are used primarily in academic articles. There are two reasons for this difference. First, the use of continuously compounded interest rates avoids a lot of minor problems with respect to market conventions. Second, much theoretical work is in continuous time for which it is convenient to use continuously compounded rates.

13.2 COUPON BONDS

Let us now discuss default-free coupon bonds. Coupon bonds are bonds with regular interest payments, called coupons, plus a principal repayment at maturity. The principal is called the face value of the bond.

Intuitively, the value of a coupon-bearing bond is determined by summing the present value of all its coupon payments and the present value of the terminal face value. To be precise, we need to introduce some notation. Suppose that the coupon bond makes coupon payments c at dates $t = 1, \ldots, T$, where T is the maturity date of the bond. Let the face value of the bond F be paid at the maturity date T. This section only considers coupon bonds with no default risk. Bonds with default risk are studied in Chapter 18.

Pricing

First we examine the pricing of default-free coupon bonds. Let $B(0, t)$ denote the present value of receiving one dollar at date t with no risk of default. This amount is the price of a zero-coupon bond. The value of the coupon-bearing bond is equal to

$$B_c(0) = \sum_{t=1}^{T} cB(0, t) + FB(0, T). \tag{13.4}$$

This expression states that the coupon bond's value, B_c, equals the sum of the present value of all the coupon payments and the face value. This is an arbitrage-free pricing relation. The right side of Expression (13.4) represents the cost of constructing a synthetic coupon bond with identical coupon payments and face value as the traded coupon bond. The synthetic coupon bond consists of c zero-coupon bonds of maturity t for $t = 1, \ldots, T$ plus F additional zero-coupon bonds of maturity T.

If the left side exceeds the right side of Expression (13.4), then the arbitrage opportunity would be to sell short the coupon bond and go long the synthetic, pocketing the difference, with no future obligations. If the right side exceeds the left side, then changing the signs of the previous trading strategy generates arbitrage profits. The only condition consistent with no arbitrage is an equality.

We now illustrate the use of Expression (13.4) to value a coupon bond.

EXAMPLE

Valuing a Coupon Bond

This example illustrates the use of Expression (13.4) to value a coupon bond. Consider a coupon bond that matures in twenty-two months' time. The next coupon payment of $3.50 per $100 face value occurs in four months' time. After that, coupon payments of $3.50 occur every six months. The final payment includes principal. Details are shown in Table 13.2.

The present value of the coupon bond, which is trading above par, is $104.5071. This represents the sum of the present value of all the remaining coupon payments plus principal. ■

TABLE 13.2 *Pricing of a Bond*

MATURITY (MONTHS)	PRICING OF A ZERO-COUPON BOND	COUPON	PRINCIPAL	PRESENT VALUE OF COUPON PLUS PRINCIPAL
4	0.9835	3.50	0	3.4422
10	0.9592	3.50	0	3.3572
16	0.9355	3.50	0	3.2743
22	0.9124	3.50	100	94.4334
				104.5071

Yield-to-Maturity

The **yield-to-maturity** is defined as an interest rate per annum that equates the present value of future cash flows to the current market value. We can express this definition algebraically.

A bond that pays interest annually
For a bond that pays interest annually, the yield-to-maturity, y, is defined as

$$B_c(0) \equiv \sum_{t=1}^{T} \frac{c}{(1+y)^t} + \frac{F}{(1+y)^T}, \tag{13.5}$$

where B_c denotes the price of the coupon-bearing bond, c is the coupon at date t, F is the face value, and T is the total number of coupon payments.

In general, solving Expression (13.5) for the yield-to-maturity is a difficult task, since it is a nonlinear equation. Consequently, the yield-to-maturity is most often calculated numerically.

EXAMPLE **Yield-to-Maturity**

This example illustrates the calculation of a bond's yield-to-maturity. Let the market value of a bond be 104.52. Suppose that the bond has a maturity of two years and a coupon of 7 percent, which is paid on an annual basis. By definition, the yield-to-maturity, y, is defined to be the solution to

$$104.52 = \frac{7}{(1+y)} + \frac{7}{(1+y)^2} + \frac{100}{(1+y)^2}.$$

Let us guess at the solution, setting $y = 0.05$. The right side is 103.72, implying our initial guess was too high. If we try $y = 0.045$, the right side is 104.68, implying the yield-to-maturity is too low. Thus, the correct value is between 4.5 and 5.0 percent. By repeating this process, we will find that $y = 4.584$ percent. ■

A bond that pays interest semiannually
For a bond that pays interest semiannually, the yield-to-maturity, y, is defined as

$$B_c(0) \equiv \sum_{t=1}^{2T} \frac{c}{(1+y/2)^t} + \frac{F}{(1+y/2)^{2T}}. \tag{13.6}$$

In this expression, there are twice the compounding periods ($2T$), and the yield over each semiannual period is divided by 2 ($y/2$). Because of the ability to reinvest the semiannual coupon, the effective annual yield-to-maturity, y_A, is

$$y_A \equiv (1 + y/2)^2 - 1. \tag{13.7}$$

EXAMPLE

Semiannual Yield-to-Maturity

In this example we illustrate the use of Expression (13.6). Consider a bond with a maturity of two years that pays a coupon on a semiannual basis. The coupon is 7.00 percent per annum, implying that every six months of the dollar value of the coupon payment is $3.50 per $100 face value. Let the market value of the coupon bond be $103.79. The yield-to-maturity, y, is defined by

$$103.79 \equiv \sum_{t=1}^{4} \frac{3.50}{(1 + y/2)^t} + \frac{100}{(1 + y/2)^4}.$$

Again, by a trial and error basis, we find that $y/2 = 2.49$ percent. The effective annual yield-to-maturity is

$$y_A \equiv (1 + 0.0249)^2 - 1$$
$$= 5.04 \text{ percent.}$$

The yield-to-maturity is the holding period return per year on the coupon bond only if the coupons can be reinvested at the same rate as the yield-to-maturity.

To see this result, consider a bond that matures in one year and has a coupon of $3.00 that is paid semiannually. Let the bond sell at par. The yield-to-maturity, y, is defined as

$$100 = \frac{3}{(1 + y/2)} + \frac{3}{(1 + y/2)^2} + \frac{100}{(1 + y/2)^2},$$

implying that $y = 0.06$.

Let us compute the holding period return on this bond assuming reinvestment at the yield-to-maturity. At the end of the first six months, the investor receives the coupon and the calculation assumes that the investor can reinvest this coupon at the yield-to-maturity rate. At the end of one year when the bond matures, the investor receives the final coupon payment and principal, giving a total of $103 and the proceeds from reinvesting the first coupon. The total value is

$$103 + 3 (1 + 0.03) = 106.09.$$

The holding period return on this investment is

$$\frac{106.09 - 100}{100} = 6.09 \text{ percent,}$$

which agrees with the effective annual yield-to-maturity in Expression (13.7):

$$y_A = (1 + 0.06/2)^2 - 1$$
$$= 6.09 \text{ percent.}$$

The important point is that the effective yield implicitly assumes reinvestment of the coupon payments at the yield-to-maturity over the life of the bond. We should question the validity of this assumption in a world with changing interest rates.

Continuous compounding

The yield-to-maturity using continuous compounding, y_c, is defined by

$$B_c(0) \equiv \sum_{t=1}^{T} c \exp(-y_c \times t) + F \exp(-y_c \times T). \tag{13.8}$$

If $t = 1, \ldots, T$ are expressed in years, then y_c is an annual continuously compounded yield-to-maturity.

EXAMPLE   **Continuously Compounded Yield to Maturity**

This example illustrates the computation of the continuously compounded yield-to-maturity. Let the market value of a bond be 104.52. Let the bond have a maturity of two years and a coupon of 7 percent, which is paid on an annual basis. The annual continuously compounded yield-to-maturity is defined by

$$104.52 = 7 \exp(-y_c) + 7 \exp(-2y_c) + 100 \exp(-2y_c),$$

implying that $y_c = 4.48$ percent, which, as would be expected, is slightly lower than the discretely compounded yield-to-maturity of 4.58 percent.   ∎

Quotes

U.S. Treasury bonds and notes are coupon-bearing bonds issued by the U.S. government. Both are normally considered to be default-free. Treasury notes are issued with maturities up to ten years, and Treasury bonds have maturities greater than ten years. All Treasury notes and bonds have semiannual coupon payments. Face value denominations range from $1,000 to $1 million. Table 13.3 gives some examples of market quotes for Treasury notes and bonds.

The convention is that prices are quoted assuming a face value of $100. An explanation of bid/ask quotes is best given via an example.

EXAMPLE   **Bid/Ask Quotes**

This example illustrates the computation of bid/ask prices from bid/ask quotes on Treasury bonds and notes. Suppose we have a bid or ask quote of 100:05. The figures on the right-hand side of the colon refer to 32nds of a dollar. Thus the dollar value is $100^{5}/_{32}$ or 100.15625.

Bond prices are quoted "flat." This means that the price does not include accrued interest. For example, consider the $11^{5}/_{8}$ November 2004 bond. Using

TABLE 13.3 *Treasury Note and Bond Quotes, Thursday, May 28, 1998**

TREASURY BONDS, NOTES & BILLS

Thursday, May 28, 1998

Representative and Indicative Over-the-Counter quotations based on $1 million or more.

Treasury bond, note and bill quotes are as of mid-afternoon. Colons in bond and note bid-and-asked quotes represent 32nds; 101:01 means 101 1/32. Net changes in 32nds. Treasury bill quotes in hundredths, quoted in terms of a rate discount. Days to maturity calculated from settlement date. All yields are based on a one-day settlement and calculated on the offer quote. Current 13-week and 26-week bills are boldfaced. For bonds callable prior to maturity, yields are computed to the earliest call date for issues quoted above par and to the maturity date for issues quoted below par. n-Treasury note. i-Inflation-indexed. wi-When issued. iw-Inflation-indexed when issued; daily change is expressed in basis points.

Source: Dow Jones/Cantor Fitzgerald.

U.S. Treasury strips as of 3 p.m. Eastern time, also based on transactions of $1 million or more. Colons in bid-and-asked quotes represent 32nds; 99:01 means 99 1/32. Net changes in 32nds. Yields calculated on the asked quotation. ci-stripped coupon interest. bp-Treasury bond, stripped principal. np-Treasury note, stripped principal. For bonds callable prior to maturity, yields are computed to the earliest call date for issues quoted above par and to the maturity date for issues below par.

Source. Bear, Stearns & Co. via Street Software Technology Inc.

GOVT. BONDS & NOTES

Rate	Maturity Mo/Yr	Bid	Asked	Chg.	Ask Yld.
5 3/8	May 98n	99:30	100:00	....	5.24
6	May 98n	99:31	100:01	....	0.30
5 1/8	Jun 98n	99:31	100:01	....	4.67
6 1/4	Jun 98n	100:02	100:04	....	4.71
8 1/4	Jul 98n	100:13	100:15	....,	4.48
5 1/4	Jul 98n	100:00	100:02	+ 1	4.81
6 1/4	Jul 98n	100:06	100:08	+ 1	4.71
5 7/8	Aug 98n	100:03	100:05	....	5.06
9 1/4	Aug 98n	100:28	100:30	....	4.73
4 3/4	Aug 98n	99:26	99:28	....	5.19
6 1/8	Aug 98n	100:06	100:08	....	5.06
4 3/4	Sep 98n	99:24	99:26	....	5.27
6	Sep 98n	100:06	100:08	....	5.20
7 1/8	Oct 98n	100:22	100:24	+ 1	5.07
4 3/4	Oct 98n	99:20	99:22	....	5.49
5 7/8	Oct 98n	100:04	100:06	+ 1	5.39
5 1/2	Nov 98n	99:31	100:01	....	5.42
8 7/8	Nov 98n	101:18	101:20	....	5.25
5 1/8	Nov 98n	99:26	99:28	....	5.38
5 5/8	Nov 98n	100:02	100:04	....	5.37
5 1/8	Dec 98n	99:24	99:26	....	5.44
5 3/4	Dec 98n	100:04	100:06	....	5.41
6 3/8	Jan 99n	100:16	100:18	....	5.44
5	Jan 99n	99:19	99:21	....	5.51
5 7/8	Jan 99n	100:06	100:08	....	5.48
5	Feb 99n	99:19	99:21	....	5.48
8 7/8	Feb 99n	102:10	102:12	− 1	5.42
5 1/2	Feb 99n	99:30	100:00	....	5.49
5 7/8	Feb 99n	100:06	100:08	− 1	5.52
5 7/8	Mar 99n	100:08	100:10	....	5.48
6 1/4	Mar 99n	100:18	100:20	....	5.47
7	Apr 99n	101:07	101:09	....	5.48
6 3/8	Apr 99n	100:26	100:28	....	5.38
6 1/2	Apr 99n	100:26	100:28	− 1	5.51
6 3/8	May 99n	100:23	100:25	....	5.53
9 1/8	May 99n	103:10	103:12	....	5.47
6 1/4	May 99n	100:24	100:26	− 1	5.41
6 3/4	May 99n	101:04	101:06	....	5.52
6	Jun 99n	100:13	100:15	− 1	5.54
6 3/4	Jun 99n	101:07	101:09	....	5.51
6 3/8	Jul 99n	100:27	100:29	....	5.53
5 7/8	Jul 99n	100:08	100:10	− 1	5.59
6 7/8	Jul 99n	101:12	101:14	− 1	5.58
6	Aug 99n	100:13	100:15	− 1	5.59
8	Aug 99n	102:24	102:26	− 1	5.56
5 7/8	Aug 99n	100:09	100:11	− 1	5.58
6 7/8	Aug 99n	101:16	101:18	− 1	5.56
5 3/4	Sep 99n	100:04	100:06	− 2	5.60
7 1/8	Sep 99n	101:29	101:31	− 1	5.57
6	Oct 99n	100:15	100:17	− 2	5.59
5 5/8	Oct 99n	99:30	100:00	− 2	5.62

Rate	Maturity Mo./Yr.	Bid	Asked	Chg.	Ask Yld.
7 1/2	Oct 99n	102:16	102:18	− 2	5.59
5 7/8	Nov 99n	100:10	100:12	− 2	5.60
7 7/8	Nov 99n	103:04	103:06	− 2	5.57
5 5/8	Nov 99n	99:31	100:01	− 2	5.60
7 3/4	Nov 99n	103:01	103:03	− 2	5.58
5 5/8	Dec 99n	99:31	100:01	− 2	5.60
7 3/4	Dec 99n	103:05	103:07	− 2	5.60
6 3/8	Jan 00n	101:03	101:05	− 3	5.62
5 3/8	Jan 00n	99:18	99:20	− 2	5.61
7 3/4	Jan 00n	103:10	103:12	− 3	5.60
5 7/8	Feb 00n	100:11	100:13	− 3	5.62
8 1/2	Feb 00n	104:20	104:22	− 3	5.59
5 1/2	Feb 00n	99:24	99:26	− 3	5.61
7 1/8	Feb 00n	102:14	102:16	− 3	5.60
5 1/2	Mar 00n	99:24	99:25	− 4	5.62
6 7/8	Mar 00n	102:04	102:06	− 3	5.60
5 1/2	Apr 00n	99:24	99:26	− 3	5.60
5 5/8	Apr 00n	99:30	100:00	− 4	5.62
6 3/4	Apr 00n	101:30	102:00	− 4	5.63
6 3/8	May 00n	101:10	101:12	− 4	5.62
8 7/8	May 00n	105:30	106:00	− 4	5.60
5 1/2	May 00n	99:28	99:29	....	5.55
6 1/4	May 00n	101:07	101:09	....	5.57
5 7/8	Jun 00n	100:14	100:16	− 4	5.61
6 1/8	Jul 00n	100:31	101:01	− 3	5.61
6	Aug 00n	100:23	100:25	− 4	5.62
8 3/4	Aug 00n	106:13	106:15	− 4	5.60
6 1/4	Aug 00n	101:08	101:10	− 4	5.62
6 1/8	Sep 00n	101:01	101:03	− 4	5.61
5 3/4	Oct 00n	100:08	100:10	− 3	5.61
5 3/4	Nov 00n	100:08	100:10	− 3	5.61
8 1/2	Nov 00n	106:17	106:19	− 3	5.59
5 5/8	Nov 00n	99:31	100:01	− 3	5.61
5 1/2	Dec 00n	99:21	99:23	− 3	5.62
5 1/4	Jan 01n	99:02	99:04	− 2	5.60
5 3/8	Feb 01n	99:12	99:13	− 2	5.61
7 3/4	Feb 01n	105:09	105:11	− 2	5.60
11 3/4	Feb 01	115:11	115:15	− 3	5.53
5 5/8	Feb 01n	100:00	100:02	− 2	5.60
6 3/8	Mar 01n	101:29	101:31	− 2	5.61
6 1/4	Apr 01n	101:21	101:23	− 1	5.60
5 5/8	May 01n	100:05	100:06	− 1	5.55
8	May 01n	106:08	106:10	− 6	5.65
13 1/8	May 01	120:02	120:08	− 7	5.61
6 1/2	May 01n	102:12	102:14	− 1	5.61
6 5/8	Jun 01n	102:24	102:26	− 1	5.62
6 5/8	Jul 01n	102:26	102:28	− 1	5.62
7 7/8	Aug 01n	106:17	106:19	− 1	5.60
13 3/8	Aug 01	122:18	122:24	− 2	5.55
6 1/2	Aug 01n	102:17	102:19	− 1	5.61
6 3/8	Sep 01n	102:06	102:08	− 1	5.62
6 1/4	Oct 01n	101:27	101:29	− 2	5.63

Mat.	Type	Bid	Asked	Chg.	Ask Yld.
7 1/2	Nov 01n	105:25	105:27	− 1	5.62
15 3/4	Nov 01	131:18	131:24	− 2	5.54
5 7/8	Nov 01n	100:23	100:25	− 1	5.63
6 1/8	Dec 01n	101:17	101:19	− 1	5.63
6 1/4	Jan 02n	101:31	102:01	− 2	5.63
14 1/4	Feb 02	128:17	128:23	− 2	5.58
6 1/4	Feb 02n	102:00	102:02	− 1	5.63
6 5/8	Mar 02n	103:10	103:12	− 1	5.63
6 5/8	Apr 02n	103:19	103:21	− 2	5.57
7 1/2	May 02n	106:16	106:18	− 2	5.63
6 1/2	May 02n	103:07	103:09	− 2	5.57
6 1/4	Jun 02n	102:05	102:07	− 1	5.63
3 5/8	Jul 02i	98:25	98:26	− 2	3.94
6	Jul 02n	101:09	101:11	− 1	5.63
6 3/8	Aug 02n	102:22	102:24	− 2	5.63
6 1/4	Aug 02n	102:06	102:08	− 2	5.64
5 7/8	Sep 02n	100:27	100:29	− 1	5.63
5 3/4	Oct 02n	100:12	100:14	− 2	5.64
11 5/8	Nov 02	123:10	123:16	− 2	5.60
5 3/4	Nov 02n	100:11	100:13	− 2	5.65
5 5/8	Dec 02n	99:29	99:31	− 2	5.63
5 1/2	Jan 03n	99:15	99:17	− 2	5.61
6 1/4	Feb 03n	102:15	102:17	− 2	5.63
10 3/4	Feb 03	120:25	120:31	− 2	5.62
5 1/2	Feb 03n	99:16	99:18	− 2	5.60
5 1/2	Mar 03n	99:17	99:18	− 2	5.60
5 3/4	Apr 03n	100:21	100:22	− 2	5.59
10 3/4	May 03	121:24	121:30	− 2	5.62
	May 03wi	5:58	5:57	+ 1	....
5 3/4	Aug 03n	100:17	100:19	− 1	5.61
11 1/8	Aug 03	124:11	124:17	− 1	5.63
11 7/8	Nov 03	128:25	128:31	+ 1	5.64
5 7/8	Feb 04n	101:07	101:09	+ 2	5.61
7 1/4	May 04n	108:01	108:03	+ 3	5.63
12 3/8	May 04	133:17	133:23	+ 4	5.64
7 1/4	Aug 04n	108:09	108:11	+ 5	5.64
13 3/4	Aug 04	141:26	142:00	+ 6	5.65
7 7/8	Nov 04n	111:25	111:29	+ 6	5.65
11 5/8	Nov 04	131:25	131:31	+ 7	5.65
7 1/2	Feb 05n	110:02	110:04	+ 7	5.67
6 1/2	May 05n	104:24	104:26	+ 10	5.65
8 1/4	May 00-05	104:25	104:27	+ 3	5.61
12	May 05	135:28	136:02	+ 12	5.66
6 1/2	Aug 05n	104:25	104:27	+ 11	5.67
10 3/4	Aug 05	129:16	129:22	+ 12	5.68
5 7/8	Nov 05n	101:04	101:06	+ 12	5.68
5 5/8	Feb 06n	99:20	99:22	+ 15	5.67
9 3/8	Feb 06	122:25	122:31	+ 16	5.66
6 7/8	May 06n	107:15	107:17	+ 17	5.69
7	Jul 06n	108:10	108:12	+ 19	5.70
6 1/2	Oct 06n	105:08	105:10	+ 21	5.69
3 3/8	Jan 07i	97:00	97:01	− 1	3.78
6 1/4	Feb 07n	103:27	103:29	+ 24	5.67
7 5/8	Feb 02-07	106:09	106:11	+ 12	5.70
6 5/8	May 07n	106:15	106:17	+ 26	5.68
6 1/8	Aug 07n	103:04	103:06	+ 28	5.67
7 7/8	Nov 02-07	109:02	109:04	+ 17	5.54
3 5/8	Jan 08i	98:31	99:00	− 2	3.75
5 1/2	Feb 08n	99:10	99:11	+ 32	5.59
5 5/8	May 08n	100:12	100:13	+ 35	5.57
8 3/8	Aug 03-08	112:08	112:12	+ 22	5.60
8 3/4	Nov 03-08	113:30	114:02	+ 23	5.72
9 1/8	May 04-09	116:27	116:31	+ 24	5.72
10 3/8	Nov 04-09	124:21	124:27	+ 27	5.72
11 3/4	Feb 05-10	133:02	133:08	+ 28	5.72
10	May 05-10	124:01	124:07	+ 27	5.73
12 3/4	Nov 05-10	141:31	142:05	+ 30	5.73
13 7/8	May 06-11	151:09	151:15	+ 33	5.73
14	Nov 06-11	154:19	154:25	+ 34	5.74
10 3/8	Nov 07-12	133:01	133:07	+ 31	5.77
12	Aug 08-13	147:10	147:16	+ 34	5.78
13 1/4	May 09-14	159:24	159:30	+ 36	5.79
12 1/2	Aug 09-14	154:17	154:23	+ 35	5.80
11 3/4	Nov 09-14	149:04	149:10	+ 34	5.80
11 1/4	Feb 15	157:12	157:18	+ 45	5.82

TABLE 13.3 *(Continued)*

Maturity Rate	Mo/Yr	Bid	Asked	Chg.	Ask Yld.
10 5/8	Aug 15	150:30	151:04	+43	5.87
9 7/8	Nov 15	143:01	143:07	+41	5.88
9 1/4	Feb 16	136:14	136:20	+39	5.89
7 1/4	May 16	114:23	114:27	+34	5.90
7 1/2	Nov 16	117:18	117:22	+34	5.91
8 3/4	May 17	131:29	132:03	+36	5.91
8 7/8	Aug 17	133:17	133:23	+35	5.91
9 1/8	May 18	137:03	137:09	+34	5.92
9	Nov 18	136:02	136:08	+33	5.92
8 7/8	Feb 19	134:23	134:29	+33	5.93
8 1/8	Aug 19	126:04	126:10	+30	5.93
8 1/2	Feb 20	130:31	131:05	+29	5.93
8 3/4	May 20	134:07	134:13	+29	5.93
8 3/4	Aug 20	134:13	134:19	+29	5.93
7 7/8	Feb 21	123:27	124:01	+25	5.94
8 1/8	May 21	127:02	127:08	+25	5.94
8 1/8	Aug 21	127:06	127:12	+24	5.94
8	Nov 21	125:25	125:31	+24	5.93
7 1/4	Aug 22	116:22	116:26	+20	5.93
7 5/8	Nov 22	121:17	121:23	+20	5.93
7 1/8	Feb 23	115:10	115:14	+18	5.93
6 1/4	Aug 23	104:08	104:10	+16	5.92
7 1/2	Nov 24	120:27	121:01	+13	5.92
7 5/8	Feb 25	122:19	122:25	+13	5.92
6 7/8	Aug 25	112:23	112:27	+10	5.92
6	Feb 26	101:06	101:08	+ 9	5.91
6 3/4	Aug 26	111:10	111:14	+ 7	5.91
6 1/2	Nov 26	108:02	108:04	+ 6	5.91
6 5/8	Feb 27	109:29	109:31	+ 6	5.90
6 3/8	Aug 27	106:26	106:27	+ 4	5.88
6 1/8	Nov 27	104:04	104:05	+ 3	5.83
3 5/8	Apr 28i	99:14	99:15	- 4	3.65

U.S. TREASURY STRIPS

Mat.	Type	Bid	Asked	Chg.	Ask Yld.
Aug 98	ci	98:29	98:29	+ 1	5.27
Aug 98	np	98:29	98:29	+ 1	5.32
Nov 98	ci	97:20	97:20	+ 1	5.35
Nov 98	np	97:18	97:19	+ 1	5.45
Feb 99	ci	96:08	96:08	+ 1	5.46
Feb 99	np	96:06	96:07	+ 1	5.54
May 99	ci	94:30	94:30	+ 1	5.52
May 99	np	94:28	94:29	+ 1	5.57
Aug 99	ci	93:19	93:20	....	5.53
Aug 99	np	93:18	93:19	+ 1	5.57
Nov 99	ci	92:11	92:12	....	5.53
Nov 99	np	92:10	92:11	....	5.56
Feb 00	ci	91:02	91:03	....	5.54
Feb 00	np	91:01	91:02	....	5.56
May 00	ci	89:28	89:29	....	5.52
May 00	np	89:26	89:27	- 1	5.57
Aug 00	ci	88:19	88:20	- 1	5.54
Aug 00	np	88:18	88:19	- 1	5.56
Nov 00	ci	87:12	87:14	- 1	5.55
Nov 00	np	87:11	87:12	- 1	5.57
Feb 01	ci	86:06	86:07	- 1	5.55
Feb 01	np	86:04	86:05	- 1	5.58
May 01	ci	84:31	85:00	- 1	5.57
May 01	np	84:29	84:31	- 1	5.59
Aug 01	ci	83:25	83:27	- 2	5.57
Aug 01	np	83:22	83:24	- 2	5.61
Nov 01	ci	82:21	82:23	- 2	5.57
Nov 01	np	82:17	82:19	- 2	5.62
Feb 02	ci	81:16	81:18	- 2	5.57
May 02	ci	80:12	80:14	- 2	5.59
May 02	np	80:08	80:10	- 2	5.62
Aug 02	ci	79:11	79:13	- 2	5.56
Aug 02	np	79:04	79:06	- 2	5.63
Nov 02	ci	78:15	78:19	- 4	5.49
Feb 03	ci	77:02	77:05	- 2	5.59
Feb 03	np	77:00	77:03	- 2	5.60
May 03	ci	75:30	76:02	- 2	5.60
Aug 03	ci	74:28	75:00	- 3	5.60
Aug 03	np	74:31	75:03	- 3	5.58
Nov 03	ci	73:28	73:31	- 3	5.60
Feb 04	ci	72:25	72:29	- 2	5.62
Feb 04	np	72:30	73:02	- 2	5.58
May 04	ci	71:23	71:27	- 2	5.63
May 04	np	71:26	71:30	- 2	5.61

Maturity Mo./Yr.	Type	Bid	Asked	Chg.	Ask Yld.
Aug 04	ci	70:25	70:29	- 2	5.61
Aug 04	np	70:25	70:29	- 2	5.62
Nov 04	ci	69:21	69:25	- 3	5.65
Nov 04	bp	69:19	69:24	- 2	5.66
Nov 04	np	69:22	69:26	- 2	5.65
Feb 05	ci	68:20	68:25	- 2	5.66
Feb 05	np	68:22	68:27	- 2	5.65
May 05	ci	67:20	67:25	- 2	5.67
May 05	bp	67:17	67:21	- 3	5.70
May 05	np	67:27	67:31	- 3	5.63
Aug 05	ci	66:22	66:27	- 3	5.67
Aug 05	bp	66:18	66:22	- 3	5.70
Aug 05	np	66:24	66:28	- 3	5.66
Nov 05	ci	65:24	65:29	- 4	5.67
Nov 05	np	65:25	65:30	- 3	5.67
Feb 06	ci	64:23	64:28	- 2	5.70
Feb 06	np	64:27	65:00	- 2	5.67
Feb 06	np	64:28	65:01	- 2	5.66
May 06	ci	63:24	63:29	- 2	5.71
Aug 06	ci	62:28	63:01	- 2	5.71
Nov 06	ci	62:00	62:04	- 2	5.71
Feb 07	ci	61:00	61:05	- 2	5.73
May 07	ci	60:04	60:09	- 3	5.74
Aug 07	ci	59:10	59:15	- 3	5.72
Nov 07	ci	58:15	58:21	- 3	5.73
Feb 08	ci	57:15	57:20	- 2	5.76
May 08	ci	56:18	56:24	- 2	5.78
Aug 08	ci	55:24	55:29	- 2	5.78
Nov 08	ci	54:26	55:00	- 2	5.80
Feb 09	ci	53:31	54:04	- 2	5.82
May 09	ci	53:04	53:10	- 2	5.83
Aug 09	ci	52:11	52:16	- 2	5.83
Nov 09	ci	51:17	51:23	- 2	5.84
Nov 09	bp	51:06	51:12	- 2	5.90
Feb 10	ci	50:23	50:28	- 2	5.86
May 10	ci	49:30	50:03	- 2	5.87
Aug 10	ci	49:05	49:11	- 2	5.87
Nov 10	ci	48:15	48:20	- 2	5.87
Feb 11	ci	47:22	47:28	....	5.88
May 11	ci	46:31	47:05	....	5.89
Aug 11	ci	46:08	46:13	....	5.90
Nov 11	ci	45:17	45:23	....	5.91
Feb 12	ci	44:26	45:00	....	5.91
May 12	ci	44:05	44:10	+ 1	5.92
Aug 12	ci	43:15	43:21	+ 1	5.92
Nov 12	ci	42:26	43:00	+ 2	5.93
Feb 13	ci	42:05	42:10	+ 1	5.93
May 13	ci	41:16	41:22	+ 1	5.94
Aug 13	ci	40:28	41:02	+ 1	5.94
Nov 13	ci	40:08	40:14	+ 1	5.95
Feb 14	ci	39:20	39:26	+ 1	5.95
May 14	ci	39:02	39:07	+ 1	5.95
Aug 14	ci	38:14	38:20	+ 1	5.95
Nov 14	ci	37:28	38:02	+ 1	5.96
Feb 15	ci	37:10	37:16	....	5.96
Feb 15	bp	38:09	38:15	....	5.80
May 15	ci	36:24	36:30	+ 1	5.96
Aug 15	ci	36:06	36:11	....	5.97
Aug 15	bp	36:18	36:24	....	5.91
Nov 15	ci	35:20	35:26	....	5.97
Nov 15	bp	35:27	36:01	+ 1	5.94
Feb 16	ci	35:02	35:08	....	5.97
Feb 16	bp	35:07	35:13	+ 1	5.95
May 16	ci	34:18	34:24	+ 1	5.98
May 16	bp	34:27	35:01	+ 1	5.93
Aug 16	ci	34:01	34:07	+ 1	5.98
Nov 16	ci	33:17	33:22	+ 1	5.98
Nov 16	bp	33:21	33:27	+ 1	5.96
Feb 17	ci	33:00	33:05	+ 2	5.99
May 17	ci	32:16	32:22	+ 1	5.99
May 17	bp	32:17	32:23	+ 1	5.98
Aug 17	ci	32:00	32:06	+ 1	5.99
Aug 17	bp	32:02	32:08	+ 1	5.98
Nov 17	ci	31:17	31:23	+ 2	5.99
Feb 18	ci	31:00	31:06	+ 1	6.00
May 18	ci	30:18	30:23	+ 1	6.00
May 18	bp	30:19	30:24	+ 1	6.00
Aug 18	ci	30:03	30:09	+ 1	6.00
Nov 18	ci	29:20	29:26	+ 1	6.01
Nov 18	bp	29:21	29:27	+ 1	6.00

Mat.	Type	Bid	Asked	Chg.	Ask Yld.
Feb 19	ci	29:05	29:11	+ 2	6.01
Feb 19	bp	29:07	29:12	+ 1	6.00
May 19	ci	28:23	28:29	+ 1	6.01
Aug 19	ci	28:10	28:15	+ 1	6.01
Aug 19	bp	28:11	28:17	+ 1	6.00
Nov 19	ci	27:28	28:02	+ 1	6.01
Feb 20	ci	27:14	27:20	+ 1	6.01
Feb 20	bp	27:17	27:22	+ 1	6.00
May 20	ci	27:02	27:07	+ 1	6.01
May 20	bp	27:03	27:09	+ 1	6.01
Aug 20	ci	26:21	26:26	+ 1	6.01
Aug 20	bp	26:22	26:28	+ 1	6.00
Nov 20	ci	26:11-	26:16	+ 1	6.00
Feb 21	ci	25:28	26:01	+ 1	6.01
Feb 21	bp	25:30	26:04	+ 1	6.00
May 21	ci	25:16	25:21	+ 1	6.01
May 21	bp	25:17	25:23	+ 1	6.01
Aug 21	ci	25:05	25:10	+ 2	6.01
Aug 21	bp	25:05	25:10	+ 1	6.01
Nov 21	ci	24:28	25:01	+ 1	5.99
Nov 21	bp	24:25	24:31	+ 1	6.01
Feb 22	ci	24:13	24:18	+ 1	6.01
Feb 22	bp	24:02	24:08	+ 1	6.00
Aug 22	ci	23:24	23:30	+ 1	6.00
Aug 22	bp	23:26	24:00	+ 1	5.99
Nov 22	ci	23:16	23:21	+ 1	5.98
Nov 22	bp	23:14	23:20	+ 1	5.99
Feb 23	ci	23:04	23:09	+ 1	5.99
Feb 23	bp	23:07	23:12	+ 1	5.97
Aug 23	ci	22:18	22:23	+ 1	5.97
Aug 23	bp	22:23	22:29	+ 1	5.93
Nov 23	ci	22:09	22:15	+ 1	5.95
Feb 24	ci	21:27	22:00	+ 1	5.97
May 24	ci	21:18	21:23	+ 1	5.97
Aug 24	ci	21:08	21:13	+ 1	5.97
Nov 24	ci	20:31	21:04	+ 1	5.96
Nov 24	bp	21:00	21:05	+ 1	5.96
Feb 25	ci	20:22	20:28	+ 1	5.95
Feb 25	bp	20:24	20:29	+ 1	5.95
May 25	ci	20:14	20:19	+ 1	5.95
Aug 25	ci	20:05	20:11	+ 1	5.94
Aug 25	bp	20:05	20:10	+ 1	5.95
Nov 25	ci	19:29	20:02	+ 1	5.93
Feb 26	ci	19:22	19:27	+ 1	5.92
Feb 26	bp	19:25	19:31	+ 1	5.90
May 26	ci	19:13	19:18	+ 1	5.92
Aug 26	ci	19:04	19:09	+ 1	5.92
Aug 26	bp	19:05	19:10	+ 1	5.91
Nov 26	ci	18:28	19:01	+ 1	5.92
Nov 26	bp	18:30	19:03	+ 1	5.91
Feb 27	ci	18:22	18:27	+ 1	5.90
Feb 27	bp	18:24	18:29	+ 1	5.89
May 27	ci	18:17	18:22	+ 1	5.88
Aug 27	ci	18:15	18:20	+ 1	5.84
Aug 27	bp	18:18	18:23	+ 1	5.82
Nov 27	ci	18:19	18:25	+ 1	5.76
Nov 27	bp	19:02	19:07	+ 1	5.68

*Source: The *Wall Street Journal*, May 29, 1998.

hypothetical data, suppose that the bid price is 129:28 and the ask price 130:00. The accrued interest, AI, is determined by the formula

$$AI \equiv C\left(\frac{\text{Number of Days Since Last Coupon Was Paid}}{\text{Total Number of Days in Current Coupon Period}}\right), \qquad (13.9)$$

where C is the semiannual coupon payment. In this case, suppose that the number of days in the current coupon period is 182 and the number of days since the last coupon was paid is 85. The accrued interest is

$$AI = \left(\frac{11.625}{2}\right)\left(\frac{85}{182}\right) = 2.7145.$$

If the bond is purchased at the bid price, the total cost is

$$129\left(^{28}\!/_{32}\right) + 2.7145 = 132.5895.$$

If the bond is purchased at the ask price, the total cost is

$$130 + 2.7145 = 132.7145. \qquad \blacksquare$$

The final column of Table 13.3 refers to **stripped Treasuries**. A Treasury note or bond is composed of two components: coupon payments and a final payment of principal. These two components can be sold separately as synthetic zero-coupon bonds, which are the Treasury strips. The notation **np** or **bp** means it is a Treasury note or Treasury bond principal payment underlying the strip and **ci** means the instrument is a claim on coupon payments.

Floating Rate Notes

A **floating rate note** is a debt contract with specified face value, maturity, and coupon payment dates. The interest payments change over time, and they are based on the current interest rate times the principal. A floating rate note's interest payments are reset at each coupon date.

Let us consider a one-year floating rate note with semiannual interest payments and unit face value. Today, the coupon for the first six months is based on the date-0 six-month rate. Let the six-month rate at date 0 be 5.25 percent per annum; the coupon is then $c = 0.0525/2 = 0.02625$. Let us move forward six months: The first coupon has been paid and a new coupon is set. The next coupon is based on the new six-month rate. For example, suppose in six months that the new six-month rate is 5.60 percent expressed on a per annum basis; the next coupon is then

$$c = 0.056/2$$
$$= 0.028.$$

The computation of interest payments in this way results in the floating rate note always being valued at par (a dollar value) at each reset date. To see this, we start at the last payment date and work backward in time. Six months from now, the floating rate note has one coupon payment remaining plus a principal repayment. The coupon payment is $0.028 and the principal repayment is $1.00. The present value of these cash flows is a dollar, that is,

$$\frac{0.028 + 1}{[1 + 0.056 \times (1/2)]} = 1.$$

This occurs because the discount rate corresponds to the interest earned.

Similarly, at date 0, the value of the floating rate loan is again a dollar. The floating rate note receives the next coupon payment of 0.02625, and it can be retired at a dollar at the next reset date. The present value of these cash flows is again a dollar, that is,

$$\frac{0.02625 + 1}{[1 + 0.0525 \times (1/2)]} = 1.$$

At reset dates the floating rate note sells at its par value. In this example, the par value is a dollar.

13.3   THE TERM STRUCTURE OF DEFAULT-FREE INTEREST RATES

Now we study the term structure of interest rates, which is defined as the relationship between the yield-to-maturity on a zero-coupon bond and the bond's maturity. Figure 13.1 shows a typical term structure. In this figure, the term structure is upward sloping, which is the most common shape. Historically, however, both flat and downward sloping term structures have been observed.

Forward Rates

Here we examine forward rates. Before giving the formal definition, we explain forward rates through a simple example.

Suppose that the yield on a one-year zero-coupon bond is 5.85 percent per annum, and 6.03 percent per annum on a two-year zero-coupon bond. If we invest one dollar for two years in the two-year zero-coupon bond, we earn

$$\$(1 + 0.0603)^2$$

at the end of two years. Alternatively, we could invest one dollar in a series of one-year zero-coupon bonds, rolling over the investment at the end of the first year. At the end of the first year, the value of the investment is

$$\$(1 + 0.0585).$$

FIGURE 13.1   *A Typical Term Structure of Interest Rates*

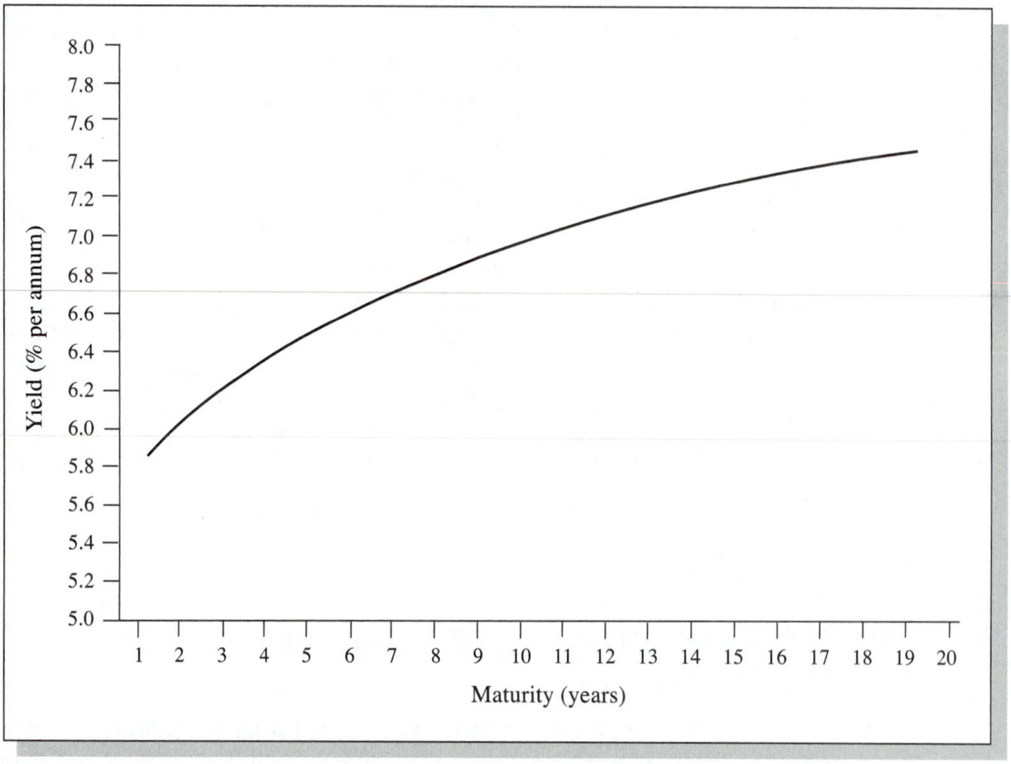

The one-year rate of interest from year one to year two is not yet known today, given that interest rates are random. But we can always find an implied one-year "break-even" interest rate to equate the value of the two investment strategies. Above this break-even rate, the rollover strategy is better; below this break-even rate, the two-year strategy is better. By definition, the one-year break-even rate from year one to year two is

$$(1 + 0.0603)^2 \equiv (1 + 0.0585)[1 + f(0,1,2)],$$

implying that the break-even rate is

$$f(0,1,2) = 0.0621.$$

This break-even rate is called the **forward interest rate** at date zero from year one to year two. The first argument of zero in the notation $f(0,1,2)$ is used to denote the fact that the forward rate is implied by the term structure at date zero. The second argument denotes the date the forward rate starts, and the third argument denotes the date

the forward rate ends. To summarize, given the term structure of interest rates at date 0, the forward rate from date 1 to date 2 is denoted by $f(0,1,2)$.

We could determine the forward rate in terms of bond prices. The value of a one-year zero-coupon bond is

$$B(0,1) = \frac{1}{1 + 0.0585}$$

and the value of a two-year zero-coupon bond is

$$B(0,2) = \frac{1}{(1 + 0.0603)^2} .$$

Therefore, the forward rate can be computed by

$$B(0,2) \equiv B(0,1) \frac{1}{1 + f(0,1,2)} .$$

This completes the simple example. The next section formalizes the above definition for arbitrary future time periods.

Formalization

Here we give the formal definition of a forward rate. The one-year forward rate from year T to year $T + 1$ implied by today's term structure is defined by

$$B(0,T + 1) \equiv B(0,T) \frac{1}{1 + f(0,T,T + 1)} . \tag{13.10}$$

Figure 13.2 shows the one-year forward rates for an upward sloping term structure. For an upward sloping term structure, observe that the forward rate is never less than the zero-coupon yield, a consequence of the mathematical definition in Expression (13.10).

In Figure 13.3, the term structure is inverted or downward sloping. In this case, the forward curve is always below the zero-coupon yield curve.

Expression (13.10) gives the definition of the one-year forward rate. In practice, it is often necessary to define forward rates for other intervals such as one month, three months, or six months. It is a straightforward exercise to generalize Expression (13.10).

Given the term structure of interest rates at date 0, the Δ period forward rate from date T to date $T + \Delta$ is defined by

$$B(0,T + \Delta) \equiv B(0,T) \frac{1}{1 + f(0,T,T + \Delta) \Delta} , \tag{13.11}$$

where Δ is measured in units of a year.

For a six-month forward rate, $\Delta = 1/2$; for a three-month forward rate, $\Delta = 1/4$; and for a one-month forward rate, $\Delta = 1/12$. We illustrate this definition via an example.

FIGURE 13.2 *Forward Curve Upward Sloping Term Structure*

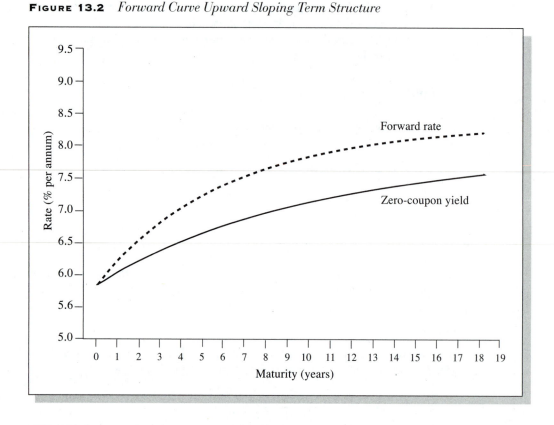

EXAMPLE **Forward Rate Calculations**

This example illustrates the use of Expression (13.11). We are given the following information.

Maturity	T-bill Price
12 months	91.5042
18 months	87.6083
24 months	83.9256

The one-year forward rate, from year one to year two, is given by

$$f(0, 12, 24) \equiv \frac{91.5042}{83.9256} - 1 = 0.0903.$$

The six-month rate, from 12 to 18 months, is given by

$$f(0, 12, 18) \equiv 2\left(\frac{91.5042}{87.6083} - 1\right) = 0.0889.$$

The six-month rate, from 18 to 24 months, is given by

$$f(0,18,24) \equiv 2\left(\frac{87.6083}{83.9256} - 1\right) = 0.0878.$$

Note that the relation between the six-month rates and the one-year rate is

$$[1 + f(0, 12, 18)\,(1/2)][1 + f(0, 18, 24)\,(1/2)] = 1.0903$$
$$= 1 + f(0, 12, 24).\quad\blacksquare$$

Par Bond Yield Curve

Consider a coupon bond. Let the coupon on the bond be set such that the bond sells at par. The curve showing the relation between the bond's maturity and the coupon rate is called the **par bond yield curve**, which is usually abbreviated to **par yield curve**. We will use an example to illustrate how to calculate the par yield curve.

FIGURE 13.3   *Forward Curve Downward Sloping Term Structure*

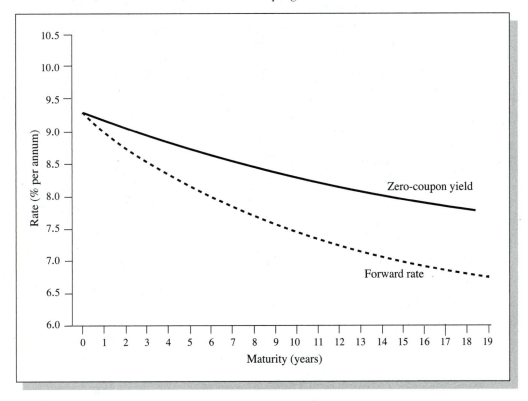

EXAMPLE

Par Yield Curve

This example illustrates the computation of a par yield curve. We are given the following information.

Maturity (Years)	T-bill Price
1	94.94
2	89.82
3	84.70

For a bond of maturity one year with face value 100 and paying an annual coupon c, the value of the bond is

$$c \times (0.9494) + 100 \times 0.9494$$
$$= 100.$$

We want to select the coupon so that the bond sells at par. This gives the equation for the par yield:

$$c = 100(1 - 0.9494)/0.9494$$
$$= 5.33.$$

For a bond with maturity two years with face value 100 and paying an annual coupon of c, the par yield equation is

$$c \times (0.9494 + 0.8982) + 100 \times 0.8982$$
$$= 100.$$

Therefore:

$$c = 100(1 - 0.8982)/1.8476$$
$$= 5.51.$$

For a bond with maturity three years and face value 100 paying an annual coupon of c, the par yield equation is

$$c \times (0.9494 + 0.8982 + 0.8470) + 100 \times 0.8470$$
$$= 100.$$

Therefore:

$$c = 100(1 - 0.8470)/2.6946$$
$$= 5.68.$$

Generalizing this example, given a bond with maturity T years, a face value of F, and which pays an annual coupon of c dollars at dates $1, 2, \ldots, T$, the par yield equation is

$$\sum_{t=1}^{T} c \times B(0,t) + F \times B(0,T) = F. \tag{13.12}$$

Hence the par coupon yield is

$$c = F \times [1 - B(0,T)]/\sum_{t=1}^{T} B(0,t). \tag{13.13}$$

Note that to calculate the par coupon yield, it is necessary to know the entire term structure of interest rates. The discussion of the par yield curve is now complete.

Computing the Zero-Coupon Yield Curve

We now discuss some practical difficulties that arise in computing the zero-coupon yield curve using market prices. To construct the zero-coupon yield curve, we require a complete set of zero-coupon bond prices out to twenty or thirty years. Unfortunately, these zero-coupon bonds do not trade. The longest maturity for a Treasury bill is one year, implying that we must extract zero-coupon bond prices with maturities greater than one year from coupon bond prices (or use the Treasury strips). We illustrate this calculation through an example.

EXAMPLE   **Implicit Zero-Coupon Bond Prices**

In this example we illustrate a "bootstrapping" technique for calculating the zero-coupon yields using coupon bond prices. Suppose that we know the price of a six-month T-bill, $B(0, 6) = 0.9748$, and a twelve-month T-bill, $B(0, 12) = 0.9493$. A Treasury note with maturity 18 months and paying a semiannual coupon of 8.0 percent per annum is trading at 103.77. Given this information, we can determine the implied price of a zero-coupon bond with maturity 18 months via the equation

$$103.77 = 4 \times B(0,6) + 4 \times B(0,12) + (4 + 100) \times B(0,18)$$
$$= 4 \times (0.9748 + 0.9493) + 104 \times B(0,18),$$

implying that

$$B(0,18) = 0.9238. \qquad \blacksquare$$

This type of "bootstrapping" technique, illustrated in the previous example, can be used to determine the whole term structure of zero-coupon yields. For example,

with a two-year Treasury note we can determine the value of the two-year zero-coupon bond's yield.

In practice, however, many complications arise. First, the maturity structure of existing Treasury notes and bonds is not equally spaced. For example, we may have a Treasury note with maturity of two years. The next Treasury note may have a maturity of two years and nine and a half months. This necessitates using different econometric techniques to generate the curve. Second, we may want to use only prices for the **on-the-run** bonds, that is, prices for the last auctioned bonds, which are usually the most actively traded. While we may have quotes for all the available bonds, both on-the-run and off-the-run, some of these quotes may be "old" and not reflect current conditions. Third, some bonds have special tax treatments that affect the price. These bonds should be omitted from the computation. Unfortunately, due to these three observations, constructing a term structure of interest rates is not an easy exercise.

13.4 TRADITIONAL MEASURES OF INTEREST RATE RISK

We now study the traditional measures of interest rate risk—duration and convexity—and their limitations. These traditional measures currently enjoy widespread use by commercial and investment banks. However, they will eventually be replaced by the techniques presented in Chapter 15 through Chapter 17.

Duration

Duration is often used to measure the risk of a bond. To see why, let B_c denote the current value of a coupon bond with yield-to-maturity y. Let the bond pay an annual coupon of c dollars at dates $t = 1, \ldots, T$, and have a face value of F dollars.[2] From Expression (13.5) we can write the bond's value as

$$B_c(y) = \sum_{t=1}^{T} \frac{c}{(1+y)^t} + \frac{F}{(1+y)^T}. \tag{13.14}$$

If the yield-to-maturity changes by a small amount, Δy, by how much does the bond's price change?

Let ΔB_c denote the change in the bond's price, that is,

$$\Delta B_c \equiv B_c(y + \Delta y) - B_c(y).$$

For a small change in the yield-to-maturity, the change in the bond's price can be written as

$$\Delta B_c \simeq -\frac{1}{(1+y)} \left[\sum_{t=1}^{T} \frac{tc}{(1+y)^t} + \frac{TF}{(1+y)^T} \right] \Delta y. \tag{13.15}$$

---

[2]The analysis for a bond that pays a semiannual coupon is given in the Appendix of this chapter.

We obtain this expression by using a Taylor series expansion of the bond's price around the bond's yield.[3] Expression (13.15) shows the sensitivity of the bond's price to changes in the bond's yield. The coefficient preceding Δy is a measure of this sensitivity, that is, a measure of risk. We now show how this coefficient relates to duration.

The classical definition of duration is

$$D_c \equiv \left[\sum_{t=1}^{T} \frac{tc}{(1+y)^t} + \frac{TF}{(1+y)^T} \right] / B_c , \qquad (13.16)$$

which is often referred to as Macauley's Duration.

Substituting Expression (13.16) into Expression (13.15) gives

$$\Delta B_c \simeq -B_c D_c \frac{\Delta y}{1+y} . \qquad (13.17)$$

The proportional change in the bond's price is related to the duration multiplied by the change in the yield-to-maturity divided by one plus the initial yield-to-maturity. If we change the definition of duration, we can obtain a simpler relation. The second definition is referred to as **modified duration**[4]:

$$D_M = D_c / (1+y). \qquad (13.18)$$

When we substitute the expression for modified duration into Expression (13.17), we find that the bond's return is directly proportional to modified duration, that is,

$$\Delta B_c \simeq -B_c \times D_M \times \Delta y. \qquad (13.19)$$

For a given change in the yield-to-maturity, the change in the bond's value is the multiplicative product of the three terms on the right side of Expression (13.19). The minus sign reflects the inverse relationship between yield and price. This expression explains why modified duration is used as a measure of a bond's risk. It measures the sensitivity of the bond's return to changes in the bond's yield.

EXAMPLE

Duration and Modified Duration for a Zero-Coupon Bond

Here we show how the definitions of duration simplify for a zero-coupon bond. Consider a zero-coupon bond with a maturity of T years. The yield-to-maturity is defined by

$$B_c(y) = \frac{F}{(1+y)^T} .$$

---

[3]For people with a knowledge of calculus use of Taylor's series expansion implies
$$B_c(y + \Delta y) - B_c(y) = \frac{dB_c}{dy}(\Delta y) + \frac{1}{2}\frac{d^2 B_c}{dy^2}(\Delta y)^2 + \dots .$$
[4]This definition is used in the CBOT publication *Understanding Duration and Convexity*.

The change in the bond's value from Expression (13.15) is

$$\Delta B_c(y) = -\frac{TF}{(1+y)^T}\frac{\Delta y}{1+y}$$

$$= -B_c(y) \times T\frac{\Delta y}{1+y}.$$

Therefore, the classical duration is

$$D_c = T$$

and the modified duration is

$$D_M = T/(1+y).$$ ∎

EXAMPLE   **Computation of Duration**

This example illustrates the computation of a coupon bond's duration. Consider a two-year bond with an annual coupon of $8.00 and a face value of $100. The annual yield-to-maturity is 8.12 percent and the bond's price is $99.7864.

Table 13.4 shows the calculations necessary to determine the modified duration of the bond. The classical duration is 1.9258 years and the modified duration is 1.7812. This coupon bond is said to be "more risky" than a one-year zero-coupon bond and "less risky" than a two-year zero-coupon bond because a one-year zero-coupon bond has a duration of one year and a two-year zero-coupon bond has a duration of two years.

TABLE 13.4   *Calculating Modified Duration of a Bond's Annual Coupon Payments*

TIME, t (YEARS)	COUPON	PRINCIPAL	DISCOUNTED VALUE	$t \times$ DISCOUNTED VALUE
1	8	0	7.3992	7.3992
2	8	100	92.3872	184.7743
			99.7864	192.1735

$$\text{Classical Duration} = \frac{192.1735}{99.7864} = 1.9258$$

$$\text{Modified Duration} = \frac{1.9258}{1.0812} = 1.7812$$

We next demonstrate that for small changes in yields, Expression (13.19) works well. Suppose that the yield-to-maturity increased by one basis point to 8.13 percent. The new bond price is

$$\frac{8.00}{(1 + 0.0813)} + \frac{8}{(1 + 0.0813)^2} + \frac{100}{(1 + 0.0813)^2} = 99.7686,$$

implying that the change in the bond's price is -0.0178.

We can use Expression (13.19) to approximate the change in the bond's price as

$$-B_c \times D_M \times \Delta y$$
$$= -99.7864 \times 1.7812 \times [(8.13 - 8.12)/100]$$
$$= -0.0178.$$

The two changes are identical, showing that Expression (13.19) works well. ∎

Convexity

Here we study the concept of a coupon bond's **convexity**. The use of modified duration to describe changes in the bond's price due to changes in the yield-to-maturity is accurate only for small changes in the yield-to-maturity. This can be illustrated with the help of Figure 13.4.

Figure 13.4 shows the relationship between yield and the bond's price. Modified duration only considers linear changes in the bond's price because it is obtained from a linear approximation. This is represented by the straight line on Figure 13.4. The relationship between yield and the bond's price, however, is nonlinear. In fact, the relationship between the bond's price and yield is convex. For small changes in yields, this nonlinearity is unimportant. But, for large changes in yields, it is necessary to take this nonlinear relationship into account.

For example, suppose that the yield-to-maturity in Table 13.4 increases to 8.50 percent from 8.12 percent per annum. The new bond price[5] is 99.1144. The change in the bond's price is

$$\Delta B_c = 99.1144 - 99.7864$$
$$= -0.6720. \tag{13.20}$$

---

[5]The bond price is

$$\frac{8}{1 + 0.085} + \frac{8}{(1 + 0.085)^2} + \frac{100}{(1 + 0.085)^2}$$

$$= 99.1144.$$

FIGURE 13.4   *Convexity*

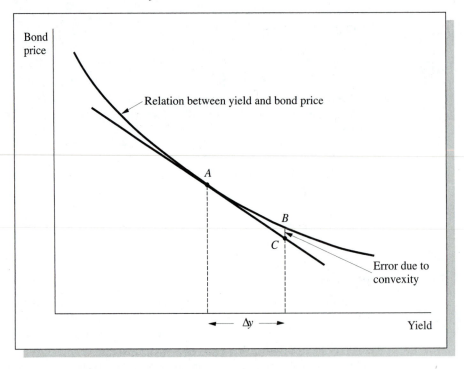

From Expression (13.19), we can approximate this change as

$$-B_c \times D_M \times \Delta y = -99.7864 \times 1.7812 \times (0.0850 - 0.0812)$$
$$= -0.6754, \tag{13.21}$$

which is not equal to the change in the bond's value. In fact, Expression (13.21) underestimates the value of the bond.

This value is illustrated in Figure 13.4. Given the change in yield, the bond's price moves from point A to point B. Expression (13.19) predicts the bond's price to be at point C, which is below point B. Point C will always lie below point B because the true relation between the bond's price and yield is a convex function.

The change in the bond's price, correcting for the convex relation between price and yield, is[6]

$$\Delta B_c = -B_c \times D_M \times (\Delta y) + (1/2) \times B_c \times (\text{Convexity}) \times (\Delta y)^2, \tag{13.22}$$

---

[6]See footnote 3.

where

$$\text{Convexity} \equiv \frac{1}{(1 + y)^2} \left[\sum_{t=1}^{T} \frac{t(t + 1)c}{(1 + y)^t} + \frac{T(T + 1)F}{(1 + y)^T} \right] / B_c .$$

The necessary steps to calculate convexity are shown in Table 13.5. The bond's convexity is 4.8155. Substituting the convexity into Expression (13.22) gives

$$\Delta B_c = -0.6754 + \frac{1}{2} \times 99.7864 \times 4.8789 \times (0.0038)^2$$
$$= -0.6754 + 0.0035$$
$$= -0.6719,$$

which is almost equal to the actual change of -0.6720.

Limitations of Analysis

The use of these simple forms of duration as risk measures implicitly assumes that only small and parallel shifts in the term structure can occur. To understand why this is true, note that Expressions (13.19) or (13.17) relate to changes in the bond's *own* yield to maturity. But, to measure risk *across* different coupon bonds, the change in each bond's yield must be assumed to be equal across the different bonds. This assumption is valid only if the change in the term structure of interest rates (the relation between yields on zero-coupon bonds and maturity) is a parallel shift.

In addition, using duration as a risk measure assumes that the approximation in Expression (13.19) or (13.17) provides a good estimate, which was shown to be true only for small changes in yields. Combined, these two arguments explain why duration is a valid risk measure only for small and parallel shifts in the term structure of interest rates.

TABLE 13.5   *Calculating the Convexity Correction Annual Coupon Payments*

TIME, t (YEARS)	COUPON	PRINCIPAL	DISCOUNTED VALUE	$t(t + 1) \times$ DISCOUNTED VALUE
1	8	0	7.3992	14.7984
2	8	100	92.3872	554.3232
			99.7864	569.1216

$$\text{Convexity} = \frac{1}{(1 + 0.0812)^2} [569.1216]/99.7864$$
$$= 4.8789$$

In practice, this never happens. Short-term rates are more volatile than long-term rates. The long and short sections of the term structure may even move in opposite directions. Furthermore, for large parallel shifts in the term structure, convexity adjustments help, but even these leave errors.

This same insight can be obtained using the techniques of Chapter 15. From a different perspective, we show that the problem with using Expression (13.19) to describe changes in the bond's price is that we are making a strong implicit assumption about the probability distribution describing bond price changes. This implicit assumption is equivalent (over infinitesimal intervals) to assuming that only small and parallel shifts in the term structure of interest rates are possible. We will expand on this issue in Chapter 15.

13.5 TREASURY BILL FUTURES

We now study the **Treasury bill futures contract**. For the Treasury bill futures contract, the underlying asset is a Treasury bill with face value of one million dollars and a maturity of 91 days. The last trading day on the T-bill futures contract is the business day immediately preceding the first delivery day. Under the terms of the contract, delivery may occur on one of three successive business days, implying that the underlying Treasury bill may have a maturity of 89, 90, or 91 days when delivered.

The price of a T-bill futures contract is quoted in terms of an index, which depends on a futures discount rate for a 90-day Treasury bill. The index value is computed as follows:

Index Value = 100 − Futures Discount Rate (%).

For example, if the index value is 96.81, then the futures discount rate is 3.19 percent. The futures contract price is defined by

$$1{,}000{,}000\left[1 - \frac{3.19}{100} \times \frac{90}{360}\right] = 992{,}025,$$

where by convention a 90-day maturity and a 360-day year is used.

A one-point change in the index implies a $25 change in the T-bill futures price. For example, suppose the index increases by one point to 96.82 from 96.81, implying the futures discount rate decreased from 3.19 to 3.18. The new contract delivery price is

$$1{,}000{,}000\left[1 - \frac{3.18}{100} \times \frac{90}{360}\right] = 992{,}050.$$

The change in the T-bill futures price is $25 (= 992,050 − 992,025).

Observe that there is a positive relationship between changes in the value of the index and the T-bill futures price, implying that the bid-quote is below the ask-quote.

TABLE 13.6 *Treasury Bill Futures Quotes, Thursday, May 28, 1998**

```
          TREASURY BILLS (CME)-$1 mil.; pts. of 100%
                                          Discount     Open
                 Open High Low Settle Chg Settle Chg Interest
          June   94.99 95.00 94.98 94.99 + .01  5.01 − .01  2,274
          Sept   94.98 94.98 94.96 94.96 − .02  5.04 + .02  2,003
              Est vol 463; vol Wed 587; open int 4,324, +118.
```

*Source: *The Wall Street Journal*, May 29, 1998.

Typical bid/ask quotes for T-bill futures are shown in Table 13.6. These quotes are from the T-bill futures contracts trading on the Chicago Mercantile Exchange (CME) on Thursday, May 28, 1998. For the June contract, the settlement index value is 94.99 and the futures discount rate is 5.01.

The final marking-to-market at the expiration of the futures contract sets the T-bill futures contract price equal to the value of a 90-day T-bill:

$$1,000,000\left[1 - i_d \times \frac{90}{360}\right]. \tag{13.23}$$

Thus, at delivery, the futures discount rate converges to the spot T-bill rate. Our description of the T-bill futures contract is now complete.

13.6 EURODOLLAR CONTRACTS

We study Eurodollar contracts in this section. A **Eurodollar** is a U.S. dollar-denominated deposit held by a bank outside the U.S. The rate at which a bank is willing to lend Eurodollars is referred to as the London Interbank Offer Rate (LIBOR). The rate at which a bank is willing to borrow is known as the London Interbank Bid Rate (LIBID). Eurodollar rates are generally higher than corresponding Treasury rates because Eurodollar rates are commercial lending rates containing credit risk. There are institutional factors such as reserve requirements that can also affect the spread between Eurodollar and Treasury rates.

Eurodollar Deposits

Here we study Eurodollar deposits in detail. We need to define a term structure of Eurodollar rates. This is done by first defining a term structure of "zero-coupon Eurodollar bonds." Let $L(0, T)$ denote the time-0 value of a Eurodollar deposit that pays one dollar at time T. Alternatively stated, $L(0, T)$ represents the present value of

a Eurodollar paid at time T. The graph of $L(0, T)$ versus T is called the term structure of Eurodollar zero-coupon bond prices.

The T-period **LIBOR** (or Eurodollar) rate can be defined from these zero-coupon bond prices. The T-period LIBOR rate $\ell(T)$ is defined as the simple interest rate using a 360-day-year convention for the Eurodollar deposit with maturity T, that is,

$$L(0, T) \equiv \frac{1}{1 + \ell(T)\,(T/360)},$$

where T is measured in days.

The graph of $\ell(T)$ versus T is the term structure of Eurodollar rates.[7] Figure 13.5 contains a typical upward sloping term structure for these Eurodollar deposits.

Table 13.7 gives LIBOR rates on Thursday, May 28, 1998, as reported in the *Wall Street Journal* on Friday, May 29. One-month rates are 5.65234 percent, three-month

FIGURE 13.5   *A Typical Term Structure of Eurodollar Rates*

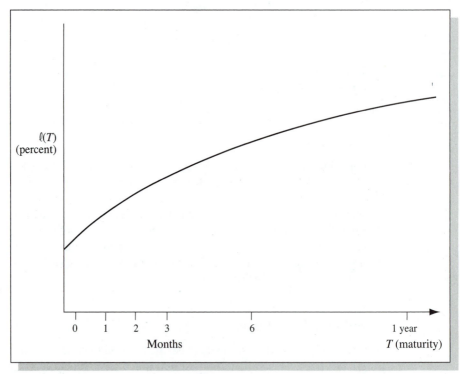

---

[7]In fact, $\ell(T)$ should be subscripted by a zero to indicate the current date. We avoid this subscript to simplify the notation.

TABLE 13.7 *Money Market Rates, Thursday, May 28, 1998**

LONDON INTERBANK OFFERED RATES (LIBOR):
5.65234% one month; 5.68750% three months; 5.75000% six months; 5.87500% one year. British Bankers' Association average of interbank offered rates for dollar deposits in the London market based on quotations at 16 major banks. Effective rate for contracts entered into two days from date appearing at top of this column.

*Source: The Wall Street Journal, May 29, 1998.

5.6875 percent, six-month 5.75000 percent, and one-year 5.87500 percent. These rates give an increasing term structure as illustrated in Figure 13.5.

Forward Rate Agreements (FRAs)

A **forward rate agreement** (FRA) is a contract written on LIBOR that requires a cash payment at maturity based on the difference between a realized spot rate of interest and a prespecified forward rate. We first give an example, which will be generalized, and then describe some of the properties of FRAs.

EXAMPLE

FRA

This example illustrates the payoff to an FRA. Consider a two-month (61-day) FRA, with principal one million dollars. The FRA is written on the three-month (91-day) LIBOR rate. Such a contract is referred to as a 2×5 FRA. The FRA rate is set today at 5.63 percent per annum. In two months' time, at the maturity of the contract, the payoff by definition is

$$\text{Principal} \times \frac{[\ell(91) - 0.0563] \times (91/360)}{1 + \ell(91) \times (91/360)},$$

where $\ell(91)$ is the spot three-month LIBOR rate at maturity.

Suppose that at maturity, $\ell(91)$ is 5.90 percent per annum. In this case, the payoff is

$$\$1,000,000 \times \frac{(0.0590 - 0.0563) \times (91/360)}{1 + 0.0590 \times (91/360)}$$

$$= \$682.50/1.0149$$

$$= \$672.47.$$

Four points should be noted from this FRA example. First, a 360-day-per-year convention is used in computing rates, in keeping with other Eurodollar contracts.

Second, the payment is discounted with the realized LIBOR rate. Third, we have assumed that there is no risk of default on the part of the writer of the FRA, implying that the payment contracted is the payment received. Fourth, the value of the contract can be positive or negative, depending on whether $\ell(91)$ is greater than or lesser than 0.0563. Thus, an FRA is a "bet" on the futures movements of the three-month LIBOR rate. Table 13.8 shows typical bid/ask quotes for forward rate agreements. FRAs typically range from 1×4 to 12×18, as illustrated in Table 13.8.

Formalization

This section formalizes the previous example.

Let us consider an FRA that matures in T months' time. The contract is written on the m month LIBOR rate. This contract is referred to as a $T \times (T + m)$ FRA. At maturity, the value of the contract is, by definition,

$$V(T) \equiv \text{Principal} \times \left[\frac{(\ell(m) - \text{FRA})\,(m/360)}{1 + \ell(m)\,(m/360)} \right], \tag{13.24}$$

where $\ell(m)$ is the m month period LIBOR rate at date T, m is months measured in days, and FRA is the $T \times (T + m)$ forward rate agreement's rate that was set when the contract was initiated.

When an FRA contract is initiated, the FRA rate is set such that the value of the contract is zero. This convention ensures that no cash is exchanged at the time the FRA contract is initiated.

We will prove that this condition implies that the FRA rate is set such that

$$\frac{1}{1 + \text{FRA}(m/360)} = \frac{L(0, T + m)}{B(0,T)}. \tag{13.25}$$

TABLE 13.8   *Forward Rate Agreement Rates*

FRAS	BID	OFFER
1–4	3.34	3.38
2–5	3.36	3.40
3–6	3.58	3.62
4–7	3.66	3.70
5–8	3.74	3.78
6–9	3.67	3.71
3–9	3.65	3.69
6–12	3.82	3.86
12–18	4.39	4.43

Before we prove this, consider Expression (13.24). This can be written in the form

$$V(T) = \frac{1 + \ell(m)(m/360) - [1 + \text{FRA}(m/360)]}{1 + \ell(m)(m/360)}$$

$$= 1 - [1 + \text{FRA}(m/360)]\frac{1}{1 + \ell(m)(m/360)},$$

where for simplicity we have set the principal equal to unity.

PROOF

Proof of Expression (13.25)

To prove Expression (13.25), we construct a portfolio whose payoffs match an FRA's. First, buy a Treasury bill that pays one dollar at date T. The cost of this position is $B(0,T)$.

To finance this purchase, write $1 + x \times (m/360)$ Eurodollar deposits, each deposit promising to pay one dollar at date $T + m$. The number x will be determined shortly. The price of one deposit is $L(0, T + m)$, so the price of $[1 + x \times (m/360)]$ deposits is $[1 + x \times (m/360)]L(0, T + m)$. The number x is chosen so that the initial value of the portfolio is zero, that is,

$$V_p(0) \equiv B(0,T) - [1 + x \times (m/360)] \times L(0, T + m) = 0.$$

We leave it as an exercise to determine x. We use the variable x as determined by this solution in the subsequent equations.

Now, the value of this portfolio at date T is

$$V_p(T) = 1 - [1 + x \times (m/360)] \times L(T, T + m).$$

But the value of a Eurodollar deposit that pays one dollar at date $T + m$ is (by definition) equal to

$$L(T, T + m) \equiv \frac{1}{1 + \ell(m)(m/360)}.$$

Therefore,

$$V_p(T) = 1 - [1 + x \times (m/360)]\frac{1}{1 + \ell(m)(m/360)}.$$

Notice that the value of the portfolio, $V_p(T)$, and the value of the FRA contract are identical in structure except that the portfolio has an "x" and the FRA contract has an "FRA." Since both the FRA contract and the portfolio have zero initial value, to avoid arbitrage, $x = \text{FRA}$ must be true. Expression (13.25) then follows from $V_p(0) = 0$ and the fact that $x = \text{FRA}$. ∎

Futures Contracts

The Eurodollar futures contract is written on a one-million dollar, three-month Eurodollar deposit. Settlement is in cash. Eurodollar futures prices are shown in Table 13.9. These quotes are from Eurodollar futures contracts trading on the Chicago Mercantile Exchange. Delivery dates for the Eurodollar futures contracts range from three months to ten years. The largest open interest occurs for the shortest maturity contracts (three months to three years).

The Eurodollar futures prices are quoted in the form of an index as follows:

Index Value = 100 − Futures Deposit Rate (%).

TABLE 13.9   *Eurodollar Futures Contracts,*
Thursday, May 28, 1998*

EURODOLLAR (CME)-$1 million; pts of 100%

	Open	High	Low	Settle	Chg	Yield Settle	Chg	Open Interest
June	94.32	94.32	94.31	94.31	− .01	5.69 +	.01	432,277
July	94.31	94.31	94.27	94.31	− .01	5.69 +	.01	11,391
Aug	94.30	94.30	94.30	94.30	− .01	5.70 +	.01	4,268
Sept	94.30	94.30	94.28	94.29	− .02	5.71 +	.02	467,651
Oct	....	....	....	94.25	− .01	5.75 +	.01	1,440
Dec	94.23	94.24	94.21	94.22	− .02	5.78 +	.02	390,001
Mr99	94.26	94.26	94.23	94.25	− .02	5.75 +	.02	295,502
June	94.22	94.23	94.20	94.21	− .02	5.79 +	.02	227,688
Sept	94.20	94.20	94.16	94.18	− .01	5.82 +	.01	207,276
Dec	94.08	94.08	94.06	94.07	− .02	5.93 +	.02	179,281
Mr00	94.15	94.15	94.12	94.14	− .01	5.86 +	.01	142,431
June	94.11	94.12	94.10	94.11	− .02	5.89 +	.02	125,166
Sept	94.09	94.10	94.08	94.09	− .02	5.91 +	.02	86,942
Dec	94.03	94.03	94.01	94.02	− .02	5.98 +	.02	71,681
Mr01	94.07	94.07	94.05	94.06	− .02	5.94 +	.02	54,897
June	94.05	94.05	94.03	94.04	− .02	5.96 +	.02	55,097
Sept	94.03	94.03	94.01	94.02	− .02	5.98 +	.02	46,142
Dec	93.96	93.96	93.94	93.95	− .02	6.05 +	.02	40,950
Mr02	93.99	94.00	93.98	93.99	− .02	6.01 +	.02	45,494
June	93.98	93.98	93.96	93.97	− .02	6.03 +	.02	46,519
Sept	93.96	93.96	93.95	93.95	− .02	6.05 +	.02	40,486
Dec	93.89	93.90	93.87	93.88	− .02	6.12 +	.02	29,986
Mr03	93.92	93.93	93.91	93.91	− .02	6.09 +	.02	24,958
June	93.89	93.90	93.88	93.89	− .02	6.11 +	.02	13,336
Sept	93.87	93.88	93.87	93.87	− .02	6.13 +	.02	15,532
Dec	93.80	93.81	93.80	93.80	− .02	6.20 +	.02	8,186
Mr04	93.83	93.84	93.83	93.83	− .02	6.17 +	.02	7,964
June	93.80	93.81	93.80	93.80	− .02	6.20 +	.02	8,151
Sept	93.78	93.79	93.78	93.78	− .02	6.22 +	.02	6,965
Dec	93.71	93.72	93.71	93.71	− .02	6.29 +	.02	6,838
Mr05	93.74	93.75	93.74	93.74	− .02	6.26 +	.02	4,893
June	93.71	93.72	93.71	93.71	− .02	6.29 +	.02	4,130
Sept	93.69	93.70	93.69	93.69	− .02	6.31 +	.02	4,074
Dec	....	....	....	93.62	− .02	6.38 +	.02	3,767
Mr06	93.65	93.66	93.65	93.65	− .02	6.35 +	.02	5,813
June	93.62	93.63	93.62	93.62	− .02	6.38 +	.02	3,440
Sept	93.60	93.61	93.60	93.60	− .02	6.40 +	.02	3,890
Dec	93.53	93.54	93.53	93.53	− .02	6.47 +	.02	4,320
Mr07	....	....	....	93.56	− .02	6.44 +	.02	3,538
June	....	....	....	93.53	− .02	6.47 +	.02	3,515
Sept	....	....	....	93.51	− .02	6.49 +	.02	3,923
Dec	....	....	....	93.44	− .02	6.56 +	.02	2,931
Mr08	....	....	....	93.47	− .02	6.53 +	.02	2,777

Est vol 294,288; vol Wed 665,333; open int 3,145,587, +12,050.

*Source: The Wall Street Journal, May 29, 1998.

For example, if the index value is 94.12, the Eurodollar futures deposit rate is 5.88 percent per annum. The contract price, by definition, is

$$1,000,000 \left[1 - \frac{5.88}{100} \times \frac{90}{360} \right]$$
$$= 985,300.$$

A one-basis-point change in the index value causes a $25 change in the Eurodollar futures price. For example, if the index value increases by one basis point to 94.13 from 94.12, the futures deposit rate decreases by one point to 5.87, and the new Eurodollar futures contract price is

$$1,000,000 \left[1 - \frac{5.87}{100} \times \frac{90}{360} \right]$$
$$= 985,325.$$

The change in the value of the Eurodollar futures contract is therefore $25 per one-point change in the index.

The final marking-to-market at the expiration of the Eurodollar futures contract sets the contract price equal to

$$1,000,000 \left[1 - \ell(90) \times \frac{90}{360} \right], \tag{13.26}$$

where $\ell(90)$ is the 90-day LIBOR rate[8] at the expiration of the contract. The Eurodollar futures deposit rate converges to the Eurodollar spot rate at the delivery date of the contract.

Expression (13.26) looks similar in form to Expression (13.23) for the T-bill futures contract, but there is an important difference. In Expression (13.23) for Treasury bill futures, i_d is a discount rate. In contrast, in Expression (13.26), $\ell(90)$ is a simple interest rate.

Recall that there is a simple linear relationship between the value of a Treasury bill and the discount rate:

$$\text{Value of Treasury Bill} = 1,000,000 \left[1 - i_d \times \frac{90}{360} \right].$$

An inverse relationship exists between the value of a Eurodollar deposit and the LIBOR rate (a simple interest rate):

$$\text{Value of Eurodollar Deposit} = 1,000,000 \left[\frac{1}{1 + \ell(90) \times \frac{90}{360}} \right].$$

---

[8]The rate used is an average rate. For contracts traded on the London Exchange, the settlement price is computed by using the quotes between 9:30 a.m. and 11:00 a.m. on the last trading day stated by a random sample of 16 from a list of designated banks. The three highest and three lowest quotes are disregarded. The settlement price will be 100 minus the average of the remaining 10 rates.

For contracts traded on the CME, a slightly different averaging procedure is used.

This difference between using a discount rate versus a simple interest rate has important ramifications for the pricing of these contracts. Our description of Eurodollar futures contracts is now complete.

13.7 TREASURY BOND AND NOTE FUTURES

Here we examine Treasury bond and Treasury note futures contracts. These futures contracts have complicated delivery features that are explained below. The delivery features make the T-bond and T-note futures contracts difficult to price and to hedge.

Treasury bond futures

The basic trading unit is a Treasury bond with a face value of $100,000. The futures contract is written on any U.S. Treasury bond that, if callable, is not callable for at least 15 years from the first day of the delivery month or, if not callable, has a maturity of at least 15 years from the first business day of the delivery month.

Because any one of many Treasury bonds can be used to satisfy the delivery requirements of the futures contract, the Chicago Board of Trade has developed a procedure for adjusting the price of the deliverable bond so that it is equivalent to a bond trading with a nominal coupon of 8 percent. We will explain this in more detail later.

Treasury bond futures contract delivery months are March, June, September, and December. The **last trading day** in the futures contract is the seventh business day preceding the last business day of the delivery month. The **last delivery day** is the last business day of the delivery month.

Price quotes are in terms of dollars and 32nds of a dollar for a $100 par value. For example, a quote of 114-26 means $114\frac{26}{32}$ or $114.8125 per $100 par value. See Table 13.10 for price quotes on T-bond futures contracts on the Chicago Board of Trade (CBT). These are listed in the first five rows of this table. The settlement price for the September contract trading on the CBT is 121-09. The open interest for this contract is 394,564 contracts.

10-Year U.S. Treasury note futures

The basic trading unit is a U.S. Treasury note with a face value of $100,000. The futures contract is written on any U.S. Treasury note maturing in at least $6\frac{1}{2}$ years, but not more than 10 years from the first business day of the delivery month. Details about the contract delivery month, the last trading day, and last delivery day are similar to those of Treasury bond futures. Table 13.10 contains price quotes on these Treasury note futures. For example, the settlement price for the June contract is 112-29.

5-Year U.S. Treasury note futures

The basic trading unit is a U.S. Treasury note with a face value of $100,000. The futures contract is written on any of the four most recently auctioned 5-year U.S.

TABLE 13.10   *Treasury Bond and Notes Features,*
Thursday, May 28, 1998*

```
           TREASURY BONDS (CBT)-$100,000; pts. 32nds of 100%
                                              Lifetime       Open
             Open High Low Settle Change High Low Interest
   June   121-15 121-21 121-08 121-15  –    3 123-28 104-03 474,040
   Sept   121-08 121-15 121-02 121-09  –    2 123-10 103-22 394,564
   Dec    120-30 121-04 120-27 121-00  –1   2 122-30 103-13  61,254
   Mr99    ....   ....   ....  120-24  –    2 121-26 103-04     51
     Est vol 500,000; vol Wed 662,618; open int 929,947, –2,140.
            TREASURY BONDS (MCE)-$50,000; pts. 32nds of 100%
   June   121-17 121-22 121-09 121-18  +    6 123-27 114-08   8,252
     Est vol 6,000; vol Wed 9,487; open int 8,770, –842.
            TREASURY NOTES (CBT)-$100,000; pts. 32nds of 100%
   June   112-29 113-01 112-25 112-29  –    2 115-06 106-26 329,439
   Sept   113-00 113-06 112-28 113-02  –    2 114-22 110-25 206,805
   Dec    112-29 112-30 112-26 112-30  –    2 114-21 111-11   9,462
     Est vol 201,000; vol Wed 316,572; open int 545,707, +11,802.
            5 YR TREAS NOTES (CBT)-$100,000; pts. 32nds of 100%
   June   09-055 109-07 09-025 09-045  – 2.5 111-00 107-28 187,753
   Sept   09-075 09-085 109-04 09-055  – 3.0 09-175 108-09  95,596
     Est vol 92,212; vol Wed 140,243; open int 283,434, –6,150.
            2 YR TREAS NOTES (CBT)-$200,000; pts. 32nds of 100%
   June   04-017 04-045 04-005 104-01  – 1.2 04-175 103-21  27,643
   Sept   104-01 04-025 104-01 04-012  – 1.7 04-042 03-225  24,910
     Est vol 7,500; vol Wed 21,155; open int 52,553, –2,322.
```

*Source: *The Wall Street Journal*, May 29, 1998.

Treasury notes that have an original maturity of not more than 5 years and 3 months and remaining maturity of not less than 4 years and 3 months, as of the first business day of the delivery month.

The remaining details, with the exception of price quotes, are similar to those of Treasury bond futures. Prices are quoted in terms of dollars and one half of 1/32 of a dollar. For example, a quote of 111-205 means $111(20.5/32)$ or $111.640625 per $100 par value. Table 13.10 contains price quotes on the 5-year Treasury note futures. The June contract has a settlement price of 109-045.

2-Year U.S. Treasury note futures

For the 2-year Treasury note futures, the basic trading unit is a U.S. Treasury note with a face value of $200,000. The futures contract is written on any U.S. Treasury note with an original maturity of not more than 5 years and 3 months and a remaining maturity of not less than 1 year and 9 months from the first day of the delivery month but not more than 2 years from the last day of the delivery month.

The remaining details, with the exception of the price quotes, are similar to those of Treasury bond futures. Prices are quoted in terms of dollars and one quarter of 1/32 of a dollar; for example,

106-230 means 106 (23/32)   = 106.718750
106-232 means 106 (23.25/32) = 106.726563

106-235 means 106 (23.50/32) = 106.734375
106-237 means 106 (23.75/32) = 106.742188.

Table 13.10 contains price quotes for the 2-year Treasury note futures. The June contract has a settlement price of 104-01.

The Delivery Process

We now discuss the delivery process of Treasury bond and Treasury note futures contracts. This is a particular example of the process described in Chapter 1. Delivery for these futures contracts is a three-day process. This provides the three parties—the buyer or long, the seller or short, and the clearing corporation—time to make the necessary notifications, delivery, and payment arrangements.

The short can initiate the three-day sequence any time during a period that begins two business days prior to the first business day of the delivery month and ends two business days before the last business day of the month. Trading in the deliverable futures contract stops on the seventh business day preceding the last business day of the delivery month.

The three-day delivery sequence begins when the short notifies the clearing corporation of the intention to deliver. This day is called the **Position Day**. On the second day of the delivery sequence, the clearing corporation matches the oldest long to the delivering short. The corporation notifies both parties to the trade.

TABLE 13.11 *The Delivery Process in Futures Markets*

DAY 1: POSITION DAY
The short informs the clearing corporation of the intent to make delivery.
DAY 2: NOTICE OF INTENTION DAY
The clearing corporation matches the oldest long to the delivering short and then notifies both parties.
The short invoices the long.
DAY 3: DELIVERY DAY
The short delivers the financial instruments to the long.
The long makes payment to the short.
TITLE PASSES
The long assumes all ownership rights and responsibilities.

After receiving this information, the short invoices the long. The second day is called the **Notice of Intention Day**. On the third day, the long takes possession of the instrument and the short receives the invoice amount. The third day is called the **Delivery Day**. For future reference, we summarize the delivery process in Table 13.11.

13.8 TREASURY BOND FUTURES

Now we return to the Treasury bond futures contract to discuss its delivery features in more detail. Recall that the Treasury bond futures contract is a commitment to deliver a nominal 8 percent, $100,000 face value U.S. Treasury bond with at least fifteen years to maturity or to the first call date, whichever comes first. The seller of the futures contract has a choice of eligible bonds that can be used for delivery. In an attempt to neutralize the effects of bonds with different coupons, the Chicago Board of Trade (CBT) designed a system of conversion factors, which we now explain.

Conversion Factors

Basically, conversion factors provide a means of equating bonds with different coupons and maturities so as to allow the seller of the futures contract a choice of eligible bonds to use for delivery, thus minimizing the possibility of price distortions, illiquidities, and manipulation.

The CBT system adjusts the T-bond futures price based on an 8 percent, fifteen-year Treasury bond with a semiannual coupon. The amount the short invoices the long is computed as follows:

$$\begin{array}{l}\text{Cash Received}\\ \text{by the Short}\end{array} \equiv \text{Quoted Futures Price} \times \begin{array}{l}\text{Conversion Factor for the}\\ \text{Bond Delivered}\end{array}$$

$$+ \text{ Accrued Interest on the Bond Delivered.}$$

For example, suppose the quoted T-bond futures price is 95-19. Remember that this is quoted in units of 32nds, so the actual price is 95 (19/32) or 95.59375 per $100 face value. Suppose that for the particular Treasury bond the short picks to deliver, the conversion factor is 1.0514, and the accrued interest is $2.85 per $100 face value. Each T-bond futures contract is for delivery of $100,000 face value of bonds. Therefore, the total dollar amount that the short invoices the long is

$$\left(\frac{100,000}{100}\right)(95.59375 \times 1.0514 + 2.85)$$
$$= 103,357.27.$$

The conversion factor for the Treasury bond delivered by the short is given by a formula, explained in the following text, as described by the Chicago Board of Trade. The maturity of the bond is rounded down to the nearest three months for the purpose of the calculation. If the maturity of the bond is an exact number of half years after the rounding, the first coupon is assumed to be paid in six months. If the maturity of the bond after rounding is not an exact number of half years—there is an extra three months—the first coupon is assumed to be paid after three months. We will use two examples to show how to calculate the conversion factor.

EXAMPLE   **Example One (Conversion Factor Calculation)**

Consider an $8\frac{1}{2}\%$ Treasury bond with a maturity of 22 years and 2 months. For the purposes of calculating the conversion factor, the bond is assumed to have a maturity of 22 years. The first coupon payment of 4.25 is assumed to be paid after six months. The value of the bond is defined to be

$$\sum_{t=1}^{44} \frac{4.25}{(1+.04)^t} + \frac{100}{(1+0.4)^{44}} = 105.1372,$$

assuming semiannual coupon payments and a face of 100. The conversion factor is defined to be 1.0514, using four-decimal-place accuracy. ∎

EXAMPLE   **Example Two (Conversion Factor Calculation)**

This example illustrates the conversion factor calculation for a more difficult situation. Consider an $8\frac{1}{2}\%$ Treasury bond with a maturity of 22 years and 11 months. The semiannual coupon payment is 4.25. For the purpose of calculating the conversion factor, the bond is assumed to have a maturity of 22 years and 9 months. The value of this bond in three months' time, the maturity being 22 years and 6 months, is defined to be

$$4.25 + \sum_{t=1}^{45} \frac{4.25}{(1+.04)^t} + \frac{100}{(1+.04)^{45}} = 109.4300.$$

Recall that the coupon is assumed to be paid in three months' time. This value is discounted back for the three-month period. The discount rate is $\sqrt{1.04} - 1 = 0.0198$. The bond's value today is

$$\frac{1}{1.0198}\, 109.4300 = 107.3049.$$

For purposes of consistency, the accrued interest, 2.125, is subtracted from the price of the bond to give 105.1799. The conversion factor is 1.0518. ∎

The Chicago Board of Trade publishes tables of conversion factors (see Table 13.12). Check the conversion factors calculated in the above two examples to see that they match those in Table 13.12.

Cheapest to Deliver

This section discusses an embedded option within the Treasury bond futures contract known as the **cheapest to deliver option**, or the **quality option**. For contracts traded on the Exchange of the Chicago Board of Trade, the investor who is short at any given time has a choice of bonds that satisfy the conditions of the futures contract. The short invoices the long for the amount:

(Quoted Futures Price × Conversion Factor) + Accrued Interest.

TABLE 13.12 *Conversion Factor to Yield 8.000 Percent**

	COUPON RATE							
YRS-MOS:	**8%**	**$8\frac{1}{8}\%$**	**$8\frac{1}{4}\%$**	**$8\frac{3}{8}\%$**	**$8\frac{1}{2}\%$**	**$8\frac{5}{8}\%$**	**$8\frac{3}{4}\%$**	**$8\frac{7}{8}\%$**
22-0	1.0000	1.0128	1.0257	1.0385	1.0514	1.0642	1.0771	1.0899
22-3	.9998	1.0127	1.0256	1.0385	1.0514	1.0643	1.0772	1.0901
22-6	1.0000	1.0130	1.0259	1.0389	1.0518	1.0648	1.0777	1.0907
22-9	.9998	1.0128	1.0258	1.0388	1.0518	1.0648	1.0778	1.0908
23-0	1.0000	1.0131	1.0261	1.0392	1.0522	1.0753	1.0783	1.0914
23-3	.9998	1.0129	1.0260	1.0391	1.0522	1.0653	1.0784	1.0915
23-6	1.0000	1.0132	1.0263	1.0395	1.0526	1.0658	1.0789	1.0921
23-9	.9998	1.0130	1.0262	1.0394	1.0526	1.0658	1.0790	1.0922
24-0	1.0000	1.0132	1.0265	1.0397	1.0530	1.0662	1.0795	1.0927
24-3	.9998	1.0131	1.0264	1.0397	1.0530	1.0663	1.0795	1.0928
24-6	1.0000	1.0133	1.0267	1.0400	1.0534	1.0667	1.0800	1.0934
27-9	.9998	1.0132	1.0266	1.0399	1.0533	1.0667	1.0801	1.0935
25-0	1.0000	1.0134	1.0269	1.0403	1.0537	1.0671	1.0806	1.0940
25-3	.9998	1.0133	1.0267	1.0402	1.0537	1.0671	1.0806	1.0941
25-6	1.0000	1.0135	1.0270	1.0405	1.0540	1.0676	1.0811	1.0946
25-9	.9998	1.0134	1.0269	1.0405	1.0540	1.0675	1.0811	1.0946
26-0	1.0000	1.0136	1.0272	1.0408	1.0544	1.0680	1.0816	1.0951
26-3	.9998	1.0134	1.0271	1.0407	1.0543	1.0679	1.0816	1.0952
26-6	1.0000	1.0137	1.0273	1.0410	1.0547	1.0684	1.0820	1.0957
26-9	.9998	1.0135	1.0272	1.0409	1.0546	1.0683	1.0820	1.0957
27-0	1.0000	1.0137	1.0275	1.0412	1.0550	1.0687	1.0825	1.0962
27-3	.9998	1.0136	1.0274	1.0411	1.0549	1.0687	1.0825	1.0963
27-6	1.0000	1.0138	1.0276	1.0415	1.0553	1.0691	1.0829	1.0967
27-9	.9998	1.0137	1.0275	1.0414	1.0552	1.0691	1.0829	1.0968

*Source: Chicago Board of Trade, *Treasury Futures for Institutional Investors*, Table 2.1.

The cost to the short of purchasing the bond to deliver is

Quoted Bond Price + Accrued Interest.

Therefore, the net return to the short is

Quoted Futures Price × Conversion Factor − Quoted Bond Price.

It is in the interest of the short to pick the bond that maximizes this difference.

For example, suppose that the quoted futures price is 94-2, or 94.0625. There are three bonds with the following prices and conversion factors:

Bond	Price	Conversion Factor
1	94.25	1.0820
2	126.00	1.4245
3	142.125	1.5938.

The net return to the short is

Bond 1	94.0625 × 1.0820 − 94.25 = 7.53
Bond 2	94.0625 × 1.4245 − 126.00 = 7.99
Bond 3	94.0625 × 1.5938 − 142.125 = 7.79.

It would be in the interest of the short to deliver Bond 2, as it is the cheapest bond to deliver.

Over time, the identity of the cheapest-to-deliver Treasury bond changes. The conversion factor system tends to favor the delivery of relatively low-coupon, long-maturity bonds when yields are in excess of 8 percent. When yields are less than 8 percent, the conversion factor system favors high-coupon, short-maturity bonds. The shape of the term structure affects the outcome. For an upward sloping curve, a positive relationship exists between maturity and yield, implying a negative relationship between maturity and price. This causes a tendency for long maturity bonds to be the cheapest to deliver.

Wild Card Option

There is another embedded option within the Treasury Bond futures option known as the **wild card option**. The Chicago Board of Trade interest rate futures markets stop trading at 2:00 P.M. (C.S.T.), while the cash market for Treasury bonds continues to trade past this time. The deadline for notifying the clearing corporation of an intent to deliver is 8:00 P.M. (C.S.T.). This difference of six hours creates a window each day within the delivery period during which the short may potentially take advantage of a decline in the cash market prices. This window generates the "wild card option." The futures price reflects the value of this option: the greater the value of the option, the lower the futures price.

Timing Option

The third embedded option within the Treasury bond futures contract is known as the **timing option**. The deliverable contract will stop trading on the seventh business day preceding the last business day of the delivery month. During this seven-business-day period, all open positions must be settled by delivery. The short has the flexibility of determining when to deliver during this period and can take advantage of any decline in the cash market. This timing option is valuable to the short, and the greater the value, the lower the Treasury bond futures price will be prior to the time the future ceases to trade.

13.9 SUMMARY

In this chapter, we discussed the basic instruments underlying the term structure of interest rates: Treasury bills, Treasury notes, and Treasury bonds. We described how Treasury bills are quoted in terms of discount rates. We also gave definitions for simple interest rates, money market rates, and continuously compounded rates. We described market yields on Treasury bonds and notes, and the valuation of floating rate notes.

Duration has a long history as a tool for hedging interest rate risk. We introduced duration for bonds and explained some of its properties. As a hedging tool, duration assumes that the term structure of interest rates shifts by small parallel amounts. In practice, this rarely happens. We will discuss in Chapter 15 a better method for measuring risk that avoids these limitations.

We also examined additional instruments related to the term structure of interest rates, including Eurodollar deposits, FRAs, Eurodollar futures contracts, and Treasury bill, note, and bond futures contracts.

In Treasury bond and Treasury note futures contracts, the writer of the futures contract has three embedded options:

1. quality option—the choice of the cheapest-to-deliver bond;
2. wild card option—on any day during the delivery month, deadline for the notice of intention to deliver is 8:00 P.M., six hours after the futures market stops trading; and
3. timing option—option to deliver during the last seven business days of the delivery month at a price based on the last settlement price at the end of trading.

These options all tend to reduce the Treasury futures price and make futures contract pricing difficult.

REFERENCES

Burghardt, G., T. Belton, M. Lane, G. Luce, and R. McVey, 1991. *Eurodollar Futures and Options*. Chicago: Probus Publishing Company.

Chicago Board of Trade Publications:

Treasury Futures for Institutional Investors

Two Year Treasury Note Futures

Five Year Treasury Note Futures

The Delivery Process in Brief: Treasury Board and Treasury Note Futures

Understanding Duration and Convexity

The London International Financial Futures Exchange, *Eurodollar Interest Rate Futures and Options*.

Stigum, M., 1981. *Money Market Calculations*. Homewood, IL: Dow Jones-Irwin.

QUESTIONS

Question 1

The current discount rate is 3 percent on a 90-day T-bill, face value $1 million. What is the price of the T-bill? If the discount rate increases by one basis point to 3.01 percent, what is the *change* in the price of the T-bill?

Question 2

The continuously compounded yield on a deposit that pays one million dollars in 365 days' time is 4.5 percent. What is the current value of the deposit? What is the yield expressed as a simple interest rate, assuming a 365-day year?

Question 3

The current discount rate on a 91-day T-bill is 3.65 percent, assuming a 360-day year. What is the simple interest rate, assuming a 365-day year?

Question 4

A bond pays interest on an annual basis. The maturity of the bond is 4 years, the coupon is 6.25 percent, the face value of the bond is 100, and its market value is 104.33. Determine the discretely compounded yield-to-maturity and the continuously compounded yield-to-maturity.

Question 5

A bond pays interest semiannually. The coupon is 5.50 percent per annum, implying that the amount paid every six months is 2.75 dollars per 100 dollar face value. The maturity of the bond is 3 years and its market value is 100.05. Determine the effective yield-to-maturity and the continuously compounded yield-to-maturity.

Question 6

Let the quote on the 15 July 1999 $6^3/_8$% Treasury note be Bid 105:26 Ask 105:28. If you purchased this bond on May 25, 1994 at the ask price, what would be the total cost? The total number of days in the current coupon period is 182.

Question 7

Consider a $12^1/_2$% Treasury bond with a maturity of 20 years. Show that the conversion factor is 1.4452.

Question 8

The quoted futures price is 114-26. Which of the following three bonds is cheapest to deliver?

Bond	Price	Conversion Factor
1	162:20	1.3987
2	138:31	1.2870
3	131.02	1.273

Question 9

Consider a Treasury note with a maturity of 5 years and a coupon of 10 percent per annum. The coupon is paid semiannually. You are given the following information about the term structure of interest rates:

Maturity	0.5	1.0	1.5	2.0	2.5
T-bill Price	0.9748	0.9494	0.9238	0.8982	0.8725

Maturity	3.0	3.5	4.0	4.5	5.0
T-bill Price	0.8470	0.8216	0.7965	0.7717	0.7472

a)   What is the market price of the Treasury note?
b)   What is the annual yield-to-maturity?
c)   What is the modified duration of the Treasury note?

Question 10

Use the information in Question 9 to answer the following questions.

a)   Determine the continuously compounded yield-to-maturity for the T-bills.
b)   Determine the continuously compounded six-month forward rates.
c)   Plot the term structure of zero-coupon yields and the term structure of forward rates.

APPENDIX: DURATION AND CONVEXITY CORRECTION FOR A SEMIANNUAL COUPON BOND

Let y denote the semiannual yield-to-maturity defined by Expression (13.6). The definition of modified duration is

$$D_M \equiv \frac{(1/2)}{(1 + y/2)} \left[\sum_{t=1}^{2T} \frac{tc}{(1 + y/2)^t} + \frac{2TF}{(1 + y/2)^{2T}} \right] / B_c.$$

EXAMPLE

Modified Duration

Consider a $2\frac{1}{2}$-year bond with a semiannual coupon of $4.00. The semiannual yield-to-maturity is 8.12 percent and the bond price is $99.6733. Table A1 shows the calculations necessary to determine the modified duration of the bond. Using the figures in Table A1 and substituting into Expression (13.16) gives

$$\Delta B_c = -99.6733 \times 2.2251 \times \Delta y$$
$$= -221.78 \Delta y.$$

If the semiannual yield-to-maturity increases by one basis point to 8.13 percent, the bond price is

$$\sum_{t=1}^{5} \frac{4.00}{(1 + 0.04065)^t} + \frac{100}{(1 + 0.04065)^5}$$
$$= 99.6500,$$

TABLE A1 *Calculating Modified Duration of a Bond with Semiannual Coupon Payments*

TIME, t (YEARS)	COUPON	PRINCIPAL	DISCOUNTED VALUE*	$t \times$ DISCOUNTED VALUE $\times$ 0.5
1	4.00	0	3.8439	1.9220
2	4.00	0	3.6340	3.6340
3	4.00	0	3.5498	5.3248
4	4.00	0	3.4113	6.8227
5	4.00	100	85.2343	213.0858
			99.6733	230.7893

$$\text{Classical Duration} = \frac{230.7893}{99.6733} = 2.3155$$

$$\text{Modified Duration} = \frac{2.35155}{1.0406} = 2.2251$$

*The semiannual yield-to-maturity is 4.06 percent.

implying that the bond price has changed by -0.02. Alternatively, we could compute an approximation to this change using modified duration to give

$$B_c = -221.78 \times [(8.13 - 8.12)/100]$$
$$= -0.02.$$

For this small change in yield, the two values are identical.   ■

Convexity correction

The convexity correction is defined by

$$\text{Convexity} \equiv \frac{(1/4)}{(1 + y/2)^2}\left[\sum_{t=1}^{2T}\frac{t(t+1)c}{(1+y/2)^t} + \frac{2T(2T+1)F}{(1+y/2)^{2T}}\right]/B_c.$$

EXAMPLE

(Continued)

Suppose that the semiannual yield-to-maturity increased to 8.50 percent. The new bond price is

$$\sum_{t=1}^{5}\frac{4}{(1 + 0.0425)^t} + \frac{100}{(1 + 0.0425)^5}$$
$$= 98.8948,$$

TABLE A2 *Calculating the Convexity Correction for a Semiannual Coupon Bond*

TIME, t (YEARS)	COUPON	PRINCIPAL	PRESENT VALUE*	$t(t+1) \times$ PRESENT VALUE
1	4.00	0	3.8439	7.6878
2	4.00	0	3.6340	21.8040
3	4.00	0	3.5498	42.5976
4	4.00	0	3.4113	68.2260
5	4.00	100	85.2343	2,557.0290
			99.6733	2,697.3444

$$\text{Convexity} = \left[\frac{(1/4)}{(1 + 0.0406)^2}\,2{,}697.3444\right]/99.6733$$
$$= 6.2478$$
$$\text{Price Correction} = (1/2)\,B_c\,\text{Convexity}\,(\Delta y)^2$$
$$= (1/2) \times 99.6733 \times 6.2478(0.0850 - 0.0812)^2$$
$$= 0.0045.$$

*The semiannual yield-to-maturity is 4.06 percent.

implying that the change in the bond price is

$$\Delta B_c = 98.8948 - 99.6733$$
$$= -0.7785.$$

The steps to calculate the convexity term are shown in Table A2. Using Expression (13.19), the change in the bond price is

$$-99.6733 \times 2.2251 \times (0.0038) + \tfrac{1}{2} \times 99.6733 \times 6.2478 \times (0.0038)^2$$
$$= -0.8428 + 0.0045$$
$$= -0.8383.   \blacksquare$$

SWAPS

14.0 INTRODUCTION

A financial **swap** is a contract between two individuals, called **counterparties**, to exchange a series of cash payments. Contained in the swap contract is a specification of the rate of interest applicable to each cash payment, the currency in which each cash payment will be made, the time table for the payments, provisions to cover the contingency that a counterparty might default, and other issues that affect the relationship between the counterparties. The first interest rate swap contracts were negotiated in 1981. Since then, the growth in the size of the swap market has been rapid. Today, the size of the swap market is measured in hundreds of billions of dollars.[1]

In this chapter, we will first discuss the structure and valuation of interest rate swaps. We also discuss foreign currency swaps, commodity swaps, and equity swaps. All of these different types of swaps have a common structure involving the mechanism for exchanging cash flows.

A swap contract involves the risk that one or either party to the swap may default.[2] This default or credit risk is often referred to as counterparty risk. For the present we will ignore counterparty risk. In Chapter 18, we will show how to incorporate counterparty risk into the analysis.

14.1 INTEREST RATE SWAPS

First let us study interest rate swaps. We start by considering a simple form of the generic or "plain vanilla" interest rate swap. We will refer to the two counterparties to the swap as A and B.

In an interest rate swap, counterparty A agrees to make fixed semiannual payments to counterparty B. The magnitude of each fixed rate-based payment is determined by a

---

[1] Among users of swaps and regulators there is a debate about the size of the swap market. In calculating the size of the market, notional principal is typically used. This is misleading, because in interest rate swaps principal is not exchanged and the value of each component in a swap is substantially less than the notional principal.

[2] While defaults in swaps are not common, major defaults do occur: for example, the Hammersmith town council in the United Kingdom in 1988–89 and Drexel Burnham Lambert in the United States.

prespecified fixed rate of interest on a notional principal. In return, counterparty B agrees to make semiannual floating rate payments to counterparty A. The magnitude of each floating rate-based payment is determined by a semiannual floating rate of interest on the same notional principal for the same period of time. Payments are made in the same currencies. The payments are netted and only the party with the positive difference owed makes a payment equal to the netted amount.

EXAMPLE

Plain Vanilla Swap

We consider a simple example to illustrate the different issues involved in plain vanilla interest rate swaps.

Consider the following swap. Party A pays a fixed rate 7.19 percent per annum on a semiannual basis, and receives from Party B LIBOR + 30 basis points (the details are represented in Figure 14.1). The current six-month LIBOR rate is 6.45 percent per annum. The notional principal is 35 million dollars.

The fixed rate in a swap is usually quoted on a semiannual bond equivalent yield basis. Therefore, the amount that is paid every six months is

$$\text{(Notional Principal)} \left(\frac{\text{Days in Period}}{365} \right) \left(\frac{\text{Interest Rate}}{100} \right)$$

$$= (\$35,000,000) \left(\frac{182}{365} \right) \left(\frac{7.19}{100} \right)$$

$$= \$1,254,802.74,$$

where it is assumed that there are 182 days in this particular period.

The floating side is quoted on a money market yield basis. The difference between the two rate computations is in the number of days in a year convention employed.[3] Therefore, the payment is

$$\text{(Notional Principal)} \left(\frac{\text{Days in Period}}{360} \right) \left(\frac{\text{Interest Rate}}{100} \right)$$

$$= (\$35,000,000) \left(\frac{182}{360} \right) \left(\frac{(6.45 + 0.30)}{100} \right)$$

$$= \$1,194,375.$$

---

[3]The money market yield can be converted to a semiannual bond equivalent yield. Let L^* be the converted bond equivalent yield and, recognizing that the amount paid remains unchanged,

$$\text{(Notional Principal)} \left(\frac{\text{Days in Period}}{360} \right) \left(\frac{L/2}{100} \right)$$

$$= \text{(Notional Principal)} \left(\frac{\text{Days in Period}}{365} \right) \left(\frac{L^*/2}{100} \right),$$

which implies

$$L^* = L(365/360),$$

where L is semiannual money market yield.

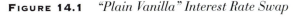

FIGURE 14.1   *"Plain Vanilla" Interest Rate Swap*

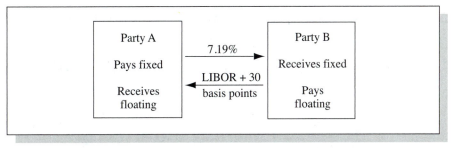

In a swap, the payments are netted. In this case, Party A pays Party B the net difference:

$1,254,802.74 − 1,194,375
= $60,427.74.   ∎

This example illustrates four points. First, payments are netted in interest rate swaps. In the example, Party A sent Party B a payment for the net amount. Second, principal is not exchanged. This is why the term "notional principal" is used. Third, Party A is exposed to the risk that Party B might default, and conversely, Party B is exposed to the risk of Party A defaulting. If one party defaults, the swap usually terminates. Fourth, on the fixed-payment side a 365-day year is assumed, while on the floating payment side a 360-day year is used. The number of days in the year is one of the issues specified in the swap contract.

Pricing Schedules

Table 14.1 shows a typical pricing schedule for swaps with various maturities. The prices are for fixed floating interest rate par swaps, assuming semiannual compounding. We will give a definition of the term "par swap" later. If a bank is negotiating a seven-year swap to receive six-month LIBOR and pay fixed, Table 14.1 shows that the fixed rate should be set at 48 basis points above the rate on a seven-year Treasury note, which is 7.10 percent per annum. Therefore, the bank will pay 7.58 percent per annum on the fixed side and receive six-month LIBOR on the floating side.

When the bank is negotiating a seven-year swap to receive fixed and pay six-month LIBOR for seven years, the pricing schedule indicates that the fixed rate is set at 50 basis points above the seven-year Treasury note yield, that is, 7.60 percent per annum. The bank's profit from negotiating two completely offsetting seven-year swaps would be 2 basis points per annum. This is called the "bid/ask" spread. Competition in the swap market has forced spreads to be very tight, even out to 30-year swaps.

TABLE 14.1 *Typical Pricing for Interest Rate Swaps*

MATURITY (YEARS)	BANK PAYS FIXED RATE	BANK RECEIVES FIXED RATE	CURRENT TN RATE
2	2 yr TN + 31 bps	2 yr TN + 32 bps	6.79
3	3 yr TN + 32 bps	3 yr TN + 33 bps	6.86
5	5 yr TN + 41 bps	5 yr Tn + 42 bps	7.06
7	7 yr TN + 48 bps	7 yr TN + 50 bps	7.10
10	10 yr TN + 57 bps	10 yr TN + 59 bps	7.22

The schedule assumes semiannual rates and also assumes that the counterparty to the swap is a triple A credit.

TN denotes the Treasury note rate quoted on a semiannual bond equivalent yield basis (actual/365 days).

All rates are quoted against six-month LIBOR.

Warehousing

In practice, a bank making a market in swaps may not be able to find an offsetting swap. Most financial institutions will warehouse the swap and use interest rate derivatives to hedge their risk exposure until they can find an offsetting swap to hedge their position. It is not always possible to find a second swap with the same maturity and notional principal as the first swap, implying that the institution making a market in the initial swap has a residual interest rate risk exposure. The relatively narrow bid/ask spread in the interest rate swap market implies that to make a profit, effective interest rate risk management is essential.

Valuation

We examine here the valuation of interest rate swaps. The valuation of the fixed side of a swap is straightforward, while the valuation of the floating side of a swap is slightly more complicated. Before providing a general analysis, we start with an example.

EXAMPLE **Swap Valuation**

This example illustrates the valuation of a two-year interest rate swap. Consider a financial institution that is receiving fixed payments at the rate 7.15 percent per annum and paying floating payments in a two-year swap. Payments are made every six months. Details are shown in Table 14.2 about the payment dates, the term structure of Treasury rates, and the term structure of LIBOR rates.

Consider first the fixed side of the swap. At the first payment date, t_1, the dollar value of the payment is

$$N_P \times 0.0715 \times (182/365),$$

TABLE 14.2 *Pricing an Interest Rate Swap*

PAYMENT DATES	DAYS BETWEEN PAYMENT DATES	TREASURY BILL PRICES $B(0, T)$	EURODOLLAR DEPOSIT $L(0, T)$
$t_1 = 182$	182	0.9679	0.9669
$t_2 = 365$	183	0.9362	0.9338
$t_3 = 548$	183	0.9052	0.9010
$t_4 = 730$	182	0.8749	0.8684

$B(0, T)$ denotes the present value of receiving for sure one dollar at date T.

$L(0, T)$ denotes the present value of receiving one Eurodollar at date T.

These prices are respectively derived from the Treasury and Eurodollar term structures.

where N_P denotes the notional principal. The present value today of receiving one dollar for sure at date t_1 is $B(0, t_1) = 0.9679$. Therefore, the present value of the first fixed swap payment is

$$N_P \times 0.9679 \times 0.0715 \times (182/365).$$

By repeating this analysis, the present value of all fixed payments is

$$
\begin{aligned}
V_R(0) = N_P\{ & 0.9679 \times 0.0715 \times (182/365) \\
+ & 0.9362 \times 0.0715 \times (183/365) \\
+ & 0.9052 \times 0.0715 \times (183/365) \\
+ & 0.8749 \times 0.0715 \times (182/365)\} \\
= & N_P \times 0.1317.
\end{aligned}
\tag{14.1}
$$

Now let us consider the floating side of the swap. The pattern of payments is similar to that of a floating rate bond, with the important proviso that there is no principal payment in a swap. From the last chapter we know that on the date when the interest rate is reset, the bond sells at par value. Hence at time 0, the present value of the sequence of floating rate payments is the notional principal, N_P. But, given that there is no principal payment in a swap, we must subtract the present value of principal repayment that would normally occur at time t_4. The present value of the floating rate payments is thus

$$
\begin{aligned}
V_F(0) \equiv & N_P - N_P \times L(0, t_4) \\
= & N_P[1 - 0.8684] \\
= & N_P \times 0.1316,
\end{aligned}
\tag{14.2}
$$

where $L(0, t_4)$ is the present value of receiving one Eurodollar at date t_4.

> The value of the swap to the financial institution receiving fixed and paying floating is
>
> $$\text{Value of Swap} \equiv V_R(0) - V_F(0)$$
> $$= N_P \times [0.1317 - 0.1316]$$
> $$= N_P \times 0.0001.$$
>
> If the notional principal is 25 million dollars, the value of the swap is $2,500.
>
> In this example, the Treasury bond prices are used to discount the cash flows based on the Treasury note rate, and the Eurodollar discount factors are used to measure the present value of the LIBOR cash flows. This incorporates the different risks implicit in these different cash flow streams. ■

To generalize this example, we simply replace algebraic symbols for the numbers. Consider a plain vanilla interest rate swap in which there are n payments with maturity t_n and principal N_P. The dates of each payment are denoted by t_j for $j = 1$, ..., n measured in days. The value of the fixed payments is

$$V_R(0) = N_P \sum_{j=1}^{n} B(0, t_j) \times \{(\overline{R}/100) \times [(t_j - t_{j-1})/365]\}, \qquad (14.3)$$

where $\overline{R}$ is the swap rate expressed as a percent. The quantity $(t_j - t_{j-1})$ represents the days between the jth and $(j-1)$th payment. The preceding equation is a generalization of Expression (14.1).

The value of the floating rate payments requires more care. If the swap is already in existence,[4] then let $\overline{\ell}$ denote the prespecified LIBOR rate for the next payment at date t_1. At date t_1 the payment is

$$N_P \times [\overline{\ell} \times (t_1/360)]$$

and a new LIBOR rate is set. The value at date t_1 of the remaining floating rate payments is

$$N_P - N_P \times L(t_1, t_n).$$

This represents the present value of a floating rate note paying the principal at time t_n, N_P, less the present value of the omitted principal payment $N_P L(t_1, t_n)$.

The total value of the floating rate payments at date t_1 is

$$V_F(t_1) = N_P \times [\overline{\ell} \times (t_1/360)] + N_P - N_P \times L(t_1, t_n).$$

---

[4]This means that time 0 is between the last payment date and the next at time t_1.

The value of the floating rate payments at date 0 is

$$V_F(0) = N_P\{[\bar{\ell} \times (t_1/360) + 1] \times L(0,t_1) - L(0,t_n)\}. \tag{14.4}$$

This expression uses the fact that the time-0 value of $L(t_1,t_n)$ is $L(0,t_n)$.

Now, if the swap is initiated at date 0, then we replace $\bar{\ell}$ with the time-0 LIBOR rate. In this case, Expression (14.4) simplifies. Let $\ell(t_1)$ denote the current LIBOR rate. By definition,

$$L(0,t_1) \equiv \frac{1}{1 + \ell(t_1)(t_1/360)}.$$

So, the value of the floating rate payment is

$$\begin{aligned} V_F(0) &= N_P\{[\ell(t_1) \times (t_1/360) + 1] \times L(0,t_1) - L(0,t_n)\} \\ &= N_P \times [1 - L(0,t_n)], \end{aligned} \tag{14.5}$$

which is a generalization of Expression (14.2).

The value of a swap receiving fixed and paying floating is $V_R(0) - V_F(0)$. This value can be positive, zero, or negative depending on current rates.

Par Swaps

A **par swap** is a swap for which the present value of the fixed payments equals the present value of the floating payments, implying that the net value of the swap is zero. Equating the value of the fixed payments (Expression (14.3)) and the value of the floating rate payments (Expression (14.5)) gives

$$N_P \sum_{j=1}^{n} B(0,t_j) \times \{(R/100) \times [(t_j - t_{j-1})/365]\} = N_P \times [1 - L(0,t_n)]. \tag{14.6}$$

The par swap rate is that rate R which satisfies Expression (14.6).

EXAMPLE **Par Swap Rate**

Using the information in Table 14.2, the par swap rate is determined by substituting these values into Expression (14.6):

$$\begin{aligned} (R/100) &\times [0.9679 \times (182/365) + 0.9362 \times (183/365) + 0.9052 \\ &\times (183/365) + 0.8749 \times (182/365)] \\ &= 1 - 0.8684, \end{aligned}$$

implying

$$(R/100) = 0.1316/1.8421$$

or

$$R = 7.14 \text{ percent per annum.} \qquad \blacksquare$$

In an upward sloping term structure environment, forward rates are increasing. For a par swap, the value of the individual fixed rate payments will be greater than the value of the individual floating rate payments over the first part of the swap. The converse is true over the remaining part of the swap, given that the value of a par swap is zero, and is illustrated in Figure 14.2, Part A.

In a downward sloping term structure environment, forward rates are decreasing. For a par swap, the value of the individual fixed rate payments over the first part of the swap will be less than the value of the individual floating rate payments. The converse is true over the remaining part of the swap and is illustrated in Figure 14.2, Part B.

A common practice is to add the present value of the principal to both the left and right sides of Expression (14.6) and to define the par swap rate as

$$N_P \sum_{j=1}^{n} B(0,t_j) \times \{(R_I/100) \times [(t_j - t_{j-1})/365]\} + N_P \times B(0,t_n) = N_P.$$

FIGURE 14.2   *Value of the Fixed and Floating Sides of a Swap*

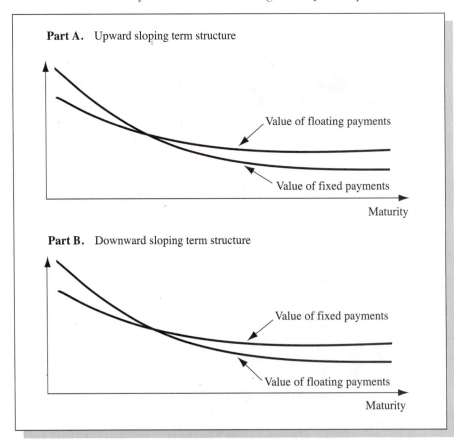

We have added the subscript I to the swap rate to indicate that this practice is, in general, *incorrect*. It only makes sense if the risk of the two cash flows is the same as that of the Treasury notes so that $L(0, t_n) = B(0, t_n)$. This is rarely the case.

Let us use the data from the last example to compute the swap rate using the incorrect formula. Substituting into the preceding equation, we have

$$(R_I/100)1.8421 + 0.8749 = 1,$$

implying

$$R_I = 6.79 \text{ percent per annum.}$$

Comparing this to the correct value of the swap rate, 7.14 percent per annum, we see that the error can be substantial.

Variants of Interest Rate Swaps

Here we discuss various different interest rate swaps seen in the markets. In the basic plain vanilla interest rate swap, illustrated in Figure 14.1, the notional principal is fixed. In one variant, an **index amortized swap**, the notional principal is reduced over the life of the swap. The schedule for reductions in the notional principal may be predefined or depend on the level of interest rates.

Constant yield swaps are swaps in which both parts are floating. For example, one part may be tied to the yield on the 30-year Treasury bond and the other part tied to the yield on the 10-year Treasury note.

Rate-capped swaps are swaps in which the floating rate is capped. Note that a plain vanilla swap can be converted into a capped swap via the use of interest rate caps. Interest rate caps are studied in Chapter 17.

Putable and **callable swaps** are swaps that give one or both counterparties the right to cancel the swap at certain times without additional costs.

Forward swaps are swaps in which the swap rate is set but the swap does not commence until a later date. These swaps are sometimes called **deferred swaps**. Other variants are also possible.

Our discussion of interest rate swaps is now complete.

14.2 FOREIGN CURRENCY SWAPS

Now we examine foreign currency swaps. Unlike interest rate swaps, a **foreign currency swap** usually involves the exchange of principal. Let us start by considering a "plain vanilla" foreign currency swap.

Counterparty A has issued bonds with face value of 50 million pounds with a coupon of 11.5 percent per annum, paid semiannually, and a maturity of seven years. Counterparty A would prefer to have dollars and to be making interest payments in

dollars. Thus counterparty A enters into a foreign currency swap with counterparty B (usually a financial institution).

In the first phase of the swap, counterparty A exchanges principal worth 50 million pounds with counterparty B and, in return, receives an approximately equivalent principal in dollars, worth 72.5 million dollars. In the second phase of the swap, counterparty A agrees to make to counterparty B semiannual interest rate payments at the rate of 9.35 percent per annum based on the dollar-denominated principal for a seven-year period. In return, counterparty A receives from counterparty B a semiannual interest rate at the rate of 11.5 percent per annum based on the sterling-denominated principal for a seven-year period. This swap is illustrated in Figure 14.3. The final phase of the swap occurs at the maturity of the swap when the principals are again exchanged, but this time in reverse. Counterparty A receives principal worth 50 million pounds and counterparty B receives principal worth 72.5 million dollars.

By entering into the foreign currency swap, counterparty A has transferred its sterling liability into a dollar liability. In this case, counterparty A was able to completely offset the sterling interest rate payments. This is not always the case. In Figure 14.4, the interest rate payments counterparty A receives from counterparty B only partially offsets the sterling expense. With the exchange of principal, the issue of counterparty risk assumes greater importance than in the case of interest rate swaps.

FIGURE 14.3   *A Plain Vanilla Foreign Currency Swap*

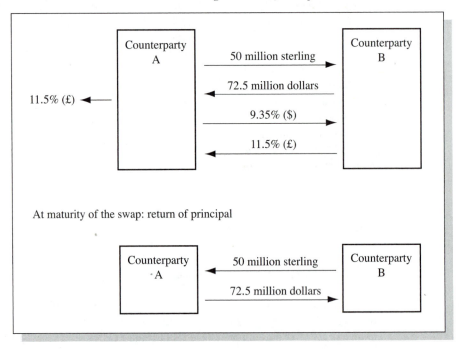

FIGURE 14.4 *Foreign Currency Swap: Counterparty A Bears Some Foreign Exchange Risk*

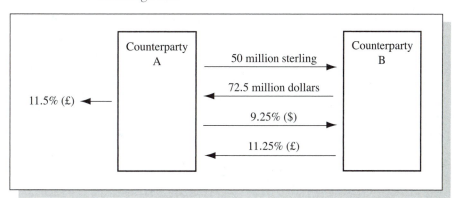

We will show how to incorporate counterparty risk into the pricing of swaps in Chapter 18.

Valuation of Currency Swaps

Here we examine how to value foreign currency swaps. Consider the position of counterparty A as shown in Figure 14.3. Under the terms of the swap, counterparty A is receiving sterling interest rate payments and making dollar interest payments. If sterling is the numeraire for counterparty A, the value of the swap to counterparty A in terms of sterling is

$$V_£(0) \equiv B_£(0) - S(0)B_\$(0), \tag{14.7}$$

where $B_£(0)$ denotes the present value in terms of sterling of the interest rate payments from counterparty B, including the principal payment at maturity. $B_\$(0)$ denotes the present value in terms of dollars of the interest rate payments to be made to counterparty B, including the principal payment at maturity. $S(0)$ is the sterling/dollar spot exchange rate at date 0. Note that the value of the swap depends on the shape of the domestic term structure of interest rates and the foreign term structure of interest rates.

EXAMPLE   **Valuing a Plain Vanilla Foreign Currency Swap**

Consider a financial institution that enters into a foreign currency swap for which the institution receives 5.875 percent per annum semiannually in French francs and pays 3.75 percent per annum semiannually in U.S. dollars. The tenor of the swap is two years and the current spot exchange rate is 0.1709 U.S.$/FF. The principals in the two currencies are 58.5 million francs and 10 million

Table 14.3   *Domestic and Foreign Term Structure*

Maturity (Months)	Price of a Zero-Coupon Bond $	Price of a Zero-Coupon Bond FF
6	0.9840 (3.22%)	0.9699 (6.09%)
12	0.9667 (3.38%)	0.9456 (5.59%)
18	0.9467 (3.65%)	0.9190 (5.63%)
24	0.9249 (3.90%)	0.8922 (5.70%)

Figures in parentheses are continuously compounded yields.

dollars. At the spot exchange rate, the dollar values of both principals are approximately equal: 58.5 mFF $\times$ 0.1709 \$/FF = 9.99765 m\$.

Information about the U.S. and French term structures of interest rates is given in Table 14.3. The coupon payment of the semiannual interest payments in French francs is

$$(58.5m)\left(\frac{5.875}{100}\right)\left(\frac{1}{2}\right) = 1,718,437.5 \text{FF}.$$

Therefore, the present value of the interest rate payments in francs plus principal translated into dollars is

$$
\begin{aligned}
S(0)\, B_{FF}(0) &= (0.1709) \{1,718,437.5 \times [0.9699 + 0.9456 + 0.9190 \\
&\quad + 0.8922] + 58,500,000 \times 0.8922\} \\
&= (0.1709) \{58,597,801\text{FF}\} \\
&= \$10,014,364.
\end{aligned}
$$

The coupon payment of the semiannual interest rate payments in U.S. dollars is

$$10,000,000\left(\frac{3.75}{100}\right)\left(\frac{1}{2}\right) = \$187,500.$$

The present value of the interest rate payments in dollars plus principal is

$$
\begin{aligned}
B_\$(0) &= 187,500 \times [0.9840 + 0.9667 + 0.9467 + 0.9249] \\
&\quad + 10,000,000 \times 0.9249 \\
&= \$9,965,681.
\end{aligned}
$$

The dollar value of the foreign currency swap is therefore

$$
\begin{aligned}
S(0)\, B_{FF}(0) - B_\$(0) &= 10,014,364 - 9,965,681 \\
&= \$48,683.
\end{aligned}
$$

Expression (14.7) for the value of the foreign currency swap can be written in terms of forward exchange rates. We first compute the present value (in the numeraire, which is sterling) of receiving the spot exchange rate at some future date t_1. Then we review some needed results from Chapter 2 on forward prices.

Consider a forward contract that expires at date T. The value in terms of sterling of this forward contract at date T is

$$V(T) = S(T) - F(0,T),$$

where $S(T)$ is the sterling/dollar spot exchange rate at date T and $F(0,T)$ is the sterling/dollar forward exchange rate. The value of the forward contract in sterling at date 0 is therefore

$$V(0) = PV_0[S(T) - F(0,T)]$$
$$= PV_0[S(T)] - F(0,T)B_£(0,T),$$

where $B_£(0,T)$ is the value at date 0 of receiving one pound for sure at date T.

By market convention, the forward exchange rate, $F(0,T)$, is set such that the initial value of the forward contract is zero:

$$V(0) = 0,$$

which implies

$$PV_0[S(T)] = F(0,T)B_£(0,T). \tag{14.8}$$

This gives us the result needed from Chapter 2.

Now, consider a foreign currency swap of sterling for dollars where $N_£$ denotes the sterling principal, $N_\$$ denotes the dollar principal, $\overline{R}_£$ is the fixed sterling rate, and $\overline{R}_\$$ is the fixed dollar rate. In the foreign currency swap, suppose payments occur at dates $t_1, t_2, \ldots, t_n$ where t_n is the maturity of the swap.

At date t_1, the net payment is

$$\overline{R}_£ N_£ - S(t_1)\overline{R}_\$ N_\$,$$

assuming sterling is the numeraire.

The sterling value of this payment at date 0 is

$$B_£(0,t_1)\overline{R}_£ N_£ - PV_0[S(t_1)]\overline{R}_\$ N_\$.$$

Substituting Expression (14.8) into this expression gives

$$B_£(0,t_1)\overline{R}_£ N_£ - F(0,t_1)B_£(0,t_1)\overline{R}_\$ N_\$.$$

Repeating the argument for the remaining payments gives the sterling value of the swap at date 0:

$$V_{£}(0) = \sum_{j=1}^{n} B_{£}(0,t_j)[\overline{R}_{£}N_{£} - F(0,t_j)\overline{R}_{\$}N_{\$}] + B_{£}(0,t_n)[N_{£} - F(0,t_n)N_{\$}]. \quad (14.9)$$

The last term in Expression (14.9) represents the payment of principals at date t_n. Expression (14.9) gives the value of the plain vanilla foreign currency swap to counterparty A in terms of forward exchange rates and the zero-coupon bond prices, all of which are observable at date 0.

Variants of Foreign Currency Swaps

Here we note some different types of foreign currency swaps. In the plain vanilla foreign currency swap, illustrated in Figure 14.3, the interest rate payments were fixed. A variant to Figure 14.3 would be that counterparty A pays the floating U.S. LIBOR rate and counterparty B pays the floating U.K. LIBOR rate. A further variant on this last type of swap is that average LIBOR rates can be used in setting the floating rates. For example, the floating rate could be set using the weekly average LIBOR rate over the last month.

In the plain vanilla foreign currency swap, the principals are fixed. Another variant is for the principals to be amortized over the life of the swap. Although this does not exhaust the various possibilities, it completes our discussion of foreign currency swaps.

14.3 COMMODITY SWAPS

Now we examine commodity swaps. In a typical commodity swap, one counterparty makes periodic payments to the second counterparty at a fixed price per unit for a given notional quantity of some commodity. The second counterparty pays the first counterparty a floating price per unit for a given notional quantity of some commodity. The commodities are usually the same. The floating price is usually defined as an average price, the average being calculated using spot commodity prices over some predefined period.

EXAMPLE   **A Commodity Swap**

Consider an airline that has a constant demand for 20,000 barrels of oil per month and is concerned about volatile oil prices. It enters into a three-year commodity swap with a swap dealer. The current spot oil price is $18.10 per barrel. The airline agrees to make monthly payments to the swap dealer at a rate of $18.20 per barrel. The notional principal is 20,000 barrels. The swap dealer agrees to pay the airline the average daily price for oil during the preceding month. The details are shown in Figure 14.5.

FIGURE 14.5   *Commodity Swap*

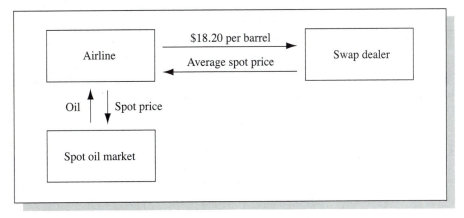

Note that in the commodity swap no exchange of notional commodities takes place between the counterparties.

The airline has reduced, but has not eliminated, its exposure to the volatile oil prices in the markets. This is because there may be a difference between the spot price and the average spot price in Figure 14.5. The airline is buying oil and paying the spot price, and from the swap dealer it receives the last month's average spot price. It also pays to the swap dealer $18.20 per barrel over the life of the contract. ■

Valuation of Commodity Swaps

A plain vanilla **commodity swap** is one in which counterparty A agrees to pay counterparty B a fixed amount X per unit of the commodity at dates $t_1, t_2, \ldots, t_n$ where t_n is the maturity of the swap. The notional principal is N_P units of the commodity. Counterparty B agrees to pay counterparty A the spot price of the commodity at dates $t_1, t_2, \ldots, t_n$.

We now value this commodity swap. Consider the first payment at time t_1. The net payment to counterparty A at date t_1 is

$$[S(t_1) - X]N_P.$$

Here, $S(t_1)$ is the spot price of the commodity at date t_1. The value of this payment at date 0 is

$$\{PV_0[S(T_1)] - XB(0,t_1)\}N_P. \tag{14.10}$$

In the absence of carrying costs and convenience yields, the present value of the spot price $S(t_1)$ would be equal to the current spot price. In practice, there are carrying costs and convenience yields.

As shown in Chapter 2, the use of forward prices incorporates these carrying costs and convenience yields. Drawing on this insight, we compute an alternative expression for the present value of the spot price $PV_0[S(t_1)]$ in terms of forward prices.

Consider a forward contract that expires at date t_1 written on this commodity. The cash flow to the forward contract when it expires at date t_1 is

$$S(t_1) - F(0, t_1),$$

where $F(0, t_1)$ is the forward price. The value of the forward contract at date 0 is

$$PV_0[S(t_1)] - F(0, t_1)B(0, t_1).$$

The forward price is set such that no cash is exchanged when the contract is written. This implies that the value of the forward contract when initiated is zero, that is,

$$PV_0[S(t_1)] = F(0, t_1)B(0, t_1). \tag{14.11}$$

This gives us the desired result. Using Expression (14.11), the value at date 0 of the first swap payment is therefore

$$[F(0, t_1) - X]B(0, t_1)N_P.$$

Repeating this argument for the remaining payments, we can show that the value of the commodity swap at date 0 is

$$V(0) = \sum_{j=1}^{n} [F(0, t_j) - X]B(0, t_j)N_P. \tag{14.12}$$

The value of the commodity swap in Expression (14.12) depends only on the forward prices of the underlying commodity and the zero-coupon bond prices, all of which are observable at date 0.

Variants of Commodity Swaps

We note here some different types of commodity swaps. In Figure 14.5, the oil price is quoted in dollars. However, the domestic currency for the airline may be, say, Deutsche marks, implying that the airline has a foreign currency exposure. The swap could be modified so that the swap dealer pays the airline the average Deutsche mark price of oil, averaged over the last month. This reduces, but does not remove, the foreign exchange exposure due to the difference remaining between the spot commodity price and the average spot commodity price.

Another variant of a commodity swap is that counterparty A pays counterparty B the average spot commodity price, averaged over a prespecified period. In return, counterparty B pays counterparty A the average spot price for a different commodity. Other modifications are possible. Our discussion of commodity swaps is now complete.

14.4 EQUITY SWAPS

Here we examine **equity swaps**. In a plain vanilla equity swap, one counterparty makes periodic fixed interest rate payments to the second counterparty for a given notional principal for a fixed period of time, the maturity of the swap. The second counterparty pays the first counterparty a floating rate pegged to the total return on some stock index. Total return includes dividends and capital gains, though in some equity swaps returns are defined to mean the price change in the index excluding any dividend payments. Notional principals are not exchanged. The index may be a broadly based index, such as the New York Stock Exchange index, the S&P 500 index, or the Nikkei index, or it could be a specific industry group, such as an oil industry index or a utility index.

EXAMPLE   **Plain Vanilla Equity Swap**

We illustrate here the use of an equity swap. Consider the portfolio of an equity fund the return of which is highly correlated to the S&P 100 stock index. The fund manager is concerned about the risk exposure and decides to enter into an equity swap.

The fund manager agrees to pay the swap dealer the S&P 100 return and receive from the swap dealer a fixed rate of 8.75 percent per annum. These payments are to be made quarterly and the notional principal is fixed at 100 million dollars. This arrangement is illustrated in Figure 14.6. ∎

FIGURE 14.6   *Plain Vanilla Equity Swap*

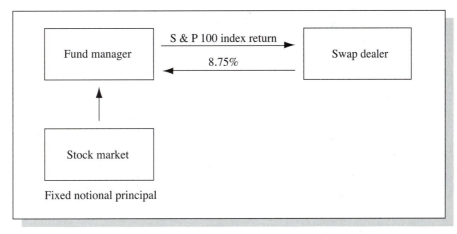

This simple example demonstrates that the fund manager can alter the risk exposure of the fund by using an equity swap. In the example, the fund manager transformed an equity portfolio into a riskless return of 8.75%, ignoring counterparty risk Note that the return on the index can be positive or negative. In the example, if it is positive, the fund manager pays the swap dealer. If it is negative, the swap dealer pays the fund manager.

Valuation

In a plain vanilla equity swap let N_P be the notional principal and let t_n be the maturity date of the swap. Let counterparty A agree to pay counterparty B the return on an index at dates $t_1, t_2, \ldots, t_n$. The return on the index at date t_j is defined by

$$R(t_j) \equiv \frac{I(t_j) + d(t_j)}{I(t_{j-1})} - 1, \tag{14.13}$$

where $I(t_j)$ denotes the value of the index at date t and $d(t_j)$ denotes the dividends paid over the period t_{j-1} to t_j by the stocks in the index.

On the other side of the swap, counterparty B agrees to pay counterparty A a fixed return $\bar{R}$ at dates $t_1, t_2, \ldots, t_n$.

We now value this swap at date 0 where $t_0 \le 0 < t_1$. For the moment, we put aside the valuation of the first payment at date t_1 and consider the payment at date t_n for $n > 1$. The dollar value of the net payment to counterparty A at date t_n is

$$[\bar{R} - R(t_n)]N_P. \tag{14.14}$$

The present value of this payment at date t_{n-1} is

$$\{\bar{R}B(t_{n-1}, t_n) - PV_{t_{n-1}}[R(t_n)]\}N_P. \tag{14.15}$$

To simplify Expression (14.15) we need to evaluate the present value at date t_{n-1} of the return on the index. First, the present value of the index plus the dividends paid by the stocks in the index equals the current value of the index:

$$PV_{t_{n-1}}[I(t_n) + d(t_n)] = I(t_{n-1}). \tag{14.16}$$

This can be written in the form

$$PV_{t_{n-1}}\left[\frac{I(t_n) + d(t_n)}{I(t_{n-1})}\right] = 1. \tag{14.17}$$

We see that, in equilibrium, the present value at date t_{n-1} of the return from investing one dollar in the index must equal one. The present value of the rate of return, using Expression (14.17), is thus

$$PV_{t_{n-1}}[R(t_n)] = PV_{t_{n-1}}\left[\frac{I(t_n) + d_n(t_n)}{I(t_{n-1})}\right] - PV_{t_{n-1}}[1]$$

$$= 1 - B(t_{n-1}, t_n), \tag{14.18}$$

which gives us our first result.

Substituting Expression (14.18) into (14.15), the present value at date t_{n-1} of the net payment to counterparty A is

$$\{\overline{R}B(t_{n-1}, t_n) - [1 - B(t_{n-1}, t_n)]\}N_P$$

and the present value of this net payment at date 0 is

$$\{\overline{R}B(0, t_n) - [B(0, t_{n-1}) - B(0, t_n)]\}N_P. \tag{14.19}$$

This computation uses the fact that $PV_0[B(t_{n-1}, t_n)] = B(0, t_n)$.

The valuation of the first payment is slightly more complicated. The return on the index is

$$\overline{R}(t_1) = \frac{I(t_1) + d(t_1)}{I(t_0)} - 1.$$

Using Expression (14.17),

$$PV_0[I(t_1) + d_1(t_1)] = I(0),$$

implying

$$PV_0[R(t_1)] = \frac{I(0)}{I(t_0)} - B(0, t_1).$$

The present value of the net payment at date 0 is

$$\left\{\overline{R}B(0, t_1) - \left[\frac{I(0)}{I(t_0)} - B(0, t_1)\right]\right\}N_p.$$

The value at date 0 of all the net payments to counterparty A is

$$V(0) = \left\{\overline{R}\sum_{j=1}^{n} B(0, t_j) - \left[\frac{I(0)}{I(t_0)} - B(0, t_n)\right]\right\}N_p.$$

When the swap is initiated, the fiscal rate $\overline{R}$ is usually set such that the initial value of the swap is zero; that is, $\overline{R}$ is set such that

$$\overline{R}\sum_{j=1}^{n} B(0, t_j) - [1 - B(0, t_n)] = 0, \tag{14.20}$$

given that date 0 is equal to date t_0.

Variants of the Basic Equity Swap

There are many variants on the basic equity swap. In Figure 14.6, the swap dealer is paying a fixed interest rate. An alternative structure is to use a floating LIBOR rate instead of a fixed rate. The notional principal in Figure 14.6 is also fixed. An alternative structure is for the notional principal to fluctuate either with the level of net payments made in the swap or with the level of the market index.

A third variant is for a cap to be put on the equity return. Referring to Figure 14.6, if the return on the S&P 100 index goes above the cap rate, the fund manager pays the swap dealer the cap rate. Given that the return on the index can be negative, a floor can also be put on the equity return.

A fourth variant is for the swap to have two equity legs rather than one. For example, the fund manager pays the swap dealer the return on, say, the S&P 100 index and receives, say, the return on the Nikkei index. The returns on the foreign index may involve the incorporation of the foreign spot exchange rate. Alternatively, the foreign exchange rate can be artificially set at unity.

A final variant is for the swap to have two equity legs, with each leg being defined as the return on an individual stock. For example, a financial institution pays the return on, say, IBM shares and receives the return on, say, Ford Motor Company shares. Such a swap is sometimes called a **credit swap**. This is a misnomer, because what is being swapped is not only credit risk but also the idiosyncratic return of one stock for the idiosyncratic return of another stock. Our discussion of equity swaps is now complete.

14.5 SUMMARY

In an **interest rate swap**, counterparty A agrees to pay counterparty B interest at a fixed rate and receive interest at a floating rate. The same notional principal is used in determining the size of the payments, and there is no exchange of principal. An interest rate swap can be used to transform a fixed rate loan extending over many years into a floating rate loan and vice versa.

In a **foreign currency swap**, one counterparty agrees to pay the second counterparty interest on a principal amount in one currency and receive interest on a principal amount in another currency. Principal amounts are exchanged at the beginning and the end of the life or tenor of the swap. A foreign currency swap can be used to transform a loan in one currency into a loan in another currency.

In a **commodity swap**, one counterparty agrees to pay the second counterparty a fixed rate per unit for a given notional quantity of some commodity and to receive a floating rate per unit for the same notional quantity. The floating rate is usually averaged over some prespecified period. The notional quantities of the commodity are not exchanged. A commodity swap can be used to transform variable spot market transactions into a quasi-fixed price series of transactions and vice versa.

In an **equity swap**, one counterparty agrees to pay the second counterparty a fixed rate of interest based on a notional principal and to receive the total returns

from some market index. There is no exchange of principal. An equity swap can be used to transform a fixed income stream into an equity investment and vice versa.

In all cases a swap is a mechanism to transform a series of cash flows with a set of particular characteristics into a series of cash flows with a different set of characteristics. In a swap there is the risk that a counterparty might default. We discuss counterparty risk in Chapter 18.

REFERENCES

A detailed description of swaps:

Marshall, J. F., and K. R. Kapner, 1993. *The Swap Market.* Miami, Florida: Kolb Publishing.

General references:

Chance, D., and D. Rich, 1998. "The Pricing of Equity Swaps and Swaptions." *The Journal of Derivatives* 5, 19–31.

Falloon, W., 1993. "Burnt Offerings." *Risk* 6, 21–27.

Marshall, J. F., E. H. Sorensen, and A. L. Tucker, 1992. "Equity Derivatives: The Plain Vanilla Equity Swap and Its Variants." *Journal of Financial Engineering* 1, 219–241.

Rendleman, R. J., 1992. "How Risks Are Shared in Interest Rate Swaps." *Journal of Financial Services Research* 7, 5–34.

Schwartz, R. J., and C. W. Smith, 1993. *Advanced Strategies in Financial Risk Management.* Englewood Cliffs, N.J.: New York Institute of Finance.

Smith, C. W., C. W. Smithson, and L. M. Wakeman, 1986. "The Evolving Market for Swaps." *Midland Corporate Finance Journal* 3, 20–32.

Turnbull, S. M., 1987. "Swaps: A Zero Sum Game?" *Financial Management* 16, 15–21.

Turnbull, S. M., 1993. "Pricing and Hedging Diff Swaps." *Journal of Financial Engineering* 2, 297–333.

QUESTIONS

Question 1

Using the information below, determine the swap rate on a five-year swap, receiving fixed payments and paying floating rate payments. The floating payments are determined using LIBOR.

PAYMENT DATES (YEARS)	TREASURY BILL PRICES $B(0, T)$	EURODOLLAR DEPOSIT $L(0, T)$
0.5	0.9772	0.9748
1.0	0.9539	0.9492

1.5	0.9302	0.9227
2.0	0.9063	0.8960
2.5	0.8821	0.8687
3.0	0.8578	0.8413
3.5	0.8335	0.8136
4.0	0.8093	0.7857
4.5	0.7851	0.7577
5.0	0.7611	0.7302

Question 2

An institution has sold a swap for which it receives fixed payments and pays floating payments. The current tenor of the swap is five years. The swap rate is 6.50 percent per annum. Use the information in Question 1 to determine the value of the swap. The notional principal is $20 million.

Question 3

In Question 2, what is the value of the swap if the notional principal decreases by half a million dollars for each payment?

Question 4

In a four-year interest rate swap, counterparty A receives floating rate payments priced using the six-month LIBOR rate and agrees to make floating rate payments priced using the six-month Treasury bill rate plus a spread, Δ. The reset dates are every six months. Use the information in Question 1 to determine the spread Δ such that the initial value of the swap is zero.

Question 5

A U.S. firm is making fixed semiannual payments in Japanese yen. The firm would like to swap these fixed yen payments for a series of fixed semiannual dollar payments. Note that there is no exchange of principal. Describe a variant of a foreign currency swap that would meet the firm's needs.

Question 6

In a foreign currency swap, counterparty A is receiving fixed sterling interest rate payments at an interest rate of $7\frac{1}{4}$ percent per annum on a principal of 50 million pounds sterling. Counterparty A agrees to make fixed dollar interest rate payments on a principal of 80.5 million dollars. Interest rate payments are made every six months and the tenor of the swap is four years. The current spot exchange rate is 1.6095 $/£. Use the information below to determine the swap rate for the dollar payments.

MATURITY (YEARS)	DOLLAR TREASURY BILL PRICE	STERLING ZERO-COUPON DEFAULT-FREE BOND PRICE
T	$B(0,T)$	$B_£(0,T)$
0.5	0.9772	0.9688
1.0	0.9539	0.9372
1.5	0.9302	0.9055
2.0	0.9063	0.8738
2.5	0.8821	0.8423
3.0	0.8578	0.8112
3.5	0.8335	0.7805
4.0	0.8093	0.7504

Question 7

A U.S. company is selling equipment to a country with little foreign reserves. The country pays for the equipment by supplying the U.S. company with a fixed amount of minerals, which the U.S. company can then sell on the world markets to generate dollar inflows. This exposes the U.S. company to uncertainty about the dollar size of the inflows. Explain how a commodity swap could remove this risk.

Question 8

A firm uses gold in its production process. The firm enters into a two-year swap contract. The current spot price for gold is $382 per troy ounce. The firm agrees to make payments every six months at a rate of X per troy ounce to the swap dealer. The notional principal is 10,000 troy ounces. The swap dealer agrees to pay the firm the spot price at the payment date. The price X is set such that the initial value of the swap is zero. Use the information below to determine the price X.

DATE T (YEARS)	FORWARD PRICE FOR GOLD $F(0,T)$	TREASURY BILL PRICE $B(0,T)$
0.5	392.50	0.9660
1.0	402.60	0.9434
1.5	413.00	0.9147
2.0	423.70	0.8863

Question 9

Using the information in Question 8, suppose that the firm enters into a deferred commodity swap, with the first payment occurring in one year's time. The firm will make three fixed rate payments, with the last payment occurring in two years' time. What is price X such that the value today of the deferred swap is zero?

Question 10

A bond portfolio manager wants to enhance the performance of the portfolio by adding a variable equity return. Explain how an equity swap could achieve this objective.

The bond portfolio's lawyers are concerned that the use of an equity swap will increase the risk of the portfolio by an unacceptable amount, given that returns on an index can be negative. Describe how the use of options could alleviate these concerns.

CHAPTER 15

INTEREST RATE DERIVATIVES

15.0 INTRODUCTION

When we price equity derivatives, the initial value of the stock is given, and we construct a lattice of future stock prices. An analogous procedure works for pricing **interest rate derivatives**. Consider pricing an option written on a Treasury bill. Given the initial price of the Treasury bill, we must model its possible values over the life of the option. We must do this in a way that (1) is consistent with the absence of arbitrage, (2) is consistent with the initial term structure, and (3) recognizes that the Treasury bill pays a known fixed amount (the principal) at maturity.

Describing this arbitrage-free evolution of the Treasury bill's price is equivalent to modeling the evolution of the term structure of interest rates. This presents a more difficult problem than that encountered for equity derivatives. A number of different solutions exist for this problem. We choose to model the evolution of the term structure by concentrating on the short-term interest rate.

In modeling the short-term interest rate, it is essential to specify how many sources of uncertainty affect its evolution. For this chapter we assume that there is only one source of uncertainty, giving a **one-factor model**. If we assumed that there are two sources of uncertainty affecting the evolution of the interest rate, this would create a **two-factor model**.[1] Using a one-factor model is a strong assumption because the empirical evidence suggests that there is more than one factor. Nonetheless, we choose the one-factor model to illustrate the procedure. Once this case is mastered, the multiple-factor extension follows similarly in a straightforward fashion.

15.1 CONSTRUCTION OF THE LATTICE

Here we explain how to construct a lattice of future spot interest rates. We use the binomial model of Chapter 4, but this time for interest rate movements. In the next section, we will formalize our discussion about the underlying assumptions.

---

[1] The difference between a one- and two-factor model can be understood as follows. A one-factor model has one source of uncertainty. The randomness underlying its evolution at any node can be generated via tossing *one* (unbiased) coin. A two-factor model has two sources of uncertainty. The generation of the evolution of the term structure at any node necessitates the tossing of at least *two* (unbiased) coins.

For pricing interest rate derivatives, we must construct a lattice of spot interest rates that is consistent with the observed initial term structure. For clarity, we choose the time between changes in the spot rate of interest to be one year. In practice, a shorter interval would be used, depending on the degree of accuracy required.

The spot rate of interest corresponds to the rate of interest over the interval in the lattice. Because our interval length is one year, we are modeling the one-year spot interest rate. If our interval length had been one week, we would be modeling the one-week spot interest rate.

To illustrate the construction, let us consider the initial term structure in Table 15.1. In this table, the first column gives the years until maturity. The second column gives the zero-coupon bond prices. The third column gives the yield-to-maturity for each bond. The last column refers to the volatility of the spot rate of interest. In the last column, the first number, 0.017, refers to the volatility of the spot interest rate at the end of the first year. The second number, 0.015, refers to the volatility of the spot interest rate at the end of the second year, given that the spot interest rate at the end of the first year is known. This specification of the volatility at the different future intervals is referred to as the **term structure of volatilities**.

Let $B(0, t)$ denote the date-0 value of a zero-coupon default-free bond that matures at the end of year t. From Table 15.1, observe that $B(0, 1) = 0.9399$. For convenience, we use continuously compounded interest rates. The current one-year rate of interest, $r(0)$, is defined by

$$0.9399 = \exp[-r(0)],$$

implying

$$r(0) = 6.1982 \text{ percent.}$$

TABLE 15.1 *Interest Rates Are Assumed to Be Normally Distributed*

INITIAL DATA			
MATURITY (YEARS)	BOND PRICES* $B(0, T)$	YIELD** (PERCENT)	VOLATILITY***
1	0.9399	6.1982	0.017
2	0.8798	6.4030	0.015
3	0.8137	6.8721	0.011
4	0.7552	7.0193	0.0075

*All bonds have zero coupons and are default-free.

**Continuously compounded yield.

***Volatility refers to the volatility of the spot interest rate.

FIGURE 15.1 *Finding the Short-Term Rates to Price a Two-Year Zero-Coupon Treasury Bond*

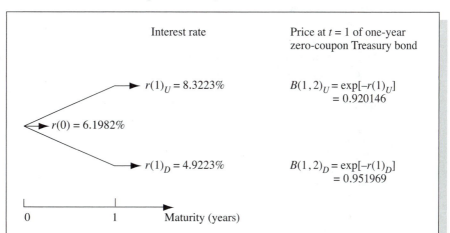

At the end of the first year, we assume that the one-year spot interest rate can take one of only two possible values, denoted by $r(1)_U$ and $r(1)_D$, respectively. This is the one-factor assumption. We must pick these values to be consistent with the initial term structure as shown in Table 15.1; we do this by trial and error. Let us guess the values

$$r(1)_U = 8.3223 \text{ percent}$$

and

$$r(1)_D = 4.9223 \text{ percent}$$

as shown in Figure 15.1.

Let $B(1,2)$ denote the value at date 1 of a zero-coupon default-free bond that matures at date 2. As shown in Figure 15.1, using the date-1 spot interest rates, we can compute the possible date-1 bond prices as

$$B(1,2) = \begin{cases} 0.920146 & \text{if} \quad r(1)_U \text{ occurs.} \\ 0.951969 & \text{if} \quad r(1)_D \text{ occurs.} \end{cases}$$

In building this lattice, it is essential to construct it so that there are no arbitrage opportunities implicitly within it. We showed in Chapter 6 that in a binomial lattice for equity derivatives, there is no arbitrage between the stock and the money market account if and only if there exists a unique probability such that the stock price normalized by the money market account's value follows a martingale.

We referred to this probability as a martingale probability. Fortunately, this theorem can be generalized to apply to the term structure of zero-coupon default-free bond prices as well.

Although we do not prove this result here, we use the insight. Analogously stated, in a one-factor model, there is no arbitrage among all the zero-coupon bonds and the money market account if and only if there exists a unique probability such that all the zero-coupon bond prices normalized by the money market account's value follow a martingale.[2] We utilize the "if" part of this theorem for the subsequent analysis.

We want to ensure that the evolution of the term structure of interest rates is arbitrage-free. That is, we want to ensure that no arbitrage opportunities exist among the zero-coupon bonds and the money market account. To do this via the above-stated theorem, we assume that there exists a unique martingale probability such that normalized zero-coupon bond prices follow a martingale.

This condition is that

$$B(0,2)/A(0) = E^{\pi}[B(1,2)/A(1)], \tag{15.1}$$

where $A(t)$ denotes the value of the money market account at date t.

Without loss of generality, we assume that the martingale probability of each state occurring is 0.5.[3]

By definition, $A(0) \equiv 1$ and $A(1) = \exp(r(0)) = \exp(0.061982)$. Substituting into Expression (15.1) gives

$$B(0,2) = \exp(-0.061982)(0.5 \times 0.920146 + 0.5 \times 0.951969)$$
$$= 0.8798,$$

which agrees with the value in Table 15.1. Our guess on the possible values for the spot interest rate at date 1 is correct.

We must also check that our estimates are consistent with the volatility given in Table 15.1. The volatility of the spot interest rate at time t is defined to be the standard deviation of the change in the spot interest rate over the next time interval. In symbols,

$$\sigma(t) \equiv \sqrt{\text{var}}^{\pi}(\Delta r(t)) \equiv \sqrt{E^{\pi}\{[\Delta r(t) - E^{\pi}(\Delta r(t))]^2\}}.$$

---

[2]For a proof of this result, see Jarrow (1995).

[3]This assumption is without loss of generality because in constructing a lattice there are usually three unknowns: (i) the magnitude of the spot rate "up," (ii) the magnitude of the spot rate "down," and (iii) the martingale probability. We usually have two constraints: (i) the expected change in the spot rate, and (ii) the volatility of the spot rate. Three unknowns-and two constraints gives 1 degree of freedom, and this degree of freedom allows the specification of $\pi = \frac{1}{2}$.

The volatility is computed using the martingale probabilities. Volatility measures the dispersion or the variability in spot rates across time. As such, it is an important statistic for understanding the term structure of the interest rate's evolution. The volatility is determined[4] by

$$\sigma(0) = [r(1)_U - r(1)_D]/2. \tag{15.2}$$

By convention, $r(1)_U$ is greater than $r(1)_D$.

Substituting for $r(1)_U$ and $r(1)_D$ gives

$$[r(1)_U - r(1)_D]/2 = (0.083223 - 0.049223)/2$$
$$= 0.017,$$

which agrees with Table 15.1. Had we been wrong, we would have revised $r(1)_U$ and $r(1)_D$ by iteration until these two conditions were satisfied.

Continuing, at the end of the first year, if the one-year rate of interest is $r(1)_U$, then at the end of the second year the one-year spot rate can have one of two possible values: $r(2)_{UU}$ or $r(2)_{UD}$. Similarly, if the one-year rate of interest at date 1 is $r(1)_D$, then the spot rate at date 2 can take the values $r(2)_{DU}$ or $r(2)_{DD}$, shown in Figure 15.2. The lattice is constructed so that it recombines.

We need to choose $r(2)_{UU}$, $r(2)_{DU}$, and $r(2)_{DD}$ to be consistent with the observed term structure of interest rates and volatilities, as shown in Table 15.1.

We first match the volatilities. Let us guess that $r(2)_{UU} = 10.8583$ percent. From Table 15.1, the spot rate volatility is 0.015, implying that for $r(2)_{UU}$ greater than $r(2)_{UD}$,

$$\sigma(1) = 0.015 = [r(2)_{UU} - r(2)_{UD}]/2, \tag{15.3}$$

which in turn implies that

$$r(2)_{UD} = 0.108583 - 2 \times 0.015$$
$$= 7.8583 \text{ percent.}$$

---

[4]If a random variable can take one of two possible values, a or b, with probability p and $(1 - p)$, respectively, then

    1) expected value $= a \times p + b \times (1 - p)$

and

    2) variance, σ^2
$$= \{a - [ap + b(1 - p)]\}^2 p + \{b - [ap + b(1 - p)]\}^2 (1 - p)$$
$$= (a - b)^2 p(1 - p).$$

In this example, $p \equiv \frac{1}{2}$, $a \equiv r(1)_U$, and $b \equiv r(1)_D$.

FIGURE 15.2   *Finding the Short-Term Rates to Price a Three-Year*
            Zero-Coupon Treasury Bond

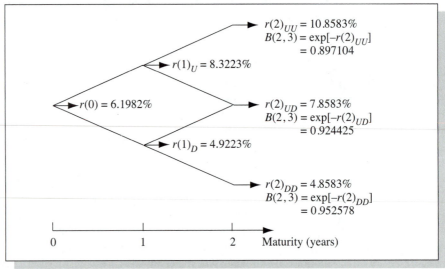

If at date 1 the one-year spot interest rate is $r(1)_D$, then because $r(2)_{DU}$ is greater than $r(2)_{DD}$,

$$\sigma(1) = 0.015 = [r(2)_{DU} - r(2)_{DD}]/2,$$

implying

$$r(2)_{DD} = 0.078583 - 2 \times 0.015$$
$$= 4.8583 \text{ percent.}$$

These choices of the date-2 spot rates match the term structure of volatilities. We next check to see if these values are consistent with the initial term structure of interest rates.

Using the three different spot rates previously computed, the three values for the bond prices for $B(2,3)$ are shown in Figure 15.2.

To ensure no arbitrage, the bond prices in the lattice must satisfy the following condition:

$$B(1,3)/A(1) = E^{\pi}[B(2,3)/A(2)].\qquad (15.4)$$

We compute these values. At the end of the first year, the spot interest rate can either be 8.3223 percent or 4.9223 percent. Suppose that we are at the upper node in the lat-

tice, where $r(1)_U = 8.3223$ percent. The value of the money market account at the end of the first year is

$$A(1) = \exp(0.061982), \tag{15.5}$$

and at the end of the second year it is

$$A(2)_U = \exp(r(0)) \times \exp(r(1)_U) = \exp(0.061982) \times \exp(0.083223). \tag{15.6}$$

It is important to realize that at the end of the first year, given that we are at the upper node, this value of $A(2)_U$ is known. Therefore, substituting Expressions (15.5) and (15.6) into Expression (15.4) and simplifying gives

$$\begin{aligned}
B(1,3)_U &\equiv \exp(-0.083223)E^{\pi}[B(2,3)] \\
&= \exp(-0.083223) \times (0.5 \times 0.897104 + 0.5 \times 0.924425) \\
&= 0.838036.
\end{aligned}$$

FIGURE 15.3 *Lattice of Short-Term Rates*

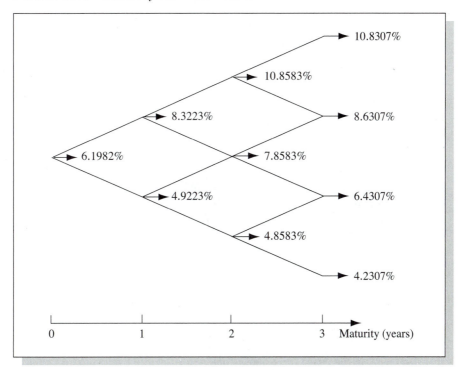

FIGURE 15.4   *Evolution of the Term Structure*

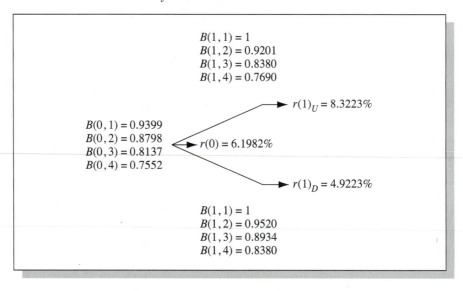

Suppose that at the end of the first year we are at the lower node in the lattice, so the spot interest rate $r(1)_D$ is 4.9223 percent. The value of the money market account at the end of the first year is

$$A(1) = \exp(0.061982)$$

and at the end of the second year it is

$$A(2)_D = \exp(r(0)) \times \exp(r(1)_D) = \exp(0.061982) \times \exp(0.049223).$$

Again, $A(2)_D$ is known at this node. Substituting into Expression (15.4) and simplifying gives

$$B(1,3)_D = \exp(-0.049223) \times (0.5 \times 0.924425 + 0.5 \times 0.952578)$$
$$= 0.893424.$$

Finally, at time 0, to ensure no arbitrage, the price of $B(0, 3)$ must satisfy the following condition:

$$B(0,3)/A(0) = E^\pi[B(1,3)/A(1)].$$

We check to see if the above condition is satisfied. Substituting in the relevant quantities gives

$$B(0,3) = \exp(-0.061982) \times (0.5 \times B(1,2)_U + 0.5 \times B(1,2)_D)$$
$$= \exp(-0.061982) \times (0.5 \times 0.838036 + 0.5 \times 0.893424)$$
$$= 0.8137,$$

which agrees with the initial value in Table 15.1.

We leave to the reader to verify that the spot interest rates given in Figure 15.3 correctly price the four-year zero-coupon Treasury bill in Table 15.1.

Figure 15.3 describes the spot interest rate process given the initial term structure of interest rates and volatilities. It also implies the evolution of the term structure of interest rates, illustrated in Figure 15.4, in which the initial term structure is shown and its evolution is given up to date 1.

Our discussion of lattice construction is now complete.

15.2   SPOT RATE PROCESS

Here we present the general model for the spot rate process. We formalize our previous example and explain the underlying structure. For the most part, this involves little more than replacing numbers with algebraic symbols.

First we need to make some assumptions about the probability distribution approximated by the evolution of the spot interest rates in our lattice. We consider two possible cases: (1) changes in interest rates follow a normal probability distribution, and (2) changes in interest rates follow a lognormal probability distribution. Both cases are used in practice.

Normal Distribution

If one believes that changes in spot interest rates are normally distributed,[5] then the evolution of the spot interest rate can be described by

$$\Delta r(t) = [a(t) - b(t)r(t)]\Delta + \sigma(t)\Delta W(t), \tag{15.7}$$

where $\Delta r(t) \equiv r(t + \Delta) - r(\Delta)$, Δ is the length of the time interval, $a(t)$, $b(t)$ are parameters, $\sigma(t)$ is the volatility at date t, and $\Delta W(t)$ is a normally distributed random variable with zero mean and variance Δ.

Expression (15.7) is under the equivalent martingale probabilities and implies that spot interest rates are normally distributed. This normality assumption is a continuous time limit of the Ho-Lee (1986) model.

The parameters $a(t)$, $b(t)$, and $\sigma(t)$ are deterministic functions of time and are independent of the spot rate, $r(t)$. This functional dependence on date t is necessary for the implied zero-coupon bond prices to be calibrated to match the observed initial term structure of interest rates.

---

[5]As discussed in the following text, this belief is under the martingale probabilities, *not* the actual or empirical probabilities.

Under Expression (15.7) we have

$$E^{\pi}(\Delta r(t)) = [a(t) - b(t)r(t)]\Delta$$

and

$$\sqrt{\mathrm{var}}^{\pi}(\Delta r(t)) = \sigma(t)\sqrt{\Delta}.$$

The expected change in spot rates is determined by the parameters $a(t)$ and $b(t)$. The volatility of the change in the spot rate is $\sigma(t)\sqrt{\Delta}$. These parameters can be estimated from historic time series observations of changes in spot rates using standard statistical procedures. Alternatively, they can be implicitly estimated by calibrating the model's values for bonds and derivatives to market prices.

Analogously to Chapter 4, we can approximate this process with a binomial model:

$$r(t + \Delta) - r(t) = \begin{cases} [a(t) - b(t)r(t)]\Delta + \sigma(t)\sqrt{\Delta} & \text{with probability } \frac{1}{2} \\ [a(t) - b(t)r(t)]\Delta - \sigma(t)\sqrt{\Delta} & \text{with probability } \frac{1}{2} \end{cases}. \quad (15.8)$$

For example, if today's spot interest rate is $r(0)$, at the end of the first interval the spot interest rate takes one of two values:

$$r(1)_U \equiv r(0) + [a(0) - b(0)r(0)]\Delta + \sigma(0)\sqrt{\Delta} \quad \text{with probability } \frac{1}{2}$$

and

$$r(1)_D \equiv r(0) + [a(0) - b(0)r(0)]\Delta - \sigma(0)\sqrt{\Delta} \quad \text{with probability } \frac{1}{2}. \quad (15.9)$$

Note that $r(1)_U > r(1)_D$, given that the volatility $\sigma(0)$ is positive.

From Expression (15.9) we have

$$[r(1)_U - r(1)_D]/2 = \sigma(0)\sqrt{\Delta}. \quad (15.10)$$

We can now recognize Expression (15.2) in the previous example as being a special case of Expression (15.10) in which the time interval Δ is set equal to one.

It is easy to generalize Expression (15.10). At date t, if the spot interest is $r(t)$, then one period later, using Expression (15.8), the interest rate will be either

$$r(t + \Delta)_U - r(t) = [a(t) - b(t)r(t)]\Delta + \sigma(t)\sqrt{\Delta}$$

or

$$r(t + \Delta)_D - r(t) = [a(t) - b(t)r(t)]\Delta - \sigma(t)\sqrt{\Delta}.$$

Subtracting the above two equations gives

$$[r(t + \Delta)_U - r(t + \Delta)_D]/2 = \sigma(t)\sqrt{\Delta}. \quad (15.11)$$

This expression shows how the term structure of volatilities determines the *spread* between the two possible spot interest rates at date $t + \Delta$.

The *level* of the spot interest rates at date $t + \Delta$ is determined by the initial term structure of interest rates via the martingale relation satisfied by the normalized zero-coupon bond prices.

The path of the short-term interest rate over two intervals is shown in Figure 15.5. Referring to Figure 15.5, we investigate when the lattice recombines, that is, whether $r(2)_{UD}$ equals $r(2)_{DU}$.

For these two rates to be equal, we require that

$$r(1)_U + [a(1) - b(1)r(1)_U]\Delta - \sigma(1)\sqrt{\Delta}$$
$$= r(1)_D + [a(1) - b(1)r(1)_D]\Delta + \sigma(1)\sqrt{\Delta},$$

which implies

$$[r(1)_U - r(1)_D]/2 - b(1)\Delta[r(1)_U - r(1)_D]/2 = \sigma(1)\sqrt{\Delta}.$$

Substituting Expression (15.10) into this equation gives, after simplification,

$$[1 - b(1)\Delta]\sigma(0) = \sigma(1). \tag{15.12}$$

This equation determines the parameter $b(1)$.

FIGURE 15.5 *The Short-Term Rate Process*

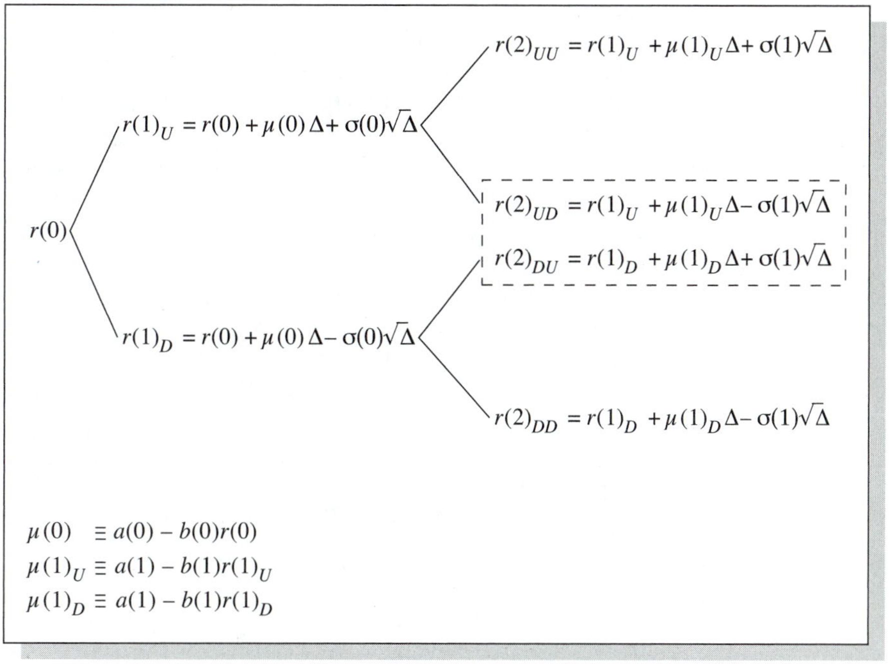

$$r(2)_{UU} = r(1)_U + \mu(1)_U\Delta + \sigma(1)\sqrt{\Delta}$$

$$r(1)_U = r(0) + \mu(0)\Delta + \sigma(0)\sqrt{\Delta}$$

$$r(2)_{UD} = r(1)_U + \mu(1)_U\Delta - \sigma(1)\sqrt{\Delta}$$
$$r(2)_{DU} = r(1)_D + \mu(1)_D\Delta + \sigma(1)\sqrt{\Delta}$$

$$r(0)$$

$$r(1)_D = r(0) + \mu(0)\Delta - \sigma(0)\sqrt{\Delta}$$

$$r(2)_{DD} = r(1)_D + \mu(1)_D\Delta - \sigma(1)\sqrt{\Delta}$$

$$\mu(0) \equiv a(0) - b(0)r(0)$$
$$\mu(1)_U \equiv a(1) - b(1)r(1)_U$$
$$\mu(1)_D \equiv a(1) - b(1)r(1)_D$$

Expression (15.12) implies that the parameters $b(1)$, $\sigma(0)$, and $\sigma(1)$ are related. In Expression (15.12), for $b(1)$ to be positive, that is, $b(1) > 0$, the volatility of the spot rate at date 1, $\sigma(1)$ must be less than the volatility at date 0, $\sigma(0)$, that is, the volatility of the spot rate of interest must decrease over time. If $b(1) = 0$, volatilities are constant across time. Finally, if $b(1) < 0$, volatilties increase.

We can show that if $b(t)$ is positive, that is, $b(t) > 0$, the time-conditional variance of $r(t)$ is bounded. This follows because $\sigma(t)$ is decreasing in t, so its largest value (the upper bound) occurs at date 0. It is not the case if $b(t)$ is zero for all t, for then the variance is proportional to t. The Ho-Lee (1986) model, for example, assumes $b(t)$ is zero.

In the financial economics literature, Expression (15.7) is usually thought of as implying **mean reversion**, that is, spot interest rates tend toward a long-run mean. This is misleading because Expression (15.7) describes the interest rate movements under the equivalent martingale probabilities and not the empirical or true probabilities. The behavior of spot rates differ under these two different probabilities. An alternative and more precise way of describing Expression (15.7) is to say that the unconditional variance of the spot interest rate is finite.[6]

Given that we have determined the spot rate at each node of the lattice, we do not need to explicitly calculate the actual values of the parameters $\{a(t)\}$ and $\{b(t)\}$. They are implied by the lattice. It should be noted that the term structure of volatilities implicitly determines the parameter $\{b(t)\}$, while the term structure of interest rates implicitly determines the parameter $\{a(t)\}$.

EXAMPLE   **Normal Distribution**

We illustrate here the calculation of the parameters $a(t)$, $b(t)$ for normally distributed spot rates. We use the information in Figure 15.3 and Table 15.1 to compute the values of $a(t)$ and $b(t)$. The length of each interval is one year, implying $\Delta = 1$.

Recall that Figure 15.3 gives the spot interest rate evolution consistent with the initial term structure of interest rates and volatilities in Table 15.1. For the first period, using Expression (15.9),

$$a(0) - b(0)r(0) = r(1)_U - r(0) - \sigma(0)$$
$$= 0.083223 - 0.061982 - 0.017$$
$$= 0.004241$$

and

$$a(0) - b(0)r(0) = r(1)_D - r(0) + \sigma(0)$$
$$= 0.049223 - 0.061982 + 0.017$$
$$= 0.004241.$$

---

[6]This is explained in Musiela *et al.* (1993).

This is one equation in two unknowns. Without additional information we do not have an unique solution, so arbitrarily[7] we set

$a(0) = 0.004241$
$b(0) = 0.0.$

For the second period, if $r(1)_U = 8.3223$ percent,

$$a(1) - b(1) \times r(1)_U = r(2)_{UU} - r(1)_U - \sigma(1)$$
$$= 0.108583 - 0.083223 - 0.015$$
$$= 0.01036$$

and

$$a(1) - b(1) \times r(1)_U = r(2)_{UD} - r(1)_U + \sigma(1)$$
$$= 0.078583 - 0.083223 + 0.015$$
$$= 0.01036.$$

From Expression (15.12),

$$b(1) = 1 - \sigma(1)/\sigma(0)$$
$$= 1 - 0.015/0.017$$
$$= 0.117647.$$

Therefore,

$a(1) = 0.02015094.$

If the spot interest is $r(1)_D = 4.9223$ percent, we need to check that we get the same values for $a(1)$ and $b(1)$. Similar computations yield

$$a(1) - b(1) \times r(1)_D = r(2)_{DU} - r(1)_D - \sigma(1)$$
$$= 0.078583 - 0.049223 - 0.015$$
$$= 0.01436$$

and

$$a(1) - b(1) \times r(1)_D = r(2)_{DD} - r(1)_D + \sigma(1)$$
$$= 0.048583 - 0.049223 + 0.015$$
$$= 0.01436.$$

---

[7]Rather than arbitrarily determining $a(0)$, $b(0)$, we could have calibrated them to some other market observable.

Given the value of $b(1)$, then

$$a(1) = 0.01436 + b(1) \times 0.049223$$
$$= 0.02015094,$$

implying that we have consistency.
We leave it to the reader to verify that

$$a(2) = 0.01767947$$

and

$$b(2) = 0.2666667.$$ ∎

Lognormal Distribution

In the previous section we studied a model in which spot interest rates are normally distributed. This is a convenient assumption, for it allows us to derive closed form solutions for many types of interest rate derivatives. However, this assumption implies that spot interest rates can be negative. We can see this via Expression (15.7) by noticing that if $\Delta W(t)$ takes on a large negative value (by chance), then $r(t + \Delta)$ can be negative. Negative spot rates generate zero-coupon bond prices above their face value. This situation is inconsistent with the availability of cash currency, which can be stored at no cost.[8] For this reason, it is usually considered an undesirable property.

One way to avoid this implication is to assume that the logarithm of the spot interest rate is normally distributed. Let

$$v(t) \equiv \ln [r(t)].$$

Assuming that $v(t)$ is normally distributed implies that the interest rate $r(t)$ cannot be negative and is lognormally distributed.[9]

Based on this insight, we assume that

$$\Delta v(t) = [a(t) - b(t)v(t)]\Delta + \sigma(t)\Delta W(t), \tag{15.13}$$

where $\Delta v(t) \equiv v(t + \Delta) - v(t) \equiv \ln r(t + \Delta) - \ln r(\Delta)$. This assumption underlies the Black, Derman, and Toy (1990) model.

---

[8] Surprisingly, in November of 1998, Japanese yen deposits in Western banks paid negative interest rates. News reports attributed this to credit risk, an issue we discuss in Chapter 18.
[9] For example, given that $r(t) = \exp[v(t)]$, if $v(t) = -2.5$, then $r(t) = 0.082$, which is positive.

Under Expression (15.13) we have

$$E^{\pi}(\Delta v(t)) = [a(t) - b(t)v(t)]\Delta$$

and

$$\sqrt{\text{var}}^{\pi}(\Delta v(t)) = \sigma(t)\sqrt{\Delta}.$$

The expected change in the $\ln r(t)$ is determined by the parameters $a(t)$ and $b(t)$. The volatility of the change in $\ln r(t)$ is $\sigma(t)\sqrt{\Delta}$. These parameters can be estimated historically using time series data or implicitly using market prices.

Because Expression (15.13) is similar to Expression (15.7), the binomial lattice of spot interest rates approximating Expression (15.13) can be constructed in a similar manner.

We illustrate this construction now. Given the spot interest rate at date t, $r(t)$, we compute $v(t) = \ln r(t)$. Using Expression (15.13), the value of v at the next interval is

$$v(t + \Delta) - v(t) = \begin{cases} [a(t) - b(t)v(t)]\Delta + \sigma(t)\sqrt{\Delta} & \text{with probability } 1/2 \\ [a(t) - b(t)v(t)]\Delta - \sigma(t)\sqrt{\Delta} & \text{with probability } 1/2. \end{cases}$$

(15.14)

In the "up state"

$$v(t + \Delta)_U - v(t) = [a(t) - b(t)v(t)]\Delta + \sigma(t)\sqrt{\Delta}$$

and in the "down state"

$$v(t + \Delta)_D - v(t) = [a(t) - b(t)v(t)]\Delta - \sigma(t)\sqrt{\Delta}.$$

Subtracting the above two equations gives

$$[v(t + \Delta)_U - v(t + \Delta)_D]/2 = \sigma(t)\sqrt{\Delta}, \tag{15.15}$$

which is analogous to Expression (15.11). In terms of the spot interest rate, this becomes

$$\{\ln[r(t + \Delta)_U/r(t + \Delta)_D]\}/2 = \sigma(t)\sqrt{\Delta}. \tag{15.16}$$

Compare Expression (15.11) with Expression (15.16). The difference in these expressions implies that the magnitude of the volatilities for the lognormal distribution can be substantially greater than those for the normal distribution. In

TABLE 15.2 *Interest Rates Are Assumed to Be Lognormally Distributed*

INITIAL DATA			
MATURITY (YEARS)	BOND PRICES* $B(0,T)$	YIELD (PERCENT)	VOLATILITY**
1	0.9399	6.1982	0.2
2	0.8798	6.4030	0.18
3	0.8137	6.8721	0.17

*All bonds have zero coupons and are default-free.

**Volatility refers to the volatility of the logarithm of the spot interest rate.

Table 15.2, a term structure of volatilities is shown, assuming that interest rates are lognormally distributed. Compare the magnitude of the numbers in this table to those in Table 15.1. The numbers in Table 15.1 are approximately equal to $r(t)$ times the numbers in Table 15.2. This makes sense, as $\sqrt{\text{var}(\Delta r(t))} = \sigma(t)\sqrt{\Delta}$ in Table 15.1, using Expression (15.7), and $\sqrt{\text{var}(\Delta r(t))} = r(t)\sigma(t)\sqrt{\Delta}$ in Table 15.2, using Expression (15.13).[10]

---

[10]Using Expression (15.13),

$$\text{var}[\Delta v(t)] = \sigma(t)^2 \Delta.$$

By definition,

$$\Delta v(t) \equiv \ln r(t + \Delta) - \ln r(t).$$

We can write

$$r(t + \Delta) \equiv r(t) + \Delta r(t)$$
$$= r(t)[1 + \Delta r(t)/r(t)]$$

so that

$$\ln r(t + h) = \ln r(t) + \ln[1 + \Delta r(t)/r(t)].$$

Hence

$$\Delta v(t) = \ln[1 + \Delta r(t)/r(t)]$$
$$\simeq \Delta r(t)/r(t).$$

Therefore,

$$\text{var}[\Delta v(t)] = \{\text{var}[\Delta r(t)]\}/r(t)^2,$$

implying

$$\sqrt{\text{var}[\Delta r(t)]} = r(t)\sigma(t)\sqrt{\Delta}.$$

EXAMPLE **Lognormal Distribution**

We illustrate in this example the computation of the parameters for lognormally distributed spot rates. We use the information in Table 15.2 to construct the lattice of spot interest rates for the lognormal case. The current spot interest rate is given by

$$0.9399 = \exp[-r(0)],$$

implying

$$r(0) = 6.1982 \text{ percent.}$$

At date 1, let us guess that

$$r(1)_U = 7.9221 \text{ percent, which implies that } B(1,2)_U = 0.923836,$$

and

$$r(1)_D = 5.3103 \text{ percent, which implies that } B(1,2)_D = 0.948282.$$

The current value of the two-year zero-coupon bond, using Expression (15.1), is

$$B(0,2) = \exp(-0.061982) \times [0.923836 \times (^1\!/_2) + 0.948282 \times (^1\!/_2)]$$
$$= 0.8798.$$

This agrees with the value in Table 15.2.

We must also check that our estimates are consistent with the volatilities given in Table 15.2:

$$v(1)_U \equiv \ln[r(1)_U] = \ln(0.079221)$$

and

$$v(1)_D = \ln[r(1)_D] = \ln(0.053103).$$

Substituting into Expression (15.15) gives

$$\sigma(0) = [\ln(0.079221) - \ln(0.053103)]/2$$
$$= 0.20,$$

which agrees with Table 15.2. This completes the spot rate determination at date 1.

At date 2, let us guess that

$r(2)_{UU} = 10.8922$ percent, which implies that $B(2,3)_{UU} = 0.896800$,
$r(2)_{UD} = 7.5993$ percent, which implies that $B(2,3)_{UD} = 0.926823$,

and

$r(2)_{DD} = 5.3018$ percent, which implies that $B(2,3)_{DD} = 0.948363$.

Substituting into Expression (15.15) gives the volatility for the upper node in the lattice:

$$\sigma(1) = [\ln(0.108922) - \ln(0.075993)]/2$$
$$= 0.18$$

and, for the lower node in the lattice,

$$\sigma(1) = [\ln(0.075993) - \ln(0.053018)]/2$$
$$= 0.18.$$

These estimates match the volatility specification in Table 15.2.
At $t = 1$,

$$B(1,3)_U = \exp{(-0.079221)} \times [0.896800 \times (\tfrac{1}{2}) + 0.926823 \times (\tfrac{1}{2})]$$
$$= 0.842364$$

and

$$B(1,3)_D = \exp(-0.053103) \times [0.926823 \times (\tfrac{1}{2}) + 0.948363 \times (\tfrac{1}{2})]$$
$$= 0.889103.$$

The current value of the three-year zero-coupon bond is

$$B(0,3) = \exp(-0.061982) \times [0.842364 \times (\tfrac{1}{2}) + 0.889103 \times (\tfrac{1}{2})]$$
$$= 0.8137,$$

which agrees with Table 15.2. The binomial lattice is shown in Figure 15.6.
We leave it to the reader to verify that over the first period, the values of the parameters for the spot interest rate process are given by

$$a(0) = 0.0454$$

and

$$b(0) = 0.0.$$

FIGURE 15.6   *Short-Term Interest Rates,*
Lognormal Distribution

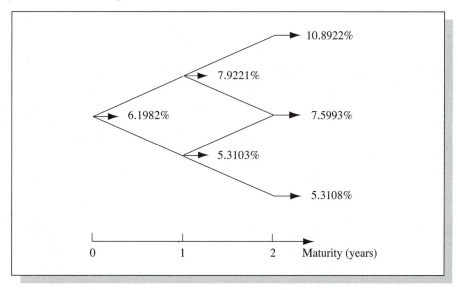

For the second period,

$$a(1) = -0.1152$$

and

$$b(1) = 0.1.$$

15.3 VALUING OPTIONS ON TREASURY BILLS

Given the arbitrage-free evolution of the spot interest rate process, the risk-neutral valuation procedure of Chapter 6 enables us to price interest rate derivatives. In this section we show how to use the material in Chapter 6 to price and hedge options on Treasury bills.

Consider a European call option that matures at date T, with strike price K, written on a Treasury bill that matures at a later date, T_1. The value of the call option at expiration is

$$c(T) \equiv \begin{cases} B(T,T_1) - K & \text{if} & B(T,T_1) > K \\ 0 & \text{if} & B(T,T_1) \le K. \end{cases} \tag{15.17}$$

The value of a put option with the same expiration date, strike price, and written on the same Treasury bill is

$$p(T) \equiv \begin{cases} 0 & \text{if} & B(T,T_1) \geq K \\ K - B(T,T_1) & \text{if} & B(T,T_1) < K. \end{cases} \tag{15.18}$$

Given an initial term structure of interest rates and volatilities, the first step in valuing these options is to construct an arbitrage-free lattice of short-term interest rates consistent with these volatilities. This procedure was illustrated in the previous sections. The second step is to use the constructed lattice and the risk-neutral valuation procedure of Chapter 6. We illustrate this procedure here.

Put Options

Here we study put option valuation using the risk-neutral valuation procedure of Chapter 6. Consider a two-year European put option written on a Treasury bill with a maturity of one year when the option expires. Let the strike price be 0.925.

We use the lattice of short-term interest rates shown in Figure 15.2 and reproduced in Figure 15.7. This lattice is based on the initial term structure of volatilities

FIGURE 15.7 *Pricing a European Put Option on Treasury Bills*
(Based on Figure 15.2)

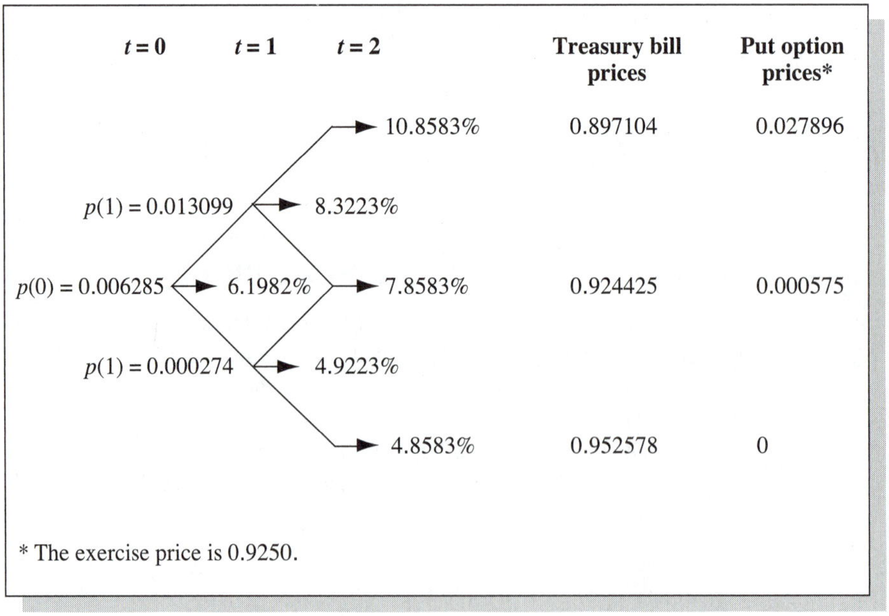

	$t = 0$	$t = 1$	$t = 2$	Treasury bill prices	Put option prices*
			10.8583%	0.897104	0.027896
	$p(1) = 0.013099$	8.3223%			
	$p(0) = 0.006285$	6.1982%	7.8583%	0.924425	0.000575
	$p(1) = 0.000274$	4.9223%			
			4.8583%	0.952578	0

* The exercise price is 0.9250.

given in Table 15.1. We observe in Figure 15.7 that there are three possible Treasury bill prices at date 2 and thus three possible put option prices (0.027896, 0.000575, 0).

At the end of the first year, if the spot interest rate is 8.3223 percent, the value of the put option is

$$
\begin{aligned}
p(1)_U &= \exp(-0.083223)E^{\pi}[p(2)] \\
&= \exp(-0.083223) \times (0.5 \times 0.027896 + 0.5 \times 0.000575) \\
&= 0.013099
\end{aligned}
$$

and, if the spot rate is 4.9223 percent, the value of the put option is

$$
\begin{aligned}
p(1)_D &= \exp(-0.049223) \times (0.5 \times 0.000575 + 0.5 \times 0) \\
&= 0.000274.
\end{aligned}
$$

The value of the put option today is

$$
\begin{aligned}
p(0) &= \exp(-0.061982)E^{\pi}[p(1)] \\
&= \exp(-0.061982) \times (0.5 \times 0.013099 + 0.5 \times 0.000274) \\
&= 0.006285.
\end{aligned}
$$

This completes the valuation procedure.

A Replicating Portfolio

Suppose we want to construct a portfolio to replicate this option. From Table 15.1, we have the one-, two-, three-, and four-year zero-coupon bonds at our disposal. How many assets do we need to replicate the option? At date $t = 1$, the end of the first interval, the option takes one of two possible (different) values, either 0.013099 or 0.000274. Therefore, we need at least two different assets in the replicating portfolio. But which two assets should we use? We could use any pair of the bonds—either

a) the one-year and two-year zero-coupon bonds,
b) the one-year and three-year zero-coupon bonds,

or

c) the two-year and three-year zero-coupon bonds.

For simplicity we ignore the four-year zero-coupon bond, but it could also be included. We could use the money market account as one of our assets, but it would be equivalent to rolling over the one-year zero-coupon bond in the replicating portfolio and is therefore omitted.

Consider using the one-year and two-year zero-coupon bonds to form the synthetic put. At date 0, the value of this replicating portfolio is

$$V(0) = n_1 \, 0.9399 + n_2 \, 0.8798,$$

where n_1 is the number of one year zero-coupon bonds and n_2 the number of two-year zero-coupon bonds.

By construction, the value of the replicating portfolio at the end of the first period must equal the value of the put option. Referring to Figures 15.1 and 15.7, this implies that

$$n_1 1 + n_2 \, 0.920146 = 0.013099$$
and
$$n_1 1 + n_2 \, 0.951969 = 0.000274,$$

which gives two equations in two unknowns. The solution is

$$n_1 = 0.383927$$
and
$$n_2 = -0.40301. \tag{15.19}$$

The cost of constructing the replicating portfolio gives the value of the synthetic put option, that is,

$$\begin{aligned} V(0) &= n_1 \, 0.9399 + n_2 \, 0.8798 \\ &= 0.006285, \end{aligned}$$

which must be the value of the traded put option to avoid arbitrage.

If we use one-year and three-year zero-coupon bonds to form the replicating portfolio, the portfolio holdings can be shown to be

$$n_1 = 0.207145$$
and
$$n_3 = -0.231548, \tag{15.20}$$

where n_1 is the number of one-year zero-coupon bonds and n_3 the number of three-year zero-coupon bonds. The cost of constructing the replicating portfolio is

$$\begin{aligned} V(0) &= n_1 \times 0.9399 + n_3 \times 0.8137 \\ &= 0.006285, \end{aligned}$$

which represents the arbitrage-free value of the traded put. Of course, this is the same value computed earlier.

Finally, if we use two-year and three-year zero-coupon bonds to form the replicating portfolio, then

$$n_2 = 0.472227$$

and

$$(15.21)$$

$$n_3 = -0.502965,$$

where n_2 is the number of two-year zero-coupon bonds and n_3 the number of three-year zero-coupon bonds. The cost of constructing the synthetic put is

$$V(0) = n_2 \times 0.8798 + n_3 \times 0.8137$$
$$= 0.006285,$$

which is the value of the put option.

Each portfolio, by construction, replicates the payoff to the put option. From a theoretical viewpoint we should be indifferent in choosing among the three different replicating portfolios. In practice, however, other considerations may indicate a preference for a particular replicating portfolio. We will return to this topic in the next chapter.

Call Options

The valuation procedure for European call options on Treasury bills is identical to that used for European puts. To gauge your understanding, you should check the values given in Figure 15.8 for a two-year European call option with strike price 0.925 written on a zero-coupon bond that has a maturity of one year when the option expires.

Put-Call Parity

Here we discuss put-call parity between options on Treasury bills. Consider a European call option and a European put option, both written on a Treasury bill that matures at date T_1. The options expire at date T and have a strike price of K.

The put-call parity relationship between the options is

$$p(t) + B(t, T_1) = c(t) + K \times B(t, T). \qquad (15.22)$$

The proof of this put-call parity relation is identical to that contained in Chapter 3 and is therefore omitted.

Let us use the results in Figures 15.7 and 15.8 and Table 15.1 to verify Expression (15.22). From Figure 15.7 and Table 15.1, the left side of Expression (15.22) is

$$p(0) = 0.0063$$
$$B(0, 3) = 0.8137$$
$$\text{Total} = 0.82.$$

FIGURE 15.8 *Pricing a European Call Option on Treasury Bills (Based on Figure 15.2)*

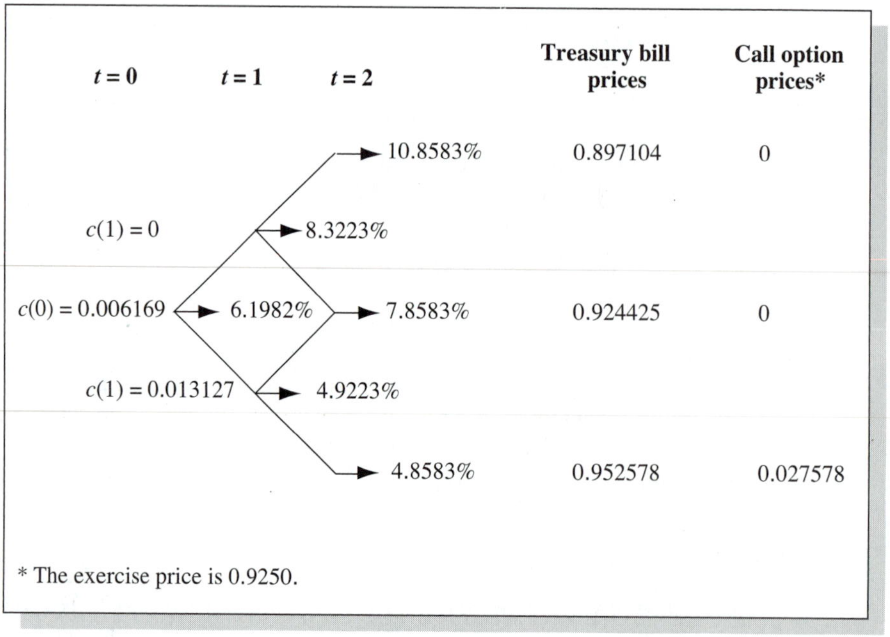

			Treasury bill prices	Call option prices*
$t = 0$	$t = 1$	$t = 2$		
		10.8583%	0.897104	0
$c(1) = 0$	8.3223%			
$c(0) = 0.006169$	6.1982%	7.8583%	0.924425	0
$c(1) = 0.013127$	4.9223%			
		4.8583%	0.952578	0.027578

* The exercise price is 0.9250.

From Figure 15.8 and Table 15.2, the right side of Expression (15.22) is

$$c(0) = 0.006169$$
$$K \times B(0,2) = 0.925 \times 0.8798$$
$$\text{Total} = 0.82.$$

These values are the same, which verifies Expression (15.22).

15.4 TREASURY BILL FUTURES

We now show how to price and hedge using Treasury bill futures. In practice, futures contracts are often more liquid securities than the Treasury bills themselves, making them a better hedging instrument.

Given the arbitrage-free lattice of short-term interest rates, the determination of futures prices is relatively straightforward.

Pricing

Let us demonstrate how to determine Treasury bill futures prices. Consider a futures contract that is written on a one-year Treasury bill. Let the futures contract delivery

date be at the end of the second year. Let $\mathcal{F}(t,2)$ denote the futures price of this contract at date $t = 0, 1, 2$.

At the delivery date of the contract, the futures price equals the spot price of the one-year Treasury bill. Hence

$$\mathcal{F}(2,2) = B(2,3).$$

In Figure 15.9, we see that three values are possible: 0.897104, 0.924425, and 0.952578.

At the end of the first year, two spot interest rates are possible: 8.3223 percent and 4.9223 percent. Suppose that we are at the upper node with a spot interest rate of 8.3223 percent.

Under the martingale probabilities, we know from Chapter 6 that futures prices are martingales. Therefore, from Expression (6.25) of Chapter 6,

$$
\begin{aligned}
\mathcal{F}(1,2)_U &= E^{\pi}[\mathcal{F}(2,2)] \\
&= 0.5 \times 0.897104 + 0.5 \times 0.924425 \\
&= 0.910765.
\end{aligned}
$$

If we are at the lower node so that the spot interest rate is 4.9223 percent, the futures price is similarly determined:

$$
\begin{aligned}
\mathcal{F}(1,2)_D &= E^{\pi}[\mathcal{F}(2,2)] \\
&= 0.5 \times 0.924425 + 0.5 \times 0.952578 \\
&= 0.938502.
\end{aligned}
$$

FIGURE 15.9 *Treasury Bill Futures Prices (Based on Figure 15.2)*

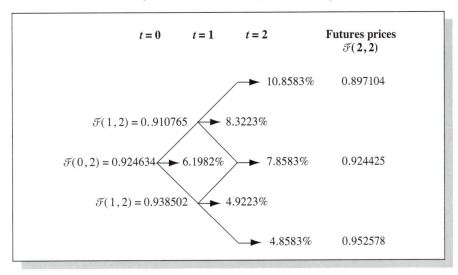

Today, the futures price is

$$\mathcal{F}(0,2) = E^\pi[\mathcal{F}(1,2)]$$
$$= 0.5 \times 0.910765 + 0.5 \times 0.938502$$
$$= 0.924634.$$

This completes the calculation of the Treasury bill futures prices.

Hedging

We now study hedging with Treasury bill futures. We have derived futures prices (Figure 15.9) and put option prices (Figure 15.7) for contracts written on one-year Treasury bills. These results are summarized in Figure 15.10.

We define the put option's delta with respect to this futures contract in the same way as we define deltas for equity options. It is the ratio of the change in the option prices across the two possible states to the change in the futures prices. For the put option, the delta is

$$\Delta_p = (1.3099 - 0.0274)/(0.910765 - 0.938502)$$
$$= -0.4624.$$

Suppose that we want to form a portfolio using the futures contract to replicate the option. Today we invest B dollars in the short-term riskless asset and enter into m

FIGURE 15.10   *Treasury Bill Futures Prices and Put Option Prices (Based on Figures 15.7 and 15.9)*

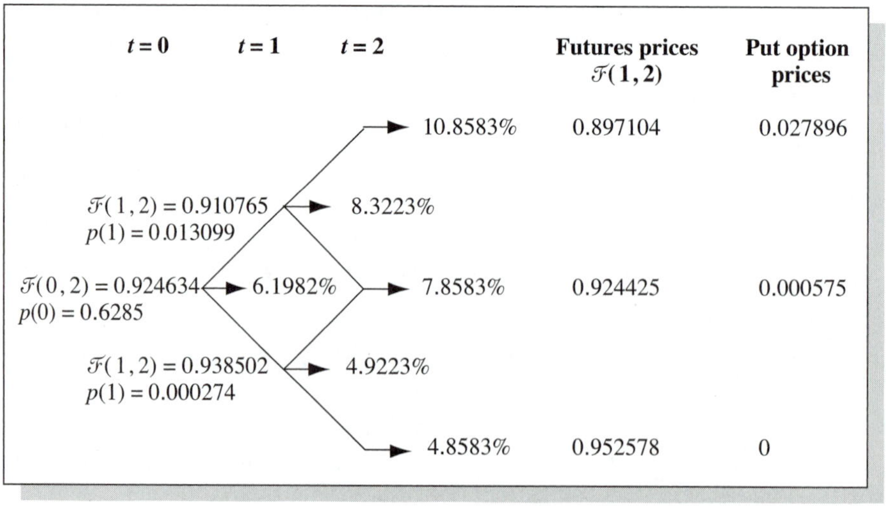

futures contracts.[11] Each dollar invested in the short-term riskless asset yields 1.0639 ($= \exp(0.061982)$). The initial cost of constructing the portfolio is

$$V(0) = m \times 0 + B,$$

given that the initial value of the futures contract is zero.

If the short-term interest rate goes to 8.3223 percent, the option value is 0.013099. By construction, we need

$$0.013099 = m(0.910765 - 0.924634) + B(1.0639),$$

where the first term on the right side is the cash flow from the investment in the futures contracts.

If the spot interest rate goes to 4.9223 percent, the option value is 0.000274. By construction, we need

$$0.000274 = m(0.938502 - 0.924634) + B(1.0639).$$

This gives two equations in two unknowns. Solving for m and B gives

$$m = (0.013099 - 0.000274)/(0.910765 - 0.938502)$$
$$= -0.4624$$

and

$$B = 0.6285.$$

The solution is to short 0.4624 futures contracts and invest 0.6285 dollars in the riskless asset.

Given that this portfolio replicates the payoffs to the put option, the value of the traded option must equal the cost of constructing this synthetic option:

$$p(0) = V(0) = B.$$

If we had written the traded put option as well, this synthetic put held in conjunction with the traded option would yield a hedged portfolio. Indeed, by writing 0.4624 futures contracts and investing 0.6285 dollars in the riskless asset, we can completely offset the risk of writing the option. This would be a zero-investment position because the investment in the short-term riskless asset is financed by the proceeds from writing the option.

Our discussion of Treasury bill futures contracts is now complete.

---

[11]This is equivalent to forming the portfolio using n_1 one-year Treasury bills and m futures contracts.

15.5 SUMMARY

We show in this chapter how to construct an arbitrage-free lattice of spot interest rates that is consistent with the following: (1) the current term structure of interest rates, and (2) the current term structure of volatilities. In constructing this lattice, we must specify the process describing the evolution of the spot interest rate. We consider two distributions; the first has interest rates normally distributed, which implies that

$$[r(t + \Delta)_U - r(t + \Delta)_D]/2 = \sigma(t)\sqrt{\Delta}.$$

The second distribution has interest rates that are lognormally distributed, which implies that

$$\{\ln[r(t + \Delta)_U/r(t + \Delta)_D]\}/2 = \sigma(t)\sqrt{\Delta}.$$

Once we construct the lattice of spot interest rates using the risk-neutral valuation procedure of Chapter 6, it is possible to price interest rate derivatives such as options on Treasury bills, Treasury bonds, and interest rate futures contracts.

We have also shown how to hedge interest rate derivatives with other types of interest rate derivatives. For example, to hedge an option written on a Treasury bill, we showed how to use either other Treasury bills or Treasury bill futures contracts. The lattice approach can also be applied to (1) price American type options, where it may be optimal to prematurely exercise the option, and (2) price interest rate exotics to which early exercise or boundary conditions are attached.

As we mentioned in the introduction to this chapter, there are a number of different approaches available for pricing interest rate derivatives in an arbitrage-free manner. The approach we use here is to model the spot interest rate process. An alternative approach is to model the evolution of the entire forward rate curve. This alternative approach is identified with Heath, Jarrow, and Morton (1992). A discrete time description of this model can be found in Jarrow (1995). In Chapter 16 we study the Heath-Jarrow-Morton approach in the context of a continuous trading model.

REFERENCES

Black, F., E. Derman, and W. Toy, 1990. "A One Factor Model of Interest Rates and Its Application to Treasury Bond Options." *Financial Analysts Journal* 46, 33–39.

Heath, D., R. Jarrow, and A. Morton, 1992. "Bond Pricing and the Term Structure of Interest Rates: A New Methodology for Contingent Claims Valuation." *Econometrica* 60, 77–105.

Ho, T., and S. Lee, 1986. "Term Structure Movements and Pricing Interest Rate Contingent Claims." *Journal of Finance* 41, 1011–1029.

Jarrow, R. A., 1997. *Modelling Fixed Income Securities and Interest Rate Options*. New York: McGraw-Hill.

Musiela, M., S. M. Turnbull, and L. M. Wakeman, 1993. "Interest Rate Risk Management." *Review of Futures Markets* 12, 221–261.

Turnbull, S. M., 1992. "Pricing Interest Rate Derivatives." *Handbook for Canadian Investment Bankers*. Toronto: McGraw-Hill.

QUESTIONS

Question 1 Put-Call Parity for European Treasury Bill Options

Consider a call option and a put option that mature at date T and with strike price K. The options are written on a Treasury bill that matures at date T_1. Prove the following:

$$p(t;T) + B(t,T_1) = c(t;T) + K \times B(t,T).$$

(Hint: The proof is very similar to the put-call parity result in Chapter 3.)

Question 2

In the following figure, you are given the lattice of six-month continuously compounded interest rates, which have been derived using the lognormal spot rate model. The time interval used in the lattice is six months.

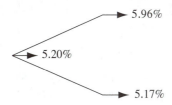

The equivalent martingale probability of an up or down state occurring is $\frac{1}{2}$. The payoff to an interest rate cap that matures in six months' time is defined by

$$\text{cap}(0) \equiv \text{Max}\left\{ \frac{[R(6) - K](1/2)}{1 + R(6)(1/2)}, 0 \right\} \times \text{Principal},$$

where $R(6)$ is the six-month (simple) interest rate when the option matures, K is the strike price, and Principal is the principal amount.

a) The interest rates in the lattice are continuously compounded rates, while the payoff to the cap is defined in terms of simple interest rates. Show that the payoff to the cap can be written in the form

$$\mathrm{cap}(0) = [1 + K(1/2)]\mathrm{Max}\{k - B(6, 12), 0\} \times \mathrm{Principal},$$

where $k \equiv 1/[1 + K(1/2)]$, and $B(6, 12)$ is the value at date six months of a T-bill that matures at date twelve months and is defined by

$$B(6, 12) \equiv 1/[1 + R(6)(1/2)].$$

b) What is the value of the cap today if $K = 0.054$ and Principal $= \$10$ million?

Question 3 Interest Rate Caps

Using the lognormal spot rate model (Black, Derman, and Toy (1990)), you are given the following information (see figure) about one-year interest rates (all rates are continuously compounded).

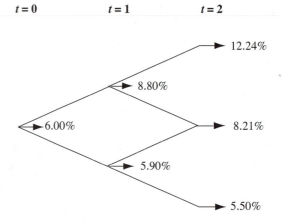

The current one-period interest rate is 6%. Next year the interest rate will be either 8.80% or 5.90%. If the rate goes down to 5.90%, then in year two it could be either 5.50% or 8.21%. Alternatively, if the rate goes up to 8.80%, then in year two it will be either 12.24% or 8.21%. The equivalent martingale probability of an up or down state occurring is $\frac{1}{2}$.

a) Price a two-year European interest rate cap. The payoff to the cap at maturity is defined by

$$\mathrm{cap}(0) = \mathrm{Max}\left\{\frac{R_1(2) - k}{1 + R_1(2)}, 0\right\}100,$$

where $R_1(2)$ is the one-year simple interest rate at year two and k is the cap rate. It is assumed that $k = 0.087$. (Hint: See Question Two.)
   What is the value of the cap today (*e.g.*, cap(2))?

b) Suppose that a futures contract matures at year two. The contract is written on a one-year Treasury bill. Determine the futures price today.
c) How would you hedge the cap (at $t = 0$) using a one-year Treasury bill and the futures contract? Determine the number of Treasury bills and futures contracts and show that you are completely hedged in each state at year one.

Question 4   *Hedging a Treasury Bill Option*

You are given the following information (see figure) about one-year interest rates.

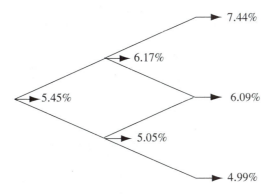

The current one-period interest rate is 5.45% per year (continuously compounded). Next year the one-period rate will be either 6.17% or 5.05% with an equivalent martingale probability of 0.5 for each state. If at $t = 1$ the rate is 6.17%, then in year two it could be either 7.44% or 6.09% with equal (martingale) probability. If the one-year rate at $t = 1$ is 5.05%, then in year two it could be either 6.09% or 4.99% with equal probability.

a) At $t = 0$, what is the price of
   1) a one-year Treasury bill,
   2) a two-year Treasury bill, and
   3) a three-year Treasury bill?
b) What is the value of a two-year European call option written on a one-year Treasury bill? The payoff to the option at maturity is defined by

$$c(2) \equiv 10 \, \text{Max} \, \{B(2,3) - 0.9450, 0\},$$

where $B(2, 3)$ is the value at year two of a one-year Treasury bill. The strike price is 0.9450.
c) What is the replicating portfolio at $t = 0$ if you decide to use Treasury bills with maturities of two and three years? Derive the investments in each Treasury bill.

d) In theory, the choice of the maturities of the Treasury bills is irrelevant: Pick two Treasury bills with different maturities and you can replicate the options. In practice, this is not the case. Why?

Question 5

You are given the following information.

T-Bill	Price	Yield	Volatility
$B(0,1)$	0.869358	14%	7.14%
$B(0,2)$	0.755029	14.05%	6.75%
$B(0,3)$	0.668527	13.42%	

Assume that the conditions of the lognormal spot rate model (Black, Derman, and Toy (1990)) hold, and that the time period is measured in years. The equivalent martingale probability of an up or down state occurring is $\frac{1}{2}$.

a) Determine the (combining) lattice of one-year interest rates.
b) Determine the futures price of a contract that matures at $t = 2$ and is written on a one-period Treasury bill.
c) How does the futures price compare to the one-year forward price from year two to year three?

CHAPTER 16

PRICING TREASURY BILLS, TREASURY BONDS, TREASURY FUTURES, AND HEDGING WITH MODEL MISSPECIFICATION

16.0 INTRODUCTION

In Chapter 15, we demonstrated how to construct a lattice of spot interest rates to be consistent with the initial term structure of interest rates and volatilities, and how to price and hedge interest rate derivatives. We considered two cases: normally distributed and lognormally distributed spot interest rates. For the first case, it is possible to generate closed form solutions for many types of interest rate derivatives. For the second case, it is not.

For institutions with large interest rate portfolios, models that generate closed form solutions significantly reduce computing time. In this chapter and the next, we will study various closed form solutions for pricing and hedging interest rate derivatives. There are two ways of doing this. One approach models the evolution of spot interest rates as we described in Chapter 15. This must be done in such a way as to match the initial term structure of interest rates.[1] An alternative and more flexible approach is to take the initial term structure as given and to model the evolution of forward rates. This approach is known as the Heath-Jarrow-Morton model (see Heath, Jarrow, and Morton, 1992). In this chapter, we study a special case of this second approach.

In Chapter 15, we showed how to hedge an interest rate option by forming a portfolio that perfectly replicates the option's payoffs. In practice, many things can (and do) happen that makes this impossible. **Model misspecification** occurs when the replicating portfolio cannot be implemented as theory requires due to transaction costs

---

[1]Vasicek (1977) models the evolution of the term structure of interest rates, assuming that the spot interest rate is normally distributed. Unfortunately, he does not incorporate the initial term structure of interest rates. Cox, Ingersoll, and Ross (1985, p. 395) demonstrate how to modify the method used by Vasicek to incorporate the initial term structure. This modified approach is used by Hull and White (1990).

or other market frictions. In this chapter, we extend to interest rate derivatives the insights gained in Chapter 10 on hedging equity derivatives in the presence of model misspecification.

16.1 THE HEATH-JARROW-MORTON MODEL

Here we introduce the continuous-time Heath-Jarrow-Morton model for pricing and hedging interest rate derivatives.

The Heath-Jarrow-Morton model starts with the initial forward rate curve described by $f(0, T)$ for all T, where $f(0, T)$ is the date-0 continuously compounded forward interest rate for the future interval $[T, T + \Delta]$, and where we think of Δ as small ($\Delta \to 0$). In the notation of Chapter 13, we have $f(0, T) \equiv \log f(0, T, T + \Delta)$. We simplify the notation here because the future time period will always be of constant length Δ.

As in the Black-Scholes model, the Heath-Jarrow-Morton model is formulated in continuous time, where the length of the trading interval Δ is infinitesimal.[2] In terms of bond prices, $B(0, T + \Delta) = B(0, T)e^{-f(0, T)\Delta}$.

The Forward Rate Evolution

Let us describe the evolution of the forward rate curve in the Heath-Jarrow-Morton model.

Consider a particular forward rate with maturity T denoted by $f(0, T)$. We want to model the evolution of this forward rate as it moves through time. That is, we want to model the values for $f(t, T)$ as t varies from 0 to T.

In order to derive closed form solutions, we assume that the change in the forward rate is normally distributed and described by the following equation:

$$\Delta f(t, T) = \alpha(t, T)\Delta + \sigma(t, T)\Delta W(t), \tag{16.1}$$

where $\Delta f(t, T) \equiv f(t + \Delta, T) - f(t, T)$ is the change in the forward rate over the interval t to $t + \Delta$ and $\Delta W(t)$ is a normally distributed random variable with zero mean and variance Δ. This evolution is under the martingale probabilities π.

Given Expression (16.1), the expected change in the forward rate is

$$E^\pi[\Delta f(t, T)] = \alpha(t, T)\Delta$$

and the variance of the change in the forward rate is

$$\mathrm{var}^\pi[\Delta f(t, T)] = \sigma(t, T)^2\Delta.$$

---

[2] Thus we have

$$f(0, T) = \lim_{\Delta \to 0}[\log f(0, T, T + \Delta)],$$

using the notation from Chapter 13.

These equations give meaning to the parameters $\alpha(t, T)$ and $\sigma(t, T)$ in Expression (16.1). The first term, $\alpha(t, T)$, is called the drift of the forward rate process and the second term, $\sigma(t, T)$, is called the volatility. Observe that there is only one source of uncertainty represented by $\Delta W(t)$ in Expression (16.1), implying that this is a single-factor model.

For implementation (statistical estimation) reasons, we assume that the forward rate's volatility is of the form

$$\sigma(t, T) = \sigma \times \exp[-\lambda(T - t)], \tag{16.2}$$

where $\sigma > 0$ is a positive constant and $\lambda \geq 0$ is a non-negative constant. This means that the volatility is stationary because it depends only on time to maturity $(T - t)$ and not on both T and t separately.

If λ is zero, then the volatility of the forward rate is a constant, $\sigma(t, T) = \sigma$. If λ is positive, it implies that the volatility of the forward rate increases as the maturity, $(T - t)$, decreases. As a consequence, short-term forward rates will be more volatile than long-term forward rates, as shown in Table 16.1. Table 16.1 illustrates the computation of the volatility in Expression (16.2) for $\sigma = 0.02$, $\lambda = 0.1$, and various time to maturity $(T - t)$ values.

We can rewrite the time-t forward rate in the following way

$$
\begin{aligned}
f(t, T) &= f(0, T) + [f(\Delta, T) - f(0, T)] + [f(2\Delta, T) - f(\Delta, T)] + \ldots \\
&\quad + [f(t, T) - f(t - \Delta, T)] \\
&= f(0, T) + \sum_{v=0}^{t - \Delta} \Delta f(v, T).
\end{aligned}
$$

This simply says that the time-t forward rate for date T is the time-0 forward rate for date T plus all accumulated changes in this rate up to that date. Next, substitution of this expression into (16.1) gives

$$f(t, T) = f(0, T) + \sum_{v=0}^{t - \Delta} \alpha(v, T)\Delta + \sum_{v=0}^{t - \Delta} \sigma(v, T)\Delta W(v). \tag{16.3}$$

TABLE 16.1 *Volatility of Changes in the Forward Rate as a Function of Maturity*

MATURITY $(T - t)$ (YEARS)	VOLATILITY
0.1	0.0198
0.5	0.0109
1.0	0.0181
2.0	0.0164

	$\sigma(t, T) = \sigma \times \exp[-\lambda(T - t)]$
Volatility	$\sigma = 2.0$ percent
Volatility Reduction Factor	$\lambda = 0.1$

Expression (16.3) describes the evolution of the forward rate at time t in terms of the initial forward rate curve $f(0, T)$, the drifts, and the volatilities of the intermediate changes in forward rates.

The Spot Rate and Money Market Account Evolution

We now derive the evolution of the spot interest rate and the money market account's value from the forward rate process.

Recall that the continuously compounded spot interest rate at time $t, r(t)$ is defined by the expression

$$B(t, t + \Delta) = 1 \cdot e^{-r(t)\Delta}.$$

Using the definition of the continuously compounded forward rate, we also have

$$B(t, t + \Delta) = 1 \cdot e^{-f(t, t)\Delta}.$$

Combined, this implies that $r(t) = f(t, t)$, that is, the spot rate of interest is the forward rate at date t for maturity t.

Given this insight, Expression (16.3) directly gives us the spot rate process by setting $T = t$:

$$r(t) = f(0, t) + \sum_{v=0}^{t-\Delta} \alpha(v, t)\Delta + \sum_{v=0}^{t-\Delta} \sigma(v, t)\Delta W(v) \quad \text{for } t \geq \Delta. \tag{16.4}$$

To obtain the money market account's evolution, we need only recall its definition. The money market account's value at time t accumulates at the spot rate of interest, starting from a dollar deposit at time 0, $A(0) = 1$. In symbols,

$$A(t) = A(t - \Delta)e^{r(t - \Delta)\Delta} \quad \text{for all } t, \text{ or}$$

$$A(t) = 1 \cdot e^{\sum_{u=0}^{t-\Delta} r(u)\Delta}. \tag{16.5}$$

Substitution of Expression (16.4) into (16.5) gives the evolution of the money market account's value:

$$A(t) = 1 \cdot e^{\sum_{u=0}^{t-\Delta} f(0, u)\Delta + \sum_{u=\Delta}^{t-\Delta} \left[\sum_{v=0}^{u-\Delta} \alpha(v, u)\Delta \right] \Delta + \sum_{u=\Delta}^{t-\Delta} \left[\sum_{v=0}^{u-\Delta} \sigma(v, u)\Delta W(v) \right] \Delta}.$$

By reversing the order of summation, we can write

$$\sum_{u=\Delta}^{t-\Delta} \left(\sum_{v=0}^{u-\Delta} \alpha(v, u)\Delta \right) \Delta = \sum_{v=0}^{t-\Delta} \left(\sum_{u=v}^{t-\Delta} \alpha(v, u)\Delta \right) \Delta \quad \text{and}$$

$$\sum_{u=\Delta}^{t-\Delta} \left(\sum_{v=0}^{u-\Delta} \sigma(v, u)\Delta W(v) \right) \Delta = \sum_{v=0}^{t-\Delta} \left(\sum_{u=v}^{t-\Delta} \sigma(v, u)\Delta \right) \Delta W(v).$$

Substitution yields

$$A(t) = 1 \cdot e^{\sum_{u=0}^{t-\Delta} f(0,u)u + \sum_{v=0}^{t-\Delta} \left(\sum_{u=v}^{t-\Delta} \alpha(v,u)\Delta \right) \Delta + \sum_{v=0}^{t-\Delta} \left(\sum_{u=v}^{t-\Delta} \sigma(v,u)\Delta \right) \Delta W(v)}. \tag{16.6}$$

This is a perplexing-looking expression involving double sums of drifts and volatilities. Nonetheless, it was simply obtained. Do not let the complexity of Expression (16.6) be disturbing. We will not use Expression (16.6) in any fashion that involves a fine understanding of double sums.

Zero-Coupon Bond Price Evolution

Here we derive the zero-coupon bond price's evolution from the forward rate process.

Again, this derivation starts with the definition of the forward rate:

$$B(t,T) = B(t,T - \Delta)e^{-f(t,T-\Delta)\Delta}.$$

We can rewrite this[3] as

$$B(t,T) = 1 \cdot e^{-\sum_{u=t}^{T-\Delta} f(t,u)\Delta}. \tag{16.7}$$

Using Expression (16.3) for the evolution of the forward rate process gives us the evolution of the zero-coupon bond price, that is,

$$B(t,T) = 1 \cdot e^{-\sum_{u=t}^{T-\Delta} f(0,u)\Delta - \sum_{u=t}^{T-\Delta} \left[\sum_{v=0}^{t-\Delta} \alpha(v,u)\Delta \right] \Delta - \sum_{u=t}^{T-\Delta} \left[\sum_{v=0}^{t-\Delta} \sigma(v,u)\Delta W(v) \right] \Delta}.$$

Interchanging the double summation gives

$$B(t,T) = 1 \cdot e^{-\sum_{u=t}^{T-\Delta} f(0,u)\Delta - \sum_{v=0}^{t-\Delta} \left[\sum_{u=t}^{T-\Delta} \alpha(v,u)\Delta \right] \Delta - \sum_{v=0}^{t-\Delta} \left(\sum_{u=t}^{T-\Delta} \sigma(v,u)\Delta \right) \Delta W(v)}. \tag{16.8}$$

Although complicated-looking, Expression (16.8) is really quite simple. The current bond price is determined by the evolution of the current forward rates. This implies a discount factor (the exponent) equal to the forward rates at time 0, a drift term, and a random term that is normally distributed,[4] implying that the zero-coupon bond's price is lognormally distributed. This fact will be useful in Chapter 17 when pricing options on Treasury bills.

---

[3]Successive substitution gives this expression. Note that $B(t,T - \Delta) = B(t,T - 2\Delta)e^{-f(t,T-2\Delta)\Delta}$. Substitution into the expression for $B(t,T)$ yields $B(t,T) = B(t,T - 2\Delta)e^{-f(t,T-\Delta)\Delta - f(t,T-2\Delta)\Delta}$. Continuing in this fashion generates Expression (16.7).

[4]Recall from probability theory that sums of normal random variables are normally distributed.

For the next section, we need the evolution of $B(t,T)/A(t)$. It follows by using Expressions (16.6) and (16.8):

$$\frac{B(t,T)}{A(t)} = \frac{e^{-\sum\limits_{u=t}^{T-\Delta} f(0,u)\Delta - \sum\limits_{v=0}^{t-\Delta}\left(\sum\limits_{u=t}^{T-\Delta}\alpha(v,u)\,\Delta\right)\Delta - \sum\limits_{v=0}^{t-\Delta}\left(\sum\limits_{u=t}^{T-\Delta}\sigma(v,u)\,\Delta\right)\Delta W(v)}}{e^{\sum\limits_{u=0}^{t-\Delta} f(0,u)\Delta + \sum\limits_{v=0}^{t-\Delta}\left(\sum\limits_{u=v}^{t-\Delta}\alpha(v,u)\,\Delta\right)\Delta + \sum\limits_{v=0}^{t-\Delta}\left(\sum\limits_{u=v}^{t-\Delta}\sigma(v,u)\,\Delta\right)\Delta W(v)}}.$$

Combining the numerator and denominator, and also recognizing that

$$B(0,T) = e^{-\sum\limits_{u=0}^{T-\Delta} f(0,u)\Delta},$$

gives

$$\frac{B(t,T)}{A(t)} = B(0,T)\, e^{-\sum\limits_{v=0}^{t-\Delta}\left(\sum\limits_{u=v}^{T-\Delta}\alpha(v,u)\,\Delta\right)\Delta - \sum\limits_{v=0}^{t-\Delta}\left(\sum\limits_{u=v}^{T-\Delta}\sigma(v,u)\,\Delta\right)\Delta W(v)}. \qquad (16.9)$$

This is the equation for the evolution of the normalized bond price process.

Arbitrage-Free Restrictions

A contribution of the Heath-Jarrow-Morton model is to provide the restrictions needed on the drift and volatility parameters of the forward rate process such that the evolution is arbitrage-free. This section provides this derivation.

From Chapter 6, martingale pricing, we know that the zero-coupon bond price processes are arbitrage-free if and only if the normalized zero-coupon bond prices $B(t,T)/A(t)$ are martingales. Alternatively stated,

$$B(0,T) = E^{\pi}(B(t,T)/A(t)) \quad \text{for all } T. \qquad (16.10)$$

We can simplify this expression to discover what it implies for forward rates. Substitution of Expression (16.9) into (16.10) gives

$$B(0,T) = B(0,T)e^{-\sum\limits_{v=0}^{t-\Delta}\left(\sum\limits_{u=v}^{T-\Delta}\alpha(v,u)\,\Delta\right)\Delta}\, E^{\pi}\!\left(e^{-\sum\limits_{v=0}^{t-\Delta}\left(\sum\limits_{u=v}^{T-\Delta}\sigma(v,u)\,\Delta\right)\Delta W(v)}\right).$$

But this is true if and only if

$$e^{\sum\limits_{v=0}^{t-\Delta}\left(\sum\limits_{u=v}^{T-\Delta}\alpha(v,u)\,\Delta\right)\Delta} = E^{\pi}\!\left(e^{-\sum\limits_{v=0}^{t-\Delta}\left(\sum\limits_{u=v}^{T-\Delta}\sigma(v,u)\,\Delta\right)\Delta W(v)}\right).$$

Using a standard property of a normal distribution, it is shown in the Appendix of this chapter that

$$E^{\pi}\left(e^{-\sum_{v=0}^{t-\Delta}\left(\sum_{u=v}^{T-\Delta}\sigma(v,u)\Delta\right)\Delta W(v)}\right) = e^{\sum_{v=0}^{t-\Delta}\left(\sum_{u=v}^{T-\Delta}\sigma(v,u)\Delta\right)^2}/2 .$$

Hence, the zero-coupon bond price evolution is arbitrage-free if and only if

$$e^{\sum_{v=0}^{t-\Delta}\left(\sum_{u=v}^{T-\Delta}\alpha(v,u)\Delta\right)\Delta} = e^{\sum_{v=0}^{t-\Delta}\left(\sum_{u=v}^{T-\Delta}\sigma(v,u)\Delta\right)^2}/2$$

or equivalently

$$\sum_{u=v}^{T-\Delta}\alpha(v,u)\Delta = \left[\sum_{u=v}^{T-\Delta}\sigma(v,u)\Delta\right]^2/2 .$$

It can be shown (see the Appendix) that this implies

$$\alpha(v,T-\Delta) = \sigma(v,T-\Delta)\sum_{u=v}^{T-\Delta}\sigma(v,u)\Delta$$

or, taking limits as $\Delta \to 0$,

$$\alpha(v,T) = \sigma(v,T)\int_v^T \sigma(v,u)\,du.$$

Under the martingale probabilities, the expected change in the forward rate must be this particular function of the volatility. This is the arbitrage-free forward rate drift restriction.

If it is not of this form, then the process would not be arbitrage-free. For the subsequent analysis, we will impose this arbitrage-free restriction on the drift term in Expression (16.1). Under this restriction, the pricing and hedging of interest rate derivatives can proceed in the manner as described earlier in Chapter 6. This analysis forms the content of the remaining sections.

Before that analysis, however, we pause to discuss mean reversion in the context of the Heath-Jarrow-Morton model.

Mean Reversion/Volatility Reduction

We now discuss **mean reversion** in the context of the Heath-Jarrow-Morton model. Empirically we observe that if current interest rates are unusually "high," they eventually fall back to a "normal" level. Conversely, if interest rates are unusually "low," they tend to increase to a "normal" level. This is often summarized by saying that interest rates are **mean reverting**. The importance of incorporating mean reversion into the pricing of interest rate derivatives is often stressed by practitioners.

In the last chapter we described a binomial lattice for the spot interest rate process. We introduced mean reversion via the specification of the term structure of volatilities. In this chapter, we introduce mean reversion indirectly through the volatility of forward rates. Indeed, an alternative way of describing mean reversion is to say that interest rates tend to move within some finite range. Equivalently, the variance of spot interest rates is bounded as a function of time.

We next show that Expression (16.2) has the spot rate variance bounded as a function of time. Given the volatility function in Expression (16.2), it can be shown that

$$\text{var}^\pi[r(t)] = (\sigma^2/2\lambda)[1 - \exp(-2\lambda t)].$$

For $\lambda > 0$, the variance of the spot interest rate is bounded by $\sigma^2/2\lambda$ for all t. The larger the value of λ, the lower is the variance of the spot interest rate. For this reason, λ is referred to as the **volatility reduction factor**. Thus the specification of the volatility function as given in Expression (16.2) has embedded within it mean reversion of spot interest rates. Our introduction to the Heath-Jarrow-Morton model is now complete.

16.2 HEDGING TREASURY BILLS

Here we describe how to price and hedge Treasury bills using the Heath-Jarrow-Morton model.

We first derive a closed form solution for the price of a Treasury bill. Heath, Jarrow, and Morton (1992) show that Expression (16.8) can be manipulated to yield (taking limits as $\Delta \to 0$) a closed form solution for the zero-coupon bond's price:

$$B(t,T) = \frac{B(0,T)}{B(0,t)} \exp[-X(t,T)r(t) + X(t,T)f(0,t) - a(t,T)], \qquad (16.11)$$

where $X(t,T) \equiv \{1 - \exp[-\lambda(T - t)]\}/\lambda$ and $a(t,T) \equiv (\sigma^2/4\lambda)X(t,T)^2 [1 - \exp(-2\lambda t)]$ for $\lambda > 0$.[5] Note that at the maturity date, when $t = T$, these parameters simplify to

$$X(T,T) = 0$$
and
$$a(T,T) = 0,$$

---

[5]If the volatility reduction factor, lambda, is zero, $\lambda = 0$, then

$$X(t,T) \equiv (T - t)$$

and

$$a(t,T) \equiv (\sigma^2/2)(T - t)^2 t.$$

yielding

$$B(T,T) = \frac{B(0,T)}{B(0,T)} = 1$$

as required.

In the zero-coupon bond's price, the spot rate $r(t)$ is the only random factor; see Expression (16.11). This insight allows us to quantify changes in the zero-coupon bond's price as a result of changes in the spot rate $r(t)$ and time t. If $r(t)$ and t change by finite amounts $\Delta r(t)$ and Δ, respectively, then the change in the zero-coupon bond value can be written (using a Taylor series expansion) as

$$\Delta B(t,T) = \frac{\partial B}{\partial t} \Delta + \frac{\partial B}{\partial r} \Delta r + \frac{1}{2} \frac{\partial^2 B}{\partial r^2} (\Delta r)^2 + \dots, \tag{16.12}$$

where

$$\frac{\partial B}{\partial r} = -B(t,T)X(t,T) \le 0 \tag{16.13}$$

and

$$\frac{\partial^2 B}{\partial r^2} = B(t,T)X(t,T)^2 \ge 0. \tag{16.14}$$

Expression (16.12) is analogous to the material we covered in Chapter 10 on the delta and gamma hedging of equity options.

Expressions (16.13) and (16.14) are generalizations of the concepts of duration and convexity, respectively, introduced in Chapter 13. Recall that *duration* attempts to measure the sensitivity of bond price changes to a common factor. Here, the common factor is the spot rate $r(t)$ and the sensitivity is its first derivative $\partial B/\partial r$. Similarly, *convexity* attempts to measure changes in duration. Here, the second derivative $\partial^2 B/\partial r^2$ measures the change in the first derivative with respect to the spot rate $r(t)$. As $r(t)$ is common to all bonds, the limitations of the traditional measures of duration and convexity do not apply to Expressions (16.13) and (16.14).

There is one circumstance where the classical notions of duration and convexity can be shown to apply. Suppose the volatility reduction factor, λ, is zero; then

$$X(t,T) = T - t,$$

which is the classical definition of duration for a zero-coupon bond; see Expression (13.16) of Chapter 13. Here $\partial B/\partial r$ is proportional to duration, showing that classical duration is indeed an appropriate measure of risk, but only in this special case.

For this special case, from Expression (16.13), we see that for small Δ and Δr— that is, ignoring all but the first two terms on the right side of Expression (16.12)—

the entire term structure shifts in a parallel fashion. The term structure shift is $\Delta B(t, T)$ and the parallel shift is induced by the spot rate Δr.

Therefore, this gives an alternative proof, based on the Heath-Jarrow-Morton model, of the statement made in Chapter 13 that classical duration is a valid risk measure for bonds only if there are parallel shifts in the zero-coupon yield curve, and if the shifts are small—that is, ignoring all terms except the first two on the right side of Expression (16.12).

Hedge Ratio (Delta)

We discuss here the hedging of zero-coupon bonds based on Expressions (16.12) through (16.14) of the preceding section. The **hedge ratio** or **delta** for a zero-coupon bond is defined to be Expression (16.3), that is,

$$\text{Hedge Ratio} \equiv \frac{\partial B(t, T)}{\partial r}$$

$$= -B(t, T) \times X(t, T) \leq 0. \tag{16.15}$$

The hedge ratio is negative or zero, which makes sense because as the spot rate $r(t)$ increases, "discount" rates increase, implying that zero-coupon bond prices will fall.

The **gamma** for a zero-coupon bond is defined to be Expression (16.14), that is,

$$\text{Gamma} \equiv \frac{\partial^2 B(t, T)}{\partial r^2}$$

$$= B(t, T) \times X(t, T)^2 \geq 0. \tag{16.16}$$

The gamma is positive or zero because of the convexity of $B(t, T)$ in $r(t)$, which implies that as the spot rate $r(t)$ increases, the hedge ratio increases, everything else being constant.

Substituting the definitions for the hedge ratio and the gamma into Expression (16.12) implies that the change in the zero-coupon bond price can be written in a more intuitive fashion:

$$\Delta B(t, T) = \frac{\partial B}{\partial t} \Delta + (\text{Hedge Ratio}) \times \Delta r$$

$$+ \frac{1}{2} (\text{Gamma}) \times (\Delta r)^2 + \dots . \tag{16.17}$$

The change in the zero-coupon bond's price is decomposable into three terms: (1) the time decay ($\partial B/\partial t \, \Delta$), (2) the delta term (Hedge Ratio $\times \Delta r$), and (3) the gamma term [$(1/2)$ Gamma $\times (\Delta r)^2$]. Expression (16.17) ignores all higher-order terms.

For continuous trading, as $\Delta \to 0$, the only random term in Expression (16.17) is the delta term involving the spot rate Δr. The gamma terms involving $(\Delta r)^2$ can be shown to approach a deterministic function of time, which is analogous to the argu-

ment used in Chapter 8. Thus, for continuous trading, only delta hedging is relevant. This is the theoretical ideal under which the Heath-Jarrow-Morton model was derived. In contrast, Expression (16.17) is derived for discrete-time (non-continuous) hedging, which is important because continuous hedging is impossible due to transaction costs and market frictions. This is the form of model misspecification that Expression (16.17) implicitly addresses.

EXAMPLE **Delta Neutral Hedging**

Consider a financial institution that wants to hedge a one-year zero-coupon bond using two other zero-coupon bonds with maturities of half a year and one and a half years. The institution wants to design this portfolio to be delta neutral. Pricing details are given in Table 16.2, including the current zero-coupon bond price curve, the hedge ratios, and gammas for all the zero-coupon bonds.

Let n_1 be the number of half-year zero-coupon bonds and n_2 be the number of one-and-a-half-year zero-coupon bonds in the hedge portfolio. Let $V(0)$ represent the initial cost of the hedged portfolio.

The portfolio is assumed to be self-financing, implying that the initial value is zero:

$$V(0) \equiv 0.954200 + n_1 \times 0.977300 + n_2 \times 0.930850 = 0.$$

This can be rewritten in the form

$$n_1 \times 0.977300 + n_2 \times 0.930850 = -0.954200,$$

which gives us our first equation.

To be **delta neutral** the portfolio must, by definition, be insensitive to small changes in the spot rate $r(t)$. The sensitivity of the zero-coupon bond

---

TABLE 16.2 *Hedging Zero-Coupon Bonds*

MATURITY (YEARS)	DISCOUNT RATE	PRICE $B(0,T)$	$X(0,T)$	HEDGE RATIO	GAMMA
0.5	4.54%	0.977300	0.4877	−0.476635	0.232458
1.0	4.58%	0.954200	0.9516	−0.908041	0.864116
1.5	4.61%	0.930850	1.3929	−1.296600	1.806060
2.0	4.64%	0.907200	1.8127	−1.644475	2.980927

	$\sigma(t,T) = \sigma \times \exp[-\lambda(T-t)]$
Volatility	$\sigma = 1.0$ percent
Volatility Reduction Factor	$\lambda = 0.1$

price to small changes in $r(t)$ is given by Expression (16.13). To see this, note that Expression (16.12) demonstrates that, when $\Delta r(t)$ is small (say, 0.01), $\Delta r(t)^2$ is orders of magnitude smaller (0.0001) and the third term in Expression (16.12) can be ignored.

For the one-year zero-coupon bond, Expression (16.13) is

$$\frac{\partial B(0, 1)}{\partial r} = -B(0,1)X(0, 1) = -0.954200 \times [1 - \exp(-\lambda. 1)]/\lambda$$
$$= -0.954200 \times 0.9516$$
$$= -0.908041.$$

The numbers from Table 16.2 are generated using the program Bond/Hedge Ratio/Treasury Bills.[6] Therefore, for the hedge portfolio to be delta neutral,

$$n_1 \frac{\partial B(0, 0.5)}{\partial r} + n_2 \frac{\partial B(0, 1.5)}{\partial r} + \frac{\partial B(0, 1)}{\partial r} = 0,$$

that is,

$$n_1 \times 0.476635 + n_2 \times 1.29660 = -0.908041.$$

This gives us our second equation in two unknowns (n_1, n_2). Solving for n_1 and n_2 gives the solution:

$$n_1 = -0.4760$$

and

$$n_2 = -0.5254.$$

Thus, to hedge the one-year zero-coupon bond, it is necessary to short 0.4760 of the half-year and short 0.5254 of the one-and-a-half-year zero-coupon bonds. If we had wanted to construct a synthetic one-year zero-coupon bond, we would go long in these two zero-coupon bonds.

Notice that according to the traditional measure of duration, to hedge this one-year zero-coupon bond the duration of the portfolio must sum to 1, which

---

[6]Note that $-0.954200 \times 0.9516 = -0.908017$. This figure differs from that in Table 16.2 due to round-off error. Quoting $X(0, 1)$ to seven decimal places gives

$$X(0, 1) = 0.9516258$$

so that

$$-0.9542 \times X(0, 1) = -0.908041,$$

which agrees with the number in Table 16.2.

is the duration of the zero-coupon bond being hedged. This would give a different second equation in n_1 and n_2. We can calculate the duration of our correct hedging portfolio and show that it is not 1. The duration of our hedging portfolio is

$$0.4760(0.5) + 0.5254(1.5) = 1.0261.$$

It is not 1, and it emphasizes the fact that there is error in using classical duration as a risk measure. ■

In the preceding example, the face value of all instruments is \$1. In practice, the face value of the instrument to be hedged is typically many orders of magnitude larger. The adjustment for this modification is straightforward. For example, suppose that the instrument to be hedged has a face value of 10 million dollars and the face value of the two zero-coupon bonds used to construct the hedge is \$100,000. In this case, the two equations used to determine the hedge become

$$n_1 \times 0.977300 \times 100,000 + n_2 \times 0.930850 \times 100,000$$
$$= -0.954200 \times 10,000,000$$

and

$$n_1 \times 0.476635 \times 100,000 + n_2 \times 1.29660 \times 100,000$$
$$= -0.908040 \times 10,000,000.$$

Solving for n_1 and n_2 gives

$$n_1 = -476$$

and

$$n_2 = -525.4.$$

Rounding the last figure to an integer gives $n_2 = -525$. We have completed the discussion of the adjustments necessary for different face value zero-coupon bonds. We will use this insight later on in the text.

Formalization (delta hedging)

This section formalizes the procedure of delta hedging. The formalization involves little more than replacing numbers in the above example with algebraic symbols.

Suppose that we want to hedge a zero-coupon bond, $B(t, T)$, using two other zero-coupon bonds that mature on dates T_1 and T_2 with prices $B(t, T_1)$ and $B(t, T_2)$, respectively. We also want the portfolio to be self-financing at date 0. Thus the initial cost of the hedged portfolio must be zero, that is,

$$V(0) \equiv B(t, T) + n_1 \times B(t, T_1) + n_2 \times B(t, T_2) = 0, \tag{16.18}$$

where n_1 is the number of zero-coupon bonds with maturity T_1 and n_2 is the number of zero-coupon bonds with maturity T_2. This gives us our first equation in the two unknowns (n_1, n_2).

To get our second equation we consider Expression (16.17). A small change in the spot rate implies that $(\Delta r)^2$ is small enough so that we can ignore it. In this case, the third term on the right side of Expression (16.17) involving gamma can be omitted.

The sensitivity of the price of a zero-coupon bond to small changes in the spot rate is thus given by

$$\text{(hedge ratio)} \times \Delta r = -B(t, T) \times X(t, T) \times \Delta r.$$

Therefore, the change in the value of the hedged portfolio is approximated by

$$\Delta V = [-B(t, T) \times X(t, T) - n_1 \times B(t, T_1) \times X(t, T_1) \\ -n_2 \times B(t, T_2) \times X(t, T_2)]\Delta r.$$

To be insensitive to small changes in the spot rate $r(t)$, the term inside the square brackets [ ] on the right side of the above expression must be zero:

$$B(t, T) \times X(t, T) + n_1 \times B(t, T_1) \times X(t, T_1) + n_2 \times B(t, T_2) \times X(t, T_2) = 0.$$
$$(16.19)$$

This gives us our second equation in the two unknowns.

Solving Expressions (16.18) and (16.19) for n_1 and n_2 allows us to construct a portfolio that hedges the zero-coupon bond $B(t, T)$ against small changes in the spot rate $r(t)$. Such a portfolio is called delta neutral.

In the limit as Δ approaches zero, only small changes in $r(t)$ are possible, and the above delta neutral portfolio is (instantaneously) riskless. This is the idea underlying the construction of synthetic bonds in a continuous time model. However, in markets with transaction costs or market frictions, continuous hedging is not possible. This is a case where discrete hedging is needed because Δ is finite. This observation implies that large changes in the spot rate become relevant, and the third term in Expression (16.17) involving gamma cannot be ignored.

Gamma Hedging

Now we examine gamma hedging. A delta neutral portfolio is constructed to be insensitive to small changes in the spot rate $r(t)$. However, it is not insensitive to large changes in $r(t)$. For large changes in $r(t)$ we cannot ignore the $(\Delta r)^2$ term in Expression (16.17). To see this, note that if $\Delta r = 0.01$, a small change, then $(\Delta r)^2 = 0.0001$ and can be ignored as insignificant. But, if $\Delta r = 1$, a large change, then $(\Delta r)^2 = 1$ is of the same order of magnitude and cannot be ignored.

To construct a portfolio to be both delta and gamma neutral, we must introduce an additional bond into the hedged portfolio. The following example illustrates this procedure.

EXAMPLE
Gamma Hedging (Continued)

This example illustrates the procedure for gamma hedging a self-financed, delta neutral portfolio.

Consider the previous example involving a self-financed, delta hedged portfolio. Let n_3 denote the number of two-year zero-coupon bonds used in the hedge to make it gamma neutral. We need to modify all the previous equations to include this third zero-coupon bond.

From Expression (16.18), to be self-financed the initial value of the portfolio is constructed to be zero, implying (using Table 16.2)

$$n_1 \times 0.977300 + n_2 \times 0.930850 + n_3 \times 0.907200 = -0.954200.$$

To be delta neutral requires, using Expression (16.19), that

$$n_1 \times 0.476635 + n_2 \times 1.296600 + n_3 \times 1.644475 = -0.908041.$$

To be gamma neutral requires, in addition, that

$$n_1 \times 0.232458 + n_2 \times 1.806060 + n_3 \times 2.980927 = -0.864116.$$

Solving the preceding three equations gives

$$n_1 = -0.3093,$$
$$n_2 = -1.0776,$$

and

$$n_3 = 0.3872.$$

Because all the zero-coupon bonds have non-negative gamma, for the portfolio to be gamma neutral requires taking a positive position in some zero-coupon bond. In this case, it turns out to be the three-year zero-coupon bond ($n_3 = 0.3872$). All the other bonds are held short. In order to overcome this positive position in the third bond, the total quantities of zero-coupon bonds held short must exceed those in the case of the delta neutral portfolio alone. ∎

Gamma and Convexity

Here we reemphasize the fact that gamma is the appropriate generalization of convexity needed to account for large changes in the spot rate $r(t)$. For large changes in the spot rate $r(t)$, and neglecting the Δ term, Expression (16.17) implies that the change in the zero-coupon bond's price is approximately equal to

$$\text{(Hedge Ratio)} \times \Delta r + \frac{1}{2}\text{(Gamma)} \times (\Delta r)^2. \tag{16.20}$$

FIGURE 16.1   *Convexity*

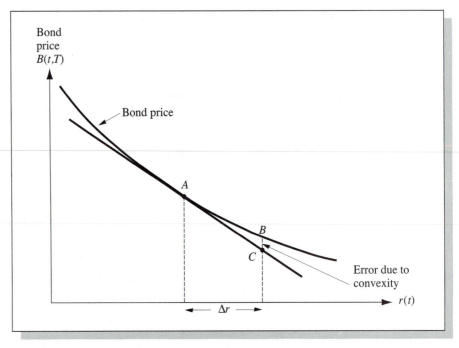

For small changes in the spot rate $r(t)$ we can ignore the term involving $(\Delta r)^2$ in Expression (16.20), and the change in the bond price is approximately linear. For large changes in $r(t)$ we cannot ignore Gamma $\times (\Delta r)^2$ in Expression (16.20), as shown in Figure 16.1. The gamma term is the correct adjustment necessary for the convexity in the bond's price due to the spot rate $r(t)$. However, this convexity is different from the traditional convexity measure defined in Chapter 13, which was based on the yield to maturity and not the spot rate.

EXAMPLE   **Importance of Gamma**

In this example we illustrate the importance of gamma in approximating changes in a zero-coupon bond's price due to changes in the spot rate $r(t)$.

Consider an over-the-counter, default-free, zero-coupon bond. The maturity of the zero-coupon bond is three years (1,080 days, assuming a 360-day year) and its current price is 84.8502, assuming a face value of $100. The instantaneous spot interest rate is 5.00 percent.

Suppose that the instantaneous spot interest rate changes by 150 basis points to 6.50 percent. The price of the zero-coupon bond changes to 81.6147, a change of −3.2355.

Given that the volatility is 1.50 percent and the volatility reduction factor is 0.1, then, using the program Bond/Hedge Ratio/Treasury Bills to calculate the Hedge Ratio and Gamma,

Hedge Ratio (Delta) = −219.9165

and

Gamma = 569.9835.

(The Treasury bill price 84.8502 implies a discount rate of 5.0499 percent.) Therefore,

Hedge Ratio (Delta) × Δr = −219.9165 × (0.015) = −3.2987

and

$0.5 \times \text{Gamma} \times (\Delta r)^2 = 0.5 \times 569.9835 \times (0.015)^2 = 0.0641$.

Hence Expression (16.20) yields

$$\begin{aligned}
\text{Hedge Ratio (Delta)} \times \Delta r & \\
+0.5 \times \text{Gamma} \times (\Delta r)^2 &= -3.2987 + 0.0641 \\
&= -3.2346,
\end{aligned}$$

which is the approximate change in the value of the Treasury bill. The error with these two adjustments is only 0.0009; without the gamma adjustment, the error would be −0.0632. ■

Expression (16.20) is a generalization of Expression (13.22) in Chapter 13, where we introduced the terms "duration" and "convexity." We prefer not to use the term "duration," since the duration and convexity formulas in Chapter 13 implicitly assume that interest rates are normally distributed with the volatility reduction factor, λ, being identically zero.[7] More importantly, we use the terms "hedge ratio" (delta) and "gamma" throughout this text. Bonds are just one simple example of a derivative security, and there is no reason to use terms such as duration and convexity, which only apply as risk measures under limited circumstances.

EXAMPLE **Comparison of Classical Duration and the Hedge Ratio**

In this example we illustrate the difference between the classical duration measure and the hedge ratio introduced above.

---

[7]This point was formally shown earlier in the chapter; see also Ingersoll, Skelton, and Weil (1978).

Consider a Treasury bill with a maturity of 0.5 years, a face value of $100, and a price of 97.7272. The Macauley duration for this bill is 0.5 years. Let the volatility be 2.0 percent and the volatility reduction factor be zero. In this case, duration and our hedge ratio should coincide.

Using the program Bond/Hedge Ratio/Treasury Bill Futures, the hedge ratio (delta) is -48.8636. The ratio of the absolute value of delta to the price of the Treasury bill is 0.5, which is identical to the Macauley duration, as it should be.

If the volatility reduction factor is positive, however, then this is no longer the case. The difference between the duration of 0.5 and the correct measure (absolute value of delta/T-bill price) is given in the following table.

VOLATILITY REDUCTION FACTOR	DELTA	ABSOLUTE VALUE OF DELTA/TREASURY BILL PRICE	DIFFERENCE
0	−48.8636	0.5000	0.0
0.1	−47.6621	0.4877	0.0123
0.2	−46.4999	0.4758	0.0242
0.3	−45.3754	0.4643	0.0357

16.3 HEDGING TREASURY BONDS

We examine here the pricing and hedging of Treasury bonds. Our analysis is similar to that used for Treasury bills, except that Treasury bonds pay coupons.

Consider a Treasury bond that makes n coupon payments. The first coupon, c_1, is paid at date T_1, the second coupon, c_2, is paid at date T_2, and so on. We allow the coupons to differ across time, although for most bonds, $c_1 = c_2 \ldots = c_n = c$. The face value F is paid at date T_n.

The value of the bond today is

$$B_c(t) \equiv \sum_{j=1}^{n} c_j \times B(t, T_j) + F \times B(t, T_n).$$

Using an equation similar to Expression (16.4), the change in the value of the Treasury bond for finite changes in date t and the spot rate $r(t)$ is given by

$$\Delta B_c(t) = \left[\sum_{j=1}^{n} c_j \times \frac{\partial B}{\partial t}(t, T_j) + F \times \frac{\partial B}{\partial t}(t, T_n) \right] \Delta$$
$$+ (HR_c) \times \Delta r + \frac{1}{2}(\text{Gamma}_c) \times (\Delta r)^2,$$

where the hedge ratio for the coupon bond is defined by

$$HR_c \equiv -\left[\sum_{j=1}^{n} c_j \times B(t, T_j) \times X(t, T_j) + F \times B(t, T_n) \times X(t, T_n) \right]$$

and the gamma for the coupon bond is defined by

$$\text{Gamma}_c \equiv \sum_{j=1}^{n} c_j \times B(t, T_j) \times X(t, T_j)^2 + F \times B(t, T_n) \times X(t, T_n)^2.$$

Both the hedge ratio and the gamma for the coupon bond are the weighted averages of the hedge ratios and gammas of the zero-coupon bonds underlying the coupon bond. The weights are the number of each zero-coupon bond in the synthetic coupon bond valuation formula.

EXAMPLE

Coupon Bond Calculations

This example illustrates the computation of a coupon bond's hedge ratio and gamma.

   Consider a coupon bond with a maturity of two years, paying a coupon of $4.50 every six months. Let the face value be $100. The details of the term structure are given in Table 16.3. The value of the coupon bond is

$$B_c(0) = 4.50 \times [0.9773 + 0.9542 + 0.9308 + 0.9072] + 100 \times 0.9072$$
$$= 107.68.$$

The hedge ratio for the coupon bond is

$$\text{HR}_c = -4.50 \times [0.4766 + 0.9080 + 1.2965 + 1.6445] - 100 \times 1.6445$$
$$= -183.9159.$$

TABLE 16.3   *Hedge Ratio and Gamma for a Treasury Bond*

MATURITY (YEARS) T	PRICE $B(0,T)$	$X(0,T)$	HEDGE RATIO* $B(0,T)X(0,T)$
0.5	0.977272	0.4877	−0.476621
1.0	0.954164	0.9516	−0.908007
1.5	0.930780	1.3929	−1.296502
2.0	0.907214	1.8127	−1.644500

$$\sigma(t, T) = \sigma \times \exp[-\lambda(T - t)]$$

Volatility $\sigma = 1.0$ percent
Volatility Reduction Factor $\lambda = 0.1$
Coupon = $4.50 every six months
Face Value = $100

*These results are generated using the program Bonds/Hedge Ratio/Treasury Bill Futures.

> You should check these calculations using the program Bonds/Hedge Ratio/Treasury Bond. The gamma for the coupon bond is calculated as
>
> $Gamma_c = 324.57.$ ∎

The procedure for delta and gamma hedging a coupon bond is identical to the procedure for delta and gamma hedging a zero-coupon bond. The only difference is that in constructing the relevant equations, we use the coupon bond's hedge ratio and gamma instead of those of the zero-coupon bond. As the analysis is otherwise identical, we leave the details to the reader. Our discussion of coupon bonds is now complete.

16.4 TREASURY BILL FUTURES

Now we study the pricing and hedging of Treasury bill futures contracts. In Chapter 15, we demonstrated that given the lattice of spot interest rates and the term structure of volatilities, we can also determine futures prices. Let $\mathcal{F}(t; T_{\mathcal{F}}, T_B)$ denote the futures price at date t of a futures contract that expires at date $T_{\mathcal{F}}$. The futures contract is written on a Treasury bill with maturity at date $T_B \geq T_{\mathcal{F}}$. The dates and maturities are illustrated in Figure 16.2.

At the delivery date $T_{\mathcal{F}}$ of the futures contract, the futures price equals the value of the underlying Treasury bill:

$$\mathcal{F}(T_{\mathcal{F}}; T_{\mathcal{F}}, T_B) = B(T_{\mathcal{F}}, T_B), \tag{16.21}$$

where $B(T_{\mathcal{F}}, T_B)$ is the value at date $T_{\mathcal{F}}$ of a Treasury bill that matures at date T_B.

Using the risk-neutral valuation methodology, we can show, using arguments similar to those described in Chapter 15, that the futures price is a martingale under the martingale probabilities. Therefore, the futures price at date 0 is given by the following equation:

$$\mathcal{F}(0; T_{\mathcal{F}}, T_B) = E^{\pi}[B(T_{\mathcal{F}}, T_B)]. \tag{16.22}$$

FIGURE 16.2 *Treasury Bill Futures*

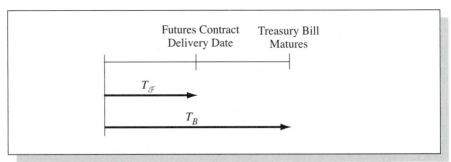

Evaluating this expression (see Musiela, Turnbull, and Wakeman (1993) for the derivation) gives

$$\mathcal{F}(0;T_{\mathcal{F}},T_B) = [B(0,T_B)/B(0,T_{\mathcal{F}})]\exp(\theta), \tag{16.23}$$

where

$$\theta \equiv -(\sigma^2/\lambda^3)\{[1 - \exp[-\lambda(T_B - T_{\mathcal{F}})]][1 - \exp(-\lambda T_{\mathcal{F}})]$$
$$- \frac{1}{4}[1 - \exp[-2\lambda(T_B - T_{\mathcal{F}})]][1 - \exp(-2\lambda T_{\mathcal{F}})]\}$$
$$+ (\sigma^2/4\lambda^3)\{[1 - \exp(-2\lambda T_{\mathcal{F}})][1 - \exp[-\lambda(T_B - T_{\mathcal{F}})]]^2\}.$$

The term $B(0,T_B)/B(0,T_{\mathcal{F}})$ is the forward price from date $T_{\mathcal{F}}$ to date T_B implied by the current term structure. Thus, the second term on the right of Expression (16.23), $\exp(\theta)$, represents the divergence between forward and futures prices. If interest rates are non-random ($\sigma \equiv 0$), then $\exp(\theta) = 1$, and forward and futures prices are identical. This situation, although unrealistic, is a special case of our earlier result from Chapter 2 on the equality of forward and futures prices.

EXAMPLE   **Treasury Bill Futures Price**

This example illustrates the computation of a Treasury bill futures price.

Consider a futures contract with delivery in 90 days' time. The contract is written on a 91-day Treasury bill. In comparison to Figure 16.2, this implies that $T_{\mathcal{F}} = 90$ and $T_B = 181$ (= 90 + 91). Let the discount rate for a Treasury bill that matures in 90 days' time be 4.524 percent and for a Treasury bill that matures in 181 days' time be 4.546 percent. Let the volatility be $\sigma = 1.2$ percent and the volatility reduction factor be $\lambda = 0.1$.

Using the program Bonds/Hedge Ratio/Treasury Bill Futures, the T-bill futures price is

$$\mathcal{F}(0;90,181) = 98.8321.$$

The futures price is quoted in terms of an index, as explained in Chapter 13. The futures discount rate i_f is determined by

$$98.8321 = 100\left[1 - \frac{i_f}{100} \times \frac{90}{360}\right],$$

implying that

$$i_f = 4.6716 \text{ percent.}$$

The T-bill futures index value is

$$\text{Futures Index Value} \equiv 100 - 4.67$$
$$= 95.33.$$

It is interesting to compare the futures price to the forward price. The price of a 90-day Treasury bill is

$$B(0,90) = 1 - \frac{4.524}{100} \times \frac{90}{360}$$
$$= 0.98869$$

and the price of a 181-day Treasury bill is

$$B(0,181) = 1 - \frac{4.546}{100} \times \frac{181}{360}$$
$$= 0.97714.$$

Therefore, the forward price is (see Chapter 13)

$$F(0,90,181) = 100[0.97714/0.98869]$$
$$= 98.8322,$$

which differs in the fourth decimal place from the futures price. ■

We glean two points from this example. First, as already mentioned, given the term structure and volatility, the futures price can be determined. Second, as mentioned in Chapter 2, for futures contracts with relatively short maturity there is little difference between forward and futures prices. This is not necessarily the case for long-dated contracts (see Question 16.9 at the end of the chapter).

Hedging

Here we study the hedging of Treasury bill futures contracts. The T-bill futures price prior to the delivery date can be expressed in the form[8]

$$\mathcal{F}(t;T_\mathcal{F},T_B) = \mathcal{F}(0;T_\mathcal{F},T_B)\exp[-X(t;T_\mathcal{F},T_B)r(t) + X(t;T_\mathcal{F},T_B)f(0,t) + a_\mathcal{F}(t,T)], \quad (16.24)$$

where

$$X(t;T_\mathcal{F},T_B) \equiv \{\exp[-\lambda(T_\mathcal{F}-t)] - \exp[-\lambda(T_B-t)]\}/\lambda \quad \text{and}$$
$$a_\mathcal{F}(t,T) \equiv (\sigma^2/2\lambda^2)X(t;T_\mathcal{F},T_B)[1 - \exp(-\lambda t)]^2$$
$$- (\sigma^2/4\lambda)X(t;T_\mathcal{F},T_B)^2[1 - \exp(-2\lambda t)].$$

---

[8]If the volatility reduction factor λ is zero, then

$$X(t;m,T) = (T - m)$$

and

$$a_\mathcal{F}(t,T) = (\sigma^2/2)(T - m)t^2 - (\sigma^2/2)(T - m)^2 t.$$

If date t and the spot rate $r(t)$ change by finite amounts of Δ and $\Delta r(t)$, respectively, the change in the futures price can be written, using a Taylor series expansion, as

$$\Delta \mathcal{F}(t; T_{\mathcal{F}}, T_B) = \frac{\partial \mathcal{F}}{\partial t} \Delta + \frac{\partial \mathcal{F}}{\partial r} \Delta r + \frac{1}{2} \frac{\partial^2 \mathcal{F}}{\partial r^2} (\Delta r)^2 + \ldots, \tag{16.25}$$

where

$$\frac{\partial \mathcal{F}}{\partial r} = -\mathcal{F}(t; T_{\mathcal{F}}, T_B) X(t; T_{\mathcal{F}}, T_B) \le 0 \tag{16.26}$$

and

$$\frac{\partial^2 \mathcal{F}}{\partial r^2} = \mathcal{F}(t; T_{\mathcal{F}}, T_B) X(t; T_{\mathcal{F}}, T_B)^2 \ge 0. \tag{16.27}$$

As before, in the limit of continuous trading as Δ approaches zero, the quantity $(\Delta r)^2$ approaches a deterministic function of time, and only the change in the spot rate, Δr, remains random. In this case, only delta hedging is required to replicate the futures contract.

For discrete changes in time $\Delta > 0$, however, both Δr and $(\Delta r)^2$ are random. In this case, hedging requires consideration of all three terms in Expression (16.25). Discrete trading becomes relevant when there are either transaction costs or market frictions that make continuous trading impossible. Unfortunately, both transaction costs and market frictions are present in Treasury bill futures markets.

Hedge Ratio (Delta)

Now we discuss the delta hedging of interest rate derivatives using T-bill futures contracts. The hedge ratio or delta for a Treasury bill futures contract is defined to be

$$\text{Hedge Ratio} \equiv \frac{\partial \mathcal{F}}{\partial r}$$
$$= -\mathcal{F}(t; T_{\mathcal{F}}, T_B) \times X(t; T_{\mathcal{F}}, T_B) \le 0. \tag{16.28}$$

The gamma for a Treasury bill futures contract is defined to be

$$\text{Gamma} \equiv \frac{\partial^2 \mathcal{F}}{\partial r^2}$$
$$= \mathcal{F}(t; T_{\mathcal{F}}, T_B) \times X(t; T_{\mathcal{F}}, T_B)^2 \ge 0. \tag{16.29}$$

Substituting these definitions into Expression (16.25) implies that the change in the futures price can be alternatively written as

$$\Delta \mathcal{F}(t; T_{\mathcal{F}}, T_B) = \frac{\partial \mathcal{F}}{\partial t} \Delta + (\text{Hedge Ratio}) \times \Delta r + \frac{1}{2} (\text{Gamma}) \times (\Delta r)^2 + \ldots.$$

EXAMPLE

Delta Hedging

This example illustrates delta hedging of a zero-coupon bond with a T-bill futures contract.

Consider a financial institution that wants to hedge a one-year zero-coupon bond with face value $100 using a zero-coupon bond with a maturity of 180 days and a face value of $100, and a 180-day futures contract written on a 91-day Treasury bill. Pricing details are given in Table 16.4. (Note the Treasury bill prices are the same as those in Table 16.2 but multiplied by 100.)

The institution wants the hedging portfolio to be self-financing at date 0. Let n_1 denote the number of 180-day Treasury bills used and n_2 denote the number of futures contracts used to hedge the one-year zero-coupon bond. By construction, the initial value of the hedged portfolio is zero, that is,

$$V(0) \equiv 95.4200 + n_1 \times 97.7300 = 0.$$

Recall that the initial value of the futures contract is zero, so the term involving n_2 does not appear in this expression.

To be neutral to small changes in the spot rate $r(t)$, the hedge ratio of the portfolio must be zero. Using the numbers from Table 16.4 gives

$$-90.8041 - n_1 \times 47.6635 - n_2 \times 23.4607 = 0.$$

TABLE 16.4 *Hedging Zero-Coupon Bonds**

TREASURY BILLS				
MATURITY (DAYS)	**DISCOUNT RATE**	**PRICE × 100**	**HEDGE RATIO**	**GAMMA**
180	4.54	97.7300	−47.6635	23.2458
360	4.58	95.4200	−90.8041	86.4116
540	4.61	93.0850	−129.6600	180.6060

FUTURES CONTRACT					
MATURITY (DAYS)	**INDEX VALUE**	**FUTURES**	**X(0; 180, 271)****	**HEDGE RATIO**	**GAMMA PRICE**
180	95.23	98.8084	0.2374	−23.4607	5.5704

$$\sigma(t, T) = \sigma \times \exp[-\lambda(T - t)]$$

Volatility $\sigma = 1.0$ percent
Volatility Reduction Factor $\lambda = 0.1$
A 360-day year is used.

---

*The program Bonds/Hedge Ratio/Treasury Bill Futures is used to generate these results.
**$X(0; 180, 271) = [\exp(-\lambda 0.5) - \exp(-\lambda 0.7528)]/\lambda.$

The delta for the futures contract is calculated using Expression (16.28), which gives us our second equation. Solving for n_1 and n_2 gives

$$n_1 = -0.9764$$

and

$$n_2 = -1.8869.$$

To hedge the one-year zero-coupon bond one needs to short 0.9764 units of the 180-day Treasury bill and write 1.8869 T-bill futures contracts. ∎

Formalization (delta hedging)

Here we formalize the analysis in the previous example. We want to hedge a Treasury bill $B(t, T)$ that matures on date T, using another Treasury bill $B(t, T_1)$ and a Treasury bill futures contract. The futures contract delivery date is date $T_{\mathcal{F}}$ and it is written on a Treasury bill that matures at date T_2. Let n_1 be the number of Treasury bills that mature at date T_1 and n_2 be the number of futures contracts used in the hedge.

First, the portfolio is required to be self-financed at date 0. By construction, therefore, the initial value of the hedged portfolio must be zero, that is,

$$V(t) \equiv B(t, T) + n_1 \times B(t, T_1) + n_2 \times 0 = 0. \tag{16.30}$$

Note that the value of the T-bill futures contract is zero. This gives us our first equation in the two unknowns (n_1, n_2).

Second, the portfolio should be neutral to small changes in the spot rate $r(t)$. The sensitivity of the portfolio to a small change in $r(t)$ is

$$[-B(t, T) \times X(t, T) - n_1 \times B(t, T_1) \times X(t, T_1) - n_2 \times \mathcal{F}(t; T_{\mathcal{F}}, T_2) \\ \times X(t; T_{\mathcal{F}}, T_2)]\Delta r.$$

To be neutral to small changes in $r(t)$ the term inside the square brackets [ ] must be zero, that is,

$$B(t, T) \times X(t, T) + n_1 \times B(t, T_1) \times X(t, T_1) + n_2 \times \mathcal{F}(t; T_{\mathcal{F}}, T_2) \\ \times X(t; T_{\mathcal{F}}, T_2) = 0, \tag{16.31}$$

which is our second equation. Solving Expressions (16.30) and (16.31) for n_1 and n_2 allows us to construct a self-financed portfolio that is neutral to small changes in the spot rate $r(t)$. Such a portfolio is called delta neutral. The example in the previous section shows how to solve these equations. A solution almost always exists.

Gamma Hedging

Here we show how to gamma hedge a portfolio. A self-financed delta neutral portfolio is sensitive to large changes in the spot rate $r(t)$. In this case, we must consider the gamma term involving $(\Delta r)^2$ in Expressions (16.12) and (16.25).

EXAMPLE   **Gamma Hedging (Continued)**

This example illustrates how to augment a self-financed, delta neutral portfolio to make it gamma neutral as well. To do this, we introduce an additional hedging instrument: an eighteen-month Treasury bill. Let n_3 denote the number of eighteen-month Treasury bills used. See Table 16.4 for the necessary inputs.

The date-0 self-financed condition implies that the initial value of the hedged portfolio is zero:

$$95.4200 + n_1 \times 97.7300 + n_2 \times 0 + n_3 \times 93.0850 = 0,$$

giving us our first equation in three unknowns. To be delta neutral implies, generalizing (16.31), that

$$90.8041 + n_1 \times 47.6635 + n_2 \times 23.4607 + n_3 \times 129.6600 = 0.$$

This gives our second equation. To be gamma neutral implies

$$86.4116 + n_1 \times 23.2458 + n_2 \times 5.5704 + n_3 \times 180.6060 = 0.$$

We have our third equation. Solving for n_1, n_2, and n_3 gives

$$n_1 = -0.6104,$$
$$n_2 = -0.5067,$$

and

$$n_3 = -0.3843.$$

This portfolio will be both delta and gamma neutral.   ■

16.5 TREASURY BOND FUTURES

We now examine the pricing and hedging of Treasury bond futures contracts. The difference is that Treasury bonds pay coupons while Treasury bills do not.

Let $\mathcal{F}_c(t; T_{\mathcal{F}})$ denote the futures price at date t of a T-bond futures contract with delivery at date $T_{\mathcal{F}}$. The subscript c denotes the fact that the underlying Treasury bond

has coupon payments. The futures contract is written on a Treasury bond that pays n coupons and matures at date $T_n \geq T_{\mathscr{F}}$ with a face value F.

At the delivery date of the T-bond futures contract, the futures price equals the price of the underlying Treasury bond, that is,

$$\mathscr{F}_c(T_{\mathscr{F}}; T_{\mathscr{F}}) = B_c(T_{\mathscr{F}}), \tag{16.32}$$

where $B_c(T_{\mathscr{F}})$ is the date-$T_{\mathscr{F}}$ value of the Treasury bond, given by

$$B_c(T_{\mathscr{F}}) = \sum_{j=1}^{n} c_j \times B(T_{\mathscr{F}}, T_j) + F \times B(T_{\mathscr{F}}, T_n), \tag{16.33}$$

where c_j is the coupon at date $T_j (T_j \geq T_{\mathscr{F}})$ and F is the face value of the bond.

From the risk-neutral valuation methodology of Chapter 6, it can be shown that the futures price is a martingale under the martingale probabilitites. Thus the futures price at date 0 is given by

$$\mathscr{F}_c(0; T_{\mathscr{F}}) = E^{\pi}[B_c(T_{\mathscr{F}})]. \tag{16.34}$$

If we substitute Expression (16.33) into the above equation and use Expression (16.22), we have the result that the futures price on a Treasury bond is the sum of futures prices on Treasury bills:

$$\mathscr{F}_c(0; T_{\mathscr{F}}) = \sum_{j=1}^{n} c_j \times \mathscr{F}(0; T_{\mathscr{F}}, T_j) + F \times \mathscr{F}(0; T_{\mathscr{F}}, T_n). \tag{16.35}$$

This result is important because it implies that all of the results from the last section on T-bill futures contracts can be used here. Before defining the hedge ratio and gamma for T-bond futures contracts, we remark that we have not considered any of the options implicit in the futures contract discussed in Chapter 13. These options do affect the futures price, especially near maturity.[9] We have omitted these embedded options to simplify the analysis.

EXAMPLE   **Treasury Bond Futures**

This example illustrates the computation of a T-note futures price. Consider a futures contract that is written on a two-year Treasury note. The delivery date of the futures contract is 180 days. The underlying Treasury note has a coupon of 8 percent per annum and a face value of $100. Given the information in Table 16.5, we use the program Bonds/Hedge Ratio/Treasury Bond Futures to determine the futures price:

Treasury Bond Futures Value = 105.4527.

---

[9]The valuation of these options is discussed in Carr and Chen (1994).

TABLE 16.5 *Treasury Bill Prices**

MATURITY (DAYS)	TREASURY BILL DATA			
	DISCOUNT RATE	PRICE × 100	HEDGE RATIO*	GAMMA*
180	4.5455	97.7272	−47.6621	23.2451
360	4.5836	95.4164	−90.8007	86.4083
540	4.6147	93.0780	−129.6502	180.5923
720	4.6393	90.7214	−164.4500	298.0973
900	4.6579	88.3553	−195.4411	432.3142

Volatility
Volatility Reduction Factor
A 360-day year is used.

$$\sigma(t,T) = \sigma \times \exp[-\lambda(T-t)]$$
$\sigma = 1.0$ percent
$\lambda = 0.1$

*The program Bonds/Hedge Ratio/Treasury Bill Futures is used to generate these results.

Alternatively, we could determine this value by using Expression (16.35). The delivery date of all the Treasury bill futures contracts is 180 days. The first contract is written on a Treasury bill that matures in 360 days' time, the time of the first coupon payment. The second contract is written on a Treasury bill that matures in 540 days' time, the time of the second coupon payment, and so on. Using the program Bonds/Hedge Ratio/Treasury Bill Futures, the Treasury bill futures prices are computed.

MATURITY OF UNDERLYING TREASURY BILL	TREASURY BILL FUTURES PRICE
360	97.6348
540	95.2415
720	92.8292
900	90.4081

Substituting into Expression (16.35) (the coupon is 4.00 every six months) gives

$$4.00 \times \{[97.6348 + 95.2415 + 92.8292 + 90.4081]/100\} + 100 \times (90.4081/100) = 105.4527.$$

This is the same value obtained earlier. ■

Hedge ratio (delta)

Here we examine delta hedging using the T-bond futures contract. Let $HR(t; T_{\mathcal{F}}, T_j)$ represent the hedge ratio at date t for a Treasury bill futures contract with delivery at date $T_{\mathcal{F}}$. The futures contract is written on a Treasury bill that matures at

date T_j. Let $\mathrm{HR}_c(t;T_{\mathscr{F}})$ denote the hedge ratio for the Treasury bond futures contract; then

$$\mathrm{HR}_c(t;T_{\mathscr{F}}) \equiv \sum_{j=1}^{n} c_j \times \mathrm{HR}(t;T_{\mathscr{F}},T_j) + F \times \mathrm{HR}(t;T_{\mathscr{F}},T_n). \qquad (16.36)$$

Using a similar notation, the gamma for the Treasury bond futures is

$$\mathrm{Gamma}_c(t;T_{\mathscr{F}}) \equiv \sum_{j=1}^{n} c_j \times \mathrm{Gamma}\,(t;T_{\mathscr{F}},T_j) + F \times \mathrm{Gamma}\,(t;T_{\mathscr{F}},T_n). \quad (16.37)$$

Delta and gamma hedging follow the analogous procedure studied for delta and gamma hedging with T-bill futures. Consequently, we only illustrate delta hedging. We leave gamma hedging to the reader as an exercise.

EXAMPLE   **Delta Hedging**

This example illustrates delta hedging using the T-bond futures contract. Suppose a financial institution wants to hedge a one-year Treasury bill using a Treasury bill with a maturity of 180 days and a futures contract written on a two-year Treasury note. The delivery date of the futures contract is 180 days. Pricing data are given in Table 16.5. Let n_1 be the number of 180-day Treasury bills used in the hedged portfolio and n_2 be the number of futures contracts.

The institution wants the portfolio to be self-financing at date 0. By construction, the initial value of the hedged portfolio is zero, implying

$$95.4164 + n_1 \times 97.7272 = 0,$$

the value of the futures contract being zero. This provides the first equation.

To be insensitive to small changes in the spot rate $r(t)$, the hedge ratio or delta of the portfolio must be zero. Using the program Bonds/Hedge Ratio/Treasury Bill Futures to calculate the hedge ratio for the two Treasury bills, we have

$$90.8007 + n_1 \times 47.6621 + n_2 \times 172.3054 = 0.$$

The hedge ratio for the futures contract is calculated using the program Bonds/Hedge Ratio/Treasury Bond Futures. This gives the second equation.

Solving for n_1 and n_2 gives

$$n_1 = -0.9764$$

and

$$n_2 = -0.2569.$$

To hedge the one-year T-bill, a short position of 0.9764 units of the 180-day T-bill and a short position in 0.2569 T-note futures contracts are needed. ■

16.6 SUMMARY

This chapter uses the Heath-Jarrow-Morton model to describe the evolution of bond prices and futures prices. The model takes as given the initial term structure of interest rates and a specification of the volatility of forward rates. For simplicity, we describe the evolution of bond prices and futures in terms of a one-factor model. The generalization to multiple factors is straightforward and can be found in the references at the end of the chapter.

We also defined the hedge ratio (delta) and gamma for Treasury bills, Treasury bonds, and for futures contracts on these instruments, and constructed delta neutral and gamma neutral portfolios. Gamma neutral portfolios are needed because market frictions make continuous delta hedging impossible. In the next chapter we apply the continuous-time Heath-Jarrow-Morton model to examine the pricing and hedging of interest rate options.

REFERENCES

Carr, P., and R. R. Chen, 1994. "Valuing Bond Futures and the Quality Option." Working Paper, School of Business, Cornell University.

Cox, J. C., J. E. Ingersoll, and S. A. Ross, 1985. "A Theory of the Term Structure of Interest Rates." *Econometrica* 53, 385–407.

Heath, D., R. A. Jarrow, and A. Morton, 1992. "Bond Pricing and the Term Structure of Interest Rates: A New Methodology for Contingent Claims Valuation." *Econometrica* 60, 77–105.

Hull, J., and A. White, 1990. "Pricing Interest Rate Derivative Securities." *Review of Financial Studies* 3, 573–592.

Ingersoll, J. E., J. Skelton, and R. L. Weil, 1978. "Duration Forty Years Later." *Journal of Financial and Quantitative Analysis* 13, 627–650.

Jarrow, R. A., and S. M. Turnbull, 1994. "Delta, Gamma and Bucket Hedging of Interest Rate Derivatives." *Applied Mathematical Finance* 1, 21–48.

Musiela, M., S. M. Turnbull, and L. M. Wakeman, 1993. "Interest Rate Risk Management." *Review of Futures Markets* 12, 221–261.

Vasicek, O., 1977. "An Equilibrium Characterization of the Term Structure." *Journal of Financial Economics* 5, 177–186.

QUESTIONS

Question 1

The price of a 235-day Treasury bill with $100 face value is 96.3745. The volatility is 2.00 percent, the volatility reduction factor 0.15, and the discount rate 5.5539 percent, assuming a 360-day year.

a) Use the program Bonds/Hedge Ratio/Treasury Bill to compute the hedge ratio (delta) and gamma of the Treasury bill.

b) The current instantaneous spot rate is 5.50 percent. If the spot rate changes to
6.50 percent, the Treasury bill changes to 95.7774. Is this what you would expect, given the delta and gamma of the Treasury bill?

Question 2

A bank wants to hedge a 180-day Treasury bill with face value $100 using 90-day and
270-day Treasury bills.

a) Construct a delta neutral portfolio using the following information.

MATURITY (DAYS)	DISCOUNT RATE* (PERCENT)	ZERO-COUPON BOND PRICE
90	4.9872	98.7532
180	4.9737	97.5123
270	4.9595	96.2803

*A 360-day year is assumed.
Volatility   1.50 percent
Volatility Reduction Factor   0

Use the program Bonds/Hedge Ratio/Treasury Bill.
b) If the volatility reduction factor is 0.1, what is the delta neutral portfolio?
c) If the volatility reduction factor is 0.2, what is the delta neutral portfolio?
d) What effect does the volatility reduction factor have on delta and the nature of
the hedged portfolio?

Question 3

A financial institution wants to hedge an eighteen-month (540-day) Treasury bill with
face value $100 such that the hedged portfolio is delta and gamma neutral. The hedge
is constructed using three other Treasury bills with maturities of 90, 180, and 270
days. Using the following information, construct the hedge portfolio.

MATURITY (DAYS)	DISCOUNT RATE* (PERCENT)	ZERO-COUPON BOND PRICE
540	5.2559	92.1162
90	5.0523	98.7369
180	5.1015	97.4492
720	5.3101	89.3799

*A 360-day year is assumed.
Volatility   2.00 percent
Volatility Reduction Factor   0.23

Use the program Bonds/Hedge Ratio/Treasury Bill.

Question 4

Using the information in Table 16.3 and the program Bonds/Hedge Ratio/Treasury Bill, compute the gamma for the bond. Verify your result using the program Bonds/Hedge Ratio/Treasury Bond.

Question 5

A financial institution wants to hedge a two-year bond that pays a coupon of $4.00 every six months, using a Treasury bill with a maturity of half a year and a three-year bond that pays a coupon of $2.125 every six months. The face value of all bonds is $100. The term structure is described below.

MATURITY (YEARS) T	ZERO-COUPON BOND PRICE $B(0, T) \times 100$
0.5	97.3185
1.0	94.1950
1.5	90.7237
2.0	86.9913
2.5	83.0761
3.0	79.0472
Volatility	2.00 percent
Volatility Reduction Factor	0.19

a) Determine the delta and gamma of the Treasury bill.
b) Determine the value of the two-year bond and its delta and gamma. Use the program Bonds/Hedge Ratio/Treasury Bond.
c) Determine the value of the three-year bond and its delta and gamma.
d) The hedged portfolio is designed to be delta neutral. Describe the construction of the portfolio.
e) By construction, the delta of the hedged portfolio is zero. What is the gamma of the hedged portfolio?

Question 6

Using the information in Question 5, determine the hedge portfolio using Redington's duration. Is the delta of your hedged portfolio zero? What is the gamma of your hedged portfolio?

Question 7

Using the information in Question 5, a financial institution wants to hedge the two-year bond using a one-year Treasury bond that pays a coupon of $2.75 every six

months and a three-year bond that pays a coupon of $3.00 every six months. The face value of all bonds is $100.

a) Determine the value of the one-year Treasury bond and its delta and gamma. Use the program Bonds/Hedge Ratio/Treasury Bond.
b) Determine the value of the three-year Treasury bond and its delta and gamma.
c) The hedged portfolio is designed to be delta neutral. Describe the construction of the portfolio.
d) By construction, the delta of the hedge portfolio is zero. What is the gamma of the hedged portfolio?

Question 8

A financial institution wants to hedge a two-and-a-half-year bond that pays a coupon of $3.125 every six months. The institution wants to hedge this bond using a Treasury bill futures contract with a maturity of 135 days, written on a 91-day Treasury bill, and a three-year bond that pays a coupon of $2.875 every six months. The face value of all bonds is $100.

You are given the following information about the term structure of interest rates.

MATURITY (YEARS) T	ZERO-COUPON BOND PRICE $B(0,T) \times 100$	DISCOUNT RATE* (PERCENT)
0.5	97.0089	5.9822
1.0	94.0401	5.9599
1.5	91.1003	5.9331
2.0	88.1955	5.9023
2.5	85.3308	5.8677
3.0	82.5110	5.8297
3.5	79.7400	5.7886
4.0	77.0214	5.7447

*Assuming a 360-day year.
Volatility is 1.5 percent.
Volatility Reduction Factor is 0.1.

a) The discount rate for a 135-day Treasury bill is 5.9871 percent and for a 226-day Treasury bill 5.9770 percent, assuming a 360-day year. Determine the delta and gamma for the futures contract. Use the program Bonds/Hedge Ratio/Treasury Bill Futures.
b) Determine the value of the two-and-a-half-year bond and its delta and gamma.
c) Determine the value of the three-year bond and its delta and gamma.
d) The hedged portfolio is constructed to be delta neutral. Describe the construction of the portfolio.
e) What is the gamma of the hedged portfolio?

Question 9

A common practice used in constructing the term structure of forward rates is to assume that there is no difference between forward rates and futures rates. Using the data below and the program Bonds/Hedge Ratio/Treasury Bill Futures:

a) Determine the three-month forward price.
b) Determine the three-month forward rate, the rate being expressed as a simple interest rate.
c) Determine the futures price for a contract written on a three-month (90-day) Treasury bill. The maturity of the futures contract is 1, 2, . . . , 9 years.
d) Express the futures price as a simple interest rate.
e) Do you think that treating the forward rate as being equal to the futures rate is a good approximation?
f) If volatility is 2.00 percent, what effect does this have on your analysis?

	ZERO-COUPON BOND PRICE		DISCOUNT RATES*	
MATURITY (YEARS) T	$B(0, T) \times 100$	$B(0, T + 0.25) \times 100$	T	$T + 0.25$
1	94.3251	92.7019	5.6749	5.8385
2	87.5033	85.6901	6.2483	6.3600
3	80.1161	78.2349	6.6280	6.6970
4	72.5974	70.7352	6.8506	6.8858
5	65.2502	63.4652	6.9500	6.9590
6	58.2712	56.5990	6.9548	6.9442
7	51.7762	50.2358	6.8891	6.8640
8	45.8225	44.4212	6.7722	6.7368
9	40.4265	39.1639	6.6193	6.5769

Volatility   1.50 percent
Volatility Reduction Factor   0.24
*A 360-day year is assumed.
Face value of all bonds is $100.

APPENDIX: PROOF OF THE RESULTS ON PAGES 492–493

Let us prove the fact that

$$E^\pi\left(e^{-\sum_{v=0}^{t-\Delta}\left(\sum_{u=v}^{T-\Delta}\sigma(v,u)\Delta\right)\Delta W(v)}\right) = e^{\sum_{v=0}^{t-\Delta}\left(\sum_{u=v}^{T-\Delta}\sigma(v,u)\Delta\right)^2/2}.$$

First,

$$\sum_{v=0}^{t-\Delta}\left(\sum_{u=v}^{T-\Delta}\sigma(v,u)\Delta\right)\Delta W(v)$$

is normally attributed with mean 0 and variance

$$\sum_{v=0}^{t-\Delta}\left[\sum_{u=v}^{T-\Delta}\sigma(v,u)\Delta\right]^2\Delta.$$

The variance follows since $\{\Delta W(v)\}$ are independent random variables with zero mean and variance Δ. Second, given a normal $(0, \Delta)$ random variable x, using the result from the Appendix in Chapter 4, $E(e^x) = e^{\text{var}(x)/2}$. This is the moment-generating function. Letting

$$x=\sum_{v=0}^{t-\Delta}\left(\sum_{u=v}^{T-\Delta}\sigma(v,u)\Delta\right)\Delta W(v)$$

gives the result.

Now we demonstrate the derivation of

$$\alpha(v,T) = \sigma(v,T)\int_v^T \sigma(v,u)du.$$

The condition derived in the text is

$$\sum_{u=v}^{T-\Delta}\alpha(v,u)\Delta = \left[\sum_{u=v}^{T-\Delta}\sigma(v,u)\Delta\right]^2/2.$$

Taking limits as $\Delta \to 0$ gives

$$\int_v^T \alpha(v,u)du = \left[\int_v^T \sigma(v,u)du\right]^2/2.$$

Take the derivative with respect to T to obtain

$$\alpha(v,T) = 2\left[\int_v^T \sigma(v,u)du\right]\sigma(v,T)/2$$

$$= \left[\int_v^T \sigma(v,u)du\right]\sigma(v,T).$$

Discretizing again gives

$$\alpha(v,T-\Delta) = \sigma(v,T-\Delta)\sum_{u=v}^{T-\Delta}\sigma(v,u)\Delta.$$

■

Pricing Interest Rate Options and Hedging with Model Misspecification

17.0 INTRODUCTION

This chapter continues our study of closed form solutions for interest rate derivatives by extending the analysis contained in Chapter 16. In Chapter 16 we examined the pricing and hedging of Treasury bills, Treasury bonds, and Treasury futures. In the present chapter, we consider the pricing and hedging of interest rate options. We start with the pricing and hedging of options on Treasury bills, and then we examine interest rate caps and floors. We price and hedge caps and floors by showing that they are equivalent to options on zero-coupon bonds. Next we study the valuation of options on Treasury bonds. **Swaptions** are options on interest rate swaps. We show how to value swaptions as options on bonds. Finally, in the last two sections we address the pricing of options on Treasury bill futures and Treasury bond futures.

Given a closed form solution for any interest rate option, the risk management techniques of delta and gamma hedging are implemented as in Chapter 16. First, we use a Taylor series expansion of the option's value around finite changes in time (Δ) and spot rates ($\Delta r(t)$). Second, we identify terms involving Δ, (Δr), and (Δr)^2. Finally, when combined into a portfolio, delta hedging requires setting the coefficients preceding the (Δr) terms to zero. Gamma hedging requires setting the coefficients preceding the (Δr)^2 terms to zero.

The technique of gamma hedging is often employed to reduce model misspecification risk when continuous delta hedging is impossible due to market frictions and transaction costs. This analysis and these computations are straightforward once valuation formulas are obtained. For this reason, this chapter concentrates on the derivation of the closed form solutions for various interest rate options. We discuss delta and gamma hedging only briefly.

17.1 OPTIONS ON TREASURY BILLS

Here we examine the pricing and hedging of options on Treasury bills. Suppose a bank asks us to price a European call option with a maturity of 35 days written on a 91-day Treasury bill. This request is ambiguous. At the maturity of the option, can we

buy a Treasury bill with a maturity of 56 days ($= 91 - 35$) or with a maturity of 91 days? The answer is 91 days. By convention, the maturity of the underlying Treasury bill is fixed at 91 days over the life of the option.

The strike price for an option on a Treasury bill is usually quoted in terms of a discount rate. Suppose the strike price is 4.50 percent. We can convert this discount rate into a dollar value. The dollar value of the strike is

$$K = \left[1 - \frac{4.50}{100} \times \frac{91}{360}\right] 100$$
$$= 98.8625,$$

assuming the underlying Treasury bill has a face value of $100 and a 360-day year is used to compute the discount rate.

There is an inverse relationship between the strike discount rate and the dollar strike price. As the strike discount rate increases, the strike price in terms of dollars decreases. Conversely, as the strike discount rate decreases, the strike price in terms of dollars increases.

The payoff to the European call option at expiration is defined to be

$$c(35) \equiv \begin{cases} 100\, B(35, 126) - K & \text{if} & 100\, B(35, 126) \geq K \\ 0 & \text{if} & 100\, B(35, 126) < K, \end{cases}$$

where $B(35, 126)$ is the value at date 35 of a Treasury bill that matures at date 126. At the maturity of the option, the maturity of the Treasury bill is 91 days ($91 = 126 - 35$).

Pricing

Let us price European options on Treasury bills by generalizing the previous example.

Consider a European option that expires at date T. The option is written on a Treasury bill with maturity m days. The strike price of the option k is expressed as a discount rate. The strike price in terms of dollars is

$$K \equiv \left[1 - \frac{k}{100} \times \frac{m}{360}\right] 100, \tag{17.1}$$

using a 360-day-per-year convention in the definition of the discount rate.

The payoff to the call option at expiration is

$$c(T) \equiv \begin{cases} 100\, B(T, T_m) - K & \text{if} & 100\, B(T, T_m) \geq K \\ 0 & \text{if} & 100\, B(T, T_m) < K, \end{cases} \tag{17.2}$$

where $T_m \equiv T + m$.

The payoff to a European put option that expires at date T on a Treasury bill with maturity m and a strike k, expressed as a discount rate, is defined by

$$p(T) \equiv \begin{cases} 0 & \text{if} & 100\, B(T, T_m) > K \\ K - 100\, B(T, T_m) & \text{if} & 100\, B(T, T_m) \leq K. \end{cases} \tag{17.3}$$

Given the assumption that forward rates follow the stochastic process given in Chapter 16, Expressions (16.1) and (16.2), then forward rates and spot interest rates are normally distributed under the martingale probabilities. This implies that prices of zero-coupon bonds are lognormally distributed (see Expression (16.8) and the discussion thereafter) similar to the situation involving equity options in the Black-Scholes setting. Consequently, similar valuation formulas will apply.

The date-t value of the call option prior to maturity is given by

$$c(t) = 100\, B(t, T_m)N(d_1) - KB(t, T)N(d_2), \tag{17.4}$$

where

$$d_1 \equiv \{\ln\,[100\, B(t, T_m)/KB(t, T)] + \sigma_c^2/2\}/\sigma_c$$
$$d_2 \equiv d_1 - \sigma_c$$
$$\sigma_c^2 \equiv (\sigma^2/2\lambda)\{1 - \exp[-2\lambda(T - t)]\}X(T, T_m)^2$$
$$X(T, T_m) \equiv \{1 - \exp[-\lambda(T_m - T)]\}/\lambda$$
$$T_m \equiv T + m.$$

The date-t value of a put option is

$$p(t) = KB(t, T)N(-d_2) - 100\, B(t, T_m)N(-d_1). \tag{17.5}$$

As expected, both of these expressions look similar to the Black-Scholes option formula because Treasury bill prices are lognormally distributed. However, this similarity masks some important differences in the definition of the Treasury bill's volatility and the definition of hedge ratios.

Let us first consider the Treasury bill's volatility. Assume that the volatility reduction factor for forward rates, λ, is zero. Then, for $t = 0$, the Treasury bill's volatility is

$$\sigma_c = \sigma \times \sqrt{T} \times m. \tag{17.6}$$

In the Black-Scholes model, the analogous term is $\sigma\sqrt{T}$. The additional quantity m on the right side of Expression (17.6) is the Treasury bill's maturity. It arises because the description of the evolution of Treasury bill prices differs from the description for the evolution of equity prices used in the Black-Scholes model. The volatilities for the two financial securities differ. Treasury bill volatilities must decline as the Treasury bill approaches maturity ($m \to 0$) because the Treasury bill pays a fixed amount at maturity. This consideration is not present in the pricing of equities.

EXAMPLE   **Treasury Bill Options**

This example illustrates the calculation of Treasury bill option prices.

For a range of strike prices, we price a European call option with a maturity of 35 days written on a 91-day Treasury bill. The range of strike prices is

TABLE 17.1 *Pricing Treasury Bill Call Options*

PART A		
INPUT DATA		
TREASURY BILL PRICES		
MATURITY (DAYS)	**DISCOUNT RATE %**	**PRICE × 100**
35	4.5095	99.5616
126	4.5327	98.4136

Volatility $\sigma = 1.0$ percent
Volatility Reduction Factor $\lambda = 0.1$

PART B				
OUTPUT DATA				
EXERCISE PRICE	**DISCOUNT PRICE**	**OPTION VALUE***	**DELTA**	**GAMMA**
98.8625	4.50	0.0233	−10.2087	3038.7627
98.7993	4.75	0.0598	−17.8425	2559.7351
98.7361	5.00	0.1128	−22.5447	1094.7031
98.6729	5.25	0.1735	−24.0656	243.3669
98.6097	5.50	0.2362	−24.3268	35.8919

*These prices are generated using the program Bonds/Treasury Bills.

4.50 to 5.50 percent, in increments of 0.25. Note that in Expression (17.4) we must know the prices of both a 35-day Treasury bill and a 126-day Treasury bill. The relevant information is given in Table 17.1, Part A. We use the program Bonds/Treasury Bills to price these options.

We can see in Table 17.1, Part B, that as the strike price expressed as a discount rate increases (implying that the strike price expressed in dollar terms decreases), the option value increases. ∎

Hedging

Here we study the hedging of European options on Treasury bills.

The expressions for the put and call option prices depend on the prices of zero-coupon bonds, $B(t, T)$ and $B(t, T_m)$. From Expression (16.3) of Chapter 16, we see that both zero-coupon bond prices depend on the spot rate $r(t)$. Following an argument similar to that used to derive Expression (16.4), for finite changes in date t and the spot rate $r(t)$, the change in the option price is

$$\Delta c = \frac{\partial c}{\partial t}\,\Delta + \frac{\partial c}{\partial r}\,\Delta r + \frac{1}{2}\frac{\partial^2 c}{\partial r^2}\,(\Delta r)^2 + \ldots . \tag{17.7}$$

Thus we may define the hedge ratio (delta) and gamma in the following manner:

$$\text{Hedge Ratio} \equiv \frac{\partial c}{\partial r} \tag{17.8}$$

and

$$\text{Gamma} \equiv \frac{\partial^2 c}{\partial r^2} \tag{17.9}$$

EXAMPLE   **Computation of Delta and Gamma (Continued)**

This example provides the delta and gamma for options on Treasury bills. As in the previous example, the delta and gamma are calculated in Table 17.1, Part B, for the European call options on Treasury bills. Observe that for a call option, the delta is negative and the gamma is positive. ∎

The hedge ratio for a call option is, using Expression (17.4),

$$\text{Hedge Ratio} = -X(t, T_m)100\, B(t, T_m)N(d_1) + KX(t, T)B(t, T)N(d_2).$$

The hedge ratio for an equity call option using the Black-Scholes model is of the form $N(d)$. The difference arises because, in the Black-Scholes model, the stock price is the only source of uncertainty. Interest rates are constant. In Expression (17.4), random changes in the term structure affect both the underlying Treasury bill $B(t, T_m)$ and the discount factor $B(t, T)$.

EXAMPLE   **Hedging a Treasury Bill Put Option**

Consider an institution that wants to hedge a Treasury bill put option. The maturity of the option is 35 days and is written on a 91-day Treasury bill. The details of the term structure are as given in Table 17.1. The strike price of the option is 4.75 percent. The face value of the option is $10 million. In forming the hedge, the institution uses n_1 Treasury bills with a maturity of 35 days and n_2 Treasury bills with a maturity of 126 days.

Using the program Bonds/Treasury Bills, the value of the put option is 0.0124, assuming the Treasury bill has a face value of $100. Details are shown in Table 17.2. The face value of the option is $10 million, so the value is $1,240.

The hedged portfolio is constructed to be self-financing, so its initial value is zero, that is,

$$1,240 + n_1 \times 99.5616 + n_2 \times 98.4136 = 0,$$

giving us our first equation. To be neutral to small changes in the spot rate $r(t)$, the hedge ratio of the portfolio must also be zero:

$$648,940 - n_1 \times 9.6327 - n_2 \times 33.8489 = 0,$$

TABLE 17.2 *Hedging a Put Option on a Treasury Bill*

From the program Bonds/Treasury Bills:

OPTION VALUE	DELTA	GAMMA
0.0124	6.4894	2549.01

From the program Bonds/Hedge Ratio/Treasury Bills:

		TREASURY BILLS		
MATURITY (DAYS)	DISCOUNT RATE	PRICE × 100	HEDGE RATIO	GAMMA
35	4.5095	99.5616	−9.6327	0.9320
126	4.5327	98.4136	−33.8489	11.6422
Volatility		$\sigma = 1.0$ percent		
Volatility Reduction Factor		$\lambda = 0.1$		

giving us our second equation. Solving for n_1 and n_2 gives

$$n_1 = -26,385.2$$

and

$$n_2 = 26,680.3.$$

These holdings result in a self-financed, delta neutral portfolio. To obtain a gamma neutral portfolio, an additional hedging instrument would be needed. This extension is similar to gamma hedging as discussed in the previous chapter and is left to the reader as an exercise. ■

17.2 CAPS, FLOORS, AND COLLARS

Now we study the pricing and hedging of interest rate caps, floors, and collars. These instruments are actively traded in the over-the-counter markets among financial institutions.

Caps and Caplets

This section describes **interest rate caps**. Interest rate caps are contracts that provide insurance against the rate of interest on a floating rate note going above some pre-specified level, called the **cap rate**. We start with a simple example.

EXAMPLE

Interest Rate Cap

This example illustrates the payoff to an interest rate cap.

Consider an institution that has issued a floating rate note for which the interest rate is reset every 90 days, using the prevailing 90-day spot interest rate. The next reset day is in 42 days' time. The institution has purchased an interest rate cap with a maturity of 42 days and cap rate of 5.50 percent.

In 42 days, at maturity, the payoff to the cap is defined by

$$\text{cap}(42) \equiv \text{Max}\left\{\frac{i_s(90) - 0.055}{1 + i_s(90) \times (90/360)}, 0\right\}(90/360)\ \text{Principal},$$

where $i_s(90)$ is the 90-day spot interest observed in 42 days[1], and Principal is the principal amount of the floating rate note. The cap payoff is discounted because the payoff to the cap is received 90 more days further into the future than the maturity date of the cap. In this example, a 360-day year convention is used in the definition of the spot interest rate, and simple interest rates are used.

For example, if the 90-day spot interest rate at 42 days is 5.80 percent, principal $10 million, then the payoff to the cap is

$$\text{cap}(42) = \text{Max}\left\{\frac{0.058 - 0.055}{1 + 0.058 \times (90/360)}, 0\right\} \times (90/360) \times 10,000,000$$

$$= \text{Max}\{0.002957, 0\} \times (90/360) \times 10,000,000$$
$$= \$7,392.80.$$

The institution can take the money at the maturity of the cap and invest it for 90 days at the 90-day spot interest. Therefore, in 90 days the institution pays the interest on its floating rate note and receives the money from its cap investment.

The net payment is

$$10,000,000 \times 0.058 \times (90/360) - 7,392.80 \times [1 + 0.058 \times (90/360)]$$
$$= \$137,550,$$

implying that the effective interest rate the institution pays is the cap rate of 5.50 percent.[2] ∎

Formalization

We now formalize the preceding example. The formalization involves little more than replacing numbers with symbols.

---

[1]Formally, $i_s(90)$ should have a subscript indicating the date the spot rate is observed, in this case at date 42 days.

[2]For an interest rate of 5.50 percent, the payment is $10,000,000 \times 0.055 \times (90/360) = \$137,550$.

Consider a cap that matures at date T. The cap is written on the m period spot interest rate. By definition, the payoff to the cap at time T is given by

$$\text{cap}(T) \equiv \text{Principal} \begin{cases} \dfrac{[i_s(m) - k] \, (m/360)}{1 + i_s(m) \times (m/360)} & \text{if} \quad i_s(m) \geq k \\ 0 & \text{if} \quad i_s(m) < k, \end{cases} \qquad (17.10)$$

where k is the cap rate expressed in terms of a simple interest rate, and $i_s(m)$ is the m period spot interest rate observed at time T. Thus a cap is a call option on a simple interest rate.

We next show that an interest rate cap is equivalent to a put option on a Treasury bill. This demonstration needs to use the relation between simple interest rates and T-bill prices. By definition of the simple interest rate,

$$B(T, T_m) \equiv \frac{1}{1 + i_s(m)(m/360)},$$

where $T_m \equiv T + m$, and a 360-day year convention is assumed.

Using this definition, we can write the cap's payoff, Expression (17.10), in the form[3]

$$\text{cap}(T) = \text{Principal} \times [1 + k(m/360)] \begin{cases} K - B(T, T_m) & \text{if} \quad B(T, T_m) \leq K \\ 0 & \text{if} \quad B(T, T_m) > K, \end{cases} \qquad (17.11)$$

where $K \equiv 1/[1 + k(m/360)]$.

Comparing Expression (17.11) with the payoff to a put option on the Treasury bill described by Expression (17.3), we see that

$$\text{cap}(T) = \text{Principal} \times [1 + k(m/360)] \times p(T), \qquad (17.12)$$

where the put is written on the Treasury bill $B(t, T_m)$ with strike price K and maturity T. This is an important observation. A cap, which is a call option on a simple interest rate, is equivalent to valuing a put option on a Treasury bill that matures at date T_m.

The value of the cap at any time prior to maturity is thus equal to the value of the put option on the Treasury bill multiplied by the appropriate adjustment, that is,

$$\text{cap}(t) = \text{Principal} \times [1 + k(m/360)] \times p(t). \qquad (17.13)$$

---

[3]We can write

$$\frac{(i_s(m) - k)(m/360)}{1 + i_s(m)(m/360)} = \frac{1 + i_s(m)(m/360) - [1 + k(m/360)]}{1 + i_s(m)(m/360)}$$

$$= 1 - \frac{1 + k(m/360)}{1 + i_s(m)(m/360)}$$

$$= [1 + k(m/360)] \left[\frac{1}{1 + k(m/360)} - \frac{1}{1 + i_s(m)(m/360)} \right]$$

$$= [1 + k(m/360)][K - B(T, T_m)].$$

EXAMPLE   **Pricing a Simple Cap**

This example illustrates the computation of a cap's value.

We want to price a cap with a maturity of 90 days written on the 90-day Treasury bill rate. The cap rate is 4.50 percent. Information about the term structure of interest rates is given in Table 17.3.

To price the cap we use its relation to the T-bill put option in Expression (17.13). To price the put option in (17.13) we must first determine the strike price K:

$$K = 1/[1 + 0.045 \times (90/360)]$$
$$= 0.9889.$$

To use the program Bonds/Treasury Bills to price the option, we must express the strike price as a discount i_d, implying

$$0.9889 \equiv 1 - i_d \times (90/360).$$

Therefore[4],

$$i_d = 4.4499 \text{ percent.}$$

Substituting into the computer program gives the value of the put option as 0.0714. Therefore, the value of the cap is

$$\text{cap}(0) = [1 + 0.045 \times (90/360)] \times 0.0714$$
$$= 0.0723. \quad \blacksquare$$

TABLE 17.3   *Pricing an Interest Rate Cap*

	MATURITY (DAYS)	DISCOUNT RATE
	90	4.5237
	180	4.5455
Volatility	$\sigma = 1.0$ percent	
Volatility Reduction Factor	$\lambda = 0.1$	

The term interest rate cap usually refers to a series of individual caps called **caplets**. We will use an example to clarify this distinction. A company has issued floating rate debt with a maturity of one year. The floating rate is reset every 90

---

[4]In the next example, we use the program Bonds/Caps/Normal to price a cap. The program does this calculation for us.

FIGURE 17.1 *One-Year Cap*

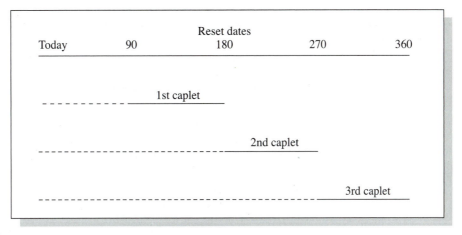

days. To insure against the consequences of rising interest rates, the company purchases a one-year cap. This cap is composed of three caplets. The first caplet expires in 90 days' time and provides insurance at the first reset date. The second caplet expires in 180 days' time and provides insurance at the second reset date. The third caplet expires in 270 days' time and provides insurance at the third and last reset date. See Figure 17.1. The payoff of each caplet is defined by Expression (17.10). The value of the cap is the sum of the values of the individual caplets.

EXAMPLE **Caps versus Caplets**

This example illustrates the pricing of a cap by decomposing it into its caplets. We want to price the preceding cap using the term structure information provided in Table 17.4 on p. 532. The term structure and the cap rate is the same as in the last example. We use the program Bonds/Caps/Normal to price the cap.

The output is shown in Table 17.4, Part B. The price and delta of the cap are given, along with the price and delta of the individual caplets. The cap's value, 0.3057, is the sum of the three caplets' values (0.0723 + 0.1038 + 0.1297). Similarly, the cap's delta is the sum of the three caplets' deltas. The value of the first caplet is identical to that derived in the previous example. ■

Floors and Collars

Here we examine floors and collars. A **floor** is analogous to a cap with the exception that a floor places a lower limit on the interest rate that is charged.

TABLE 17.4   *Pricing an Interest Rate Cap Using the Heath-Jarrow-Morton Model*

PART A		
INPUT DATA		
MATURITY (DAYS)	DISCOUNT RATE	PRICE × 100
90	4.5237	98.8691
180	4.5455	97.7272
270	4.5654	96.5759
360	4.5836	95.4164

Volatility $\sigma = 1.0$ percent
Volatility Reduction Factor $\lambda = 0.1$
Cap Rate $k = 4.50$ percent

PART B
OUTPUT DATA*

Number of Reset Dates   3
Cap Principal   100.0000
Cap Rate   4.5000
Time to First Reset Date (days)   90.0000
Cap Period (days)   90.0000
Cap Days (days)   360

RESET DATES	MARKET VALUE OF T-BILL × 100	VOLATILITY	VOLATILITY REDUCTION FACTOR	VALUE OF CAPLET	VALUE OF DELTA
90	98.8691	1.0000	0.1000	0.0723	15.1533
180	97.7272	1.0000	0.1000	0.1038	14.8874
270	96.5759	1.0000	0.1000	0.1297	14.6485
			Total Value	0.3057	44.6892

*These prices are generated using the program Bonds/Caps/Normal.

Consider a floor with strike price k that matures at date T. The floor is written on the m period spot rate computed as a simple interest rate. By definition, the payoff to the floor is given by

$$\text{floor}(T) \equiv \text{Principal} \begin{cases} \dfrac{[k - i_s(m)](m/360)}{1 + i_s(m) \times (m/360)} & \text{if} \quad i_s(m) \leq k \\ 0 & \text{if} \quad i_s(m) > k, \end{cases} \quad (17.14)$$

where k is the floor rate expressed in terms of a simple interest rate and $i_s(m)$ is the m period spot interest rate observed at time T.

Thus a floor is a put option on simple interest rates. To an institution owning a floating rate note, a floor provides insurance that its income will not fall below the floor rate.

A similar analysis to that used for caps shows that a floor's payoff can be written in terms of a Treasury bill maturing at date $T_m \equiv m + T$, that is,

$$\text{floor}(T) \equiv \text{Principal} \times [1 + k(m/360)] \begin{cases} B(T,T_m) - K & \text{if } B(T,T_m) - K \geq 0 \\ 0 & \text{if } B(T,T_m) - K < 0, \end{cases}$$
(17.15)

where $K \equiv 1/[1 + k(m/360)]$.

Comparing Expression (17.15) with the payoff to a call option on the Treasury bill in Expression (17.2) gives the following relation:

$$\text{floor}(T) = \text{Principal} \times [1 + k(m/360)] \times c(T),$$

where the call option is on the Treasury bill $B(t, T_m)$ with strike price K and maturity T. This is an important observation. A floor, which is a put option on a simple interest rate, is equivalent to a call option on the Treasury bill's price.

The date-t value of the floor at any time prior to maturity is thus

$$\text{floor}(t) = \text{Principal} \times [1 + k(m/360)] \times c(t),$$
(17.16)

where the call option is valued in Expression (17.4).

The term interest rate floor usually refers to a series of individual floors called **floorlets**, just as with caps and caplets. A floor is then valued as the sum of a series of floorlets where each floorlet is valued using Expression (17.16). Delta and gamma hedging proceeds in a straightforward fashion.

A **collar** is a combination of a cap and a floor. A collar specifies the upper and lower limits on the interest that will be charged. A corporation that has issued a floating rate note and is concerned about its interest rate exposure can purchase a collar. In one form of a collar, the corporation picks the cap rate and the institution selling the collar picks the floor rate such that the net cost of the collar is zero.

Valuation formulas for collars are just the sum of the valuation formulas for a cap and floor combined. Delta and gamma hedging proceeds in a straightforward fashion. It is interesting to note that a floating rate note with a cap and floor both with the same strike k is identical to a fixed rate note at the rate k. Thus a plain vanilla interest rate swap receiving floating and paying fixed that is used to swap a floating rate note into a fixed rate note is equivalent to purchasing a collar with the same strikes on the floating rate note. This equivalence is, in fact, put-call parity in disguise.

The Black Model for Caps and Floors

This section presents Black's model for pricing caps and floors and discusses its limitations. Recall that the Black model prices options on forward contracts as explained in Chapter 9, Expression (9.16). This model is often used for pricing caps. The application

of the model involves a number of approximations and a set of assumptions different from those used in the preceding text. The model, in fact, is inconsistent with an arbitrage-free term structure of interest rates. We include this model in the text because it is widely used in practice. Consequently, its benefits and limitations need to be understood.

Consider the payoff at maturity of a simple cap, for which there is only one caplet. The cap matures at date T and is written on the m period spot interest rate with strike k. Using Expression (17.10), the payoff is defined by

$$cap(T) \equiv P \times \text{Max}\left\{ \frac{[i_s(m) - k]q}{1 + i_s(m)q}, 0 \right\},$$

where $q \equiv m/360$, P denotes the principal, and $i_s(m)$ is the m period spot rate observed at time T computed as a simple interest rate.

Let $f(0, T, T_m)$ denote the m period forward rate from date T to date $T_m \equiv T + m$ implied by the initial term structure. The first approximation involved in using Black's formula involves changing the payoff to the cap. Suppose that we approximate the payoff to the cap to be

$$cap(T) = \frac{P \times q}{1 + f(0, T, T_m)q} \, \text{Max}\{i_s(m) - k, 0\}.$$

In this approximation, we replace the spot rate $i_s(m)$ in the denominator with the forward rate $f(0, T, T_m)$.

Now consider the second term on the right side of this equation. If we rewrite this term in the form

$$\begin{cases} i_s(m) - k & \text{if} & i_s(m) \geq k \\ 0 & \text{if} & i_s(m) < k, \end{cases}$$

it represents the payoff to a call option written on the rate $i_s(m)$ with strike price k. Now, by definition, at date T the m period forward rate implied by the term structure at that date, $f(T, T, T_m)$, equals the spot rate:

$$f(T, T, T_m) = i_s(m).$$

Therefore, we can regard this payoff as describing a call option on a forward rate.

Finally, if we assume that forward rates are lognormally distributed, with constant volatility σ_B, we can use the Black model. Hence the value of the cap today is

$$cap(0) = \frac{P \times q}{1 + f(0, T, T_m)q} \{B(0, T)[f(0, T, T_m)N(d_1) - kN(d_2)]\}, \tag{17.17}$$

where

$$d_1 \equiv \{\ln[f(0, T, T_m)/k] + \sigma_B^2 T/2\}/\sigma_B \sqrt{T}$$
$$d_2 \equiv d_1 - \sigma_B \sqrt{T}.$$

Expression (17.17) is the Black model applied to pricing interest rate caps. It is quick to compute and, given the assumption that forward rates are lognormally distributed, rules out negative interest rates.

Expression (17.17) has been derived under a number of assumptions different from those used elsewhere in this chapter. These assumptions are the basis for its limitations.

First, the denominator of Expression (17.14), $(1 + i_s(m)q)$, which is random, is approximated by the non-random term $(1 + f(0, T, T_m)q)$. This is a crude approximation that leads to incorrect deltas (see the next example).

Second, the Black model is derived under the assumption that interest rates are constant, yet it is used here to price caps that derive their value because m period interest rates are stochastic. These two assumptions are inconsistent with an arbitrage-free term structure evolution. Indeed, there is no way that instantaneous spot rates can be constant across time but m-period interest rates be random. Why? In this case, the m-period rate is just the constant spot rate times m.

Third, the assumption of a constant volatility for forward rates over the life of the contract is contrary to the evidence. For a forward contract with long maturity, the volatility is relatively small given that the forward rate is relatively insensitive to changes in the current term structure. The forward rate becomes more sensitive to changes in the term structure as the time to maturity decreases. This point is shown in Figure 17.2. The

FIGURE 17.2 *Forward Rate Volatility*

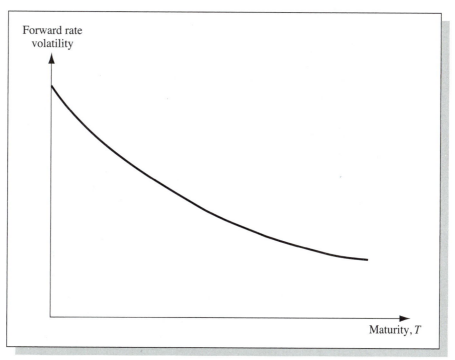

volatility structure of forward rates that we used in the Heath-Jarrow-Morton model of Chapter 16, Expression (16.2), is consistent with Figure 17.2. The volatility assumption underlying Black's model is not.

It is possible to derive the Black model for pricing individual caplets in an alternative fashion by assuming that the discrete m period spot rate is lognormally distributed.[5] This alternative approach can be shown to be a special case of the Heath-Jarrow-Morton model. Unfortunately, the assumptions underlying this alternative derivation provide no guidance on how to hedge a cap using futures contracts. To obtain these insights, one must utilize the general Heath-Jarrow-Morton framework, which is beyond the scope of this text.

TABLE 17.5 *Pricing an Interest Rate Cap Using the Black Model*

PART A
INPUT DATA

TERM STRUCTURE DATA			VOLATILITY DATA
MATURITY (DAYS)	DISCOUNT RATE	PRICE × 100	
90	4.5237	98.8691	21.5
180	4.5455	97.7272	21.1
270	4.5654	96.5759	20.6
360	4.5836	95.4164	

Cap Rate $k = 4.50$ percent

PART B
OUTPUT DATA*

Number of Reset Dates	3
Cap Principal	100.0000
Cap Rate	4.5000
Time to First Reset Date (days)	90.0000
Cap Period (days)	90.0000
Cap Days (days)	360

RESET DATES	MARKET VALUE OF T-BILL × 100	VOLATILITY	FORWARD RATE	VALUE OF CAPLET	VALUE OF DELTA
90	98.8691	21.5000	4.6738	0.0722	16.0699
180	97.7272	21.1000	4.7685	0.1039	16.3773
270	96.5759	20.6000	4.8608	0.1297	16.6739
			Total Value	0.3058	49.1211

*These prices are generated using the program Bonds/Caps/Black.

[5] See the recent work of Miltersen, Sandmann, and Sondermann (1997).

| EXAMPLE | **Black Model** |

We illustrate here the differences between Black's model and the Heath-Jarrow-Morton model derived earlier.

We price a one-year cap using the Black model. Term structure data are shown in Table 17.5, Part A, which are identical to that given in Table 17.4 where we priced the same cap using the Heath-Jarrow-Morton model. Also given in Table 17.5, Part A, is the term structure of volatilities.

The price and delta for the cap and the individual caplets are shown in Table 17.5, Part B, using the program Bonds/Caps/Black. Note that the prices of the caplets are almost identical to those given in Table 17.4, Part B, which are calculated using the Heath-Jarrow-Morton model under the assumption of normality with a positive volatility reduction factor.

The deltas in the two sets of tables are, however, quite different. In the Black model, delta measures the change in the cap value for a unit change in the forward rate $f(t, T, T_m)$, while the delta in the Heath-Jarrow-Morton model measures the change in the cap value for a unit change in the spot rate $r(t)$. There is no reason why these two deltas should be equal. To hedge with the Black model, it is necessary to determine how the different instruments used in the hedge portfolio vary for changes in the forward rate $f(t, T, T_m)$. ∎

17.3 OPTIONS ON TREASURY BONDS

We now examine the pricing and hedging of options on Treasury bonds. The difference from the preceding section is that Treasury bonds have coupons while Treasury bills do not.

Consider a European put option with a maturity of 150 days written on an eighteen-month Treasury note. At the maturity of the option you can sell a Treasury note with a maturity of just over a year. Unlike options on Treasury bills, for options on Treasury bonds and notes the maturity of the underlying Treasury bond or note declines over the life of the option, and the strike price of the option is quoted directly in terms of dollars.

Consider an option with expiration date T and strike price K written on a Treasury bond. Suppose that the Treasury bond makes n semiannual coupon payments $c_1, c_2, \ldots, c_n$ at dates $T_1, T_2, \ldots, T_n$, respectively. The bond matures at date T_n and its face value is F.

The market value of the bond at date T is

$$B_c(T) \equiv \sum_{j=1}^{n} c_j \times B(T, T_j). \tag{17.18}$$

For convenience, we let c_n represent the coupon plus principal payment at date T_n. Including the principal repayment plus coupon in the last payment c_n considerably simplifies the subsequent formulas.

The payoff at maturity for the call option on the Treasury bond is given by

$$c(T) \equiv \begin{cases} B_c(T) - K & \text{if} \quad B_c(T) \geq K. \\ 0 & \text{if} \quad B_c(T) < K, \end{cases} \qquad (17.19)$$

where K is the strike price.

Similarly, the payoff at maturity T for a put option with strike K on the same Treasury bond is defined by

$$p(T) \equiv \begin{cases} 0 & \text{if} \quad B_c(T) > K \\ K - B_c(T) & \text{if} \quad B_c(T) \leq K. \end{cases} \qquad (17.20)$$

For European options, any coupon payments paid prior to the maturity of the option are not received by the holder of the option.

Closed form solutions can be derived for European Treasury bond options, though they are more complicated than those given in Expressions (17.4) and (17.5) for Treasury bill options. We now derive these expressions.

Substituting Expression (16.3) from Chapter 16 into Expression (17.18) gives

$$B_c(T) = \sum_{j=1}^{n} c_j \frac{B(0, T_j)}{B(0, T)} \exp[-X(T, T_j) r(T) + X(T, T_j) f(0, T) - a(T, T_j)]. \qquad (17.21)$$

Let $\bar{r}$ be the value of the spot rate $r(t)$ for which

$$B_c(T) = K. \qquad (17.22)$$

The critical value $\bar{r}$ can be found using an iterative procedure.

If $r(T) > \bar{r}$, then $B_c(T) < K$, and if $r(T) < \bar{r}$, then $B_c(T) > K$. Given this relation, we can rewrite the payoff to the call option in terms of $\bar{r}$. This rewritten payoff is

$$c(T) = \begin{cases} B_c(T) - K & \text{if} \quad r(T) \leq \bar{r} \\ 0 & \text{if} \quad r(T) > \bar{r}. \end{cases}$$

The value of a call option under the Heath-Jarrow-Morton model is

$$c(T) = \sum_{j=1}^{n} c_j \times B(0, T_j) \times N(d_j) - K \times B(0, T) N(d), \qquad (17.23)$$

where

$$\sigma_R d_j \equiv \bar{r} + X(T, T_j) \sigma_R^2 \qquad \text{for} \qquad j = 1, \ldots, n$$
$$\sigma_R d \equiv \bar{r}$$

and

$$\sigma_R^2 \equiv (\sigma^2/2\lambda)[1 - \exp(-2\lambda T)].$$

An analogous argument shows that the value of a put option is

$$p(T) = K \times B(0,T) \times N(-d) - \sum_{j=1}^{n} c_j \times B(0,T_j) \times N(-d_j). \qquad (17.24)$$

To value these options, it is necessary to have information about the entire term structure, that is, the values of the zero-coupon bonds $B(0,T)$, $B(0,T_1)$, ..., $B(0,T_n)$. We illustrate the computation of these formulas through an example.

EXAMPLE   **European Put Options**

This example illustrates the computation of Expression (17.24).

We want to price four European put options written on a two-year Treasury note. The options have a maturity of 150 days. Strike prices are 99, 100, 101, and 102. Details of the term structure of interest rates are given in Table 17.6, Part A on p. 540.

The coupon on the bond is 4.50 percent per annum, implying a payment of $2.25 every six months, assuming a face value of $100. We use the program Bonds/Treasury Bonds to price these options. The output is shown in Table 17.6, Part B. ■

Swaptions

Now we study the pricing and hedging of swaptions. Swaptions are options on interest rate swaps. A swaption gives the holder the right to enter into a prespecified swap at a fixed time in the future. We first illustrate the meaning of a swaption with an example.

EXAMPLE   **Swaptions**

Consider a company that is planning to issue a floating rate bond in three months' time. The company is concerned about the future level of interest rates. It purchases a three-month European option on a swap, giving the company the option to receive floating rate payments and to make fixed rate payments at the swap rate of 7 percent per annum. Treasury rates are used in determining the fixed and floating rate payments. The length of the swap is three years. Note that the swap rate and the length of the swap, measured from the date the option expires, are prespecified.

Now consider the value of this swaption at maturity. The value of the floating rate payments, using the results from Chapter 14, is

TABLE 17.6 *Pricing Treasury Bond Put Options*

PART A INPUT DATA

TERM STRUCTURE DATA

MATURITY (MONTHS)	PRICE × 100
6	97.7272
12	95.4164
18	93.0780
24	90.7214

150-day Discount Rate	4.5384 percent
Volatility	1.0 percent
Volatility Reduction Factor	0.1

PART B
OUTPUT DATA*

Type of Option	Put Option
Maturity of Option (days)	150.00
Exercise Price	99.0000
Standard Deviation	0.0100
Volatility Reduction Factor	0.1000

EXERCISE PRICE	OPTION VALUE	DELTA	GAMMA
99.0000	0.0027	1.2188	500.1101
100.0000	0.0468	14.7444	3823.8449
101.0000	0.3088	61.4945	8004.2709
102.0000	0.9666	112.8586	4667.4728

*These prices are generated using the program Bonds/Treasury Bonds.

$$N_P \times [1 - B(T, T_6)],$$

where N_P is the notional principal, T denotes the date the option expires, and T_6 is the date of the last payment.

The value at date T of the fixed rate payments, which are made on a semi-annual basis, is

$$N_P \times (0.07/2) \sum_{j=1}^{6} B(T, T_j),$$

where T_j denotes the date of the jth payment for $j = 1, \ldots, 6$. The first payment is made six months from the expiry of the option, the second payment is made twelve months from the expiry of the option, and so on.

The net value of the swap at date T is

$$V_S(T) \equiv N_P \times [1 - B(T, T_6)] - N_P \times (0.07/2) \sum_{j=1}^{6} B(T, T_j),$$

given that the company will receive floating rate payments and make fixed rate payments.

Alternatively, the company could enter into a new swap that by market convention has zero value. Therefore, it will be in the best interests of the company to exercise the swaption at date T if

$$V_S(T) \geq 0.$$

If $V_S(T)$ is negative, the swaption is worthless. ∎

Formalization

This section formalizes the preceding example. This involves little more than replacing numbers with algebraic symbols.

The swap rate, on a per annum basis, specified in the swaption is denoted by R_S. The swaption expires at date T. The swap specified in the option contract involves n fixed rate payments at dates $T_1, T_2, \ldots, T_n$ and floating rate payments. The swap terminates at date T_n.

There are two types of swaptions. In the first case, the swap involves receiving floating rate payments and making fixed rate payments and was described above. The second type of swap involves receiving fixed rate payments and making floating rate payments. We will consider both types of swaptions and show that they are analogous to a put option on a bond in the first case and a call option on a bond in the second case.

First Type of Swaption (Receive Floating, Pay Fixed). Let us value the first type of swaption. The first swap involves receiving floating rate payments and paying fixed rate payments. The value of the floating rate payments at date T when the swaption matures is

$$N_P \times [1 - B(T, T_n)].$$

The value of the fixed rate payments is

$$N_P \times (R_S/2) \sum_{j=1}^{n} B(T, T_j).$$

The net value of the swap is thus

$$V_{S1}(T) \equiv N_P \times [1 - B(T, T_n)] - N_P \times (R_S/2) \sum_{j=1}^{n} B(T, T_j). \tag{17.25}$$

Because a newly issued swap at date T has zero value, the swaption is only exercised if $V_{S1}(T) \geq 0$. It implies that the payoff to the swaption at maturity T is

$$\text{swaption}_1(T) \equiv \begin{cases} V_{S1}(T) & \text{if} & V_{S1}(T) \geq 0 \\ 0 & \text{if} & V_{S1}(T) < 0. \end{cases} \tag{17.26}$$

We now show that this swaption is equivalent to a put option on a bond with strike price N_P. We rewrite the swap's value, Expression (17.25), in the form

$$V_{S1}(T) = N_P - \left[\sum_{j=1}^{n} N_P \times (R_S/2) \times B(T, T_j) + N_P \times B(T, T_n) \right].$$

The term inside the square brackets on the right side represents the value of a Treasury bond with coupon R_S and face value N_P. Let $B_c(T)$ denote the value of this Treasury bond:

$$B_c(T) \equiv \sum_{j=1}^{n} N_P \times (R_S/2) \times B(T, T_j) + N_P \times B(T, T_n).$$

Then the expression for the swaption's payoff at maturity can be rewritten as

$$\text{swaption}_1(T) = \begin{cases} N_P - B_c(T) & \text{if} & N_P \geq B_c(T) \\ 0 & \text{if} & N_P < B_c(T). \end{cases} \tag{17.27}$$

A comparison with Expression (17.20) shows that this equation is the payoff to a put option with strike N_P written on a Treasury bond with coupon R_S. Because we have already discussed the pricing and hedging of these Treasury bond options, the analysis for the first type of swaption is complete.

Second Type of Swaption (Received Fixed, Pay Floating). Now we value the second type of swaption. The second swap involves receiving fixed rate payments and paying floating rate payments. The value of the swap when the swaption matures at date T is

$$V_{S2}(T) \equiv N_P \times (R_S/2) \sum_{j=1}^{n} B(T, T_j) - N_P \times [1 - B(T, T_n)], \tag{17.28}$$

which is the negative of the value of the first type of swap, given in Expression (17.25).

Because the swaption is only exercised if its value is positive at maturity, the payoff to the swaption at date T can be written as

$$\text{swaption}_2(T) \equiv \begin{cases} V_{S2}(T) & \text{if} & V_{S2}(T) \geq 0 \\ 0 & \text{if} & V_{S2}(T) < 0. \end{cases} \tag{17.29}$$

We now show that this swaption is equivalent to a call option on a Treasury bond with strike price N_P. We rewrite the swap's value, Expression (17.28), in the form

$$V_{S2}(T) = \left[\sum_{j=1}^{n} N_P \times (R_S/2) \times B(T,T_j) + N_P \times B(T,T_n) \right] - N_P$$

$$= B_c(T) - N_P.$$

Using this expression, the payoff to the swaption can be written as

$$\text{swaption}_2(T) = \begin{cases} B_c(T) - N_P & \text{if} & B_c(T) \geq N_P \\ 0 & \text{if} & B_c(T) < N_P. \end{cases} \tag{17.30}$$

Comparing this expression with Expression (17.19), this payoff represents a call option with strike price N_P written on a Treasury bond with coupon R_S and face value N_P.

Because Treasury bond options have already been analyzed, we know how to price and hedge this second type of swaptions. We illustrate this valuation through an example.

EXAMPLE | **Valuation of a Swaption**

Consider a European swaption with a maturity of 120 days (four months). The underlying swap is one in which the swap owner receives a fixed rate of 4.60 percent per annum over a three-year period on a semiannual basis, and pays a floating rate. From Expression (17.30), this is equivalent to a call option with strike 100 written on a Treasury bond with coupon 4.60 per annum. Details about the underlying term structure are given in Table 17.7, Part A on p. 544.

Note that if the swaption is exercised, the first coupon payment of $2.30 is received six months later, implying that we need the price today of a ten-month Treasury bond.

We use the program Bonds/Treasury Bonds to price this swaption. The results are given in Table 17.7, Part B. The delta and gamma are also provided for hedging purposes. ■

In valuing the swaptions in this section we have made the implicit assumption that the fixed and floating rate components are priced off the same Treasury curve. This is a strong assumption, as explained in Chapter 13. It is possible to relax this assumption at the expense of additional complexity.

We have only addressed the pricing of European swaptions. In practice, swaptions can be American or European, or a combination of the two.[6] For example, for a swaption with a maturity of three years, it may be European for the first year and then American over the remaining two years. To value such contracts it is necessary to use the lattice techniques discussed in Chapter 15 or a lattice approximation to the

---

[6]This is called a Bermuda option (see Gastineau (1992)).

TABLE 17.7 *Pricing Swaptions*

PART A
INPUT DATA

TERM STRUCTURE DATA

MATURITY (MONTHS)	PRICE × 100
10	96.1903
16	93.8599
22	91.5084
28	89.1446
34	86.7767
40	84.4119

120-day Discount Rate	4.5312 percent
Volatility	1.0 percent
Volatility Reduction Factor	0.1

PART B
OUTPUT DATA*

Type of Option	Call Option
Maturity of Option (days)	120.00
Exercise Price	100.0000
Standard Deviation	0.0100
Volatility Reduction Factor	0.1000

EXERCISE PRICE	OPTION VALUE	DELTA	GAMMA
100.0000	0.0752	−26.6350	7780.1002

*The program Bonds/Treasury Bonds is used.

Heath-Jarrow-Morton model utilized above (see Jarrow (1995) for such an approximation). Our study of swaptions is now complete.

17.4 OPTIONS ON TREASURY BILL FUTURES

Here we study the pricing and hedging of Treasury bill futures options. We first illustrate a Treasury bill futures option with an example.

Consider a European option that matures in 35 days' time and is written on a Treasury bill futures contract with delivery in 90 days. At the maturity of the call (put) option, the option holder can buy (sell) a 90-day futures contract at a fixed strike price. The futures contract is written on a 90-day Treasury bill. For easy reference, the dates and maturities are shown in Figure 17.3.

FIGURE 17.3   *Options on Treasury Bill Futures*

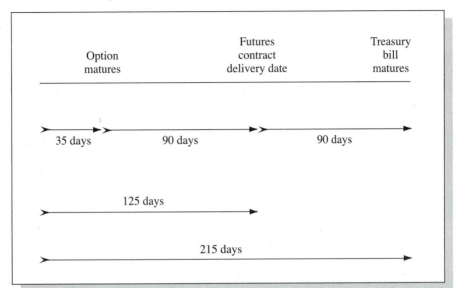

Treasury bill futures prices are quoted in terms of index values. The strike price of an option on a Treasury bill futures contract is also quoted in terms of an index value. For example, if the strike price is 95.5, it implies a futures discount rate of 4.5 percent ($= 100 - 95.5$) and a dollar value of

$$100 \times \left[1 - \frac{4.5}{100} \times \frac{90}{360} \right] = 98.8750,$$

assuming a 360 day year convention.

Formalization

This section formalizes the previous discussion. Consider a European option that matures at date T and is written on a Treasury bill futures contract with delivery at date $T_{\mathscr{F}}$. The T-bill futures contract is written on a Treasury bill that matures at date T_B. In comparison to Figure 17.3, it would imply that $T = 35$, $T_{\mathscr{F}} = 125$, and $T_B = 215$.

The strike price of the option is k, quoted in terms of an index value. This implies a futures discount rate of $100 - k$ and a dollar value of

$$K \equiv 100 \times \left[1 - \frac{(100 - k)}{100} \times \frac{(T_{\mathscr{F}} - T)}{360} \right], \tag{17.31}$$

assuming a 360-day year convention.

The payoff at maturity T to the call option on the Treasury bill futures is

$$c(T) \equiv \begin{cases} \mathcal{F}(T;T_{\mathcal{F}},T_{B}) - K & \text{if} & \mathcal{F}(T;T_{\mathcal{F}},T_{B}) \geq K \\ 0 & \text{if} & \mathcal{F}(T;T_{\mathcal{F}},T_{B}) < K, \end{cases} \tag{17.32}$$

where $\mathcal{F}(T;T_{\mathcal{F}},T_{B})$ is the Treasury bill futures price at date T expressed in terms of dollars.

The payoff at maturity T to a put option on the Treasury bill futures is

$$p(T) \equiv \begin{cases} K - \mathcal{F}(T;T_{\mathcal{F}},T_{B}) & \text{if} & \mathcal{F}(T;T_{\mathcal{F}},T_{B}) \leq K \\ 0 & \text{if} & \mathcal{F}(T;T_{\mathcal{F}},T_{B}) > K. \end{cases} \tag{17.33}$$

Using the risk-neutral valuation approach, it can be shown that the date-0 value of the call option is

$$c(0) = B(0,T)[\mathcal{F}(0;T_{\mathcal{F}},T_{B})\exp(\theta)N(d) - KN(d - \sigma_1)] \tag{17.34}$$

and the date-0 value of the put option is

$$p(0) = B(0,T)[KN(-d + \sigma_1) - \mathcal{F}(0;T_{\mathcal{F}},T_{B})\exp(\theta)N(-d)], \tag{17.35}$$

where

$$\sigma_1 d \equiv \ln[\mathcal{F}(0;T_{\mathcal{F}},T_{B})/K] + \theta + \sigma_1^2/2$$
$$\theta \equiv X(0,T)^2 \{\exp[-\lambda(T_{\mathcal{F}} - T)] - \exp[-\lambda(T_B - T)]\}(\sigma^2/\lambda)$$
$$\sigma_1^2 \equiv \{\exp[-\lambda(T_{\mathcal{F}} - T)] - \exp[-\lambda(T_B - T)]\}^2 [1 - \exp(-2\lambda T)](\sigma^2/2\lambda^3)$$
$$X(0,T) \equiv [1 - \exp(-\lambda T)]/\lambda.$$

These formulas are easily programmed on a computer. We illustrate the computation through an example.

EXAMPLE   **Treasury Bill Futures Option**

This example illustrates the valuation of Expression (17.34).

Consider a European call option on a Treasury bill futures contract. The maturity is 35 days. The strike price of the option is 94 (Index Value). The delivery date of the futures contract is in 90 days, and the contract is written on a 90-day Treasury bill. Relevant price data are given in Table 17.8, Part A.

The value of the option is shown in Table 17.8, Part B, using the program Bonds/Treasury Bill Futures. Note that its delta is negative. If interest rates increase, futures prices will decrease and the value of the call option will also decrease. ■

TABLE 17.8   *Pricing Options on Treasury Bill Futures*

PART A
INPUT DATA

Maturity of Option	35 days
Maturity of Futures Contract	90 days
Maturity of Treasury Bill	90 days
Discount rate for Treasury bill with maturity of 35 days is 4.5095 percent (360-day year).	
Futures Price (Index Value)	95.3434
Volatility	1.0 percent
Volatility Reduction Factor	0.1

PART B
OUTPUT DATA*

Type of Option	Call Option
Maturity of Option (days)	35.00
Maturity of Futures (days)	90.00
Maturity of Treasury Bill (days)	90.00
Exercise Price	94.00
Standard Deviation	0.0100
Volatility Reduction Factor	0.1000

EXERCISE PRICE	OPTION VALUE	DELTA	GAMMA
94.000	0.3344	−23.4988	10.2330

*The program Bonds/Treasury Bill Futures is used.

17.5 OPTIONS ON TREASURY BOND FUTURES

Now we examine pricing and hedging options on Treasury bond futures. We first illustrate options on Treasury bond futures with an example.

Consider a European call option written on a Treasury note futures contract. The maturity of the option is 35 days. The futures contract delivery date is in 125 days' time. At the maturity of the option, the delivery date of the Treasury futures contract will be in 90 days.

Treasury bond and note futures prices are quoted in terms of dollars. The strike prices of options on Treasury bond and note futures are also quoted in terms of dollars. At maturity of the option, if the Treasury bond futures price exceeds the strike price the option is exercised. Otherwise, it expires worthless.

We now study the valuation of Treasury bond futures options. The derivation of pricing formulas for European call and put options on Treasury bond futures is similar to that for options on Treasury bonds. This similarity should help one's understanding of the following derivation.

Consider a futures contract with delivery at date $T_{\mathcal{F}}$. The contract is written on a Treasury bond. The Treasury bond makes n coupon payments c_j at date T_j for $j = 1$, $\ldots, n$. For convenience, we define the last coupon payment to include the principal payment. We are only concerned with coupon payments after the maturity date of the futures contract, implying that date T_1 is after date $T_{\mathcal{F}}$.

From the last chapter we know that we can write the Treasury bond futures price as a sum of futures prices on Treasury bills. Writing Expression (16.35) of Chapter 16 in a slightly more compact form yields

$$\mathcal{F}_c(T; T_{\mathcal{F}}) \equiv \sum_{j=1}^{n} c_j \times \mathcal{F}(T; T_{\mathcal{F}}, T_j), \tag{17.36}$$

where $\mathcal{F}_c(T; T_{\mathcal{F}})$ is the futures price at date T on the Treasury bond and $\mathcal{F}(T; T_{\mathcal{F}}, T_j)$ is the Treasury bill futures price at date T.

The T-bill futures contract $\mathcal{F}(T; T_{\mathcal{F}}, T_j)$ has delivery at date $T_{\mathcal{F}}$ and is written on a Treasury bill that matures at date T_j for $j = 1, \ldots, n$.

Consider a call option on a Treasury bond futures contract that matures at date T with strike price K. The payoff to the call option at maturity T is defined to be

$$c(T) \equiv \begin{cases} \mathcal{F}_c(T; T_{\mathcal{F}}) - K & \text{if} & \mathcal{F}_c(T; T_{\mathcal{F}}) \geq K \\ 0 & \text{if} & \mathcal{F}_c(T; T_{\mathcal{F}}) < K. \end{cases} \tag{17.37}$$

We know from equation (16.24) of Chapter 16 that we can write the Treasury bill futures price at date T for a contract with delivery at date $T_{\mathcal{F}}$ that is written on a Treasury bill that expires at date T_j in the form

$$\mathcal{F}(T; T_{\mathcal{F}}, T_j) = \mathcal{F}(0; T_{\mathcal{F}}, T_j)\exp[-X(T; T_{\mathcal{F}}, T_j)r(T) - X(T; T_{\mathcal{F}}, T_j)\, f(0, T) \\ + a_{\mathcal{F}}(T, T_j)], \tag{17.38}$$

where

$$X(T; T_{\mathcal{F}}, T_j) \equiv \{\exp[-\lambda(T_{\mathcal{F}} - T)] - \exp[-\lambda(T_j - T)]\}/\lambda \\ a_{\mathcal{F}}(T, T_j) \equiv (\sigma^2/2\lambda^2)X(T; T_{\mathcal{F}}, T_j)[1 - \exp(-\lambda T)]^2 \\ - (\sigma^2/4\lambda)X(T; T_{\mathcal{F}}, T_j)^2[1 - \exp(-2\lambda T)].$$

Substituting Expression (17.38) into Expression (17.36) gives

$$\mathcal{F}_c(T; T_{\mathcal{F}}) = \sum_{j=1}^{n} c_j \mathcal{F}(0; T_{\mathcal{F}}, T_j)\exp[-X(T; T_{\mathcal{F}}, T_j)r(T) \\ + X(T; T_{\mathcal{F}}, T_j)f(0, T) + a_{\mathcal{F}}(T, T_j)]. \tag{17.39}$$

Let $\bar{r}$ denote the critical value of the spot rate $r(T)$ for which the T-bond futures price equals the strike price, that is,

$$\mathcal{F}_c(T; T_{\mathcal{F}}) = K. \tag{17.40}$$

We can determine this critical value $\bar{r}$ by an iterative procedure.

Given the definition of $\bar{r}$, the payoff to the T-bond futures call option at maturity T can be written

$$c(T) \equiv \begin{cases} \mathcal{F}_c(T;T_{\mathcal{F}}) - K & \text{if} \quad r(T) \leq \bar{r} \\ 0 & \text{if} \quad r(T) > \bar{r}. \end{cases} \qquad (17.41)$$

Using the risk-neutral valuation technique, it can be shown that the date-0 value of the call option is

$$c(0) = B(0,T)\left[\sum_{j=1}^{n} c_j \mathcal{F}(0;T_{\mathcal{F}},T_j)\exp(\theta_j)N(d_j) - KN(d)\right], \qquad (17.42)$$

where

$$\sigma_R d_j \equiv \bar{r} + X(T;T_{\mathcal{F}},T_j)\sigma_R^2 \qquad \text{for} \qquad j = 1,\ldots,n$$
$$\sigma_R d \equiv \bar{r}$$
$$\sigma_R^2 \equiv (\sigma^2/2\lambda)[1 - \exp(-2\lambda T)]$$
$$\theta_j \equiv (\sigma^2/2)X(T;T_{\mathcal{F}},T_j)\{[1 - \exp(-\lambda T)]/\lambda\}^2$$
$$X(T;T_{\mathcal{F}},T_j) \equiv \{\exp[-\lambda(T_{\mathcal{F}} - T)] - \exp[-\lambda(T_j - T)]\}/\lambda.$$

Similarly, the value of a Treasury bond futures put option with the same contractual conditions as the call is given by

$$p(0) = B(0,T)\left[KN(-d) - \sum_{j=1}^{n} c_j \mathcal{F}(0;T_{\mathcal{F}},T_j)\exp(\theta_j)N(-d_j)\right]. \qquad (17.43)$$

FIGURE 17.4 *Pricing Options on Treasury Bond Futures*

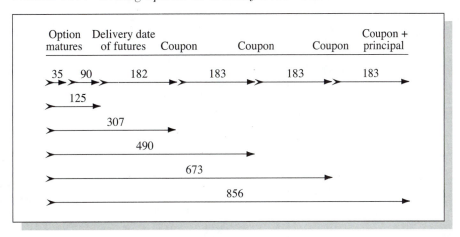

A potential difficulty with using Expressions (17.42) and (17.43) to price options on Treasury bond futures is that they involve futures prices on Treasury bills. Unfortunately, Treasury bill futures do not always trade for all the delivery dates needed. For example, suppose that we wanted to price an option on a Treasury bond futures contract written on a fifteen-year Treasury bond. Treasury bill futures are written only on 91-day Treasury bills, implying that we cannot use these formulas in their current form. Fortunately, we can transform these formulas into expressions involving only zero-coupon bond prices.

TABLE 17.9 *Pricing Options on Treasury Bond Futures*

PART A		
INPUT DATA		
MATURITY **(DAYS)**	**DISCOUNT*** **RATE**	**PRICE × 100**
35	4.5093	99.5676
125	4.5320	98.4479
Coupon per Period	2.2500	
Face Value	100.0000	
Time to First Coupon	307.0000	
Time to Subsequent Coupons	183.0000	

*A 365-day year is assumed.

PAYMENT NO.	**PAYMENT DATE** **DAYS**	**CASH AMOUNT**	**TREASURY** **BILL PRICE × 100**
1	307	2.2500	96.15430
2	490	2.2500	93.81719
3	673	2.2500	91.45880
4	856	102.2500	89.10130

PART B			
OUTPUT DATA*			
Type of Option	Call Option		
Maturity of Option (days)	35.00		
Maturity of Futures (days)	90.00		
Exercise Price	94.0000		
Standard Deviation	0.0100		
Volatility Reduction Factor	0.1000		
EXERCISE PRICE	**OPTION VALUE**	**DELTA**	**GAMMA**
94.0000	4.9520	−167.8685	321.4810

*The program Bonds/Treasury Bond Futures is used.

This transformation is done using Expression (16.23) of Chapter 16, which gives the relevant expression for transforming Treasury bill futures prices into those involving only the zero-coupon bond prices. Direct substitution yields the desired result. Our discussion of Treasury bond futures options is now complete. We finish this section with an example.

EXAMPLE | **Treasury Bond Futures Options**

This example illustrates the valuation of an option on a Treasury note futures contract. We want to price a European call option with a maturity of 35 days. The option is written on a Treasury note futures contract. The delivery date of the futures contract, when the option matures, is in 90 days. The underlying Treasury note is a two-year note with a coupon of 4.50 percent per annum and face value of $100, implying that a coupon of $2.25 is paid semiannually.

To price this option, first we need to determine what term structure data are required. After the futures contract matures, the first coupon payment is made 182 days later. Subsequent coupon payments are made every 183 days. The timing is shown in Figure 17.4 on p. 549. Using the information from Figure 17.4, the relevant term structure data are shown in Table 17.9, Part A.

The strike price of the option is 94. The program Bonds/Treasury Bond Futures is used to price the option. The results are shown in Table 17.9, Part B. ■

17.6 SUMMARY

In this chapter we use the Heath-Jarrow-Morton model to price (1) options on Treasury bills, (2) options on Treasury bonds, (3) options on Treasury bill futures, and (4) options on Treasury bond futures. The Heath-Jarrow-Morton model takes as given the initial term structure of interest rates and a specification of the volatility of forward rates. We have also described the pricing of interest rate caps, floors, collars, and swaptions. A common model used for pricing caps is the Black model. We explain this model and discuss its limitations. This chapter completes our study of interest rate derivatives using the Heath-Jarrow-Morton model.

REFERENCES

Carr, P., and R. R. Chen, 1994. "Valuing Bond Futures and the Quality Option." Working Paper, Cornell University.

Constantinides, G. M., 1992. "A Theory of the Nominal Term Structure of Interest Rates." *Review of Financial Studies* 5, 531–552.

Cox, J. C., J. E. Ingersoll, and S. A. Ross, 1985. "A Theory of the Term Structure of Interest Rates." *Econometrica* 53, 385–407.

Gastineau, G. L., 1992. *Dictionary of Financial Risk Management*. Chicago: Probus Publishing Company.

Heath, D., R. A. Jarrow, and A. Morton, 1992. "Bond Pricing and the Term Structure of Interest Rates: A New Methodology for Contingent Claim Valuation." *Econometrica* 60, 77–105.

Hull, J., and A. White, 1990. "Pricing Interest Rate Derivative Securities." *Review of Financial Studies* 3, 573–592.

Ingersoll, J. E., J. Skelton, and R. L. Weil, 1978. "Duration Forty Years Later." *Journal of Financial and Quantitative Analysis* 13, 627–650.

Jarrow, R., 1995. *Modelling Fixed Income Securities and Interest Rate Options*. New York: McGraw-Hill Book Company.

Jarrow, R. A., and S. M. Turnbull, 1994. "Delta, Gamma and Bucket Hedging of Interest Rate Derivatives." *Applied Mathematical Finance* 1, 21–58.

Longstaff, F. A., and E. S. Schwartz, 1992. "Interest Rate Volatility and the Term Structure: A Two Factor General Equilibrium Model." *Journal of Finance* 47, 1259–1282.

Miltersen, K. R., K. Sandmann, and D. Sondermann, 1997. "Closed Form Solutions for Term Structure Derivatives with Lognormal Interest Rates." *Journal of Finance* 52, 409–430.

Musiela, M., S. M. Turnbull, and L. M. Wakeman, 1990. "Interest Rate Risk Management." *Review of Futures Markets* 12, 221–261.

Turnbull, S. M., 1995. "Interest Rate Digital Options and Range Notes." *Journal of Derivatives* 3, 92–101.

Vasicek, O., 1977. "An Equilibrium Characterization of the Term Structure." *Journal of Financial Economics* 5, 177–186.

QUESTIONS

Question 1

Use the information in Table 17.1 to answer the following questions.

a) Determine the current 91-day forward price starting at day 35. Express this forward price in terms of a discount rate.

b) Consider pricing a call option and a put option with a maturity of 35 days written on a 91-day Treasury bill. The strike prices of the options are set at the forward price. What is the value of the call option and its delta and gamma? What is the value of the put option and its delta and gamma? Use the program Bonds/ Treasury Bills.

c) Explain your results.

Question 2

An institution wants to construct a synthetic call option. The option has a maturity of 35 days and is written on a 91-day Treasury bill. The strike price, expressed as a dis-

count rate, is 4.85 percent assuming a 360-day year. The institution plans to use a futures contract with a maturity of 35 days written on a 91-day Treasury bill and a Treasury bill with a maturity of 126 days. Use the information in Table 17.1.

a) Determine the delta and gamma of the futures contract. Use the program Bonds/ Hedge Ratio/Treasury Bill Futures.
b) Determine the delta and gamma of the Treasury bill with a maturity of 126 days. Use the program Bonds/Hedge Ratio/Treasury Bills.
c) Determine the value of the call option and its delta and gamma. Use the program Bonds/Treasury Bills.
d) Describe the construction of the synthetic option.
e) What is the gamma of the synthetic option?

Question 3

a) Use the information in Table 17.4 to value a one-year floor. The floor rate is 4.50 percent. Use the program Bonds/Floors/Normal.
b) If volatility increased to 1.50 percent, what effect would this have on the floor price?

Question 4

a) Use the information in Table 17.5 to value a one-year floor. The floor rate is 4.50 percent. Use the program Bonds/Floors/Black.
b) How do your answers compare to the answers in Question 3(a)?

Question 5

Using the information in Table 17.6, consider a two-year bond that pays a coupon of $2.375 every six months, assuming a face value of $100. An institution has written a put option on this bond. The maturity of the put option is 150 days and the strike price is $102. The institution wants to hedge this option using the two-year bond and a Treasury bill with a maturity of 150 days.

a) What is the delta and gamma of the Treasury bill? Use the program Bonds/Hedge Ratio/Treasury Bills.
b) What is the value of the two-year bond and its delta and gamma? Use the program Bonds/Hedge Ratio/Treasury Bonds.
c) What is the value of the put option and its delta and gamma? Use the program Bonds/Treasury Bonds.
d) Describe the hedged portfolio.
e) The delta of the hedged portfolio is zero. What is its gamma?

Question 6

Consider a European swaption with a maturity of 120 days (four months). The underlying swap is one in which the swap owner receives floating and pays fixed at the rate of $4.625 per annum over a three-year period on a semiannual basis. Use the information in Table 17.7 to price this swaption.

Question 7

Consider a European put option on a Treasury bill futures contract. The maturity of the option is 45 days. The strike price of the option is 96.50 (index value). The delivery date of the futures contract is 90 days and it is written on a 90-day Treasury bill. Input data is summarized below.

Maturity of Option	45 days
Maturity of Futures Contract	90 days
Maturity of Treasury Bill	90 days

Discount rate for Treasury bill with maturity of 45 days is 4.1152 percent.
Discount rate for Treasury bill with maturity of 135 days is 4.1830 percent.
Discount rate for Treasury bill with maturity of 225 days is 4.2498 percent.

Futures Price (Index Value)	95.7488
Volatility	1.50 percent
Volatility Reduction Factor	0.1

a) Check the futures price, quoted as an index value.
b) Determine the value of the option and its delta and gamma.

(A 360-day year is assumed.)

Question 8

A financial institution has written the option described in Question 7. It wants to hedge the option using a Treasury bill with a maturity of 45 days and a Treasury bill with a maturity of 135 days.

a) Determine the delta and gamma of the 45-day Treasury bill. Use the program Bonds/Hedge Ratio/Treasury Bills.
b) Determine the delta and gamma of the 135-day Treasury bill.
c) Describe the hedge portfolio.
d) What is the gamma of the hedged portfolio?

Question 9

A financial institution has written the option described in Question 7. It wants to hedge the option using a Treasury bill with a maturity of 45 days and a Treasury bill

futures contract with delivery in 61 days' time. The contract is written on a 91-day Treasury bill. The discount rate for a Treasury bill that matures in 61 days' time is 4.1273 percent, and for a Treasury bill that matures in 152 days' time it is 4.1957 percent.

a) Determine the price, delta, and gamma of the 45-day Treasury bill. Use the program Bonds/Hedge Ratio/Treasury Bills.
b) Determine the delta and gamma of the futures contract with delivery in 61 days' time. Use the program Bonds/Hedge Ratio/Treasury Bills.
c) Describe the hedge portfolio.
d) What is the gamma of the hedged portfolio?

(Assume a 360-day year.)

Question 10

A financial institution that has written the European call option on the Treasury bond futures contract described in Table 17.9 decides to hedge the option with the underlying futures contract and a Treasury bill with a maturity of 35 days. Use the information in Table 17.9.

a) Determine the delta and gamma of the Treasury bill. Use the program Bonds/Hedge Ratio/Treasury Bill.
b) Determine the delta and gamma of the Treasury bond futures contract. Note that the maturity of this contract is 125 days. Use the program Bonds/Hedge Ratio/Treasury Bond Futures.
c) Describe the hedge portfolio.
d) What is the gamma of the hedged portfolio?

CREDIT RISK

18.0 INTRODUCTION

The pricing and hedging models we describe in the previous chapters are based on the four fundamental assumptions we first discussed in Chapter 2.

Assumption A1.   No market frictions

Assumption A2.   No counterparty risk

Assumption A3.   Competitive markets

Assumption A4.   No arbitrage opportunities

Of these four assumptions, the second one—no counterparty risk—is perhaps the least defensible. In practice, bankruptcy and the nonexecution of contracts are of major concern in all business transactions, including the trading of financial instruments, especially over-the-counter contracts. When entities borrow and lend, Assumption A2 implies that there is only one rate—the default-free rate. However, in practice, there are many rates for borrowing. These rates differ based on the perceived ability (or likelihood) of the borrower to repay the loan.

For exchange-traded derivative securities, such as options and futures, there is the risk that the writer of the security will be unable to meet the obligations of the contract. As a consequence, exchanges have set up clearing corporations to reduce concern about this counterparty risk (see Chapter 1). A clearing corporation is the counterparty to all exchange-traded derivatives. In the United States the triple-A-credit rated Options Clearing Corporation helps reduce counterparty risk in the execution of exchange-traded option contracts. Many investment banks have also set up triple-A-credit rated derivative product companies in response to concern about creditworthiness in the over-the-counter market.

These observations suggest that if we want to understand corporate bond markets and over-the-counter contracts, we need to understand the pricing and hedging of derivatives in the presence of counterparty risk, that is, the relaxation of Assumption A2.

The pricing and hedging of financial securities under the relaxation of Assumption A2 is an exciting and new area of research in financial economics. Here we present the modeling paradigm formulated by Jarrow and Turnbull (1995). This paradigm

can be shown to include all other modeling approaches as special cases, hence its suitability for presentation. The material is no more difficult than any of the other areas studied in this text. However, the notation is slightly more complicated in order to keep track of bankruptcy and its likelihood of occurrence.

This model considers pricing and hedging of derivatives under two forms of credit risk. The first form we examine is the pricing of derivatives written on assets subject to default risk. An example is the pricing of derivatives written on corporate bonds, where default may occur on the part of the corporation. The second form we examine is the pricing of derivatives where the writer of the derivative might default. For example, consider an over-the-counter option written on a Treasury bond. There is no default risk arising from the underlying asset—the Treasury bond. However, default risk arises from the fact that the writer of the option may not be able to honor the obligation if the option is exercised. This form of risk is referred to as **counterparty risk**. We will describe a simple approach to the pricing and hedging of both forms of credit risk. We will give a number of examples, including the pricing of credit-risky annuities, floating rate debt, swaps, and derivatives.

In the over-the-counter market counterparty risk is a major concern to financial institutions and regulatory bodies. One of the main concerns of bank regulators is to evaluate management's ability to measure and control risk and to determine when risk exposures become excessive relative to the institution's capital position.[1] The traditional approach of specifying minimum or maximum balance sheet ratios such as equity to total assets is inappropriate for two reasons. First, derivative securities such as swaps and options that are now a significant source of risk do not appear on the balance sheet. Second, the static nature of balance sheet ratios is woefully inadequate in assessing the risk of derivative securities. The last part of this chapter describes some recent regulatory developments in this regard.

18.1 PRICING CREDIT-RISKY BONDS

In this section we study the pricing of bonds (loans) subject to default risk, called **credit-risky bonds**. Our approach to pricing credit-risky bonds allocates firms to particular risk classes—AAA, AA, and so on—based on their current creditworthiness.[2] A typical set of credit-risky term structures is shown in Figure 18.1.

Illustrated in this figure are the yields on zero-coupon bonds issued by firms with different credit risk. The default-free curve is derived using Treasury bills, notes, and bonds, as described in Chapter 13. A corporation in credit class AAA is assumed to have the least credit risk among corporate firms. Its yields are higher than those of the Treasury's due to default risk. Firms of lower credit than AAA, such as those in credit class AA, trade at a lower price and thus at a higher yield than AAA, and so forth.

---

[1] See Part 1 of the Federal Reserve Trading Manual (1994).

[2] An extended form of this structure is for each firm to belong to its own separate credit class. In this case, the analysis applies firm by firm.

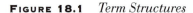

FIGURE 18.1 *Term Structures*

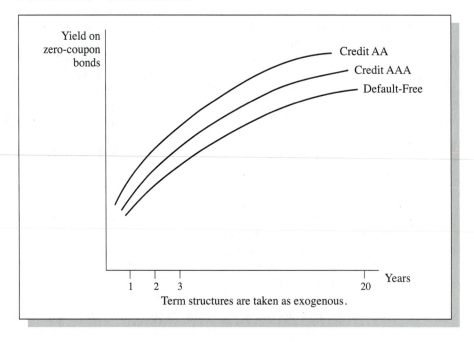

Term structures are taken as exogenous.

Given these term structures of zero-coupon bond prices for the different credit classes, pricing coupon bonds issued by the different credit classes is a straightforward exercise. For example, consider a coupon bond issued by a firm in credit class ABC with coupons c_j paid at times T_j for $j = 1, \ldots, n$ and a face value F paid at the time T_n.

Let $v(0, T)$ represent the date-0 value of a promised dollar at date T issued by the ABC credit class firm. Then, the coupon bond's value at date 0, denoted $v_c(0)$, is given by

$$v_c(0) = \sum_{j=1}^{n} c_j v(0, T_j) + Fv(0, T_n),$$

which is an arbitrage-free pricing relation. Its proof is identical to the proof of Expression (13.4) in Chapter 13. The zero-coupon term structures for the different credit classes are the only inputs necessary for pricing credit-risky coupon bonds.

In fact, we have already used this result previously in Chapter 14 when valuing plain vanilla interest rate swaps. In that case, the two different term structures were the default-free and the LIBOR curves. We used those curves to determine the present value of the swap's cash flows.

Next, suppose we want to price a derivative written on a zero-coupon bond issued by a firm with credit rating ABC. We must price this derivative in such a way that it is

(1) consistent with the absence of arbitrage, (2) consistent with the relevant initial term structures of interest rates, and (3) consistent with a positive probability of default. This is a two-step procedure. First, we need to construct a lattice of one-period interest rates to model the default-free term structure. This construction is described in Chapter 15. Second, we need to perform a similar, but more complex, construction for the zero-coupon bonds of the firm belonging to the risk class ABC. We now turn to these tasks.

Lattice of Default-Free Interest Rates

Here we recall the construction of the lattice for default-free interest rates studied in Chapter 15. The term structure for default-free zero-coupon bonds is assumed to be identical to that given in Table 15.1 of Chapter 15, and the lattice for short-term interest rates shown in Figure 15.3 is reproduced here as Figure 18.2.

We have selected the lattice approximating normally distributed interest rates. Alternatively, we could have used the Black, Derman, and Toy (1990) lognormal model given by the lattice in Figure 15.6.

We note that all of the insights concerning the pricing of default-free interest rate derivatives shown in Chapter 15 apply based on these figures. In the next section we extend this model to handle credit-risky bonds.

FIGURE 18.2 *Default-Free Spot Interest Rates*

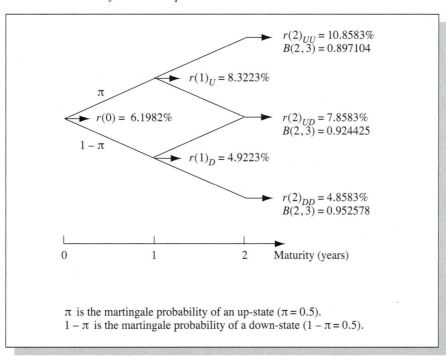

π is the martingale probability of an up-state ($\pi = 0.5$).
$1 - \pi$ is the martingale probability of a down-state ($1 - \pi = 0.5$).

Risky Debt

Let us examine the pricing of credit-risky debt. We want to value a zero-coupon bond for a firm belonging to the credit class ABC.

Let $v(t, T)$ denote the value at date t of a zero-coupon bond issued by the firm. The debt matures at date T, and the bondholders are *promised* the face value of the bond at maturity. Let the face value be \$1. Because the firm's debt is risky, there is a positive probability that the firm might default over the life of the bond. If default occurs, the bondholders will receive less than the promised amount.

It is instructive to view the pricing of credit-risky bonds in terms of a foreign currency analogy. Imagine a hypothetical currency, called *ABC*s. In terms of this currency, we can view the debt issued by the firm as default-free. Indeed, at maturity the bondholder is issued the face value of debt in *ABC*s. But this hypothetical currency is useless to the bondholder; we need to define an exchange rate that converts this hypothetical currency to dollars. After all, the bondholders are interested in the dollar value of their *ABC*s.

There are two cases to consider. If default has not occurred before or at date t, then the exchange rate is unity. If default did occur, it is assumed that we get some fraction δ of a dollar for each *ABC*. This is the same as receiving the fraction δ of the face amount of the debt in the event of default. The fraction δ is also called the **payoff ratio** or **recovery rate**.

Defining e_t as the date-t exchange rate per *ABC*s, we have

$$e_t = \begin{cases} 1 \text{ with probability } 1 - \lambda(t)\,\Delta & \text{if} & \text{no default} \\ \delta \text{ with probability } \lambda(t)\,\Delta & \text{if} & \text{default,} \end{cases} \tag{18.1}$$

where $0 \leq \delta < 1$ and $\lambda(t)\,\Delta$ is the martingale probability of default conditional upon no default at or before date $t - \Delta$.

We are interested in the martingale probabilities of default because we want to develop pricing formulas that are arbitrage-free.[3] This approach is analogous to that taken in Chapter 15 for default-free derivatives and draws upon the work in Chapter 6.

If default has occurred at or before date $t - \Delta$, it is assumed that the bond remains in default and the payoff ratio remains constant at δ dollars:

$$e_t \equiv \delta. \tag{18.2}$$

The conditional martingale probabilities of default can be estimated using the observed term structures of interest rates. We will discuss how to do this in the following text.

To simplify the analysis, we are going to assume that the default process is independent of the level of the default-free interest rate. This implies that interest rates be-

---

[3]The existence and uniqueness of these martingale probabilities of default is discussed in Jarrow and Turnbull (1995).

ing either "high" or "low" have no effect on the probability of default. This is a useful first approximation and its relaxation is discussed in Jarrow and Turnbull (1995).

Credit-Risky Debt

This section shows how to determine the martingale probabilities of default using the observed term structures of zero-coupon bond prices. We use an example to illustrate the procedure.

EXAMPLE   **Martingale Probabilities of Default**

This example illustrates the procedure for determining the martingale probabilities of default. In Table 18.1, we are given two sets of prices for zero-coupon bonds of maturities one, two, and three years. The first is for default-free bonds and the second is for bonds belonging to credit class ABC.

The default-free bonds at each maturity are seen to be more valuable than the equivalent maturity bond issued by the firm in credit class ABC. This difference reflects the likelihood of default and the recovery rate. We want to estimate the martingale probabilities of default implicit in these bond prices.

Before we make our estimate, however, we must first specify the payoff ratio δ in the event of default. This value comes from our credit risk analysts who estimate that, given the nature of the debt, we expect to receive $0.32 on the dollar in the event of default.[4]

Consider first the one-year ABC zero-coupon bond. For simplicity, we take the interval in the lattice to be one year. At maturity, the credit-risky bond's value is

$$v(1,1) = \begin{cases} 1 \text{ with probability } 1 - \lambda(0)\,\Delta & \text{if} & \text{no default} \\ \delta \text{ with probability } \lambda(0)\,\Delta & \text{if} & \text{default,} \end{cases} \quad (18.3)$$

where $\Delta = 1$ and $\delta = 0.32$.

TABLE 18.1   *Prices of Zero-Coupon Bonds*

MATURITY (YEARS) T	DEFAULT-FREE $B(0,T)$	CREDIT CLASS ABC $v(0,T)$
1	0.9399	0.9361
2	0.8798	0.8703
3	0.8137	0.7980

[4]For different types of bonds, average recovery rates are given in Moody's Special Report (1992).

The default process is shown in Figure 18.3. Given that default has not occurred at date $t = 0$, the conditional (martingale) probability that default occurs at $t = 1$ is denoted by $\lambda(0) \times \Delta$, where Δ is the time interval. In this example, $\Delta = 1$. The conditional (martingale) probability that default does not occur is $1 - \lambda(0) \Delta$.

We can use the term structures of interest rates for default-free and credit class ABC bonds to infer the value of $\lambda(0)$. We know from Chapter 6 that normalized prices are a martingale under the martingale probabilities:[5]

$$\frac{v(0,1)}{A(0)} = E^{\pi}\left[\frac{v(1,1)}{A(1)}\right], \tag{18.4}$$

where $A(t)$ denotes the value of the money market account at date t.

We use Expression (18.4) to solve for the value of $\lambda(0)$. First, by construction we have that $A(0) = 1$, and from Figure 18.2 we see that

$$A(1) = \exp\left[r(0)\right] = \exp(0.06198) = 1.0639.$$

Substituting Expression (18.3) into (18.4), given no default at time 0, we have

$$v(0, 1) = \{1 \times [1 - \lambda(0)] + \delta \times \lambda(0)\}/1.0639.$$

FIGURE 18.3   *One-Period Credit-Risky Debt Default Process*

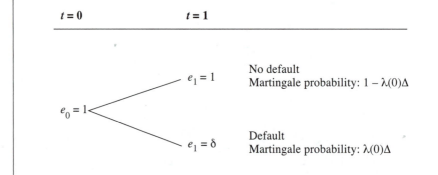

$t = 0$ $t = 1$

$e_0 = 1$

$e_1 = 1$ No default
Martingale probability: $1 - \lambda(0)\Delta$

$e_1 = \delta$ Default
Martingale probability: $\lambda(0)\Delta$

$\lambda(0)\Delta$ is the martingale probability that default occurs at date $t = 1$, conditional upon the fact that default has not occurred at date $t = 0$. In this example $\Delta = 1$.

---

[5]The reader is referred to Jarrow and Turnbull (1995) for technical details.

FIGURE 18.4   *Two-Period Credit-Risky Debt Default Process*

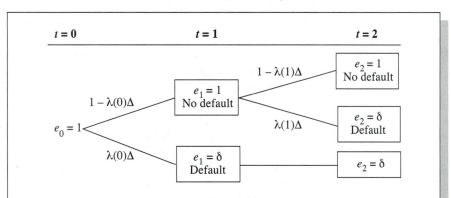

$\lambda(1)\Delta$ is the martingale probability that default occurs at date $t = 2$, conditional upon the fact that default has not occurred at date $t = 1$.

From Table 18.1, we know that $v(0,1) = 0.9361$ and $\delta = 0.32$. Therefore,

$$0.9361 = \frac{1}{1.0639} \{[1 - \lambda(0)] + 0.32 \times \lambda(0)\}. \tag{18.5}$$

Solving for the martingale probability of default gives

$$(1 - 0.32) \times \lambda(0) = 1 - (0.9361 \times 1.0639)$$

or

$$\lambda(0) = 0.0059.$$

The pricing of the two-period zero-coupon bond is slightly more complicated because, at the end of the first period, both interest rates and the default status of the firm are uncertain.

The default process is shown in Figure 18.4. If default has occurred at date $t = 1$, the bond is assumed to remain in default. If default has not occurred at date $t = 1$, then one period later, at date $t = 2$, either default occurs or it does not. The martingale probability of default occurring at date $t = 2$, conditional upon the fact that default has not occurred at date $t = 1$, is $\lambda(1)\,\Delta$. The conditional (martingale) probability that default does not occur at date $t = 2$ is $1 - \lambda(1)\,\Delta$.

Combining Figure 18.4 with Figure 18.2 gives all the possible states, as shown in Figure 18.5. There are four possible states labeled A, B, C, and D, corresponding to all combinations of interest rates going up or down combined with default or no default. The martingale probabilities of each state occurring at date 1 are given as the multiplicative product of the separate probabilities of interest rates going up or down times the probabilities of default or no default. The multiplicative product is the implication of the assumption that the interest rate process and the bankruptcy process are statistically independent.

We use an analogous argument to determine the conditional martingale probability of default $\lambda(1)$ implicit in the bond prices.

Let us start at state A, at date $t = 1$. The value of a default-free bond that matures at $t = 2$ is

$$B(1,2) = \exp(-0.0492).$$

FIGURE 18.5   *Two-Period Credit-Risky Debt: Determining the Implied Probabilities*

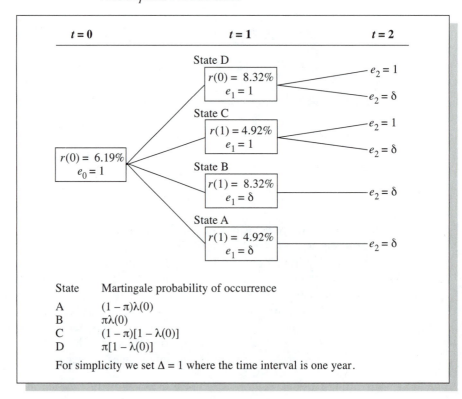

State	Martingale probability of occurrence
A	$(1 - \pi)\lambda(0)$
B	$\pi\lambda(0)$
C	$(1 - \pi)[1 - \lambda(0)]$
D	$\pi[1 - \lambda(0)]$

For simplicity we set $\Delta = 1$ where the time interval is one year.

In state A, default has occurred at date $t = 1$, so the payoff to the risky bond at date $t = 2$ is

$$v(2,2) = \delta.$$

The value in state A at date $t = 1$, given that default has occurred, is

$$\frac{v(1,2)}{A(1)} = E^\pi \left[\frac{v(2,2)}{A(2)} \right].$$

Now from Figure 18.5, in state A we have that the value of the money market is

$$A(2) = A(1)\exp(0.0492).$$

Substitution yields

$$v_A(1,2) = \frac{1}{\exp(0.0492)} \delta$$
$$= B(1,2)_d\delta.$$

The subscript d refers to the down-state for the default-free spot rate of interest.

A similar argument applies if state B occurs. In state B the firm has defaulted, so

$$v_B(1,2) = \frac{1}{\exp(0.0832)} \delta$$
$$= B(1,2)_u\delta,$$

where

$$B(1,2)_u = \exp(-0.0832).$$

The subscript u refers to the up-state for the default-free spot rate of interest.

If state C occurs, the argument is more interesting. In state C, default has not occurred, so that one period later, at maturity, one of two possible states can occur:

$$v(2,2) = \begin{cases} 1 \text{ with probability } 1 - \lambda(1) & \text{if} \quad \text{no default} \\ \delta \text{ with probability } \lambda(1) & \text{if} \quad \text{default}. \end{cases}$$

Therefore, in state C the value of the bond is

$$v_C(1,2) = \frac{1}{\exp(0.0492)}\{[1 - \lambda(1)] + \delta\lambda(1)\}$$

$$= B(1,2)_d\{[1 - \lambda(1)] + \delta\lambda(1)\}.$$

In state D, a similar argument applies because the firm has not yet defaulted:

$$v_D(1,2) = \frac{1}{\exp(0.0832)}\{[1 - \lambda(1)] + \delta\lambda(1)\}$$

$$= B(1,2)_u\{[1 - \lambda(1)] + \delta\lambda(1)\}.$$

Today we know the value of the risky bond $v(0,2) = 0.8703$ from Table 18.1. Now

$$\frac{v(0,2)}{A(0)} = E^{\pi}\left[\frac{v(1,2)}{A(1)}\right].$$

Referring to Figure 18.5, there are four possible states. Therefore,

$$v(0,2) = \frac{1}{\exp(0.0619)}\{(1 - \pi)\lambda(0)v_A(1,2) + \pi\lambda(0)v_B(1,2)$$

$$+ (1 - \pi)[1 - \lambda(0)]v_C(1,2) + \pi[1 - \lambda(0)]v_D(1,2)\}.$$

Substituting the previously computed values of the bond in the four different states gives

$$v(0,2) = \frac{1}{\exp(0.0619)}[(1- \pi)\exp(-0.0492) + \pi\exp(-0.0832)]\lambda(0)\delta$$

$$+ \frac{1}{\exp(0.0619)}[(1 - \pi)\exp(-0.0492) + \pi\exp(-0.0832)]$$

$$\times [1 - \lambda(0)]\{[1 - \lambda(1)] + \lambda(1)\delta\}.$$

The above calculation can be simplified by considering the pricing of a two-period default-free zero-coupon bond. Consider the value of the default-free bond at $t = 1$:

$$B(1,2) = \begin{cases} \exp(-0.0832) & \text{with martingale probability } \pi \\ \exp(-0.0492) & \text{with martingale probability } 1 - \pi. \end{cases}$$

The value of the default-free bond today at $t = 0$ is

$$B(0,2) = \frac{1}{\exp(0.0619)}[(1 - \pi)\exp(-0.0492) + \pi\exp(-0.0832)].$$

FIGURE 18.6 *Two-Period Credit-Risky Debt: Summary of Results*

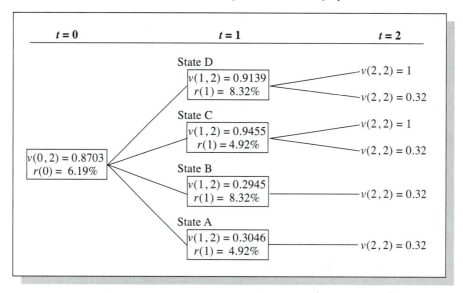

Therefore, substituting into the expression for $v(0,2)$ yields

$$v(0,2) = B(0,2)\{\lambda(0)\delta + [1 - \lambda(0)]([1 - \lambda(1)] + \lambda(1)\delta)\}. \quad (18.6)$$

This is the equation we use to solve for $\lambda(1)$.

From Table 18.1 we have $B(0,2) = 0.8798$, $v(0,2) = 0.8703$, and $\delta = 0.32$, and we have previously computed $\lambda(0) = 0.0059$. Substituting these values into Expression (18.6) and solving for $\lambda(1)$ gives

$$\lambda(1) = 0.0100.$$

The martingale probability of default at date 1 as implied by the bond prices, $\lambda(1)$, is seen to be almost twice that of default at date 0, $\lambda(0)$.

Given that $\lambda(0) = 0.0059$ and $\lambda(1) = 0.0100$, the pricing of the two-period credit-risky debt is summarized in Figure 18.6.

We leave it as an exercise for the reader, using the prices of the three-year bonds, to prove that

$$\lambda(2) = 0.0127. \quad \blacksquare$$

In summary, this example shows how to infer the martingale probabilities of default using the term structures for default-free bonds and credit-risky bonds.

Formalization

Here we formalize the preceding example. This involves little more than replacing numbers with symbols. However, this formalization provides additional insights into the pricing of credit-risky derivatives.

First we consider Expression (18.5). The value of a one-period, zero-coupon, default-free bond is given by

$$B(0,1) = \frac{1}{\exp(0.0619)}.$$

Thus, given no default at time 0, we can rewrite Expression (18.5) in the form

$$v(0,1) = B(0,1)\{[1 - \lambda(0)] + \delta\lambda(0)\}.$$

The default process is defined by Expression (18.3):

$$e_1 = \begin{cases} 1 \text{ with probability } 1 - \lambda(0)\,\Delta & \text{if} & \text{no default} \\ \delta \text{ with probability } \lambda(0)\,\Delta & \text{if} & \text{default,} \end{cases}$$

conditional upon no default at $t = 0$.

The expected value, conditional upon no default at $t = 0$, is

$$E_0^\pi[e_1 \mid \text{no default}] = [1 - \lambda(0)\,\Delta] + \delta[\lambda(0)\,\Delta].$$

In this section, for clarity of the exposition, we need to indicate via a subscript the date at which the expectation is computed. For this expectation, it is time 0, hence the zero subscript.

We can rewrite Expression (18.3) one last time as

$$v(0,1) = B(0,1)E_0^\pi[e_1 \mid \text{no default}]. \tag{18.7}$$

This is the generalized version of the risky zero-coupon bond's valuation formula. It states that the risky zero-coupon bond's date-0 price is the discounted expected payoff to the risky bond at date 1. The expectation is computed under the martingale probabilities.

A similar expression holds for the two-period credit-risky bond, for which (referring to Figure 18.5), if we are in either state A or state B, default has occurred and

$$e_2 = \delta.$$

Therefore, conditional on default having occurred at date $t = 1$,

$$E_1^\pi[e_2 \mid \text{default}] = \delta.$$

If we are in state C or state D, default has not occurred, so

$$e_2 = \begin{cases} 1 \text{ with probability } 1 - \lambda(1)\,\Delta & \text{if} & \text{no default} \\ \delta \text{ with probability } \lambda(1)\,\Delta & \text{if} & \text{default} \end{cases}$$

and the conditional expected value is

$$E_1^\pi\,[e_2\,|\,\text{no default}] = [1 - \lambda(1)\,\Delta] + \delta[\lambda(1)\,\Delta].$$

Today, at $t = 0$, default has not occurred, so

$$e_1 = \begin{cases} 1 \text{ with probability } 1 - \lambda(0)\,\Delta & \text{if} & \text{no default} \\ \delta \text{ with probability } \lambda(0)\,\Delta & \text{if} & \text{default.} \end{cases}$$

Therefore, when viewed from date 0,

$$\begin{aligned} E_0^\pi\,[e_2\,|\,\text{no default}] = {} & [1 - \lambda(0)\,\Delta]\,E_1^\pi\,[e_2\,|\,\text{no default}] \\ & + [\lambda(0)\,\Delta]E_1^\pi\,[e_2\,|\,\text{default}]. \end{aligned} \tag{18.8}$$

Using these general expressions, we can rewrite Expression (18.6) in the form

$$\begin{aligned} v(0,2) = {} & B(0,2)\{\lambda(0)\,\Delta E_1^\pi\,[e_2\,|\,\text{default}] + [1 - \lambda(0)\,\Delta]E_1^\pi\,[e_2\,|\,\text{no default}]\} \\ = {} & B(0,2)E_0^\pi[e_2\,|\,\text{no default}]. \end{aligned} \tag{18.9}$$

This expression states that the date-0 price of the two-year, credit-risky, zero-coupon bond is its discounted expected payoff at date 2 under the martingale probabilities.

Expressions (18.7) and (18.9) are special cases of the general formulas

$$v(0,T) = B(0,T)E_0^\pi\,[e_T\,|\,\text{no default}] \qquad \text{if} \qquad \text{no default} \tag{18.10a}$$

and

$$v(0,T) = B(0,T)\delta \qquad \text{if} \qquad \text{default,} \tag{18.10b}$$

both for a risky zero-coupon bond of maturity T.

Expression (18.10a) gives the risky zero-coupon bond's value if the firm is not in default, and Expression (18.10b) gives the risky zero-coupon bond's value if the firm is in default. The value not in default, Expression (18.10a), is greater than the value in default, Expression (18.10b), because $E_0^\pi\,[e_T\,|\,\text{no default}] > \delta$. This follows because if default has not yet occurred, there is some positive probability that the firm will pay its promised face value of a dollar at the bond's maturity. An example helps to clarify these calculations.

EXAMPLE   **Computations of Discounted Expected Payoffs (Continued)**

This example illustrates the computation of the discounted expected payoffs using Expressions (18.7) and (18.10a,b). Referring to the numbers in the previous example, we have

$$\lambda(0) = 0.0059,$$
$$\lambda(1) = 0.0100,$$

and

$$\lambda(2) = 0.0127.$$

To determine the value of a three-year, zero-coupon, credit-risky bond, we must first compute the expected value of the exchange rate at $t = 3$, conditional upon no default at $t = 2$:

$$\begin{aligned} E_2^\pi[e_3 \mid \text{no default}] &= [1 - \lambda(2)] + \delta\lambda(2) \\ &= (1 - 0.0127) + 0.32(0.0127) \\ &= 0.9914. \end{aligned}$$

If default has occurred at $t = 2$, then

$$E_2^\pi[e_3 \mid \text{default}] = \delta.$$

At $t = 1$, the expected value of the exchange rate at $t = 3$, conditional upon no default at $t = 1$, is given by

$$\begin{aligned} E_1^\pi[e_3 \mid \text{no default}] &= [1 - \lambda(1)]E_2^\pi[e_3 \mid \text{no default}] + \lambda(1)E_2^\pi[e_3 \mid \text{default}] \\ &= 0.9846. \end{aligned}$$

If default has occurred at $t = 1$, then

$$E_1^\pi[e_3 \mid \text{default}] = \delta.$$

At $t = 0$, the expected value of the exchange rate at $t = 3$, conditional upon no default at $t = 0$, is given by

$$\begin{aligned} E_0^\pi[e_3 \mid \text{no default}] &= [1 - \lambda(0)]E_1^\pi[e_3 \mid \text{no default}] + \lambda(0)E_1^\pi[e_3 \mid \text{default}] \\ &= 0.9807. \end{aligned}$$

Therefore, using Expressions (18.10a,b), the price of the three-year risky zero-coupon bond is

$$\begin{aligned} v(0,3) &= 0.8137 \times 0.9807 \\ &= 0.7980, \end{aligned}$$

which agrees with Table 18.1.   ■

Interpretation of Expression (18.10a,b)

We pause to discuss the interpretation of Expression (18.10a,b), which is an important and intuitive result. It is important both because it provides a practical way of computing the martingale probabilities of default using market data and because it can be used for pricing derivatives on credit-risky cash flows. It is intuitive because the second term in Expression (18.10a), $E_0^\pi [e_T \mid \text{no default}]$, is the date-0 expected value of the promised payoff at date T. We can alternatively rewrite expression (18.10a) using the form

$$E_0^\pi [e_T \mid \text{no default}] = v(0, T)/B(0, T), \qquad (18.11)$$

and the right side can be interpreted as a credit spread. This credit spread will prove useful in subsequent applications.

Value of the Claim in the Event of Default

We have assumed that if default occurs, bondholders will receive the fraction δ per promised dollar at the maturity of the bond. The present value of this payment is $\delta B(t, T)$, assuming that default has occurred by date t.

An alternative assumption is to assume that the present value of the claim to bondholders is proportional to the value of the bond just prior to default. This assumption is associated with the work of Duffie and Singleton (1997). It is a simple exercise to incorporate this assumption into our previous analysis. This proportionality assumption and others can be found in Jarrow and Turnbull (1999).

18.2 PRICING OPTIONS ON CREDIT-RISKY BONDS

We demonstrate in this section how to price options on credit-risky bonds. Consider an option written on the debt issued by *ABC* Company. We illustrate the analysis with a simple example, which we will then formalize.

EXAMPLE **Put Option**

This example illustrates the pricing of a put option on *ABC* debt. Consider a put option with a maturity of one year. At maturity, the option allows you to sell a one-year zero-coupon bond issued by the *ABC* firm for a strike price of 0.93.

To price this option, we follow the same risk-neutral valuation procedure that we have used throughout this text. For simplicity of exposition, we maintain our assumption that the length of the lattice interval is one year so that we can use all the results summarized in Figure 18.6. In practice, we would use intervals of shorter length.

We start by considering the value of the option at its maturity date. At the maturity of the option, there are four possible values for the underlying risky

zero-coupon bond in states A, B, C, and D. The option values are shown in Figure 18.7. Pricing the put option at date 0 using the risk-neutral valuation procedure gives

$$\frac{p(0)}{A(0)} = E^{\pi} \left[\frac{p(1)}{A(1)} \right],$$

(18.12)

where $p(t)$ is the value of the put option at date $t = 0, 1$.

We next discuss how to evaluate Expression (18.12). First, the values of the money market account at $t = 0$ and $t = 1$ are

$$A(0) \equiv 1$$

and

$$A(1) = \exp(0.06198) = 1.0639.$$

Next, in states A and B at date 1, default has occurred on the underlying *ABC* zero-coupon bond. The value of the put option varies over these two states because the value of the underlying *ABC* zero-coupon bond varies due to the interest rate risk.

Figure 18.7   *Pricing a Put Option Written on Credit-Risky Debt*

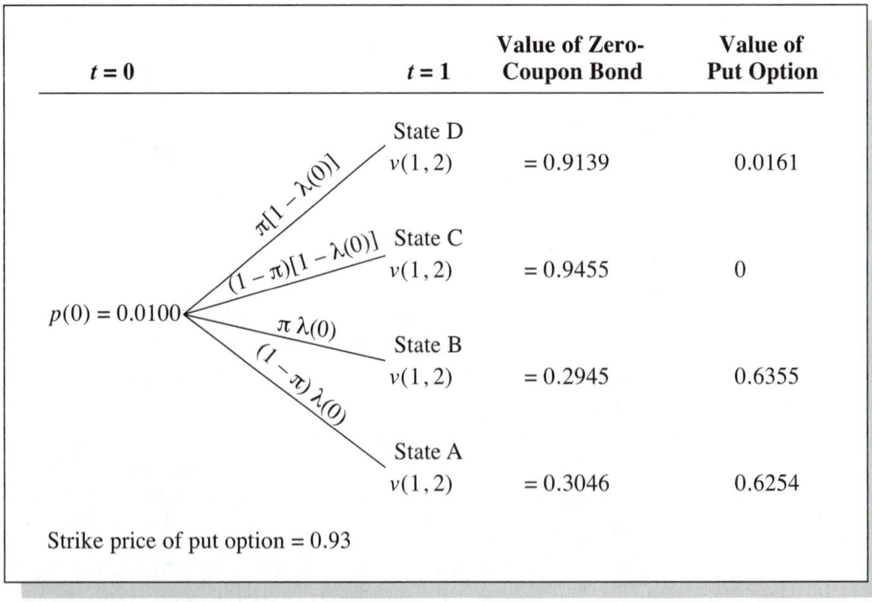

$t = 0$		$t = 1$	Value of Zero-Coupon Bond	Value of Put Option
		State D $v(1,2)$	$= 0.9139$	0.0161
		State C $v(1,2)$	$= 0.9455$	0
$p(0) = 0.0100$		State B $v(1,2)$	$= 0.2945$	0.6355
		State A $v(1,2)$	$= 0.3046$	0.6254

Branch labels: $\pi[1 - \lambda(0)]$, $(1 - \pi)[1 - \lambda(0)]$, $\pi \lambda(0)$, $(1 - \pi) \lambda(0)$

Strike price of put option = 0.93

In states C and D at $t = 1$, the underlying *ABC* bond is not in default. The date-0 value of the option based on Expression (18.12) is

$$p(0) = \frac{1}{1.0639} \{[1 - \lambda(0)][\pi 0.0161 + (1 - \pi)0]$$

$$+ \lambda(0)[\pi 0.6355 + (1 - \pi)0.6254]\}. \tag{18.13}$$

Given that $\pi = 0.5$ and $\lambda(0) = 0.0059$, then

$$p(0) = \frac{1}{1.0639} \{[1 - \lambda(0)]0.0805 + \lambda(0)0.6292\}$$

$$= 0.0110. \quad \blacksquare$$

Formalization

Here we formalize the preceding analysis. This involves little more than replacing the numerical values in the previous example with symbols.

We can write Expression (18.12) in the form

$$p(0) = [1 - \lambda(0)][\pi p(1, U; \text{no default}) + (1 - \pi)p(1, D; \text{no default})]/A(1)$$
$$+ \lambda(0)[\pi p(1, U; \text{default}) + (1 - \pi)p(1, D; \text{default})]/A(1)$$
$$= [1 - \lambda(0)][\text{Value of option, given default did not occur}]$$
$$+ \lambda(0)[\text{Value of option, given default occurs}]. \tag{18.14}$$

The preceding expression readily generalizes, which is important because it implies that we can always separate the problem of pricing an option on credit-risky debt into two simpler problems. First, we can price an option assuming that default does not occur over the life of the option. Second, we can price an option given that default does occur. Then, we take an expectation across these two values.

These two more simple problems can be solved using the methods described in Chapter 15. Indeed, if the debt never defaults, the debt is default-free and the techniques of Chapter 15 apply. If the debt defaults, there is no more default risk. Thus, after default, the debt is default-free again and the techniques of Chapter 15 apply. In the latter case, however, the payoff is $\delta < 1$ and not 1.

Hedging

Here we study the hedging of options on risky debt. To hedge and/or to construct a synthetic option, we employ the same procedures introduced in Chapter 5 for the binomial pricing model. The only difference is that instead of only two outcomes after each node in the lattice, now there are four. The modifications necessary to handle this difference are straightforward and best illustrated using the previous example.

EXAMPLE   **Put Option (Continued)**

This example illustrates constructing a synthetic option using risky debt and default-free debt.

To hedge the put option's values given in Figure 18.7, we need four assets because there are four possible outcomes given by states A, B, C, and D. We choose the two *ABC* zero-coupon risky bonds maturing at dates 1 and 2, and the two default-free zero-coupon bonds maturing at dates 1 and 2.

The initial cost of constructing this portfolio is

$$V(0) = n_1 v(0,1) + n_2 v(0,2) + n_3 B(0,1) + n_4 B(0,2),$$

where

n_1 equals the number of one-year *ABC* zero-coupon bonds,
n_2 equals the number of two-year *ABC* zero-coupon bonds,
n_3 equals the number of one-year default-free zero-coupon bonds, and
n_4 equals the number of two-year default-free zero-coupon bonds.

The prices of these bonds are contained in Table 18.1, so

$$V(0) = n_1(0.9361) + n_2(0.8703) + n_3(0.9399) + n_4(0.8798).$$

The holdings n_1, n_2, n_3, n_4 must be determined so that this portfolio's value at date 1 matches the put option's values across all possible states at date 1. That is,

(state D) $n_1 1 + n_2(0.9139) + n_3 1 + n_4(0.9201) = 0.0161$
(state C) $n_1 1 + n_2(0.9455) + n_3 1 + n_4(0.9520) = 0$
(state B) $n_1(0.32) + n_2(0.2945) + n_3 1 + n_4(0.9201) = 0.6355$
(state A) $n_1(0.32) + n_2(0.3046) + n_3 1 + n_4(0.9520) = 0.6254.$

We obtained the values for the prices in these equations as follows. The date-1 values for $v(1,1)$ are obtained from the definition of their payoff at maturity, with $\delta = 0.32$ in default. The date-1 values for $v(1,2)$ are obtained from Figure 18.7. The date-1 values of $B(1,1)$ are always 1. Finally, the date-1 values for $B(1,2)$ are available in Figure 18.8.

The solutions to these equations are

$n_1 = -0.6567$
$n_2 = -0.2791$
$n_3 = 1.1379$
$n_4 = -0.2283.$

FIGURE 18.8 *Pricing a Default-Free Treasury Bill Call Option*

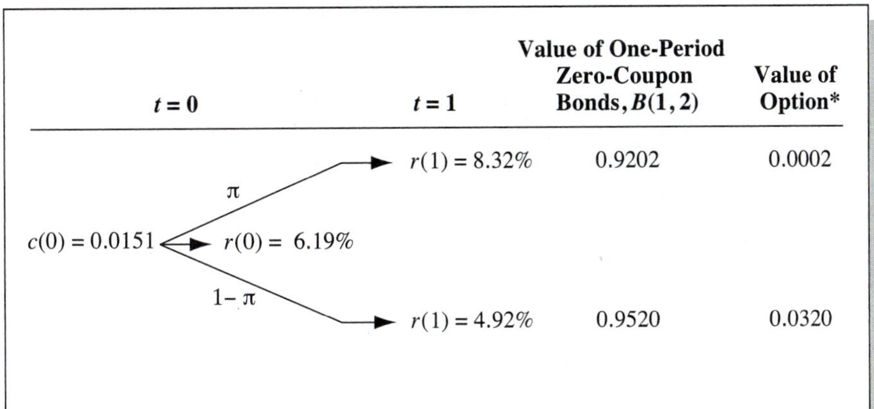

	t = 0	t = 1	Value of One-Period Zero-Coupon Bonds, $B(1,2)$	Value of Option*
		$r(1) = 8.32\%$	0.9202	0.0002
	$c(0) = 0.0151$ $r(0) = 6.19\%$			
		$r(1) = 4.92\%$	0.9520	0.0320

*Strike price is 0.92, where $\pi = 0.5$ represents the martingale probability of an up-jump in spot interest rates.

These holdings of the four bonds give the synthetic put option. The initial cost of the synthetic put is

$$V(0) = -0.6567(0.9361) - 0.2791(0.8703) + 1.1379(0.9399)$$
$$- 0.2283(0.8798)$$
$$= 0.0110,$$

which equals the value of the put option obtained from Expression (18.13), as is to be expected. ■

18.3 PRICING VULNERABLE DERIVATIVES

We examine here the pricing of vulnerable derivatives. **Vulnerable derivatives** are derivative securities subject to the additional risk that the writer of the derivative might default. For example, consider an over-the-counter (OTC) option written by a financial institution on a Treasury bill. There is no default risk associated with the underlying asset—the Treasury bill. However, the writer of the option, a financial institution, may default, so there is the risk that if the option is exercised, the writer may be unable to fulfill the obligation to make the required payment. The previous methodology can handle this situation. A simple example is used to illustrate the procedure.

EXAMPLE

Valuing a Vulnerable Call Option

This example illustrates the procedure for valuing a vulnerable call option. Initially, let's assume there is no risk of the writer defaulting.

Consider a call option written on a Treasury bill. The maturity is one year, and at expiration the option holder can purchase a one-year Treasury bill at a strike price of 0.92. The option is valued using the information summarized in Figure 18.8. The lattice of interest rates comes from Figure 18.5.

The date-0 value of the call option is

$$c(0) = \frac{1}{A(1)} [\pi \times 0.0002 + (1 - \pi) \times 0.0320]$$

$$= \frac{1}{1.0639} [0.5 \times 0.0002 + 0.5 \times 0.0320]$$

$$= 0.0151.$$

Now assume that the financial institution writing the option belongs to the ABC credit class. Consequently, we can use the results summarized in Figure 18.6 for the financial institution. When the option matures, there are four possible states, A, B, C, and D, depending on whether interest rates go up or down and whether the writer defaults. The four states are shown in Figure 18.9, which is similar in nature to Figure 18.7.

FIGURE 18.9 *Pricing a Vulnerable Call Option*

$t = 0$	$t = 1$	Value of Option
	State D No default	0.0002
	State C No default	0.0320
	State B Default	0.0002 x 0.32 = 0.000064
	State A Default	0.0320 x 0.32 = 0.010240

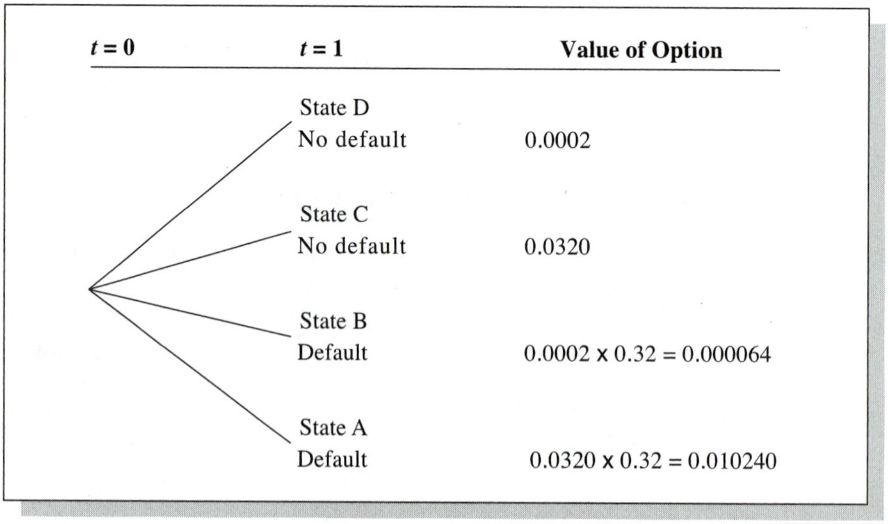

In states A and B, the writer defaults. By assumption, claimholders receive as the payoff 32 percent of the value of their option in these states. In states C and D, the writer does not default, and the entire payment is received.

The value of the vulnerable option today is the discounted expected value of these payments, that is,

$$c_V(0) = \frac{1}{1.0639}\{[1 - \lambda(0)][\pi 0.0002 + (1 - \pi)0.0320]$$

$$+ \lambda(0)[\pi 0.0002 + (1 - \pi)0.0320] \times 0.32\}. \qquad (18.15)$$

Given that $\pi = 0.5$ and $\lambda(0) = 0.0059$,

$$c_V(0) = [1 - \lambda(0)]0.0151 + \lambda(0)0.0048$$
$$= 0.0150.$$

The difference in these option prices paid to a default-free writer versus a writer in credit class ABC is small—only 0.0001—which is to be expected given that the martingale probability of default is small. ∎

Formalization

Now we formalize the analysis in the previous example, which again essentially involves replacing numbers with symbols.

Let $c(1)$ represent the date $t = 1$ value of the option in the absence of the writer defaulting, and let $c_V(1)$ represent the value of a vulnerable option.

At maturity, the payoff to the option is

$$c_V(1) = \begin{cases} c(1) & \text{if} & \text{no default} \\ \delta c(1) & \text{if} & \text{default,} \end{cases}$$

where δ represents the fractional payoff the holder receives if default occurs.

The date-0 value of the option in the absence of default is

$$c(0) = E^\pi\left[\frac{c(1)}{A(1)}\right].$$

Using Expression (18.15), the value of the vulnerable option is

$$c_V(0) = [1 - \lambda(0)]c(0) + \lambda(0)\delta c(0)$$
$$= E^\pi(e_1)c(0) \qquad (18.16)$$

because $E^\pi(e_1) = [1 - \lambda(0)] + \lambda(0)\delta$.

This expression says that the value of a vulnerable option is the value of an option written by a default-free entity times the expected payoff from the option writer at the maturity date of the option.

This result has an important implication. Given that there is a positive probability of default, the expected payoff is

$$E^{\pi}(e_1) < 1,$$

which implies that a vulnerable option must always be worth less than a non-vulnerable option, that is,

$$c_V(0) < c(0). \tag{18.17}$$

Expression (18.16) holds for any European option that matures at date T:

$$c_V(0) = E^{\pi}(e_T)c(0). \tag{18.18a}$$

Using Expression (18.11), Expression (18.18a) can be rewritten in the form

$$c_V(0) = [v(0, T)/B(0, T)]c(0). \tag{18.18b}$$

This form of the expression is useful in practice because it involves pricing a vulnerable option in terms of a credit risk spread for the writer—the term inside the square bracket on the right side—and the price of a non-vulnerable option.

EXAMPLE

Pricing a Vulnerable Option

This example illustrates the use of Expression (18.18b).

Consider a firm that wants to buy a five-year interest rate cap on the six-month default-free interest rate. Three institutions offer to sell the firm a cap. The institutions, however, have different credit ratings. Institution A belongs to credit class A, Institution B belongs to credit class B, and Institution C belongs to credit class C. Credit class A has a lower risk of default than credit class B, and credit class B has a lower risk of default than credit class C.

The term structure details are given in Table 18.2, Part A, for default-free interest rates and the three credit classes. The value of the caplets, assuming no counterparty risk, is calculated using the program Bonds/Caps/Normal. The prices of the caplets are given in Table 18.2, Part B.

To incorporate the effects of counterparty risk, we use Expression (18.18b). Consider the last caplet. The value in the absence of counterparty risk is $15,620.

For institution A belonging to credit class A, using the figures from the last row of Table 18.2, Part A,

$$v_A(0, 4.5)/B(0, 4.5) = 0.753875/0.775249$$
$$= 0.9724.$$

TABLE 18.2 *Pricing a Vulnerable Cap*

PART A
TERM STRUCTURE DATA

MATURITY (YEARS)	DEFAULT-FREE × 100	CREDIT CLASS A × 100	CREDIT CLASS B × 100	CREDIT CLASS C × 100
0.5	97.4892	97.2260	97.1870	96.1244
1.0	94.9635	94.4443	94.3320	92.3261
1.5	92.4320	91.6633	91.4518	88.6109
2.0	89.9028	88.8909	88.5610	84.9835
2.5	87.3835	86.1342	85.6727	81.6727
3.0	84.8806	83.3999	82.7984	78.0064
3.5	82.3998	80.6939	79.9480	74.9480
4.0	79.9464	78.0215	77.1301	71.4161
4.5	77.5249	75.3875	74.3521	68.2698

PART B
PRICING THE CAPLETS

MATURITY (YEARS)	VALUE OF CAPLET*	CREDIT CLASS A	CREDIT CLASS B	CREDIT CLASS C
0.5	80	79.78	79.75	78.88
1.0	1,050	1,044.26	1,043.02	1,020.84
1.5	2,890	2,865.97	2,859.35	2,770.53
2.0	5,120	5,062.37	5,043.58	4,839.84
2.5	7,450	7,343.49	7,304.14	6,963.12
3.0	9,730	9,560.26	9,491.31	8,942.00
3.5	11,880	11,634.05	11,526.51	10,805.64
4.0	13,840	13,506.77	13,352.45	12,363.27
4.5	15,620	15,189.35	14,980.73	13,755.25
Total	67,680	66,286.30	65,680.84	61,539.37
Difference		1,393.70	1,999.16	6,140.63
		2.06%	2.95%	9.07%

*Volatility — 1.0 percent
Volatility Reduction Factor — 0.1
Cap Rate — 7.00 percent
Principal — $10 million

Therefore, using Expression (18.18b), the value of the caplet is

$$\$15,620 \times 0.9724$$
$$= \$15,189.35,$$

as shown in Table 18.2, Part B.

The values of the other caplets are calculated in a similar way. The credit risk of Institution A lowers the value of the cap by approximately 2 percent, for Institution B, 2.95 percent, and for Institution C, 9.07 percent. ■

Hedging

Let us examine hedging vulnerable options. To hedge and/or construct a synthetic vulnerable option we employ the same procedure introduced in Chapter 5 for the binomial pricing model. The only difference is that instead of there being two outcomes after each node in the tree, there are now four. The modifications necessary to handle this difference are straightforward and best illustrated using the preceding example.

EXAMPLE　**Hedging a Vulnerable Option**

Consider the vulnerable call option example at the start of this section. To hedge the call option's values given in Figure 18.9 we need four assets, because there are four possible outcomes given in states A, B, C, and D. We choose the two risky zero-coupon bonds maturing at dates 1 and 2, and the two default-free zero-coupon bonds maturing at dates 1 and 2.

The initial cost of constructing this portfolio is

$$V(0) = n_1 v(0,1) + n_2 v(0,2) + n_3 B(0,1) + n_4 B(0,2),$$

where

n_1 equals the number of one-year ABC zero-coupon bonds,
n_2 equals the number of two-year ABC zero-coupon bonds,
n_3 equals the number of one-year default-free zero-coupon bonds, and
n_4 equals the number of two-year default-free zero-coupon bonds.

The prices of these bonds are contained in Table 18.1, so

$$V(0) = n_1 (0.9361) + n_2(0.8703) + n_3(0.9399) + n_4(0.8798).$$

The holdings n_1, n_2, n_3, n_4 must be determined so that this portfolio's date-1 value matches the vulnerable call's date-1 values across all possible states, that is,

(state D)　$n_1 1 + n_2(0.9139) + n_3(1) + n_4(0.9201) = 0.0002$
(state C)　$n_1 1 + n_2(0.9455) + n_3(1) + n_4(0.9520) = 0.0320$
(state B)　$n_1(0.32) + n_2(0.2945) + n_3(1) + n_4(0.9201) = 0.000064$
(state A)　$n_1(0.32) + n_2(0.3046) + n_3(1) + n_4(0.9520) = 0.010240.$

We obtained the prices in these equations as follows. The date-1 values for $v(1,1)$ are obtained from the definition of their payoff at maturity, with $\delta = 0.32$ in default. The date-1 values for $v(1,1)$ are obtained from Figure 18.7. The date-1 values of $B(1,1)$ are always 1. Finally, the date-1 values for $B(1,2)$ are available in Figure 18.8.

The solutions to these equations are

$$n_1 = -0.9160$$
$$n_2 = 1.0058$$
$$n_3 = -0.0036$$
$$n_4 = 0.0006.$$

These holdings give the synthetic vulnerable call option portfolio.
The initial cost of the synthetic vulnerable call is

$$V(0) = -0.9160(0.9361) + 1.0058(0.8703) - 0.0036(0.9399)$$
$$+ 0.0006(0.8798)$$
$$= 0.0150,$$

which agrees with the value given earlier by Expression (18.15), as it should. ∎

Risk Management

The pricing of counterparty risk is important for risk management. From this pricing one can compute the reserve that should be set aside to account for the dollar value of counterparty risk. The preceding methodology provides a simple, robust approach to measure this reserve.

18.4 VALUATION OF A SWAP

Here we study the valuation of a swap where the counterparties have different credit risk.

Consider a simple interest rate swap for which we are receiving fixed payments $\overline{R}$ from a firm in a given credit class, say, the ABC class. In return, we are making floating rate payments. Payments are due at dates $t_1, t_2, \ldots, t_N$, where the subscript N denotes the total number of payments.

To price this swap, we must price each side of the swap separately. First we value the fixed payments, and then we value the floating payments.

Fixed Payment Side

The present value of an annuity of fixed payments reflects the credit risk of default from a firm in class ABC. The present value of the payments is

$$v(0,t_1)\overline{R} + v(0,t_2)\overline{R} + \ldots + v(0,t_N)\overline{R}$$
$$\equiv v_{\overline{R}}(0). \tag{18.19}$$

Each fixed payment of $\overline{R}$ is discounted via the rate appropriate for the firm in class ABC promising the payment.

TABLE 18.3   *Value of Floating Rate Payments*

DATE	VALUE AT $t = 0$
t_1	$1 - B(0, t_1)$
t_2	$B(0, t_1) - B(0, t_2)$
.	.
.	.
.	.
t_N	$B(0, t_{N-1}) - B(0, t_N)$
SUM	$1 - B(0, t_N)$

Floating Payment Side

For reasons of simplicity, we assume that we are default-free and that we make floating rate payments using the Treasury rate as the reference interest rate. In practice, the LIBOR interest rate is used.

The value of the floating rate payments is calculated using the results from Chapter 14 and is summarized in Table 18.3.

From Table 18.3, the total value of the floating rate payments is

$$V_F(0) = 1 - B(0, t_N). \tag{18.20}$$

The value of the swap is the value of the fixed payments less the floating payments, that is,

$$\begin{aligned} V_S(0) &\equiv v_{\bar{R}}(0) - V_F(0) \\ &= v_{\bar{R}}(0) - [1 - B(0, t_N)]. \end{aligned} \tag{18.21}$$

When the swap is initiated, the swap rate $\bar{R}$ is set such that the value of the swap is zero. An example will clarify these expressions.

EXAMPLE   **Calculating the Swap Rate**

This example illustrates the valuation of a swap using Expression (18.21). The swap rate is calculated by equating the present value of the floating rate payments with the present value of the fixed rate payments.

Using the term structure data in Table 18.4, we want to determine the swap rate for a two-year swap.

The valuation of the floating rate payments is given by

$$\begin{aligned} V_F(0) &= [1 - B(0, t_N)]100 \\ &= 100 - 90.7214 \\ &= 9.2786, \end{aligned}$$

TABLE 18.4 *Determination of Swap Rate*

MATURITY (YEARS) T	DEFAULT-FREE $B(0,T) \times 100$	CREDIT CLASS ABC $v(0,T) \times 100$
0.5	97.7272	97.2508
1.0	95.4164	94.4826
1.5	93.0780	91.7064
2.0	90.7214	88.9320

assuming a notional principal of $100.

The valuation of the fixed rate payments using Table 18.4 is given by

$$(\overline{R}/2) \times (97.2508 + 94.4826 + 91.7064 + 88.9320) = \overline{R} \times 186.19,$$

where $\overline{R}$ is the annual swap rate.

The swap rate is defined to be that rate $\overline{R}$ that satisfies

$$9.2786 = \overline{R} \times 186.19,$$

implying

$$\overline{R} = 4.98\%. \quad \blacksquare$$

Note that a number of implicit assumptions are used in determining the swap rate. The swap rate assumes that if default occurs on the fixed side, payments continue on the floating rate side. This is because the floating payment side is valued at the default-free rate, which assumes that the payments occur with certainty.

On the other hand, in default, the fixed rate side pays δ for each promised payment over the life of the swap. It might be argued that it makes sense for default to occur by the counterparty only if the present value of the fixed payments is greater than the present value of the floating rate payments. If the swap is viewed in isolation, this argument makes sense. However, default can occur for many different reasons. If we have many contracts with this counterparty, default on one contract may trigger default on all the contracts, which is the case if "netting" is allowed. The issue of netting is discussed later in this chapter.

18.5 CREDIT DEFAULT SWAPS

Here we show how to use the martingale approach to price a **simple credit default swap**. We start by describing a credit default swap and then show how to price it.

Let us consider a one-year credit default swap. The basic structure is shown in Figure 18.10. In this credit default swap, the bank is buying default protection from the counterparty. The counterparty's default exposure is to two companies. These companies are specified in the contract. These companies are usually referred to as reference credits. After the first default by one of the reference credits, the counterparty's exposure to subsequent defaults is terminated. In the event of a default by one of the two reference credits, the counterparty pays a fixed amount to the bank. In return for this default insurance, the bank pays a premium to the counterparty when the swap is initiated. We will show how to determine this premium.

To illustrate how to price this form of credit default swap, a simple numerical example will be considered. The tenor of the swap is assumed to be one year. For simplicity, we divide the one year into two six-month intervals. In practice, shorter intervals would be used.

The counterparty is assumed to belong to credit class A and the two reference credits belong to credit class C, which is a lower credit class than A. We summarize the martingale default probabilities in Table 18.5.

Conditional on no defaults by the two reference credits at date $t - 1$, payment by the counterparty at date t is described by one of four mutually exclusive and exhaustive events:

1. first credit defaults, second credit does not default,
2. first credit does not default, second credit defaults,
3. first credit defaults, second credit defaults, or
4. first credit does not default, second credit does not default.

If one of the first three events occur, the counterparty makes a fixed payment, F, to the bank. If event four happens, no payment occurs.

The probability that the first (second) credit does not default at date t, conditional upon no default at date $t - 1$, is $[1 - \lambda_c(t - 1)\Delta]$, where $\lambda_c(t - 1)$ is the (martingale) conditional probability of default occurring at date t for a firm in credit class

FIGURE 18.10 *A Simple Credit Default Swap*

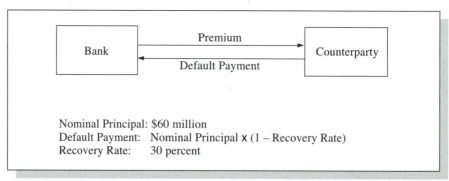

TABLE 18.5 *Term Structure Data*

| MATURITY (YEARS) | DEFAULT-FREE* × 100 | CREDIT CLASS A* | | CREDIT CLASS C | |
		PRICE × 100	MARTINGALE PROBABILITIES OF DEFAULT	PRICE × 100	MARTINGALE PROBABILITIES OF DEFAULT
0.5	97.4892	97.2260	0.01	96.1244	0.0412
1.00	94.9635	94.4443	0.0103	92.3261	0.0413
Recovery Rates			0.46		0.32

*This data comes from Table 18.2.

C, conditional upon no default at date $t - 1$ and where Δ is the length of the interval between dates $t - 1$ and t.

Assuming independence between the event of default for the first credit and the second credit, the conditional probability of event four occurring is $[1 - \lambda_c(t - 1)\Delta]^2$. Recall that both reference credits are in credit class C. This independence assumption is imposed for simplicity. Basically, it states that the defaults in the two companies would be caused by idiosyncratic events, that is, events that are not related. This assumption may be easily relaxed.

To summarize the payment by the counterparty to the bank, it will prove useful if we define the following indicator function. Conditional upon no default at date $t - 1$, we define

$$\mathbf{1}(t) \equiv \begin{cases} 0 & \text{with probability } [1 - \lambda_c(t - 1)\Delta]^2 \\ 1 & \text{with probability } 1 - [1 - \lambda_c(t - 1)\Delta]^2. \end{cases} \tag{18.22}$$

If $\mathbf{1}(t) = 0$ at date t, it implies event four has occurred and no payment is made by the counterparty to the bank; if $\mathbf{1}(t) = 1$ at date t, it implies that either event one, two, or three has occurred and the counterparty makes a payment, F, to the bank.

If a default has occurred at or prior to date $t - 1$, we define

$$\mathbf{1}(t) \equiv 0, \tag{18.23}$$

implying that the counterparty's exposure is terminated.

In this example, the credit swap has a maturity of one year. The default payment process over the two intervals is shown in Figure 18.11.

Referring to Figure 18.11, if no defaults have occurred at date $t = 1$, state A, the value of the swap is

$$V_A(1) \equiv B(1,2)[0 \times q_1 + F \times (1 - q_1)], \tag{18.24}$$

where $q_1 \equiv [1 - \lambda_c(1)\Delta]^2$.

FIGURE 18.11   *Default Payment Process*

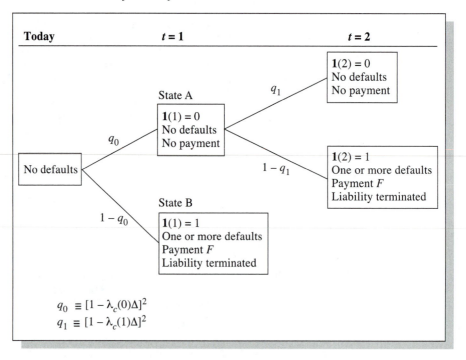

If one or more defaults occur at date $t = 1$, state B, then

$$V_B(1) \equiv F. \tag{18.25}$$

Today the value of the swap is

$$V(0) = B(0,2)q_0[0 \times q_1 + F \times (1 - q_1)] + B(0,1)(1 - q_0)F, \tag{18.26}$$

where $q_0 \equiv [1 - \lambda_c(0)\Delta]^2$.
Using the data in Table 18.5 gives

$$q_0 = [1 - 0.0412 \times 0.5]^2 = 0.95922$$
$$q_1 = [1 - 0.0413 \times 0.5]^2 = 0.95913,$$

so that

$$V(0) = 0.9496 \times 0.95922[0 + F(1 - 0.95913)] + 0.9749 \times (1 - 0.95922)F$$
$$= F(0.0770).$$

This calculation determines the value of the swap in terms of the default payment F. Note that the analysis assumes that the counterparty does not default. This assumption can be relaxed using the analysis given in Section 18.3. Our discussion of credit default swaps is now complete.

18.6 REGULATION

We now discuss the current regulatory issues involving derivative securities. The risks arising from a portfolio of derivative securities include (1) market or price risk, (2) liquidity risk, (3) credit risk, (4) clearing or settlement risk, (5) operations and systems risk, and (6) legal risk.[6] We discuss each of these risks in turn.

1. **Market or Price Risk** is the risk from unanticipated changes in the value of a financial instrument or portfolio of financial instruments. This includes the risk arising from model misspecification.
2. **Liquidity Risk** is the risk of being unable to close out open positions within a reasonable time and in sufficient quantities at a reasonable price.
3. **Credit Risk** is the risk that a counterparty defaults on its obligations.
4. **Clearing or Settlement Risk** is the risk that technical difficulties interrupt delivery or settlement despite the counterparty's ability or willingness to perform. This type of risk also occurs when a counterparty defaults.
5. **Operations and Systems Risk** is the risk of human error; fraud; inadequate internal controls; or that the systems will fail to fully record, monitor, and account for transactions or positions.
6. **Legal Risk** is the risk that an action by a court or regulatory body will invalidate a contract.[7]

These risks are not unique to derivatives, being common to many financial activities.

Regulators of the financial system act to ensure that the management of financial institutions act prudently by not assuming excessive risk and by having sufficient capital reserves. The Bank of International Settlement (B.I.S.)[8] in July 1988 issued a report containing proposals describing the minimum capital reserve requirements for banks.[9]

---

[6]This list combines and generalizes the factors identified in the Federal Reserve Board Trading Manual (1994) and the General Accounting Office Report (1994).

[7]The British House of Lords ruled on January 24, 1991 that the swap contracts entered into by the London Borough of Hammersmith and Fulham were unlawful. Because this rule affected all UK local authorities, it was estimated that international banks would lose around £600 million in the estimated closeout value of their swaps. See Shirreff (1991).

[8]The B.I.S. was established in 1930 in Basle, Switzerland, by Western European banks.

[9]Bank for International Settlements, "Proposals for International Convergence of Capital Adequacy Standards," July 1988. The report was issued by the Basle Committee on Banking Regulations and Supervisory Practices with the endorsement of the central bank governors of the Group of Ten countries (Belgium, Canada, France, Germany, Italy, Japan, the Netherlands, Sweden, Switzerland, the United Kingdom, and the United States of America).

The report states certain minimum capital standards for on- and off-balance-sheet items and assigns different capital requirements for different classes of assets. In July 1993, the Group of Thirty[10] issued a report[11] to improve the supervisory and capital requirements of the "off-balance-sheet" risks related to derivative activity for dealers and end users.[12] The United States General Accounting Office[13] in May 1994 issued a report on financial derivatives and the actions needed to protect the financial system.[14] The B.I.S. 1988 Accord was extended by the 1996 Amendment that became mandatory in 1998. We start by discussing the 1988 Accord and then the 1996 Amendment.[15]

Bank of International Settlement (B.I.S.) 1988 Accord

The B.I.S. reserve requirements start by defining two forms of capital. Tier One Capital is defined as common stockholders' equity, non-cumulative perpetual preferred stock, and minority equity interests in consolidated subsidiaries, less goodwill.[16] Tier Two Capital is defined as cumulative perpetual preferred shares, subordinated debt with an original average maturity of at least five years, and other forms of long-term capital.

Given these definitions, there are two forms of capital requirements. The first states that

$$\frac{\text{Tier One Capital}}{\text{Risk-Weighted Amount}} > 0.08$$

TABLE 18.6 *Risks Weights for On-Balance-Sheet Asset Category*

RISK WEIGHTS (%)	ASSET CATEGORY
0	Cash, gold bullion, claims on OECD Treasury bonds
20	Claims on OECD banks and OECD public sector entities
50	Uninsured residential mortgages
100	Corporate bonds, equity, real estate

[10]The Group of Thirty is an international financial policy organization whose members include representatives of central banks, international banks, and securities firms.

[11]"Derivatives: Practices and Principles," a report prepared by the Global Derivatives Study Group, the Group of Thirty, Washington, D.C., July 1993.

[12]End users typically enter into derivative transactions for many reasons, such as to reduce financing costs and/or alter their risk exposure. Dealers or intermediaries cater to the needs of end users by making markets in over-the-counter derivatives.

[13]The General Accounting Office is a branch of the U.S. Government.

[14]General Accounting Office, *Financial Derivatives*, May 1994, Washington, D.C.

[15]For a detailed description see Crouhy, Galai, and Mark (1998a).

[16]Tier One Capital includes only permanent shareholder equity (issued and fully paid ordinary shares/common stock and perpetual non-cumulative preference shares) and disclosed reserves (share premiums, retained profits, general reserves, and legal reserves).

TABLE 18.7 *Add-on Factors**

MATURITY	INTEREST RATE	EXCHANGE RATE AND GOLD	EQUITY	PRECIOUS METALS EXCEPT GOLD	OTHER COMMODITIES
One year or less	0	1.0	6.0	7.0	10.00
Over one year to five years	0.5	5.0	8.0	7.0	12.0
Over five years	1.5	7.5	10.0	8.0	15.0

*Expressed as percentages.

and the second states that

$$\frac{\text{Tier Two Capital}}{\text{Risk-Weighted Amount}} > 0.08.$$

It is required that at least 50 percent of capital must be Tier One Capital. The risk-weighted amount for on-the-balance-sheet items is defined as the sum of principal $\times$ risk weight for each asset. The B.I.S. defines the risk capital weights (see Table 18.6 for a partial list). For example, the risk weight for commercial loans is 1.00, 0.5 for residential mortgages, and 0.0 for Treasury bills.

For off-balance-sheet items, the determination is more complicated. We start by defining a number of terms.

Current exposure
The B.I.S. first calculates the current mark-to-market value of a deal and then defines the **current exposure** as follows:

$$\text{Current Exposure} \equiv \text{Max}\{\text{Mark-to-Market Value}, 0\}.$$

Add-on amount
The **add-on amount** is computed by multiplying the notional amount of the asset by the B.I.S.-required add-on factor, as shown in Table 18.7. Note that there are five categories—interest rate, exchange rate and gold, equity, precious metals except gold, and other commodities. The interest rate category includes single-currency interest rate swaps, forward rate agreements, interest rate futures, and interest rate options (purchased). The exchange rate and gold category includes foreign currency swaps, forward rate agreements, futures, and options (purchased).

In 1995, the initial B.I.S. Accord was modified to allow banks to reduce their credit equivalent when bilateral agreements are in place.[17]

---

[17]Details are given in Crouhy, Galai, and Mark (1998b).

Credit equivalent amount

The **credit equivalent amount** equals the sum of the current exposure and the add-on amount, that is,

Credit Equivalent Amount = Current Exposure + Add-on Amount.

Risk-weighted amount

The **risk-weighted amount** is the product of the credit equivalent amount and the **counterparty credit weight**, that is,

$$\text{Risk-Weighted Amount} \equiv \text{Credit Equivalent Amount} \times \text{Counterparty Credit Weight.}$$

Table 18.8 provides a partial list of the counterparty credit weights.

The risk-weighted amount is defined to equal the sum of the risk-weighted amount for the on-the-balance-sheet assets plus the risk-weighted amount for the off-balance-sheet items.

The 1998 Accord completely ignores capital adequacy for marketable securities in the trading book.[18] This issue is addressed in the 1996 Accord.

B.I.S. 1996 Amendment

In the 1996 Amendment, a bank must hold capital to cover the market risk associated with debt and equity positions in the trading book and foreign exchange and commodity positions in both the trading and banking books. Market risk is measured for on- and off-balance-sheet traded instruments. On-balance-sheet instruments are subject only to market risk capital charges. Off-balance-sheet instruments are subject to market risk and credit capital charges.

TABLE 18.8   *Risk Weights for Off-Balance-Sheet Credit Equivalents by Type of Counterparty*

RISK WEIGHTS (%)	TYPE OF COUNTERPARTY
0	OECD governments
20	OECD banks and public sector entities
50	Corporate counterparties

---

[18]The trading book means the bank's proprietary positions in financial instruments, whether on- or off-balance-sheet, that are intentionally held for short-term trading. All trading book positions must be marked-to-market or marked-to-model every day.

A bank's overall capital requirements will be the sum of the following:

1. The credit risk capital charges described by the 1988 Accord. They apply to all the positions in the trading and banking books, over-the-counter derivatives, and off-balance sheet commitments *but* exclude debt and equity traded securities in the trading book and *all* positions in commodities and foreign exchange.
2. Market risk capital charges for the debt and equity positions in the trading book and foreign exchange and commodity positions in the trading and banking books.

Market risk is defined to cover general market risk and specific risk. General market risk refers to the risk arising from general market movements, or systematic risk. Examples of general market risk are changes in the S&P 500 index, commodity prices, foreign exchange rates, and interest rates. Specific risk refers to unanticipated changes in the market value of individual positions due to factors other than general market movements. Examples of specific risk are unanticipated changes in credit quality and liquidity and events unique to the individual asset.

The Amendment also gives banks the choice, subject to certain conditions, to develop their own internal models to assess market risks or to follow a standardized approach. This means that sophisticated institutions that already have an independent risk management division in place will have the choice between using their own internal value-at-risk (VAR) model under the internal models approach or following the standardized approach. The new capital requirement related to market rates should be offset by the fact that it will no longer be necessary to cover credit risk using the 1998 Accord for debt and equity traded securities in the trading book and all positions in commodities and foreign exchange. The internal models approach will generate greater savings in capital than the standardized models approach. However, the costs of developing an internal VAR model and maintaining it to the required standard to gain regulatory approval are not insubstantial.[19]

The Amendment introduces a third tier of capital to meet market risk requirements. Tier Three Capital consists of short-term subordinated debt with an original maturity of at least two years. It must be unsecured and fully paid up. It is subject to lock-in clauses that prevent the issuer from repaying the debt before maturity. Tier Three Capital cannot support capital requirements arising from the banking book.

Limitations of the 1988 Accord and 1996 Amendment

The Amendment does not alter the main rules applying to credit risk. There are a number of significant weaknesses to these rules.

---

[19]Crouhy, Galai, and Mark (1998b) estimate these savings to be in the order of 20 to 50 percent.

Limited differentiation[20]

The 1988 Accord provides a limited differentiation of credit risk into broad categories; see Tables 18.6 and 18.8. Why does an exposure to, say, Turkey—an OECD country with a B1 Moody's credit rating—receive no charge, while exposure to a corporate credit risk with a AAA rating receives a charge? Why are all corporate credit risks treated equally, regardless of credit rating?

Static measures of default risk

The Accord uses an 8 percent-of-capital requirement as protection for corporate credit risk, regardless of the actual credit risk. If a bank must hold 8 percent of capital against corporate loans, it has an incentive to lend to high-yield issuers.

Maturity of credit risk exposure

Capital credit charges are set at the same level regardless of the maturity of the credit exposure. The current rules make no distinction between current and future credit exposures.

Simplified counterparty risk calculation

Look at Table 18.7, which gives the add-on charges for the credit equivalent amount. It treats all equity investments as having the same risk. A similar comment applies to the other categories.

Integration of credit and market risk

The current approach categorizes credit risk under three headings: (1) banking book credit risk, (2) trading book specific risk, and (3) counterparty risk. Yet with the models we have described in this chapter, market and credit risk cannot be separated.

18.7 WHAT CAN GO WRONG?

There are many reasons why losses can occur. We list a number of examples; see Table 18.9.

Wrong model

The Bank of Tokyo-Mitsubishi suffered an $80 million loss in 1997 due to swaptions that traders calibrated to market prices of at-the-money swaptions using a Black, Derman, and Toy model. The model did not correctly price out-of-the-money swaptions and was incapable of pricing Bermuda swaptions.

Operational risk

The BankBoston Corporation in 1998 discovered about $73 million in irregular loans secured by fraudulent or nonexistent collateral to friends of a bank's employee.[21]

---

[20]See the International Swaps and Derivatives Association (1988) document for a more detailed discussion.
[21]New York Times, March 19, 1998.

TABLE 18.9   *Recent Corporate Losses*

COMPANY	LOSS (PRETAX, IN MILLIONS)	TYPE OF TRANSACTION
Metallgesellschaft (Germany) (1993)	$1,340	Oil Derivatives
Procter & Gamble (U.S.) (1994)	$102	Leveraged Currency Swaps
Air Products & Chemicals (U.S.) (1993)	$60	Leveraged Interest Rate and Currency Swaps
Paine Webber (U.S.) (1994)	$180	Mortgage-Based Structured Notes

The Sumitomo Corporation recorded a loss of $2.6 billion arising from unauthorized trades by one of its commodity traders over an eleven-year period.[22] The company was also fined $150 million for allowing one of its traders to corner the copper market.

Rogue traders are not unique to financial institutions. Philip Services Corporation, a metal company in Ontario, Canada, revealed a loss of approximately US$120 million due to rogue trading in copper.[23]

Recipes for Risk[24]

Arrogance and incentives

All too frequently trouble arises when little thought is given to a particular policy and the incentives generated by the policy. To create risk, just blend arrogance and incentives together. What do we mean by arrogance? An example is picking an accounting policy for a product without adequately questioning the appropriateness of the policy's underlying assumptions. Incentives usually provide rewards based on positive accounting performance over short periods. If the adopted accounting policy creates profits that have low short-term correlation with economic profits, then the firm is at risk.

Example 1

Consider a seven-year zero-coupon bond with a yield to maturity of 6 percent, trading at $665 per $1,000 face value. Suppose accrual accounting is used, and the accrual is calculated on a straight-line basis as (1000 − 665)/7 = $48 instead of on a

---

[22]New York Times, May 12, 1998.

[23]Globe and Mail, Toronto, March 6, 1998.

[24]We are making extensive use of a talk given by Lee Wakeman, "The Changing Role of the Financial Engineer" (1996). We thank him for many helpful discussions.

compound basis of $40 over the first year. If bonuses are based on accounting profits, there is an incentive for traders to buy and hold.

Example 2

It is customary for trading desks at many banks to be funded by their treasury departments at rates close to LIBOR. Suppose the borrowing rate is 5 percent. Using the data given in Example 1, this creates a carrying charge of $665 \times 0.05 = $33 per year per $1,000 face value. If the zero-coupon bond is accrued on a compound basis, it will accrue $40 for a net holding profit of $7 per $1,000 face value.

This type of accounting policy creates an incentive for high-yield and emerging-market debt desks to maintain larger than necessary inventories. Such inventories are justified with the response that they "are necessary to maintain an inventory in order to respond quickly to customer buy orders." RAROC systems if properly designed can reduce these incentives.[25]

Credulity

Senior managers normally participate in short-term, profit-based bonus schemes as described above. Large trading profits lead to large bonuses, creating an incentive for these managers to believe the traders reporting the profits and to dismiss questions raised by risk managers.

In the fairy tale "Peter Pan," Peter asks the children in the audience to shout "I believe, I believe" in order to revive the poisoned Tinkerbell. After several repetitions at increasing volume of this "I believe" mantra, the fading light that represents a sick Tinkerbell glows bright again.

No matter how enthusiastically managers invoke this mantra, some profits insist on disappearing.

Tinkerbell 1: Kidder Peabody

Kidder Peabody dismissed the head trader of its government bond trading desk for allegedly falsely reporting over $300 million in trading profits. The "trading profits" were generated by a flaw in Kidder Peabody's accounting system.[26]

The importance of having an independent middle office and senior management that is concerned about risk exposure arises in this case. Apparently the risk manager on the trading desk notified senior management about the difficulty of making such profits in one of the world's most efficient capital markets. His concerns were ignored.

Tinkerbell 2: Barings Brothers and Co. Limited[27]

Barings Bank was the oldest merchant bank in the City of London at the time of its collapse. It was founded in 1762 and was privately controlled. On February 25, 1995,

---

[25]For an introduction to RAROC see Crouhy, Turnbull, and Wakeman (1999).

[26]See the New York Times, July 23, 1998.

[27]We draw upon the Report of the Board of Banking Supervision Inquiry into the Circumstances of the Collapse of Barings. We refer to this as the Bank of England Report. It is an excellent report and should be read by everyone interested in risk management.

Peter Baring informed the Bank of England that Barings Bank had been the victim of a massive fraud. At the end of December, 1994 the cumulative concealed losses were 208 million pounds; the loss by February 27, 1995 was 827 million pounds.

Barings Futures Singapore (BFS) was an indirect subsidiary of Barings Bank. This office executed trades in three kinds of financial futures: the Nikkei 225 contract, the ten-year Japanese government bond (JGB) contract, and the three-month Euroyen contract. It also traded options on these financial futures. These contracts could be traded on the Osaka Securities Exchange (OSE), the Tokyo Stock Exchange, the Tokyo Futures Exchange, and the Singapore International Monetary Exchange (SIMEX). The original function of the BFS office was to execute trades for its clients. In mid-1993, BFS began trading for its own account, arbitraging any differences between the SIMEX contracts and the equivalent contracts on the Japanese markets. These trades were viewed as being non-directional. If they were long in the Nikkei contracts traded on SIMEX, they would be short in Nikkei contracts traded in Japan. Until the collapse, Barings' management in London believed the trading conducted by BFS to be essentially risk-free and very profitable.

Nick Leeson moved to the BFS office in March, 1992. Account 88888, opened in July, 1992, was recorded at BFS as a client's account. Details of all client accounts were sent to London in four different reports: the trade file, the price file, the margin file, and the file containing details of positions. In July, 1992, Leeson ordered that for account 88888 only the margin file was to be sent to London. Contrary to stated policy, Leeson took directional positions. Profits were recorded in a different account and losses in account 88888. This account was also used to record trading positions. To help meet margin calls, Leeson also sold options. Again, this was contrary to stated policy. In early 1993 he was appointed as general manager. He was in charge of the front and back offices at BFS.

Barings' senior management were given a number of warning signals but chose to ignore them.

1. An initial audit report in August, 1994 identified the lack of segregation between the front and back offices in BFS's operations.
2. The high profitability of BFS's trading activities relative to the low risk as perceived and authorized by Barings' management in London was a clear signal that something was amiss.

    In one week when Leeson reported profits of US$10 million, senior management commented:[28] "Wow! That is impressive. . . . You know, if he makes US$10 million doing arbitrage in a week, what is that? About a half a billion a year. That is pretty good doing arbitrage. That guy is a turbo arbitrageur!"
3. Management in London were sent daily reports from BFS. At no time did they realize that while they received the margin report for account 88888, they did not receive the trade, price, and position reports associated with the account. This discrepancy was not noticed or appreciated.

---

[28]See p. 50, 3.63, Bank of England Report.

Why did Leeson risk sending this report to London? The margin account provided the rationale for the cash needed by Leeson to meet the Osaka and SIMEX margin calls.

4. In February, 1993, SIMEX sent a letter to BFS with respect to a transaction for account 88888. On January 11, 1995, reference was again made to account 88888 in a letter sent by SIMEX to BFS. On January 27, 1995, SIMEX sent a letter to BFS asking for assurance that it could fund margin calls arising from Leeson's trading.

Despite all these warning signals, senior management, whose bonuses depended on the level of profits, were true believers in their turbo arbitrageur. He was providing Barings Bank with most of its profits. We leave the last word to the Bank of England Report with respect to the profits reported by Leeson and management's willingness to accept them at face value:[29] "As the Exchanges were open and competitive markets, this suggests a lack of understanding of the nature of the business."

18.8 SUMMARY

This chapter takes as exogenous both the term structure of zero-coupon corporate bonds for firms within a given risk class and the term structure of zero-coupon default-free bonds. Using standard arguments, we show how to extract the conditional martingale probabilities of default. Given these probabilities, we show how to price options on credit-risky bonds and how to price vulnerable options. This analysis is then used to examine the pricing of swaps and the credit exposure in swaps. Lastly, we briefly discuss regulatory issues and capital requirements.

We make the simplifying assumption that the martingale default probabilities are independent of the martingale probabilities for the default-free spot interest rates, an assumption that can be relaxed and generalized in numerous ways. Jarrow, Lando, and Turnbull (1997) let the default probabilities for firm *ABC* depend on a current credit rating given by an external agency, like Standard & Poor's, Inc. or Moody's. This creates a Markov chain in credit ratings, in which historical default frequency data can be utilized. Lando (1994) allows the default probability to be dependent upon the level of spot interest rates. This last modification appears promising in the area of Eurodollar contracts.

REFERENCES

Basle Committee on Banking Regulations and Supervisory Practices, 1988. "Proposals for International Convergence of Capital Adequacy Standards." Basle, Switzerland: Bank for International Settlements.

Black, F., E. Derman, and W. Toy, 1990. "A One Factor Model of Interest Rates and Its Application to Treasury Bond Options." *Financial Analyst Journal* 46, 33–39.

Brickell, M., 1994. "New Tools for New Rules." *Risk* 7, 13–17.

---

[29]See p. 50, 3.66, Bank of England Report.

Cooper, I., and A. Mello, 1991. "The Default Risk of Swaps." *Journal of Finance* 46, 597–620.

Crouhy, M., D. Galai, and R. Mark, 1998a. "The New 1998 Regulatory Frameworks for Capital Adequacy: 'Standardized Approach' versus 'Internal Models'." *Risk Management and Analysis*, Vol. 1, Edited by C. Alexander. London: John Wiley & Sons, Ltd.

Crouhy, M., D. Galai, and R. Mark, 1998b. "Model Risk." Working Paper, Canadian Imperial Bank of Commerce, Toronto.

Crouhy, M., S. M. Turnbull, and L. Wakeman, 1999. "Measuring Risk Adjusted Performance." Working Paper, Canadian Imperial Bank of Commerce, Toronto.

Duffie, D., and K. Singleton, 1997. "An Econometric Model of the Term Structure of Interest Rate Swap Yields." *Journal of Finance* 52, 1287–1321.

Federal Reserve Board, 1994. *Trading Activities Manual*. Washington, D.C.: United States Government Printing Office.

General Accounting Office, 1994. *Financial Derivatives*. Washington, D.C.: United States Government Printing Office.

Global Derivatives Study Group, 1993. "Derivatives: Practices and Principles." Washington, D.C.: Group of Thirty.

Jarrow, R. A., D. Lando, and S. M. Turnbull, 1997. "A Markov Model for the Term Structure of Credit Risk Spreads." *Review of Financial Studies* 10, 481–523.

Jarrow, R. A., and S. M. Turnbull, 1995. "Pricing Options on Derivative Securities Subject to Credit Risk." *Journal of Finance* 50, 53–85.

Jarrow, R. A., and S. M. Turnbull, 1999. "The Intersection of Market and Credit Risk." *Journal of Banking and Finance*, in press.

Lando, D., 1994. "Three Essays on Contingent Claims Pricing." Ph.D. thesis, Cornell University.

Merton, R. C., 1974. "On the Pricing of Corporate Debt: The Risk Structure of Interest Rates." *Journal of Finance* 2, 449–470.

Moody's, 1992. "Special Report: Corporate Bond Defaults and Default Rates." Moody's Investors Service, New York.

Report of the Board of Banking Supervision: Inquiry into the Circumstances of the Collapse of Barings, 1995. Bank of England.

Shirreff, D., 1991. "Lords in the Jungle." *Risk* 4, 46.

Wakeman, L., 1996. "The Changing Role of the Financial Engineer." I.A.F.E. Conference, New York.

Wisener, P., 1994. "Net Errors." *Risk* 7, 26–28.

QUESTIONS

Question 1

In the accompanying figure, you are given a lattice of spot interest rates for the default-free term structure. The interval between the nodes is 0.5 year. You are also given the conditional martingale probabilitites of default for a firm in a particular credit class. If default occurs, the recovery rate is 48 cents per dollar.

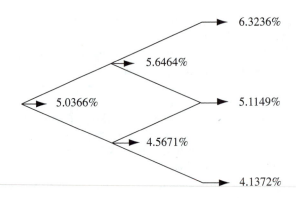

Conditional martingale probabilities of default:

$\lambda(0) = 0.007$ for the first interval,
$\lambda(1) = 0.008$ for the second interval,
$\lambda(2) = 0.010$ for the third interval.

a) Determine the prices of zero-coupon default-free bonds with maturities 0.5, 1.0, and 1.5 years.
b) Determine the prices of zero-coupon credit-risky bonds with maturities 0.5, 1.0, and 1.5 years.

Question 2

Given the information in Question 1, determine the value of a six-month put option written on a zero-coupon credit-risky bond. At the expiry of the option, the maturity of the underlying credit-risky bond is six months. The strike price of the option is $98. The face value of the zero-coupon bond is $100.

Question 3

Given the information in Question 1, determine the value of a six-month put option written on a default-free zero-coupon bond. At the expiry of the option, the maturity of the underlying default-free zero-coupon bond is six months. The strike price of the option is $98. The face value of the zero-coupon bond is $100. The writer of the option is a firm that belongs to the same credit class as that described in Question 1.

Question 4

Given the following information, please answer the following questions.

a) A three-year bond with a face value of $100 pays a coupon of $2 $^{5}/_{8}$ every six months. If the bond is default-free, what is its value?

b) If the bond is issued by a firm belonging to credit class A, what is the value of the bond?

c) If the bond is issued by a firm belonging to credit class B, what is the value of the bond?

MATURITY (YEARS) T	DEFAULT-FREE $B(0,T)$	CREDIT CLASS A $v(0,T)$	CREDIT CLASS B $v(0,T)$
0.5	0.9772	0.9751	0.9748
1.0	0.9540	0.9501	0.9492
1.5	0.9303	0.9242	0.9228
2.0	0.9065	0.8980	0.8962
2.5	0.8825	0.8713	0.8692
3.0	0.8585	0.8445	0.8419
Recovery Rate		0.45	0.38

Question 5

Use the information in Question 4 to answer the following questions.

a) Determine the conditional martingale probabilities of default for credit class A.
b) Determine the conditional martingale probabilities of default for credit class B.

Question 6

Use the information in Question 4 to answer the following. A call option with a maturity of six months is written on a zero-coupon bond by a firm belonging to credit class A. At the expiry of the option, the maturity of the zero-coupon bond is one year. The strike price of the option is 95, face value being $100. The lattice of spot interest rates for the default-free process is given in the accompanying figure.

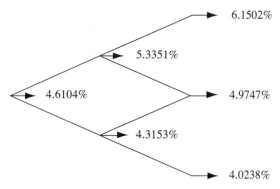

Interval length: $\Delta = 0.5$ years.

Determine the value of the option.

Question 7

Given the information in Question 4, please answer the following questions.

a) If the default-free forward rates are assumed to be normally distributed, determine the value of a three-year cap. Volatility is 1.5 percent and the volatility reduction factor 0.1. Reset dates are every six months. The cap rate is 5.50 percent. Use the program Bonds/Caps/Normal to determine the values of the caplets and cap.
b) If this cap is issued by a firm belonging to credit class A, what are the values of the caplets and cap?
c) If the cap is issued by a firm belonging to credit class B, what are the values of the caplets and cap?

Question 8

A regional bank has a loan portfolio that is undiversified with respect to geographic location and industry. Explain how a credit swap could reduce the bank's credit exposure.

Question 9   Swap Rates

You are given the following information. Determine the swap rate. The floating rate payments are assumed to be default-free.

MATURITY (YEARS) T	DEFAULT-FREE $B(0,T) \times 100$	CREDIT CLASS $v(0,T) \times 100$	MARTINGALE PROBABILITIES OF DEFAULT
0.5	97.7272	97.2508	0.0075
1.0	95.4164	94.4776	0.0077
1.5	93.0780	91.6916	0.0079
2.0	90.7214	88.9030	0.0081
2.5	88.3553	86.1212	0.0083
3.0	85.9877	83.3544	0.0085
3.5	83.6256	80.6099	0.0087
4.0	81.2752	77.8943	0.0090
4.5	78.9423	75.2135	0.0092
5.0	76.6319	72.5723	0.0095

PART V

EXOTICS

Non-Standard (Exotic) Options

19.0 INTRODUCTION

Non-standard or **exotic options** are derivative securities that in some way deviate from the standard American or European call and put option contracts. In this chapter, we describe some of the European non-standard foreign exchange options that are completely defined by their payoff at maturity. Such options are referred to as being **path-independent** because their value at maturity does not depend on the path of the foreign exchange rate during the life of the option. Path independence implies that the valuation of such options is relatively straightforward.

We start with **digital** or **binary options** written on a foreign currency. These options are perhaps the simplest form to describe and to price. Next we consider pay-later, or contingent premium, options. We show that these options are a combination of an ordinary call or put option and a digital option. We then consider different forms of compound options, which are options written on options. Chooser options, which allow the option holder at expiration to pick either a call option or a put option, are one example of compound options. Finally, we describe options on the maximum or minimum of two risky outcomes.

We employ the same assumptions as given in Chapter 11. In particular, we assume throughout this chapter that (1) the spot exchange rate (domestic per unit of foreign currency) is lognormally distributed, and (2) domestic and foreign interest rates are constant. These two assumptions facilitate the analysis of non-standard or exotic options by providing closed form solutions, which are easily programmed on a computer.

19.1 EUROPEAN DIGITAL (BINARY) OPTIONS

We first examine European digital or binary options. A European digital option pays one dollar at expiration if it is in-the-money, and pays zero otherwise. There are two types of digital options: calls and puts. We study each type of option in turn.

Digital Call

A **European digital call option** is defined by its payoff at expiration. The payoff at expiration date T to a European digital call option with strike price K is described by

$$DC(T) = \begin{cases} 1 & \text{if} & S(T) > K \\ 0 & \text{if} & S(T) \le K, \end{cases} \tag{19.1}$$

where $S(T)$ is the spot exchange rate in dollars per unit of foreign currency.

The payoff for the digital call is shown in Figure 19.1. Note that unlike an ordinary foreign currency call option, the payoff at maturity is fixed at 1, even if the option is deep-in-the-money.

Using the risk-neutral pricing methodology, the value of the option prior to maturity is given by its discounted expected value, that is,

$$\begin{aligned} DC(0) &= B(0,T)\, E^{\pi}\{DC(T)\} \\ &= B(0,T)N(d - \sigma\sqrt{T}), \end{aligned} \tag{19.2}$$

where $d \equiv \{\ln[S(0)B_f(0,T)/KB(0,T)] + (\sigma^2/2)T\}/(\sigma\sqrt{T})$, $B(0,T)$ is the date-0 value of a zero-coupon default-free bond that pays one dollar at date T, $B_f(0,T)$ is the date-0 value of a zero-coupon default-free bond that pays one unit of the foreign currency at date T, and σ is the volatility of the spot exchange rate.

Under the martingale probabilities, Expression (19.2) is the discounted probability of ending up in-the-money. This completes our discussion of European digital call options.

Digital Put

A **European digital put option** is defined by its payoff at expiration. The payoff at the expiration date T to a European digital put option with strike price K is

$$DP(T) = \begin{cases} 1 & \text{if} & S(T) < K \\ 0 & \text{if} & S(T) \ge K. \end{cases} \tag{19.3}$$

FIGURE 19.1 *European Digital Call Option Payoff at Maturity*

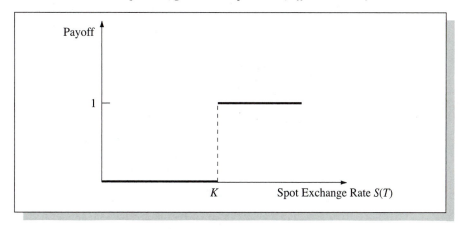

By an argument analogous to the call, the date-0 value prior to maturity is given by

$$DP(0) = B(0, T)N(-d + \sigma\sqrt{T}). \tag{19.4}$$

As with the call, the put's value in Expression (19.4) is the discounted probability of ending up in-the-money (under the martingale probabilities).

EXAMPLE

Digital Options

We illustrate here the usefulness of digital options.

Consider a U.S. firm that is committed to buying equipment from a German firm. The cost of the equipment is 10 million Deutsche marks. The U.S. firm must pay for the equipment in 49 days' time. The firm is concerned that the Deutsche mark might appreciate against the dollar, implying that the dollar cost of buying the equipment would increase.

TABLE 19.1   *Pricing Digital Options*

PART A
DATA INPUT

Spot Exchange Rate	63.03 cents/DM
Maturity	49 days
Volatility*	2.8 percent
Domestic Discount Rate**	4.04 percent
Foreign Discount Rate**	4.28 percent
Strike Price	63.05 cents/DM

*A 365-day year is assumed.

**A 360-day year is assumed.

PART B
OUTPUT
PRICE OF OPTIONS

ORDINARY FX CALL OPTION*	DIGITAL FX CALL OPTION**
$23,680	$21,162

*The program FX/Pricing/European is used. The option value is 0.2368 cents/DM, assuming a contract amount of 1 Deutsche mark. For a contract size of 10 million Deutsche marks the cost of the option is $(0.2368/100) \times 10,000,000 = \$23,680$.

**The program Exotic/Digitals is used. The option value is $47.0262 assuming a contract size of $100. For a contract size of $45,000, the cost of the option is $(47.0262/100) \times 45,000 = \$21,162$.

TABLE 19.2   *Dollar Cost of Equipment*

Spot Exchange Rate (Cents/DM)	Dollar Cost of Equipment	Value of Ordinary* FX Call	Net Cost of Equipment	Value of Digital** FX Call	Net Cost of Equipment
62.50	6,250,000	0	6,273,811	0	6,271,279
63.05	6,305,000	0	6,328,811	0	6,326,279
63.25	6,325,000	20,000	6,328,811	45,000	6,301,279
63.50	6,350,000	45,000	6,328,811	45,000	6,326,279
64.00	6,400,000	95,000	6,328,811	45,000	6,376,279

Net Cost of Equipment ≡ Dollar Cost of Equipment − Value of Option
+ Cost of Carry

*Cost of the option plus borrowing costs is $23,811.
**Cost of the option plus borrowing costs is $21,279.

One way to insure against this contingency is to buy an ordinary foreign currency call option, giving the firm the option to buy Deutsche marks at the strike price when the option matures. The firm is considering purchasing an ordinary foreign currency option with principal of 10 million Deutsche marks. Alternatively, the company could purchase a foreign currency digital call option. By definition, the digital at maturity pays one dollar if in-the-money, and pays zero otherwise. The U.S. firm decides that if it purchases a digital, the principal will be for $45,000.

We use the information in Table 19.1, Part A, to price the two options. The results are shown in Table 19.1, Part B. The cost of the ordinary foreign currency call option is $23,680, principal 10 million Deutsche marks. The cost of the foreign currency digital call option is $21,162, principal $45,000. The foreign currency digital is cheaper.

These two options have different implications for the net dollar cost of purchasing the equipment in 49 days' time as shown in Table 19.2. In determining the net cost, we must consider the carrying cost for the option. Given a domestic discount rate of 4.04 percent, the price of a default-free bond paying one dollar in 49 days is $0.9945. The cost-of-carry for the ordinary option is $23,680/0.9945 = $23,811, and for the digital option $21,162/0.9945 = $21,279.

Suppose the spot exchange rate is 64 cents/DM. The net dollar cost of the equipment when the ordinary option is used is

$$\$6,400,000 - 95,000 + 23,811 = \$6,328,811$$

and, when the digital option is used,

$$\$6,400,000 - 45,000 + 21,279 = \$6,376,279.$$

In examining Table 19.2, we see that the net costs of purchasing the equipment differ for the two options. The ordinary foreign currency option ensures that the cost will never go above $6,328,811. This is not the case for the digital option. The option we prefer to use depends on our personal risk preferences. ■

Hedging

Here we discuss hedging of digital options. Digital options can be hedged in the same way that ordinary options are hedged, although as the following example will demonstrate, delta hedging has its practical limitations.

EXAMPLE | **Digital Call Hedging**

This example illustrates the delta hedging of a digital call option. Consider a financial institution that has sold a digital call option and wants to hedge its position. Relevant information is given in Table 19.3, Part A.

To construct a self-financed, delta neutral position, the institution invests n Deutsche marks in the foreign riskless asset and B dollars in the domestic risk-

TABLE 19.3 *Hedging Digital Options*

PART A
DATA INPUT

Spot Exchange Rate	62.80 cents/DM
Maturity	5 days
Volatility*	2.8 percent
Domestic Discount Rate**	3.95 percent
Foreign Discount Rate**	4.15 percent
Strike Price	63.05 cents/DM
Principal	$100

*A 365-day year is assumed.

**A 360-day year is assumed.

PART B
CALL OPTION PRICES

SPOT EXCHANGE RATE (CENTS/DM)	OPTION PRICES*	DELTA
62.40	0.0756	1.2729
62.80	11.0708	91.7729
63.20	76.2269	149.0923

*The program Exotic/Digital is used.

less asset. Using the program Exotic/Digital, the price of the option is $11.0708 and its delta 91.7729. The initial position is

$$0 = -11.0708 + n0.6280 + B.$$

A minus appears in front of the option price because the institution has written the option. The delta of the hedged position is set to zero, implying

$$0 = -91.7729 + n.$$

Therefore,

$$n = 91.7729$$

and

$$B = -46.5626.$$

Now we want to consider the sensitivity of the hedged portfolio to small changes in the spot exchange rate. We first consider a decrease of 0.40 cents/DM in the spot exchange rate from 62.80 to 62.40 cents/DM. The value of the hedged position, using the information in Table 19.3, Part B, is

$$-0.0756 + 91.7729 \times 0.6240 - 46.5626 = \$10.63.$$

The portfolio increases in value by $10.63.

Suppose the spot exchange rate increases to 63.20 cents/DM from 62.80 cents/DM. The value of the hedged position, using the information in Table 19.3, Part B, is

$$-76.2269 + 91.7729 \times 0.6320 - 46.5626 = -\$64.79.$$

This hedge performs very poorly because it is very sensitive to small movements in the spot exchange rate.   ∎

We can understand the poor performance of the hedge in the preceding example by examining the behavior of the option's delta. The option has only five days to expiry and the spot exchange rate is close to the strike price. Recall that the delta is a measure of the change in the option value for a small change in the spot exchange rate.

Figure 19.2 shows that the delta is unstable. If the spot exchange rate is below the strike, say at 62 cents/DM, the option is so deep-out-of-the-money that the delta is approximately zero. If the exchange rate is above the strike, say at 64 cents/DM, the option is deep-in-the-money. However, the maximum value of the option is bounded and

FIGURE 19.2   *Instability of Delta*

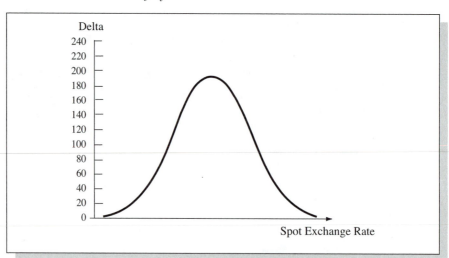

cannot be greater than the face amount. The delta is again approximately zero. For spot exchange rates between 62 cents/DM and 64 cents/DM, the option value goes from approximately zero to approximately 100, and the delta goes from approximately zero to approximately 193 and then back again to approximately zero. This instability creates significant practical problems in delta hedging digitals in actual markets, given transaction costs and discrete trading.

An alternative way to approximately hedge a digital option that avoids the delta hedging instability is to use two ordinary European call options with strike prices K_1 and K_2, for which $K_1 < K < K_2$, K being the strike price of the digital option. The expiry date for the two ordinary options must be the same as that for the digital option.

Consider a portfolio long the ordinary option with strike price K_1 and short the ordinary option with strike price K_2. The payoff at expiration to this portfolio is

$$c(T, K_1) - c(T, K_2) = \begin{cases} K_2 - K_1 & \text{if} & S(T) > K_2 \\ S(T) - K_1 & \text{if} & K_2 \geq S(T) > K_1 \\ 0 & \text{if} & S(T) < K_1. \end{cases}$$

To avoid confusion, the notation for the call option is expanded to include the strike price. This payoff is shown in Figure 19.3. The shape of the payoff is similar to that of a digital call except for its magnitude. This suggests that a portfolio of $[1/(K_2 - K_1)]$ of these options can be used to approximate a digital call option's payoff. In addition, the portfolio's value at date 0 is given by

$$[c(0, K_1) - c(0, K_2)]/(K_2 - K_1).$$

FIGURE 19.3 *Approximating the Payoff of a Digital Option*

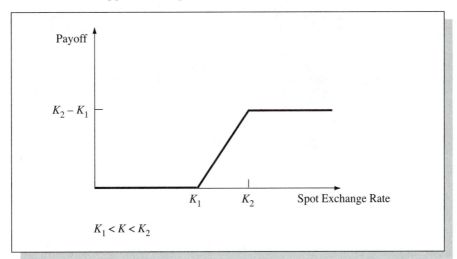

This portfolio's value can be used to approximate the date-0 value of the digital call option.

This portfolio is called a **static hedge** because the hedge consists of buying/selling and holding the ordinary calls until maturity. The accuracy of this static hedge portfolio for a particular example is shown in Table 19.4. The accuracy of the static hedge approximation is seen to improve as the spread between the strikes $(K_2 - K_1)$ decreases. The options in Table 19.4 are priced using the information from Table 19.3.

TABLE 19.4 *Accuracy of Approximation*

SPREAD* Δ	STRIKE K_1	STRIKE K_2	VALUE OF PORTFOLIO	DELTA OF PORTFOLIO
0.10	62.95	63.15	11.9590	93.4054
0.08	62.97	63.13	11.6431	92.8522
0.06	62.99	63.11	11.3942	92.3955
0.04	63.01	63.09	11.2150	92.0546
0.02	63.03	63.07	11.1075	91.8441
		Digital Call	11.0708	91.7729

*The spread, Δ, is defined such that
$$K_2 \equiv K + \Delta$$
$$K_1 \equiv K - \Delta$$
$$K = 63.05.$$

EXAMPLE **Static Hedge**

This example illustrates the valuation of a static hedge portfolio.

The static hedge portfolio consists of two ordinary options with strike prices $K_1 = 63.03$ and $K_2 = 63.07$. Given the information in Table 19.3 and using the program FX/Pricing/European Option, the values of the two ordinary call options are \$1.3482 and \$0.9039, respectively, assuming a contract size of 100 Deutsche marks. Therefore, the initial value of the static hedge portfolio is

$$(1.3482 - 0.9039)/(63.07 - 63.03) = 11.1075 \text{ dollars.} \quad \blacksquare$$

Gap Options

We discuss here the pricing of **European gap options**. There are two types of European gap options: calls and puts. We discuss each of these in turn. For pricing and hedging, we will show that a European gap option is the combination of an ordinary option and a digital option. Once this is shown, the analysis is done because we have previously studied the pricing and hedging of both of these simpler options.

Gap call option

A **European gap call option** is defined by its payoff at expiration. The payoff at the expiration date T to a European gap call option is

$$GC(T) \equiv \begin{cases} S(T) - G & \text{if} \quad S(T) > K \\ 0 & \text{if} \quad S(T) \leq K, \end{cases} \tag{19.5}$$

where in general G is different from the strike price K.

At maturity, if the spot exchange rate is greater than the strike price K, the payoff to the gap call option is defined to be $S(T) - G$, where G may be greater or less than the strike price K.

The payoff is shown in Figure 19.4. The payoff indicates why this option is called a gap option. The payoff diagram has a jump or "gap" at the strike price K.

We next show the relation between a gap call option, an ordinary call, and a digital call. Expression (19.5) can be rewritten as

$$GC(T) \equiv \begin{cases} S(T) - K & \text{if} \quad S(T) > K \\ 0 & \text{if} \quad S(T) \leq K \end{cases} + (K - G) \begin{cases} 1 & \text{if} \quad S(T) > K \\ 0 & \text{if} \quad S(T) \leq K. \end{cases} \tag{19.6}$$

The first term on the right side of this expression is the payoff to an ordinary call option with strike K, and the second term on the right side is $(K - G)$ times the payoff to a digital call option with strike K.

FIGURE 19.4 *Payoff to a Gap Call Option*

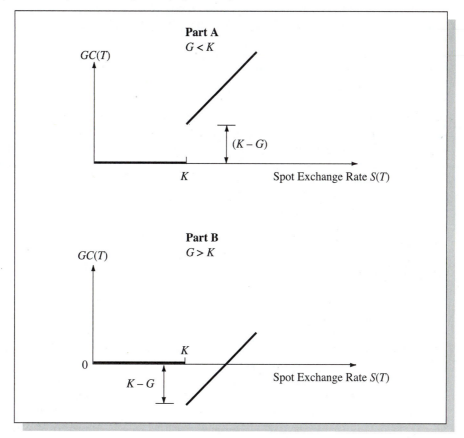

Therefore, the gap call option is equivalent to an ordinary call option plus $(K - G)$ digital call options. The value of a gap call option today is thus

$$GC(0) = c(0) + (K - G)DC(0),\tag{19.7}$$

where $c(0)$ is the value of an ordinary European foreign currency call option with strike price K and maturity T. A similar analysis applies to gap put options.

Gap put option
A **European gap put option** is defined by its payoff at expiration. The payoff at the expiration date T to a European gap put option is

$$GP(T) \equiv \begin{cases} G - S(T) & \text{if} \quad S(T) < K \\ 0 & \text{if} \quad S(T) \geq K. \end{cases}\tag{19.8}$$

As with the gap call option, we can express this payoff as the sum of the payoff of an ordinary put option with strike K plus $(G - K)$ times the payoff to a digital put option with strike K. This implies that a gap put option is equivalent to an ordinary put option plus $(G - K)$ digital put options.

The value of the gap put option is thus

$$GP(0) = p(0) + (G - K)DP(0) \tag{19.9}$$

where $p(0)$ is the date-0 value of an ordinary European foreign currency put option with strike price K and maturity T.

To hedge gap options, we can hedge using ordinary options and digital options as given in Expressions (19.7) and (19.9), or we can delta hedge. The gap option's deltas are obtained from the deltas of the ordinary calls and digital calls via Expressions (19.7) and (19.9). Just as delta hedging is difficult for digital options, it will also be so for gap options due to the linear relationship between the two. Our discussion of European digital and gap options is now complete.

19.2 PAYLATER OPTIONS

In this section we describe **paylater options**.[1] The premium for a paylater option is paid only on the exercise of the option. Paylater options are **contingent options**: The buyer must exercise the option if it is in-the-money, regardless of whether the option expires sufficiently deeply in-the-money to pay the premium and make a profit.

These options, which have been written on foreign currencies, stock indices, and commodities, provide a means to insure against large one-way price movements at zero initial cost. The option premium is set when the option is written such that the initial value of the option is zero, and the premium is paid only if the option expires in-the-money. There are two types of paylater options: calls and puts. We discuss each of these options in turn.

Call Option

A **European paylater call option** is defined by its payoff at expiration. The payoff at the expiration date T to a European paylater call option with strike price K is

$$PLC(T) \equiv \begin{cases} S(T) - K - X_c & \text{if} \quad S(T) > K \\ 0 & \text{if} \quad S(T) \leq K, \end{cases} \tag{19.10}$$

where X_c is the premium of the option.

The payoff to this option is shown in Figure 19.5. Note that payoff is negative if the spot exchange rate is between K and $K + X_c$. This is where the spot exchange rate

---

[1]These are sometimes called contingent premium options, or deferred premium options.

exceeds the strike price K but the cash flow from exercising does not exceed the deferred premium.

Figure 19.5 is similar to the payoff to a gap call option as given in Figure 19.4, Part B. However, there is an important difference in the two options. For a paylater option, the premium is only paid if the option expires in-the-money. For a gap option, the premium is paid when initiated.

As with gap options, we value the paylater call option by showing that the payoff for a paylater call option can be expressed in terms of the payoff to an ordinary call option and a digital call option. To see this, we can rewrite Expression (19.10) in the form

$$PLC(T) = \begin{cases} S(T) - K & \text{if} & S(T) > K \\ 0 & \text{if} & S(T) \le K \end{cases} - X_c \begin{cases} 1 & \text{if} & S(T) > K \\ 0 & \text{if} & S(T) \le K. \end{cases}$$
(19.11)

The first term on the right side of Expression (19.11) is the payoff to an ordinary European call option, and the second term on the right side is X_c times the payoff to a European digital call option.

Thus a paylater call option is equivalent to being long an ordinary call option and being short X_c digital call options. The value of the paylater call option prior to maturity is given by

$$PLC(t) = c(t) - X_c \times DC(t),$$
(19.12)

where the first term on the right is the value of an ordinary European call option and the second term is the value of X_c European digital calls.

FIGURE 19.5 *European Paylater Call Option Payoff at Maturity*

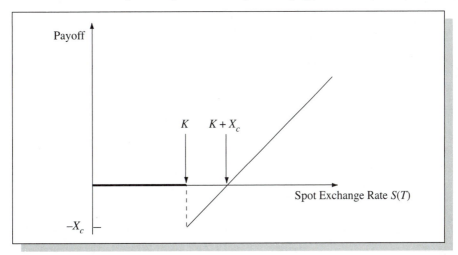

When a paylater call option is initiated, the premium is set such that the initial value of the option is zero. Using Expression (19.12), this implies that the premium is given by

$$X_c = c(0)/DC(0).\tag{19.13}$$

This premium is fixed over the life of the option and is paid only if the option expires in-the-money.

Once the premium is set, the value of the option at date t is

$$PLC(t) = c(t) - X_c \times DC(t),\tag{19.14}$$

which can be positive or negative. Figure 19.6 shows the value of the paylater call option for a range of spot exchange rates. For low values of the spot exchange rate, the paylater call's value is approximately zero. As the spot exchange rate increases, the value of the paylater call first goes negative, then eventually turns positive, and continues to increase as the spot exchange rate increases. It is negative for some values of the spot exchange rate. Why? Because for these values the paylater call will likely end up in-the-money but by less than the premium owed.

FIGURE 19.6   *Value of a Paylater Option*

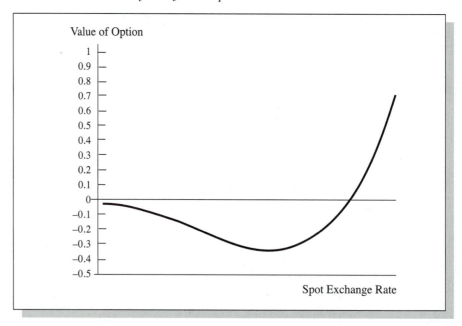

EXAMPLE **Paylater Call Option Valuation**

Using the information in Table 19.1, we want to determine the premium for a paylater call option with a strike price of 63.05 cents/DM and a maturity of 49 days. The program Exotics/Paylater/Pricing European is used. The premium is found to be $X_c = 0.5036$ cents/DM. Therefore, the premium for a paylater option with principal 10 million Deutsche marks is $50,360.

Compare this to the price of an ordinary foreign currency call option. From Table 19.1, Part B, the price is $23,680. The premium for the paylater option is more than double the price of the ordinary option. This is not unusual, and it is a drawback to paylater options. The benefit to the paylater option, of course, is that this premium is not paid if the option expires out-of-the-money.

In Table 19.5, the net cost of purchasing the equipment using a paylater option is compared to the two alternatives, examined in Table 19.2, of using an ordinary foreign currency call option and a foreign currency digital option. If the spot exchange rate never goes above the strike price of 63.05 cents/DM, the cost of the equipment using a paylater option is less than using the other two types of options. This conclusion does not hold if the spot exchange rate is greater than 63.05 cents/DM. The paylater call option is the most expensive alternative for spot exchange rates of 63.25 and 63.5 cents/DM. ■

The analysis for paylater put options is very similar to the analysis for paylater call options, thus our exposition will be brief.

Put Option

A **European paylater put option** is defined by its payoff at expiration. The payoff at expiration to a European paylater put option that matures at date T with strike price K is

TABLE 19.5 *Net Cost of Equipment*

SPOT EXCHANGE RATE (CENTS/DM)	ORDINARY FX* CALL	PAYLATER FX CALL	DIGITAL FX* CALL
62.50	6,273,811	6,250,000	6,271,279
63.05	6,328,811	6,305,000	6,326,279
63.25	6,328,811	6,355,360	6,301,279
63.50	6,328,811	6,355,360	6,326,279
64.00	6,328,811	6,355,360	6,376,279

*These figures are taken from Table 19.2.

$$PLP(T) = \begin{cases} K - S(T) - X_p & \text{if} \quad S(T) < K \\ 0 & \text{if} \quad S(T) \geq K, \end{cases} \tag{19.15}$$

where X_p is the premium.

Repeating the same form of argument, the value of the paylater put option at date t is

$$PLP(t) = p(t) - X_p \times DP(t), \tag{19.16}$$

where the first term on the right is the value of an ordinary European foreign currency put option, and the second term is the value of a European foreign currency digital put option, both with strike K and maturity T.

Thus a paylater put option is equivalent to an ordinary put option less X_p digital puts. The option premium is given by

$$X_p = p(0)/DP(0). \tag{19.17}$$

The representation of paylater options as a combination of ordinary options and digital options gives the necessary insights for static and/or delta hedging. The static hedging can be done using Expressions (19.12) and (19.16). Similarly, delta hedging can be done using the deltas obtained from Expressions (19.12) and (19.16) as well. Our study of paylater options is now complete.

19.3 COMPOUND OPTIONS

Now we study compound options. A **compound option** is an option written on another option.

Consider a company bidding on a contract to sell equipment in Germany. The sale price is in Deutsche marks. The company will learn if its bid is successful in three weeks' time. If successful, the company will receive payment four weeks later. In this case, the company faces the risk that in four weeks' time the Deutsche mark will depreciate against the dollar. One possible solution is for the company to buy a compound option. It could buy today a call option with a maturity of three weeks, giving it the right to buy a put option with a maturity of four weeks. This is one example of a compound option: a call option on a put option.

We start by describing the payoffs to compound options and we then describe the pricing and hedging of such options.

Options on a Call

We first study options on call options. This compound option is written on a call option that matures at date T_1 and has a strike price K_1.

Call on a call

The **compound call option** is defined by its payoff at maturity. The compound call option matures at date $T \leq T_1$ and the strike price is K. The payoff to the compound call option at maturity is

$$cc(T) = \begin{cases} c(T, T_1, K_1) - K & \text{if positive} \\ 0 & \text{otherwise,} \end{cases} \tag{19.18}$$

where $c(T, T_1, K_1)$ is the value at date T of a European call option with maturity T_1 and strike price K_1. The compound call is exercised at date T if the value of the underlying European call exceeds the strike price K. Otherwise, it expires worthless.

The payoff to the compound put option is similar and we discuss it next.

Put on a call

The **compound put option** is defined by its payoff at maturity. The compound put option matures at date T and the strike price is K. The payoff at maturity is

$$pc(T) = \begin{cases} K - c(T, T_1, K_1) & \text{if positive} \\ 0 & \text{otherwise.} \end{cases} \tag{19.19}$$

Having defined their payoffs, we now consider the valuation of these compound options. These values are determined using the risk-neutral pricing methodology of Chapter 6. Crucial in this procedure is the determination of the critical value for the underlying spot exchange rate S^* such that above this value the compound call option is exercised, and below this value the compound put option is exercised. This is the task to which we now turn.

We define S^* to be that spot exchange rate at date T such that

$$c(T, T_1, K_1) = K. \tag{19.20}$$

If the realized spot exchange rate at date T is greater than S^*, then the value of the underlying call is greater than the strike price K. In symbols, if $S(T) > S^*$, then $c(T, T_1, K_1) > K$. The converse is also true; if $S(T) < S^*$, then $c(T, T_1, K_1) < K$. The critical value S^* can be determined on a computer using a numerical search procedure.

Given the critical value S^*, taking the discounted expected payoff for these options under the martingale probabilities determines their prices. The value of a compound call-on-call option is given by

$$\begin{aligned} cc(0) = [&B_f(0, T_1)S(0)N_2(h + \sigma\sqrt{T}, k + \sigma\sqrt{T_1}, \rho) \\ &- K_1 B(0, T_1,)N_2(h, k, \rho)] \\ &- KB(0, T)N(h), \end{aligned} \tag{19.21}$$

where

$$h \equiv \{\ln[S(0)B_f(0,T)/S*B(0,T)] - (\sigma^2/2)T\}/(\sigma\sqrt{T})$$
$$k \equiv \{\ln[S(0)B_f(0,T_1)/K_1B(0,T_1)] - (\sigma^2/2)T_1\}/(\sigma\sqrt{T_1})$$
$$\rho \equiv \sqrt{T/T_1}.$$

$N_2(\cdot,\cdot,\cdot)$ is the cumulative bivariate normal distribution function.[2]

The value of a compound put-on-call option is given by

$$
\begin{aligned}
pc(0) = \ &KB(0,T)N(-h) \\
&- [B_f(0,T_1)S(0)N_2(-h - \sigma\sqrt{T}, k + \sigma\sqrt{T_1}, -\rho) \\
&- B(0,T_1)KN_2(-h, k, -\rho)].
\end{aligned}
\tag{19.22}
$$

Options on a Put

We next study options on a put. This compound option is written on a European put option that matures at date T_1 and has a strike price K_1.

Call on a put

The compound call option is defined by its payoff at maturity. The compound call option matures at date T and the strike price is K. The payoff to the compound call option at maturity is

$$
cp(T) \equiv \begin{cases} p(T,T_1,K_1) - K & \text{if positive} \\ 0 & \text{otherwise,} \end{cases}
\tag{19.23}
$$

where $p(T,T_1,K_1)$ is the value at date T of a European put option with maturity T_1 and strike price K_1. The compound call option is exercised at date T only if the underlying put option's value exceeds the strike price K. Otherwise, it expires worthless. A compound put option is similar and we discuss it next.

Put on a put

The compound put option is defined by its payoff at maturity. The compound put option matures at date T and the strike price is K. The payoff to the compound put option at maturity is

$$
pp(T) \equiv \begin{cases} K - p(T,T_1,K_1) & \text{if positive} \\ 0 & \text{otherwise.} \end{cases}
\tag{19.24}
$$

Having defined their payoffs at maturity, we now value these options using the risk-neutral pricing procedure from Chapter 6. This approach computes current values as the discounted expected payoffs at maturity using the martingale probabilities. Crucial in this calculation is the critical spot exchange rate's value, $\bar{S}$, such that above

---

[2]Drezner and Wesolousky (1990) describe a quick and accurate algorithm for computing the cumulative bivariate normal distribution function.

this value the compound call is exercised, and below the value the compound put is exercised. This is the task to which we now turn.

Define $\bar{S}$ to be that spot exchange rate at date T such that

$$p(T, T_1, K_1) = K. \tag{19.25}$$

If the realized spot exchange rate at date T is greater than $\bar{S}$, then the value of the underlying put option is less than the strike price K. In symbols, if $S(T) > \bar{S}$, then $p(T, T_1, K_1) < K$, and if $S(T) < \bar{S}$, then $p(T, T_1, K_1) > K$.

Given $\bar{S}$, the value of a compound call-on-put is given by

$$
\begin{aligned}
cp(0) = {} & B(0, T_1)K_1 N_2(-\bar{h}, -k, \rho) \\
& - B_f(0, T_1)S(0)N_2(-\bar{h} - \sigma\sqrt{T}, -k - \sigma\sqrt{T_1}, \rho) \\
& - KB(0, T)N(-\bar{h}),
\end{aligned} \tag{19.26}
$$

where

$$\bar{h} \equiv \{\ln[S(0)B_f(0, T)/\bar{S}B(0, T)] - (\sigma^2/2)T\}/(\sigma\sqrt{T}).$$

The value of a compound put-on-put is given by

$$
\begin{aligned}
pp(0) = {} & B(0, T)KN(\bar{h}) \\
& - [B(0, T_1)K_1 N_2(\bar{h}, -k, -\rho) \\
& - B_f(0, T_1)S(0)N_2(\bar{h} + \sigma\sqrt{T}, k + \sigma\sqrt{T_1}, -\rho)].
\end{aligned} \tag{19.27}
$$

We illustrate the use of these formulas through an example.

EXAMPLE   **Call on a Put**

This example illustrates the use of a call-on-put compound option.

Consider a firm that is bidding for a contract to sell equipment to a German firm for 10 million Deutsche marks. The firm will be informed in 25 days' time whether its bid has been accepted. If accepted, the firm will receive payment 24 days later when the equipment is delivered. The company is concerned that the Deutsche mark might depreciate against the dollar, implying the dollar value of the sale would decrease.

One possibility would be to buy a put option on Deutsche marks with a maturity of 49 days and strike price of 63.03 cents/DM. Given the information in Table 19.6, the cost of this option is 0.2669 cents/DM using the program FX/Pricing/European Option. Given that the sale price of the equipment is 10 million DM, the total cost of the option would be $26,690. This scenario does not recognize the contingency that the company's bid might not be successful.

TABLE 19.6 *Pricing a Compound Call-on-Put Option*

PART A DATA INPUTS	
Spot Exchange Rate	63.03 cents/DM
Initial Exercise Price for Compound Option	0.16
Final Exercise Price for Compound Option	0.24
Exercise Price Interval	0.02
Maturity of Compound Option	25 days
Volatility*	2.8 percent
Domestic Discount Rate**	4.04 percent
Foreign Discount Rate**	4.28 percent
Exercise Price for Underlying Put Option	63.03
Maturity for Underlying Put Option	24 days

*A 365-day year is assumed.

**A 360-day year is assumed.

PART B OUTPUT*			
EXERCISE PRICE	**OPTION PRICE**	**DELTA**	**GAMMA**
0.16	0.1485	−0.4051	0.7388
0.18	0.1377	−0.3880	0.7420
0.20	0.1277	−0.3708	0.7419
0.22	0.1184	−0.3536	0.7389
0.24	0.1096	−0.3366	0.7330

*The program Exotics/Compound/Option on a Put is used.

A second possibility is to buy a call option written on a put option. The maturity of this compound call option is set at 25 days. When this option matures, the firm can buy a put option with a maturity of 24 days and strike price of 63.03 cents/DM if its bid is successful. If the bid is not successful, it can sell the put option back to the financial institution.

What strike price should the firm choose for the compound call option? The value of an at-the-money put option with a maturity of 24 days is 0.185, so the company wants to price the compound call option for a range of strike prices. The data inputs are summarized in Table 19.6, Part A, and the prices for the compound option are given in Part B.

Note that in Part B, as the strike price increases, the value of the option decreases. Given the definition of the payoff at maturity—see Expression (19.23)—this is to be expected. Note that delta is negative. If the spot exchange

rate increases the value of the underlying put option decreases, implying that the value of the compound call decreases.

If the strike price for the compound call option is chosen to be 0.18, the cost of the option is 0.1377 cents/DM or $13,770 for 10 million DM. Thus the initial cost of the compound is far less than that of an ordinary put option ($26,690 per 10 million DM). However, if the company is successful and decides to exercise the compound option at maturity, assuming it is in-the-money, there will be a further cost of $18,000 to the company. ∎

19.4 CHOOSER OPTION

Here we examine chooser options. A **chooser option**[3] is an option to buy either a call or put option at some future date. Consider a chooser option that matures at date T. It is written on a call option that matures at date $T_1 \geq T$ with strike price K_1 and a put option that matures at date $T_2 \geq T$ with strike price K_2.

The payoff to the chooser option at maturity T is defined by

$$co(T) \equiv \text{Max}[c(T, T_1, K_1), p(T, T_2, K_2)]. \tag{19.28}$$

To understand this payoff, let us first consider a special case.

Special Case ($T_1 = T_2, K_1 = K_2$)

Suppose that the two underlying options have the same maturity date ($T_1 = T_2$) and same strike price ($K_1 = K_2$); then using the put-call parity relationship for foreign currency options, we know that

$$p(T, T_1, K_1) = c(T, T_1, K_1) + K_1 B(T, T_1) - S(T) B_f(T, T_1).$$

Substituting this result into Expression (19.28) and simplifying gives

$$co(T) = c(T, T_1, K_1) + \text{Max}[0, K_1 B(T, T_1) - S(T) B_f(T, T_1)]. \tag{19.29}$$

The first term on the right side of Expression (19.29) is the value at date T of a call option that matures at date T_1 with a strike price of K_1. We can write the second term on the right side of Expression (19.29) in the form

$$B_f(T, T_1) \text{Max}[0, K - S(T)],$$

where $K \equiv K_1 B(T, T_1)/B_f(T, T_1)$. The above expression represents the payoff to a put option with strike price K. The payoff is multiplied by $B_f(T, T_1)$. That is, a chooser

---

[3]This is sometimes called an **as-you-like option**.

option is equivalent (in this special case) to an ordinary call option with strike K_1 plus $B_f(T, T_1)$ ordinary put options with strike K. This implies that the value of the chooser option today is

$$co(0) = c(0, T_1, K_1) + B_f(T, T_1)p(0, T, K).$$
(19.30)

Determining the value of the chooser option for the general case is not so easy.

General Case

To value the chooser option for the general case, we need to determine the spot exchange rate $\overline{S}$ such that above this spot exchange rate the underlying call is more valuable, and below this spot exchange rate the underlying put is more valuable.

Define $\overline{S}$ to be the spot exchange rate at date T such that

$$c(0, T_1, K_1) = p(T, T_2, K_2).$$
(19.31)

Given $\overline{S}$, the payoff to the chooser option at maturity, given by Expression (19.28), can be rewritten as

$$co(T) = \begin{cases} c(T, T_1, K_1) & \text{if} \quad S(T) > \overline{S} \\ 0 & \text{if} \quad S(T) \leq \overline{S} \end{cases} + \begin{cases} 0 & \text{if} \quad S(T) > \overline{S} \\ p(T, T_2, K_2) & \text{if} \quad S(T) \leq \overline{S}. \end{cases}$$

The payoff to a chooser option can be decomposed into the payoff from two compound options, a call on a call plus a call on a put, each with a zero strike price. Thus a chooser option is equivalent to a call on a call plus a call on a put, each with a zero strike price.

To value the chooser option, we can use Expressions (19.21) and (19.26), that is,

$$\begin{aligned} co(0) = \ & B_f(0, T_1)S(0)N_2(h_1 + \sigma\sqrt{T}, \ k_1 + \sigma\sqrt{T_1}, \ \rho_1) \\ & - \ K_1 B(0, T_1)N_2(h_1, k_1, \rho_1) \\ & + \ B(0, T_2)K_2 N_2(-h_2, -k_2, \rho_2) \\ & - \ B_f(0, T_2)S(0)N_2(-h_2 - \sigma\sqrt{T}, \ -k_2, \ -\sigma\sqrt{T_2}, \rho_2), \end{aligned}$$
(19.32)

where

$$\begin{aligned} h_1 &= \{\ln[B_f(0, T)S(0)/B(0, T)\overline{S}] - (\sigma^2/2)T\}/(\sigma\sqrt{T}) \\ k_1 &= \{\ln[B_f(0, T_1)S(0)/B(0, T_1)K_1] - (\sigma^2/2)T_1\}/(\sigma\sqrt{T_1}) \\ \rho_1 &= \sqrt{T/T_1} \\ h_2 &= h_1 \\ k_2 &= \{\ln[B_f(0, T_2)S(0)/B(0, T_2)K_2] - (\sigma^2/2)T_2\}/(\sigma\sqrt{T_2}) \\ \rho_2 &= \sqrt{T/T_2}. \end{aligned}$$

Hedging the chooser option is equivalent to hedging a portfolio consisting of the call on a call plus the call on a put. We illustrate the valuation of a chooser option through an example.

EXAMPLE   ### Chooser Option

Let us consider a company that must make a payment in sterling in 100 days' time. It is concerned about the risk of sterling appreciating against the dollar. The company could purchase an ordinary foreign exchange call option to buy sterling. The company also expects to receive a payment in sterling in 68 days' time. In this case, the company is concerned about sterling depreciating against the dollar. The company could purchase an ordinary foreign exchange put option to sell sterling.

The company expects that economic events over the next 30 days will have a long-run effect on spot exchange rates, although the company is uncertain about the actual direction of changes. The company decides to purchase a chooser option with a maturity of 30 days. The current spot exchange rate is 158 cents/pound. The underlying call option has a maturity of $70(= 100 - 30)$ days and a strike price of 160 cents/pound. The underlying put option has a maturity of $38(= 68 - 30)$ days and a strike price of 156 cents/pound.

Volatility	12 percent	(365-day year)
Domestic Discount Rate	4.50 percent	(360-day year)
U.K. Discount Rate	5.60 percent	(360-day year)

Using the program Exotics/Chooser, the value of the chooser option is 5.48 cents/pound.   ■

19.5 OPTIONS ON THE MINIMUM OR MAXIMUM OF TWO RISKY ASSETS

Here we examine **options on the minimum or maximum of two risky assets**. We illustrate such an option through an example.

EXAMPLE   ### Call on the Maximum

Let us consider a zero-coupon bond that pays at maturity F dollars or F_1 Deutsche marks or F_2 sterling. The bondholder has the option to choose the payment currency. If dollars are the reference currency, the bondholder must compare the dollar value of F_1 Deutsche marks and the dollar value of F_2 sterling with F dollars.

Let $S_1(t)$ denote the dollar/Deutsche mark spot exchange rate at date t, and let $S_2(t)$ denote the dollar/sterling spot exchange rate at date t.

If the bond matures at date T, the bondholder will pick payment in the currency with the maximum dollar value. The dollar value of the payoff at date T, $DV(T)$, can be expressed in the form

$$DV(T) \equiv \text{Max}[F, S_1(T)F_1, S_2(T)F_2]. \tag{19.33}$$

We can write this expression in a more intuitive manner. First, we can determine whether the dollar value of F_1 Deutsche marks is greater than or less than the dollar value of F_2 sterling, choosing the greater. Second, compare this to receiving F dollars. In symbols,

$$DV(T) = F + \begin{cases} \text{Max}[S_1(T)F_1, S_2(T)F_2] - F & \text{if } \text{Max}[S_1(T)F_1, S_2(T)F_2] > F \\ 0 & \text{if } \text{Max}[S_1(T)F_1, S_2(T)F_2] \leq F. \end{cases} \tag{19.34}$$

For example, suppose the dollar value of receiving F_1 Deutsche marks is greater than the dollar value of receiving F_2 sterling or F dollars. In this case,

$$\text{Max}[S_1(T)F_1, S_2(T)F_2] = S_1(T)F_1 > F,$$

and Expression (19.34) becomes

$$\begin{aligned} DV(T) &= F + [S_1(T)F_1 - F] \\ &= S_1(T)F_1. \end{aligned}$$

Expression (19.34) is an example of a call option on the maximum of two risky assets.

Suppose the firm gets to pick the currency of payment instead of the bondholders. In this case, the firm will want to minimize the dollar outflow of funds, assuming the firm is acting in the best interests of all shareholders. From the firm's perspective, the dollar value of the payoff at date T, $DV(T)$, can be written in the form

$$DV(T) \equiv \text{Min}[F, S_1(T)F_1, S_2(T)F_2]. \tag{19.35}$$

Again, this expression can be written in a more intuitive manner. First, determine whether the dollar value of F_1 Deutsche marks is less than or greater than the dollar value of F_2 sterling, and then pick the lesser. Second, compare this to paying F dollars. In symbols,

$$DV(T) = F - \begin{cases} F - \text{Min}[S_1(T)F_1, S_2(T)F_2] & \text{if } \text{Min}[S_1(T)F_1, S_2(T)F_2] < F \\ 0 & \text{if } \text{Min}[S_1(T)F_1, S_2(T)F_2] \geq F. \end{cases} \tag{19.36}$$

For example, suppose the dollar cost of paying F_1 Deutsche marks is less than the dollar cost of paying F_2 sterling or F dollars. In this case,

$$\text{Min}[S_1(T)F_1, S_2(T)F_2] = S_1(T)F_1 < F,$$

and Expression (19.36) becomes

$$\begin{aligned} DV(T) &= F - [F - S_1(T)F_1] \\ &= S_1(T)F_1. \end{aligned}$$

Expression (19.36) is an example of a put option on the minimum of two risky assets. ∎

Formalization

Here we generalize the preceding example. Consider two foreign currency spot exchange rates, $S_1(t)$ and $S_2(t)$, the dollar being the numeraire. These spot exchange rates are, in general, correlated. We denote the correlation coefficient by ρ (rho). Given this notation, we are ready to discuss options on the minimum and maximum of these two spot exchange rates.

Call Option on the Minimum

We examine in this section a call **option on the minimum of the two spot exchange rates**.

The option expires at date T and the strike price is K. The payoff at expiration to a call option on the minimum of two spot exchange rates is defined by

$$C\,\text{Min}(T) \equiv \begin{cases} \text{Min}[S_1(T), S_2(T)] - K & \text{if} \quad \text{Min}[S_1(T), S_2(T)] > K \\ 0 & \text{if} \quad \text{Min}[S_1(T), S_2(T)] \le K. \end{cases} \tag{19.37}$$

If the minimum of the two spot exchange rates exceeds the strike price K, the call is exercised with value $\text{Min}[S_1(T), S_2(T)] - K$. Otherwise, it ends up out-of-the-money and worthless.

We can value this option using the risk-neutral pricing method of Chapter 6. In this approach, the call's value is its discounted expected payoff at maturity T under the martingale probabilities. Performing this calculation, we can show that the date-0 value of the call option today on the minimum of two spot exchange rates is

$$\begin{aligned} C\,\text{Min}(0) = {}& S_1(0)B_1(0, T)N_2[h_1, h_3, (\rho\sigma_2 - \sigma_1)/\sigma] \\ & + S_2(0)B_2(0, T)N_2[h_2, h_4, (\rho\sigma_1 - \sigma_2)/\sigma] \\ & - KB(0, T)N_2[h_1 - \sigma_1\sqrt{T}, h_2 - \sigma_2\sqrt{T}, \rho], \end{aligned} \tag{19.38}$$

where

$$h_1 \equiv \{\ln[B_1(0,T)S_1(0)/B(0,T)K] + (\sigma_1^2/2)T\}/(\sigma_1\sqrt{T})$$
$$h_2 \equiv \{\ln[B_2(0,T)S_2(0)/B(0,T)K] + (\sigma_2^2/2)T\}/(\sigma_2\sqrt{T})$$
$$h_3 \equiv \{\ln[B_2(0,T)S_2(0)/B_1(0,T)S_1(0)] - (\sigma^2/2)T\}/(\sigma\sqrt{T})$$
$$h_4 \equiv \{\ln[B_1(0,T)S_1(0)/B_2(0,T)S_2(0)] - (\sigma^2/2)T\}/(\sigma\sqrt{T})$$
$$\sigma^2 = \sigma_1^2 - 2\rho\sigma_1\sigma_2 + \sigma_2^2,$$

ρ being the correlation coefficient between proportional changes in $S_1(t)$ and $S_2(t)$.

A similar argument is applied for a put option on the minimum of two spot exchange rates. For this reason, our presentation for put options will be brief.

Put Option on the Minimum

We examine here a put option on the minimum of two spot exchange rates. The option expires at date T and the strike price is K. The payoff at expiration to a put option on the minimum of two spot exchange rates is defined by

$$P\,\text{Min}(T) \equiv \begin{cases} K - \text{Min}[S_1(T), S_2(T)] & \text{if} & K > \text{Min}[S_1(T), S_2(T)] \\ 0 & \text{if} & K \le \text{Min}[S_1(T), S_2(T)]. \end{cases} \tag{19.39}$$

With some algebra, we can rewrite this put on the minimum as a portfolio of calls on the minimum. Algebra yields

$$P\,\text{Min}(T) = \begin{cases} K - \text{Min}[S_1(T), S_2(T)] & \text{if} & K > \text{Min}[S_1(T), S_2(T)] \\ K - \text{Min}[S_1(T), S_2(T)] & \text{if} & K \le \text{Min}[S_1(T), S_2(T)] \end{cases}$$
$$- \begin{cases} 0 & \text{if} & K > \text{Min}[S_1(T), S_2(T)] \\ K - \text{Min}[S_1(T), S_2(T)] & \text{if} & K \le \text{Min}[S_1(T), S_2(T)] \end{cases}$$
$$= K - \text{Min}[S_1(T), S_2(T)] + C\,\text{Min}[S_1(T), S_2(T), 0; K]. \tag{19.40}$$

Expression (19.40) is the desired result. The put on the minimum is seen to be the sum of three terms. The first term is K dollars (a bond). The second term on the right can be considered as a call option on the minimum with a strike price of zero. The third term is a call option on the minimum. Thus a put option on the minimum is equivalent to K bonds less a call on the minimum with a strike price of 0 plus a call on the minimum with a strike price of K. Hence the value of the put option today is

$$P\,\text{Min}(0) = KB(0,T) - C\,\text{Min}(0,0) + C\,\text{Min}(0,K), \tag{19.41}$$

where $C\,\text{Min}(0,K)$ is the time-0 value of the call on a minimum of two assets with a strike price of K, and

$$C\operatorname{Min}(0,0) = S_1(0)B_1(0,T)N(h_3) + S_2(0)B_2(0,T)N(h_4).$$

This completes our analysis of put options on the minimum of two spot exchange rates.

Call Option on the Maximum

We study here a call option on the maximum of two spot exchange rates. The option expires at date T and the strike price of the option is K. The payoff at expiration to a call option on the maximum of two spot exchange rates is defined by

$$C\operatorname{Max}(T) \equiv \begin{cases} \operatorname{Max}[S_1(T), S_2(T)] - K & \text{if} & \operatorname{Max}[S_1(T), S_2(T)] > K \\ 0 & \text{if} & \operatorname{Max}[S_1(T), S_2(T)] \leq K. \end{cases} \tag{19.42}$$

If the maximum of the two spot exchange rates exceeds the strike price K, the call ends up in-the-money, and it is exercised with value $\operatorname{Max}[S_1(T), S_2(T)] - K$. Otherwise, it expires worthless.

Fortunately, we can use our previous results to price such an option. To do so, we simply manipulate the payoff Expression (19.42) until we obtain an expression we recognize. By definition,

$$\begin{aligned} \operatorname{Max}[S_1(T), S_2(T)] &= \begin{cases} S_1(T) & \text{if} & S_1(T) > S_2(T) \\ S_2(T) & \text{if} & S_1(T) \leq S_2(T) \end{cases} \\ &= S_1(T) + S_2(T) - \begin{cases} S_2(T) & \text{if} & S_1(T) > S_2(T) \\ S_1(T) & \text{if} & S_1(T) \leq S_2(T) \end{cases} \\ &= S_1(T) + S_2(T) - \operatorname{Min}[S_1(T), S_2(T)]. \end{aligned} \tag{19.43}$$

Substitution of Expression (19.43) into (19.42) yields

$$C\operatorname{Max}(T) = \begin{cases} S_1(T) + S_2(T) - \operatorname{Min}[S_1(T), S_2(T)] - K & \text{if } \operatorname{Max}[S_1(T), S_2(T)] > K \\ 0 & \text{if } \operatorname{Max}[S_1(T), S_2(T)] \leq K. \end{cases}$$

We need to consider five cases.

(i)   If $S_1(T) \geq S_2(T) > K$, then $C\operatorname{Max}(T) = S_1(T) - K$,
(ii)   if $S_2(T) \geq S_1(T) > K$, then $C\operatorname{Max}(T) = S_2(T) - K$,
(iii) if $S_1(T) > K \geq S_2(T)$, then $C\operatorname{Max}(T) = S_1(T) - K$,
(iv)   if $S_2(T) > K \geq S_1(T)$, then $C\operatorname{Max}(T) = S_2(T) - K$,   and
(v)   if $K \geq \operatorname{Max}[S_1(T), S_2(T)]$, then $C\operatorname{Max}(T) = 0$.

These five cases imply that we can rewrite the previous payoff as

$$\begin{aligned} C\operatorname{Max}(T) = {} & \operatorname{Max}[S_1(T) - K, 0] + \operatorname{Max}[S_2(T) - K, 0] \\ & - \operatorname{Max}\{\operatorname{Min}[S_1(T), S_2(T)] - K, 0\}. \end{aligned}$$

For example, suppose $S_1(T) \geq S_2(T) > K$; then the above expression yields

$$[S_1(T) - K] + [S_2(T) - K] - [S_2(T) - K] = S_1(T) - K,$$

which agrees with case (i). Cases (ii) to (v) can be verified in a similar manner.

This calculation shows that a call on the maximum of two spot exchange rates is equivalent to an ordinary call on the first spot exchange rate plus an ordinary call on the second spot exchange rate less a call on the minimum of the two spot exchange rates.

Therefore, the value of the call option on the maximum today is

$$C \, \text{Max}(0) = c[0, S_1(0)] + c[0, S_2(0)] - C \, \text{Min}(0), \tag{19.44}$$

where $c[0, S_1(0)]$ is the time-0 value of a foreign currency call option on S_1 that matures at date T and with strike K. A similar definition applies for $c[0, S_2(0)]$. Given that we have already derived pricing formulas for all the call options in Expression (19.44), our discussion of call options on the maximum of two spot exchange rates is complete.

Put Option on the Maximum

Here we discuss put options on the maximum of two spot exchange rates. Because the arguments are analogous to those used for calls, our presentation will be brief. The option expires at date T and the strike price of the option is K. The payoff at expiration to a put option on the maximum is defined by

$$P \, \text{Max}(T) \equiv \begin{cases} K - \text{Max}[S_1(T), S_2(T)] & \text{if} \quad K > \text{Max}[S_1(T), S_2(T)] \\ 0 & \text{if} \quad K \leq \text{Max}[S_1(T), S_2(T)]. \end{cases} \tag{19.45}$$

Using Expression (19.43), we can rewrite the payoff in Expression (19.45) as

$$\begin{aligned} P \, \text{Max}(T) = {} & \text{Max}[K - S_1(T), 0] + \text{Max}[K - S_2(T), 0] \\ & - \text{Max}[K - \text{Min}(S_1(T), S_2(T)), 0]. \end{aligned}$$

This calculation shows that a put option on the maximum of two spot exchange rates is equivalent to an ordinary put on the first spot exchange rate plus an ordinary put on the second spot exchange rate less a put option on the minimum of two spot exchange rates.

Therefore, the value of the put option today is

$$P \, \text{Max}(0) = p[0, S_1(0)] + p[0, S_2(0)] - P \, \text{Min}(0), \tag{19.46}$$

where $p[0, S_1(0)]$ is the time-0 value of a foreign currency put option on S_1 that matures at date T. A similar definition applies for $p[0, S_2(0)]$. Given that we have previously derived pricing formulas for the put options in Expression (19.46), this completes the derivation. We illustrate the use of these formulas through an example.

EXAMPLE

Call on the Maximum (Continued)

We now illustrate computing the value of a call option on the maximum of two spot exchange rates. We return to the example given at the start of this section.

A zero-coupon bond matures in 90 days' time and will pay either 100 dollars, 161 Deutsche marks, or 65 pounds sterling. The bondholder has the option to choose the currency of payment. As we previously explained, this option is a call option on the maximum of two spot exchange rates.

To value this option, we use the program Exotic/Maximum. Input data is summarized in Table 19.7, Part A.

To value this option, we require the correlation coefficient between the dollar/Deutsche mark spot exchange rate and dollar/sterling spot exchange rate. In practice, there can be substantial variation in the estimates one finds for the correlation coefficients. These differences are due to different estimation procedures. Consequently, we value the option over a range of correlation values.

TABLE 19.7   *Pricing Options on the Maximum of Two Risky Outcomes*

PART A DATA INPUT	$/DEUTSCHE MARK	$/STERLING
Spot Exchange Rate	0.6226	1.5305
Discount Rate*	4.56 percent	4.70 percent
Volatility**	2.8 percent	3.5 percent
Principal	161	65
Maturity	90 days	
Domestic Discount Rate*	4.11 percent	
Exercise Price	100	

*A 360-day year is assumed.
**A 365-day year is assumed.

PART B OUTPUT	
CORRELATION COEFFICIENT	OPTION VALUE*
0	0.8941
0.25	0.8472
0.50	0.7912
0.75	0.7195

*The program Exotic/Maximum is used.

The output is shown in Table 19.7, Part B. Observe that the option value is sensitive to changes in the correlation coefficient, which implies that accurate estimation of correlation coefficients will be important for pricing options on the minimum or maximum of two spot exchange rates.   ■

19.6 SUMMARY

In this chapter we examine a number of non-standard or exotic options on foreign currencies: digital options, paylater options, compound options, chooser options, and options on the maximum or minimum of two risky assets. All these options are path-independent, implying that their value at maturity does not depend on the path taken by the spot exchange rate prior to maturity. This path independence simplifies the valuation of such options. Non-standard (exotic) options that are path-dependent are studied in the next chapter.

Given the assumptions that the spot exchange rates are lognormally distributed and that the domestic and foreign term structures are constant, closed form solutions exist for the path-independent options that we consider. These solutions simplify the analysis and facilitate computer implementation. Although this chapter emphasizes foreign currency exotic options, these techniques can be applied to stock index or commodity exotic options as well. The extension is analogous to the way in which we extend the material from Chapter 11 on foreign currency options to the material in Chapter 12 on stock index and commodity options. We leave this straightforward extension to the reader.

REFERENCES

General reference:
Haug, E. G., 1997. *Option Pricing Formulas.* New York: McGraw-Hill.

Paylater options:
Turnbull, S. M., 1992. "The Price is Right." *Risk* 5, 56–57.

Compound options:
Drezner, Z., and G. O. Wesolousky, 1990. "On the Computation of the Bivariate Normal Integral." *Journal of Statistical Computer Simulation* 35, 101–107.
Geske, R., 1979. "The Valuation of Compound Options." *Journal of Financial Economics* 7, 63–81.
Rubinstein, M., 199/2. "Double Trouble." *Risk* 5, 73.

Chooser options:
Rubinstein, M., 1991. "Options For the Undecided." *Risk* 4, 43.

Options on the maximum or minimum of two risky outcomes:
Rubinstein, M., 1991. "Somewhere Over the Rainbow." *Risk* 4, 63–66.
Stulz, R. M., 1982. "Options on the Minimum or Maximum of Two Risky Assets:
Analysis and Applications." *Journal of Financial Economics* 10, 161–186.

QUESTIONS

Question 1   Digital Options

Show that for European digital options, the following results hold. For a call option,

$$DC[S(0), T; K] \le B(0, T),$$

and for a put option,

$$DC[S(0), T; K] \le B(0, T).$$

Question 2   Range Digitals

The payoff at maturity to a European range digital option is defined by

$$RD[S(T), 0; K_L, K_U] \equiv \begin{cases} 1 & \text{if} & K_U \ge S(T) > K_L \\ 0 & \text{if} & \text{otherwise,} \end{cases}$$

where $K_U > K_L > 0$. Show that this payoff can be expressed as a linear combination of two European digital calls. [Hint: Draw a figure representing the payoff.]

Question 3   Chooser Option

Consider a chooser option written on a call option that matures at date T_1 and strike price K_1, and a put option with the same maturity date and strike price. The chooser option matures at date $T \le T_1$. Show that the value of the chooser option today is given by

$$co(S, T) = p(S, T_1; K_1) + B_f(T, T_1)c(S, T; K),$$

where $K \equiv K_1 B(T, T_1)/B_f(T, T_1)$.

Question 4

An American company has issued debt with a face value of 10 million pounds sterling. The debt matures in 66 days' time. The company is concerned about the dollar cost of repaying the principal. One possibility is to purchase a European digital option.

You are given the following information.

Spot Exchange Rate	158.40 cents/pound	
Implied Volatility	11.87 percent	(365-day year)
U.S. Discount Rate	5.72 percent	(360-day year)
U.K. Discount Rate	5.99 percent	(360-day year)

a) Should the company buy a call digital option or a put digital option?
b) If the strike price is set at 159 cents/pound, what is the price of the option, assuming a face value of $100? What is the cost of carry? The face value of the option is $300,000.
c) Consider what might happen at maturity. Fill in the following table.

POSSIBLE SPOT EXCHANGE RATES	DOLLAR COST OF PRINCIPAL	VALUE OF DIGITAL FX OPTION	NET COST*
$/£		$	$
1.55			
1.58			
1.61			
1.64			

*Net Cost ≡ Dollar Cost of Principal Value of Options + Cost of Carry

Question 5

An institution has written a digital put option. The maturity of the option, its strike price, and relevant data are described in Question 4.

a) Determine the value of the put option and its delta.
b) The institution invests n pounds in the U.K. riskless asset and B dollars in the U.S. riskless asset. Use the program Exotic/Digital to describe the hedged portfolio.
c) Compute the value of the hedged position over the range of possible spot exchange rates. Fill in the following table.

SPOT EXCHANGE RATE (CENTS/£)	OPTION VALUE	VALUE OF HEDGE PORTFOLIO
155		
158.4		
160		
165		

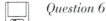

Question 6

Using the information in Question 4, an alternative strategy for the company is to buy a paylater option. The strike price is set at $1.59/£.

a) Should the company buy a call or put paylater option?
b) What is the premium of the option? Use the program Exotic/Paylater/Price European.
c) Consider what might happen at maturity. Fill in the following table. The face value of the option is chosen to be 10 million pounds.

POSSIBLE SPOT EXCHANGE RATE	DOLLAR COST OF PRINCIPAL	DOLLAR VALUE OF OPTION	NET COST
1.55			
1.58			
1.61			
1.64			
1.67			

Question 7

An institution has sold a chooser option. Details of the option follow. Information about two ordinary options is also provided.

a) Using these options, show how to construct a delta neutral position.
b) Suppose that the spot exchange rate moves from 158 cents/pound to 162 cents/pound. How does the hedge perform? Compute the value of the chooser option and the value of the hedged portfolio.

Information

Spot Exchange Rate	158 cents/pound	
Implied Volatility	12 percent	(365-day year)
U.S. Discount Rate	4.50 percent	(360-day year)
U.K. Discount Rate	5.60 percent	(360-day year)

Chooser option

Face Value   100

Maturity   135 days

Underlying Call Option
    Exercise Price   160 cents/pound
    Maturity   30 days

Underlying Put Option
    Exercise Price   160 cents/pound
    Maturity   30 days

Two ordinary options

1. Type   European Call
    Exercise Price   158 cents/pound
    Maturity   92 days

2. Type   European Put
    Exercise Price   158 cents/pound
    Maturity   92 days

 Question 8

An American firm is buying equipment costing 10 million Deutsche marks. The sale will be completed in 49 days' time. Management is concerned about the Deutsche mark appreciating against the dollar.

a) One possibility is to buy an ordinary European at-the-money FX option. Use the information in Table 19.6 and the program FX/Pricing/European Option to price such an option.
b) Some members of the management team think that over the next few weeks, the dollar will strengthen against the Deutsche mark, hence they are thinking of purchasing a compound call option written on a call. The maturity of the compound option is 30 days. The maturity of the underlying call option is 19 days and its strike price is 63.03 cents/DM. Complete the following valuation table for this compound option. Relevant volatility and interest rates are given in Table 19.6. Use the program Exotic/Compound/Option on a Call.

COMPOUND OPTION STRIKE PRICE	COMPOUND OPTION VALUE	DELTA
0.10		
0.15		
0.20		

c) Which of the two alternatives would you recommend, and why?
d) In the above table, you will find that delta is positive. Does this make intuitive sense?

Non-Standard (Exotic) Options: Path-Dependent

20.0 INTRODUCTION

In this chapter we continue our study of exotic options under the assumptions of Chapter 11. Here, we consider three types of non-standard options on foreign currencies: barrier options, lookback options, and average options. These options are path-dependent because the value of the option at its maturity date depends on the path taken by the spot exchange rate over the life of the option, complicating the valuation of such options. In all cases we use the risk-neutral valuation Expression (6.4) of Chapter 6. For the first two types of exotic options, it is possible to derive a closed form solution for the value of the option. This is not the case for average options, although it is possible to derive an approximate closed form solution. As in Chapter 19, we assume here that (1) the spot exchange rate (domestic per unit of foreign currency) is lognormally distributed, and (2) domestic and foreign interest rates are constant. These two assumptions facilitate the derivation of closed form solutions (in some cases) that are easily programmed on a computer.

20.1 BARRIER OPTIONS

Here we study **barrier options**. The value of a barrier option depends on whether the underlying spot exchange rate crosses some prespecified upper level in the case of up-and-in and up-and-out options, or some prespecified lower level in the case of down-and-in and down-and-out options. We study each of these options in turn.

Down-and-Out Options

Here we look at **down-and-out options**.[1] For a down-and-out option, a lower barrier is specified. If the spot exchange rate falls below this lower barrier during the life of the option, the option ceases to exist. An example will help illustrate the usefulness of down-and-out options.

---

[1]These options are often called **knock-out options**.

Down-and-Out Call Option

Consider a company that must make a payment in 51 days' time of 200 million French francs. The company is concerned that the franc may appreciate against the dollar over this period.

To insure against this risk the company could purchase an ordinary foreign currency European call option, allowing it to purchase French francs at a fixed price. Over the next 51 days it is quite possible that the franc may depreciate against the dollar. If this happens, the company may feel that it no longer wants the insurance provided by the ordinary call option.

Instead of purchasing an ordinary call option, the company could purchase a down-and-out call option at a lower cost. If the spot exchange rate never falls below the lower barrier over the life of the option, then at the maturity of the option the company owns an ordinary call option. If, over the life of the option, the spot exchange falls below the lower barrier, the down-and-out call option ceases to exist.

We should note that if the company purchases a down-and-out call option, it is exposed to an additional risk. It is possible over the next 51 days for the franc to first depreciate against the dollar, crossing the lower barrier, so that the down-and-out call option ceases to exist. But afterwards, and prior to 51 days, it is then possible for the franc to appreciate against the dollar. If this happens, the company may have to undertake further action to limit its exposure. ■

Figure 20.1 shows a particular history of a spot exchange rate. In this figure, the spot exchange rate crosses the lower barrier twice. When the spot exchange rate crosses the lower barrier for the first time, the down-and-out option ceases to exist.

The time it takes from the present for the barrier to be crossed is referred to as a **stopping time**. A stopping time is random because we do not know when the barrier will be crossed. The introduction of the concept of a stopping time provides us with an elegant way to describe the different forms of barrier options.

Let Γ denote the stopping time, defined as the time it takes from the present to cross the barrier for the first time. To indicate whether the down-and-out option is still in existence, we can use an indicator function. Let T denote the maturity of the option. Define the indicator function by

$$\mathbf{1}(\Gamma > T) \equiv \begin{cases} 1 & \text{if} & \text{the barrier is not crossed by date } T, (\Gamma > T) \\ 0 & \text{if} & \text{the barrier has been crossed by date } T, (\Gamma \leq T). \end{cases}$$

$$(20.1)$$

In Figure 20.1, one realization of the stopping time is shown. In this case, the stopping time is less than the maturity of the option, $(\Gamma < T)$.

For down-and-out options, sometimes a rebate is provided if the barrier is crossed. The magnitude of the rebate (possibly zero) is specified when the contract is initiated.

FIGURE 20.1 *Down-and-Out Option*

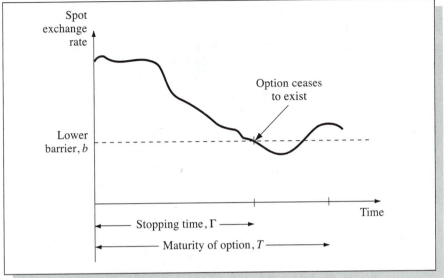

Call option

We now consider the pricing of a **down-and-out call option**. For the moment we ignore any rebate.

Consider a down-and-out call option that matures at date T with strike price K. The lower barrier is denoted by b. The value of a down-and-out call option at maturity is defined by the payoff:

$$DOC(T) \equiv \mathbf{1}(\Gamma > T)\mathrm{Max}[S(T) - K, 0]. \tag{20.2}$$

If the barrier has not been crossed, $(\Gamma > T)$, then $\mathbf{1}(\Gamma > T) = 1$ and we have the payoff to an ordinary call option. If the barrier has been crossed, $(\Gamma \leq T)$, then $\mathbf{1}(\Gamma > T) = 0$ and the payoff to the option is zero, regardless of the level of the spot exchange rate at date T.

The value of a down-and-out call option will never be greater than an ordinary call option with the same strike price and maturity because the value of the down-and-out call option depends on the probability of the barrier being crossed, and this probability is usually greater than zero. The greater the probability of the barrier being crossed, the lower the value of the option. The value of an ordinary call is independent of the probability of the barrier being crossed.

The value of a down-and-out call option is derived using the risk-neutral pricing method of Chapter 6. The down-and-out call option is the discounted expected value

of its payoff at expiration. For the lower barrier less than the strike price, that is, $b \leq K$, the value of a down-and-out call option is

$$
\begin{aligned}
DOC(0) &= B(0,T)E^{\pi}[DOC(T)] \\
&= B_f(0,T)S(0)N(d_1) - B(0,T)KN(d_1 - \sigma\sqrt{T}) \\
&\quad - \{B_f(0,T)S(0)[b/S(0)]^{2\eta+1}N(d_2) \\
&\quad - B(0,T)K[b/S(0)]^{2\eta-1}N(d_2 - \sigma\sqrt{T})\},
\end{aligned}
\tag{20.3}
$$

where

$$
\begin{aligned}
d_1 &\equiv \{\ln[B_f(0,T)S(0)/B(0,T)K] + (\sigma^2/2)T\}/(\sigma\sqrt{T}) \\
d_2 &\equiv \{\ln[B_f(0,T)b^2)/(B(0,T)S(0)K] + (\sigma^2/2)T\}/(\sigma\sqrt{T}) \\
\eta &\equiv (r - r_f)/\sigma^2, r \neq r_f.
\end{aligned}
$$

For the lower barrier greater than the strike price, that is, $b > K$, the value is

$$
\begin{aligned}
DOC(0) &= B_f(0,T)S(0)N(d_3) - B(0,T)bN(d_3 - \sigma\sqrt{T}) \\
&\quad + B(0,T)(b - K)N(d_3 - \sigma\sqrt{T}) \\
&\quad - \{B_f(0,T)S(0)[b/S(0)]^{2\eta+1}N(d_4) \\
&\quad - B(0,T)K[b/S(0)]^{2\eta-1}N(d_4 - \sigma\sqrt{T})\},
\end{aligned}
\tag{20.4}
$$

where

$$
\begin{aligned}
d_3 &\equiv \{\ln[B_f(0,T)S(0)/B(0,T)b] + (\sigma^2/2)T\}/(\sigma\sqrt{T}) \\
d_4 &\equiv \{\ln[B_f(0,T)b/B(0,T)S(0)] + (\sigma^2/2)T\}/(\sigma\sqrt{T}).
\end{aligned}
$$

If a rebate is paid to the option when the barrier is crossed, the down-and-out option's value is increased by the value of the rebate. If the rebate is denoted by R_d, the value of the rebate is given by its discounted expected value, which we can show equals

$$
R_d\{[b/S(0)]^{\alpha_1}N(d_5) - [b/S(0)]^{\alpha_2}N(d_6)\},
\tag{20.5}
$$

where

$$
\begin{aligned}
d_5 &\equiv \{\ln[b/S(0)] + T\beta_1\}/(\sigma\sqrt{T}) \\
d_6 &\equiv \{\ln[b/S(0)] - T\beta_1\}/(\sigma\sqrt{T}) \\
\alpha_1 &\equiv \eta - 1/2 + \beta_1/\sigma^2 \\
\alpha_2 &\equiv \eta - 1/2 - \beta_1/\sigma^2 \\
\beta_1 &\equiv [(r - r_f - \sigma^2/2)^2 + 2r\sigma^2]^{1/2}.
\end{aligned}
$$

We illustrate the valuation of this formula in Figure 20.2. The value of a down-and-out call option is compared to the value of an ordinary European call with the same strike and maturity in Figure 20.2. If the current spot exchange rate is far

greater than the barrier, the value of the two options is approximately equal. In this case, the probability of the barrier being crossed approaches zero and has a negligible effect. If the spot exchange rate is just slightly greater than the barrier, the probability of the barrier being crossed is significant and the value of the down-and-out call option is less than the value of the ordinary call.

Put option

We next consider the valuation of a **down-and-out put option**. Because the argument is analogous to that used for the down-and-out call option, our discussion will be brief.

Consider a down-and-out put option that matures at date T with strike K and barrier b. The value of a down-and-out put option at maturity is defined by the payoff:

$$DOP(T) \equiv \mathbf{1}(\Gamma > T)\mathrm{Max}[K - S(T), 0]. \tag{20.6}$$

If the barrier has not been crossed, $(\Gamma > T)$, then $\mathbf{1}(\Gamma > T) = 1$ and we have the payoff to an ordinary put option. If the barrier has been crossed, $(\Gamma \le T)$, then $\mathbf{1}(\Gamma > T) = 0$ and the value of the option is zero, regardless of the level of the spot exchange rate.

Closed form solutions similar in nature to Expressions (20.3) and (20.4) can be derived for the value of a down-and-out put prior to maturity. We do not list these formulas in the text; however, the formulas are computable with the software.

FIGURE 20.2 *Down-and-Out Call*

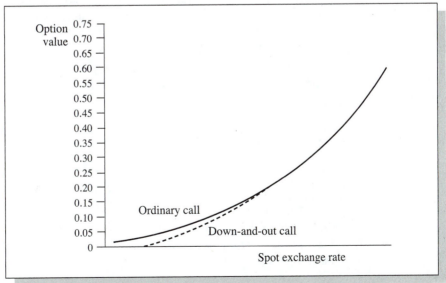

EXAMPLE

Down-and-Out Call

We illustrate in this example the computation of a down-and-out call option's value.

Consider a company that must make a payment in 51 days' time of 200 million French francs on the principal of a Euro French franc bond. The current spot exchange rate ($/FF) is 18.213 cents per French franc. The company is concerned that the French franc may appreciate against the dollar and increase the dollar cost of purchasing 200 million French francs.

The company is thinking of either purchasing an ordinary foreign currency call option or a down-and-out call. The barrier is set at 17.50 cents per French franc. The company's treasurer thinks that if the spot exchange rate went that low during the next 51 days, the spot exchange rate risk at the payment date would be acceptable.

Input data is given in Table 20.1. Using the program FX/Pricing/ European Option, the value of the ordinary call option is 0.0462 cents per French franc. Therefore, the total cost is

$$\text{Ordinary Call Option} = \$0.0462 \times (200,000,000/100)$$
$$= \$92,400,$$

where we divide by 100 to convert the price of the option from cents to dollars.

Using the program Exotic/Barrier/Down-Out, the value of the down-and-out call is 0.0453 cents per French franc. Therefore, the total cost is

$$\text{Down-and-Out Call Option} = \$0.0453 \times (200,000,000/100)$$
$$= \$90,600.$$

If the treasurer uses the down-and-out call, there is a savings of $1,800 compared to using the ordinary call. However, there is additional risk. It is always possible for the spot exchange rate to go down below the barrier level, thus knocking out the down-and-out call, and then increase. ∎

TABLE 20.1 *Down-and-Out Call*

INPUT DATA	
Spot Exchange Rate	18.213 cents/FF
Strike Price	19.50 cents/FF
Lower Barrier	17.50 cents/FF
Maturity	51 days
Volatility*	14.4 percent
Domestic Discount Rate**	4.18 percent
French Discount Rate**	5.24 percent

  *This is quoted on a 365-day basis.

**This is quoted on a 360-day basis.

Down-and-In Options

Here we examine **down-and-in options**.[2] Down-and-in options become active only if the spot exchange rate goes below the barrier b. Therefore, the payoff to the option is contingent on the event that the barrier b must be crossed at least once during the life of the option.

The value of a down-and-in option will never be greater than an ordinary option with the same strike price and maturity. Why? Because the value of the down-and-in option only matches the ordinary option's payoff if the barrier is crossed at least once. The probability that the barrier is crossed is usually less than one. We illustrate the use of down-and-in options through an example.

EXAMPLE | **Down-and-In Put Option**

Consider a company that expects to receive a payment of 100 million French francs in 47 days' time. The company is concerned that the French franc may depreciate against the dollar, given political uncertainty about upcoming presidential elections. One form of insurance would be for the firm to purchase a put option on the French franc.

Recently, the franc has been appreciating against the dollar, and the company expects this general trend to continue. The company decides to purchase a down-and-in put option. If the company is right and the franc continues to appreciate against the dollar, the put option will never come into existence. However, if the franc depreciates against the dollar such that the lower barrier is crossed, the put option will come into existence and provide the company with the required insurance. The cost of the down-and-in put option will never be greater than that of an ordinary put option with the same strike price and maturity date. ∎

Call option

Now we examine the pricing of a **down-and-in call option**. Again, it is convenient to use an indicator function. Define the indicator function by

$$\mathbf{1}(\Gamma \le T) = \begin{cases} 1 & \text{if} \quad \text{the barrier is crossed by date } T, (\Gamma \le T) \\ 0 & \text{if} \quad \text{the barrier has not been crossed by date } T, (\Gamma > T). \end{cases}$$

Consider an option that matures at date T with strike price K and barrier b. The value of a down-and-in call option at its maturity is defined by its payoff:

$$DIC(T) \equiv \mathbf{1}(\Gamma \le T)\text{Max}[S(T) - K, 0]. \tag{20.7}$$

If the barrier is crossed during the life of the option, $(\Gamma \le T)$, then $\mathbf{1}(\Gamma \le T) = 1$ and we have the payoff to an ordinary call option. If the barrier is not crossed, $(\Gamma > T)$,

---

[2]These options are often called **knock-in options**.

then $\mathbf{1}(\Gamma \leq T) = 0$ and the payoff to the option is zero, regardless of the level of the spot exchange rate.

We value the down-and-in call option by showing its equivalence to an ordinary call option less a down-and-out call option. There is an intrinsic relation between down-and-in and down-and-out options, assuming that for both options the rebate is zero. This relation can be seen as follows. During the life of the option, either the barrier is crossed or it is not crossed. Using the indicator functions defined by Expressions (20.1) and (20.7), we can write

$$1 = \mathbf{1}(\Gamma \leq T) + \mathbf{1}(\Gamma > T). \tag{20.8}$$

Substituting Expression (20.8) into Expression (20.7) enables us to rewrite the payoff to a down-and-in call option as

$$
\begin{aligned}
DIC(T) &= [1 - \mathbf{1}(\Gamma > T)]\text{Max}[S(T) - K, 0] \\
&= \text{Max}[S(T) - K, 0] - \mathbf{1}(\Gamma > T)\text{Max}[S(T) - K, 0]. \tag{20.9}
\end{aligned}
$$

The first term on the right represents the payoff to an ordinary call option, and the second term is the payoff to a down-and-out call option. This gives us the desired equivalence relation between a down-and-in call option and an ordinary call option less a down-and-out call.

Let us check the validity of Expression (20.9). Suppose that over the life of the down-and-in option the barrier is never crossed, $(\Gamma > T)$. Therefore, by definition the left side of Expression (20.9), the value of the option, is zero: it never kicks in. On the right side of Expression (20.9) we are long an ordinary call option and short a down-and-out call. This down-and-out option has not been kicked out, $(\Gamma > T)$, so its payoff is identical to an ordinary call option. Hence the two options cancel out and the net value is zero. Both sides of Expression (20.9) are equal to zero.

Now suppose that over the life of the down-and-in option, the barrier is crossed, $(\Gamma \leq T)$. Therefore, the left side of Expression (20.9), the value of the option, is equal to that of an ordinary call option. On the right side of Expression (20.9) the down-and-out option ceases to exist, $(\Gamma \leq T)$, so we are left with an ordinary call option. Again, both sides of Expression (20.9) are equal, which completes our check of the validity of Expression (20.9).

Therefore, given Expression (20.9) at any date t prior to maturity, the value of a down-and-in option is given by

$$DIC(0) = c(0) - DOC(0), \tag{20.10}$$

where $c(0)$ is the value of a European call option with strike price K and maturity date T. This equation shows that the value of a down-and-in call option is equivalent to the value of an ordinary call option less a down-and-out call option with the same strike price, maturity date, and barrier.

Put option

We next study **down-and-in put options**. Because the argument is analogous to that given for the call option, our presentation will be brief. The value of a down-and-in put option at maturity T with strike price K and barrier b is defined by

$$DIP(T) \equiv \mathbf{1}(\Gamma \leq T)\text{Max}[K - S(T), 0]. \tag{20.11}$$

Repeating the logic used to derive Expression (20.9) gives

$$DIP(T) = \text{Max}[K - S(T), 0] - \mathbf{1}(\Gamma > T)\text{Max}[K - S(T), 0]. \tag{20.12}$$

The first term on the right represents the payoff to an ordinary put option, and the second term is the payoff to a down-and-out put option. Therefore, prior to maturity,

$$DIP(0) = p(0) - DOP(0), \tag{20.13}$$

where $p(0)$ is the value of a European put option with strike price K and maturity date T. This expression shows the equivalence between a down-and-in put option and an ordinary put option less a down-and-out put option with the same strike price, maturity date, and barrier.

Up-and-Out Options

Here we study **up-and-out options**. For an up-and-out option an upper barrier is specified. If the spot exchange rate goes above this barrier during the life of the option, the option ceases to exist, as shown in Figure 20.3. For up-and-out options, a rebate may be provided if the barrier is crossed. The magnitude of the rebate (possibly zero) is specified when the contract is initiated. We illustrate the usefulness of up-and-out options through an example.

EXAMPLE

Up-and-Out Put Option

Consider a U.S. company that is receiving a payment of 100 million Japanese yen in 30 days' time. The current spot exchange rate is $0.011009 per yen. The company faces the risk that the yen will depreciate against the dollar. Recently, the yen has been appreciating against the dollar, and the company feels that if the spot exchange rate reaches the level $0.011047 per yen, its risk exposure will be negligible. The company decides to buy an up-and-out put option, the upper barrier being $0.011047 per year. If this barrier is not reached, the company effectively owns a put option that provides it with the insurance against the yen depreciating.

FIGURE 20.3 *Up-and-Out Option*

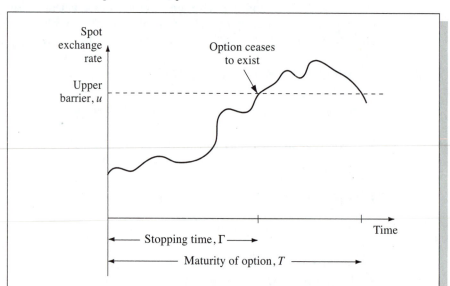

Note that the purchase of an up-and-out put option still leaves the company exposed to risk. It is quite possible over the next 30 days for the yen to appreciate, crossing the barrier so that the up-and-out put option ceases to exist, and then for the yen to depreciate against the dollar. If this happens, the company may have to undertake additional measures to reduce its exposure. ∎

Call option

Let us value an **up-and-out call option**. For the moment we ignore any rebate. Consider an up-and-out call option that matures at date T with strike price K. The upper barrier is denoted by u. The value of an up-and-out call option at maturity is defined by its payoff:

$$UOC(T) \equiv \mathbf{1}(\Gamma > T)\,\mathrm{Max}\,[S(T) - K, 0]. \tag{20.14}$$

If the barrier has not been crossed, $(\Gamma > T)$, then $\mathbf{1}(\Gamma > T) = 1$ and we have the payoff to an ordinary call option. If the barrier has been crossed, $(\Gamma \le T)$, then $\mathbf{1}(\Gamma > T) = 0$ and the payoff to the option is zero, regardless of the level of the spot exchange rate.

We now value the up-and-out call option at date 0. The value is determined using the risk-neutral pricing method of Chapter 6, in which the value at date t is shown to be equal to the discounted expected payoff at maturity.

For $K \geq u$, the value of an up-and-out call is always zero. Why? Because for the up-and-out call option to have value, the spot exchange rate must be greater than the strike. But this would imply that the barrier has been crossed, thus the option ceases to exist.

For $K < u$, the value of an up-and-out call option prior to maturity is given by

$$
\begin{aligned}
UOC(0) = {} & B_f(0,T)S(0)N(d_1) - B(0,T)KN(d_1 - \sigma\sqrt{T}) \\
& - [B_f(0,T)S(0)N(d_2) - B(0,T)KN(d_2 - \sigma\sqrt{T})] \\
& - [B_f(0,T)S(0)(u/S(0))^{2\eta+1}N(d_3) \\
& \quad - B(0,T)K(u/S(0))^{2\eta-1}N(d_3 - \sigma\sqrt{T})] \\
& + [B_f(0,T)S(0)(u/S(0))^{2\eta+1}N(d_4) \\
& \quad - B(0,T)K(u/S(0))^{2\eta-1}N(d_4 - \sigma\sqrt{T})],
\end{aligned}
\tag{20.15}
$$

where

$$
\begin{aligned}
d_1 & \equiv \{\ln[B_f(0,T)S(0)/KB(0,T)] + (\sigma^2/2)T\}/(\sigma\sqrt{T}) \\
d_2 & \equiv \{\ln[B_f(0,T)S(0)/uB(0,T)] + (\sigma^2/2)T\}/(\sigma\sqrt{T}) \\
d_3 & \equiv \{\ln[B_f(0,T)u^2/(B(0,T)S(0)K)] + (\sigma^2/2)T\}/(\sigma\sqrt{T}) \\
d_4 & \equiv \{\ln[B_f(0,T)u/B(0,T)S(0)] + (\sigma^2/2)T\}/(\sigma\sqrt{T}) \\
\eta & \equiv (r - r_f)/\sigma^2,\ r \neq r_f.
\end{aligned}
$$

If the up-and-out call option earns a rebate when the barrier is crossed, we need to value this rebate and add it to the value of the option. If the rebate is denoted by R_U, the value of the rebate is given by

$$
R_U\{[u/S(0)]^{\alpha_1}N(d_5) - [u/S(0)]^{\alpha_2}N(d_6)\},
\tag{20.16}
$$

where

$$
\begin{aligned}
\alpha_1 & \equiv \eta - 1/2 + \beta_1/\sigma^2 \\
\alpha_2 & \equiv \eta - 1/2 - \beta_1/\sigma^2 \\
d_5 & \equiv -\{\ln[u/S(0)] + \beta_1 T\}/(\sigma\sqrt{T}) \\
d_6 & \equiv -\{\ln[u/S(0)] - \beta_1 T\}/(\sigma\sqrt{T}) \\
\beta_1 & \equiv [(r - r_f - \sigma^2/2)^2 + 2r\sigma^2]^{1/2}.
\end{aligned}
$$

This is the discounted expected value of the rebate, paid if the barrier is crossed.

Put option

Here we price an **up-and-out put option**. Because the analysis is identical to the call, our presentation will be brief. Consider an up-and-out put option that matures at date T with strike K and barrier u.

The payoff of an up-and-out put option at maturity is given by

$$
UOP(T) \equiv \mathbf{1}(\Gamma > T)\operatorname{Max}[K - S(T), 0].
\tag{20.17}
$$

We can derive closed form solutions similar to Expression (20.15) for the value of the option prior to maturity. We do this by taking the discounted expected value of Expression (20.17). We do not provide the formula in this text, although the software can be used to compute its value.

Up-and-In Options

We now examine up-and-in options. An up-and-in option is worthless at maturity unless the spot exchange rate goes above the upper barrier u during the life of the option. An example illustrates the usefulness of up-and-in options.

EXAMPLE   **Up-and-In Call Option**

Consider a company that must pay the principal of 50 million Deutsche marks on a Eurobond that matures in 76 days' time. The company is concerned that the Deutsche mark may appreciate against the dollar. However, the company has observed that the Deutsche mark has been depreciating against the dollar, and it expects this decline to continue over the near term. If the company's expectations are correct, there would be no need for the company to buy insurance against the appreciation of the Deutsche mark.

The company decides to purchase an up-and-in call option. If the company's predictions are correct and the Deutsche mark declines against the dollar, the call option will never come into existence. If the company's predictions are incorrect and the Deutsche mark appreciates, the call option will come into existence as the upper barrier is crossed, providing the firm with insurance.   ∎

Call option

Here we show how to price an **up-and-in call option**. Consider an up-and-in call option that matures at date T with strike price K and barrier u. The payoff of an up-and-in call option at maturity is defined by

$$UIC(T) \equiv \mathbf{1}(\Gamma \leq T)\text{Max}[S(T) - K, 0]. \tag{20.18}$$

If the barrier is crossed during the life of the option, $(\Gamma \leq T)$, then $\mathbf{1}(\Gamma \leq T) = 1$ and we have the payoff to an ordinary call option. If the barrier is not crossed, $(\Gamma > T)$, then $\mathbf{1}(\Gamma \leq T) = 0$ and the payoff to the option is zero, regardless of the level of the spot exchange rate.

We value an up-and-in call option by showing that it is equivalent to an ordinary call option less an up-and-out call option. This derivation is based on an intrinsic relation between up-and-in and up-and-out options, assuming that for both options the rebate is zero. Using Expression (20.8), we can rewrite the payoff to an up-and-in call option as

$$UIC(T) = \text{Max}[S(T) - K, 0] - \mathbf{1}(\Gamma > T)UOC(T). \tag{20.19}$$

Given Expression (20.19), for any date t prior to maturity, the value of an up-and-in call option is given by

$$UIC(t) = c(t) - UOC(t), \tag{20.20}$$

where $c(t)$ is the value of a European call option with strike price K and maturity date T. This shows that the up-and-in call option is equivalent to an ordinary call option less an up-and-out call option with the same strike price, maturity date, and barrier.

Put option

Let us value an **up-and-in put option**. Since the argument is analogous to the call, our presentation will be brief. The payoff of an up-and-in put option at maturity T with strike price K and barrier u is defined by

$$UIP(T) \equiv \mathbf{1}(\Gamma \leq T)\mathrm{Max}[K - S(T), 0]. \tag{20.21}$$

Repeating what is now a familiar argument gives the value of the up-and-in put option prior to maturity as

$$UIP(0) = p(0) - UOP(0), \tag{20.22}$$

where $p(0)$ is the value of a European put option with strike price K and maturity date T. Thus an up-and-in put option is equivalent to an ordinary put option less an up-and-out put option with the same strike price, maturity date, and barrier. Our discussion of barrier options is now complete.

20.2 LOOKBACK OPTIONS

Now let us examine **lookback options**. There are two common forms of lookback options: standard lookback options and extrema lookback options (options on extrema). We discuss each of these in turn.

Standard Lookback Options

Here we study **standard lookback options**. These options are often called **no regret options** for reasons that will be apparent once they are described.

Call option

We first study a **standard lookback call option**. Consider a standard lookback call option that was initiated at date T_0, prior to the present date 0. During that time the minimum value of the spot exchange rate is observed to be m_0. Let the option mature at date T.

Let m denote the minimum value of the spot exchange rate from now until the maturity date T. We will only know the value of m when the option matures. At that

FIGURE 20.4   *Standard Lookback Call Option*

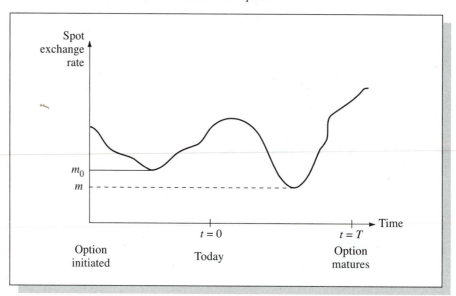

point we can look back and determine the value of m, as is shown in Figure 20.4, for example.

The payoff to the standard lookback call option at maturity is defined by

$$SLB(T) \equiv S(T) - \text{Min}(m_0, m). \tag{20.23}$$

For example, referring to Figure 20.4, the minimum value of the spot exchange rate from $t = 0$ to $t = T$ is m, which is less than m_0. In this case, therefore, the value of the standard lookback call option at maturity would be $S(T) - m$, which is positive.

In general, the payoff to the standard lookback call option will always be positive unless the minimum occurs at the maturity date. The value of the option can never be negative.

To value the standard lookback call option, we use the risk-neutral valuation method of Chapter 6. The value of the option is the expected discounted value of its payoff, as given in Expression (20.23). Thus it can be shown that the value of the option today is given by

$$\begin{aligned}
SLB(0) = &\; B_f(0, T)S(0)N(d_1) - B(0, T)m_0 N(d_1 - \sigma\sqrt{T}) \\
&+ \{B(0, T)S(0)[m_0/S(0)]^{2\eta}N(-d_1 + 2\eta\sigma\sqrt{T}) \\
&- B_f(0, T)S(0)N(-d_1)\}/(2\eta),
\end{aligned} \tag{20.24}$$

where

$$d_1 \equiv \{\ln[S(0)B_f(0,T)/m_0 B(0,T)] + (\sigma^2/2)T\}/(\sigma\sqrt{T})$$
$$\eta = (r - r_f)/\sigma^2, \qquad r \neq r_f.$$

Note that if the option is initiated at date 0, then $m_0 \equiv S(0)$. We illustrate the computation of this formula through an example.

EXAMPLE

Lookback Call

This example illustrates the valuation of a standard lookback call option.

We want to value a standard lookback call option and compare its value to that of an ordinary call option, using the information in Table 20.1. The value of the ordinary call option with the strike price set equal to the spot exchange rate is 0.3749 cents per French franc.

To value the lookback option, we use the program Exotic/Lookback/ Standard. Given that we are pricing a new lookback option, the minimum is set to the current spot exchange rate. The value of the option is 0.7504 cents per French franc. The lookback is much more expensive. The lookback option will, in general, always expire in-the-money, and the owner pays for this privilege. ■

Put option

Now we value a **standard lookback put option**. Let us consider an option that was initiated at date T_0, prior to the present date. During that time, the maximum value of the spot exchange rate that is observed is M_0. Let the option mature at date T.

Let M denote the maximum value of the spot exchange rate from now until date T. We will only know the value of M when the option matures. At that point we can look back and determine the value of M, as is shown in Figure 20.5, for example.

The payoff to the standard lookback put option at maturity is defined by

$$SLBP(T) \equiv \text{Max}(M_0, M) - S(T). \tag{20.25}$$

For example, referring to Figure 20.5, the maximum value of the spot exchange rate from $t = 0$ to $t = T$ is M. In this case it is less than M_0, so the value of the standard lookback put option at maturity would be $M_0 - S(T)$, which is positive. In general, the payoff to the lookback put option will always be positive unless the maximum occurs at the maturity date. The value of the option can never be negative.

Using the risk-neutral pricing method of Chapter 6, we can show that the value of the standard lookback put option today is given by

$$SLBP(0) = B(0,T)M_0 N(-d_2 + \sigma\sqrt{T}) - B_f(0,T)S(0)N(-d_2)$$
$$- \{B(0,T)S(0)[M_0/S(0)]^{2\eta}N(d_2 - 2\eta\sigma\sqrt{T})$$
$$- B_f(0,T)S(0)N(d_2)\}/(2\eta), \tag{20.26}$$

FIGURE 20.5 *Standard Lookback Put Option*

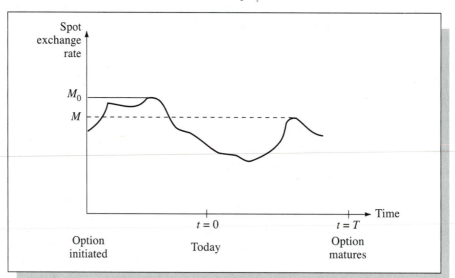

where

$$d_2 \equiv \{\ln[S(0)B_f(0,T)/M_0 B(0,T)] + (\sigma^2/2)T\}/(\sigma\sqrt{T})$$
$$\eta = (r - r_f)/\sigma^2, \qquad r \neq r_f.$$

Note that if the option is initiated at date 0, then $M_0 \equiv S(0)$.

Options on Extrema

We now examine **options on extrema**, both calls and puts.

Call option

First we study an **extrema lookback call option**. Let us consider an extrema lookback call option that was initiated at date T_0, prior to the present date. During that time the maximum value of the spot exchange rate that is observed is M_0. Let the option mature at date T and let the strike price be K. Let M denote the maximum value of the spot exchange rate from now until date T.

The payoff at maturity to an extrema lookback call option is defined by

$$ELBC(T) \equiv \begin{cases} \text{Max}(M_0, M) - K & \text{if} \quad \text{Max}(M_0, M) > K \\ 0 & \text{if} \quad \text{Max}(M_0, M) \leq K. \end{cases} \qquad (20.27)$$

For example, referring to Figure 20.5, the maximum value of the spot exchange rate from $t = 0$ to $t = T$ is M, which is less than M_0. Therefore, in this case the value of the

extrema lookback call option at maturity would be $\text{Max}\{M_0 - K, 0\}$. We illustrate the usefulness of these extrema lookback call options with an example.

EXAMPLE   **Extrema Lookback Call Options**

Consider a company that is buying Deutsche marks on a daily basis. The average quantity of marks to be purchased each day can be predicted with a high degree of accuracy, based upon experience. However, this is not the case for the spot exchange rate. The company does its accounting on a monthly basis and is concerned with the dollar amount it spends each month on its Deutsche mark purchases. If the mark appreciates against the dollar, the cost to the firm will increase.

One possible solution is for the company to purchase each month a call option on the extremum. This will provide the company with protection against the largest spot exchange rate over each month. ■

To value an extrema lookback call option, we use the risk-neutral valuation approach of Chapter 6. The value of the extrema lookback call is its discounted expected payoff. In doing this, we must consider two cases. First, if $M_0 \leq K$,

$$
\begin{aligned}
ELBC(0) = \ &B_f(0,T)S(0)N(d_3) - B(0,T)KN(d_3 - \sigma\sqrt{T}) \\
&+ \{S(0)B_f(0,T)N(d_3) \\
&\quad - B(0,T)S(0)[K/S(0)]^{2\eta}N(d_3 - 2\eta\sigma\sqrt{T})\}/(2\eta),
\end{aligned}
\tag{20.28}
$$

where

$$
\begin{aligned}
&d_3 \equiv \{\ln[S(0)B_f(0,T)/KB(0,T)] + (\sigma^2/2)T\}/(\sigma\sqrt{T}) \\
&\eta \equiv (r - r_f)/\sigma^2, \qquad r \neq r_f.
\end{aligned}
$$

Second, if $M_0 > K$, the extrema lookback call option will always mature in-the-money because

$$
\text{Max}(M_0, M) \geq M_0 > K.
$$

For this case,

$$
\begin{aligned}
ELBC(0) = \ &B(0,T)(M_0 - K) \\
&+ S(0)B_f(0,T)N(d_2) - M_0 B(0,T)N(d_2 - \sigma\sqrt{T}) \\
&+ \{S(0)B_f(0,T)N(d_2) \\
&\quad - B(0,T)S(0)[M_0/S(0)]^{2\eta}N(d_2 - 2\eta\sigma\sqrt{T})\}/(2\eta),
\end{aligned}
\tag{20.29}
$$

where

$$
d_2 \equiv \{\ln[S(0)B_f(0,T)/M_0 B(0,T)] + (\sigma^2/2)T\}/\sigma\sqrt{T}.
$$

Note that if the option is initiated at date 0, then $M_0 \equiv S(0)$.

Put option

Next we examine an **extrema lookback put option**. Consider an extrema lookback put option that was initiated at date T_0, prior to the present date. During that time, the minimum value of the spot exchange rate observed is m_0. Let the option mature at date T and let the strike price be K. Let m denote the minimum value of the spot exchange rate from now until date T.

The payoff at maturity to an extrema lookback put option is defined by

$$ELBP(T) \equiv \begin{cases} K - \text{Min}(m_0, m) & \text{if} \quad K > \text{Min}(m_0, m) \\ 0 & \text{if} \quad K \leq \text{Min}(m_0, m). \end{cases} \qquad (20.30)$$

For example, referring to Figure 20.4, the minimum value of the spot exchange rate from $t = 0$ to $t = T$ is m, which is less than m_0. Therefore, in this case the value of the extrema lookback put option at maturity is $\text{Min}\{K - m, 0\}$.

As before, we use the risk-neutral valuation procedure of Chapter 6 to price this option prior to maturity. We need to consider two cases. First, if $K \leq m_0$, then

$$\begin{aligned} ELBP(0) = {} & B(0,T)KN(-d_3 + \sigma\sqrt{T}) - B_f(0,T)S(0)N(-d_3) \\ & + \{B(0,T)S(0)[K/S(0)]^{2\eta}N(-d_3 + 2\eta\sigma\sqrt{T}) \\ & - B_f(0,T)S(0)N(-d_3)\}/(2\eta), \end{aligned} \qquad (20.31)$$

where

$$d_3 \equiv \{\ln[S(0)B_f(0,T)/KB(0,T)] + (\sigma^2/2)T\}/(\sigma\sqrt{T})$$
$$\eta \equiv (r - r_f)/\sigma^2, \qquad r \neq r_f.$$

Second, if $K > m_0$, the option will always be in-the-money because

$$K > m_0 \geq \text{Min}(m_0, m).$$

In this case, the value of the option is

$$\begin{aligned} ELBP(0) = {} & B(0,T)(K - m_0) \\ & + B(0,T)m_0 N(-d_1 + \sigma\sqrt{T}) - B_f(0,T)S(0)N(-d_1) \\ & + \{B(0,T)S(0)[m_0/S(0)]^{2\eta}N(-d_1 + 2\eta\sigma\sqrt{T}) \\ & - B_f(0,T)S(0)N(-d_1)\}/(2\eta), \end{aligned} \qquad (20.32)$$

where

$$d_1 \equiv \{\ln[S(0)B_f(0,T)/m_0 B(0,T)] + (\sigma^2/2)T\}/(\sigma\sqrt{T}).$$

Our study of lookback options is now complete.

20.3 AVERAGE OPTIONS

We turn now to **average options**. Average options are options for which the payoff depends on the average price of the underlying asset over some prespecified period. There are two forms of average options: fixed strike and floating strike. We will concentrate on the first form since it is by far the most common.

Average options have proved to be very popular and are used in many different markets. They are used in foreign exchange contracts, commodity contracts, and interest rate contracts. For example, long-dated over-the-counter oil options may be based on an average price. In floating rate interest rate notes, at the reset date the new interest rate may be based on the average rate over, say, the last five trading days. A similar comment applies to interest rate caps. The use of an average reduces the sensitivity of a contract to price changes at the maturity of a contract, which is especially important in markets that may be illiquid, such as many commodity markets.

EXAMPLE   **Use of Average Options**

Consider a U.S. company that is selling merchandise in Germany. It receives weekly inflows of Deutsche marks. The manufacturing costs to the firm are in terms of dollars. Thus the firm has a foreign exchange exposure. If the Deutsche mark depreciates against the dollar, the dollar profits of the firm will decrease.

One way for the firm to reduce its exposure, should it so desire, is to purchase a series of average put options on the Deutsche mark. For example, a weekly average could be used. Such a contract does not eliminate the firm's exposure, although it can greatly reduce it.   ■

Fixed strike

We look now at **fixed strike average options**. Let us consider an average option that matures at date T. The strike price of the option is fixed and denoted by K. Let $S(t)$ denote the spot exchange rate at date t. The option contract will specify the dates and times of the prices used to define the average.

EXAMPLE   **Definition of Average**

Consider an option that matures on Friday, November 25 at 11.00 A.M. The average is defined over a month using weekly observations of the dollar/sterling spot exchange rate observed at 11.00 A.M. or just prior to this time in New York.

Using the information given in Table 20.2, the average spot exchange rate is defined to be

$$A \equiv (1.5705 + 1.5609 + 1.5804 + 1.5750 + 1.5675)/5$$
$$= 1.5709. \quad ■$$

TABLE 20.2   *Average Spot Exchange Rate*

NEW YORK 11:00 A.M. FIXINGS	
DATE	**SPOT EXCHANGE RATE**
November 25	1.5705
November 18	1.5609
November 10	1.5804
November 4	1.5750
October 28	1.5675

We pause to note three points from this example. First, an arithmetic average is used. Second, the number, the date, and the timing of price observations used in the average are prespecified. Third, the interval between the observations is not necessarily constant. In Table 20.2, there is no observation on the 11th, as might be expected given the use of weekly observations, because the New York market was closed.

Let $A(T)$ denote the value of the average at date T. The payoff to an average fixed strike call option at maturity is defined by

$$AC(T) \equiv \text{Max} \{A(T) - K, 0\}. \tag{20.33}$$

For a put option,

$$AP(T) \equiv \text{Max} \{K - A(T), 0\}. \tag{20.34}$$

In both cases, the underlying asset is the average and the strike price is fixed.[3]

Valuation

Given the payoff to the option, we next move to valuation. Consider an average option based on three spot exchange rates:

$$A(T) \equiv [S(T) + S(T - 1) + S(T - 2)]/3, \tag{20.35}$$

---

[3]For a **floating strike average call option**, the value at maturity is defined by

$$\text{Max} \{S(T) - A(T), 0\}$$

and, for a put option,

$$\text{Max} \{A(T) - S(T), 0\}.$$

where $S(t)$ is the spot exchange rate at date t. It is assumed that the spot exchange rate is lognormally distributed.

To value the average option, we use the risk-neutral valuation method of Chapter 6. The price is the discounted expected value of the payoff at maturity. To compute this expected value we need to know the probability distribution for the average.

The sum of two lognormal random variables is not lognormal, implying that the distribution of $A(T)$ is not lognormal. Unfortunately, it is not possible to obtain a simple representation of the probability density of the average. Therefore, it has not been possible to derive an exact closed form solution for (discrete) average options.

We could use a binomial lattice to approximate the distribution of $A(T)$. But, in practice, we encounter a complication. We illustrate this complication through the simple lattice shown in Figure 20.6. At the maturity of the option, there are three possible spot exchange rates. We use the numbers in the lattice to calculate the average defined by Expression (20.35). The results are shown in Figure 20.7. You will notice that there are four different possible values of the average. For the average, the lattice does not recombine and we must consider each individual path, which is the problem.

If we had n intervals, we might have to keep track of 2^n price paths. If $n = 25$, $2^n = 33,554,432$, implying that this approach is not really feasible to implement on a computer.

While it is not possible to derive the probability density function for the average, all its moments can be calculated. It is, however, possible to approximate the distribution of the average and to match the moments of the approximate distribution to the moments of the average. This approach provides a quick and accurate way to price these types of options.

FIGURE 20.6   *Standard Lattice*

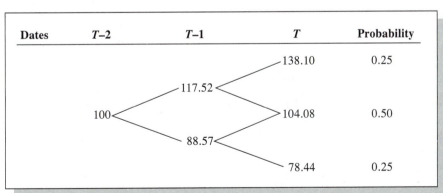

Dates	$T-2$	$T-1$	T	Probability
			138.10	0.25
		117.52		
	100		104.08	0.50
		88.57		
			78.44	0.25

Figure 20.7 *Average Option: Possible Paths*

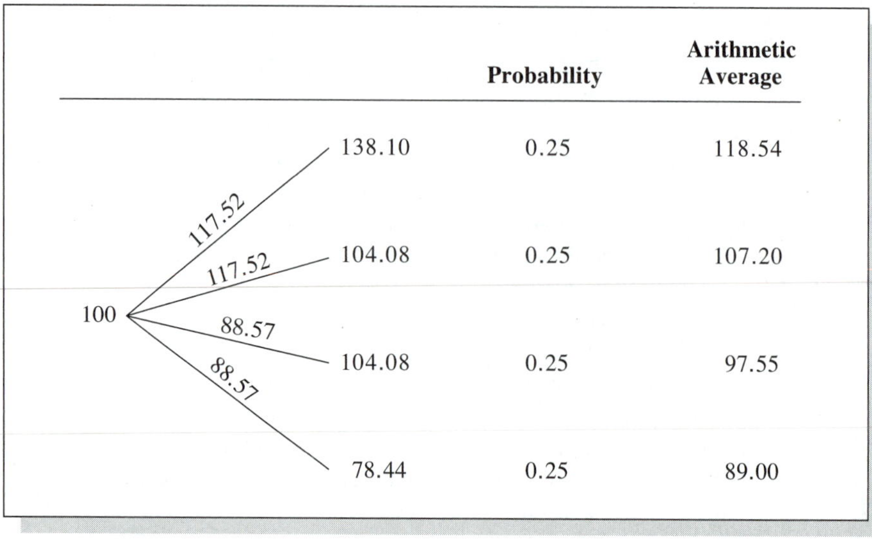

		Probability	Arithmetic Average
138.10		0.25	118.54
104.08		0.25	107.20
104.08		0.25	97.55
78.44		0.25	89.00

(Tree diagram: 100 branches via 117.52 and 88.57 nodes. Upper branch 117.52 leads to 138.10 and 104.08; lower branch 88.57 leads to 104.08 and 78.44.)

Example

Average Option Valuation

A company is planning a special sales promotion in Germany. The promotion starts in 21 days' time and will last for four weeks. During that time, the company will receive revenues in Deutsche marks. The company is concerned that the mark will depreciate against the dollar. It decides to purchase an average put option. The maturity of the option is 49 days (= 21 + 28). The company spec-

Table 20.3 *Average Option*

Spot Exchange	62.26 cents/Deutsche mark
Strike Price	62.26 cents/Deutsche mark
Maturity	49 days
Volatility*	14.9 percent
Domestic Discount Rate**	4.18 percent
German Discount Rate**	4.63 percent
Exchange Rates in Average	4
Interval Between Prices	7
Average of Past Prices	0

*This is quoted on a 365-day basis.

**This is quoted on a 360-day basis.

ifies that a weekly averaging period is to be used, and the average is to be calculated over the last four weeks. The average is defined by

$$A(49) \equiv [S(49) + S(42) + S(35) + S(28)]/4.$$

Table 20.3 gives the relevant input data. The program Exotic/Average is used to price the option. This program is based on an approximation to the distribution of the average, as first described in Turnbull and Wakeman (1991). The time interval between prices is 7 days. The averaging period starts in the future, so the average of past prices is set to zero. The value of the option is found to be 1.1398 cents per Deutsche mark. ∎

In the preceding example, the maturity of the average option is 49 days and the averaging is over the last four weeks. This is an example of what is referred to as a **forward starting average option**. The average period starts in the future.

The effect of averaging is to reduce the volatility of the terminal value of the average. Therefore, it might be tempting to state that the value of a forward starting average option is always less than that of an ordinary option with the same maturity and strike price. However, this is not the case, as we demonstrate using the data given in Table 20.4. The value of an ordinary call option is 5.76 using the program FX/European Option. The value of an average call option is 5.78 using the program Exotic/Average.

Inside the averaging period

The behavior of average options once inside the averaging period can be quite different from that of ordinary options. Let us consider an average call option, where the average is calculated using daily prices over the last eight days. The strike price is 100. The option will expire tomorrow, implying that seven of the prices used to compute the average have been observed; they are shown in Table 20.5.

TABLE 20.4   *Pricing a Forward Starting Average Call Option*

Spot Exchange Rate	156
Strike Price	150
Maturity	100 days
Volatility	2.8 percent
Domestic Discount Rate	4.20 percent
Foreign Discount Rate	4.60 percent
Exchange Rates in Average	29
Interval Between Prices	1
Average of Past Prices	0

TABLE 20.5   *Pricing Inside the Averaging Period: Computing the Average*

DATE	0	−1	−2	−3	−4	−5	−6
PRICE	120	117	115	116	114	112	113

Total of the 7 prices = 807.

Suppose that the stock price tomorrow is zero. The value of an ordinary call is, of course, zero. The value of the average is

$(0 + 807)/8$
$= 100.875.$

The value of the average option is 0.875 (= 100.875 − 100). The use of an average makes average options less sensitive to unusual price movements at the maturity date of the option.

EXAMPLE

Average Call Valuation

This example illustrates the average call option's valuation inside the averaging period.

Let us consider an average call option that was sold some months ago. The option has a remaining maturity of 2 days. The average for the option is specified to be the daily average over the last 5 days:

TABLE 20.6   *Pricing Inside the Averaging Period*

DATA INPUTS	
Spot Exchange Rate	62.26
Strike Price	63.00
Maturity	2 days
Volatility*	14.9 percent
Domestic Discount Rate**	4.08 percent
German Discount Rate**	4.49 percent
Spot Exchange Rate Yesterday	63.15
Spot Exchange Rate Two Days Ago	64.04
Average of Past Prices	(62.26 + 63.15 + 64.40)/3 = 63.15
Exchange Rates in Average	5
Interval Between Prices	1

*This is quoted on a 365-day basis.

**This is quoted on a 360-day basis.

$$A(2) \equiv [S(2) + S(1) + S(0) + S(-1) + S(-2)]/5.$$

The spot exchange rates $S(0)$, $S(-1)$, and $S(-2)$ have been observed.

Table 20.6 gives the relevant input data. The program Exotic/Average is again used. The program asks for the average of past prices, which is defined to be the average of all observed prices that contribute to the average. In this case we have observed three spot exchange rates, so the average of past prices is, by definition,

$$(62.26 + 63.15 + 64.04)/3$$
$$= 63.15.$$

The value of the average option is 0.0201. ∎

20.4 SUMMARY

In this chapter, we have discussed three types of path-dependent non-standard options: barrier options, lookback options, and average options. In the first two cases, under the assumptions of lognormally distributed spot exchange rates and constant domestic and foreign interest rates, it is possible to derive exact closed form solutions. It is not, in general, possible for average options.[4] However, accurate approximations have been developed. The Turnbull and Wakeman (1991) approximation is illustrated in the text. Although in this chapter we have focused on foreign currency options, the results apply to any underlying asset the structure of which satisfies the assumptions of Chapter 11, including stock indexes and commodity options (see Chapter 12).

REFERENCES

Lookback options:

Conze, A., and Viswanathan, 1991. "Path Dependent Options: The Case of Lookback Options." *Journal of Finance* 46, 1893–1907.

Barrier options:

Boyle, P. P., 1992. "Barrier Options." Working Paper, University of Waterloo.
Rubinstein, M., and E. Reiner, 1991. "Breaking Down the Barriers." *Risk* 4, 31–35.

---

[4]Geman and Yor (1993) have derived a closed form expression for the case in which the average is defined by an integral. Unfortunately, for OTC options, the average is always defined using a discrete sum and not an integral.

Pricing of average options:

Curran, M., 1992. "Beyond Average Intelligence." *Risk* 5, 60−62.

Geman, H., and M. Yor, 1993. "Bessel Processes, Asian Options and Perpetuities." *Mathematical Finance* 3, 349−375.

Levy, E., 1992. "Pricing European Average Rate Currency Options." *Journal of International Money and Finance* 11, 474−491.

Ritchken, P., L. Sankarasubramanian, and A.M. Vijh, 1993. "The Valuation of Path Dependent Contracts on the Average." *Management Science* 39, 1202−1213.

Turnbull, S. M., and L. M. Wakeman, 1991. "A Quick Algorithm for Pricing European Average Options." *Journal of Financial and Quantitative Analysis* 26, 377−389.

Accuracy of pricing formulas for average options:

Levy, E., and S. M. Turnbull, 1992. "Average Intelligence." *Risk* 5, 53−59.

QUESTIONS

Question 1

A financial institution has written the down-and-out call option described in Table 20.1. The call option is to buy 10 million French francs. The institution decides to hedge this option with two ordinary European options. The first option is a call option with a strike price of 18.00 cents/FF and maturity of 51 days. The second option is a call option with a strike price of 17.50 cents/FF and a maturity of 51 days. The contract size for these two options is 62,500 French francs. Fill in the following table.

a) Using the program FX/Pricing/European Option, determine the prices and deltas of the two ordinary options.
b) Using the program Exotic/Barrier/Down-and-Out, determine the price and delta of the down-and-out call option.
c) Describe the hedged portfolio.
d) To analyze the portfolio of the hedge, consider the value of the hedged portfolio if the spot exchange rate changes.

POSSIBLE FUTURE SPOT EXCHANGE RATE (CENTS/FF)	VALUE OF DOWN-AND-OUT CALL	VALUE OF ORDINARY OPTIONS		VALUE OF HEDGED PORTFOLIO
		STRIKE 18.00	STRIKE 17.50	
16				
17				
18				
18.213				
19				
20				
21				

Question 2

A company expects to receive payment of 150 million French francs in 51 days' time. The company is concerned that the franc may depreciate against the dollar. It could purchase an ordinary foreign exchange European put option or it could purchase a down-and-in put option. Use the information in Table 20.1 to answer the following questions.

a) What is the value of an ordinary foreign exchange European put option with a strike price of 19.50 cents/FF? Use the program FX/Pricing/European Option.
b) What is the value of a down-and-in put option? Use the program Exotic/Barrier/Down-In.
c) What is the advantage of the down-and-in put compared to an ordinary put?

Question 3

Given the information in Table 20.1, plot the value of a down-and-in call option over a range of spot exchange rates.

Initial Spot Exchange Rate	17.30 cents/FF
Final Spot Exchange Rate	20.00 cents/FF
Spot Exchange Rate Interval	0.10 cents/FF

Use the program Exotic/Barrier/Down-and-In.

a) Plot option value against the spot exchange rate. Explain the shape of this curve.
b) Plot delta against the spot exchange rate. Explain the shape of this curve.

Question 4

a) Using the following information, determine the value of an up-and-out put option. Use the program Exotic/Barrier/Up-Out.

Spot Exchange Rate	110.09 (1/100) cents/yen
Strike Price	100.00 (1/100) cents/yen
Upper Barrier	111.047 (1/100) cents/yen
Maturity	30 days
Volatility*	15.50 percent
Domestic Discount Rate**	5.65 percent
Foreign Discount Rate**	1.53 percent
Face Value	6,250,000 yen
Rebate	0

*Assuming a 365-day year.
**Assuming a 360-day year.

b)   Determine the value of an ordinary put option with the same strike and maturity. Comment on the relative magnitudes. Is this a general result? Explain.

Question 5

A standard lookback put option written on the French franc matures in 51 days' time. To date, the observed maximum spot exchange rate has been 21.25 cents per French franc.

a)   Given the information in Table 20.1, value this option. Use the program Exotic/ Lookback/Standard.

b)   Compare the value of this option to an ordinary put option with the same maturity and a strike price of 21.25 cents per French franc. Comment on the relative values and explain whether this is an example of a general result.

Question 6

A company is selling Deutsche marks on a daily basis. The average quantity of marks that are sold is one million each day. The company does its accounting on a monthly basis and is concerned about the total dollar amount it receives each month on its Deutsche mark sales. If the mark depreciates against the dollar, the company's dollar revenues will fall.

a)   Value a 30-day option on the extremum written on the Deutsche mark. Should the company buy a call option or a put option on the extremum? Use the program Exotic/Lookback/Extrema.

Spot Exchange Rate	0.7062 dollars/DM
Strike Price	0.7062 dollars/DM
Maturity	30 days
Volatility*	14.6 percent
Domestic Discount Rate**	5.65 percent
Foreign Discount Rate**	4.47 percent

   *A 365-day year is assumed.
   **A 360-day year is assumed.

b)   What amount of options should the company buy?

Question 7

Plot the value of an extrema lookback call option using the following information.

Initial Spot Exchange Rate	69 cents/DM
Final Spot Exchange Rate	80

Spot Exchange Rate Interval	0.50
Current Observed Maximum	74 cents/DM
Strike Price	70 cents/DM
Maturity	30 days
Volatility*	14.6 percent
Domestic Discount Rate**	5.65 percent
Foreign Discount Rate**	4.47 percent

*A 365-day year is assumed.

**A 360-day year is assumed.

Use the program Exotic/Lookback/Extrema.

a) Plot the graph of option value against the spot exchange rate. What happens as the exchange rate exceeds 74 cents/DM?

b) Plot the graph of delta against the spot exchange rate. What happens as the exchange rate exceeds 74 cents/DM?

Question 8

Referring to Question 6, the company decides to use an average put option. The averaging is to start immediately.

a) How many observations will be used to compute the average?

b) Compute the value of the option. If the option is to sell 30 million Deutsche marks, what is the total cost? Use the program Exotic/Average. Note that the average of past prices is 0.7062, given that the current spot exchange rate is known and is included in the average.

c) How does your answer compare to Question 6?

GLOSSARY OF SYMBOLS

$A(t)$	The value of the money market account at date t. Denotes the value at date t of investing one dollar in the short-term riskless asset and rolling the investment over.
AI	Accrued interest.
$AC(0)$	Average fixed strike call option.
$AP(0)$	Average fixed strike put option.
$B(t, T)$	The value at date t of a zero-coupon bond that pays one dollar for sure at date $(T \geq t)$.
$B_f(t, T)$	The value at date t of a zero-coupon bond that pays one unit of a foreign currency for sure at date T.
$B_c(t)$	The value of a coupon-paying bond at date t.
$c(t)$	Value of a European call option at date t written on an asset with price $S(t)$. The strike price of the option is K and the option expires at date T, the maturity of the option being $T - t$.
$C(t)$	Value of an American call option at date t written on an asset with price $S(t)$. The strike price of the option is K and the option expires at date T.
$cc(0)$	Compound call-on-call option.
$cp(0)$	Compound call-on-put option.
$co(0)$	Chooser option.
$C\operatorname{Min}(0)$	Call option on the minimum of two risky outcomes.
$C\operatorname{Max}(0)$	Call option on the maximum of two risky outcomes.
Δ	(delta) Time interval.
d_t	Dividend per share at date t.
d_y	Constant dividend yield.
D	The value of the down factor in the binomial model.
D_C	Macauley's duration.
D_M	Modified duration.
$DOC(0)$	Down-and-out call option.
$DOP(0)$	Down-and-out put option.
$DIC(0)$	Down-and-in call option.
$DIP(0)$	Down-and-in put option.
$DC(0)$	Digital call option.
$DP(0)$	Digital put option.
$E^\pi[\cdot]$	The expected value using the martingale probabilities.

$ELBC(0)$	Extrema lookback call option.
$ELBP(0)$	Extrema lookback put option.
e_t	Describes the default process at date t.
$f(t_1, t_2, t_3)$	The forward rate of interest implied by the term structure at date t_1, for the period from date t_2 to date t_3, $t_1 \leq t_2 \leq t_3$.
$F(t, T_F)$	The forward price at date t for delivery at date T_F.
$\mathcal{F}(t, T_{\mathcal{F}})$	The futures price at date t for delivery at date $T_{\mathcal{F}}$.
$\mathcal{F}_c(t, T_{\mathcal{F}})$	The futures price at date t for delivery at date $T_{\mathcal{F}}$. The contract is written on a coupon-paying bond.
FRA	Forward rate agreement.
g	Proportional storage costs.
G	Total storage costs.
$GC(0)$	Gap call option.
$GP(0)$	Gap put option.
$H(t)$	Value of the stock at date t net of the present value of the dividend payments.
i_c	Discretely compounded rate over the period $[0, T]$.
i_d	Discount rate over the period $[0, T]$.
i_s	Simple interest rate over the period $[0, T]$.
i_I	Implied repro rate.
$I(t)$	Index value at date t.
λ	(lambda) The volatility reduction factor.
$\lambda(T)$	The martingale probability of default occurring at date T conditional on default not having occurred up to and including date $T - 1$.
$\ell(T)$	The spot LIBOR rate for the period T.
$LIBID$	London Interbank Bid Rate.
$LIBOR$	London Interbank Offer Rate.
$L(0, T)$	The date-0 value of a Eurodollar deposit that promises to pay one dollar at date T.
μ	(mu) The instantaneous expected rate of return per unit time on an asset computed using the original probability distribution.
$\tilde{\mu}$	(mu tilde) The instantaneous expected rate of return per unit time on an asset compounded using the equivalent martingale probabilities.
N_p	Notional principal.
π	(pi) The martingale probability of an up-state occurring next period in the binomial model.
$pc(0)$	Compound put-on-call option.
$pp(0)$	Compound put-on-put option.
$p(t)$	Value of a European put option written on an asset with price $S(t)$. The strike price of the option is K and the option expires at date T, the maturity of the option being $T - t$.
$P(t)$	Value of an American put option written on an asset with price $S(t)$. The strike price of the option is K and the option expires at date T, the maturity of the option being $T - t$.

$PLC(0)$	Paylater call option.
$PLP(0)$	Paylater put option.
$P\text{Max}(0)$	Put option on the maximum of two risky outcomes.
$P\text{Min}(0)$	Put option on the minimum of two risky outcomes.
$PV_t[\cdot]$	The present value at date t.
r	Continuously compounded domestic spot interest rate.
r_f	Continuously compounded foreign spot interest rate.
R	The amount earned from investing one dollar in the riskless asset for the period Δ.
R_d	Rebate.
R_f	The amount earned from investing one unit of foreign currency in the foreign riskless asset for the period Δ.
$\overline{R}$	Swap rate.
$\overline{R}_I$	The swap rate if principal is added to the fixed and floating sides. Note that this is in general incorrect.
σ	(sigma) The volatility of the rate of return on an asset.
$SLBC(0)$	Standard lookback call option.
$SLBP(0)$	Standard lookback put option.
U	The value of the up factor in the binomial model.
$UIC(0)$	Up-and-in call option.
$UIP(0)$	Up-and-in put option.
$UOC(0)$	Up-and-out call option.
$UOP(0)$	Up-and-out put option.
$v(0, T)$	Value at date 0 of a zero-coupon bond that promises to pay one dollar at date T.
$W(t)$	Normal random variable with zero mean and variance t.
y	Yield-to-maturity (semiannual).
y_A	Effective annual yield-to-maturity.
y_c	Continuously compounded yield-to-maturity.
y_n	Continuously compounded net convenience value.
y_y	Continuously compounded convenience value.
$Y(0, T)$	Convenience value.
z_n	$\ln[S(n)/S(n-1)]$.
$Z(T)$	$\ln[S(T)/S(0)]$.

GLOSSARY OF TERMS

Accrued interest   The interest earned on a bond since the last coupon payment date.

American option   An option that can be exercised from the date of purchase until the expiration date.

AMEX   American Stock Exchange, New York.

Amortizing swap   A swap in which the notional principal decreases through time.

Arbitrage   A trading strategy that makes riskless profits from a zero investment.

Ask price   The price at which one can buy an asset.

Asian option   See average option.

At-the-money   A term referring to an option when the market value of the asset on which the option is written is equal to the strike price of the option.

Average option   An option in which the final payoff is determined by the average price of the asset during a specified period. In a fixed strike average option, the payoff at maturity depends on the difference of the average and a fixed strike price. In a floating strike average option, the payoff at maturity depends on the difference of the spot price and the average.

Backward induction   A technique used in pricing derivative securities. The value of the option is first determined at maturity, and then, by working backwards, the current value of the derivative is calculated.

Barrier option   A path-dependent option the payoff of which depends on the payoff to an ordinary option and whether a prespecified barrier has been crossed. Common examples include down-and-in options, down-and-out options, up-and-in options, and up-and-out options.

Basis   The difference between the spot price and the futures price of a commodity.

Basis point   Defined as being equal to one-hundredth of one percent (0.01 percent).

Basle Accord   An international agreement to establish capital adequacy standards for banks.

Bearish   A position in an asset that decreases in value when the asset's price decreases.

Bermuda option   An option that can only be exercised at a fixed number of intervals over its life. It is a cross between a European and an American option.

Beta   A measure of risk for an individual asset.

Bid price   The price at which one can sell an asset.

Bid-ask spread   The difference between the ask price and the bid price.

Binary option   See digital option.

Binomial model   A model that describes the random evolution of the price of an asset over time. The model assumes that at the end of each interval the asset price can have one of two possible values.

B.I.S.   Bank of International Settlement.

Black's model   A model for pricing a futures option using a lognormal distribution for the underlying futures price.

Black-Scholes model   A model for pricing stock options using a lognormal distribution for the underlying stock price.

Block trades   Trades in a common stock over 10,000 shares.

Bullish   A position in an asset that increases in value when the price of the asset increases.

Boundary condition   The payoff to a derivative security at expiration or at an exercise date.

Brownian motion   A stochastic process the increments of which are normally distributed with zero mean and variance proportional to time.

Butterfly spread   A combination of a vertical bull spread and vertical bear spread with the same expiration date on all options and the same strike price on all short options.

Call option   An option to buy an underlying asset.

Callable swap   An interest rate swap where one party has the right to cancel the swap at a certain time without any additional costs.

Cap   A series of European interest rate call options, often used by a party that has issued a floating rate note. The cap ensures that the effective interest rate paid on the debt is capped at a fixed rate.

Caplet   One of the component interest rate call options in a cap.

Cash-and-carry   An investment strategy that duplicates the payoff to a forward contract.

CBOE   Chicago Board of Options Exchange.

CBOT   Chicago Board of Trade.

CBT   Chicago Board of Trade.

Cheapest to deliver   The bond in a futures contract that is least expensive to deliver on the contract.

Chooser option   An option for which during the life of the option, the option owner can pick either a call option or a put option.

Circuit breakers   Trading halts in the stock market or stock index futures market when the price changes in the index or futures are large.

Clearing house   The firm that guarantees the performance of exchange-traded derivative security contracts.

Closed form solution   A formula that can easily be computed.

CME   Chicago Merchantile Exchange.

Collar   An interest rate contract that establishes a cap (maximum) and a floor (minimum) on a specified rate of interest that is to be paid. Can also be used in commodity, foreign currency, and equity markets.

COMEX   Commodity Exchange, New York.

Commodity derivative   A derivative written on a commodity.

Commodity futures   A futures contract written on a commodity.

Commodity Futures Trading Commission   The federal agency responsible for regulating futures markets in the United States.

Commodity swap   A swap in which counterparties exchange cash flows based on at least one commodity price.

Competitive markets   A market where all traders act as price takers.

Compound option   An option written on one or more options.

Condor   An option portfolio: Purchase a call option and a put option, both equally out-of-the-money. Write a call option and a put option, each further out-of-the-money than

the call and put options that were purchased. All options have the same time to expiration.

Constant yield swap   An interest rate swap in which both parts are floating.

Contingent premium option   See paylater option.

Continuous trading   A market where trading can take place continuously in time.

Continuously compounded interest rates   Interest rates in which interest is compounded continuously.

Convenience value   The value to storing a commodity for its use in production.

Convenience yield   The convenience value expressed as a percent.

Conversion factor   The adjustment factor in Treasury bond futures contracts for bonds of different maturities and coupon rates.

Convexity   A measure of the bond's sensitivity to large changes in the bond's yield.

Corner   A market situation where a trader or group of traders acting in unison own the available supply of an asset.

Cost-of-carry   A trading strategy that duplicates the payoff to a forward contract.

Counterparty   The opposite party to a financial contract.

Counterparty risk   The risk that a counterparty to a contract might default.

Coupon   The interest payment made on a bond.

Coupon bond   A bond that makes coupon payments.

Coupon rate   The coupon on a bond divided by the face value of the bond.

Covered call   A position in a call option with an opposite position in the underlying asset.

Credit risk   Exposure to the risk of a loss arising from default or credit downgrade.

Cross rate option   A foreign currency option for which the numeraire is not dollars but a foreign currency.

CSCE   Coffee, Sugar, and Cocoa Exchange, New York.

CTN   Cotton Exchange, New York.

Cum-dividend   A stock trading before a dividend is paid.

Daily price limits   The maximum and minimum daily price movement allowed on a futures contract.

Default-free   A payoff to a security that has no possibility of default.

Deferred swap   A forward swap.

Delivery date   The date on which the underlying asset is exchanged for a cash payment on a forward contract or a futures contract.

Delivery price   The price used in determining the value of a contract held to maturity.

Delta   The change in a derivative's value for a unit change in the underlying asset's price.

Delta neutral   A portfolio position that has a delta of zero.

Derivative security   A financial contract the value of which is derived from some underlying asset.

Deterministic interest rates   Future interest rates that are known with certainty.

Digital option   An option that at maturity pays one dollar if in-the-money, zero otherwise.

Discount bond   A zero-coupon bond.

Discount rate   The interest rate in which Treasury bills are quoted.

Discretely compounded interest rates   Interest rates that include compounding over discrete time periods.

Displaced lognormal distribution   A lognormal distribution the mean of which is translated along the horizontal axis.

Dividend   A cash payment made to a common stock.

Dividend yield   The ratio of the dividend payment to the stock price.

Dollar return   One plus the percent return.

Down-and-in option   For down-and-in options, a lower level (barrier) is specified for the asset price on which the option is written. For a down-and-in call (put) option the contract becomes a standard call (put) option if the price of the underlying asset falls below the barrier. If the price of the underlying asset never falls below the barrier during the life of the contract, the contract expires worthless.

Down-and-out option   For down-and-out options, a lower level (barrier) is specified for the asset price on which the option is written. For a down-and-out call (put) option the contract ceases to exist if the price of the underlying asset falls below the barrier. If the price of the underlying asset never falls below the barrier during the life of the contract, the contract expires as an ordinary call (put) option.

DTB   Deutsche Terminborse, Frankfurt, Germany.

Duration   A measure of the average life of a bond.

Dynamically complete   A market where any derivative can be synthetically replicated using a dynamic trading strategy.

ECU   European Currency Unit; based on a basket of community currencies.

Efficient markets   A theory that states that asset prices accurately reflect relevant information.

Equity swap   A swap in which one series of cash flows that are linked to equity are swapped for a series of cash flows that may or may not be linked to equity.

Equivalent martingale probabilities   The probabilities for computing the risk-neutral value.

Euro   The legal currency of the eleven participating countries of the European Union.

Eurodollar contracts   Derivative securities written on Eurodollar deposits.

Eurodollar futures contract   A futures contract written on a Eurodollar deposit.

Eurodollars   Dollars deposited in a non-U.S. bank.

European option   An option that can be exercised only on the expiration date.

Exchange rate   The rate at which a unit of one currency is exchanged for another currency.

Ex-dividend date   The day on which a common stock makes a dividend payment.

Exercise price   The price at which the underlying asset may be purchased or sold when an option is exercised.

Exotic option   A non-standard option.

Expected value   A measure of the central tendency of a probability distribution.

Expiration date   The maturity date of a derivative security.

Ex-split date   The day on which the stock split occurs.

Extendible bonds   A bond for which the bondholder has an option to extend the maturity of the bond.

Extrema lookback options   For a call (put) option, the payoff at maturity depends on the maximum (minimum) value of the price of the underlying asset over the life of the option.

Face value The principal payment on a bond at maturity.

FINEX Financial Instruments Exchange, New York.

Floating rate note A debt instrument that pays interest based on a changing (floating) rate of interest.

Floor A series of European interest rate put options, often used by a party that has purchased a floating rate note. The floor ensures that the effective interest rate received from the note never falls below a fixed level.

Floorlet One of the component interest rate put options in a floor.

Foreign currency derivative A derivative security written on foreign currency spot exchange rates.

Foreign currency forward price The forward price of a foreign currency.

Foreign currency futures A futures contract written on a foreign currency spot exchange rate.

Foreign currency futures option An option written on a foreign currency futures.

Foreign currency option An option written on a foreign currency spot exchange rate.

Foreign currency swap An exchange of payments converting a series of cash flows in one currency to a series of cash flows in another currency.

Forward contract A financial contract that obligates the owner to purchase some underlying asset for a fixed price (the delivery price) at a fixed future date. Usually no cash flows are exchanged until the delivery date.

Forward exchange rate The value in a domestic currency of a unit of a foreign currency delivered at a future date.

Forward option An option on a forward contract.

Forward price The delivery price written in a forward contract such that the initial value of the forward contract is zero.

Forward rate The interest rate one can contract for today for riskless borrowing at a future date.

Forward rate agreement (FRA) A contract written on LIBOR that requires a cash payment at maturity based on the difference between a spot rate and a forward rate of interest.

Forward swap An interest rate swap in which the swap rate is set but the swap does not commence until a later date.

Frictionless markets Markets where there are no restrictions nor costs to trading assets.

Futures contract A financial contract that obligates the owner to purchase some underlying asset for a fixed price at a fixed future date. The financial contract is marked-to-market.

Futures option An option on a futures contract.

Futures price The delivery price written in a futures contract.

Gamma The change in the option's delta for a unit change in the underlying asset's price.

Gamma neutral A portfolio position that has a zero gamma.

Grade The measured quality of a commodity.

Greeks The option's partial derivatives with respect to its input parameters.

Group of Thirty An international financial policy organization the members of which include representatives of central banks, international banks, and securities firms.

Heath-Jarrow-Morton (HJM) model A model for pricing interest rate derivatives.

Hedge   A position in an asset designed to remove the price risk from another position in a different instrument.

Hedge ratio   The number of shares of the underlying asset used to create a hedged portfolio.

Historic volatility   The volatility estimated from using past observations of the underlying asset's price.

Implicit volatility   The volatility implied from option prices.

Implied repo rate   The interest rate implicit in a forward contract.

Index amortized swap   An interest rate swap for which the notional principal is amortized over the life of the swap. The rate of amortization is related to the level of interest rates.

Index options   Option contracts written on a stock index.

Initial margin   The initial margin that is required in a margin account.

Interest rate derivative   A derivative security the value of which depends on the evolution of the term structure of interest rates.

Interest rate parity   An arbitrage relation that holds between foreign currency spot prices and interest rates.

Interest rate swap   A swap based on interest rates.

In-the-money   A term referring to a call (put) option when the market value of the asset on which the option is written is greater (less) than the strike price.

Intrinsic value   For a call option, the difference of the asset price less the strike price if positive, zero otherwise. For a put option, the difference of the strike price less the asset price if positive, zero otherwise.

IPE   International Petroleum Exchange.

ISDA   International Swaps and Derivatives Association.

Kappa   See vega.

KC   Kansas City Board of Trade.

Known dividend model   An extension of the Black-Scholes model for pricing European options when the underlying asset pays dividends.

Lattice   A tree describing the evolution of an asset price or interest rate over time. The branches in the lattice recombine. If the branches do not recombine, the lattice is usually called a bushy lattice.

LEAPS   Long Term Equity Anticipation Securities (long-term options on the S&P 500 index).

Leverage   A portfolio position using borrowing to finance a purchase.

LIBID   London Interbank Bid Rate. The rate at which a bank is willing to borrow Eurodollars.

LIBOR   London Interbank Offer Rate. The rate at which a bank is willing to lend Eurodollars.

LIFFE   London International Financial Futures Exchange.

LME   London Metals Exchange.

Lognormal distribution   A probability distribution for a random variable x such that the natural logarithm of x follows a normal distribution.

Long position   A position in an asset that has been purchased.

Maintenance margin   The minimum amount of margin that must be kept in a margin account after its initiation.

Margin The dollar amount of cash or securities used as collateral to purchase some derivative security or asset.

Market frictions Conditions in the market that make trading costly or restrict trading.

Mark-to-market The process to record daily price changes in futures markets and to debit or credit accounts.

Martingale A stochastic process the expected value of which equals the current value.

Martingale pricing A pricing method that uses martingale probabilities to compute present values.

Martingale probabilities The probabilities used in the risk-neutral valuation technique.

MATIF Marche a Terme International de France.

Maturity date The date on which a derivative security contract matures.

MCE MidAmerica Commodity Exchange.

ME Montreal Exchange, Canada.

Model misspecification The error in a given model.

Modified duration Duration divided by one plus the bond's yield.

Money market account An investment that earns interest at the spot rate of interest.

MPLS Minneapolis Grain Exchange.

Naked option position An option position with no associated position in the underlying asset.

Net convenience yield The convenience yield less the spot rate of interest.

Netting A contractual agreement to aggregate all payments between two counterparties.

Netting by novation A single agreement to combine the obligations of multiple contracts

with a single counterparty all of which are denominated in the same currency.

Normal distribution The standard bell-shaped, symmetric probability distribution.

NYFE New York Futures Exchange, subsidiary of New York Cotton Exchange.

NYM New York Mercantile Exchange.

NYSE New York Stock Exchange.

Open interest The total number of outstanding futures or options contracts.

Option A contract granting the right to buy or sell an asset at a stated price over a specified period.

OTC derivatives Derivative securities traded in the over-the-counter market.

Out-of-the-money A term referring to a call (put) option when the market value of the asset on which the option is written is less (greater) than the strike price.

Over-the-counter market An off-exchange market between commercial and investment banks for trading in an asset.

Par bond yield The coupon that makes the price of a bond price equal to its face value. The yield-to-maturity equals the coupon rate, given that the bond is selling at par.

Par bond yield curve The graph of the par bond yields for bonds of different maturities.

Par swap rate The fixed rate on a plain vanilla interest rate swap that sets the value of the swap to zero.

Path-dependent option An option the value of which depends on the path of the price of the underlying asset over the life of the option.

Paylater option An option in which the premium is paid at expiration, contingent on the option being in-the-money.

Payoff diagram   A graph that illustrates the payoff to a derivative security at expiration.

PHLX   Philadelphia Stock Exchange.

Plain vanilla swap   An interest rate swap where one side receives fixed rate payments and the other side makes floating rate payments every period for a fixed period of time. Notional principals are not exchanged.

Portfolio insurance   The use of stock index derivatives to protect the value of a portfolio of common stocks.

Position limit   The maximum number of futures contracts an individual can hold.

Premium   The purchase price of an option contract.

Price taker   An individual who buys or sells an asset without changing its price.

PSE   Pacific Stock Exchange.

Pseudo-American option   An option that at initiation gives the choice of the exercise date from a set of possible dates.

Pseudo-American option model   An extension of the Black-Scholes model for pricing American options when the underlying asset pays dividends.

Put-call parity   A relation between a put and a call option.

Put option   An option to sell an underlying asset.

Putable swap   An interest rate swap for which one side has the right to cancel the swap at a fixed time.

Rate-capped swap   An interest rate swap in which the floating rate is capped.

Replicating portfolio   A portfolio of assets that replicates the cash flow and values of some derivative security.

Rho   The change in the option's value for a unit change in the interest rate.

Risk-free rate   A default-free interest rate.

Risk-neutral valuation   A present value technique that computes the present value as the expected discounted future cash flows.

Roll model   An American call option model with one known dividend paid on the underlying asset.

SDR   Special Drawing Rights.

Seagull   An option portfolio: Write a call option and a put option, both equally out-of-the-money. Buy an at-the-money call option. All options have the same time to expiration.

SEC   Securities Exchange Commission; a federal agency responsible for regulating securities markets and listed option markets in the United States.

Self-financing trading strategy   A trading strategy that has no cash inflows or outflows prior to its liquidation.

Settlement price   The price at which futures contracts are settled at the end of a trading date.

SFE   Sydney Futures Exchange, Australia.

Short position   A position in an asset that is sold short. Also refers to a transaction where an investor has written a derivative.

Short sale   A transaction in which an investor borrows a security from a broker and sells the security. At a later date, the investor must buy the security back and return it to the broker.

Short squeeze   A situation in a market where a corner exits and the outstanding shorts must cover their positions at prices determined by the entity holding the corner.

SIMEX   Singapore International Monetary Exchange.

Simple interest rate   An interest rate that does not include compounding.

Speculation A position in an asset designed to perform well if some random variable, such as the asset's price, achieves a certain value.

Spot exchange rate The current value of one unit of a currency in terms of a second currency.

Spot price The price on some asset for immediate delivery.

Standard and Poor's 500 index A stock price index consisting of 500 selected stocks.

Standard deviation The square root of the variance.

Standard lookback option At the maturity of the option, the payoff for a call option depends on the difference between the spot price of the underlying asset and the minimum value of the asset price over the life of the option. The payoff for a put option depends on the difference between the maximum value of the asset price over the life of the option and the spot price of the underlying asset.

Static hedge A hedge that consists of buying/selling securities that are held until the maturity date of the derivative being hedged.

Stock dividend A dividend paid to a common stock in units of additional share of the stock.

Stock index futures A futures contract written on a stock market index.

Stock market index A portfolio of common stocks.

Stock option An option on a common stock.

Stock split A situation in which a company changes the number of outstanding shares of common stock by issuing to each existing shareholder a multiple number of units of the shares originally held.

Storage costs The costs of storing a commodity.

Straddle An option portfolio consisting of a long call and a long put option with the same exercise price and exercise date.

Strangle An option portfolio consisting of a long call and long put option position with the same exercise date and different exercise prices.

Strike price The price at which the underlying asset may be purchased or sold when an option is exercised.

Swap A financial contract that obligates both counterparties to a series of cash payments for a fixed period of time.

Swaption An option on a swap.

Synthetic derivative A portfolio of traded securities that duplicates the cash flows and payoffs to a derivative.

Synthetic replication The process of forming a synthetic derivative.

Term structure of interest rates The graph of various maturity interest rates versus their maturities.

TFE Toronto Futures Exchange, Canada.

Theta The change in the option's value for a unit change in time.

Theta neutral A portfolio position that has a theta of zero.

Tick size The smallest price change allowed for trading an asset.

TIFFE Tokyo International Financial Futures Exchange.

Time spread An option portfolio: Write a call (put) and buy another call (put) with a longer time to expiration. The options have the same strike price.

Time value The part of the option's value above its price if it is exercised for certain at the maturity date.

Timing option   The right to deliver a bond on any day in the delivery month of a Treasury bond futures contract.

Trading strategy   A portfolio position that can change over time.

Transaction costs   The costs involved in buying or selling an asset.

Treasury bill   A zero-coupon bond issued by the U.S. government with maturity of less than one year.

Treasury bill futures   A futures contract written on Treasury bills.

Treasury bond   A coupon bond issued by the U.S. government with maturity of greater than ten years.

Treasury bond futures   A futures contract written on Treasury bonds.

Treasury note   A coupon bond issued by the U.S. government with maturity less than ten years.

Treasury note futures   A futures contract written on Treasury notes.

Treasury strips   A synthetic zero-coupon bond constructed from Treasury notes and bonds.

TSE   Toronto Stock Exchange, Canada.

Up-and-in option   For up-and-in options, an upper level (barrier) is specified for the asset price on which the option is written. For a up-and-in call (put) option, the contract becomes a standard call (put) option if the price of the underlying asset never goes above the barrier during the life of the contract, otherwise the contract expires worthless.

Up-and-out option   For up-and-out options, an upper level (barrier) is specified for the asset price on which the option is written. For a up-and-out call (put) option, the contract ceases to exist if the price of the underlying asset goes above the barrier. If the price

of the underlying asset never goes above the barrier during the life of the contract, the contract expires as an ordinary call (put) option.

Up-tick rule   A rule in the stock market that prohibits short sales except when the last transaction in the stock had a price increase.

Variance   A measure of the dispersion of a probability distribution.

Vega   The change in the option's value for a unit change in the volatility.

Vega neutral   A portfolio position that has a vega of zero.

Vertical bear spread   Buy a call (put) option and sell a call (put) with a lower strike price. All options have the same maturity.

Vertical bull spread   Buy a call (put) option and sell a call (put) with a higher strike price. All options have the same maturity.

Volatility   The standard deviation of an asset's return.

Vulnerable derivative   A derivative for which there is the risk that the writer of the derivative might default.

Wildcard option   The right to deliver on a futures contract after the close of trading but before the start of the next trading day.

WPG   Winnipeg Commodity Exchange, Canada.

Writer   A person who issues a derivative security.

Yield   The yield-to-maturity of a bond.

Yield curve   The graph of the yield on bonds of different maturities.

Yield-to-maturity   The internal rate of return on a bond.

Zero-coupon bond   A bond that makes no interest or coupon payments.

INDEX